WORLD GEOGRAPHY

BUILDING A GLOBAL PERSPECTIVE

PRENTICE HALL

WORLD GEOGRAPHY

BUILDING A GLOBAL PERSPECTIVE

Thomas J. Baerwald

Celeste Fraser

Prentice
Hall

Upper Saddle River, New Jersey
Glenview, Illinois
Needham, Massachusetts

Authors

Thomas J. Baerwald received a B.A. degree in geography and history from Valparaiso University in Indiana and earned his M.A and Ph.D degrees in geography at the University of Minnesota. He has served on the boards of the Association of American Geographers and the National Council for Geographic Education and has lectured at many universities across the country. Currently Dr. Baerwald is Deputy Assistant Director for Geosciences at the National Science Foundation in Arlington, Virginia.

Celeste Fraser received her B.A and M.A degrees at the University of Colorado. She has served on the board of the National Council for Geographic Education and the Geographic Society of Chicago. Ms. Fraser is the Geography Specialist and Exhibit Developer at the Chicago Children's Museum and has taught at the middle and high school levels.

Area Specialists

Mexico and Countries of South America
Dr. Louis B. Casagrande
Senior Vice President
Science Museum of Minnesota
St. Paul, Minnesota

Central America and the Caribbean
Dr. Sam Sheldon
Associate Professor of Geography
Department of Sociology and Social Sciences
St. Bonaventure University
St. Bonaventure, New York

Southwest Asia
John Voll
Professor of Islamic History
Deputy Director,
Center for Muslim-Christian Understanding
Georgetown University
Washington, D.C.

South Asia
Leonard A. Gordon
Professor of History
Brooklyn College
City University of New York
New York, New York

Mel Bacon
Brighton High School
Brighton, Colorado

Henry Dircks
Mepham High School
Long Island, New York

Judith Ellis
Saratoga High School
Saratoga, California

Keith Has-Ellison
Livingston High School
Livingston, California

Karen Hausdorf
North Cobb High School
Kennesaw, Georgia

Peggy Sorenson
Lawrence High School
Lawrence, Kansas

Barbara Vallejo-Doten
Huntington Park High School
Huntington Park, California

Robert Weaver
Snider High School
Fort Wayne, Indiana

The World Geography Team

Alison Anholt-White, Tom Barber, Jackie Bedoya, Bruce Bond, Patrick Connolly, David Graham, Mary Ann Gundersen, Joan McCulley, Luess Sampson-Lizotte, Holly Schuster, Olena Serbyn, Carol Signorino, John Springer

Reviewers

Cheli Armstrong
Hamilton Southeastern High School
Fishers, Indiana

ISBN 0-13-052955-9

2 3 4 5 6 7 8 9 10   05 04 03 02 01

TABLE of contents

Unit 1

Physical and Human Geography 30

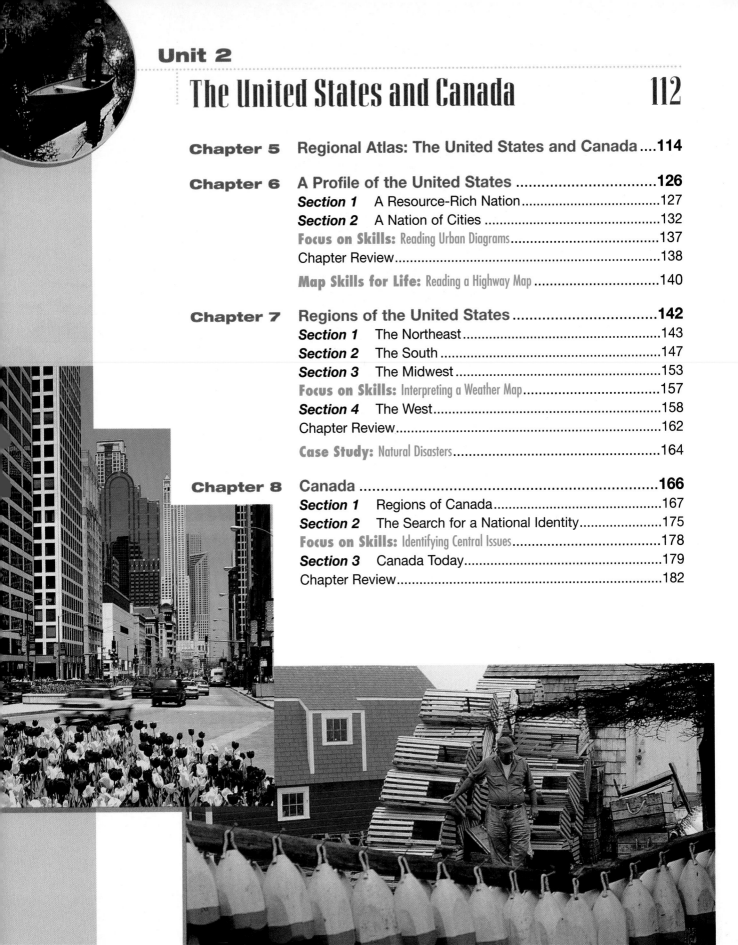

Unit 2

The United States and Canada　　112

Unit 3

Latin America   186

Unit 4

Western Europe 266

Unit 5

Eastern Europe 346

Unit 6

Northern Eurasia 384

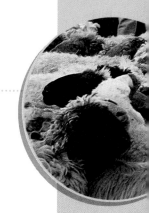

Unit 7

Southwest Asia 422

Unit 10

East Asia and the Pacific World   594

Maps

Charts, Graphs, and Diagrams

Of Special Interest

Lab work involves students in active learning

Case Study ON GLOBAL ISSUES

Helps build a global perspective

Map Skills
for Life

Real-life application of geography to students' lives

Focus on Skills

Balances instruction in three skill areas

Map and Globe

Social Studies

Critical Thinking and Problem Solving

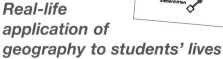

HISTORY
shapes the present

An in-depth look at the links between geography and history

A WORLD OF eXtremes

Amazing facts about the physical world

Skills
HANDBOOK

What does it mean to learn world geography? It means more than gathering the facts, names, and data about the nations and lands of the earth. It means gaining a feel for, or an appreciation of, the richness and variety of the face of our planet.

From the
National Geographic Society Archives

Few people get to travel across the whole earth, seeing all the world's sights. Yet everyone can explore the world through photographs and maps. Many of the pictures in this book are taken from the National Geographic Society's archives. These images come from every corner of the world and show the earth in all its immense variety. Photos from the archives are indicated with the label "Appeared in *National Geographic.*"

APPEARED IN *NATIONAL GEOGRAPHIC*

Munda refugee camp, Pakistan

APPEARED IN *NATIONAL GEOGRAPHIC*

APPEARED IN *NATIONAL GEOGRAPHIC*

South Dakota, United States

Stockholm, Sweden

Shanghai, China

The Andes, Colombia

Artibonite Valley, Haiti

Serengeti National Park, Tanzania

The Geographer's Craft

Geography is the study of "place and space" across the surface of the earth. Geographers ask many questions. What are different places like? How do places change over time? How do people change the world around them? To answer these questions, geographers need to collect information, analyze it, then display their findings for others.

Collecting Information

A geographer's first job is to gather information or data. They might count the number of people in a town through a **census**, a detailed counting of the population, or use data collected by computers or satellites to create **remote sensing images**. These computer-generated images reveal many different views of the earth's surface.

▼ *Scientists collect data in Antarctica.*

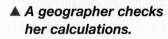

▲ *A geographer checks her calculations.*

Analyzing Information

After collecting information, geographers must analyze it. They study the information looking for patterns as well as possible causes and consequences of the information they gather.

▲ *Population density patterns are shown in this nighttime satellite photograph.*

▲ *A color-enhanced satellite image shows land use patterns.*

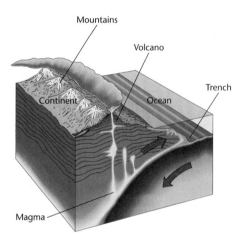

Displaying Information

All geographers want to share their findings with other people. What is the best way to do that? Geographers often use maps to show what they have learned, but diagrams, tables, and graphs are also helpful.

skills
PRACTICE

1. **Name one way that geographers collect information.**

2. **Why do geographers analyze information?**

3. **How do geographers display the information they have collected?**

Using Maps
Basic Map Components

Most maps have basic map components that help you interpret the contents of the map: a legend or key, a scale, and a directional indicator.

Compass Rose

The compass rose, or directional indicator, shows where the **cardinal directions** (north, east, south, and west) lie on the map.

Legend

The legend, or key, tells the user about the symbols used on the map. In this map the legend tells you that highways are symbolized by a red line, and railroads by a cross-hatched black line.

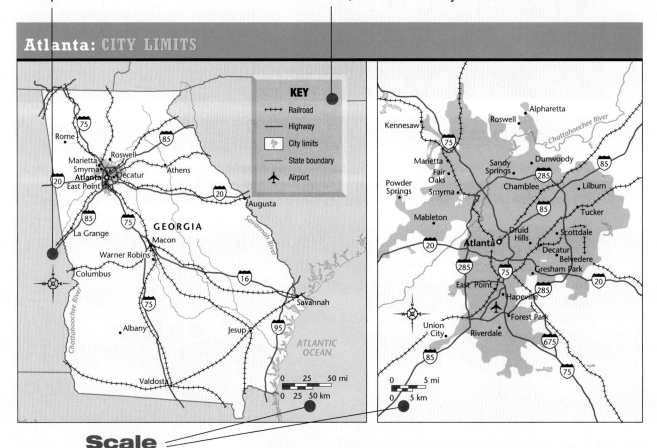

Atlanta: CITY LIMITS

KEY
- ┼┼┼ Railroad
- ── Highway
- ▭ City limits
- ── State boundary
- ✈ Airport

Scale

A scale tells the user about the size of a map in relation to the size of the real world by giving the ratio between distances on the map and actual distances on the earth. The map on the left shows the state of Georgia. The map on the right shows a more detailed view of the area surrounding Atlanta.

Global Grid

North Pole

South Pole

Parallels of Latitude

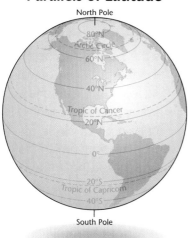

North Pole

South Pole

Meridians of Longitude

North Pole

South Pole

Latitude and Longitude

Lines of latitude and longitude are imaginary lines that form a grid covering the whole globe. This grid helps geographers find the location of places anywhere in the world.

The Grid

Lines of latitude, like the Equator, run east to west around the globe. Lines of longitude, like the Prime Meridian, run north to south, meeting at the poles. Taken together, latitude and longitude lines form a grid. Every place on earth has a unique position on this grid, like a street address in a big city.

Parallels

Lines of latitude are often called parallels because they run parallel to the Equator. Although not every line of latitude is shown on a map, every place does have a specific latitude.

Meridians

Lines of longitude, called meridians, run from pole to pole, crossing the lines of latitude. Every place is located at a specific longitude. You will learn more about using latitude and longitude to estimate distances on page 237.

skills
PRACTICE

1. *What does a map scale indicate?*

2. *What are the four cardinal directions?*

3. *In what direction do lines of longitude run?*

Displaying Information

A globe is the most accurate method of showing the entire surface of the earth. However, globes are bulky and you can't carry one in your pocket. Cartographers, or mapmakers, face a difficult problem: how do you represent the features of our round planet on a flat page? Different map projections, ways of showing the earth on a flat page, are efforts to make the best possible representation with the least distortion.

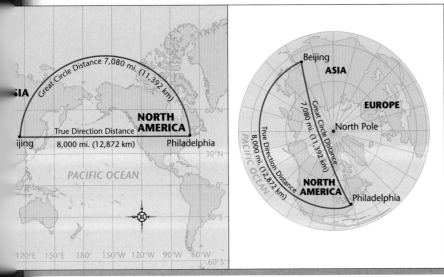

Mercator Projection

Orthographic Projection

Great Circle Route

A globe provides accurate information about distances and directions between two points. A round globe is the best tool to help you find the shortest distance between two places. If you stretched a string around the entire globe, it would make a **great circle**, or an imaginary line that circles the earth. Airplanes flying a great distance use great circle routes to save fuel and to reduce travel time.

Global Gores

With the help of mathematics, cartographers can take the information from a globe and flatten the surface of the earth. Size, shape, and distance are distorted when curves become straight lines.

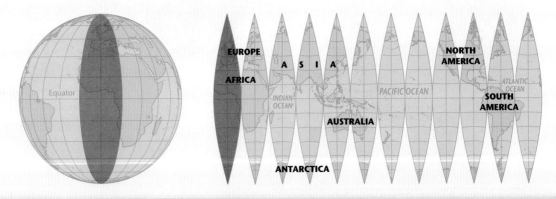

Mercator Projection

This is one of the simplest projections, but also one of the more distorted. The Mercator projection spreads the image near the poles in order to flatten the representation of the globe. This makes images near the poles appear much bigger than they really are. However, all images on a Mercator map have accurate, well-defined shapes. In short, shapes are more accurate but areas or sizes are not.

Robinson Projection

Shape and size on a map using a Robinson projection are both somewhat distorted, but not so much as on a Mercator projection map. Areas near the poles appear flatter than they really are. Land on the western and eastern edges of the map are fairly accurate in size and shape.

skills PRACTICE

1. **What is the most accurate way to display information about the earth?**

2. **Compare a straight route with a great circle route. How much shorter is the great circle route?**

3. **What is the advantage of a Robinson projection?**

Types of Maps

General purpose maps show the information that is most often used by readers. Special purpose maps relay information about specific types of data.

Physical Maps

Physical maps depict many kinds of physical features, including mountains, rivers, and lakes. Areas of water are usually colored blue. **Relief**—the changing elevation of the land—is represented either by shading or by changing colors, usually green at lower elevations and orange and brown at the higher elevations.

Political Maps

Political maps show political features. These are not natural or physical features, but rather features that are determined by people. Political features that are depicted on maps include state and national boundaries and capital cities. A capital is often represented by a star within a circle.

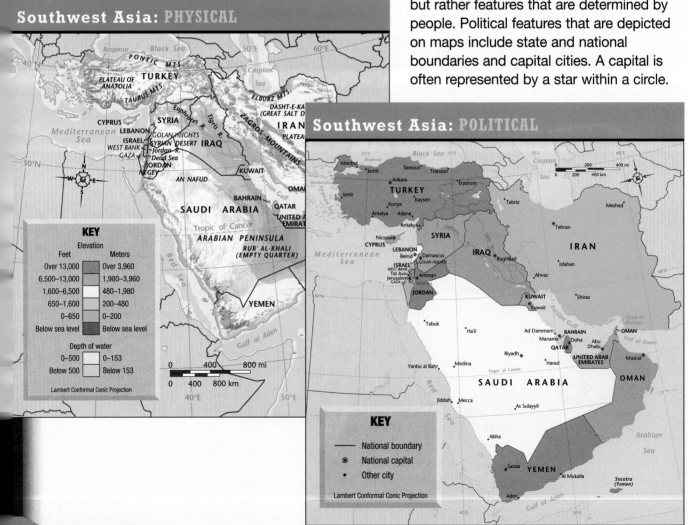

Special Purpose Maps

Some maps are designed to display very specific data or information. These are called special purpose maps. Road maps, which show the roads in a given region, are one example. There are many other kinds, including climate, vegetation, natural resources, and population density maps.

Climate Maps

Climate maps show information about general temperature and precipitation patterns in a region. This map is shaded to show seven different climate zones.

Australia: NATURAL RESOURCES AND ECONOMY

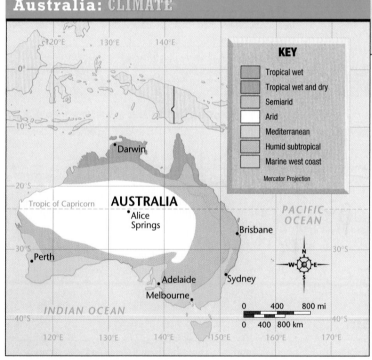

Australia: CLIMATE

Natural Resources and Economic Activity Maps

Natural resources are the materials found in the natural world that people use in various ways. Economic activity shows how people in an area make their living. These maps are marked by symbols that show where different resources and activities are located.

skills
PRACTICE

1. **How does a natural resources map show where different resources are found?**

2. **What is the climate zone found in Brisbane?**

3. **What is the difference between a natural resource and an economic activity?**

Using Charts
Graphs, Diagrams, and Tables

Graphs, diagrams, and tables are devices that organize and present information in patterns that are easy to see and read. Charts like those shown on these pages are especially helpful for making comparisons between two or more similar sets of facts.

South Asia: Major Religions

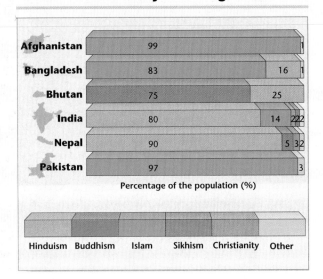

Percentage of the population (%)

Hinduism   Buddhism   Islam   Sikhism   Christianity   Other

Bar Graphs

Bar graphs are a simple way to compare information in a visual way.

Availability of Electricity in India

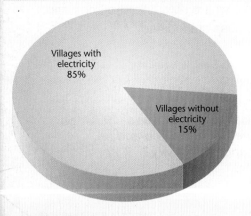

Villages with electricity 85%

Villages without electricity 15%

Line Graphs

Line graphs show the relationship between two sets of information, in this case employment and time.

Unemployment in France

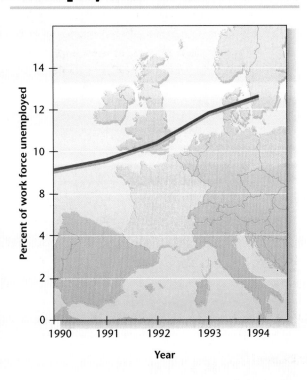

Percent of work force unemployed

Year

Circle Graphs

Circle graphs are an easy way to show the size of parts in relation to a single whole. In these graphs the whole or total is represented by a circle, which is broken into pie-shaped sections. Each section represents a part of the whole.

Cross Section: The United States

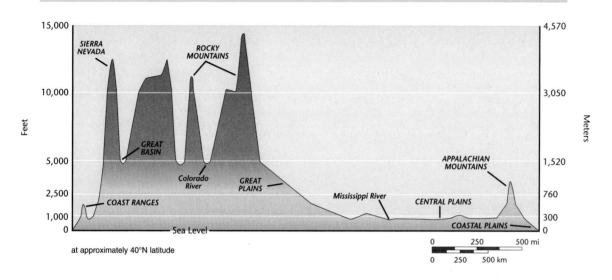

at approximately 40°N latitude

Cross-Sectional Diagrams

A cross-sectional diagram enables you to view something as if the subject has been cut and you are viewing one slice from the side. This diagram shows a cross section of the mountain ranges, basins, valleys, and plains that are located in the United States.

Country	Population	Life Expectancy (years)	Per Capita GNP (in U.S. $)
Canada	29,600,000	78	$20,670
United States	263,200,000	76	24,750

Source: Population Reference Bureau

Tables

Tables organize information into rows and columns. Tables allow the reader to find information quickly and make comparisons between similar sets of facts. This table shows facts about population, per capita GNP, and life expectancy in years.

skills PRACTICE

1. **What is one advantage of using graphs, charts, or tables to display information?**

2. **According to the circle graph, what percentage of villages in India have electricity?**

3. **Use the cross-sectional diagram to determine which large portion of the United States lies below an elevation of 1,000 feet.**

180° 160°W 140°W 120°W 100°W 80°W 60°W

80°N

60°N

ALASKA
(U.S.)

CANADA

NORTH
AMERICA

Ottawa ⊛

40°N

UNITED STATES

Washington, D.C. ⊛

Azores Islands
(Port.)

Bermuda
(U.K.)

Tropic of Cancer

See Inset Below

MEXICO

Mexico City ⊛

20°N

HAWAII
(U.S.)

CAPE
VERDE

Caracas
VENEZUELA   GUYANA
Georgetown ⊛   Paramaribo ⊛
Bogotá ⊛   SURINAME
COLOMBIA   ⊛ Cayenne
FRENCH
GUIANA
(FR.)

PACIFIC OCEAN

P O L Y N E S I A

Equator

Quito ⊛
Galápagos Is.   ECUADOR
(Ec.)

SOUTH
AMERICA

Wallis and
Futuna
(Fr.)

KIRIBATI

BRAZIL

TOKELAU (N.Z.)

PERU
Lima ⊛   La Paz ⊛   Brasília ⊛
AMERICAN
SAMOA COOK
(U.S) ISLANDS
(N.Z.)

FRENCH
POLYNESIA
(FR.)

BOLIVIA
Sucre ⊛   PARAGUAY

SAMOA

Tropic of Capricorn

Asunción ⊛

TONGA

CHILE   ARGENTINA   URUGUAY

PITCAIRN IS.
(U.K.)

Santiago ⊛   Buenos   Montevideo ⊛
Aires ⊛

International Date Line

0   1,000   2,000 mi

0   1,000   2,000 km

Falkland Is.
(U.K.)

40°S

60°S

Antarctic Circle

80°S

160°W 140°W 120°W 100°W 80°W 60°W

Central America and the Caribbean

90°W   80°W   70°W

Tropic of Cancer

Nassau ⊛   BAHAMAS

Gulf of Mexico

Havana ⊛

60°W

ATLANTIC OCEAN   20°N

20°N

CUBA

HAITI DOMINICAN
REPUBLIC   PUERTO RICO   VIRGIN ISLANDS
Port-au-Prince ⊛   (U.S.)   (U.K., U.S.)

MEXICO   BELIZE
⊛ Belmopan

Santo
Domingo

ANTIGUA AND BARBUDA

JAMAICA   Kingston   ST. KITTS   GUADELOUPE (FR.)
AND NEVIS
DOMINICA

GUATEMALA

Guatemala ⊛   HONDURAS
Tegucigalpa ⊛
San Salvador ⊛   EL SALVADOR
NICARAGUA

Caribbean Sea

MARTINIQUE (FR.)
ST. VINCENT AND   ST. LUCIA
THE GRENADINES   BARBADOS
ARUBA   GRENADA
(NETH.)   NETHERLANDS ANTILLES
(NETH.)

Managua ⊛

N
W   E
S

Port of Spain ⊛   TRINIDAD AND   10°N
TOBAGO

PACIFIC OCEAN   10°N

San José ⊛
COSTA   PANAMA
RICA   Panama ⊛

VENEZUELA

SOUTH AMERICA

0   200   400 mi

0   200   400 km

COLOMBIA   GUYANA

90°W   80°W   70°W   60°W   SURINAME

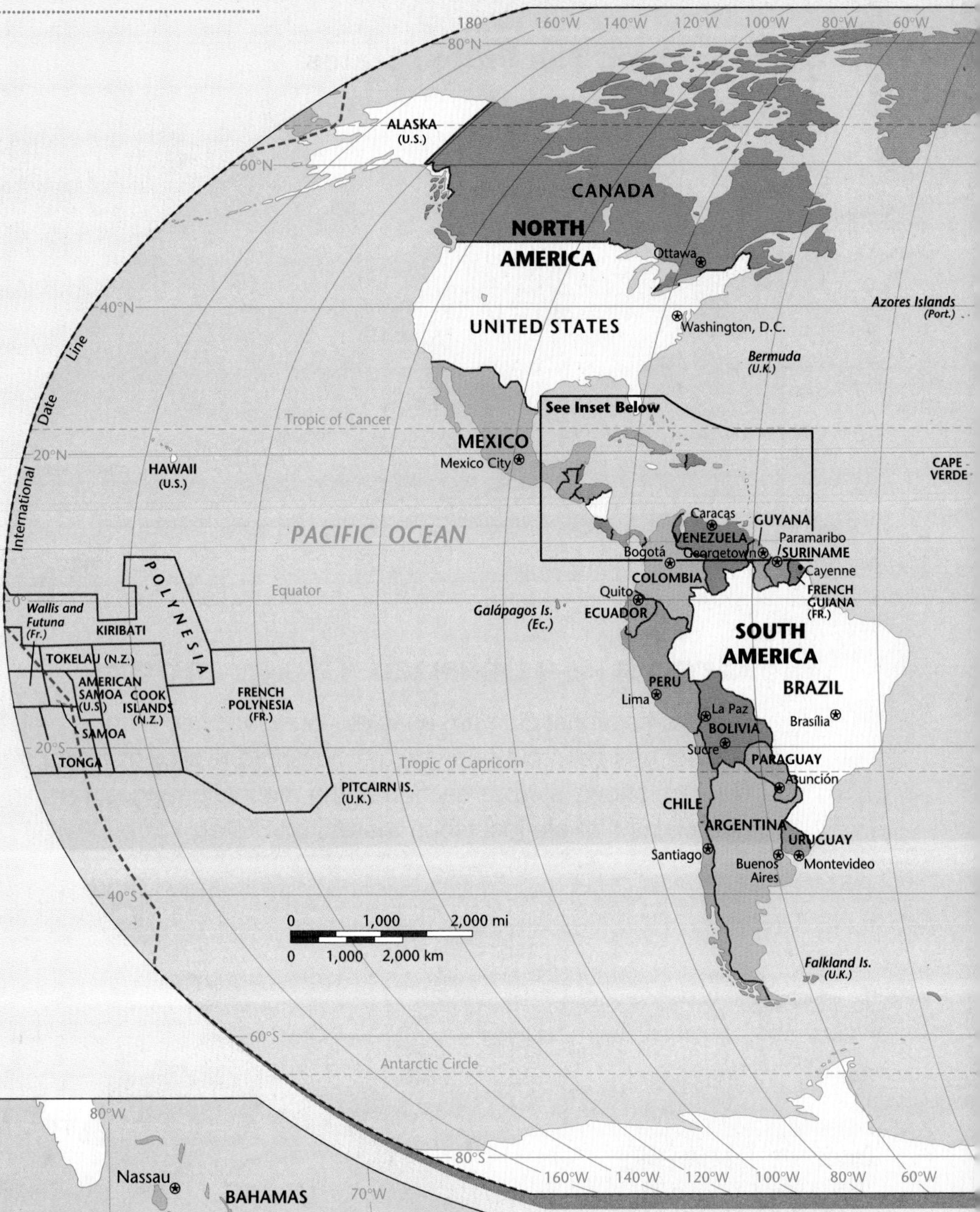

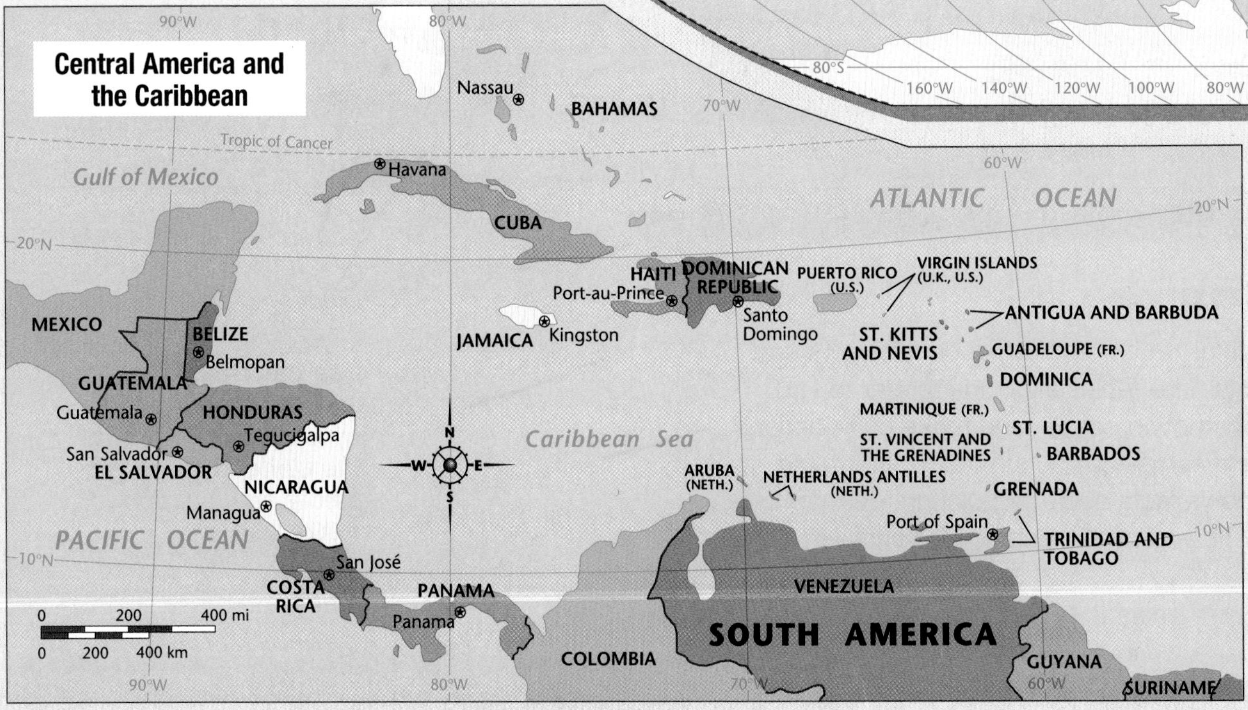

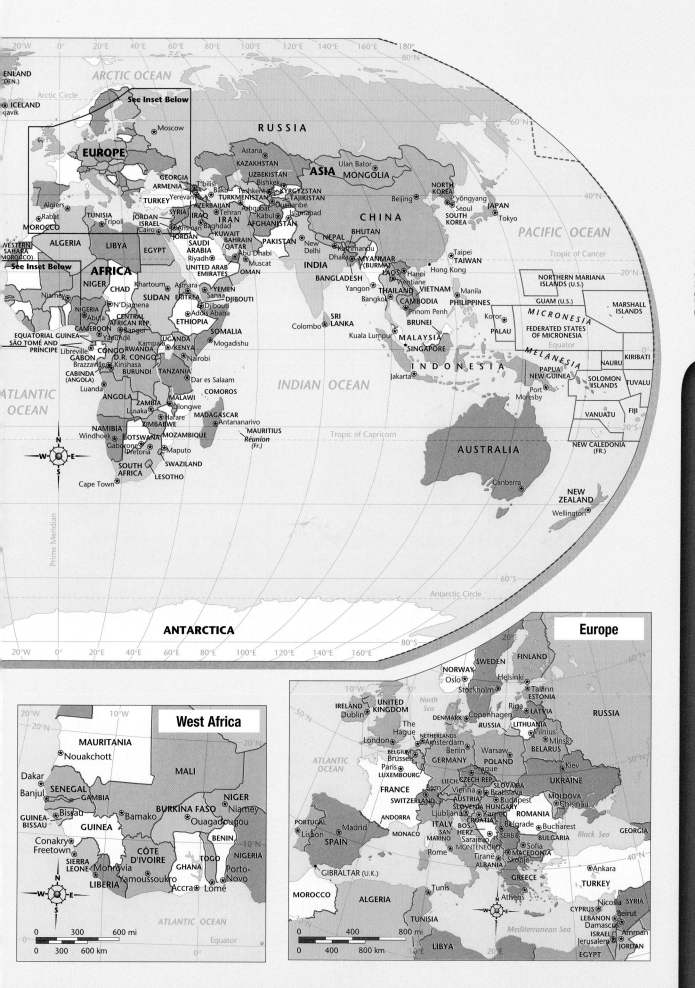

ARCTIC OCEAN

Arctic Circle

ICELAND
kjavik

See Inset Below

EUROPE

Moscow

RUSSIA

ASIA

Astana
KAZAKHSTAN

UZBEKISTAN
Bishkek

Ulan Bator

MONGOLIA

GEORGIA
ARMENIA
T'bilisi
Baku
Tashkent
KYRGYZSTAN
TAJIKISTAN
TURKMENISTAN
Yerevan
Ashgabat
Dushanbe
AZERBAIJAN
Islamabad
Kabul

Beijing

NORTH
KOREA
P'yŏngyang
Seoul

JAPAN

SOUTH
KOREA

Tokyo

PACIFIC OCEAN

Algiers
Rabat
TUNISIA
Tripoli

TURKEY

JORDAN
ISRAEL
Cairo

SYRIA
IRAQ
Amman
Baghdad
KUWAIT

IRAN

Tehran

AFGHANISTAN

PAKISTAN

CHINA

New
Delhi
NEPAL
Kathmandu
BHUTAN

TAIWAN

Taipei

Tropic of Cancer

MOROCCO

JORDAN

SAUDI
ARABIA
Riyadh
BAHRAIN
QATAR

UNITED ARAB
EMIRATES
Muscat

Abu Dhabi

OMAN

Dhaka
INDIA

BANGLADESH

MYANMAR
(BURMA)

Hong Kong

NORTHERN MARIANA
ISLANDS (U.S.)

WESTERN
SAHARA
(MOROCCO)

EGYPT

Hanoi
LAOS
Vientiane

GUAM (U.S.)

See Inset Below

AFRICA

NIGER
CHAD

Khartoum
Asmara
YEMEN
Sanaa

Yangon
THAILAND

VIETNAM

Manila

MARSHALL
ISLANDS

MICRONESIA

Niamey

NIGERIA
Abuja

N'Djamena

CENTRAL
AFRICAN REP.

SUDAN

ERITREA

DJIBOUTI
Djibouti

Addis Ababa

ETHIOPIA

SOMALIA

Bangkok
CAMBODIA
Phnom Penh

BRUNEI

PHILIPPINES

Koror
PALAU

FEDERATED STATES
OF MICRONESIA

KIRIBATI

NAURU

EQUATORIAL GUINEA
SÃO TOMÉ AND
PRÍNCIPE

CAMEROON
Yaoundé

UGANDA
Kampala
KENYA

Colombo
SRI
LANKA

MALAYSIA
Kuala Lumpur
SINGAPORE

Equator

MELANESIA

Libreville
GABON
CONGO
Brazzaville
Kinshasa
D.R. CONGO

RWANDA
BURUNDI

Nairobi

INDONESIA

PAPUA
NEW GUINEA

SOLOMON
ISLANDS

TUVALU

CABINDA
(ANGOLA)
Luanda

TANZANIA
Dar es Salaam

Jakarta

Port
Moresby

ANGOLA

ZAMBIA
Lusaka

MALAWI
Lilongwe

COMOROS

INDIAN OCEAN

VANUATU

FIJI

NAMIBIA
Windhoek

ZIMBABWE
Harare

MADAGASCAR
Antananarivo

MAURITIUS
Réunion
(Fr.)

Tropic of Capricorn

NEW CALEDONIA
(FR.)

BOTSWANA
Gaborone
Pretoria

MOZAMBIQUE
Maputo

AUSTRALIA

**ATLANTIC
OCEAN**

SOUTH
AFRICA
SWAZILAND
LESOTHO

Cape Town

Canberra

N
W   E
S

NEW
ZEALAND

Wellington

60°S

Antarctic Circle

ANTARCTICA

80°S

Europe

SWEDEN
FINLAND

NORWAY
Oslo
Helsinki
Stockholm

Talinn
ESTONIA

RUSSIA

IRELAND
Dublin
UNITED
KINGDOM
North
Sea
DENMARK
Copenhagen
Riga
LATVIA

LITHUANIA
Vilnius
Minsk

The
Hague
London
NETHERLANDS
Amsterdam
Berlin
RUSSIA

BELARUS

ATLANTIC
OCEAN

BELGIUM
Brussels
Paris
LUXEMBOURG
GERMANY
Warsaw
POLAND
Prague
Kiev

UKRAINE

FRANCE
Bern
LIECH.
SWITZERLAND
CZECH REP.
Vienna
AUSTRIA
SLOVAKIA
Bratislava
Budapest
HUNGARY
MOLDOVA
Chişinău

PORTUGAL
Lisbon
Madrid
ANDORRA
MONACO
SLOVENIA
Ljubljana
ITALY
CROATIA
Zagreb
ROMANIA
Belgrade
Bucharest
GEORGIA

SAN
MARINO
BOS.
HERZ.
Sarajevo
SERBIA
Black Sea

SPAIN
Rome
MONTENEGRO
MACEDONIA
Skopje
BULGARIA
Sofia

Ankara

GIBRALTAR (U.K.)
Tirané
ALBANIA

MOROCCO
ALGERIA
Tunis
GREECE
TURKEY

CYPRUS
Nicosia
SYRIA
LEBANON
Beirut
Damascus

Athens

TUNISIA

Mediterranean Sea

ISRAEL
Jerusalem
JORDAN
Amman

LIBYA
EGYPT

0   400   800 mi
0   400   800 km

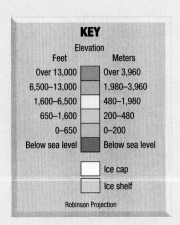

KEY

Elevation

Feet	Meters
Over 13,000	Over 3,960
6,500–13,000	1,980–3,960
1,600–6,500	480–1,980
650–1,600	200–480
0–650	0–200
Below sea level	Below sea level

Ice cap

Ice shelf

Robinson Projection

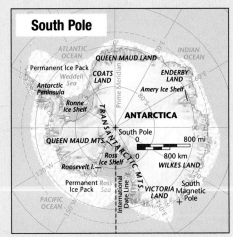

South Pole

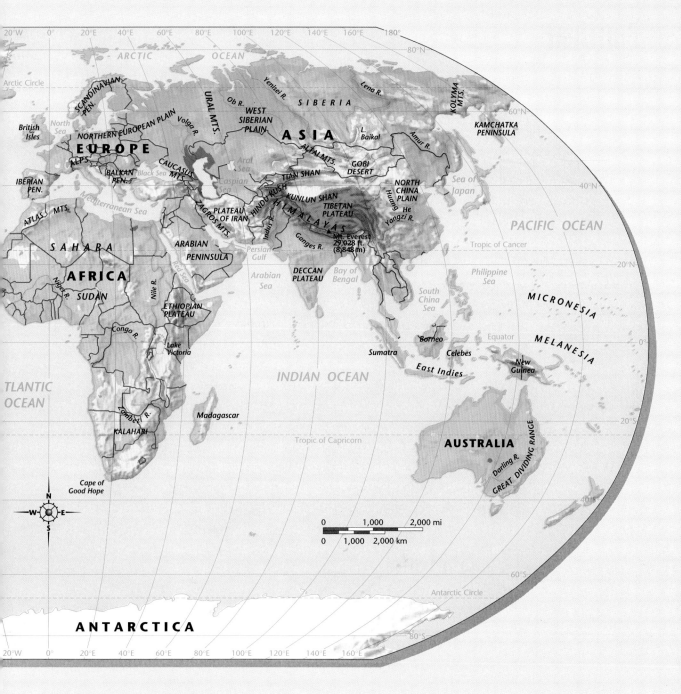

ARCTIC OCEAN

20°W 0° 20°E 40°E 60°E 80°E 100°E 120°E 140°E 160°E 180°

80°N

Arctic Circle

SCANDINAVIAN PEN.

British Isles

North Sea

NORTHERN EUROPEAN PLAIN

URAL MTS.

Ob R.

WEST SIBERIAN PLAIN

Yenisei R.

SIBERIA

Lena R.

60°N

KOLYMA MTS.

KAMCHATKA PENINSULA

EUROPE

ALPS

Volga R.

ASIA

L. Baikal

ALTAI MTS.

Amur R.

CAUCASUS MTS.

BALKAN PEN.

Black Sea

Aral Sea

TIAN SHAN

GOBI DESERT

Sea of Japan

40°N

IBERIAN PEN.

Caspian Sea

HINDU KUSH

KUNLUN SHAN

NORTH CHINA PLAIN

ATLAS MTS.

Mediterranean Sea

ZAGROS MTS.

PLATEAU OF IRAN

TIBETAN PLATEAU

H I M A L A Y A S

Huang He

PACIFIC OCEAN

Indus R.

Yangzi R.

SAHARA

ARABIAN PENINSULA

Persian Gulf

Ganges R.

Mt. Everest 29,028 ft. (8,848 m)

Tropic of Cancer

20°N

AFRICA

Niger R.

SUDAN

Nile R.

Red Sea

Arabian Sea

DECCAN PLATEAU

Bay of Bengal

Philippine Sea

South China Sea

MICRONESIA

ETHIOPIAN PLATEAU

Congo R.

Lake Victoria

INDIAN OCEAN

Borneo

Sumatra

Celebes

East Indies

Equator

MELANESIA

New Guinea

0°

ATLANTIC OCEAN

Zambezi R.

Madagascar

20°S

KALAHARI

Tropic of Capricorn

AUSTRALIA

Darling R.

GREAT DIVIDING RANGE

Cape of Good Hope

N
W E
S

0   1,000   2,000 mi
0   1,000   2,000 km

60°S

Antarctic Circle

80°S

A N T A R C T I C A

20°W 0° 20°E 40°E 60°E 80°E 100°E 120°E 140°E 160°E

Atlas

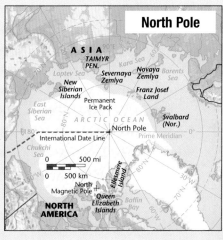

North Pole

ASIA

TAIMYR PEN.

Laptev Sea

Kara Sea

New Siberian Islands

Severnaya Zemlya

Novaya Zemlya

Barents Sea

East Siberian Sea

Permanent Ice Pack

Franz Josef Land

ARCTIC OCEAN

Svalbard (Nor.)

North Pole

International Date Line

Prime Meridian

Chukchi Sea

0   500 mi
0   500 km

North Magnetic Pole

Ellesmere Island

Queen Elizabeth Islands

Baffin Bay

NORTH AMERICA

15

United States
Political

CANADA

Lake Superior

Duluth

Sault Ste. Marie

MINNESOTA

MICHIGAN

Lake Huron

Lake Michigan

Minneapolis • St. Paul

WISCONSIN

Lansing

Milwaukee

Madison

Detroit

Lake Erie

Lake Ontario

Buffalo

Presque Isle

MAINE

Augusta

Portland

Montpelier

VERMONT

NEW HAMPSHIRE

Concord

NEW YORK

Boston

MASSACHUSETTS

Albany

Hartford

Providence

RHODE ISLAND

New Haven

CONNECTICUT

Chicago

IOWA

Cedar Rapids

Des Moines

ILLINOIS

Springfield

St. Louis

INDIANA

Indianapolis

OHIO

Columbus

Cincinnati

PENNSYLVANIA

Cleveland

Harrisburg

Pittsburgh

New York City

Trenton

NEW JERSEY

Philadelphia

Baltimore

Dover

DELAWARE

Annapolis

Washington, D.C.

MARYLAND

Omaha

Lincoln

Topeka

NSAS

Wichita

Kansas City

Jefferson City

MISSOURI

Frankfort

Louisville

KENTUCKY

WEST VIRGINIA

Charleston

VIRGINIA

Richmond

Norfolk

Raleigh

NORTH CAROLINA

Ohio River

Tennessee River

Mississippi River

Missouri River

LAHOMA

Tulsa

Oklahoma City

ARKANSAS

Little Rock

Pine Bluff

Nashville

TENNESSEE

Memphis

Charlotte

Columbia

SOUTH CAROLINA

Charleston

Atlanta

GEORGIA

Columbus

Savannah

ATLANTIC OCEAN

Red River

Dallas

Shreveport

MISSISSIPPI

Jackson

ALABAMA

Montgomery

Birmingham

Hattiesburg

KAS

Austin

San Antonio

Houston

Baton Rouge

LOUISIANA

New Orleans

Tallahassee

Jacksonville

FLORIDA

Tampa

Lake Okeechobee

Miami

Gulf of Mexico

0 150 300 mi
0 150 300 km

90°W

80°W

70°W

40°N

30°N

90°W

80°W

North and South America

Political

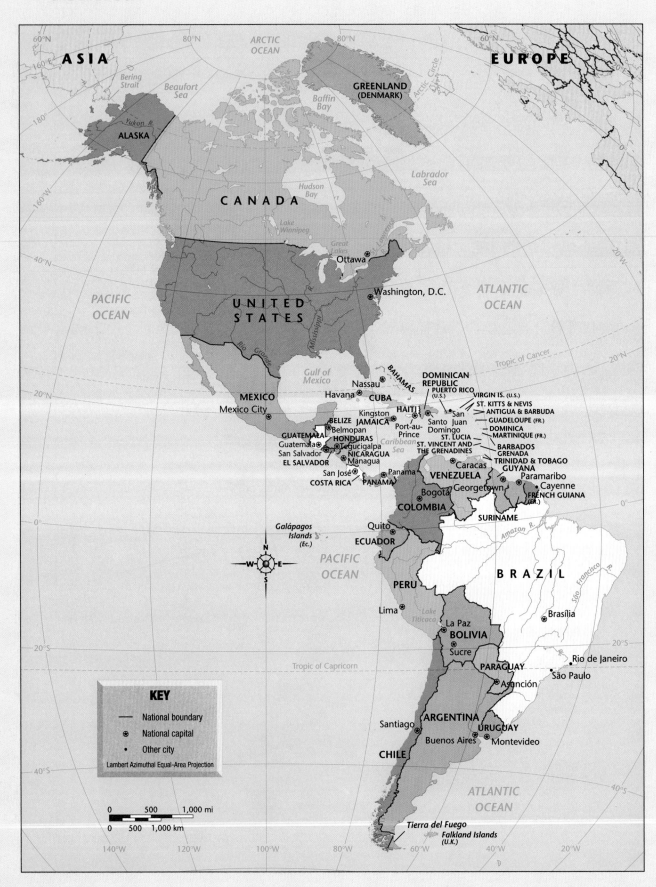

KEY

— National boundary

⊛ National capital

• Other city

Lambert Azimuthal Equal-Area Projection

0   500   1,000 mi

0   500 1,000 km

ASIA

ARCTIC OCEAN

EUROPE

Bering Strait

Beaufort Sea

Baffin Bay

Yukon R.

Mackenzie R.

Labrador Sea

Hudson Bay

CANADIAN SHIELD

Lake Winnipeg

Great Lakes

St. Lawrence R.

ROCKY MOUNTAINS

GREAT PLAINS

CASCADES

Great Salt Lake

SIERRA NEVADA

Missouri R.

Colorado R.

Ohio R.

Mississippi R.

APPALACHIAN MTS.

PACIFIC OCEAN

ATLANTIC OCEAN

BAJA CALIFORNIA

SIERRA MADRE OCCIDENTAL

SIERRA MADRE ORIENTAL

Rio Grande

Gulf of Mexico

Tropic of Cancer

YUCATÁN PENINSULA

Hispaniola

Caribbean Sea

ISTHMUS OF PANAMA

Orinoco R.

Amazon R.

AMAZON BASIN

PACIFIC OCEAN

ANDES MOUNTAINS

Lake Titicaca

ATACAMA DESERT

São Francisco R.

BRAZILIAN HIGHLANDS

Paraguay R.

Paraná R.

Tropic of Capricorn

PAMPAS

PATAGONIA

ATLANTIC OCEAN

Tierra del Fuego

KEY

Elevation

Feet	Meters
Over 13,000	Over 3,960
6,500–13,000	1,980–3,960
1,600–6,500	480–1,980
650–1,600	200–480
0–650	0–200
	Ice cap

Lambert Azimuthal Equal-Area Projection

0   500   1,000 mi

0   500   1,000 km

N W E S

Atlas

KEY
— National boundary
⊛ National capital
• Other city

Lambert Azimuthal Equal-Area Projection

Physical

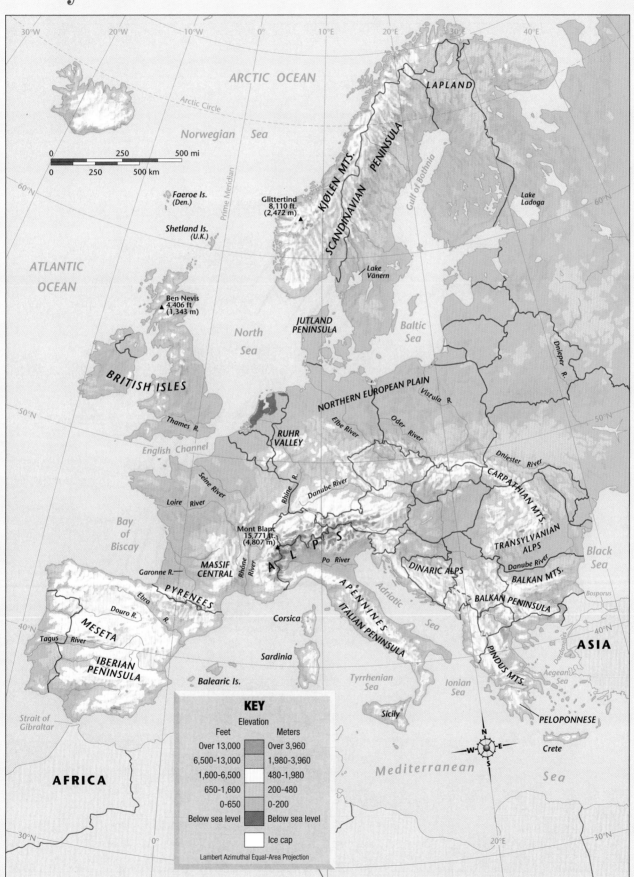

ARCTIC OCEAN

Arctic Circle

Norwegian Sea

LAPLAND

KJØLEN MTS.

SCANDINAVIAN PENINSULA

Gulf of Bothnia

Lake Ladoga

Faeroe Is. (Den.)

Glittertind 8,110 ft. (2,472 m)

Shetland Is. (U.K.)

ATLANTIC OCEAN

Prime Meridian

Lake Vänern

Ben Nevis 4,406 ft (1,343 m)

JUTLAND PENINSULA

Baltic Sea

North Sea

Dnieper R.

BRITISH ISLES

NORTHERN EUROPEAN PLAIN

Vistula R.

Thames R.

Elbe River

Oder River

English Channel

RUHR VALLEY

Dniester River

CARPATHIAN MTS.

Seine River

Rhine R.

Danube River

Loire River

Bay of Biscay

Mont Blanc 15,771 ft. (4,807 m)

A L P S

Po River

TRANSYLVANIAN ALPS

Rhône River

Danube River

MASSIF CENTRAL

Garonne R.

DINARIC ALPS

BALKAN MTS.

Black Sea

PYRENEES

BALKAN PENINSULA

Ebro R.

Douro R.

Adriatic Sea

Bosporus

MESETA

A P E N N I N E S

Corsica

ITALIAN PENINSULA

PINDUS MTS.

Tagus River

IBERIAN PENINSULA

Sardinia

Tyrrhenian Sea

Ionian Sea

Aegean Sea

Dodecanese

ASIA

Balearic Is.

PELOPONNESE

Sicily

Strait of Gibraltar

N W E S

Crete

AFRICA

Mediterranean Sea

KEY

Elevation

Feet		Meters
Over 13,000		Over 3,960
6,500–13,000		1,980–3,960
1,600–6,500		480–1,980
650–1,600		200–480
0–650		0–200
Below sea level		Below sea level
	Ice cap	

Lambert Azimuthal Equal-Area Projection

0 250 500 mi
0 250 500 km

30°W 20°W 10°W 0° 10°E 20°E 30°E 40°E

60°N 50°N 40°N 30°N

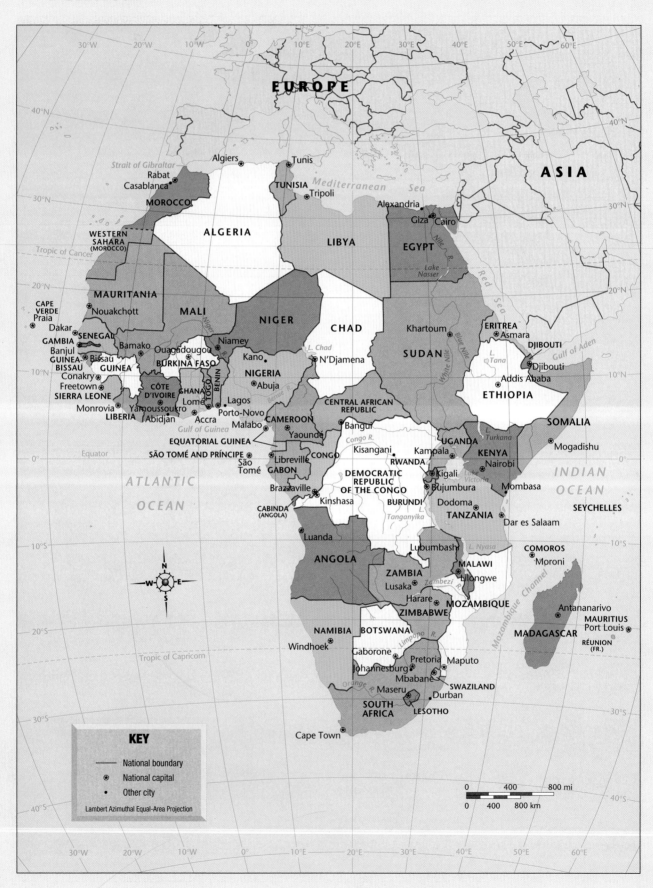

KEY

— National boundary

⊛ National capital

• Other city

Lambert Azimuthal Equal-Area Projection

0   400   800 mi

0   400   800 km

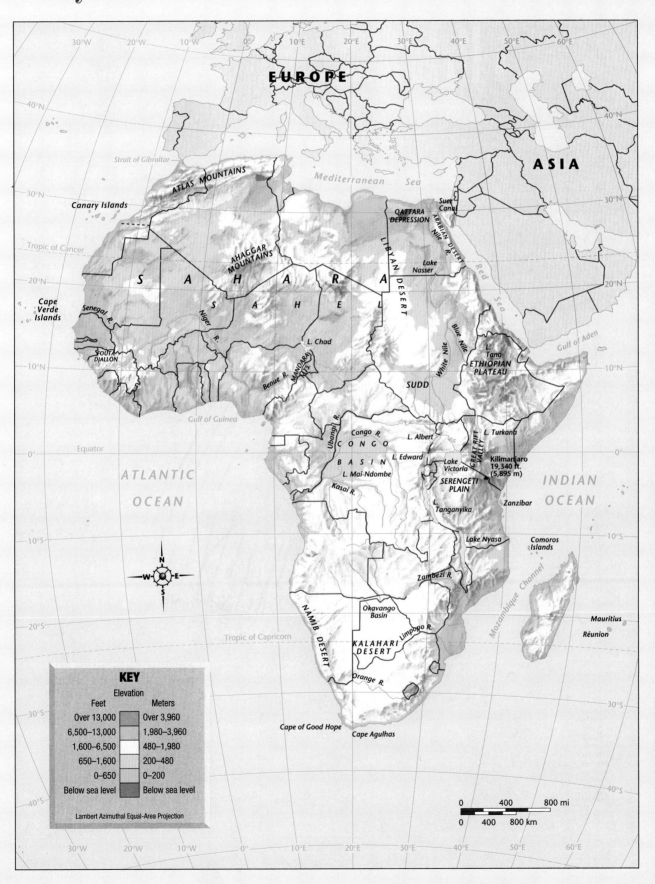

EUROPE

ASIA

Strait of Gibraltar

Mediterranean Sea

Canary Islands

ATLAS MOUNTAINS

QATTARA DEPRESSION

Suez Canal

Tropic of Cancer

AHAGGAR MOUNTAINS

LIBYAN DESERT

ARABIAN DESERT

Lake Nasser

Nile R.

Red Sea

S A H A R A

Cape Verde Islands

Senegal R.

S A H E L

Niger R.

FOUTA DJALLON

L. Chad

White Nile

Blue Nile

Gulf of Aden

L. Tana

ETHIOPIAN PLATEAU

Benue R.

MANDARA MTS.

SUDD

Gulf of Guinea

Ubangi R.

Congo R.

C O N G O

L. Albert

L. Turkana

GREAT RIFT VALLEY

Kilimanjaro
19,340 ft.
(5,895 m)

Equator

B A S I N

L. Edward

Lake Victoria

SERENGETI PLAIN

L. Mai-Ndombe

ATLANTIC OCEAN

Kasai R.

INDIAN OCEAN

L. Tanganyika

Zanzibar

Lake Nyasa

Comoros Islands

Zambezi R.

Mozambique Channel

Mauritius

Réunion

Okavango Basin

Limpopo R.

Tropic of Capricorn

NAMIB DESERT

KALAHARI DESERT

Orange R.

Cape of Good Hope

Cape Agulhas

KEY

Elevation

Feet	Meters
Over 13,000	Over 3,960
6,500–13,000	1,980–3,960
1,600–6,500	480–1,980
650–1,600	200–480
0–650	0–200
Below sea level	Below sea level

Lambert Azimuthal Equal-Area Projection

0	400	800 mi

0	400	800 km

KEY
National boundary
National capital
Other city
Two-Point Equidistant Projection

170°W
180°
170°E
160°E
150°E
140°E
130°E
120°E
110°E
100°E
90°E
80°E
70°E
60°E
50°E
40°E

70°N
60°N
50°N
40°N
30°N
20°N
10°N

PACIFIC OCEAN

Port Moresby
PAPUA NEW GUINEA
New Guinea

PALAU
Koror

Bandar Seri Begawan
BRUNEI
Celebes
Borneo
INDONESIA
Tanimbar
Timor
Java Sea
Java
Jakarta
Sumatra

MALAYSIA
Kuala Lumpur
SINGAPORE
Singapore

PHILIPPINES
Manila

Philippine Sea

Ryukyu Islands
East China Sea
Taipei
TAIWAN
Hong Kong
Macau
Fuzhou

South China Sea

VIETNAM
Hanoi
LAOS
Vientiane
THAILAND
Bangkok
CAMBODIA
Phnom Penh

MYANMAR (BURMA)
Yangon

Bay of Bengal

Tropic of Cancer

Kuril Islands (Russia)
Sakhalin Island
Sea of Japan
Vladivostok
JAPAN
Tokyo
N. KOREA
P'yŏngyang
S. KOREA
Seoul
Yellow Sea
Beijing
Harbin

Sea of Okhotsk

CHINA
Xi'an
Huang He
Yangtze R.

MONGOLIA
Ulan Bator

Lake Baikal
Irkutsk
Bratsk

Verkhoyansk

East Siberian Sea

RUSSIA

Lena R.
Ob R.
Yenisei R.
Irtysh R.

North Pole
ARCTIC OCEAN

Barents Sea

Arctic Circle

St. Petersburg
Moscow
Samara
Volga
Yekaterinburg
Omsk
Astana
KAZAKHSTAN
Qaraghandy
Aral Sea
Lake Balkhash
UZBEKISTAN
Tashkent
Almaty
Bishkek
KYRGYZSTAN
TAJIKISTAN
Dushanbe
TURKMENISTAN
Ashkhabad
Caspian Sea
Baku
AZERBAIJAN
GEORGIA
T'bilisi
ARMENIA
Yerevan
Tehran
IRAN
Shiraz

AFGHANISTAN
Kabul
Islamabad
PAKISTAN

NEPAL
Kathmandu
New Delhi
BHUTAN
Thimphu
BANGLADESH
Dhaka
Ganges R.
INDIA

Mumbai (Bombay)
Madras

Arabian Sea

SRI LANKA
Colombo
Male
MALDIVES

INDIAN OCEAN

EUROPE
(RUSSIA)

Black Sea
TURKEY
Ankara
CYPRUS
Nicosia
LEBANON
Beirut
SYRIA
Damascus
Amman
JORDAN
ISRAEL
Jerusalem
IRAQ
Baghdad
KUWAIT
Kuwait
BAHRAIN
QATAR
UNITED ARAB EMIRATES
Abu Dhabi
Persian Gulf
Gulf of Oman
Muscat
OMAN
Socotra (Yemen)

SAUDI ARABIA
Riyadh
YEMEN
Sanaa
Mecca
Red Sea
Gulf of Aden

Mediterranean Sea

AFRICA

Tropic of Cancer
Equator

N
W E
S

1,000 mi
0 500 1,000 km
0 500

Asia
Physical

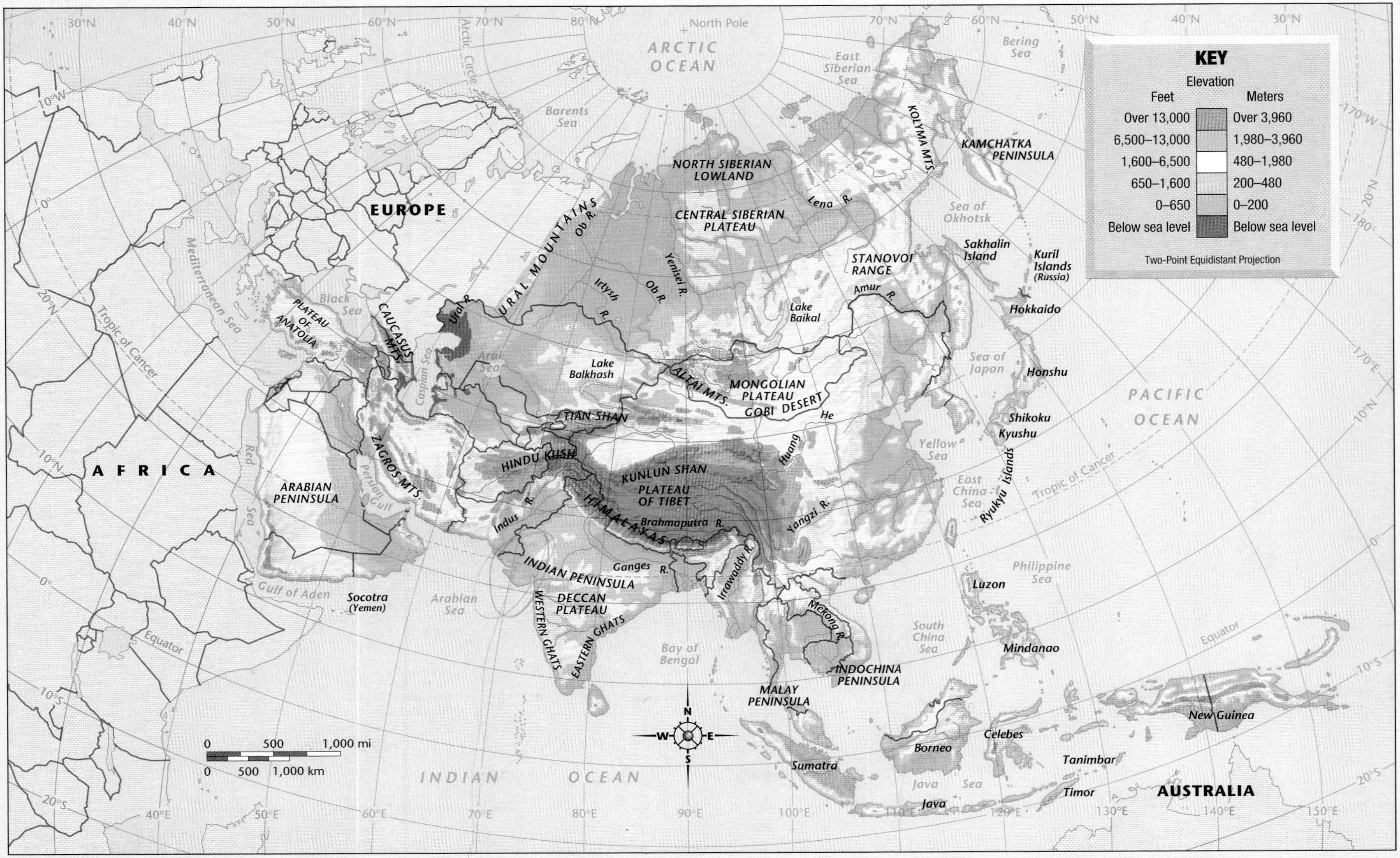

KEY

Elevation

Feet	Meters
Over 13,000	Over 3,960
6,500–13,000	1,980–3,960
1,600–6,500	480–1,980
650–1,600	200–480
0–650	0–200
Below sea level	Below sea level

Two-Point Equidistant Projection

ARCTIC OCEAN

North Pole

Barents Sea

East Siberian Sea

Bering Sea

KOLYMA MTS.

KAMCHATKA PENINSULA

Sea of Okhotsk

Sakhalin Island

Kuril Islands (Russia)

Hokkaido

Honshu

Shikoku

Kyushu

Sea of Japan

Ryukyu Islands

Yellow Sea

East China Sea

PACIFIC OCEAN

Tropic of Cancer

Philippine Sea

Luzon

Mindanao

Celebes

Borneo

Java Sea

Java

Sumatra

MALAY PENINSULA

South China Sea

INDOCHINA PENINSULA

Mekong R.

Bay of Bengal

Tanimbar

Timor

New Guinea

AUSTRALIA

Equator

STANOVOI RANGE

Amur R.

Lena R.

Lake Baikal

He

Huang

Yangtzi R.

MONGOLIAN PLATEAU GOBI DESERT

ALTAI MTS.

NORTH SIBERIAN LOWLAND

CENTRAL SIBERIAN PLATEAU

Yenisei R.

Ob R.

Irtysh R.

Lake Balkhash

TIAN SHAN

KUNLUN SHAN

PLATEAU OF TIBET

HIMALAYAS

HINDU KUSH

Brahmaputra R.

Ganges R.

Indus R.

INDIAN PENINSULA

DECCAN PLATEAU

EASTERN GHATS

WESTERN GHATS

Irrawaddy R.

URAL MOUNTAINS

Ob R.

Aral Sea

Caspian Sea

CAUCASUS MTS.

ZAGROS MTS.

Persian Gulf

Socotra (Yemen)

ARABIAN PENINSULA

Gulf of Aden

Arabian Sea

INDIAN OCEAN

EUROPE

Black Sea

PLATEAU OF ANATOLIA

Mediterranean Sea

Red Sea

Tropic of Cancer

AFRICA

Equator

Arctic Circle

N W E S

0 500 1,000 mi
0 500 1,000 km

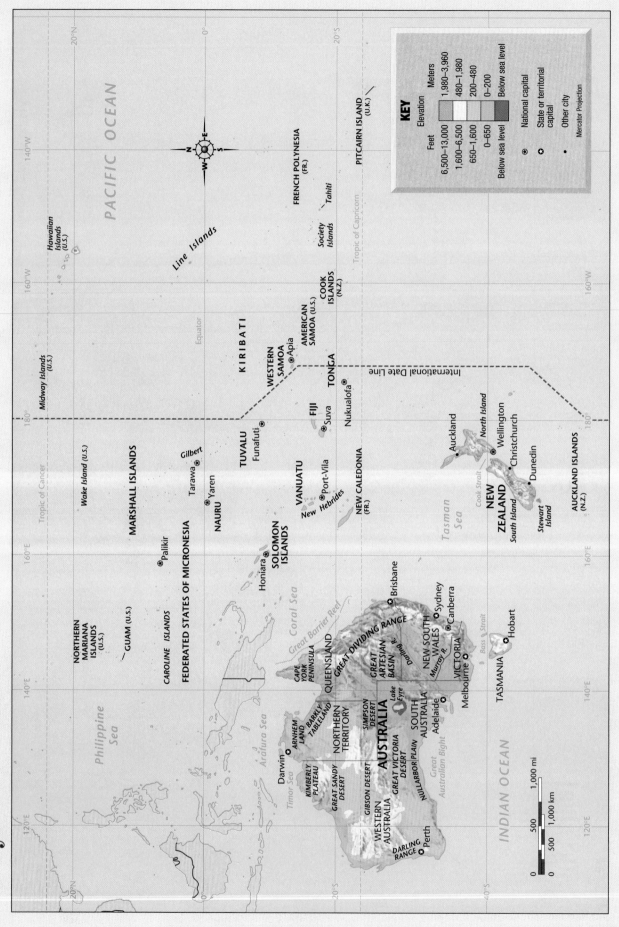

KEY

Elevation

Feet	Meters
6,500–13,000	1,980–3,960
1,600–6,500	480–1,980
650–1,600	200–480
0–650	0–200
Below sea level	Below sea level

⊛ National capital

⊛ State or territorial capital

• Other city

Mercator Projection

PACIFIC OCEAN

Midway Islands (U.S.)

Hawaiian Islands (U.S.)

Line Islands

FRENCH POLYNESIA (FR.)

Society Islands

Tahiti

PITCAIRN ISLAND (U.K.)

Tropic of Capricorn

KIRIBATI

COOK ISLANDS (N.Z.)

AMERICAN SAMOA (U.S.)

WESTERN SAMOA

Apia

TONGA

Nukualofa

Equator

Tropic of Cancer

Wake Island (U.S.)

MARSHALL ISLANDS

Gilbert

Tarawa

NAURU

Yaren

TUVALU

Funafuti

FIJI

Suva

VANUATU

Port-Vila

New Hebrides

NEW CALEDONIA (FR.)

International Date Line

North Island

Auckland

Wellington

Christchurch

NEW ZEALAND

South Island

Dunedin

Stewart Island

AUCKLAND ISLANDS (N.Z.)

Cook Strait

Tasman Sea

NORTHERN MARIANA ISLANDS (U.S.)

GUAM (U.S.)

CAROLINE ISLANDS

FEDERATED STATES OF MICRONESIA

Palikir

SOLOMON ISLANDS

Honiara

Coral Sea

Great Barrier Reef

Philippine Sea

Arafura Sea

Timor Sea

CAPE YORK PENINSULA

QUEENSLAND

Brisbane

GREAT DIVIDING RANGE

GREAT ARTESIAN BASIN

Darling R.

NEW SOUTH WALES

Sydney

Canberra

Murray R.

VICTORIA

Melbourne

Bass Strait

TASMANIA

Hobart

Darwin

ARNHEM LAND

BARKLY TABLELAND

NORTHERN TERRITORY

SIMPSON DESERT

Lake Eyre

SOUTH AUSTRALIA

Adelaide

AUSTRALIA

KIMBERLEY PLATEAU

GREAT SANDY DESERT

GIBSON DESERT

GREAT VICTORIA DESERT

NULLARBOR PLAIN

Great Australian Bight

WESTERN AUSTRALIA

DARLING RANGE

Perth

INDIAN OCEAN

1,000 mi

1,000 km

500

500

0

0

The Arctic

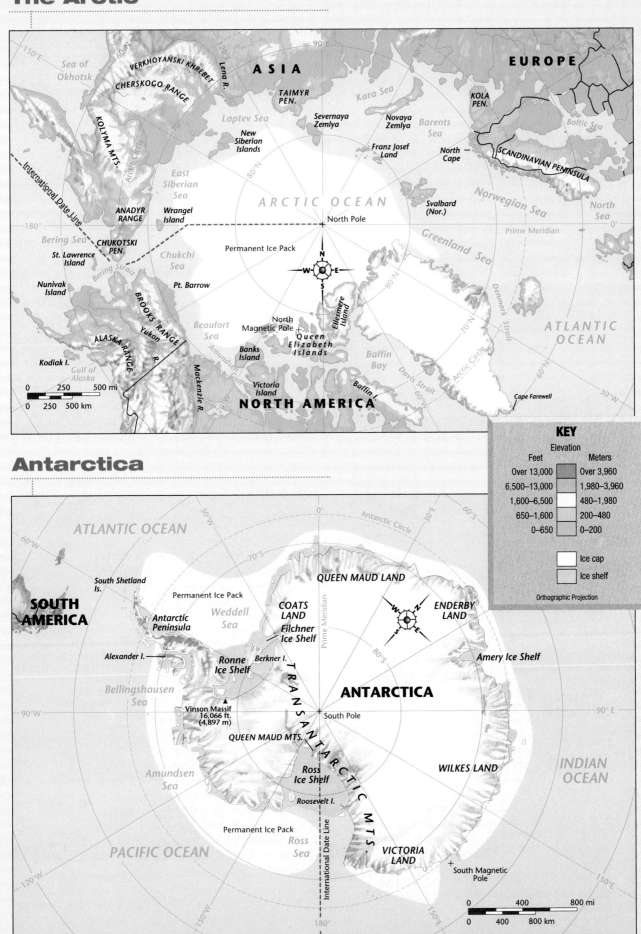

Sea of Okhotsk

VERKHOYANSKI KHREBET

CHERSKOGO RANGE

Lena R.

ASIA

EUROPE

KOLYMA MTS.

Arctic Circle

Laptev Sea

TAIMYR PEN.

Severnaya Zemlya

Kara Sea

Novaya Zemlya

KOLA PEN.

Baltic Sea

New Siberian Islands

Franz Josef Land

Barents Sea

North Cape

SCANDINAVIAN PENINSULA

East Siberian Sea

ANADYR RANGE

Wrangel Island

ARCTIC OCEAN

80°N

Svalbard (Nor.)

Norwegian Sea

North Sea

International Date Line

180°

Bering Sea

CHUKOTSKI PEN.

North Pole

Prime Meridian

Greenland Sea

ATLANTIC OCEAN

St. Lawrence Island

Chukchi Sea

Permanent Ice Pack

Nunivak Island

Pt. Barrow

70°N

Denmark Strait

BROOKS RANGE

Yukon R.

Beaufort Sea

North Magnetic Pole

Ellesmere Island

ALASKA RANGE

Banks Island

Queen Elizabeth Islands

Baffin Bay

Arctic Circle

Kodiak I.

Gulf of Alaska

Amundsen Gulf

Mackenzie R.

Victoria Island

Baffin I.

Davis Strait

60°N

Cape Farewell

30°W

NORTH AMERICA

0   250   500 mi
0   250   500 km

Antarctica

ATLANTIC OCEAN

Antarctic Circle

60°S

30°W

0°

30°E

60°S

70°S

South Shetland Is.

Permanent Ice Pack

QUEEN MAUD LAND

ENDERBY LAND

SOUTH AMERICA

Antarctic Peninsula

Weddell Sea

COATS LAND

Filchner Ice Shelf

Prime Meridian

Alexander I.

Ronne Ice Shelf

Berkner I.

Amery Ice Shelf

Bellingshausen Sea

Vinson Massif 16,066 ft. (4,897 m)

TRANSANTARCTIC MTS.

80°S

ANTARCTICA

90°E

90°W

South Pole

QUEEN MAUD MTS.

Amundsen Sea

WILKES LAND

INDIAN OCEAN

Ross Ice Shelf

Roosevelt I.

PACIFIC OCEAN

Permanent Ice Pack

Ross Sea

International Date Line

VICTORIA LAND

South Magnetic Pole

120°W

150°W

180°

150°E

0   400   800 mi
0   400   800 km

KEY

Elevation

Feet	Meters
Over 13,000	Over 3,960
6,500–13,000	1,980–3,960
1,600–6,500	480–1,980
650–1,600	200–480
0–650	0–200

Ice cap

Ice shelf

Orthographic Projection

Ocean Floor

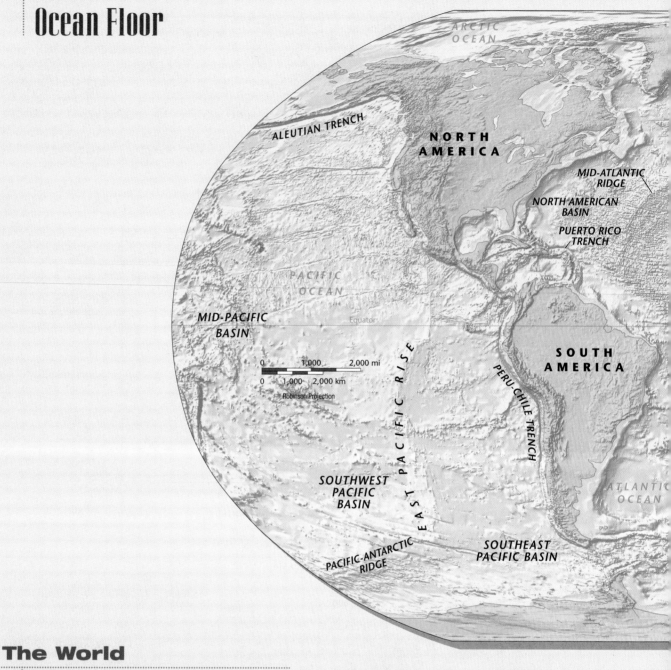

ARCTIC OCEAN

ALEUTIAN TRENCH

NORTH AMERICA

MID-ATLANTIC RIDGE

NORTH AMERICAN BASIN

PUERTO RICO TRENCH

PACIFIC OCEAN

Equator

MID-PACIFIC BASIN

0   1,000   2,000 mi

0   1,000   2,000 km

Robinson Projection

SOUTH AMERICA

PERU-CHILE TRENCH

ATLANTIC OCEAN

E A S T   P A C I F I C   R I S E

SOUTHWEST PACIFIC BASIN

SOUTHEAST PACIFIC BASIN

PACIFIC-ANTARCTIC RIDGE

Ocean Floor Profile

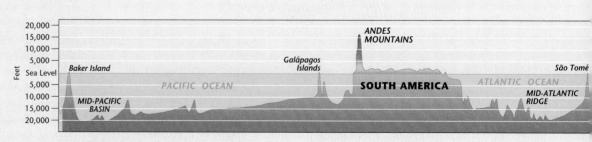

Feet		
20,000		
15,000		*ANDES MOUNTAINS*
10,000		
5,000		
Sea Level	*Baker Island*	*Galápagos Islands* **SOUTH AMERICA** *São Tomé*
5,000	*PACIFIC OCEAN*	*ATLANTIC OCEAN*
10,000	*MID-PACIFIC BASIN*	*MID-ATLANTIC RIDGE*
15,000		
20,000		

Profile drawn along the Equator

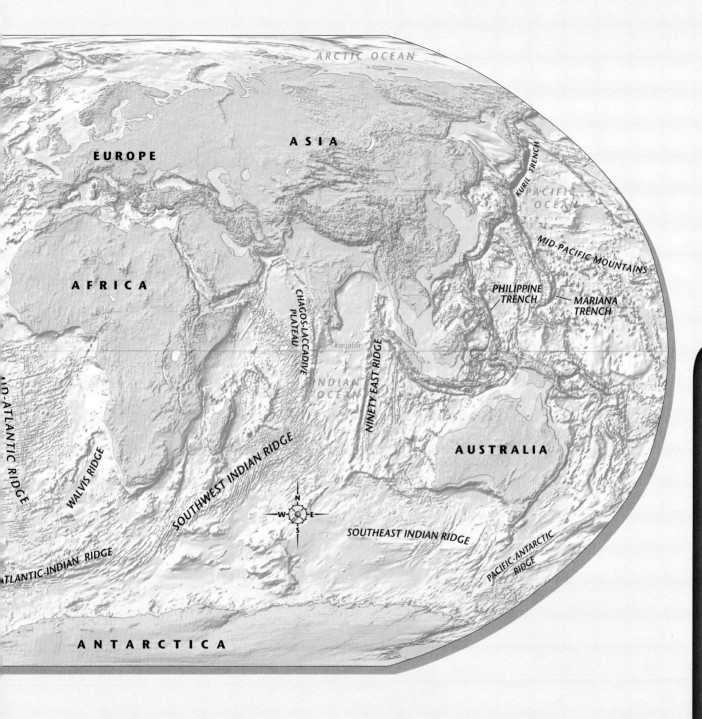

ARCTIC OCEAN

EUROPE

ASIA

AFRICA

KURIL TRENCH

PACIFIC
OCEAN

MID-PACIFIC MOUNTAINS

CHAGOS-LACCADIVE PLATEAU

PHILIPPINE
TRENCH

MARIANA
TRENCH

Equator

INDIAN
OCEAN

NINETY EAST RIDGE

MID-ATLANTIC RIDGE

WALVIS RIDGE

SOUTHWEST INDIAN RIDGE

AUSTRALIA

N
W   E
S

ATLANTIC-INDIAN RIDGE

SOUTHEAST INDIAN RIDGE

PACIFIC-ANTARCTIC
RIDGE

ANTARCTICA

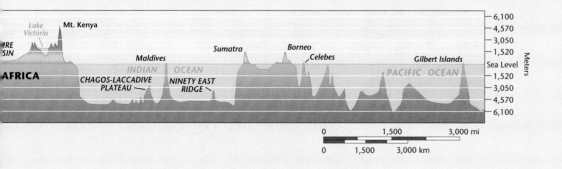

Lake
Victoria   Mt. Kenya

IRE
SIN

Maldives

Sumatra

Borneo

Celebes

Gilbert Islands

6,100
4,570
3,050
1,520

AFRICA

INDIAN   OCEAN

CHAGOS-LACCADIVE
PLATEAU

NINETY EAST
RIDGE

PACIFIC OCEAN

Sea Level

Meters

1,520
3,050
4,570
6,100

0   1,500   3,000 mi

0   1,500   3,000 km

29

Physical and Human Geography

CHAPTERS

A Global Perspective

Geography allows people to find answers to questions about the world. Through the study of geography, you will explore and discover the processes that shape the earth, the relationships between people and environments, and the links between people and places. Geography will help you to build a global perspective and to understand the connections between global and local events.

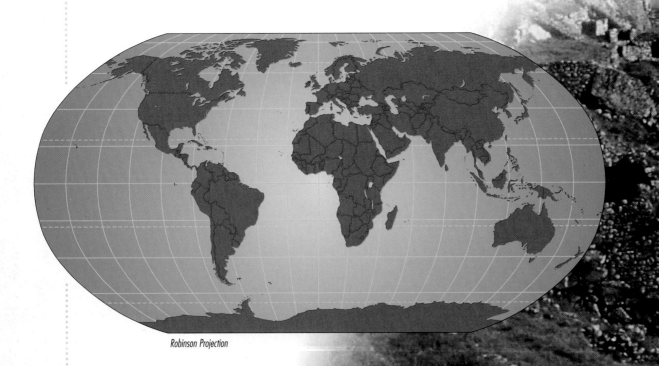

Robinson Projection

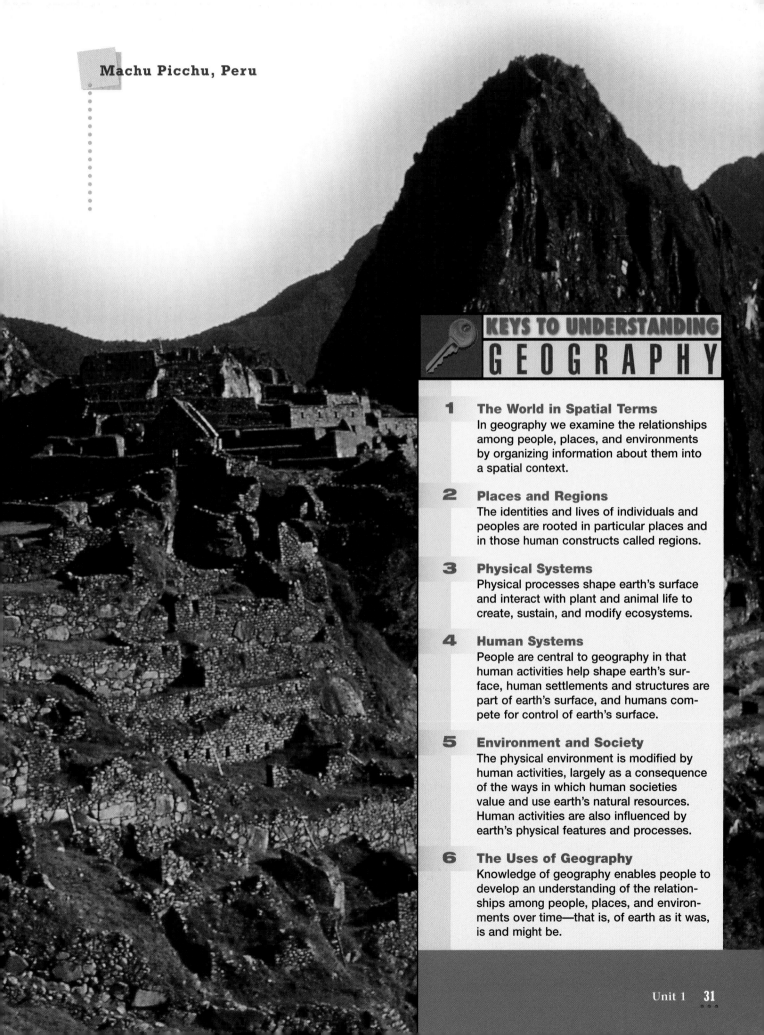

Machu Picchu, Peru

KEYS TO UNDERSTANDING
GEOGRAPHY

1 The World in Spatial Terms
In geography we examine the relationships among people, places, and environments by organizing information about them into a spatial context.

2 Places and Regions
The identities and lives of individuals and peoples are rooted in particular places and in those human constructs called regions.

3 Physical Systems
Physical processes shape earth's surface and interact with plant and animal life to create, sustain, and modify ecosystems.

4 Human Systems
People are central to geography in that human activities help shape earth's surface, human settlements and structures are part of earth's surface, and humans compete for control of earth's surface.

5 Environment and Society
The physical environment is modified by human activities, largely as a consequence of the ways in which human societies value and use earth's natural resources. Human activities are also influenced by earth's physical features and processes.

6 The Uses of Geography
Knowledge of geography enables people to develop an understanding of the relationships among people, places, and environments over time—that is, of earth as it was, is and might be.

Exploring Geography

The World: CONTINENTS, OCEANS, AND SEAS

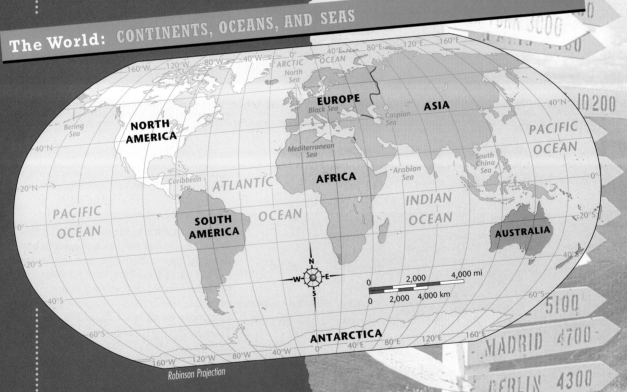

Robinson Projection

learning LOCATIONS

Mapping the World

Create a map like the one above, lightly shading each continent a different color. Then add labels for the continents, oceans, and seas that are shown on this map.

1 The Five Themes of Geography

Section Preview

Main Ideas

- Places may be described as having absolute and relative locations, and physical and human characteristics.

- Interactions between people and their environments have both positive and negative consequences.

Vocabulary

geography, absolute location, Equator, hemisphere, latitude, longitude, Prime Meridian, relative location, formal region, functional region

Hang gliding provides a unique look at the earth for both man and beast.

What is your world? Is it the small area where you spend most of your time—your home, school, favorite hangout, stores, and the routes that connect them?

Or is it those locations you have visited, read about, or seen on television?

Or is it the entire earth—the small blue planet that provides a life-sustaining balance of resources for a wide range of living species?

Through the study of geography you will learn to see your world from many different perspectives. Whether you are looking at global patterns or the finer details of neighborhood patterns, you will develop valuable insights about the earth, its people, and the many different kinds of relationships between them.

The Study of Geography

We know about the world around us because people are—and always have been—curious about their surroundings. In a sense, people have always wanted to be geographers.

What is geography? *Geography* comes from a Greek word meaning "writing about," or

"describing," the earth. **Geography** is the study of where people, places, and things are located and of the ways in which things relate to each other. Geography provides a way to discover and organize information regarding many aspects of the world. It explores the earth's surface and the various processes that shape it. Geography also examines the people of the world, their distinct cultures and economies, and the complex relationships that develop between people and their environments.

Does the world seem bigger than it did in ancient times because our understanding of it has greatly increased? Or does it seem smaller because it is no longer so mysterious and unknown? As we learn, our perspective changes, and so does the focus of geography. Now that we have explored almost all of the earth's land areas, geographers are paying more attention to the complex relationships and interactions between humans and natural forces around the globe.

Satellite images show the whole world looking like a small and fragile crystal ball, and in many ways, the earth is fragile. Rapidly

A WORLD OF eXtremes

Mariana Trench

Extremely Deep

The Mariana Trench's Challenger Deep, the deepest spot in the world, drops 35,802 ft (10,912 m) below the ocean surface.

Under Pressure

The pressure in Challenger Deep is over 8 tons per square inch—equal to an average-sized woman holding up 48 jumbo jets.

Deep-sea Creatures

Sea slugs, tube worms, and shrimp were all captured on film by a Japanese robot that journeyed down to this most inhospitable place on earth.

Researchers explored the trench in a special submarine

growing populations, greater demands on resources, and elevated levels of pollution threaten global environments. By studying how people and natural phenomena interact at specific places and by examining movement between places, geographers can better understand the ways in which each of us operates as part of a greater whole.

Geography's Five Themes

The study of geography is fueled by human curiosity. Why are places on the earth so amazingly different from each other? Five important questions can help organize information about places:

- What is the location of a place?
- What is the character of a place?
- How do people interact with the natural environment of a place?
- How do people, goods, and ideas move between places?
- How are places similar to and different from other places?

Each of these questions is related to one of five themes that geographers use to organize their study of the world. The five themes are location, place, human-environment interaction, movement, and regions. Each theme offers a way of looking at the world and its people. The themes are not mutually exclusive. To thoroughly understand a place or problem, you need to know how the different themes relate to each other.

For example, the tiny principality of Monaco occupies steep hillsides on three sides of a beautiful natural harbor of the Mediterranean Sea. This breathtaking site is a popular destination for thousands of tourists who flock yearly to the Côte d'Azur region of southern France. However, continued movements of people into the area are causing steadily increasing pressures on the region's fragile environment.

In using the five themes to study places, geographers learn from advances and discoveries made in other natural and social sciences, such as biology and history. According to geographer B. L. Turner II:

Geographers focus on anything and everything but relate their investigations to place and space. A linkage to other disciplines is basic to addressing and answering the why of where.

Location

Geographers studying a place usually begin by finding its location. A place's location can be described in either absolute or relative terms.

Absolute Location Where is a place? One way to answer this question is by describing its **absolute location**—its position on the globe.

The most common way to find a place's absolute location is by using the imaginary lines marking positions on the surface of the earth. The **Equator** is one such line. It circles the globe halfway between the North and South poles. The Equator divides the world into two halves, or **hemispheres**. All land and water between the Equator and the North Pole is located in the Northern Hemisphere. Likewise, everything that lies between the Equator and the South Pole is located in the Southern Hemisphere.

Imaginary lines that run parallel to the Equator are called lines of **latitude**, or parallels. They measure distances north or south of the Equator. The Equator is designated 0°, while the poles are 90° north (N) and 90° south (S).

Because the earth is tilted about 23½° as it revolves around the sun, the Tropic of Cancer at 23½°N and the Tropic of Capricorn at 23½°S mark the boundaries of the places on the earth that receive the most direct sunlight and the greatest heat energy from the sun. Find the Equator and the tropics in the diagram on page 5.

Another set of imaginary lines are lines of **longitude**, or meridians, which run north and south between the two poles. The **Prime Meridian**, at 0°, runs through the Royal Observatory in Greenwich, England. Other meridians are measured in degrees from 0 to 180 east (E) or west (W) from Greenwich. Unlike lines of latitude, meridians are not parallel to each other. As you can see on the diagram on page 5, the dis-

tance between meridians is greatest at the Equator but decreases as you approach the poles.

Using the grid formed by lines of latitude and longitude, you can name the precise or absolute location of any place on earth. Mogadishu, Somalia, is located at 2°N latitude and 45°E longitude. Atlanta, Georgia, is at 34°N and 84°W. See page 237 to read more about this grid system.

Getting Around

- **Location** A map is a flat drawing representing all or part of the earth's surface. The tourists shown here are using a city map to find their way around Trafalgar Square in London, England. *What is the difference between absolute and relative location?*
- **Critical Thinking** *Will these tourists be using absolute or relative location to find their way around London?*

Relative Location The second way to find where a place is located is by describing its **relative location**—where it is located in relation to other places. Atlanta, Georgia, for example, can be described as being southwest of Columbia, South Carolina.

Each place has only one absolute location and that location never changes. In contrast, each place has many relative locations and these can change over time. For example, while Atlanta once was many days' travel away from Los Angeles, now—thanks to the airplane—it is only a few hours away.

Place

Every place on the earth has features that distinguish it from other places. One challenge of geography is to understand how places are similar to and distinct from one another.

Physical Characteristics Places have unique physical characteristics, including landforms, vegetation, and climate. These physical characteristics vary around the world. Land may be mountainous, flat, or anywhere in between. Vegetation ranges from leafy tropical rain forests to the sparse, moss-covered tundra. Climate includes not only normal weather patterns but more dramatic occurrences like hurricanes, blizzards, droughts, and floods.

Human Characteristics Places can also be described in terms of their human characteristics. How many people live, work, and visit a place? What are their languages, customs, and beliefs? How does their economy work? How are they governed? In answering questions such as these, geographers study all aspects of human activity, such as urban growth, farming techniques, architectural styles, and politics.

Each place on the earth has a unique combination of physical and human characteristics. Returning travelers do not describe the longitude and latitude of a vacation spot. Instead they tell of the interesting people, sites, and customs that made their visit memorable. But they may also report having spoken the same language, used the same credit cards, and watched the same television shows as at home. This mix of unique and common features is what geographers mean when they talk about place.

A Modern Mosaic

● **Human-Environment Interaction** Color-enhanced satellite imagery demonstrates the land-use patterns along the Canada–United States border. The dark-tinted land indicates Canadian grazing land, while the light-colored land indicates United States wheat fields. The red areas are land left in its natural state. *To what degree have humans altered the landscape?*

City at Night

● **Movement** This time-lapsed photograph shows movement of traffic in and out of Atlanta. The yellow streaks were made by car headlights, and the red streaks by car taillights. *What role has transportation played in Atlanta's development?*

Human-Environment Interaction

The third geographic theme involves how people use their environment. Have they changed it? What are the consequences of those changes? How have people responded to changes in their environment?

Human beings have made enormous changes in their environment. Some changes are intentional and others are accidental; some changes are favorable and others are destructive. The American Southwest is one example. Before the era of swimming pools, air-conditioning, massive irrigation, and automobiles, this hot, dry region had few residents. Today it is one of the fastest-growing regions in the country. People from all over the country have flocked to this area, looking for a comfortable place to retire. New buildings and roads have altered the region's natural environment. The rapid growth in the region's population is straining the already limited supplies of water. This change may cause problems in the future.

Movement

Places do not exist in isolation. Because places have different characteristics, it follows that people, goods, and ideas will move between them.

The fourth geographic theme explores the impact geography has on this movement.

Atlanta's history illustrates the importance of movement. The city was established in 1837 at the terminus, or end, of a section of railroad and was even named Terminus at first. During the Civil War, Atlanta served as a major Confederate supply center because of its rail connections. Rebuilt after the Civil War, Atlanta remained an important transportation hub in the Southeast.

Modern Atlanta still depends on movement. The city's transportation links have attracted not only manufacturers, but also companies that handle distribution tasks such as warehousing and trucking. These new jobs, in turn, have helped the city grow. In addition, Atlanta's Hartsfield International Airport is one of the nation's largest and busiest.

Regions

The last of the five geographic themes deals with regions. A region is a group of places with at least one common characteristic. Geographers divide the world into many diverse regions.

Formal regions are areas in which a certain characteristic is found throughout the area. For example, states, countries, and cities are all political regions. Within these formal regions,

South Pacific

Regions The village of Luatuanuu is located in Western Samoa. This area is known for its scenic beauty. *What regional characteristics can you determine from this photograph?*

all people are subject to the same laws and are ruled by the same government. Formal regions can also be defined using other characteristics. The steppe region in Northern Eurasia consists of temperate grasslands with rich soils. The Corn Belt is the part of the United States where corn is grown in abundance. Chinatown is a part of San Francisco, California, containing many Chinese-American people, restaurants, and stores.

Functional regions consist of one central place and the surrounding places affected by it. As is true of formal regions, functional regions can be defined using several different criteria. The Amazon drainage basin in South America is the region drained by the Amazon River. The Denver, Colorado, metropolitan region consists of the city of Denver plus its surrounding suburbs.

Because various criteria can be used to define regions, the same place may be found in several different regions. From a physical perspective, Mexico is part of the North American continental region. Culturally, Mexico is linked to the Spanish-speaking nations of Central and South America.

Section 1 Review

Vocabulary and Main Ideas

1. **Define:** a. geography b. absolute location c. Equator d. hemisphere e. latitude f. longitude g. Prime Meridian h. relative location i. formal region j. functional region

2. **Describe the physical and human characteristics of the place where you live.**

3. **Give one example of the effect of movement on the history of your community.**

4. Critical Thinking: *Making Comparisons* **How does the study of a place's human characteristics differ from the study of its physical characteristics?**

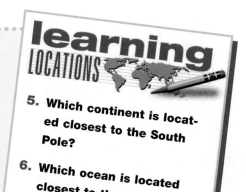

learning LOCATIONS

5. Which continent is located closest to the South Pole?

6. Which ocean is located closest to the North Pole?

Focus on Skills

☑ Social Studies
☐ Map and Globe
☐ Critical Thinking
  and Problem Solving

Demonstrating Visual Literacy

The Rock of Gibraltar climbs 1,400 feet into the air to guard the narrow passage between the Atlantic Ocean and the Mediterranean Sea. Use the five geographic themes to analyze the map and photo below.

1. Identify the location of Gibraltar. An English colony since 1713, Gibraltar sits at the entrance to the Mediterranean Sea. Look on the map to find the location of Gibraltar. Then answer the following questions: (a) What is the absolute location of Gibraltar? (b) Describe Gibraltar's relative location.

2. Describe the characteristics that make the Strait of Gibraltar a unique place. Every place on earth has both physical and human characteristics that make it unique. Answer the following questions: (a) What physical feature distinguishes Gibraltar? (b) If you were standing on the Rock of Gibraltar, what two continents would you be able to see?

3. Consider the impact people have had on Gibraltar. Gibraltar has been settled since Neolithic times. It has been influenced by many cultures and races, including Phoenicians, Romans, Carthaginians, Moors, Spanish, and British. Why do you think so many different people have contributed to Gibraltar's culture?

4. Analyze how movement through the Strait of Gibraltar impacts the surrounding area. Seeking to control passage into the Mediterranean Sea, the Spanish developed Gibraltar as an important military and naval base. It was seized by the British in 1704 and remains under British control, despite several Spanish attempts to regain possession of the territory. (a) Why would a country want to control Gibraltar? (b) What water bodies can be accessed by the Strait of Gibraltar?

5. Determine the common characteristics that identify the region in which Gibraltar is located. A region is defined by a group of places that share some common characteristics. In what regions would you place Gibraltar?

Rock of Gibraltar

2 Changes Within the Earth

Section Preview

Main Ideas

- Earth is a changing planet, affected by geologic processes.

- Forces inside the earth create and change landforms on the surface.

- The theory of plate tectonics suggests answers to many questions about the earth's landforms.

Vocabulary

geology, core, mantle, crust, continent, relief, lava, fold, fault, plate tectonics, continental drift theory, Ring of Fire

APPEARED IN *NATIONAL GEOGRAPHIC*

Volcanic eruptions betray the dynamic forces at work within the earth.

One of geographers' biggest tasks is to understand the earth's constant changes. Earth is not a quiet planet. Earthquakes topple buildings and open up great cracks in the ground. Volcanoes erupt with red-hot lava and dangerous gases. While these are some of the more spectacular ways in which the earth is changing, they are not the only ways. Many processes—some dramatic like these, others less noticeable—are always at work shaping the earth on which we live.

The Earth's Structure

Geology—the study of the earth's physical structure and history—is a relatively new science. It deals, however, with very ancient history—that of the earth itself. This history, scientists now think, goes back about 4.6 billion years. Since it began, the earth has been changing. Geologists try to learn what those changes were, to understand why they occurred, and to predict any future changes.

Inside the Earth Scientists have developed an idea of what the interior of the earth is like. The diagram on page 41 shows the earth's layers as geologists envision them.

The **core**, or center, of the earth consists of very hot metal, mainly iron mixed with some nickel. The inner core is thought to be dense and solid, while the metal of the outer core is molten, or liquid. Around the core is the **mantle**, a thick layer of rock. Scientists speculate that the mantle is about 1,800 miles (2,896 km) thick. Mantle rock is mostly solid, but some upper layers may be pliable. The mantle also contains pockets of magma, or melted rock.

The earth's **crust**, the rocky surface layer, is surprisingly thin, like frosting on a cake. The thinner parts of the crust, which are only about 5 miles (8 km) thick, are below the oceans. The crust beneath the continents is thicker and very uneven, averaging about 22 miles (35 km) in thickness. Natural forces interact with and affect the earth's crust, creating the landforms, or natural features, found on the surface of the earth.

Land and Water Photographs of the earth taken from space show clearly that it is truly a "watery planet." More than 70 percent of the earth's surface is covered by water, mainly the salt water of oceans and seas. The large landmasses in the oceans are the **continents**. Although some of these landforms are not completely separated by ocean waters, geographers define seven separate continents. Asia is the largest, Australia the smallest. All the continents have a variety of landforms, although those in Antarctica are hidden by ice.

Landforms are commonly classified according to differences in **relief**—the difference in elevation between the highest and lowest points. Another important characteristic is whether they rise gradually or steeply.

The major types of landforms are mountains, hills, plateaus, and plains. Mountains have high relief, rising at least 2,000 feet (610 m) above the surrounding terrain. Hills are lower, rounded, and generally less steep than mountains. The elevation of the surrounding land determines whether a landform is called a mountain or a hill. What is referred to as a mountain in the British Isles might be called a hill in western North America. It all depends on the relative height of other nearby landforms. A plateau is also a raised area, but its surface is generally level. Many plateaus, however, have deep gulleys or canyons, making the surface seem rough rather than flat. At least one side of a plateau rises steeply above the surrounding land.

Plains are landforms, too. A plain is a flat or gently rolling area where there are few changes in elevation. Many plains are along coasts.

Other landforms include valleys, canyons, and basins. Various geographical features of landscapes include rivers, peninsulas, and islands. Many of the earth's landforms are shown on the diagram on page 42.

Internal Forces

When a geologist or geographer looks at a piece of land they often ask, "What forces shaped the mountains, plains, and other landforms that are here?" Landforms are shaped first by internal forces that originate in the earth's interior. One of these forces is volcanism, which involves the movement of magma inside the earth. Other major internal forces

The Earth's Layers

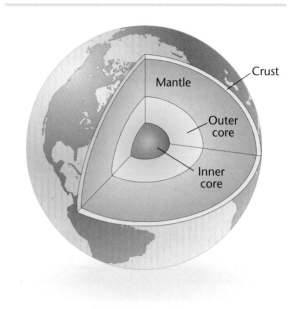

Crust

Mantle

Outer core

Inner core

DIAGRAM STUDY

This diagram shows what geologists believe is the internal structure of the earth. Recent discoveries suggest that the inner core may be spinning at a different rate from the rest of the earth. *What is the outermost layer called?*

consist of movements that fold, lift, bend, or break the rock of the earth's crust.

Volcanoes The ancient Romans believed that a god named Vulcan worked with hot iron and gold at his forge beneath the earth. In his honor, a fiery island off the coast of Italy was named Vulcano, and all mountains formed by molten rock were called volcanoes.

Volcanoes form when magma—molten rock inside the earth—breaks through the earth's crust. On the surface the molten rock, or **lava**, may flow evenly, producing a plateau-like shield volcano. Ash and cinders erupting from a break in the ground may produce small cinder cones. Alternating sequences of explosive eruptions and smooth lava flows create distinctive cone-shaped mountains. One example of this type of volcano is Japan's Mount Fuji.

Changes in the Earth's Crust The movements that bend and break the earth's crust are varied and complex. When rock layers bend and buckle the result is a **fold.** Other stresses on rocks cause **faults,** or breaks in the earth's crust. Sometimes the rock on either side of a fault slips or moves suddenly. Rock on one side of a fault may move sideways, up, or down in relation to the rock on the other side of the fault. Slow movements along a fault will produce subtle, almost unnoticeable changes. A large, sudden movement along a fault can send out shock waves through the earth, causing an earthquake. Whether rock layers fault or fold is determined by the hardness of the rock and the strength of the movement.

Geologic History

Most changes in the earth's surface take place so slowly that they are not immediately noticeable to the human eye. Geologists have reconstructed much of the earth's history from the record they read in the rocks. For many years scientists assumed that the basic arrangement of oceans and continents was stable and permanent.

Today, however, most accept the idea that the earth's landmasses have broken apart, rejoined, and moved to other parts of the globe. This concept forms part of the plate tectonic theory, which suggests answers to many puzzling questions about the earth's landforms.

Plate Tectonics According to the theory of **plate tectonics,** the earth's outer shell is not one solid piece of rock. Instead, the lithosphere—the earth's crust and the brittle, upper layer of the mantle—is broken into a number of moving plates. The plates vary in size and thickness. The North American Plate stretches from the mid-Atlantic Ocean to the northern tip of Japan. The Cocos Plate covers a small area in the Pacific Ocean just west of Central America. These plates are not anchored in place, but slide over a hot and pliable layer of the mantle.

The earth's oceans and continents ride atop the plates as they move in different directions. The map on page 43 shows the boundaries of

Landforms and Water Bodies

DIAGRAM STUDY

- The diagram shows many of the earth's most common landforms. Examine the landforms and their labels. *How does a plateau differ from a plain?*

- *What is a delta?* Use the glossary beginning on page 721 to check your answer.

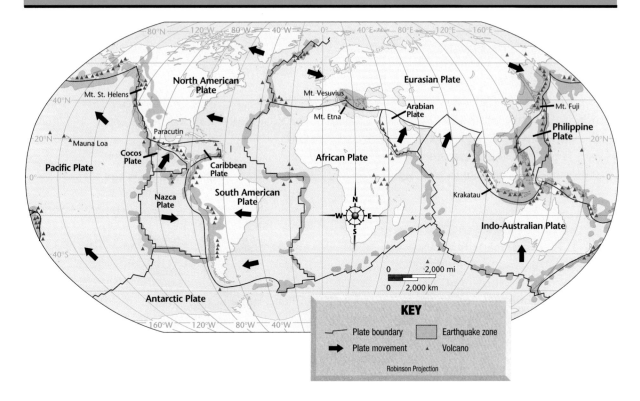

APPLYING THE GEOGRAPHIC THEMES

● **Place** The world's continents and oceans ride atop moving tectonic plates. *In which direction are the Nazca and South American plates moving?*

● **Critical Thinking** *What are some results of the movement of these plates?*

the different plates. It also shows the direction in which the plates are moving. The Pacific Plate and the Nazca Plate, for example, are moving apart. The Nazca Plate and the South American Plate, however, are moving toward each other. It is along the boundaries where plates meet that most earthquakes, volcanoes, and other geologic events occur.

The plate tectonic theory began to be widely accepted in the 1960s. It was based on earlier ideas and research, however, and encompasses two other theories: continental drift and seafloor spreading.

Continental Drift As early as the 1600s, people looking at maps noticed that several continents seemed to fit together like jigsaw puzzle pieces. Could they once have been joined as one gigantic landmass?

In the early 1900s a German explorer and scientist named Alfred Wegener suggested the **continental drift theory**. Wegener proposed that there was once a single "supercontinent." He called it Pangaea (pan JEE uh), from the Greek words *pan*, meaning "all," and *gaia*, personifying the earth. Wegener theorized that about 180 million years ago, Pangaea began to break up into separate continents.

To support his theory, Wegener found evidence that showed that fossils—the preserved remains of ancient animals and plants—from South America, Africa, India, and Australia were almost identical. The rocks containing the fossils were also much alike. Still, many scientists remained unconvinced by these arguments.

Seafloor Spreading The other theory supporting plate tectonics emerged from study

Pangaea and the Drifting Continents

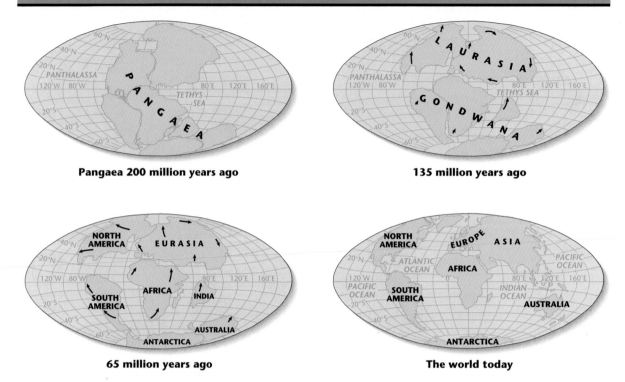

Pangaea 200 million years ago

135 million years ago

65 million years ago

The world today

Mollweide Projection

APPLYING THE GEOGRAPHIC THEMES

● **Place** Scientists theorize that the earth once supported a single "supercontinent," which they have named Pangaea. *Between which years did South America break away from Africa? What two giant landmasses do scientists believe existed 135 million years ago?*

of the ocean floor. Using sonar, scientists began to map the floor of the Atlantic Ocean. Sonar exploration revealed that the ocean floor was not flat. The landforms under water closely resembled continental landforms, including rugged mountains, deep canyons, and wide plains. Scientists were surprised to find that rocks taken from the ocean floor were much younger than those found on the continents. The youngest rocks of all were those nearest the underwater ridge system—a series of underwater mountains that extend around the world, stretching more than 40,000 miles (64,000 km).

The explanation first suggested in the 1960s is the theory of seafloor spreading. According to this theory, molten rock from the mantle rises under the underwater ridge and breaks through a split at the top of the ridge. The split is called a rift

valley. The rock then spreads out in both directions from the ridge as if it were on two huge conveyor belts. As the seafloor moves away from the ridge, it carries older rocks away. Seafloor spreading, along with the older theory of continental drift, became part of the theory of plate tectonics.

Plate Movement One reason that people in the 1920s doubted the continental drift theory was the question of just *how* the continents moved. What force is powerful enough to send gigantic plates sliding around the earth?

Today, most scientists believe this force is a process called convection. Convection is a circular movement caused when a material is heated, expands and rises, then cools and falls. This process is thought to be occurring in the mantle rock beneath the plates. The heat energy that drives convection probably comes from the slow decay of materials under the earth's crust.

When Plates Meet As mentioned earlier, the places where plates meet are some of the most restless parts of the earth. Plates can pull away from each other, crash head-on, or slide past each other.

When plates pull away from one another— a process known as spreading—they form a diverging plate boundary, or spreading zone. Such areas are likely to have a rift valley, earthquakes, and volcanic action.

What happens when plates crash into each other depends on the types of plates involved. Because continental crust is lighter than oceanic crust, continental plates "float" higher. Therefore, when an oceanic plate meets a continental plate, it slides under the lighter plate and down into the mantle. The oceanic rock then melts deep in the earth. This process is known as subduction. Molten material produced in a subduction zone can rise to the earth's surface and cause volcanic mountain building and earthquakes on the continental plate. The Andes Mountains, for example, formed over the course of millions of years as the Nazca Plate slid under the South American Plate.

When two plates of the same type meet, the result is a process called converging. When both are oceanic plates, one slides under the other.

Often an island group forms at this boundary. When both are continental plates, the plates push against each other, creating mountain ranges. Earth's highest mountain range, the Himalayas, was formed millions of years ago when the Indo-Australian Plate crashed into the Eurasian Plate. Even today, the Indo-Australian Plate continues to push against the Eurasian Plate at a rate of about 2 inches (5 cm) a year.

Finally, instead of pulling away from each other or colliding with each other, plates sometimes slip or grind past each other along faults. This process is known as faulting. The San Andreas Fault in California is a well-known example of faulting.

Explaining Volcanoes Plate tectonic theory attempts to explain many of the processes affecting the earth, such as volcanic eruptions. Most eruptions occur along plate boundaries. The **Ring of Fire** is a circle of volcanoes surrounding the Pacific Ocean. The ring includes the Cascades in North America, the islands of Japan and Indonesia, and the Andes in South America. Locate the "Ring of Fire" on the map on page 43.

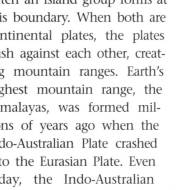

GLOBAL issues

Population

Human population is growing fastest along the "Ring of Fire," where most of the world's roughly 600 active volcanoes and many earthquake zones are found.

Where the Fault Lies

Regions California's San Andreas Fault lies on the boundary between two tectonic plates, the North American Plate and the Pacific Plate (see the map on page 43). The two plates are sliding past each other at a rate of 2 to 2¼ inches (5 to 6 centimeters) each year. The fault, which is over 750 miles (1,210 km) long, frequently plagues California with earthquakes. *How does faulting differ from subduction?*

Major Types of Plate Movement

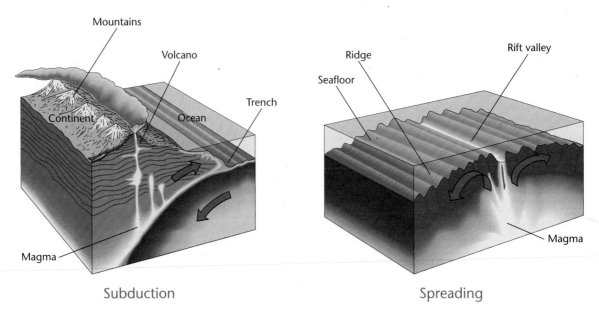

Subduction

Spreading

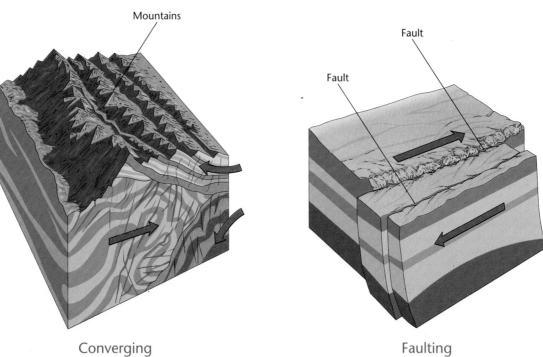

Converging

Faulting

DIAGRAM STUDY

In a subduction zone, one plate slides or dives under another. In a spreading zone, two plates move apart from each other, creating a rift, or crack, in the earth's crust. In a converging zone, two plates collide and push slowly against each other. At a fault, plates grind or slide past each other, rather than collide. *Which type of plate boundary occurs when an oceanic plate meets a continental plate?*

Letting Off Steam

Place Hot rocks heat springs deep within the earth. Steam pressure then forces the remaining water upward. Such violent eruptions of water and steam are called geysers. Old Faithful, in Yellowstone National Park, erupts at an average rate of once every 73 minutes. *How are geysers similar to volcanoes?*

Plate tectonic theory also attempts to explain how volcanic island arcs, or chains of islands, are formed far away from plate boundaries. "Hot spots" are hot regions deep within the earth's mantle that produce plumes of magma that rise toward the earth's surface. As the molten rock rises from a hot spot, the magma may heat underground water and produce hot springs or geysers such as the ones found in Iceland or in Yellowstone National Park in the United States. However, if molten rock flows out of a crack in the earth's surface, it may produce a volcanic island chain as the plate drifts over a stationary hot spot. The easterly island of Hawaii is part of an island arc that formed in the center of a plate. Hawaii, which is currently over a hot spot, is constantly erupting. Other islands to the west have remained dormant since the moving Pacific Plate removed them from the hot spot.

Section 2 Review

Vocabulary and Main Ideas

1. Define: a. geology b. core c. mantle d. crust e. continent f. relief g. lava h. fold i. fault j. plate tectonics k. continental drift theory l. Ring of Fire

2. What are the two internal processes that create landforms?

3. How can the plate tectonic theory help explain the formation of the Andes and Himalayan mountains?

4. Critical Thinking: *Making Comparisons* Use the map on pages 28 and 29 to identify three types of landforms that are found on the ocean floor.

learning LOCATIONS

5. Look at the map on page 43. Part of which continent sits on top of the Arabian Plate?

6. Look at the illustration on page 44. Which continent was Australia attached to 65 million years ago?

3 Changes on the Earth's Surface

Section Preview

Main Ideas

Mechanical and chemical weathering are forces that change landforms.

Erosion is another external process that alters the surface of the earth.

Vocabulary

weathering, mechanical weathering, chemical weathering, acid rain, erosion, sediment, loess, glacier, moraine

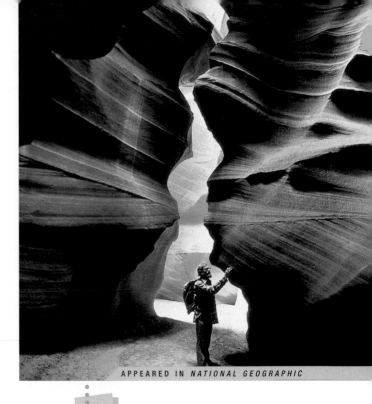

APPEARED IN *NATIONAL GEOGRAPHIC*

Portions of the earth have been sculpted into magnificent shapes by weathering and erosion.

Mixed in the soil of the Hawaiian Islands is a crumbly, gray clay that is older than the islands themselves. For years scientists wondered how this soil had formed. Now they think that the clay comes from a desert in far-off China. Blown across thousands of miles of ocean by the wind, it was deposited on the islands by centuries of rainstorms. This process is still going on today. World Watch Institute president Lester Brown explains:

> *So much soil from the Asian mainland blows over the Pacific Ocean that scientists taking air samples at the Mauna Loa observatory in Hawaii can now tell when spring plowing starts in North China.*

Wind is only one of several external agents that change the earth's surface. These forces, which can act over thousands or even millions of years, are usually grouped into two broad categories: weathering and erosion.

Weathering

Weathering is the breakdown of rock at or near the earth's surface into smaller and smaller pieces. Over millions of years, weathering can reduce a mountain to gravel. There are two kinds of weathering: mechanical and chemical.

Mechanical Weathering The process of **mechanical weathering** occurs when rock is actually broken or weakened physically. Mechanical weathering breaks large masses of rock into even smaller pieces, producing boulders, stones, pebbles, sand, silt, and dust. The most common type of mechanical weathering takes place when water freezes to ice in a crack in the rock. Because water expands when it freezes, the ice widens the crack and eventually splits the rock. This process is known as frost wedging.

Frost wedging is most likely to occur in areas where the freezing is both frequent and intense. Over time it can even cause huge parts of a mountainside to break and fall away. This form of weathering can easily be observed above the tree line in mountainous areas.

Another kind of mechanical weathering occurs when seeds take root in cracks in rocks. In the same way as sidewalks crack when tree roots grow beneath them, a rock will split as plants or trees grow within a fracture.

Chemical Weathering While mechanical weathering can destroy rock, it changes only the physical structure, not the original crystals or minerals that make up the rock. It leaves the chemical structure unchanged. One important effect of mechanical weathering is to expose bedrock to the forces of **chemical weathering**. The process of chemical weathering alters a rock's chemical makeup by changing the minerals that form the rock or combining them with new chemical elements. Unlike mechanical weathering, chemical weathering can change one kind of rock into a completely different kind.

The most important factors in chemical weathering are water and carbon dioxide. Carbon dioxide from the air or soil combines with water to make a weak solution of carbonic acid. When the acidic water seeps into cracks in certain types of rock, such as limestone, it can dissolve the rock. Many caves were formed in this way.

Moisture is an important element in chemical weathering. In dry regions where water is scarce, there is little chemical weathering. But in a damp or wet area, chemical weathering occurs quickly and is widespread. Chemical weathering is also more likely to occur under high temperature conditions than in cooler regions.

Another type of chemical weathering is **acid rain**. Chemicals in the polluted air combine with water vapor and fall back to earth as acid rain. Acid rain not only destroys forests and pollutes water, but also eats away the surfaces of stone buildings and natural rock formations. Industrial pollution, acid-producing agents from the ocean, and volcanic activity are among the known causes of acid rain. For more information about the effects of acid rain, see the Geographer's Lab on pages 382 and 383.

Rock Unsolid

● **Human-Environment Interaction**
Chemical weathering has contributed to the bedraggled look of this stone traveler. *What impact has human activity had on acid rain?*

Observing Weathering The effects of weathering can be seen on almost any old stone structure. Weathering blurs the lettering on old tombstones, softens the sharp features on carved stone statues, and breaks down the mortar that holds together stone or brick walls.

Weathering changes natural landforms, too. Over millions of years, mountains can be worn from jagged peaks to rounded hills. In an area where temperature changes cause frost wedging, the south side of a mountain in the Northern Hemisphere is likely to be more rugged than the north slope. Because the south side receives more sunlight, water in the cracks of rocks thaws and freezes more often than on the cold north

Rising Waters

Regions Water can make dramatic changes to the earth's surface. Some changes, such as the creation of canyons, are made slowly over time. Other changes are more immediately felt. Water overflowing the Mississippi River can flood homes and farms located on the flood plain. *What do river waters carry?*

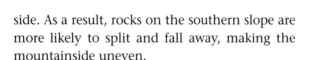

side. As a result, rocks on the southern slope are more likely to split and fall away, making the mountainside uneven.

Erosion

Erosion is the movement of weathered materials such as gravel, soil, and sand. The three most common causes of erosion are water, wind, and glaciers.

Erosion is an important part of the cycle that has made and kept the earth a place where living things can survive. Without this process, the earth's surface would be barren rock, with no soil where plants can grow. Erosion is actually a significant agent in mechanical weathering. The erosive forces that caused the "weathering away" that created Niagara Falls and the Grand Canyon, for example, are all part of mechanical weathering.

Water The largest canyons and the deepest valleys on the earth were created in part by moving water. Moving water—rain, rivers, streams, and oceans—is the greatest cause of erosion. Over time, water can cut into even the hardest rock and wear it away.

It is not water alone that carves out valleys and canyons. Water moving swiftly down a streambed carries **sediment**—small particles of soil, sand, and gravel. Like sandpaper, the sedi-

ment helps grind away the surface of rocks along the stream's path.

The rocks and soil carried away by water are eventually deposited somewhere else. When the stream or river slows down, sediment settles out of the water and lands on the banks or streambed, creating new kinds of landforms. A broad flood plain, or alluvial plain, may form on either side of the river, or a delta may form. A delta is a flat, low-lying plain that is sometimes formed at the mouth of a river—the place where the river enters a lake, a larger river, or an ocean.

The Mississippi River, for example, carries an estimated 500 million tons (454 million metric tons) of sediment a year. The river deposits some of this rich sand, silt, gravel, and clay along its flood plain, which is as much as 80 miles (129 km) wide in some places. The rest of the sediment builds up in the delta where the river empties into the Gulf of Mexico.

Rivers and streams play the largest role in water erosion. But crashing ocean surf or the gentler waves along a lakeshore can also erode beach cliffs, carve steep bluffs, and pile up sand dunes. As bluffs are undercut by the force of water, rocks tumble down cliffs into the water. Continuing erosion wears rocks into sandy beaches, then carries the sand farther down the shoreline.

Ocean waves may move sand away from the shore. For example, the barrier islands off the coast of North Carolina, known as the Outer Banks, have been slowly eroding due to wave action. The Cape Hatteras Lighthouse, built in 1870 on the Outer Banks, once stood over 1,500 feet (457 m) from the ocean. Erosion brought the shore to within 100 feet (30 m) of the lighthouse. In 1999, the lighthouse was moved to a point 3,000 feet (914 m) from the shore.

Wind Wind is a second major cause of erosion, especially in areas with little water and few plants to hold the soil in place. In the 1930s wind erosion devastated the Great Plains in the central United States. As the population grew farmers plowed under more farmland. More land was stripped of its plant life and was exposed to the wind. The upper layers of soil that are usually rich in minerals and nutrients were dry from a long drought. As a result, the wind picked up and carried away the soil in great dust storms. As their farms' fertile soil blew away, several states became part of what was called a "dust bowl." Writer George Greenfield described it in this way:

In this country there is now no life for miles upon miles; no human beings, no birds, no animals. Only a dull brown land with cracks showing. Hills furrowed with eroded gullies—you have seen pictures like that in ruins of lost civilizations.

On the other hand, the windblown deposits of mineral-rich dust and silt called **loess** (luss) have benefited farmers in China, the American Midwest, and other parts of the world. Loess is valued in part because it is extremely porous. This allows it to absorb and hold on to great amounts of water. Because its particles are so fine, loess may be blown thousands of miles.

Sandstorms, or windblown sand, are major causes of erosion, especially near deserts. Just as sandblasting cleans stone buildings, windblown sand carves or smoothes the surfaces of both rock formations and objects made by humans.

Sand and dust carried by the wind are eventually deposited when the wind dies down. The cumulative effects of windblown sand can be seen both in the desert and along ocean shores in the form of sand dunes, loose windblown sand heaped into a mound or a low hill. Winds may move shifting dunes so far that they bury any vegetation or human

Winds of Change

• **Human-Environment Interaction** Strong winds have caused sands to drift like snow, nearly burying this Texas farm. *How has human activity contributed to erosion?*

• **Regions** In the 1930s, the Great Plains suffered severe effects of drought and erosion. Much of its rich top soil was lost to scouring winds. *What was this area called?*

Ice Sculpture

Regions Columbia Glacier in the Canadian Rocky Mountains is an example of an alpine glacier. Alpine glaciers form on mountainsides and move downhill by the force of gravity. *How do glaciers alter the landscape?*

Critical Thinking *Explain why you think Columbia Glacier will bring great or small changes to the landscape.*

settlements in their path. Grasses that take root in ocean dunes help prevent further wind erosion. Human development along the shoreline has contributed to beach erosion. When natural vegetation barriers are removed for construction, wind erosion occurs at a faster pace.

Glaciers Another major agent of erosion is **glaciers**—huge, slow-moving sheets of ice. They form over many years as layers of unmelted snow are pressed together, thaw slightly, and then turn to ice. As glaciers move, they carry dirt, rocks, and boulders. The terrain is worn away by the rock debris dragged along with the moving ice.

When the earth was cooler than it is today, much of the planet's water became locked up in immense glaciers that covered up to a third of the earth's surface. Over thousands of years the glaciers melted back, then grew again when the earth became colder. Long periods of these colder temperatures are known as Ice Ages. Geologists believe that there have been at least four Ice Ages in the past 600 million years, the last of which peaked about 18,000 years ago.

If you live in the northern part of the United States you might see the effects of Ice Age glaciers. Like giant bulldozers, glaciers scooped out the basins of the Great Lakes, as well as thousands of smaller lakes elsewhere in the United States and Canada. When glaciers melted and receded in some places, they left behind ridgelike piles of rocks and debris called **moraines** (muh RAYNS). In some places, moraines acted like dams, blocking valleys and creating areas where water collected into lakes. In other cases glacial debris formed long ridges of land. Long Island in New York is one such example of a moraine.

The glaciers of the Ice Ages were mainly continental glaciers, or ice sheets. Today such broad, flat glaciers exist in only a few places in the world. They cover about 80 percent of Greenland and most of the continent of Antarctica. The Greenland glacier is estimated to be 9,900 feet (3,018 m) thick. The front of the glacier usually moves forward a few feet each winter and then recedes during the summer. Great chunks of continental glaciers frequently break off from the edges of the ice sheets to produce floating icebergs.

Valley or alpine glaciers, on the other hand, are found throughout the world in high mountain valleys where the climate is not warm enough for the ice to melt. In North America,

valley glaciers snake through the Rocky and Cascade mountains, the Sierra Nevada, and the Alaskan ranges.

Although glaciers are sometimes described as "rivers of ice," they do not move and flow quickly like water. Glaciers slide forward because of their great weight. The entire mass does not move at once; rather it oozes outward down-valley from the top of an alpine glacier. Large valley glaciers in Europe may move nearly 600 feet (183 m) in a year. Glacial landscapes are distinctly different from landscapes formed by water. While rivers cut sharp-sided, V-shaped valleys, glaciers carve out valleys that are rounded and U-shaped. The amount of erosion that occurs when a glacier passes by depends partly on the size and speed of the glacier and partly on the terrain and texture of bedrock being covered. On flat land, glacial erosion is relatively minor. In mountainous areas the erosion can be significant.

Section 3 Review

Vocabulary and Main Ideas

1. Define: a. weathering b. mechanical weathering c. chemical weathering d. acid rain e. erosion f. sediment g. loess h. glacier i. moraine

2. What are the two most important forces in chemical weathering?

3. What are the three most common causes of erosion?

4. Critical Thinking: *Making Comparisons* Which process—weathering or erosion—is easier to see actually taking place? Explain your answer.

learning LOCATIONS

5. On which continent is the Great Plains, site of the "dust bowl" of the 1930s, located?

6. What continent is mostly covered by glaciers?

Summarizing Main Ideas

Section 1 The Five Themes of Geography

- The theme of location describes where a place is in absolute or relative terms.
- The theme of place describes the features that make a place unique.
- The theme of human-environment interaction describes the ways in which people and their environment have affected one another.
- The theme of movement describes how people, goods, and ideas move between places.
- The theme of regions classifies places according to characteristics that they share.

Section 2 Changes Within the Earth

- The earth consists of a hot metal core surrounded by a thick mantle and topped off by a relatively thin rock crust.
- The theory of plate tectonics states that the top layers of the earth are broken into a number of huge, moving plates.
- The movement of plates explains the formation of separate continents and the creation of volcanoes.

Section 3 Changes on the Earth's Surface

- Mechanical weathering breaks large rocks into smaller ones.
- Chemical weathering, caused mainly by water and carbon dioxide, turns rock into other substances.
- Erosion—caused by water, wind, and glaciers—moves materials such as soil and sand across the earth's surface.

Reviewing Vocabulary

Use each of the following terms in a sentence that shows its meaning.

1. geography
2. absolute location
3. Equator
4. hemisphere
5. latitude
6. longitude
7. relative location
8. formal region
9. functional region
10. continent
11. weathering
12. erosion

Applying the Geographic Themes

1. **Location** How does the theory of plate tectonics explain the location of certain mountain ranges?
2. **Place** How do wind and water alter places on the earth's surface?
3. **Human-Environment Interaction** In what ways do the houses that people build reflect the environment in which they live?
4. **Movement** What factors might cause people to want to move to a new place? What factors might force people to move?
5. **Regions** Do all the places in any given region look alike? Explain.

Critical Thinking and Applying Skills

1. **Drawing Conclusions** Explain how erosion can have both negative and positive effects and provide at least one example of each.
2. **Expressing Problems Clearly** Living near the boundaries of moving plates can be dangerous. Explain why this statement is true.
3. **Demonstrating Visual Literacy** Look again at the photograph of Atlanta on page 37. Identify how each of the five geographic themes are represented in the picture.

Writing Across Cultures

▶ 1. Using each of the five geographic themes, describe a favorite place from your childhood. Your description should also explain why that place is important to you.

▶ 2. Though acid rain is caused by industrial pollution, winds can carry acid rain thousands of miles away from the sources of that pollution. Explain how this makes the problem of acid rain more difficult to confront. Describe the problem from two points of view: a country that produces a great deal of pollution, and a country that produces little pollution but suffers from acid rain anyway.

INTERNET link

Visit the Learning Web at the U.S. Geological Survey to learn more about the world we live in. Link to this site from:

• www.phschool.com

Choose a topic which interests you and explore it. When you are done, write a paragraph stating what you learned.

Continents, Oceans, and Seas

Number from 1 to 12 on a piece of paper. Next to each number, write the letter of the place on the map that corresponds to the places listed below.

1. Africa
2. Antarctica
3. Asia
4. Australia
5. Europe
6. Mediterranean Sea
7. North America
8. South America
9. Arctic Ocean
10. Atlantic Ocean
11. Indian Ocean
12. Pacific Ocean

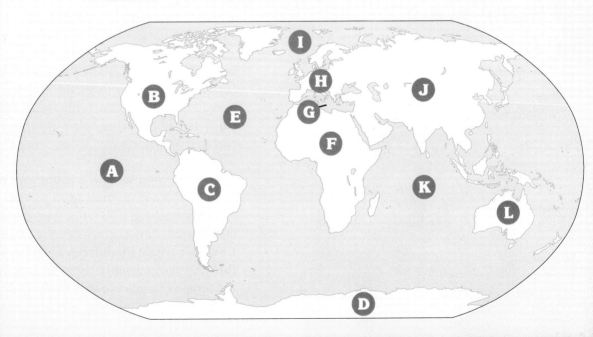

Map Skills for Life

Marcus and Teresa, along with their classmates, are on the annual school trip to Washington, D.C. As they tour the capital of the United States, they plan to visit the White House and the Lincoln Memorial. They also want to visit the Capitol building, where the Senate and the House of Representatives meet.

Since Congress is in session, this is a good time to visit the Capitol. Teresa and Marcus want to see the following places:

★ the House Chamber, where the House of Representatives meets.

★ the Senate Chamber, where the U.S. Senate meets.

★ Statuary Hall, with its many marble statues of distinguished Americans.

Reading the Map

Follow the steps to understand how Marcus and Teresa can use the floor plan to find the places they want to see.

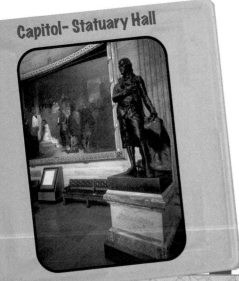

Capitol- Statuary Hall

1. Find the starting location on the map. Look over the map and get a general idea of how the building is laid out. From pictures, you know that a huge dome crowns the center of the Capitol. This dome is above the Rotunda. **(a)** What is the general plan of the Capitol? **(b)** What are in the two wings of the building? **(c)** If Teresa and Marcus enter the Capitol through the East Front, what will be in front of them?

2. Use the map and key to locate the sights they want to see. Like many visitors' guides, this map includes a key to major features, which are numbered in the key and on the map. **(a)** What number is the House Chamber? After entering the Capitol, Marcus and Teresa reach the Rotunda, facing the back of the building and the private offices. **(b)** Which way should they turn to reach the House Chamber? **(c)** Which of the other sights will they pass through on the way?

3. Use the map to plan a route that will include the sights they want to see. (a) If the Senate session is about to start, and Teresa and Marcus want to hurry directly to the Senate Chamber, where should they enter the building? **(b)** What sights would they see in walking from the Senate Chamber to the House Chamber?

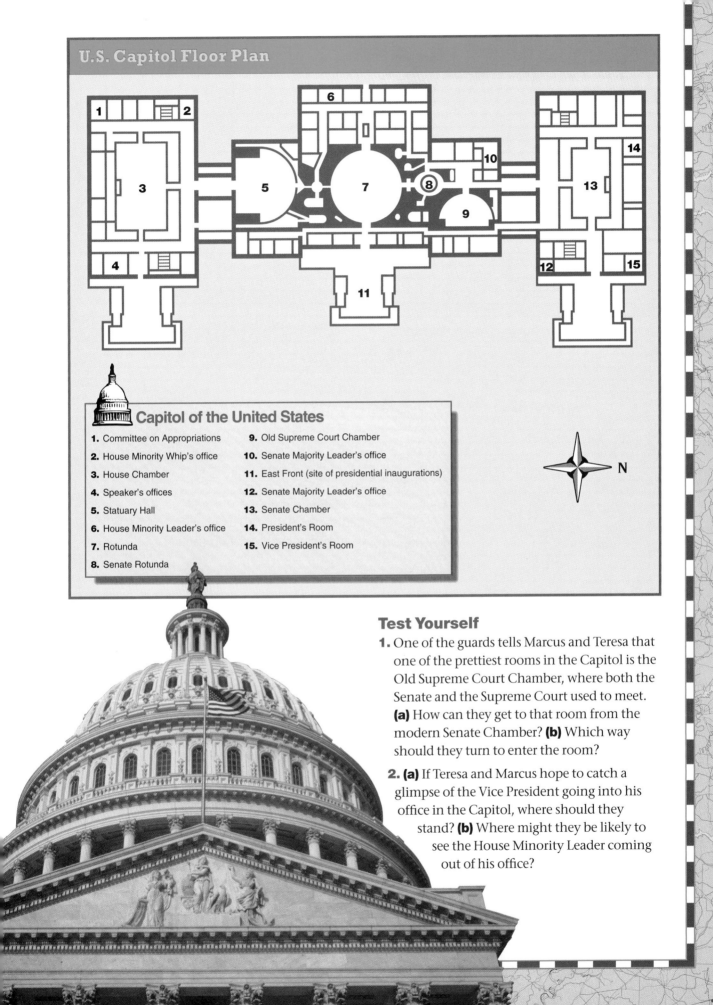

U.S. Capitol Floor Plan

Capitol of the United States

1. Committee on Appropriations
2. House Minority Whip's office
3. House Chamber
4. Speaker's offices
5. Statuary Hall
6. House Minority Leader's office
7. Rotunda
8. Senate Rotunda
9. Old Supreme Court Chamber
10. Senate Majority Leader's office
11. East Front (site of presidential inaugurations)
12. Senate Majority Leader's office
13. Senate Chamber
14. President's Room
15. Vice President's Room

N

Test Yourself

1. One of the guards tells Marcus and Teresa that one of the prettiest rooms in the Capitol is the Old Supreme Court Chamber, where both the Senate and the Supreme Court used to meet. **(a)** How can they get to that room from the modern Senate Chamber? **(b)** Which way should they turn to enter the room?

2. **(a)** If Teresa and Marcus hope to catch a glimpse of the Vice President going into his office in the Capitol, where should they stand? **(b)** Where might they be likely to see the House Minority Leader coming out of his office?

Climate and Vegetation

SECTIONS

1 Weather and Climate

2 Vegetation Regions

The World: MOUNTAINS, DESERTS, AND PENINSULAS

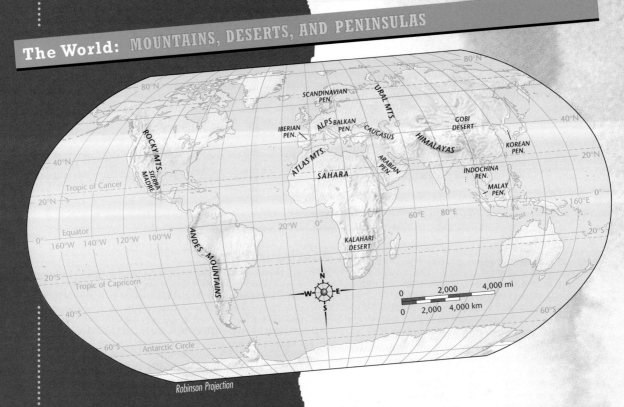

Robinson Projection

Mapping the World

Create a map like the one above, lightly shading each continent a different color. Then add labels for the mountains, deserts, and peninsulas that are shown on this map.

1 Weather and Climate

Section Preview

Main Ideas

- Climate is the weather that prevails in an area over a long period of time.

- Factors like location, latitude, elevation, and landforms influence the climate of a place.

- Convection is the process by which the sun's heat is distributed throughout the world.

- Climate regions are classified mainly by temperature and precipitation.

Vocabulary

weather, atmosphere, climate, rotation, revolution, solstice, equinox, precipitation, front, continental climate

Modest rainfall and a long growing season make the interior plains of the United States ideal for farming.

Everybody talks about the weather. No matter where you live or what language you speak, you probably know some folk sayings for predicting weather. In India, people sometimes say, "When the frog croaks in the meadow, there will be rain in three hours' time." In Britain and America, the advice is different: "Rain before seven, sun by eleven." Weather seems so important because it affects everyday life—planting, harvests, and sometimes survival.

Weather and Climate

What is "weather"? **Weather** is the condition of the bottom layer of the earth's atmosphere in one place over a short period of time. The **atmosphere** is a multilayered band of gases, water vapor, and dust above the earth. A description of the weather usually mentions temperature, moisture or precipitation, and wind. That is, a day might be "warm, dry, and calm" or "cold, snowy, and windy." Weather is in an almost constant state of change, sometimes

shifting erratically from warm to cool and back again in a short period of time. The weather in one region may influence, or be influenced by, the weather in an area far away.

Climate is the term for the weather patterns that an area typically experiences over a long period of time. The climate of an area depends on a number of factors, including its elevation, latitude, and location in relation to nearby landforms and bodies of water. Climate can change, but these changes usually take place over a longer period of time.

The concepts of weather and climate, then, are related but are not synonymous. The distinction between the two is the difference between specifics and generalities. According to an old farmer's saying, "Climate is what you expect; weather is what you get."

The Sun and the Earth

The ultimate source of the earth's climates—and of life on earth—lies some 93 million miles (150 million km) away. The sun, an intensely hot

◀ **Tornado** *(photo left)*

The Earth's Revolution and the Seasons

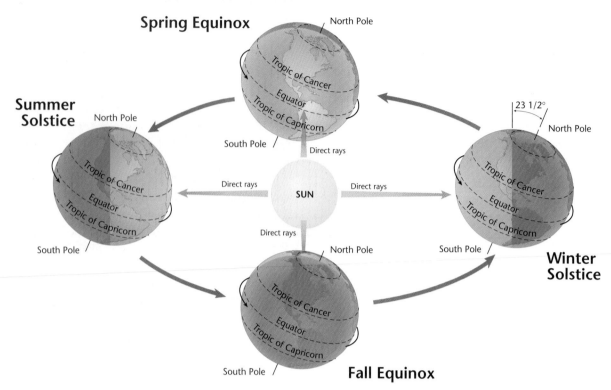

Spring Equinox
North Pole
Tropic of Cancer
Equator
Tropic of Capricorn
South Pole
Direct rays

Summer Solstice
North Pole
Tropic of Cancer
Equator
Tropic of Capricorn
South Pole

Direct rays
SUN
Direct rays

23 1/2°
North Pole
Tropic of Cancer
Equator
Tropic of Capricorn
South Pole

Winter Solstice

Direct rays
North Pole
Tropic of Cancer
Equator
Tropic of Capricorn
South Pole

Fall Equinox

DIAGRAM STUDY

It takes 365 ¼ days for the earth to make one revolution around the sun.
Because of the earth's tilt, some places receive more direct sun rays than others.
Where are the sun's rays most direct?

star, gives off energy and light that are essential for the survival of plants and animals.

The Greenhouse Effect Only a small amount of solar radiation reaches the earth's atmosphere. Some of the radiation is reflected back into space by the atmosphere and by the earth's surface, but enough remains to warm the earth's land and water. The atmosphere also prevents heat from escaping back into space too quickly.

In this sense, the earth's atmosphere has been compared to the glass walls and roof of a greenhouse, which trap the sun's warmth for growing plants. Without this so-called "greenhouse effect," the earth would be too cold for most living things.

Not all places on the earth get the same amount of heat and light from the sun. Day and night, seasonal change, and differing climates are all largely determined by the relative positions of the sun and the earth.

Rotation and Revolution As the earth moves through space it spins on its axis like a top. This movement is known as **rotation**. The axis is an invisible line through the center of the earth from pole to pole. The earth completes one rotation in approximately twenty-four hours. On the side that faces the sun, it is daytime. On the side turned away, it is night. The earth spins from west to east, so the sun appears to rise in the east and set in the west.

The earth also revolves, or moves, around the sun in a nearly circular path called an orbit. A **revolution** is one complete orbit around the sun. The earth completes one revolution every 365¼ days—the length of a year. To account for the quarter day, every four years we make the year 366 days long by adding one day to the month of February. This is known as Leap Year.

As the earth revolves, its position relative to the sun is not straight up-and-down. Rather, the earth is tilted 23½° on its axis. Because of the earth's tilt, the Tropic of Cancer at 23½°N and the Tropic of Capricorn at 23½°S mark the boundaries of the places on the earth that receive the most direct sunlight.

The earth's tilt also means that sunlight strikes different parts of the planet more directly at certain times of the year. As the diagram on page 60 shows, when the North Pole is tilted toward the sun, the sun's rays fall more directly on the Northern Hemisphere, bringing longer, warmer days. This is summer in the Northern Hemisphere and winter in the Southern Hemisphere. As the earth moves halfway around the sun, the Southern Hemisphere tilts closer to the sun, and the situation is reversed. These changes in season are marked by the summer and winter **solstices**, June 21 and December 21, the days when the sun appears directly overhead at the Tropics of Capricorn and Cancer.

The other markers for seasonal change occur on or about March 21 and September 23. These dates are known as the spring and fall **equinoxes**. On those days, the sun, at noon, appears directly overhead at the Equator. Around these dates, the lengths of day and night are nearly equal everywhere on the earth.

Latitude and Climate The angle of the sun's rays affects weather and climate in other ways. Because the earth is round, the sun's rays always fall most directly at or near the Equator. As the diagram on page 60 shows, the rays grow less and less direct as they fall closer to the North and South poles. As a result, most places near the Equator have warm climates, while the areas farthest from the Equator are cold.

Geographers use latitude, or distance from the Equator, to divide the world into zones. The tropical zones are low-latitude zones reaching 23½° north and south of the Equator. Most places in the tropics are hot year-round. The earth's two temperate zones are in the middle latitudes. They extend from 23½°N to 66½°N and from 23½°S to 66½°S. The temperate zones are generally cooler than the tropics and have a wide range of temperatures. The polar zones are in the high latitudes, from 66½°N and 66½°S to the poles. Because sunlight strikes here very indirectly, the sun's rays are spread out over a wide area. Polar climates are always cool or bitterly cold. These zones are shown in the diagram on page 62.

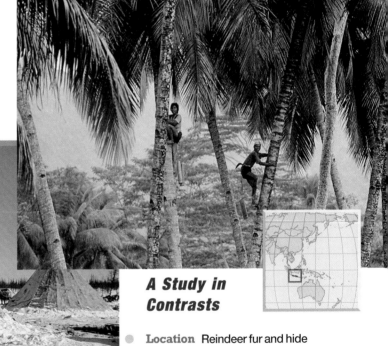

APPEARED IN *NATIONAL GEOGRAPHIC*

APPEARED IN *NATIONAL GEOGRAPHIC*

A Study in Contrasts

● **Location** Reindeer fur and hide offer people protection from the cold in Siberia, located in the far northern latitudes (left). Near the equator, people in Java (top) enjoy a tropical lifestyle. *How does location affect climate?*

Distributing the Sun's Heat

Heat from the sun does not all stay where it falls. If it did, the tropics would grow hotter each year and the polar regions colder. Instead, heat is distributed by a process called convection—the transfer of heat from one place to another.

Convection occurs because warm gases and liquids are lighter or less dense than cool gases and liquids. Therefore, warm gases and liquids tend to rise, while cooler, heavier gases and liquids sink and displace the lighter materials.

This process takes place in both air and water. Movements of air are called winds; movements of water are called currents. Warm air and warm water both flow from the Equator toward the poles. Cold air and cold water tend to move from the poles toward the Equator. Within these broad movements are complex smaller patterns.

Wind Atmospheric pressure is the weight of the atmosphere overhead. Rising warm air creates areas of low pressure; falling cool air causes areas of high pressure. Winds move from areas of high pressure into areas of low pressure. The movement of winds worldwide redistributes the sun's heat over the earth's surface.

The pattern of winds begins when light, warm air rises from the Equator and flows northward and southward toward the poles. At the same time, air from the cooler regions sinks down and moves toward the Equator.

If the world were standing still, these winds would blow in a straight line. But the earth is rotating, and its movement deflects, or bends, them. This deflection is called the Coriolis effect. In the Northern Hemisphere the path of the winds curves to the right, while in the Southern Hemisphere it curves left. The diagram below shows these patterns.

Wind Patterns In each latitude zone, temperature and pressure combine to create a pattern of prevailing, or dominant, winds. At the Equator, the rising warm air causes calm weather or very

Zones of Latitude and Prevailing Winds

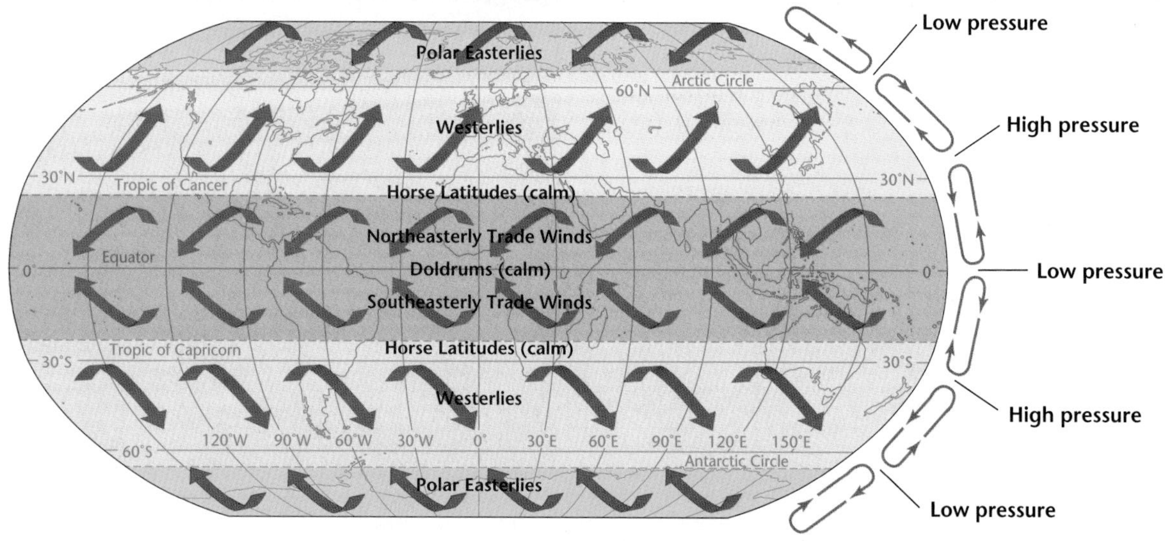

APPLYING THE GEOGRAPHIC THEMES

● **Regions** Because of the Coriolis effect, winds are deflected from their straight path toward the poles. *Which prevailing winds arise in the polar zones?*

● **Critical Thinking** *If you were to sail within the middle latitudes from the United States to Europe, in which direction would you sail to take advantage of the prevailing winds?*

KEY

Low latitudes
Middle latitudes
High latitudes
Prevailing winds
Robinson Projection

light, variable breezes. Thus the region called the "doldrums" at the Equator has light winds.

Two other regions of light and unpredictable winds are at about 30° North and South latitudes, where cool air sinks toward earth. Sailing ships had trouble getting enough wind to travel in these "horse latitudes." Supposedly, this name arose when Spaniards sailing to the Americas threw their horses overboard in order to lighten their ships and move faster.

Between the horse latitudes and the Equator, the "trade winds" blow steadily toward the Equator from the northeast and southeast. These winds got their name because merchant trading ships depended on them to push the ships laden with goods across the ocean.

Currents The waters of the oceans also help to distribute heat. Following convection patterns similar to those of winds, ocean currents, both near the ocean's surface and far below it, carry warm water from the tropics to the poles. Other currents return cold water to the Equator. Wind and the Coriolis effect influence the circular patterns of currents in the oceans. The map below shows the major warm and cold ocean currents.

Precipitation

Humidity is the amount of water vapor contained in the atmosphere. **Precipitation**, on the other hand, is all forms of water that fall from the atmosphere onto the earth's surface. Timing and volume of precipitation are important aspects of climate.

Precipitation forms as air temperature changes. Warm, less-dense air absorbs more moisture than cool air. When this air cools, it cannot retain all of its water vapor, so excess water vapor condenses into a liquid. Tiny droplets of water gather together to form clouds. Precipitation occurs when more water

Ocean Currents

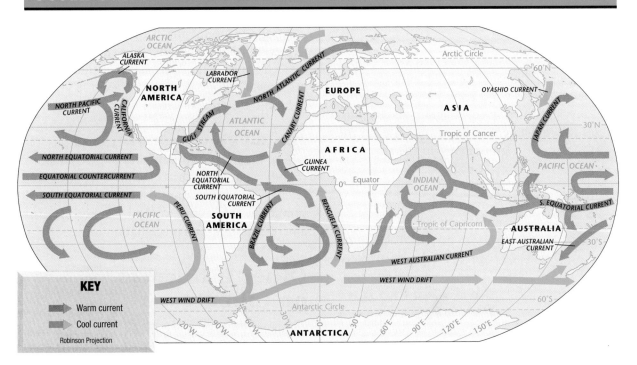

KEY
→ Warm current
→ Cool current
Robinson Projection

APPLYING THE GEOGRAPHIC THEMES
● **Movement** Warm and cold ocean currents, like the winds, help redistribute heat from the regions near the Equator to the polar regions. *Which ocean current moves north along Africa's west coast?*

Hydrologic Cycle

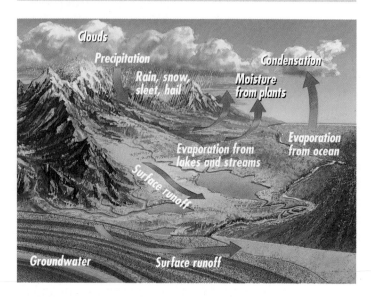

Clouds

Precipitation

Rain, snow, sleet, hail

Condensation

Moisture from plants

Evaporation from lakes and streams

Evaporation from ocean

Surface runoff

Groundwater

Surface runoff

DIAGRAM STUDY

● The movement of all of the water on the earth's surface is called the hydrologic cycle. About 97 percent of the earth's water is in the oceans. More than 2 percent is frozen in glaciers and ice sheets. Less than 1 percent is in streams and lakes, or underground. *How is the water on earth recycled?*

collects in clouds than they can hold. Snow, rain, sleet, or hail may fall, depending on air temperature and wind conditions. The hydrologic cycle, shown in the diagram above, illustrates the movement of all of the water in the ground and in the air.

Geographers divide precipitation into three types: convectional, orographic, and frontal. These types, shown in the diagram on page 65, are described below.

Convectional Precipitation

Convectional precipitation occurs when hot, humid air rises from the earth's surface and cools, thereby losing its ability to hold much water. Convectional precipitation is common near the Equator and in the tropics, where generally hot, humid surface air exists. Convectional precipitation produces nourishing rainfalls that feed lush, tropical forests.

Orographic Precipitation

Sometimes warm, moist air is forced upward when passing over high landforms, causing precipitation. This effect—called orographic precipitation—is common on seacoasts where moist, ocean winds blow toward coastal mountains. The warm winds cool as they rise up over the mountains. Clouds form and rain or snow falls. The air is cool and dry by the time it reaches the other side of the mountains. For example, winds from the Pacific Ocean deposit moisture on the windward, or wind-facing slopes, of the Cascade Range on the west coast of the United States. This thickly forested area is often foggy and rainy.

The land on the leeward side of the mountains—away from the wind—lies in what is called a rain shadow. After losing its moisture crossing the mountains, the air warms up again as elevation drops. This dry, hot air often creates dry climates behind coastal mountains. For example, California's Mohave Desert lies inland behind the Sierra Nevada.

Frontal Precipitation

Frontal precipitation, the most common kind of precipitation, occurs when two **fronts**, or air masses, of different temperatures meet. The warm air is forced upward by the heavier, cool air. The rising warm air cools, and frontal precipitation forms.

Other Influences on Climate

Temperature and precipitation are the major factors affecting weather and climate. Other influences on specific areas include nearby bodies of water, elevation, and location in relation to nearby landforms.

Nearby Bodies of Water

Land and water absorb and store heat at very different

rates. Within a few hours, land temperatures can change many degrees. Across seasons, the change is even more dramatic. In parts of Siberia on the Asian mainland, land temperatures can vary by as much as 140°F (60°C) from summer to winter. By contrast, water temperatures change much more slowly. Average temperatures on ocean surfaces, for example, vary less than 10°F (6°C) throughout the year.

Because of this difference, large bodies of water—oceans or large lakes—affect the surrounding climates. Winds that blow over water take on the water's temperature. These winds moderate land temperatures as they blow onshore. Such areas often have milder climates than other areas that are at the same latitude but far from a large body of water.

Coastal areas have specific climate types. Some mid-latitude areas on continental west coasts have mild, humid, marine climates. Prevailing westerlies supply warm, moist ocean air. Marine climates are found on the Pacific coast of North America and in southern Chile.

The British Isles and the countries of Western Europe also have a marine climate. Although these countries are located relatively far north, the winds that blow onshore from the Atlantic have been warmed by the North Atlantic Current, a branch of the warm-water Gulf Stream.

Away from the moderating influence of the oceans, the great central areas of continents in the Northern Hemisphere have what are known as **continental climates**. Most areas with continental climates have cold, snowy winters and warm or hot summers. Humidity and precipitation vary, and temperatures often reach extremes of hot and cold. Regions with this climate are the transition zones between mild and polar climates. Central Europe, Northern Eurasia, parts of China, and much of North America have continental climates.

DIAGRAM STUDY

● Precipitation occurs when rising warm air cools to form water droplets, which are then released by clouds. Examine the illustration of orographic precipitation. *Why has a desert formed on the leeward side of the mountains?*

Types of Precipitation

CONVECTIONAL PRECIPITATION

Warm air

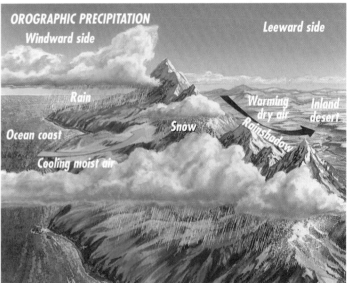

OROGRAPHIC PRECIPITATION
Windward side
Leeward side
Rain
Warming dry air
Inland desert
Ocean coast
Snow
Rainshadow
Cooling moist air

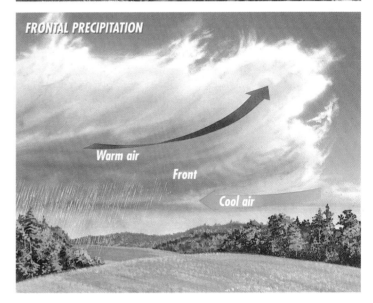

FRONTAL PRECIPITATION
Warm air
Front
Cool air

Elevation Although it is located almost on the Equator in Tanzania, Africa, Mount Kilimanjaro is capped with snow year-round. The peak's elevation of 19,340 feet (5,895 m) above sea level affects its climate much more than does its location in the tropics. Elevation has a dramatic effect on climate in highland areas throughout the world.

Air temperature decreases at a rate of about 3.5°F (2°C) for every 1,000 feet (305 m) in elevation. For this reason hikers must use caution when planning a climb. They can leave the base of a mountain in hot weather yet face a snowstorm at the peak.

Nearby Landforms Variations in climate occur naturally. Indeed no climate is ever completely uniform. Coastal mountains are not the only landforms that affect climate. Inland mountains, large desert areas, lakes, forests, and other natural features can influence climate nearby. Even a concentration of tall buildings can influence climate in the surrounding area. The pavement and concrete of large cities absorb vast amounts of solar energy. This causes the average temperature of the city proper to be greater than that of the more open areas surrounding the city. Such small variations within a region are called microclimates.

The World: CLIMATE REGIONS

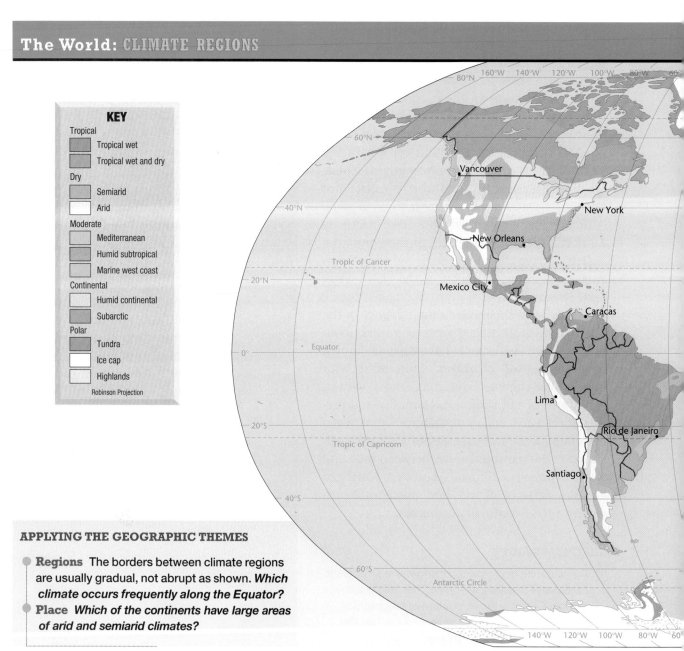

KEY

Tropical
- Tropical wet
- Tropical wet and dry

Dry
- Semiarid
- Arid

Moderate
- Mediterranean
- Humid subtropical
- Marine west coast

Continental
- Humid continental
- Subarctic

Polar
- Tundra
- Ice cap
- Highlands

Robinson Projection

APPLYING THE GEOGRAPHIC THEMES

- **Regions** The borders between climate regions are usually gradual, not abrupt as shown. *Which climate occurs frequently along the Equator?*
- **Place** *Which of the continents have large areas of arid and semiarid climates?*

World Climate Regions

Geographers and climatologists have developed many different classification systems to define the world's major climate regions. Defining these climate regions is difficult because of changing climate conditions and the lack of accurate weather data in many parts of the world. Most efforts to classify climate regions rely on two factors: temperature and precipitation.

Generally climates are classified using variations of a system developed in the early 1900s by Wladimir Köppen (VLAD uh meer KEPP pen), a German biologist. These systems identify six broad types of climate regions—Tropical, Dry, Moderate, Continental, Polar, and Highland. Most of these climate groups have specific subdivisions. For example, in the dry group there are two subdivisions: semiarid and arid.

The table on page 68 describes the climate classification system used in this book. The map on these pages shows climate regions using this system. Regional divisions on the map do not mean that climate changes abruptly. Instead, boundary lines usually mark areas of transition where one climate region merges with another. Although climate is generally constant in a region, temporary variations can and do take place.

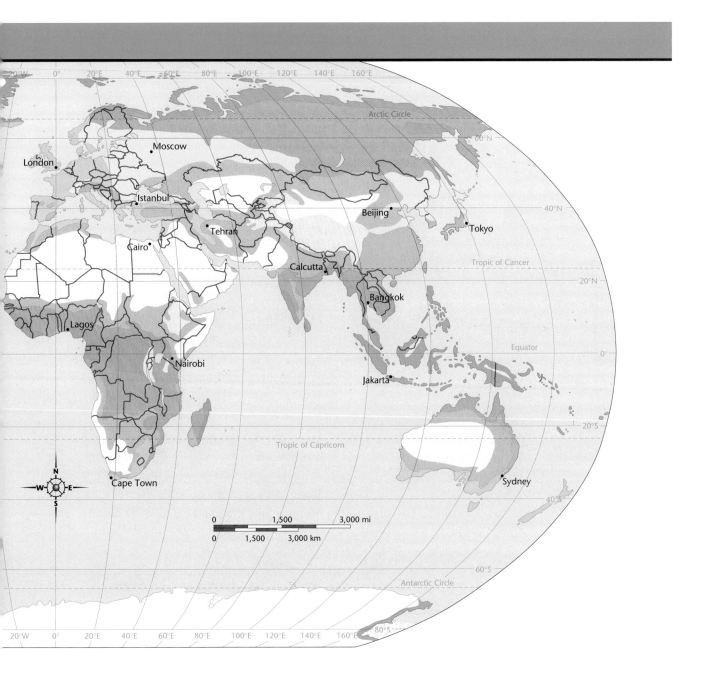

World Climate Regions

CLIMATE TYPE	TEMPERATURE	PRECIPITATION
Tropical		
Tropical Wet	Hot all year (avg.) 79°F (26°C)	*Yearly:* 100 in. (254.0 cm) *Monthly* (avg.): 8.3 in. (21.1 cm)
Tropical Wet and Dry	Hot all year 79°F (26°C)	*Yearly:* 50 in. (127.0 cm) *Summer:* 10.2 in. (25.9 cm) *Winter:* 0.5 in. (1.3 cm)
Dry		
Semiarid	Hot summers, mild to cold winters *Summer* (avg.): 78°F (26°C) *Winter* (avg.): 51°F (11°C)	*Yearly:* 18 in. (45.7 cm) *Monthly* (avg.): Summer: 3.4 in. (8.6 cm) Winter: 0.2 in. (0.5 cm)
Arid	Hot days, cold nights *Summer* (avg.): 81°F (27°C) *Winter* (avg.): 55°F (13°C)	*Yearly:* 5 in. (12.7 cm) *Monthly* (avg.): Summer: 0.6 in. (1.5 cm) Winter: 0.1 in. (0.3 cm)
Moderate		
Mediterranean	Hot summers, cool winters *Summer* (avg.): 72°F (22°C) *Winter* (avg.): 52°F (11°C)	*Yearly:* 23 in. (58.4 cm) *Monthly* (avg.): Summer: 0.4 in. (1.0 cm) Winter: 3.8 in. (9.7 cm)
Humid Subtropical	Hot summers, cool winters *Summer* (avg.): 77°F (25°C) *Winter* (avg.): 47°F (8°C)	*Yearly:* 50 in. (127.0 cm) *Monthly* (avg.): Summer: 6.2 in. (15.7 cm) Winter: 2.8 in. (7.1 cm)
Marine West Coast	Warm summers, cool winters *Summer* (avg.): 60°F (16°C) *Winter* (avg.): 42°F (6°C)	*Yearly:* 45 in. (114.3 cm) *Monthly* (avg.): Summer: 2.5 in. (6.4 cm) Winter: 5.5 in. (14.0 cm)
Continental		
Humid Continental	Warm summers, cold winters *Summer* (avg.): 66°F (19°C) *Winter* (avg.): 21°F (−6°C)	*Yearly:* 27 in. (68.6 cm) *Monthly* (avg.): Summer: 3.2 in. (8.1 cm) Winter: 1.6 in. (4.1 cm)
Subarctic	Cool summers, very cold winters *Summer* (avg.): 56°F (13°C) *Winter* (avg.): −8°F (−22°C)	*Yearly:* 17 in. (43.2 cm) *Monthly* (avg.): Summer: 1.8 in. (4.6 cm) Winter: 1.2 in. (3.0 cm)
Polar		
Tundra	Cold summers, very cold winters *Summer* (avg.): 40°F (4°C) *Winter* (avg.): 0°F (−18°C)	*Yearly:* 16 in. (40.6 cm) *Monthly* (avg.): Summer: 1.9 in. (4.8 cm) Winter: 1.2 in. (3.0 cm)
Ice Cap	Cold all year *Summer* (avg.): 32°F (0°C) *Winter* (avg.): −14°F (−26°C)	*Yearly:* 8 in. (20.3 cm) *Monthly* (avg.): Summer: 1.0 in. (2.5 cm) Winter: 0.4 in. (1.0 cm)
Highland		
	Varies depending on elevation	*Yearly:* Ranges from 3 in. (7.6 cm) to 123 in. (312.4 cm)

Source: Goode's World Atlas, Rand McNally

● Look over the chart on the opposite page.
  Which climate region receives the highest annual average precipitation?

Changing Climates

Many climate changes result from changes in nature, but more may now be caused by human action. Increasing amounts of carbon dioxide and other substances in the earth's atmosphere may lead to what scientists call "global warming"—a rise in the earth's temperature. Global warming could partially melt polar ice caps, causing a rise in the level of the oceans and flooding of densely populated low-lying areas. Other possible effects of global warming include an increase in precipitation in some areas and a decline in others. Areas that now support agriculture could become deserts.

Scientists are concerned about climatic change because past changes in climates have had a profound impact. Historians believe that ancient Scandinavian explorers called Vikings first settled on the shores of Greenland and Iceland in the tenth century when those regions were somewhat warmer. But in the mid-1500s, North Atlantic climates cooled. Lower temperatures made agriculture difficult, resulting in lower population levels. As the Greenland ice sheet expanded, the Greenland settlements were finally abandoned.

Pooling Their Resources

● **Human-Environment Interaction**
Fleeing the cold and snow of winter, millions of Americans have settled in the hot, dry climate of the nation's Southwestern states. Many, however, seem intent on altering their new environment. *What changes do you see in this photograph of an Arizona suburb?*

Section 1 Review

Vocabulary and Main Ideas

1. **Define:** a. **weather** b. **atmosphere** c. **climate**
   d. **rotation** e. **revolution** f. **solstice**
   g. **equinox** h. **precipitation** i. **front**
   j. **continental climate**

2. **How do winds help distribute the sun's heat?**

3. **How do ocean currents help distribute the sun's heat?**

4. **Critical Thinking:** *Cause and Effect* **Why do coastal mountains often have foggy, rainy climates?**

learning LOCATIONS

5. Look at the map on page 63. Near which continents does the Canary Current run?

6. Look at the map on pages 66–67. Which European mountain range has a highland climate?

Focus on Skills

☑ Social Studies
☐ Map and Globe
☐ Critical Thinking and Problem Solving

Using Climate Graphs

In most climates, temperatures slide up or down, and precipitation rises and falls depending on the season. Climate graphs usually show two kinds of basic information: average temperatures along one vertical scale and average precipitation along a second vertical scale. A time scale across the bottom of the graph indicates the months of the year by their initial letter.

The climate graphs below are for the cities of São Paulo and Beijing. Use the following steps to analyze the information in the graphs and compare climates in these cities.

1. Determine the annual variation in temperature for each city. Temperature is shown by the curved line at the top of the graphs. To find the average temperature for any month, locate the point on the temperature line directly above the name of the month. Then look at the markings for degrees on the left-hand scale. Answer the following questions: (a) Which city has the greater extremes of hot and cold temperatures? (b) Which has the more even temperatures year-round?

2. Determine the annual variation in precipitation for each city. Precipitation is shown by the bar graph at the bottom of each graph. It is measured in inches on the right-hand vertical scale. To read the graph, measure the height of the bar for any given month against that scale. (a) What is the rainiest month in Beijing? (b) About how many inches of rain fall in that month? (c) Is the amount of rainfall in Beijing's rainiest month less than, equal to, or greater than the amount of rainfall in São Paulo's rainiest month?

3. Compare the values for temperature and precipitation to describe each climate. Climate graphs show temperature and precipitation side by side because these are the two major factors that determine a climate. (a) Which city has the more variable climate—with both wet and dry seasons and great changes in temperature? (b) How would you describe São Paulo's climate?

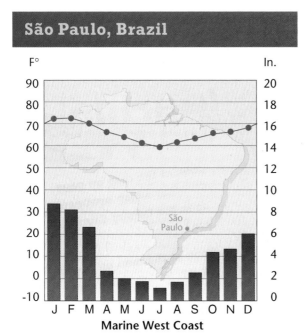

São Paulo, Brazil
Marine West Coast

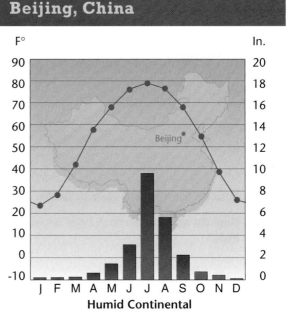

Beijing, China
Humid Continental

Line graphs show temperature. Bar graphs show precipitation.

2 Vegetation Regions

Section Preview

Main Ideas

- In similar environments, similar groups of plants grow together to form a plant community.

- There are four different kinds of vegetation regions: forests, grasslands, desert plants, and tundra.

- Plants in every region adapt to their surroundings.

Vocabulary

plant community, environment, natural vegetation, deciduous, coniferous, chaparral, savanna, tundra, permafrost

APPEARED IN *NATIONAL GEOGRAPHIC*

The forests of the northeastern United States produce spectacular fall foliage.

Except for the polar ice caps and the most barren spots of the deserts, plants grow everywhere on earth. They range from microscopic, one-celled plants to gigantic redwood trees. Plants are among the oldest and most basic forms of life on earth. Green plants are especially important because they supply food for humans and animals and help recycle the earth's water supply.

Plant Communities

Plants seldom live alone. Instead, groups of plants tend to be interdependent—that is, they depend on one another for such things as shade, support, and even nourishment. In the wild, for example, trees provide certain vines with both food and a place to grow.

The mix of interdependent plants that naturally grows in one place is called a **plant community**. Such a natural grouping consists of plants that can easily survive in a particular **environment**—the physical conditions of the natural surroundings. Climate, sunlight, temperature, precipitation, elevation, soil, and landforms are all part of the plant environment. Similar environments tend to produce similar plant communities.

Biomes and Vegetation Regions

The term *biome* (BY om) is used to describe a region in which the environment, plants, and animal life are suited to one another. For example, in any temperate forest biome, you are likely to find moderate temperatures and rainfall, oak or maple trees, and animals such as deer, squirrels, raccoons, and owls.

Geographers also classify regions by their **natural vegetation**, or the typical plant life in areas where humans have not altered the

GLOBAL issues

Rain Forests

A United Nations Food and Agriculture Organization study reports that currently nearly 1.3 acres (5,261 sq m) of tropical rain forest disappear every second. If this rate of destruction continues, all tropical forests will disappear in less than 115 years.

landscape significantly. The map below shows major vegetation regions of the world. Because these regions have similar plant life, they are often similar in climate and other characteristics on which those plants depend. Vegetation regions are of four general types: forest, grassland, desert, and tundra. Besides climate, soil type, slope, and drainage all contribute to the kind of vegetation found in each region.

Forest Regions

The word *forest* probably makes you think of whatever kind of forest is most familiar to you—giant groves of redwoods, thick clumps of oaks and maples, hillsides covered with fragrant pines. All these forests exist in North America. In different parts of the world there are other types of forest regions. Forest vegetation of one kind or another grows on every continent except Antarctica.

Tropical Rain Forest In areas near the Equator, where the temperature is warm and great amounts of rain fall, thick, tropical rain forests grow. The largest are in the Amazon River basin in South America and the Congo River basin in central Africa. Within the rain

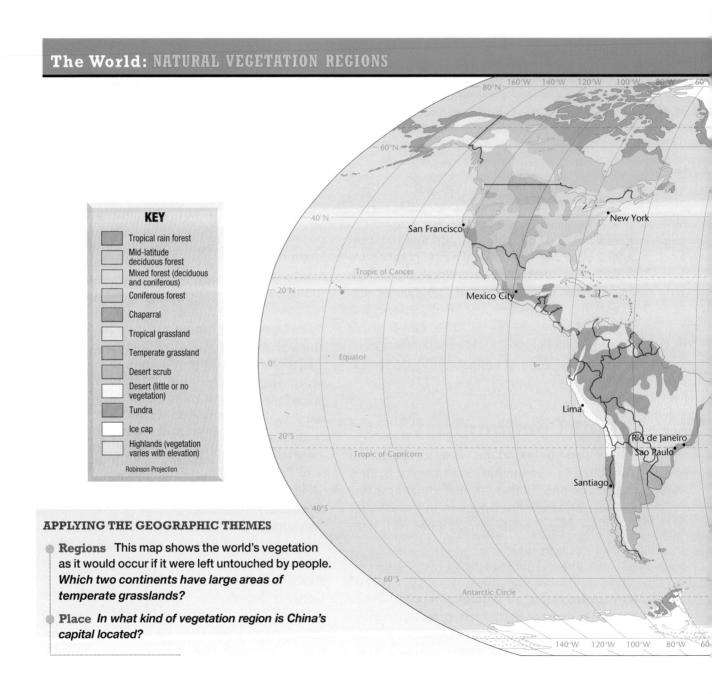

The World: NATURAL VEGETATION REGIONS

KEY

- Tropical rain forest
- Mid-latitude deciduous forest
- Mixed forest (deciduous and coniferous)
- Coniferous forest
- Chaparral
- Tropical grassland
- Temperate grassland
- Desert scrub
- Desert (little or no vegetation)
- Tundra
- Ice cap
- Highlands (vegetation varies with elevation)

Robinson Projection

APPLYING THE GEOGRAPHIC THEMES

- **Regions** This map shows the world's vegetation as it would occur if it were left untouched by people. *Which two continents have large areas of temperate grasslands?*

- **Place** *In what kind of vegetation region is China's capital located?*

forest, tall trees stretch skyward toward the sunlight. Their foliage forms a dense, green, tangled canopy of leaves that almost entirely blocks out the sun from the forest floor. Where there are gaps in the canopy, for example, along the side of a river, light reaches the ground. The result is a heavy undergrowth of twisting vines.

Mid-Latitude Forest The trees in the tropical rain forest are broadleaf evergreens, which keep their leaves year-round. By contrast, the dominant trees in the forests of the middle latitudes are **deciduous**. That is, they shed their leaves during one season, usually autumn. These forests look dramatically different depending on the season—stark and bare in the winter and lush and green in the summer. In some parts of the world, the broad leaves of these trees—such as oaks, birches, and maples—turn brilliant colors before they fall. The New England states are famous for their vibrant fall foliage.

Broadleaf deciduous forests once covered much of Europe, eastern North America, and eastern Asia. Except in relatively hilly areas, a large part of this type of forest was cleared over the centuries for agriculture and other human

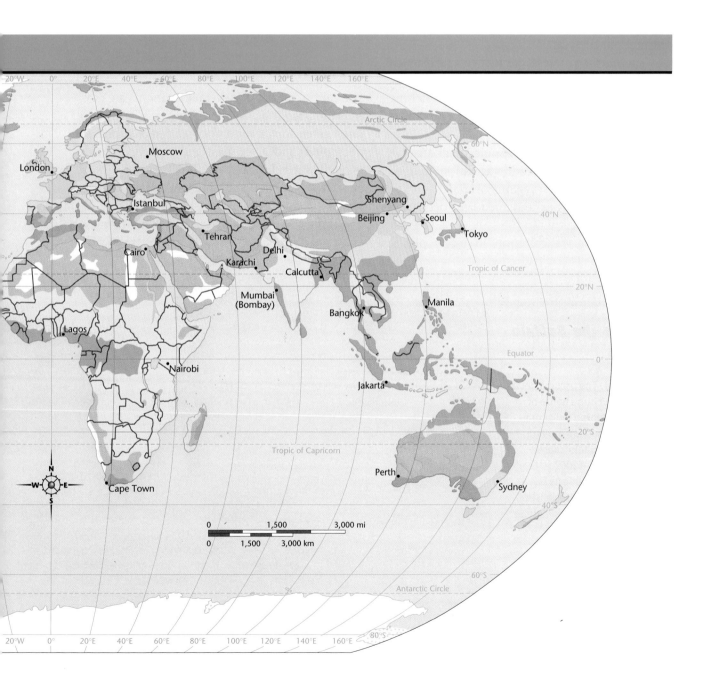

uses. Very little of the original natural vegetation remains. In some places, fields have been abandoned and the natural vegetation is reclaiming the land. These lands in the middle latitudes have a temperate climate with adequate rainfall, warm summers, and cool or cold winters.

Coniferous Forest In the colder parts of the middle latitudes grow several kinds of trees that can survive long, cold winters. Pines, spruces, firs, and their relatives have long, thin "needles" rather than broad, flat leaves. Needle leaves expose only a small surface to the cold and so can remain on the tree in winter without freezing. As a result, these needleleaf trees are "evergreen," using whatever sunlight is available throughout the year.

The northern forests are named **coniferous** after the cones that carry and protect their seeds. Coniferous forests cover huge areas stretching across northern North America, Europe, and Asia.

Other Forest Types Some small areas of the world have unique forest vegetation. In most places, however, forest regions overlap. A mixed region has coniferous and broadleaf deciduous trees growing together in the same area. Clusters of such forests are common in many places, including the northern United States. They grow in cool parts of the middle latitudes or at high elevations where winters are mild or very cold.

Another distinctive forest type is **chaparral**, which includes small evergreen trees and low bushes, or scrub. *Chaparral* is a Spanish word for "an area of small evergreen oak trees." This vegetation is uniquely adapted to a Mediterranean climate, where most of the precipitation falls during the winter and where summers are hot and dry. Many chaparral plants have leathery leaves to hold moisture over the dry summer. Regions of chaparral are found on the coasts of the Mediterranean Sea, southern California, Chile, South Africa, and Australia, as well as in a few inland areas of the American Southwest.

Grasslands

The central regions of several continents are covered by grasslands. At the edges, grasslands and forest often mix. In addition, scattered clumps of trees often grow on grasslands where there is enough water. Like forests, the characteristics of grasslands vary depending on their latitudes.

Tropical Grasslands Huge tropical grasslands, or **savannas**, grow in the warm

Where the Buffalo Roam

- **Regions** The prairies once supported huge herds of buffalo. Hunted indiscriminately by settlers moving west, the buffalo neared extinction by 1900. Conservation efforts have preserved the species, but most of their natural habitat has been converted to farmland. *What other regions of the world support temperate grasslands?*

Death Valley

Place Despite its name, Death Valley does support some life, as evidenced by this tarantula. *What might be the biggest challenge for plants and animals in this desert?*

lands nearest the Equator. Savanna grasses thrive in tropical climates. Scattered trees and other plants that can survive the dry periods of tropical climates dot the savanna. Savannas have three distinct seasons. During the wet season, the grasses grow tall and green. This is followed by a dry season, when the grasses wither, turn brown, and eventually die above ground. The third "season" is a period of naturally occurring wildfires. Although fire is usually considered destructive, it is necessary to the savanna. Fires that break out in the dry season help maintain the savanna by encouraging new grasses to grow.

Temperate Grasslands The grasslands in cooler parts of the world are known by several names. They differ in the length and kinds of grasses, which in turn vary with the amount of rainfall and soil types.

The temperate grasslands of North America are called prairies. Because rainfall decreases toward the west, the prairie grasses also are different. In the east, which gets as much as 40 inches (102 cm) of rain a year, "tallgrass" prairie once grew. This true prairie is typified by tall grasses dotted with colorful wildflowers. Grasses are shorter as you move west toward the central prairies and the dry Great Plains.

In most parts of the prairies, trees and shrubs grow along the banks of rivers and

streams. Grass fires are fairly common in the summer season. Though prairie grasses once covered the American Midwest, little of the natural prairie vegetation is now left. Much of the grassland region was plowed under to provide fertile farmland for growing grain.

The cool, dry, temperate grasslands of Northern Eurasia and central Asia—called the steppes—are similar to the Great Plains. The word "steppe" comes from a Russian word meaning "treeless plain." Other well-known and productive grasslands are the pampas of Argentina and the veld of South Africa.

Desert Vegetation

Desert regions are not just barren expanses of sand. Many plants have adapted to survive with almost no water. Cactus plants, for example, store water in thick stems. The saguaro cactus expands like an accordion to make room for water stored in its trunks and branches. It is capable of storing hundreds of gallons of water.

Cactus leaves are prickly needles, which protect them and their water supply from animals. Other desert plants have small leaves, which lose little moisture into the air through evaporation. Still others have seeds that can survive for many years until there is enough water for them to sprout. These plants have a short life cycle. After a rain they will sprout, grow, flower, produce new

Cold Comfort

- **Regions** Arctic tundra is found in the extreme northern latitudes, such as here in Denali National Park, Alaska. It supports many kinds of wildlife, such as foxes, wolves, polar bears, moose, caribou, and more than eighty species of birds. *What kinds of vegetation are found in this region?*
- **Critical Thinking** The growing season on the Arctic tundra can be less than two months long. *What factors might contribute to the short growing season?*

seeds, and die in a short period—all to ensure that their seeds will be ready for the next rainfall.

Roots also help plants find and store water in desert regions. On valley floors and in dry streambeds, long roots reach deep into the ground toward water. Other species of plants have long, shallow root systems that stretch out over a wide area to gather the water that falls during the brief rainfalls. Desert plants grow widely scattered, for the water in one area cannot support much vegetation.

Tundra

In **tundra** regions, where temperatures are always cool or cold, only specialized plants can grow. One type of tundra—alpine tundra—exists in high mountains. No trees grow at these high elevations. Small plants and wildflowers grow in sheltered spots. Tiny, brightly colored plants called lichens (LYE kenz) make patterns on the rocks.

In another type of tundra, the arctic tundra, plants must also be able to live in cold temperatures and short growing seasons. In addition, they must go without sunlight for most of the winter.

Arctic landscapes are treeless, covered with grasses, mosses, lichens, and some flowering plants. Some species have developed extremely large leaves that tilt toward the sun. This allows them to catch as much light as possible. In parts of the tundra a layer of soil just below the surface, known as **permafrost**, stays permanently frozen. The soil above this layer of permafrost is often soggy and waterlogged.

Although the tundra sounds like a bleak place, many people find it beautiful. One naturalist wrote this description of the Alaskan tundra in late June:

> *When we climbed the higher, drier [river] banks we looked over an eternal expanse of green and brown. . . . It was a glorious garden of arctic plants, this summer tundra-delta, and stiff with northern birds, so that never for a moment were we out of sight or hearing of crane, goose, duck, or wader.*

In some extreme climate regions of the world vegetation is rare. Some highland areas,

where temperatures are very low and the soil is rocky and poor, are almost completely bare of plants. The polar ice caps and the great ice sheets of Greenland and Antarctica are considered regions without vegetation. Even there, however, small and simple plants survive in some areas. As scientists explore more and more of the earth's extreme climate regions, they are finding that there are really very few places on earth with no plants growing at all.

Section 2 Review

Vocabulary and Main Ideas

1. **Define: a. plant community b. environment c. natural vegetation d. deciduous e. coniferous f. chaparral g. savanna h. tundra i. permafrost**

2. **What are the four major categories of vegetation?**

3. **In what ways have plants adapted to life in the desert?**

4. **Critical Thinking: *Formulating Questions* What questions would you have to ask in order to define a natural vegetation region?**

5. Look at the map on pages 72–73. What area is shown by the desert scrub and desert vegetation areas of northern Africa?

6. Look at the map on pages 72–73. Which northern European peninsula has tundra, highland, coniferous forest, and mixed forest vegetation?

Reviewing Vocabulary

Use each of the following terms in a sentence that shows its meaning.

1. weather
2. atmosphere
3. climate
4. rotation
5. revolution
6. equinox
7. precipitation
8. front
9. natural vegetation
10. deciduous
11. coniferous
12. chaparral
13. savanna
14. tundra
15. permafrost

Summarizing Main Ideas

Section 1 Weather and Climate

■ Climate—the weather that prevails in an area over a long period of time—is influenced by latitude, elevation, landforms, and other factors.

■ The climates at different latitudes are greatly influenced by the amount and intensity of sunlight the areas receive and by the way wind and water redistribute the sun's heat throughout the world by the process of convection.

■ Climate regions are classified mainly on the basis of seasonal temperatures and levels of precipitation.

Section 2 Vegetation Regions

■ In similar environments, similar groups of plants form a plant community.

■ Both natural events and human actions can change the environment.

■ Geographers classify natural vegetation regions based on different types of forests, grasslands, desert plants, and tundra.

■ Plants in every region adapt to the conditions in their environment.

Applying the Geographic Themes

1. **Location** How do large bodies of water affect the climate of coastal areas?
2. **Place** How does elevation affect the climate of a place?
3. **Human-Environment Interaction** How could an increase in carbon dioxide in the atmosphere cause a change in climate?
4. **Movement** How could an understanding of ocean currents aid travel?
5. **Regions** Which vegetation regions have the least plant life?

Critical Thinking and Applying Skills

1. **Analyzing Information** Why are the earth's winds and ocean currents important to life on the planet?
2. **Using Climate Graphs** Study the two climate graphs on page 70 and then answer the following questions.

   a. Which of the two climates clearly has a brief rainy season?

   b. Which of the two climates has a relatively equal amount of rainfall?

Journal Activity

Writing Across Cultures

▶ 1. Imagine that you spend one year in a place that has a climate similar to your home's but that is located in the Southern Hemisphere. Write four paragraphs—one for each season—describing the changes in the weather from month to month. (Be sure to name each month.)

▶ 2. Choose a vegetation region described in this chapter that is different from the region in which you live. Then write a paragraph explaining why you would like to visit such a region.

INTERNET link

Hurricanes strike all over the world, often causing great damage. Follow the path of one storm and read about the destruction it caused, at the National Hurricane Center page of the National Oceanic and Atmospheric Administration. Link to this site from:

• www.phschool.com

Choose Storm Archives. Then, with a regional map in front of you, track the storm. Use the data in the report to write a summary of the storm's path and its effects.

learning LOCATIONS

Mountains, Deserts, and Peninsulas

Number from 1 to 12 on a piece of paper. Next to each number, write the letter of the place on the map that corresponds to the places listed below.

1. Alps
2. Andes Mountains
3. Arabian Peninsula
4. Balkan Peninsula
5. Caucasus Mountains
6. Gobi Desert
7. Indochina Peninsula
8. Kalahari Desert
9. Himalayas
10. Sahara
11. Sierra Madre
12. Ural Mountains

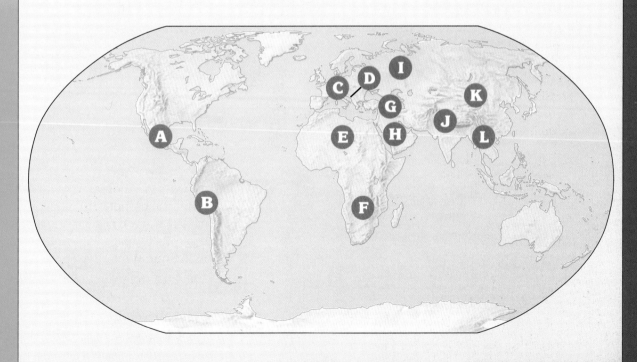

3

Population and Culture

Cities of the World

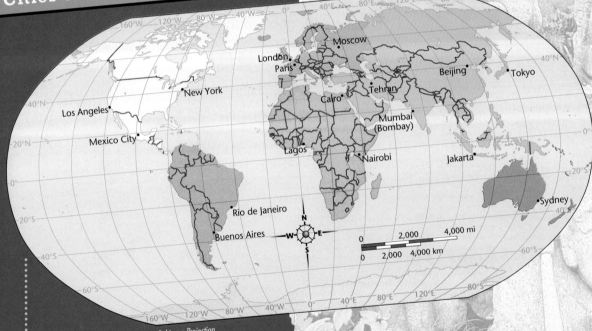

Robinson Projection

learning LOCATIONS

Mapping the World

Create a map like the one above, lightly shading each continent a different color. Then add labels for the major world cities that are shown on this map.

The Study of Human Geography

Section Preview

Main Ideas

- Population is unevenly distributed throughout the world.

- World population has increased more rapidly during the twentieth century than at any other time.

- Every group of people develops a set of customs, beliefs, and actions that make up its culture.

Vocabulary

demography, culture, population density, birthrate, death rate, immigrant, emigrant, urbanization, rural, diffusion, acculturation, culture hearth

APPEARED IN *NATIONAL GEOGRAPHIC*

Eager bathers all but obscure this beach in Tel Aviv, Israel.

Geographers are interested in human activities as well as the physical environment. Human geography includes a wide range of topics, such as the study of languages, religions, customs, and economic and political systems.

A special focus of human geography is **demography**—the study of populations—including such topics as birth, marriage, migration, and death. Human geographers also study **culture**—the beliefs and actions that define a group of people's way of life.

Where People Live

It is difficult to imagine how vast the numbers 1 million or 1 billion are. For instance, you had lived a million seconds when you were 11.6 days old. You won't have lived a billion seconds until you are 31.7 years old. Today the world's population is more than five-and-a-half *billion* people. In some areas, the **population density**—the average number of people in a square mile or a square kilometer—is very high. Other areas have few or no inhabitants.

What factors lead people to live where they do? Natural obstacles greatly restrict where people can comfortably live. More than two thirds of the earth is covered by water, and about half of the land area is almost unlivable because of harsh deserts, rugged mountains, or bitterly cold climates. As a result, almost all people live on a relatively small share of the earth's surface—areas where the soil is fertile enough, water is plentiful enough, and the climate is mild enough to grow crops.

People and Environments People have always adapted their way of life in response to the surrounding environment. For example, in colder areas they wear heavier clothes. These adaptations have allowed people to survive in areas that might appear hostile to human life.

At the same time, human activity has dramatically altered the earth's physical landscape. By cutting trees, grazing their animals on wild grasses, plowing soils, and damming rivers, people have modified the earth. Some of these modifications have been mild with minimal impact, while others have been drastic.

◀ **Hand-carved stone sculptures, Kyoto, Japan** *(photo left)*

Population Density The simple way to calculate population density is to divide the total population of a region by the region's land area. The results can be misleading, however. In Egypt, for example, more than 90 percent of the land is desert, and nearly all Egyptians live along a narrow strip beside the Nile River.

Some geographers thus prefer to figure a country's population density in terms of its arable land—land that can be farmed—rather than its total land area. Egypt had an overall population density in 1995 of about 161 people per square mile (62 per sq km). Measured in terms of arable land, the density was about 5,360 people per square mile (2,074 per sq km)!

Population Growth

As the graph on page 85 shows, the world's population has increased dramatically in the past half-century. The current yearly increase alone—more than 80 million people—is almost as big as the current population of Mexico. This overwhelming growth rate poses a special problem for poorer countries and a difficult challenge for the world as a whole.

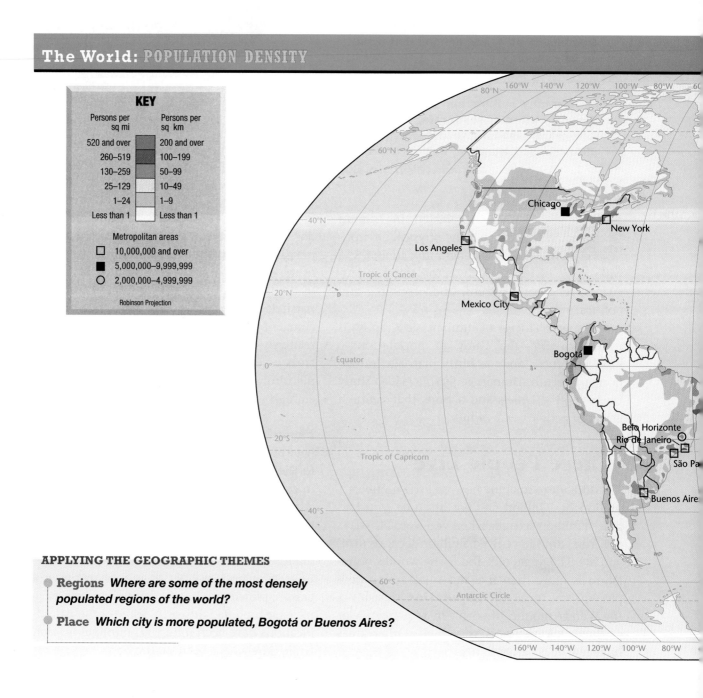

The World: POPULATION DENSITY

KEY

Persons per sq mi	Persons per sq km
520 and over	200 and over
260–519	100–199
130–259	50–99
25–129	10–49
1–24	1–9
Less than 1	Less than 1

Metropolitan areas
☐ 10,000,000 and over
■ 5,000,000–9,999,999
○ 2,000,000–4,999,999

Robinson Projection

APPLYING THE GEOGRAPHIC THEMES

● **Regions** *Where are some of the most densely populated regions of the world?*

● **Place** *Which city is more populated, Bogotá or Buenos Aires?*

The Effects of Growth What will the effects of rapid population growth be? Some demographers predict increases in famine, disease, and natural resource depletion. Others are optimistic about the future and predict that as the number of humans increases, levels of technology and creativity will also increase.

Comparing Growth Rates World population growth is very uneven. Different countries have different balances between the **birthrate**—the number of live births each year per 1,000 people—and the **death rate**—the number of deaths each year per 1,000 people. A country's population is also affected by differences in the number of **immigrants** (people who move into the country) and **emigrants** (people who leave the country to live elsewhere).

When the combined birthrate and immigration rate equals the combined death rate and emigration rate, a country is said to have reached "zero population growth." This is the case in some highly industrialized countries today. In many developing countries, however, birthrates are still high, while death rates have fallen because of improved health.

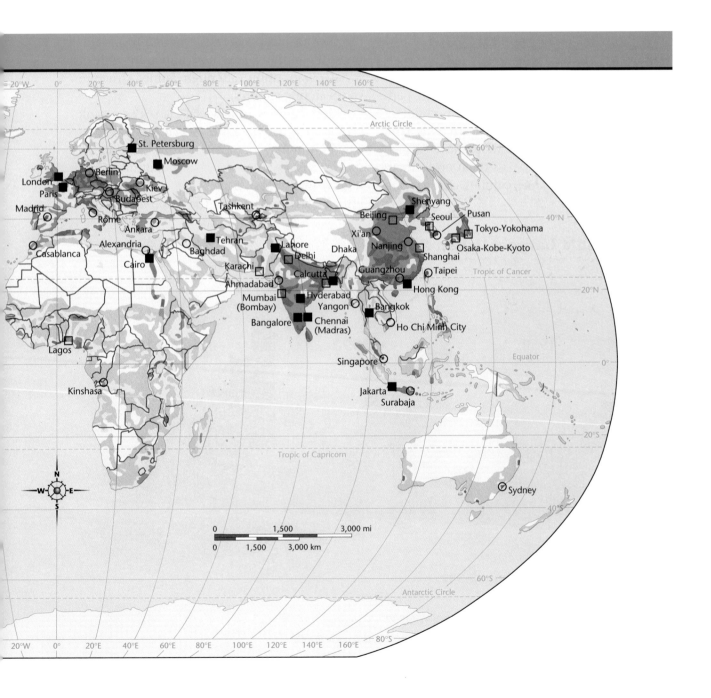

Patterns of Population

The map on page 82–83 illustrates the uneven distribution of the world population. The densest concentrations of people are in four regions: East Asia, South Asia, Europe, and eastern North America.

Many of the people in these population clusters live in metropolitan areas—central cities surrounded by suburbs. Today most Europeans and North Americans live in cities, and **urbanization**—the growth of city populations—is going on throughout the world. In many countries, urban populations are growing twice as fast as **rural**—countryside—populations.

The Nature of Culture

Differences in population patterns are in part reflections of differences in culture. As children grow up in a given culture, they learn skills, language, eating customs, and thousands of other cultural traits. Later they pass them on to their own children. Over time cultures change, but usually very slowly.

Culture is reflected in both objects and ideas—that is, in material and nonmaterial ways. Material culture includes things that people make, such as food, clothing, architecture, arts, crafts, and technology. Nonmaterial culture includes religion, language, spiritual beliefs, and patterns of behavior. Some cultures, for example, value cooperation and group activities, while others place greater value on individual achievement.

Social Organization Every culture creates a social structure by organizing its members into smaller units. This social organization is meant to help the people of a culture work together to meet their basic needs. In all cultures, the family is the most important unit of social organization, although family structure varies among cultures.

Most cultures have social classes that rank people in order of status. Social class may be based on money, occupation, education, ancestry, or any other factor that a culture values highly. In the past, a person was usually born into a class and stayed there for life. Today,

The World's Largest Urban Areas

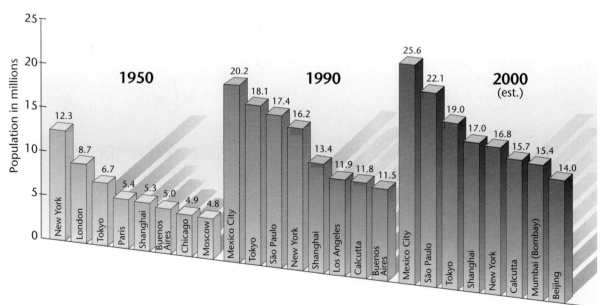

Source: United Nations Department of International Economic and Social Affairs

CHART STUDY

● *What was the world's largest urban area in 1950?*

● *Which urban area was expected to be the largest in the year 2000?*

people in most cultures have at least some degree of social mobility.

Language Language is the cornerstone of culture. Without language, people would not be able to communicate. They could not pass on what they know or believe to a new generation. All cultures have language, although not all have written languages.

Language reflects a culture's identity. People who speak the same language generally share the same customs. Many societies, however, include large groups of people who speak different languages. India, for example, has more than 700 languages. The map on pages 86–87 shows the major language families around the world.

Religion Religion is another important aspect of culture. Religion helps people answer basic questions about the meaning and purpose of life. It supports the values that a group of people consider important.

Religious beliefs vary around the world. The worship of one god is called monotheism. The worship of more than one god is called poly-theism. Religious practices such as prayers and rituals also vary from one culture to another. The map on pages 88-89 shows the major religions of the world.

Struggles over religious differences are a problem in many countries. These troubles often find their roots in the past. Religious differences are usually not the only cause of fighting, however. Lack of political power or economic opportunity often fuels rivalries.

Cultural Landscapes Technology is an important part of culture. As human beings use natural resources or alter the surface of the earth, they produce unique cultural landscapes that reflect specific cultures. Farming areas in Kansas and in China, for example, look quite different.

Cultural Change Cultures are changed by both internal and external influences. Within a culture, discoveries and inventions can bring change. Change from outside comes through **diffusion**, or the spread of cultural traits from one culture to another. The process of adapting traits from other cultures is called **acculturation**.

(Text continues on page 90)

World Population Growth: A.D. 1150 to 2000

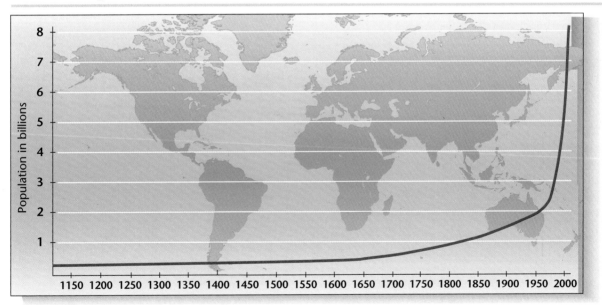

Source: Population Reference Bureau, Inc.

CHART STUDY

⬤ Rapid population growth is a recent phenomenon. *About when did the world's population begin to increase dramatically?*

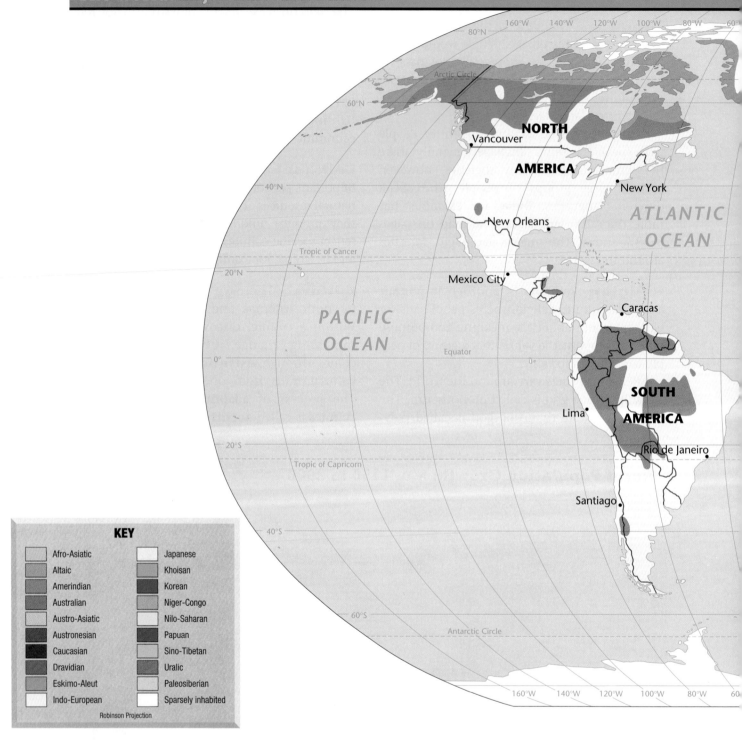

KEY

	Afro-Asiatic		Japanese
	Altaic		Khoisan
	Amerindian		Korean
	Australian		Niger-Congo
	Austro-Asiatic		Nilo-Saharan
	Austronesian		Papuan
	Caucasian		Sino-Tibetan
	Dravidian		Uralic
	Eskimo-Aleut		Paleosiberian
	Indo-European		Sparsely inhabited

Robinson Projection

APPLYING THE GEOGRAPHIC THEMES

● **Regions** Language is the system of vocal sounds and their written symbols which people use to communicate with each other. Around 3,000 languages are spoken today. Based on their similarities and ancestry, languages can be grouped into a few major categories called language families. *What is the major language family in North America?*

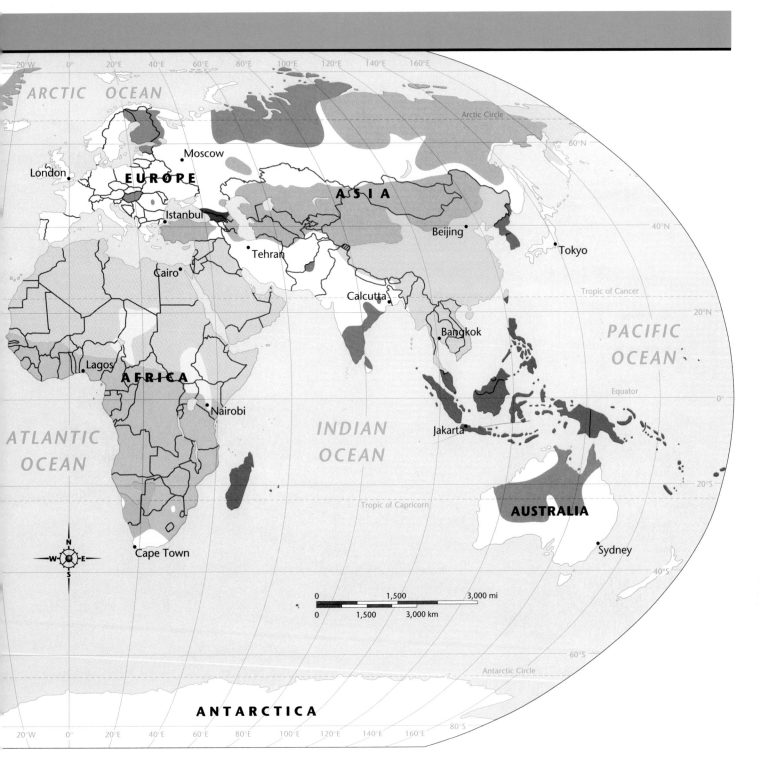

KEY

Christianity

Roman Catholic
Protestant
Eastern Churches
Other Christian

Islam

Sunni
Shiite

Other

Hinduism
Buddhism
Judaism
Traditional
Sparsely inhabited

Robinson Projection

NORTH

Vancouver

AMERICA

New York

ATLANTIC
OCEAN

New Orleans

Tropic of Cancer

PACIFIC
OCEAN

Mexico City

Caracas

Equator

SOUTH

Lima

AMERICA

Tropic of Capricorn

Rio de Janeiro

Santiago

Antarctic Circle

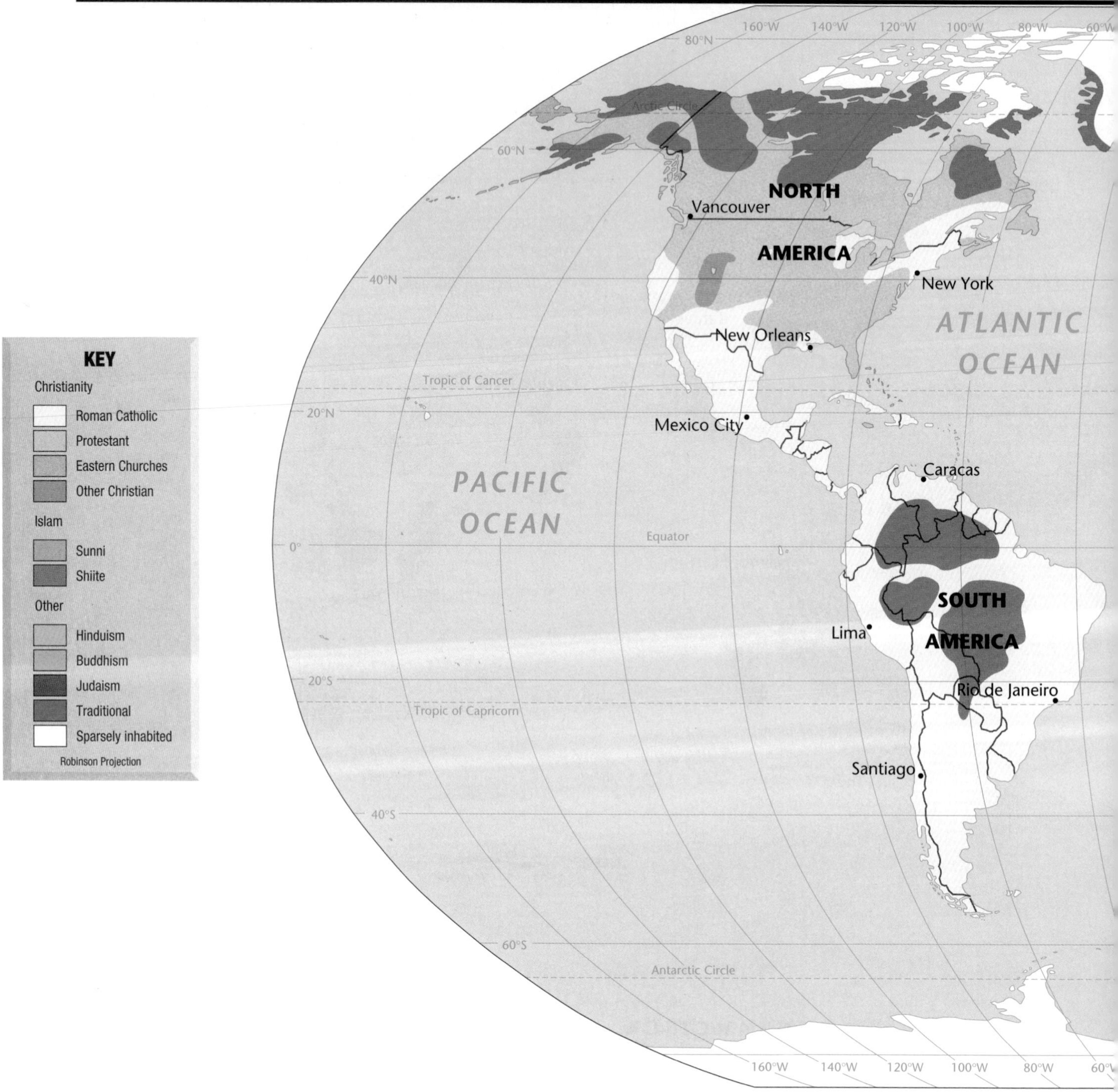

APPLYING THE GEOGRAPHIC THEMES

● **Regions** The map shows the general distribution of the major world religions, with the largest religious group shown for each region. *Which religion dominates northern Africa?*

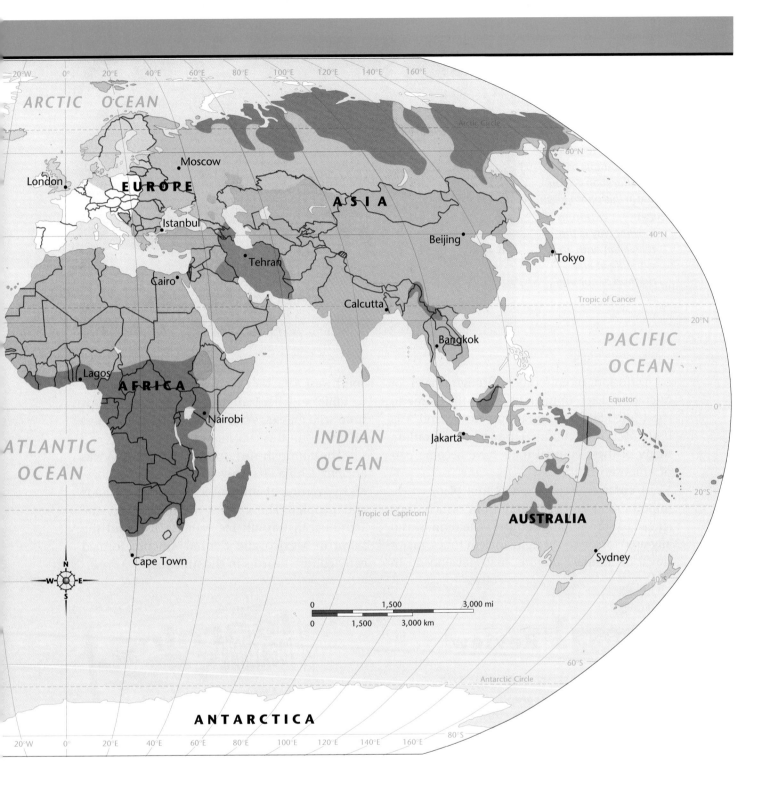

Prime Time in the Pacific

● **Movement** A Pacific Island family enjoys leisure time together. *What example of acculturation do you see in this photograph?*

● **Critical Thinking** *In what way is the television both an example of and method of cultural diffusion?*

Diffusion often occurs through travel or migration. Each immigrant group that came to the United States from Europe, Africa, and Asia brought its own culture. Through acculturation, many of these cultural traits have become part of American culture.

A **culture hearth** refers to a place where important ideas begin and from which they spread to surrounding cultures. The term is usually used for areas where, in ancient times, major traits of human culture first developed. In Southwest Asia, for example, people first learned to tame and herd animals and to grow crops from wild grasses. Writing and mathematics also originated in this culture hearth.

The culture hearth for most of East Asia was ancient China. Its language, arts, technology, and government influenced neighboring lands and peoples. The cultures of the Olmec, the Teotihuacán (tay uh tee wah KAHN), and the Maya in Mexico and Central America formed early culture hearths in the Americas.

Section 1 Review

Vocabulary and Main Ideas

1. **Define:** a. demography b. culture c. population density d. birthrate e. death rate f. immigrant g. emigrant h. urbanization i. rural j. diffusion k. acculturation l. culture hearth

2. What is zero population growth?

3. Where are the world's four areas of greatest population density?

4. **Critical Thinking:** *Making a Hypothesis* Why is cultural diffusion occurring more rapidly around the world today than in previous centuries?

learning LOCATIONS

5. List the world's largest urban areas for the year 2000 shown on the graph on page 84. Next to each urban area, list its country.

6. Look at the map on pages 82–83. Which continent has the greatest number of cities with populations over five million people?

Focus on Skills

- ☐ Social Studies
- ☑ Map and Globe
- ☐ Critical Thinking and Problem Solving

Reading a Population Density Map

Where are new roads needed? Where will a business find the most customers? Government officials, business leaders, and social scientists study population density maps to find answers to questions like these. The map on this page shows the population density of North America. Use the following steps to help you analyze it.

1. Know what information is covered on the map. Maps can show population density for small areas, such as a neighborhood or city, or for very large areas, such as a continent or the entire world.

Study the map key to find out the colors and codes that are used. Maps usually show density with shading. Other symbols may indicate the sizes of cities. (a) How many categories of population density does this map include? (b) What areas average fewer than one person per square mile?

2. Study the data to draw conclusions. A population density map can make a very dramatic first impression. It is obvious immediately that population is very unevenly distributed. In this case you can also see at a glance the overall patterns of human settlement in North America. (a) What areas of North America appear to be quite uninhabited? (b) What different physical factors do you think might keep people from settling there? (c) Name four large cities in North America that have populations greater than one million people.

3. Analyze population density patterns. Move from your general impressions to think about the data available on the map. For instance, think geographically as you consider the areas of highest population density on this map. (a) What region of the United States has the greatest concentration of people? (b) What factors contribute to the population density of this region? (c) Where are population densities lighter? Why?

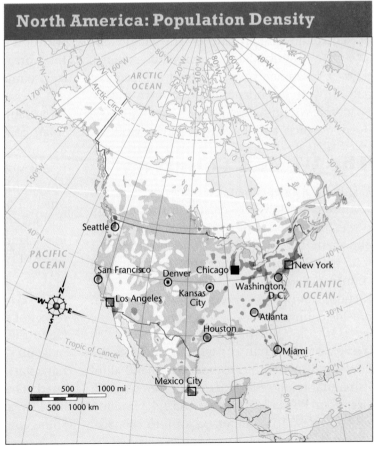

North America: Population Density

KEY

Persons per sq mi	Persons per sq km
520 and over	200 and over
260–519	100–199
130–259	50–99
25–129	10–49
1–24	1–9
Less than 1	Less than 1

Metropolitan areas
- ☐ 10,000,000 and over
- ■ 5,000,000–9,999,999
- ○ 2,000,000–4,999,999
- ◉ 1,000,000–1,999,999

Lambert Azimuthal Equal-Area Projection

2 Political and Economic Systems

Section Preview ·········

Main Ideas

● The characteristics of a country are territory, population, sovereignty, and government.

● Governments differ in their structure and in the source of their political power.

● Each economic system must decide which goods will be produced, how they will be produced, and how goods and profits will be distributed.

Vocabulary

sovereignty, unitary, federal, confederation, authoritarian, dictatorship, totalitarianism, monarchy, democracy, capitalist, communism, socialism

At 370 acres (150 hectares), the principality of Monaco is one of the world's smallest countries.

Two important traits of any culture are its political and economic systems. Governments usually reflect beliefs about authority, independence, and human rights. Economic systems reflect people's ideas about the use of resources and the distribution of wealth.

The World's Countries

Nearly 200 independent countries exist in the world today. They vary greatly in size, military power, natural resources, economic importance, and many other ways. Each one, however, has four specific characteristics that define it as a country. These are (1) clearly defined territory; (2) population; (3) **sovereignty**—freedom from outside control; and (4) a government.

Territory A country's territory includes the land and water within its boundaries and all of its natural resources. Modern countries range in size from Russia, with more than 6.5 million square miles (16.8 million sq km), to Monaco,

with less than 1 square mile (2.6 sq km). The total area of the United States is 3.7 million square miles (9.5 million sq km).

A country's resources may be even more important than its size. For example, several small countries in the Persian Gulf region are extremely wealthy because of their huge reserves of oil. The earth's natural resources are not evenly distributed around the world. This unequal distribution has led to conflict between nations. Throughout history, disputes over territory—land and resources—have been a common cause of war.

Population The size of the population does not determine the existence of a country. Countries vary widely in both the size and the makeup of their populations. Some countries have vast land areas that are largely unpopulated. Other countries are small in terms of land area, but extremely densely populated. Some countries, such as India and the United

States, contain a wide diversity of people and cultures. In others, such as Sweden or Greece, most people share a similar background, language, and culture.

As citizens of a nation, people are usually assured of protection by their government. In return, citizens usually must pay taxes, serve in the military, or carry out other obligations to the government.

Sovereignty A sovereign country is one that can rule itself by establishing its own policies and determining its own course of action. A country's sovereignty entitles it to act independently, deal equally with other sovereign countries, and protect its territory and citizens.

Types of Government

Government is the institution through which a society makes and enforces its public policies and provides for its common needs. These needs include keeping order within a society, protecting the society from outside threats, and providing some services to its people.

Though there are many countries in the world, there are only a few kinds of political systems. Each system can be classified according to its structure (How does the system divide power between the central government and smaller governments?) and its basis of authority (Who ultimately holds political power?).

Government Structure Nearly every country contains smaller units. These may be called states, provinces, or republics. One way of classifying governments is based on the relationship between these smaller units and the central government.

If one central government runs the nation, the system is said to be **unitary**. The central government makes laws for the entire nation; local governments have only those powers that the central government gives to them. Great Britain and Japan are among the countries with unitary governments.

In the United States, on the other hand, the national government shares power with the fifty state governments. Under this **federal** system, some powers are given to the national government and other powers are reserved for the states.

The third type of government structure is a **confederation**. In this system, smaller political units keep their sovereignty and give the central government only very limited powers, typically in such fields as defense and foreign commerce. A confederate system makes it possible for the several states to cooperate in common concerns and still retain their separate identities. The only currently existing confederate system is the

A Right and a Privilege

• **Place** Once a French colony, then ruled by a series of brutal dictators, Haiti now enjoys an uneasy democracy. These Haitians wait patiently in a voting line, eager to exercise their new rights. *What is a representative democracy?*

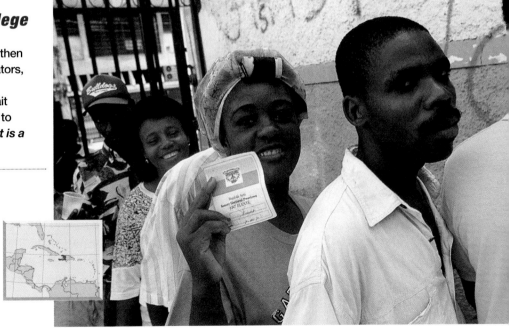

World Economic Systems

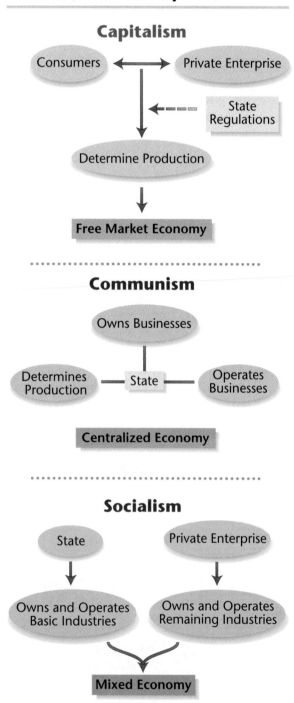

Capitalism

Consumers ⟷ Private Enterprise

State Regulations ⟶

⟶ Determine Production

⟶ **Free Market Economy**

Communism

Owns Businesses

Determines Production — State — Operates Businesses

Centralized Economy

Socialism

State   Private Enterprise

Owns and Operates Basic Industries   Owns and Operates Remaining Industries

Mixed Economy

DIAGRAM STUDY

- The main difference between economic systems is the way in which the state is involved in the production and distribution of goods and services. *In which economic system is the state least involved?*

- **Critical Thinking** *What are the advantages and disadvantages of each economic system?*

Commonwealth of Independent States. This loosely associated group was formed by several republics after the breakup of the Soviet Union.

Government Authority Another way of defining a government is according to the source of its authority. Until fairly modern times, most countries had **authoritarian** governments. The leaders held all, or nearly all, political power.

Authoritarian governments take different forms. Today the most common form of authoritarian government is **dictatorship**, in which power is concentrated in a small group or even a single person. Most dictators use military force or political terror to gain and exercise power. People are not free to express opinions.

The most extreme form of dictatorship is **totalitarianism**. In countries under totalitarian rule, the government tries to control every part of society—politics, the economy, and people's personal lives. Nazi Germany under Hitler and the Soviet Union under Stalin are examples of totalitarian rule.

Throughout much of history, the most common kind of authoritarian government has been a **monarchy**. Monarchs—kings, queens, pharaohs, shahs, sultans—inherit their positions by being born into the ruling family.

In the past, monarchs often ruled with dictatorial power. Today, however, nearly all monarchies—including the British monarchy, which is perhaps the best known—are constitutional monarchies. Real power rests with an elected lawmaking body, such as a legislature or parliament. The monarch serves primarily as a symbol of national unity.

Any country in which the people choose their leaders and have the power to set government policy is a **democracy**. (A constitutional monarchy can also be a democracy.) Today democratic countries have *representative* democracies. All of the nation's eligible adult citizens have the right to choose the representatives making the country's laws. In most representative democracies the elected legislature makes and carries out the laws. One of the world's most populous democratic nations is the United States.

Types of Economic Systems

Any economic system must answer three basic questions: What (and how many) goods and services will be produced? How will these products be produced? How will the products and the wealth gained from their sale be distributed? The main difference among modern economic systems is the degree to which government helps answer these questions.

Capitalism In a **capitalist** system, the people answer the questions. People, as consumers, help determine what will be produced by buying or not buying certain products. In response, producers make more of the products people want. Because all these decisions are made in a free market, a capitalist system is also called a "market economy."

Under a system of "pure" capitalism, government would take no part in the economy. In fact, in the United States and in other capitalist countries, governments do provide some goods and services such as a postal service, highways, and public education. To protect the public, governments also play a limited role in regulating private business. Government regulations affect such areas as worker health and safety and environmental pollution.

Communism In contrast to pure capitalism, in which the government takes no part in the economy, **communism** requires the state to make all the economic decisions. The state owns and operates all the major farms and factories, utilities, and stores. Government planners decide what products will be made, how much workers will be paid, and how much things will cost. Because of their centralized economic planning, Communist systems are also called "planned economies."

Socialism The basic philosophy of **socialism** is that, for the good of society as a whole, the state should own and run basic industries such as transportation, communications, banking, coal mining, and the steel industry. Because private enterprise operates most other parts of the economy, most socialist systems could also be described as "mixed economies." That is, the free market and the government jointly make economic decisions for the benefit of the nation.

Socialists believe that wealth should be distributed more equally and that everyone is entitled to certain goods and services. Socialist countries are sometimes known as "welfare states" because they provide many social services such as housing, health care, child care, and pensions for retired workers. To pay for these services, taxes are usually high.

Section 2 Review

Vocabulary and Main Ideas

1. Define: a. sovereignty b. unitary c. federal
   d. confederation e. authoritarian
   f. dictatorship g. totalitarianism
   h. monarchy i. democracy j. capitalist
   k. communism l. socialism

2. What is the most basic difference between authoritarian governments and democratic governments?

3. Why are socialist systems described as "mixed economies"?

4. Critical Thinking: *Demonstrating Reasoned Judgment* Why might a unitary government be more successful in a country like Japan than in the United States?

5. Look at the map on pages 82–83. Name the two most populous cities in the largest formerly Communist country.

6. Name a city shown on the map on pages 82–83 that is located in a country that has a constitutional monarchy.

Review and Activities

Summarizing Main Ideas

Section 1 The Study of Human Geography

- World population is unevenly distributed over the globe.
- Although people tend to settle where there is adequate water, soil for farming or grazing, and a moderate climate, they also have adapted their ways of living to suit a variety of environments.
- World population has increased rapidly in the last half of the twentieth century.
- Every group develops a set of learned customs, beliefs, and actions that make up its culture.
- Cultures change slowly, mainly through the exchange of ideas with other cultures.

Section 2 Political and Economic Systems

- All countries share four common characteristics: territory, population, sovereignty, and government.
- Governments can be classified by the relationship between the central government and smaller governments and by the ultimate source of political authority.
- Any country's economic system must answer three questions: What and how much shall be produced, by whom, and for whom?
- Major modern economic systems are communism (government control), capitalism (private control), and socialism (a mixture of government and private control).

Reviewing Vocabulary

Use each of the following terms in a sentence that shows its meaning.

1. culture
2. birthrate
3. death rate
4. diffusion
5. acculturation
6. sovereignty
7. authoritarian
8. dictatorship
9. totalitarianism
10. monarchy
11. democracy
12. capitalist
13. communism
14. socialism

Applying the Geographic Themes

1. **Location** Is it possible for a culture hearth to influence places that are located far away? Explain.
2. **Place** Explain the differences between a unitary system of government, a federal system, and a confederation.
3. **Movement** How does the movement of humans affect cultures?
4. **Human-Environment Interaction** What is urbanization, and what parts of the world are experiencing it?
5. **Regions** Why does population density sometimes vary a great deal across a large region?

Critical Thinking and Applying Skills

1. **Predicting Consequences** Why might rapid population growth create more difficulties for poorer countries than for wealthier countries?
2. **Reading a Population Density Map** Look at the map on page 91. List the two largest cities in the United States, and next to each city name the body of water on which it is located. How do you explain the fact that the nation's two largest cities are located next to water?

Writing Across Cultures

▶ 1. Imagine that you are about to meet some-one from a culture you have never heard of, and you want to learn as much as you can about that culture. Write ten questions that will provide you with the fullest possible understanding of that culture.

▶ 2. Imagine that you have grown up under an authoritarian dictatorship, but that your country has recently adopted a democratic form of government. What hopes would you have for life under democratic rule? What fears would you have?

INTERNET link

How much do you know about popula-tion? Learn more at the Population Reference Bureau. Link to this site from:

• www.phschool.com

When you are done, write a summary of three interesting facts you learned.

learning LOCATIONS

Cities of the World

Number from 1 to 12 on a piece of paper. Next to each number, write the letter of the place on the map that corresponds to the places listed below.

1. Beijing
2. Buenos Aires
3. Cairo
4. Jakarta
5. Lagos
6. London
7. Mexico City
8. Moscow
9. New York
10. Rio de Janeiro
11. Sydney
12. Tokyo

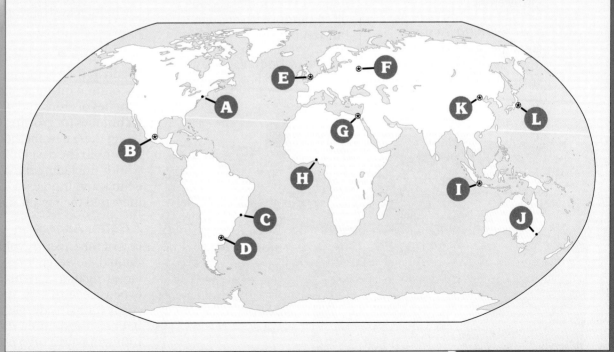

Food, Hunger, and Sustainable Agriculture

The Issue

Hunger exists everywhere in the world, but is more widespread in some regions than in others. Here are some of the reasons why.

Farmland is unevenly distributed Not all nations possess fertile land on which they can grow food. Some are covered by deserts, mountains, and rain forests. In addition, some regions of the world are plagued by regular drought and flooding, both of which destroy crops.

Overcrowding In some places the population has grown too large. Rapid urban expansion has taken over valuable farmland. Often there are simply too many people for the land to sustain. Overcultivating and overgrazing eventually deplete the soils of all their nutrients and leave them barren.

Poverty A large percentage of the world's people are hungry because they live in poverty in developing nations. They may own land, but they cannot afford the seed, fertilizers, or irrigation systems necessary to grow enough food. In the cities of these developing nations, the landless poor often cannot earn enough to buy food.

Global Impact Each day an estimated 1 billion people go hungry. Yearly millions die of starvation and hunger-related diseases. As the population continues to grow in regions where hunger is already a problem, the imbalance between available food and number of people becomes even greater.

Some Solutions

Over the years, scientists and farmers have made some progress in feeding the world's hungry. They have developed several solutions that are helping to increase the world's food supply.

The Green Revolution Begun in the 1950s, the Green Revolution introduced better varieties of crops and new techniques for growing them. Using these new methods, nations in the developing world—including India, China, and Indonesia—have increased their grain supply.

A Better Approach The success of the Green Revolution is limited, however. It relies on large irrigation systems and expensive fertilizers, and is too costly for many developing nations. In addition, the environment pays a high price. Green Revolution farming

All in a Row

Human-Environment Interaction A field of sugar beets grows in San Joaquin Valley, California. Some people consider traditional ditch irrigation to be wasteful because water is lost to evaporation.

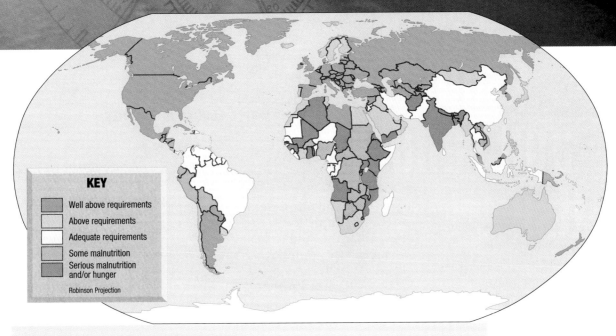

KEY

- Well above requirements
- Above requirements
- Adequate requirements
- Some malnutrition
- Serious malnutrition and/or hunger

Robinson Projection

APPLYING THE GEOGRAPHIC THEMES

● **Human-Environment Interaction** People require a certain number of calories in order to maintain good health. This map reflects general data on calorie supply and does not account for famine or wars. *What region has the largest number of countries with an insufficient calorie supply?*

methods are heavily dependent on energy, large amounts of water, and pesticides.

Sustainable Agriculture

Many scientists think a more promising solution to the problem of hunger is the practice of sustainable agriculture. Sustainable agriculture aims to preserve natural resources and maintain the fertility of the land so that it can support healthy crops indefinitely. For example, to reduce their reliance on costly and dangerous pesticides that damage the soil and water supply, farmers cultivate pest-resistant plant varieties. They also introduce predator insects that feed on pests. To save water and energy, farmers use drip irrigation—watering the roots of plants in small but steady amounts, rather than conventional methods of irrigation that require great amounts of water.

YOU DECIDE

1. Give three reasons why people are hungry in the world.

2. Why is sustainable agriculture a better alternative than conventional methods for raising food?

3. **Problem Solving** Brainstorm a list of long-term solutions to the problem of world hunger.

4. **What You Can Do** Think about how your eating habits either promote or discourage sustainable agriculture. Discuss your thoughts with your family or friends.

5. **Internet Activity** Learn how the U.S. Agency for International Development is helping people achieve economic growth. Choose a few projects to read about, then summarize each in a short paragraph. Link to this site from:
   • www.phschool.com

Resources and Land Use

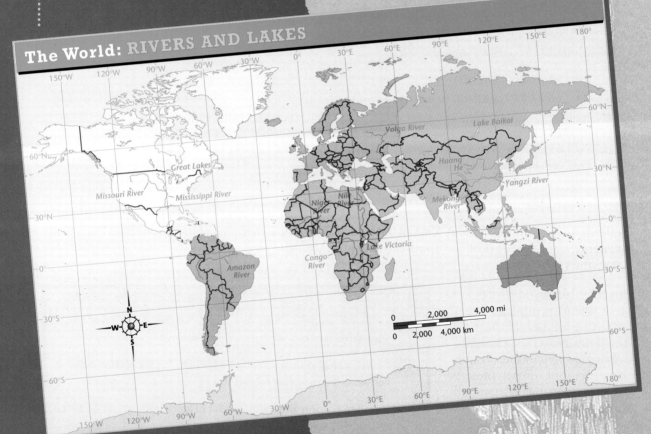

The World: RIVERS AND LAKES

Volga River · Lake Baikal · Great Lakes · Huang He · Missouri River · Mississippi River · Yangzi River · Niger River · Nile River · Mekong River · Lake Victoria · Congo River · Amazon River

0   2,000   4,000 mi

0   2,000   4,000 km

Miller Projection

learning LOCATIONS

Mapping the World

Create a map like the one above, lightly shading each continent a different color. Then add labels for rivers, lakes, and other water bodies that are shown on this map.

World Resources

Section Preview

Main Ideas

- **People use natural resources in order to survive and meet other needs.**

- **Natural resources are unevenly distributed throughout the world.**

- **Modern civilizations depend on reliable sources of energy.**

Vocabulary

natural resource, renewable resource, nonrenewable resource, fossil fuels, nuclear energy, geothermal energy, solar energy

APPEARED IN *NATIONAL GEOGRAPHIC*

Recycling is one way to conserve resources.

The earliest people used the resources they found in their environment. They breathed the air, drank the water, and caught fish to eat. Gaining skills, they made tools to shape the earth's materials into useful goods. They hammered copper into weapons and ornaments and hollowed out trees to make canoes. People today are just as dependent on the earth's resources. The ways that people use the earth's resources, where the resources are located, how resources are distributed among people, and how the use of resources affects the earth are all subjects that geographers study.

Natural Resources

Resources come in different kinds. Capital resources are the money and machines used to produce goods or services. Human resources are the people who perform various tasks. **Natural resources** are materials that people take from the natural environment to survive and to satisfy their needs.

Renewable Resources When people use certain natural resources, called **renewable**

resources, the environment continues to supply or replace them. Soil, for example, is always being created by the weathering of rocks and by decomposing plant and animal material. The hydrologic water cycle returns new supplies of fresh water to the land as rain or snow. Our most important energy resource, the sun, although not renewable, will probably keep the earth warm for 5 billion years or more.

Natural growth takes time, however, and human activities can interfere with the process of renewal. An oil spill, for example, might affect the wildlife in a bay for many years.

Nonrenewable Resources As their name suggests, **nonrenewable resources** cannot be replaced once they have been used. Nonrenewable resources are minerals formed in the earth's crust over millions of years. The earth has only a limited supply of them, and it would take millions of years to replace them.

Among the most important nonrenewable mineral resources are **fossil fuels**. These fuels are coal, oil, and natural gas, which formed from the remains of ancient plants and

◄ **Logging in the Tongass National Forest, Alaska** *(photo left)*

Chapter 4 ▪ Section 1   **101**

animals. Other important minerals include iron, copper, aluminum, uranium, and gold.

While advanced technologies may help us find new mineral deposits in the future, recycling is a way to increase nonrenewable resource supplies right now. For example, Americans recycle about 1,500 aluminum cans every second. Some experts believe half of all trash currently thrown away could be recycled. The other way to stretch the limited supply of nonrenewable resources is to reduce the overall consumption level.

Energy Sources

Modern industrial countries use energy to light cities, power cars and airplanes, and run computers and other machines. The main energy source is nonrenewable fossil fuels. Today nations are searching for new energy sources and competing for those that already exist.

Depending On Fossil Fuels Nearly all modern industrialized countries, including the United States, depend heavily on fossil fuels. Few of these nations have sufficient supplies to meet their own needs. Thus they must import much of what they use.

Oil and natural gas reserves are unevenly spread around the world. Over half of the world's known oil supply is located in just a few countries in Southwest Asia. At the present rate of use, the world's oil is likely to run out in less than a century. Reserves of natural gas are also limited. Northern Eurasia has the world's greatest reserves, which provide the region with both energy and a valuable export.

Coal deposits are larger and more widely distributed than oil reserves. The United States, China, and Russia have rich deposits. Industrial areas in Europe also arose near coal supplies. The world's reserves of coal are thought to be enough for at least two hundred years. Coal, however, has its drawbacks. Burning coal can create air pollution such as acid rain.

APPEARED IN *NATIONAL GEOGRAPHIC*

APPEARED IN *NATIONAL GEOGRAPHIC*

Power to the People

Human-Environment Interaction Industrialized nations depend on fossil fuels for their energy needs. The Canadian oil refinery shown here (immediate right) indicates the scale of oil production. *What provides energy in less developed areas of the world, as in this rural Chinese village (top right)?*

Nuclear Energy   Many countries now supply part of their energy through electricity that is created by nuclear power. **Nuclear energy** today is produced by fission—the splitting of uranium atoms in a nuclear reactor to release their stored energy.

Many questions and concerns surround the use of nuclear power. Opponents of nuclear power warn of leaks, explosions, and the disposal of radioactive wastes, that can remain toxic for thousands of years. Nuclear fission also uses uranium, a limited and nonrenewable resource. Although nuclear fission does not contribute to global warming, the process of refining uranium does. Scientists hope to find a way to generate energy through fusion, a type of nuclear reaction for which the fuel is plentiful.

Other Energy Sources   Many experts think that nations must begin to replace their dependence on fossil fuels with renewable energy sources. These sources are in limited use today around the world.

One ancient source of energy, water power, uses the energy of falling water to move machinery or generate electricity. Although new dams must be built from time to time, water power is a renewable energy source. Ocean tides are another source of power.

In areas with volcanic activity, a potential energy source is **geothermal energy**—energy that comes from the earth's internal heat. Magma heats underground water, producing steam that can be used to heat homes or make electricity. Iceland, Italy, Japan, and New Zealand all make use of geothermal energy.

Solar energy is energy produced by the sun. Systems to collect and store the sun's energy have been used for years to heat water and homes. Generating electricity from solar energy has been more difficult. Nevertheless, solar radiation is potentially the greatest renewable energy source.

GLOBAL issues

Water Usage

Although water is a renewable resource, its supplies are not unlimited. The average American uses some 100 gallons of water each day. Simply keeping the water running while brushing your teeth can waste 1 to 2 gallons.

Distribution of Resources   The earth's natural resources are not evenly distributed around the world. This unequal distribution affects the ways in which countries interact with each other and results in trade among nations. Resources that are brought into a nation are called imports; those that are shipped out are called exports. For example, Japan has few natural resources and must import the raw materials needed to build cars. In turn, it sells its finished manufactured products in other countries around the world. The need to import and export goods and resources drives the international market.

Section 1 Review

Vocabulary and Main Ideas

1. Define: a. natural resource b. renewable resource c. nonrenewable resource d. fossil fuels e. nuclear energy f. geothermal energy g. solar energy

2. What is the main source of energy for most modern industrial countries?

3. What are the advantages and disadvantages of using coal?

4. Critical Thinking: *Expressing Problems Clearly* Why are alternative energy sources important for the future?

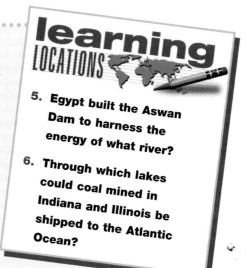

learning LOCATIONS

5. Egypt built the Aswan Dam to harness the energy of what river?

6. Through which lakes could coal mined in Indiana and Illinois be shipped to the Atlantic Ocean?

Focus on Skills

☐ Social Studies

☑ Map and Globe

☐ Critical Thinking and Problem Solving

Interpreting an Economic Activity Map

An economic activity map uses a color-coded key to communicate basic information about a given region. This type of thematic map allows us to compare data in a general way. It is easy to see, for example, that far more land in Africa is used for subsistence farming than in Europe. However, precise measurements in square miles are not shown on this map.

Use the following steps to read and analyze the world map below.

1. Identify the variety of economic activities shown. Economic activity can range from gathering nuts and berries to manufacturing cars and trucks on an assembly line. Use the key to answer the following questions: (a) What appears to be the major economic activity in Australia? (b) What appears to be the major economic activity in the northernmost region of Asia? (c) Where are the manufacturing and trade centers in South America?

2. Look for relationships among the data. Use the map to look for patterns. Answer the following questions: (a) Does more manufacturing and trade take place in countries in the northern hemisphere or in the southern hemisphere? (b) How does the amount of land used for commercial farming in the United States compare with the amount used in Australia? (c) In South America is more area used for commercial fishing or for subsistence farming?

The World: Economic Activity

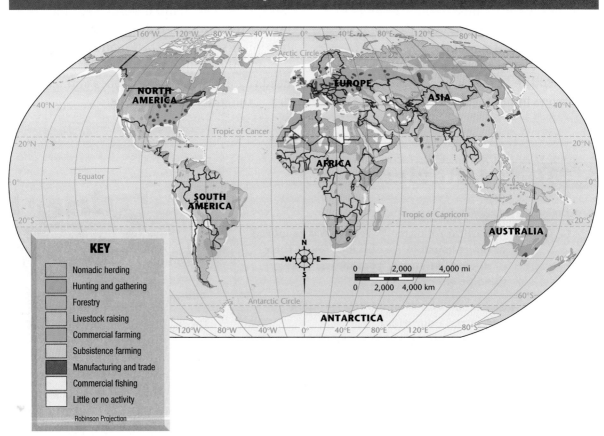

KEY

- Nomadic herding
- Hunting and gathering
- Forestry
- Livestock raising
- Commercial farming
- Subsistence farming
- Manufacturing and trade
- Commercial fishing
- Little or no activity

Robinson Projection

2 World Economic Activity

Section Preview

Main Ideas

● Economic activities are the ways in which people use land and resources to earn their living.

● Countries are at different stages of economic development.

● Agriculture is practiced differently in different parts of the world.

Vocabulary

manufacturing, developed country, developing country, gross national product (GNP), per capita GNP, subsistence farming, commercial farming

APPEARED IN *NATIONAL GEOGRAPHIC*

This man is tapping a tree for latex, an important product in the Amazon.

Every morning in the cities of Asia, Africa, Europe, and the Americas, millions of people ride trains, cars, buses, or bicycles to work in stores, factories, and offices. Every night they go home. To them this seems a natural way to live and work.

To millions of other people, this way of living would seem strange. For these people, working means farming the land where they live, traveling with herds of animals, or catching fish far out at sea.

Economic Activities

The map on page 104 gives you an idea of the varied ways in which people make their living. These categories of economic activity are related to a region's climate and natural resources.

Farming, for example, is impossible under certain land and climate conditions. Even where the land can be farmed, rainfall and temperature influence farmers' choice of crops. A

Russian farmer would probably not choose to grow coffee, while a Kenyan farmer would probably not choose to grow sugar beets.

Fishing, forestry, and mining also are limited to places where there are fish, trees, or minerals to make the activity practical. Because they use natural resources directly, activities like agriculture and forestry are called primary activities. Industries that process natural resources are termed secondary activities. They include the processing of raw materials, such as food processing, and **manufacturing**—turning raw materials into finished products.

Service industries—transportation, advertising, government, and so on—make up the third level of economic activity. Service industries are businesses that are not directly related to the gathering of raw materials or to manu-

> **GEO facts**
> Approximately 40 percent of the world's grain supply goes to feed livestock.

Hidden Treasure

● **Regions** There is very little water in Australia's outback. This Aboriginal woman is digging for moisture-rich tubers beneath the hard, cracked soil. *Critical Thinking Why have Aborigines subsisted on gathering and hunting for thousands of years?*

facturing. Service industries such as banking and health care employ millions of people.

Economic Development

How its people earn a living is one way to measure a country's economic development. Modern industrial societies, such as France, the United States, and Japan, are said to be **developed countries**. Countries that lack industries and modern technology and depend on developed countries for many of their manufactured goods are said to be **developing countries.**

Generally, developed countries are wealthier than developing countries. One way to compare the wealth of countries is to look at the **gross national product (GNP)**, which measures the total value of goods and services produced in a year. Another measure of development, **per capita GNP**, is the GNP divided by the country's total population. The average per capita GNP is more than 15 times greater in developed countries than in developing countries.

Agriculture

Although populations in world cities have soared, developing countries are still mainly rural. About half of all people living in developing countries work in agriculture, while in developed countries that figure is less than 10 percent. People around the world use a variety of agricultural methods.

Gatherers and Herders Some cultural groups do not engage in any agriculture. The Bushmen of the Kalahari and the Mountain Lapps of northern Scandinavia, for example, still follow ancient ways of hunting and gathering food and herding animals. Hunters and gatherers live in small groups in remote areas. They gather nuts and other wild foods, sometimes fishing or hunting. Herders follow large herds of animals, such as caribou, over huge expanses of grazing land. Thus herders are most often nomadic, traveling from place to place in different seasons.

Hunters, gatherers, and herders have developed well-organized cultures. Their ways of life are often based on a knowledge of the environment that has been passed down from generation to generation for hundreds of years. Some people fear this knowledge will be lost as the nomadic life style comes under increasing pressure from industrialization.

Subsistence Farming Much of the agriculture in developing countries is **subsistence farming**. People grow only enough for

March of Progress

Human-Environment Interaction In industrialized nations, such as the United States, only a small percentage of the population is engaged in agriculture. Farm size and farm output, however, have increased steadily over the years. **Critical Thinking** *How has industrialization aided agriculture?*

their own family's or village's needs. If they are lucky enough to have a very good crop or an extra animal, they may sell or trade it. Mainly, though, they grow food to eat, not to sell. Tools and agricultural methods are generally very basic and time consuming. Farm animals and family members provide the main source of labor in subsistence farming.

Commercial Farming In developed countries, nearly all farmers raise crops and live-stock to sell in the market. This is **commercial farming**. Modern techniques and equipment make these farmers more productive. As a result, only a small part of the labor force is needed in these countries to produce enough food to feed the entire population. In Japan, for example, about 7 percent of workers are in farming or fishing.

Some commercial farming takes place in developing countries, too. Large plantations in tropical regions produce coffee, sugar, and other crops. Until recently, most were owned by foreign investors.

Section 2 Review

Vocabulary and Main Ideas

1. **Define:** a. manufacturing b. developed country c. developing country d. gross national product (GNP) e. per capita GNP f. subsistence farming g. commercial farming

2. **What is the difference between subsistence farming and commercial farming?**

3. **In what ways do climate and resources influence the economic activity in an area?**

4. **Critical Thinking:** *Identifying Central Issues* **What reasons might hunters, gatherers, and herders have for moving from place to place with the seasons?**

5. The port city of Shanghai, one of China's leading economic centers, is located at the mouth of what river?

6. Which African river has its source in the nation of Guinea and provides water for agriculture to Guinea and other nations?

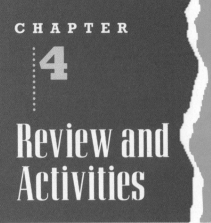

Review and Activities

Summarizing Main Ideas

Section 1 World Resources

- To meet their needs, people take natural resources from the environment—from the land, water, and air.
- Renewable resources are those that can be replenished, such as water, forests, and wildlife. Nonrenewable resources include fossil fuels, metals, and other minerals.
- Modern civilizations are dependent on nonrenewable fossil fuels.
- Alternative renewable energy sources include nuclear energy and solar energy.
- Resources are distributed unevenly around the world.

Section 2 World Economic Activity

- Economic activities—the ways in which people use land and resources to earn their living—vary greatly throughout the world.
- Economic activities depend on the land and resources available in a given area.
- Different countries are at different stages of economic development. Industrial countries are considered to be developed, while non-industrial countries are considered to be developing.
- A variety of agricultural methods are practiced around the world, including hunting and gathering, subsistence farming, and commercial farming.

Reviewing Vocabulary

Use each of the following terms in a sentence that shows its meaning.

1. natural resource
2. renewable resource
3. nonrenewable resource
4. fossil fuel
5. nuclear energy
6. geothermal energy
7. solar energy
8. manufacturing
9. developed country
10. developing country
11. gross national product (GNP)
12. per capita GNP
13. subsistence farming
14. commercial farming

Applying the Geographic Themes

1. **Location** Look at the map on page 104. In which hemisphere, the northern or southern, are most of the world's areas of manufacturing and trade located?
2. **Place** What types of economic activity depend on a place's natural resources and climate?
3. **Movement** Why is a good transportation system important for countries that have many manufacturing industries?
4. **Human-Environment Interaction** In general, how is agriculture in developed countries different from that in developing countries?
5. **Regions** Which region has the largest percentage of world oil supplies?

Critical Thinking and Applying Skills

1. **Cause and Effect** How might foreign investment both help and harm a developing country?
2. **Interpreting an Economic Activity Map** Using the economic activity map on page 104, list the major kinds of economic activity in the United States and indicate the regions in which these activities occur.

Journal Activity

Writing Across Cultures

▶ 1. List your activities in a typical day that rely on some form of external energy source, such as electricity or gasoline. Then describe how you might perform these activities if this energy were not available.

▶ 2. Write two descriptions of life on a farm. The first should describe life on a farm that practices subsistence farming. The second should describe life on a farm that practices commercial farming. Be sure to mention both the similarities and the differences between the two kinds of agriculture.

Find out more about solar energy. Visit the Energy Efficiency and Renewable Energy Network at the U.S. Department of Energy. Link to this site from:

• www.phschool.com

When you have completed your tour, write a summary of what you have learned.

Rivers and Lakes

Number from 1 to 12 on a piece of paper. Next to each number, write the letter of the place on the map that corresponds to the places listed below.

1. Amazon River	5. Lake Baikal	9. Niger River
2. Congo River	6. Lake Victoria	10. Nile River
3. Great Lakes	7. Mekong River	11. Volga River
4. Huang He	8. Mississippi River	12. Yangzi River

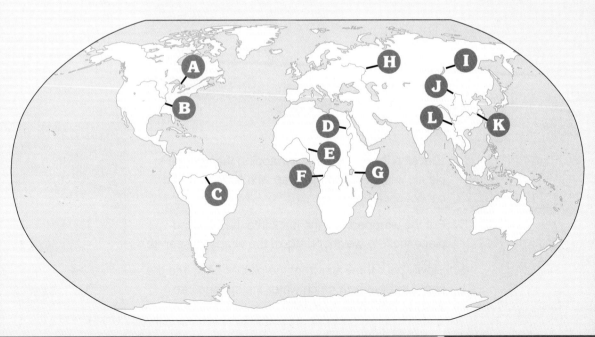

THE ROLE OF WETLANDS

Wetlands play an important role absorbing excess water as a river system swells each year with snow melt and rainfall. When wetland areas are developed and flooding takes place, who is to blame— nature or people? Think about these questions as you perform the following experiment.

MATERIALS:

- 1 Large or 2-4 small sponge(s)
- 1 Shallow plastic pan
- Water pitcher
- Water
- Plastic wrap
- Clear packing tape
- 3 lb Weight

PROCEDURES:

1. Place the dry sponge in the plastic pan. This represents a wetland area.

2. Using the pitcher, pour water into the pan until it is about 1 inch from the top. Discard any water left in the pitcher.

Step 2

3. Carefully wring out the sponge into the pitcher and pour all the water from the pan back into the pitcher. Note how much water is now in the pitcher.

Step 4

4. "Develop the wetlands" by wrapping the sponge in plastic wrap. Secure the wrap with tape so that it cannot soak up water.

5. Put the wrapped sponge back into the pan and place the 3 lb weight on top of the wrapped sponge.

6. Slowly pour the water from the pitcher back into the pan. Observe how much water the sponge can absorb after "development."

Step 6

OBSERVATIONS AND ANALYSIS:

1. Describe your results for this simulation. Explain why the container could not hold all of the water in step 6. How do wetlands prevent flooding? How does paving over and developing wetland areas affect their flood prevention properties?

2. Estimate the percentage of water that could not be absorbed by the sponge in step 6.

3. When a developed river area floods, do you think it is a natural or human-made disaster? Explain your answer.

4. Rebuilding a damaged riverside area would provide thousands of jobs and increase farming land. However, the cost could be high—nearly $12 billion dollars—and natural ecosystems would be endangered. How would you advise your congressional representative on a plan to balance wetland protection, flood prevention, and the local economy?

FLOODING DEVASTATES
the Midwest

Heavy rains continue to fall over the Midwest, adding to the worst flooding in 120 years. Environmentalists blame the manipulation of the riverside wetlands and the building of levees that have narrowed the flow of water and allowed people to live where the river should be. The commercial shipping industry that operates on the river is experiencing losses of $1 million dollars a day. Other losses include 700,000 acres of farmland which will leave many farmers financially devastated.

taking *Action*

In addition to storing floodwaters, wetlands serve a number of other ecological and commercial functions. They provide habitats for many rare and endangered plant and animal species. Consider doing the following to help protect our remaining wetlands.

✔ Contact your local chapter of The Audubon Society and request information on wetlands and how you can volunteer to protect wetlands in your area.

Mississippi River
July 4, 1988

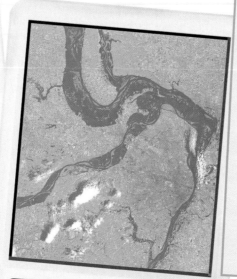

Mississippi River
July 8, 1993

two

The United States and Canada

CHAPTERS

A Global Perspective

The United States and Canada occupy most of the sprawling continent of North America. The northwestern tip of North America almost reaches the northeastern tip of Asia. The southern part of North America, which borders the United States, is a land link to another continent—South America. Seen from this perspective, the United States and Canada are right in the center of today's busy world.

Robinson Projection

Banff National Park,
Alberta, Canada

KEYS TO UNDERSTANDING THIS REGION

1 Countries and Cities *(pp. 114–115)*
The United States and Canada share the same continent and are linked by geographic, historical, cultural, and economic ties.

2 Physical Features *(pp. 116–117)*
The United States and Canada share many of the same landforms, including craggy mountains in the west, rounded mountains in the east, and rolling plains in the center.

3 People and Cultures *(pp. 118–119)*
The populations of the United States and Canada differ greatly in size but share similar characteristics, including a high standard of living and a diversity of cultural backgrounds.

4 Climate and Vegetation *(pp. 120–121)*
The climates of Canada and the United States differ greatly. Canada's climates are generally colder than those of the United States, because Canada is located at more northern latitudes. Most of the natural vegetation of the United States and Canada falls into four broad categories: tundra, forest, grassland, and desert scrub.

5 Economy and Resources *(pp. 122–123)*
The United States and Canada are highly industrialized countries with many resources. Although much land in the region is devoted to farming, most people make a living in manufacturing or trade or by providing services. The two countries have close economic ties.

VISUAL PREVIEW ACTIVITY

Each of the five keys above corresponds to a section of the Regional Atlas that follows. Number from 1 to 5 on a piece of paper. Use information from the maps, graphs, and photographs in the Regional Atlas to write one additional fact for each of the five keys above.

Chapter 5

THE UNITED STATES AND CANADA

Use the Map, Graph, and Photo Studies in the Regional Atlas to gain a better understanding of the region's physical and cultural geography.

ATLAS VOCABULARY

continental divide	cordillera	prairie
drainage basin	literacy	hydroelectric power
tributaries	standard of living	

1 COUNTRIES AND CITIES

LARGEST METROPOLITAN AREAS

New York, United States
19,342,000

Los Angeles, United States
14,532,000

Chicago, United States
8,240,000

Washington D.C., U.S.A.
6,727,000

San Francisco, United States
6,253,000

Philadelphia, United States
5,893,000

Boston, United States
5,455,000

Detroit, United States
5,187,000

Dallas, United States
4,037,000

Toronto, Canada
3,893,000

= 2,000,000 people

Source: *United Nations*

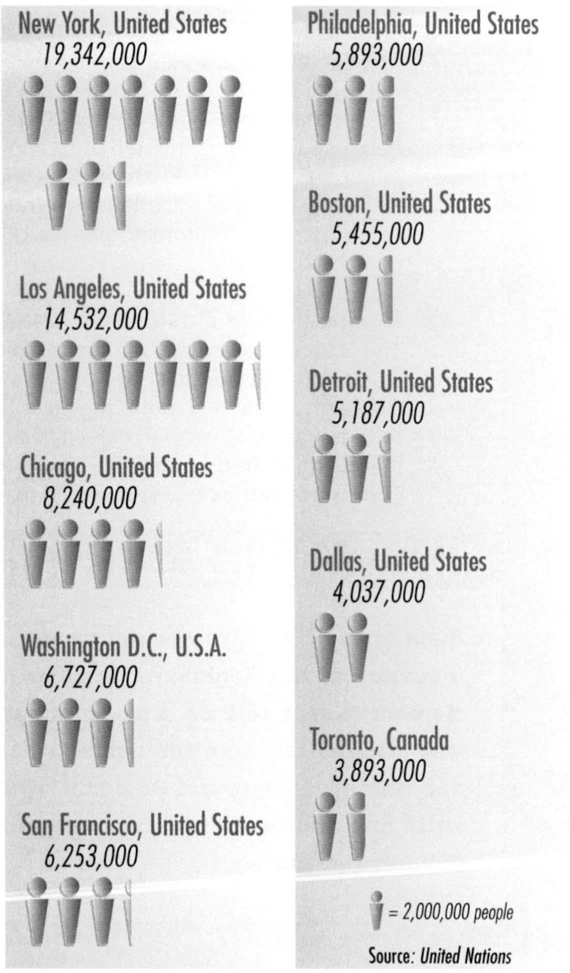

MAP STUDY
Applying the Geographic Themes

1 Location Parts of both the United States and Canada lie within the Arctic Circle. *Which country extends farther north?*

2 Place Seattle, Washington, and Vancouver, Canada, are both important port cities. *What ocean serves these two cities?*

3 Regions The Great Lakes are an important resource to both Canada and the United States. *What major cities have grown up in this region?*

CHART STUDY

4 Location The chart at left shows the population of the ten largest metropolitan areas in the United States and Canada. Locate these cities on the map on page 115. *What generalization can you make about the location of these cities?*

The United States and Canada: POLITICAL

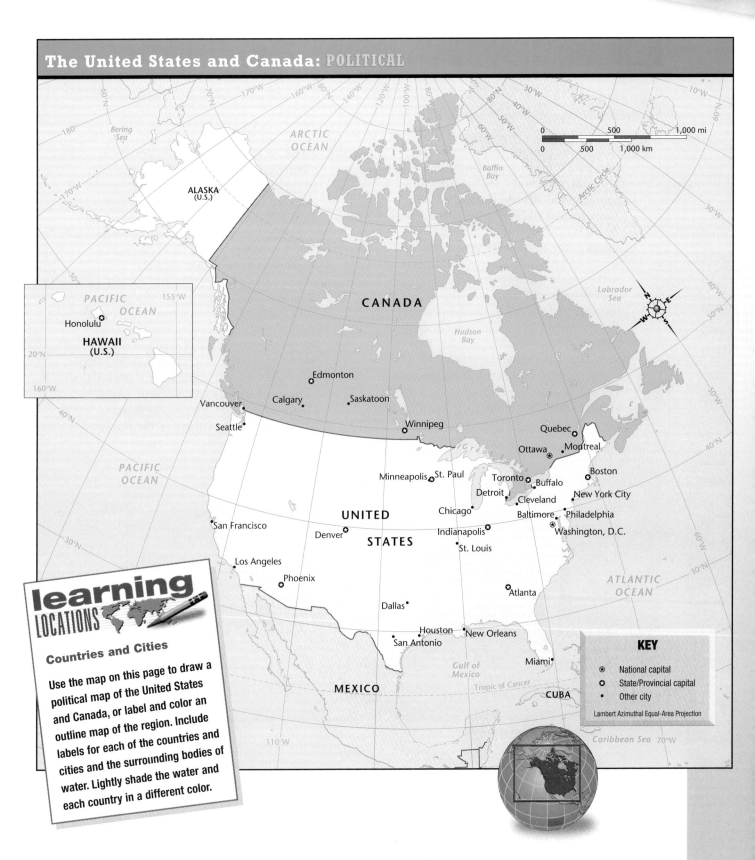

learning LOCATIONS

Countries and Cities

Use the map on this page to draw a political map of the United States and Canada, or label and color an outline map of the region. Include labels for each of the countries and cities and the surrounding bodies of water. Lightly shade the water and each country in a different color.

KEY

⊛ National capital

⊙ State/Provincial capital

• Other city

Lambert Azimuthal Equal-Area Projection

MAP STUDY
Applying the Geographic Themes

1 Place Because rivers wend their way downhill, the pattern of landforms determines the direction in which they flow. A **continental divide** is the boundary that separates rivers flowing toward opposite sides of a continent. In North America, the Rockies separate the rivers that flow west from the rivers that flow east. A divide also separates one **drainage basin** from another. A drainage basin is the entire area of land that is drained by a major river and its **tributaries**—rivers and streams that carry water to a major river. The Mississippi River and its tributaries drain the largest area in the United States. *Into which body of water does the Mississippi River drain?*

2 Region The Rocky Mountains are a **cordillera** (kawr dill YER uh), or a related set of mountain ranges, that stretches for more than 3,000 miles (4,827 km) from northern Alaska to Mexico, making it the longest mountain chain in North America. *What ranges lie between the Rockies and the Pacific coast?*

3 Region The Appalachian Mountains were formed by tectonic forces about 250 million years ago. Their once-sharp peaks have been worn down by rain, ice, and wind. Only a few reach higher than 6,000 feet (1,829 m). Compare their elevations to those of the Rockies. *Critical Thinking Which mountains do you think are older—the Appalachians or the Rockies?*

Cross Section: The United States

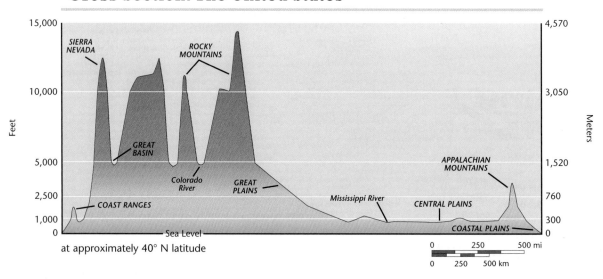

DIAGRAM STUDY

4 Physical Profile A vast plain with rich, deep soils stretches across the central part of both Canada and the United States. In the United States the plains region is divided into the Great Plains and the Central Plains. *Which of these plains has the highest elevation?*

REGIONAL *atlas*

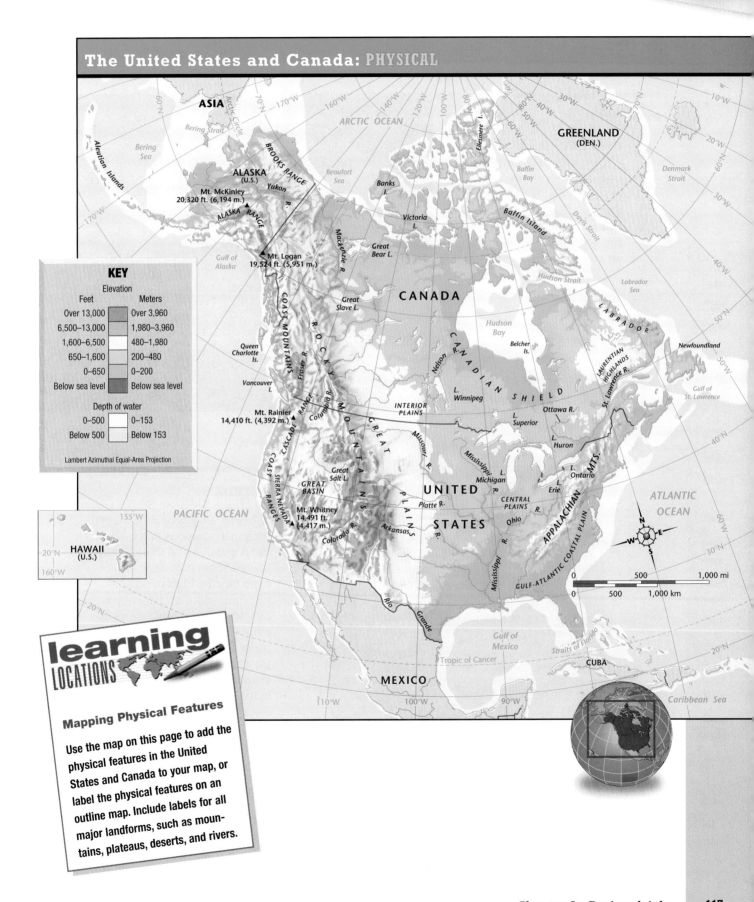

The United States and Canada: PHYSICAL

KEY

Elevation

Feet	Meters
Over 13,000	Over 3,960
6,500–13,000	1,980–3,960
1,600–6,500	480–1,980
650–1,600	200–480
0–650	0–200
Below sea level	Below sea level

Depth of water

0–500	0–153
Below 500	Below 153

Lambert Azimuthal Equal-Area Projection

ASIA

Bering Strait

Arctic Circle

ARCTIC OCEAN

GREENLAND (DEN.)

Aleutian Islands

Bering Sea

BROOKS RANGE

Beaufort Sea

Banks I.

Ellesmere I.

Denmark Strait

ALASKA (U.S.)

Mt. McKinley 20,320 ft. (6,194 m.)

Yukon R.

ALASKA RANGE

Victoria I.

Baffin Bay

Baffin Island

Davis Strait

Gulf of Alaska

Mt. Logan 19,524 ft. (5,951 m.)

Mackenzie R.

Great Bear L.

Hudson Strait

Labrador Sea

COAST MOUNTAINS

Great Slave L.

CANADA

LABRADOR

Queen Charlotte Is.

R O C K Y   M O U N T A I N S

Fraser R.

Hudson Bay

Belcher Is.

LAURENTIAN HIGHLANDS

Newfoundland

Vancouver I.

Columbia R.

INTERIOR PLAINS

L. Winnipeg

Nelson R.

C A N A D I A N   S H I E L D

St. Lawrence R.

Gulf of St. Lawrence

Mt. Rainier 14,410 ft. (4,392 m.)

CASCADE RANGE

G R E A T   P L A I N S

Missouri R.

L. Superior

Ottawa R.

APPALACHIAN MTS.

COAST RANGES

SIERRA NEVADA

GREAT BASIN

Great Salt L.

UNITED STATES

Mississippi R.

L. Michigan

L. Huron

L. Ontario

L. Erie

ATLANTIC OCEAN

PACIFIC OCEAN

Mt. Whitney 14,491 ft. (4,417 m.)

Colorado R.

Platte R.

CENTRAL PLAINS

Ohio R.

GULF-ATLANTIC COASTAL PLAIN

Arkansas R.

Mississippi R.

HAWAII (U.S.)

Rio Grande

Gulf of Mexico

Straits of Florida

CUBA

0   500   1,000 mi

0   500   1,000 km

Tropic of Cancer

MEXICO

Caribbean Sea

N E W S

learning LOCATIONS

Mapping Physical Features

Use the map on this page to add the physical features in the United States and Canada to your map, or label the physical features on an outline map. Include labels for all major landforms, such as mountains, plateaus, deserts, and rivers.

3 PEOPLE AND CULTURES

PHOTO STUDY

1 **Night Light** The pattern of electric lights reveals population density patterns in this evening satellite photograph. *Critical Thinking* **How does this photograph compare to the population density map on page 119?**

PHOTO STUDY

2 **A Land of Plenty** Compared with many nations of the world, the populations of Canada and the United States have long life expectancies, high per capita incomes, and high **literacy** rates. Literacy is the ability to read and write. These and other statistics show that people in Canada and the United States have a high **standard of living**. Standard of living is a measurement of a person's or group's education, housing, health care, and nutrition. *Critical Thinking* **How does a shopping mall reflect this high standard of living?**

THE UNITED STATES AND CANADA

The United States and Canada: POPULATION DENSITY

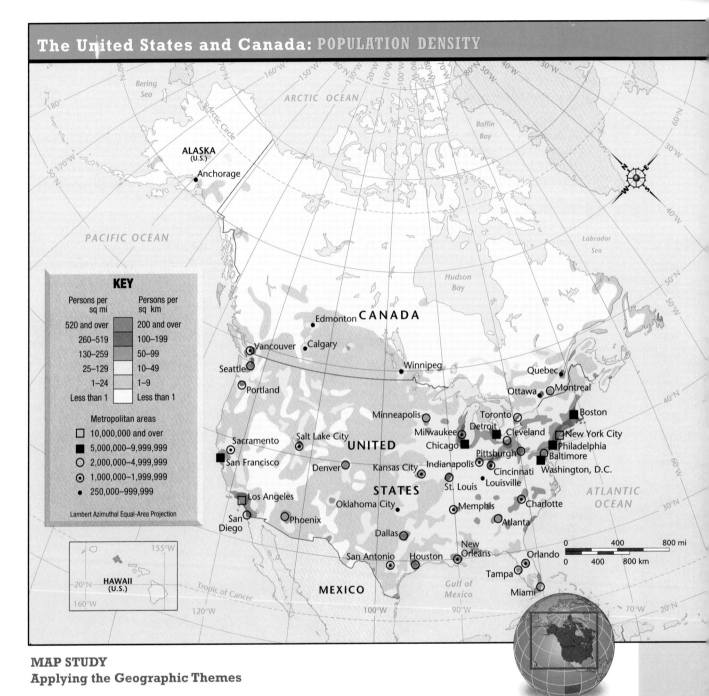

KEY

Persons per sq mi	Persons per sq km
520 and over	200 and over
260–519	100–199
130–259	50–99
25–129	10–49
1–24	1–9
Less than 1	Less than 1

Metropolitan areas

☐ 10,000,000 and over
■ 5,000,000–9,999,999
○ 2,000,000–4,999,999
◉ 1,000,000–1,999,999
• 250,000–999,999

Lambert Azimuthal Equal-Area Projection

MAP STUDY
Applying the Geographic Themes

3 Regions The populations of the United States and Canada differ greatly in size. The United States has more than 263 million people, whereas Canada has fewer than 30 million. About three fourths of the people in both countries live in urban areas. *Connections: Math About how many people live in the urban areas of Canada and the United States?*

4 Location Nearly four fifths of all Canadians live within two hundred miles (322 km) of the United States border. Few people live in the northern two thirds of Canada. Compare the population density map with the climate map on page 120. *Critical Thinking Why do you think this region is sparsely populated? Where do most Americans live?*

4 CLIMATE AND VEGETATION

MAP STUDY
Applying the Geographic Themes

1. **Regions** Canada and the United States have similar landform patterns, but differ greatly in climate. *In what ways do their climates differ?*

2. **Regions** Grasses grow well in the dry, interior plains of Canada and the United States. Blocked by the Rockies, rainfall on the plains averages 10 to 20 inches (25 to 51 cm) a year. This is just enough moisture for healthy grasses to grow. This temperate grassland is also called **prairie** and is characterized by a great variety of grasses. Compare the Natural Vegetation map to the Economic Activity and Resources map on page 122. *Critical Thinking What conclusions can you draw about temperate grasslands?*

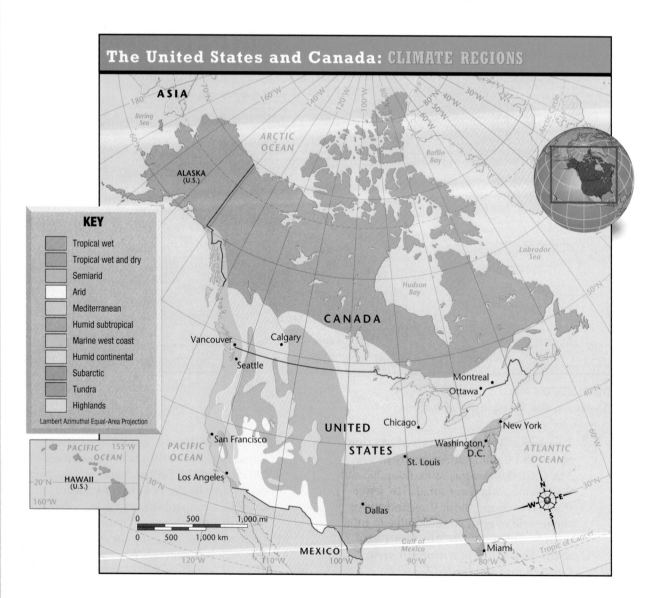

The United States and Canada: CLIMATE REGIONS

KEY
- Tropical wet
- Tropical wet and dry
- Semiarid
- Arid
- Mediterranean
- Humid subtropical
- Marine west coast
- Humid continental
- Subarctic
- Tundra
- Highlands

Lambert Azimuthal Equal-Area Projection

ASIA
Bering Sea
ARCTIC OCEAN
ALASKA (U.S.)
Baffin Bay
Labrador Sea
Hudson Bay
CANADA
Vancouver
Calgary
Seattle
Montreal
Ottawa
PACIFIC OCEAN
San Francisco
UNITED STATES
Chicago
New York
Washington, D.C.
St. Louis
ATLANTIC OCEAN
Los Angeles
Dallas
PACIFIC OCEAN
HAWAII (U.S.)
MEXICO
Gulf of Mexico
Miami
Tropic of Cancer

0 500 1,000 mi
0 500 1,000 km

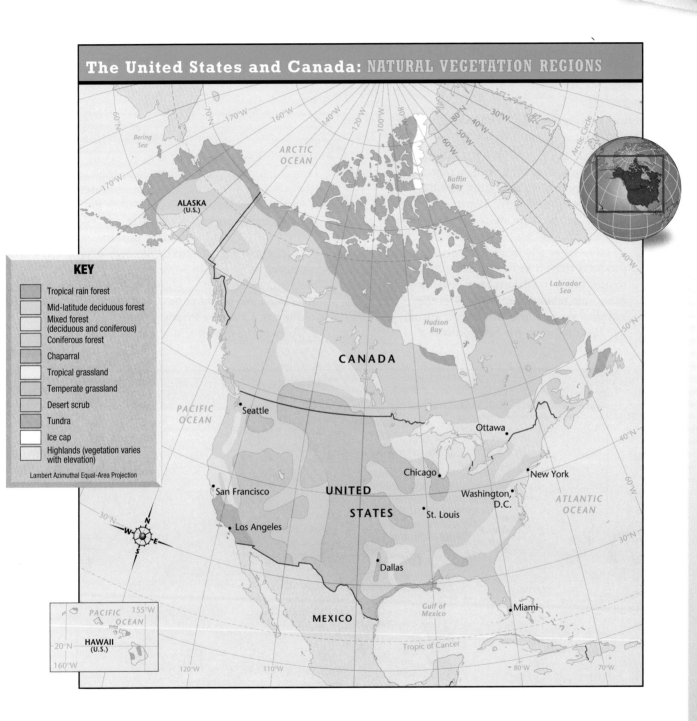

The United States and Canada: NATURAL VEGETATION REGIONS

KEY

- Tropical rain forest
- Mid-latitude deciduous forest
- Mixed forest (deciduous and coniferous)
- Coniferous forest
- Chaparral
- Tropical grassland
- Temperate grassland
- Desert scrub
- Tundra
- Ice cap
- Highlands (vegetation varies with elevation)

Lambert Azimuthal Equal-Area Projection

3 Regions The southwestern United States has a hot, dry climate, receiving less than 10 inches (25 cm) of rainfall each year. Lack of water keeps the population relatively low, but the landscape is well-suited to raising cattle and sheep on expansive ranches. *What type of vegetation does the region support?*

4 Regions Cold temperatures, strong winds, a short growing season, and permafrost characterize the Arctic tundra. The only plants that can grow on the tundra are lichens, mosses, and a few other tiny plants. *Where is the tundra region located?*

THE UNITED STATES AND CANADA

MAP STUDY
Applying the Geographic Themes

1 Human-Environment Interaction In most places, people have changed the environment so dramatically that little natural vegetation remains. *What economic activity accounts for most of this change?*

2 Movement The ability of people and products to pass easily from one country to another is important to maintaining an economic relationship. *How does the physical geography of the region encourage links between the two countries?*

3 Human-Environment Interaction Detroit is a major United States industrial city near Lake Erie. Canada's industry, and it's population, are also concentrated in the Great Lakes region and along the St. Lawrence River. **Hydroelectric power**, electricity that is generated by moving water, is used to supply power to many of these industries. *Critical Thinking In what other ways do you think the Great Lakes and the St. Lawrence River are important to industry in the United States and Canada?*

THE UNITED STATES AND CANADA

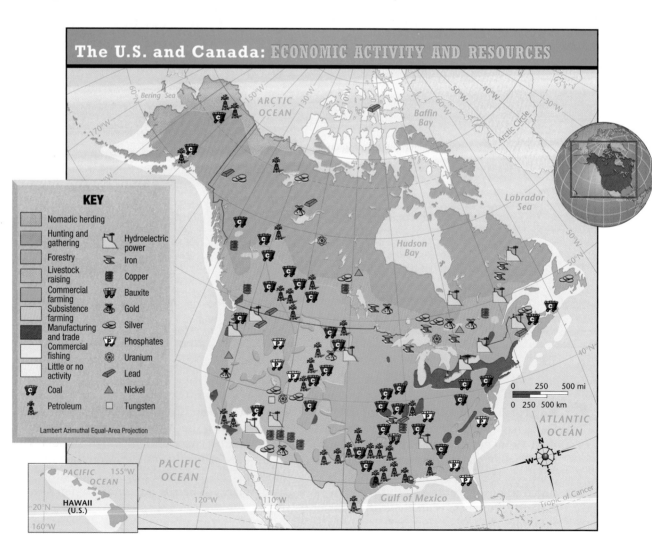

The U.S. and Canada: ECONOMIC ACTIVITY AND RESOURCES

KEY

Nomadic herding
Hunting and gathering
Forestry
Livestock raising
Commercial farming
Subsistence farming
Manufacturing and trade
Commercial fishing
Little or no activity
Coal
Petroleum

Hydroelectric power
Iron
Copper
Bauxite
Gold
Silver
Phosphates
Uranium
Lead
Nickel
Tungsten

Lambert Azimuthal Equal-Area Projection

0   250   500 mi
0   250 500 km

HAWAII (U.S.)

PHOTO STUDY

4 **Altering the Environment** Economic activities like logging in northwestern North America and mining in the Rocky Mountain region usually take place in areas of low population density. They produce major changes, however, in the environment. *Critical Thinking Why do you think there is controversy over economic activities that alter the environment?*

atlas REVIEW

Vocabulary and Main Ideas

1. Define: a. **cordillera** b. **continental divide**
   c. **drainage basin** d. **tributaries** e. **prairie**
   f. **literacy** g. **standard of living**
   h. **hydroelectric power**

2. **Name the landform that dominates the central United States and Canada.**

3. **How has human activity affected the landscape of Canada and the United States?**

4. **Critical Thinking** **What role have abundant natural resources played in the economies of the United States and Canada?**

learning LOCATIONS

5. Which country lies closer to the Equator, Canada or the United States?

6. Which Canadian city is situated southwest of Ottawa on the shores of Lake Ontario?

THE UNITED STATES AND CANADA

Native American ritual figure

Settlement of the Americas

More than any other part of the world, the countries of the Americas are nations of immigrants. Geography helps explain how and why people first migrated to those countries.

The Bering Land Bridge

For most of the past several million years, two great oceans have separated the American continents from the rest of the world. But during the Ice Ages—between about 20,000 and 12,000 years ago—geographers believe that much of the earth's water was frozen into glaciers and ice sheets. As a result, ocean levels dropped, exposing a flat bridge of land between Alaska and eastern Asia, where the Bering Strait is today.

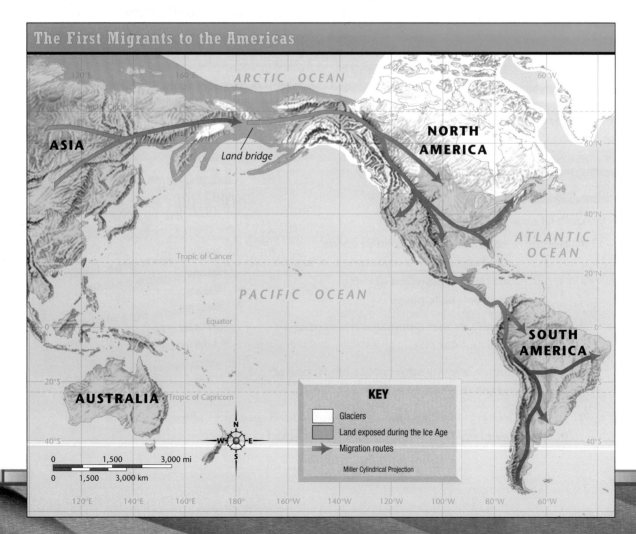

The First Migrants to the Americas

ARCTIC OCEAN

ASIA

Land bridge

NORTH AMERICA

ATLANTIC OCEAN

Tropic of Cancer

PACIFIC OCEAN

Equator

SOUTH AMERICA

AUSTRALIA · Tropic of Capricorn

KEY
- Glaciers
- Land exposed during the Ice Age
- Migration routes

0   1,500   3,000 mi
0   1,500   3,000 km

Miller Cylindrical Projection

Eastern Asia—Siberia— was home to groups of wandering hunters. When animals wandered onto the land bridge to graze, most scientists believe that the hunters followed. Both animals and hunters gradually moved onto the new land. Over thousands of years, different hunting groups gradually spread out over North and South America. These Paleo-Indians were the first humans in the Americas, ancestors of all the Native American peoples.

Worlds Apart

For thousands of years more, the Americas remained worlds apart. People traveled only on land or in small ships that did not venture far from sight of land. Isolated by rugged mountain ranges and great distances, people in different regions of the Americas developed their own distinctive language families and cultures.

Compared with Europe and Asia, the population of the Americas was small. A few settlements grew into populous towns and cities, but most Native Americans remained hunters and farmers. Thick forests and broad, tall grass prairies covered most of the land.

The Age of Exploration Brings Newcomers

In Europe and Asia, however, populations were growing and cities were becoming crowded. Good land—the main measure of wealth—was scarce. By the 1500s, better ships and navigation methods allowed European explorers to find their way to the two huge continents to the west.

The first European newcomers, mainly from Spain, settled in what are now Florida, the Southwest, and Mexico. Their first goals were gold and conquest, but in time people settled there permanently. Later Spanish settlers went south into Central and South America. About a century later, settlers from France and Great Britain set up colonies on the eastern coast of North America. North America had rich resources: forests, farmlands, and wild animals that supplied valuable furs. Europeans also settled on many Caribbean islands, and established profitable plantations in the warm climate.

Gold figurines attracted European explorers.

Changing Patterns

For several hundred years, nearly all those who chose to move to North America were Europeans. They came because of wars, religious unrest, and lack of land or opportunity at home. In addition, millions of Africans were brought unwillingly as slaves. Railroad building and gold-mining attracted the first immigrants from Asia in the mid-1800s, but for a long time, discriminatory laws kept the number of Asian immigrants low.

Dramatic changes in patterns of immigration to the United States began in the 1960s. Today the greatest number of immigrants come from Asia and from other parts of the Americas.

connecting
TO TODAY

1. **Who were the ancestors of the Native Americans?**

2. **From what country did the first European settlers in the Americas come?**

3. **Critical Thinking** **Over time, how did people's reasons for migrating to the Americas change?**

4. **Hands-On Activity** **Take a poll of the members of your class and list the countries from which their families or distant ancestors came to the United States. Place push pins on a world map at each place of origin. Then stretch a string or ribbon from each one to your community.**

A Profile of the United States

SECTIONS

1 **A Resource-Rich Nation**

2 **A Nation of Cities**

The United States: POLITICAL

learning LOCATIONS

Mapping the Region in Detail

Create a map like the one above, lightly shading each state in a different color. Then add the labels for the states and water bodies that are shown on this map.

1 A Resource-Rich Nation

Section Preview

Main Ideas

● Abundant natural resources, new technology, hard-working individuals, and a system of free enterprise led to the economic success of the United States.

● Transportation and communication systems provided links that remain vital to American industries.

Vocabulary

gross national product, telecommunications, free enterprise, rugged individualism

APPEARED IN *NATIONAL GEOGRAPHIC*

Farmers often ship their produce to distant markets.

Compared with most countries of the world, the United States is enormous. It is the world's fourth-largest country in area and is the third most populous. The United States is also wealthy. The nation's **gross national product** (GNP) is the highest in the world. The gross national product is a measure of the total value of all the goods and services produced by a country in a year.

How did the United States become such a wealthy country? At least four factors help answer this question: its abundance of natural resources, the development of new transportation and communication technology, the hard work of its people, and its political system.

An Abundance of Natural Resources

"I think in all the world the like abundance is not to be found." These were the words of Arthur Barlowe, an English sea captain, shortly after his arrival in North America in 1584. The continent seemed to offer the newcomer an unbelievable degree of plenty, and with it the promise of wealth.

Farming the Land One of the most abundant natural resources in the United States is the land itself. The prairie grasses of the Midwest and the Great Plains boast some of the richest soils in the world. The United States established early on the importance of this resource. For much of the country's history, parcels of land were given to people who promised to live on them for at least five years. In the 1700s much of that land was used for farming. When the nation's first census was taken in 1790, more than three fourths of the nation's people lived on farms.

In 1862 the government further encouraged development of the land with the passage of the Homestead Act. The act granted 160 acres of land to settlers who agreed to establish farms. The United States Department of Agriculture, which promotes and supports farming activities, was created that same year. Today, farm exports bring in $30–40 billion annually.

The land had been cultivated long before the establishment of the United States, however. Many Native American groups, such as the Cayuga, Creek, Natchez, and Cherokee, lived in permanent or semi-permanent villages. There they grew crops such as maize, squash, beans, cotton, and tobacco.

◀ **Chicago** (*photo left*)

U.S. Energy Consumption

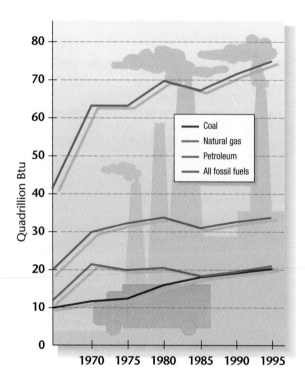

Source: The World Almanac and Book of Facts

GRAPH STUDY

● The United States is the world's biggest consumer of energy. Consumption of energy is measured in British Thermal Units, or Btu. The United States relies primarily on fossil fuels such as coal, natural gas, and petroleum, for its energy needs. *On which fossil fuel does the United States rely most?*

● **Critical Thinking** *What might account for the nation's increasing consumption of energy?*

Even uncultivated, the land provided food in the form of wild plants, fish, and game.

European colonization and later westward expansion of the United States into Native American territory caused a state of almost continual warfare for more than 300 years. Thousands of people died in these so-called Indian Wars. In the end, Native Americans were forced to give up their lands and live on reservations.

Clearing the Forests Forests are another of the United States' rich resources. They provide material for a startling array of products, including lumber for housing and furniture construction, paper, rayon, photo-

graphic film, artificial sponges, charcoal, methanol, medicinal chemicals, maple sugar, and even plastics.

The United States lumber industry began in colonial New England, which sawed timber for barrel staves and board lumber and harvested trees to make ships' masts. After American Independence, logging activity shifted to the South. Because of the South's mild climate, loggers could use rivers year-round to transport logs to the saw mills. Logging in the midwest was limited by the seasonal variations of the climate, yet the forests were quickly logged over in the late 1800s, and much of the land was converted to farmland.

By 1930, the forests of the east were depleted or converted to farmland, so the lumber industry moved west. Nearly half of the nation's lumber is now obtained west of the Rocky Mountains, primarily in California, Oregon, Washington, and Idaho.

Forests are a renewable resource, if managed carefully. A better understanding of forest ecosystems is leading to better management of the nation's timber. Grazing laws, harvesting regulations, better logging practices, and reforestation programs are helping to conserve the nation's forests. Thousands of acres of forest have been set aside as national parks, protecting not only the trees themselves, but the valuable watersheds and fish and wildlife habitats they support. Even so, only 5 percent of the nation's virgin forest remains.

Finding Wealth Underground Beneath the lush forests and rich soils of the United States lies an abundance of mineral resources. One of the country's most abundant minerals is coal, a solid fossil fuel that is used as a source of energy for industry, transportation, and homes. The United States produces about one fifth of the world's supply of coal.

Oil and natural gas are other fossil fuels found in the United States. They lie beneath the central and western plains, as well as in Alaska. In recent years, Americans have become concerned over the fact that these fuels, as well as coal, are nonrenewable. Because oil, natural gas, and coal are all extremely vital to the United States energy supply and economy, they require careful management.

The graph on page 128 shows the United States consumption of fossil fuels.

The United States produces significant amounts of copper, gold, lead, titanium, uranium, zinc, and other non-fuel minerals as well. A nation's supply of minerals is important not only for trade, but for development of its industries as well. Copper, for example, is used in building construction, electrical and electronic equipment, transportation, and consumer products.

Moving Resources, Goods, and People

The United States could not have turned its resources into wealth without the development of new technologies for transportation. Improved transportation provided more and faster links that allowed producers to move raw materials to factories and finished goods from factories to consumers.

Travel Over Water In the 1800s, transportation was faster on water than on land. But river travel was still a cumbersome process. A keelboat could take as long as six weeks to float down the Mississippi and four months to make the return trip. But the successful development of the steam engine changed all that. Steam provided boats with the power to travel against both wind and current. By the 1850s, steamboats were a common sight on rivers, steaming their way across a watery transportation network. Steamboats also turned the Great Lakes into important transportation routes.

In the early 1800s the United States also began building canals, or artificial waterways, to make even more places accessible by water. The combination of canals and the steamboat made travel of people and goods over water both speedy and cheap.

Movement Over Land Steam-powered railroads later replaced steamboats as the most efficient means of transporting goods. A transcontinental railroad linking the east and west coasts of the country was completed in 1869. By 1900, people and goods in nearly every

Santa Fe Railway

Location This busy freight yard in Kansas City, Missouri, serves twelve railroads. *Why has transportation been so important to the development of industry?*

settled part of the country were within reach of a railroad.

The invention of the automobile in the 1890s heralded the next revolution in transportation. Mass production techniques pioneered by automobile manufacturer Henry Ford made automobiles affordable to the general public. Individuals could now enjoy greater freedom of movement. By the 1950s, as more and more people owned cars, the nation began building an interstate highway system—a network of roads that link major cities across the nation.

Improving Communication

The industrial and economic growth of the United States was also closely tied to improved communications. In the early 1800s, communication required the transportation of people or paper, until Samuel F. B. Morse found a way to send messages by an electric current. In 1837 Morse demonstrated the first successful telegraph. A telegraph was capable of sending a coded message. Patterns of long and short sounds—or printed dots and dashes—were converted by the receiving telegraph operator into corresponding letters of the alphabet.

Telegraph lines were commonly strung along railroad rights of way. In exchange, telegraph offices provided free service to railroad companies. With access to speedy communication, railroads were able to coordinate train schedules, locate trains, and establish standardized time.

By the 1860s there were telegraph offices in every important city. Newspapers talked about the "mystic band" that now held the nation together. Telegraphs allowed Americans to transfer information in minutes instead of days. American businesses could now communicate more efficiently with the people who supplied raw materials and parts for their machines, as well as with their customers.

New forms of communication were the center of attention at the nation's centennial exposition in Philadelphia in 1876. The star of the show was a small device invented that year by Alexander Graham Bell—the telephone. By 1915, telephone wires connected people from coast to coast. Well over 90 percent of United States households now have telephones. Today, fiber optics, the conversion of electronic signals into light waves, is replacing the use of telephone wires. People can now communicate at the speed of light.

Many people and businesses today are also communicating via an elaborate web of computer networks. Computer, telephone, satellite, and other forms of **telecommunications**, or communication by electronic means, are becoming increasingly important to doing business.

All Lines Are Busy

Movement Complicated networks support the more than ten billion telephone calls Americans make every working day. *When was the world introduced to the telephone?*

Respecting the Individual

The interaction between production, transportation, and communication has been vital to the economic success of the country. So, too, has the political system of the United States. The government that was established by the people in 1789 reflected one of the most important shared values in the United States—the belief in individual equality, opportunity, and freedom. Important, too, was the belief that individuals acting in their own interest may also serve the interests of others. These ideals are supported by an economic system based on capitalism, or **free enterprise**. The system of free enterprise allows individuals to own, operate, and profit from their own businesses in an open, competitive market.

One of the driving notions behind free enterprise is that any hardworking individual—regardless of his or her wealth, cultural background, or religion—can find opportunity and success in the United States. It was this belief that drew, and continues to draw, many immigrants to the country. The people of the United States have long praised the quality of **rugged individualism**—the willingness of individuals to stand alone and struggle long and hard to survive and prosper, relying on their own personal resources, opinions, and beliefs.

George Washington Carver

Human-Environment Interaction Agriculturist George Washington Carver was born a slave around 1864. He eventually earned degrees in agriculture, a faculty appointment, and numerous awards. He is most famous for his research on peanuts. **Critical Thinking** *How does Carver represent the ideal of rugged individualism?*

Section 1 Review

Vocabulary and Main Ideas

1. Define: a. gross national product
   b. telecommunications c. free enterprise
   d. rugged individualism

2. What are some of the abundant resources available in the United States?

3. Describe three ways in which transportation and communication systems strengthened the nation's economy.

4. How has the United States system of government contributed to the economic success of the country?

5. Critical Thinking: *Synthesizing Information* In what ways do you think free public education has contributed to the wealth of the country?

6. What states border the Great Lakes?

7. Which two states are not part of the United States mainland?

A Nation of Cities

Section Preview

Main Ideas

Four factors affected the growth rate of United States cities: location, transportation, economy, and popular preferences.

Cities of different sizes serve different functions and are related to one another in an urban hierarchy.

Vocabulary

suburbs, hierarchy, hinterland

Chicago is the most important city in the Midwest.

As the economy of the United States grew, it also changed. It began as an economy based primarily on local agriculture. As the nation began to develop its other resources and make improvements in transportation and communication, its economic base shifted to industry and manufacturing.

Most recently, service industries have begun to make up a larger share of the nation's economy. Service industries are businesses that are not directly related to manufacturing or gathering raw materials. Health care, education, entertainment, banking, transportation, and government are all service industries. See the graph on page 135 for a description of how most Americans will soon be earning a living.

As these changes in the economy took place, life for men, women, and children living in American villages and towns was transformed. In fact, by 1890 many rural places were all but abandoned by people who had left for new jobs and homes in the country's growing cities. Cities became the centers of transportation and production in the new industrial economy.

Location: The Growth of Cities

Once a nation dominated by rural settlers, the United States is now largely a nation of city dwellers. The country has more than 260 metropolitan areas. A metropolitan area comprises a major city and its surrounding suburbs. More than half of the nation's people live in the 40 largest metropolitan areas, which have populations over 1 million. How did all these metropolitan areas grow so large? Why have some grown faster than others? To answer these questions, keep in mind an old saying: "The value of any parcel of land is determined by three factors. The first is location. The second is location. And the third is location."

The value of a city's location is affected by changes in transportation, changes in economic activities, and changes in popular preferences. As the United States economy changed, so did the circumstances of each village, town, and city within it.

Movement: The Impact of Transportation

For the first fifty years or so following American independence, sailing ships were the fastest and cheapest form of transportation. Cities functioned largely as places to carry on trade between the United States and Europe. All the major cities were busy Atlantic ports; some of the largest were Baltimore, Boston, New York, and Philadelphia.

Canals As the interior of the continent was developed, settlers came to rely on the country's abundant rivers to transport their crops. Many of the rivers the farmers used were tributaries of the Mississippi. New Orleans flourished at the mouth of the Mississippi as a steady flow of trade goods from the Midwest filled its harbor and moved out into the world.

The people of many eastern cities realized that they, too, could benefit from more direct ties to the West. In the early 1800s, the governor of New York, DeWitt Clinton, came up with a daring plan to dig a 363-mile (584 km) canal from Lake Erie to the Hudson River. Western crops could be floated east through the Great Lakes into the canal and down the Hudson River to New York City. The Erie Canal provided the best connection between the east coast and settlements near the Great Lakes.

New cities were established on the shores of the Great Lakes and also along the Ohio, Mississippi, and Missouri rivers. Buffalo, Cleveland, Detroit, and Chicago soon rivaled the older cities of the East. The success of the Erie Canal sparked a canal-building boom. Before the end of the 1800s a vast canal system, stretching for over 4,000 miles (6,436 km), linked the cities of the North and West.

Railroads The same benefits from trade that motivated the building of canals also motivated the construction of railroads. The first successful railroads were built in the United States in 1830. By 1840, there were over 1,000 miles (1,609 km) of railroad tracks. The great wave of railroad building over the next fifty years united the nation.

Early railroad tracks, however, were laid out in short, unconnected lines, and most of them existed in the East. Goods and passengers had to be moved to different cars on different lines, resulting in costly delays and inconvenience. In 1862 Congress initiated a plan to build a single rail line connecting the East to the West.

The nation's first transcontinental rail line was laid out on approximately the 42nd parallel, from Omaha to Sacramento. Building such a line proved to be a geographical challenge. Train tracks need to be level and relatively straight, rather than curved. Yet, as you can see from the physical map

Miami on the Move

● **Movement** Miami is the second largest city in Florida. Its international airport is one of the busiest in the nation, its port serves both passenger and cargo ships from many countries, and its first railroad track was laid down over 100 years ago. *Critical Thinking Why is it important for a city to have many forms of transportation?*

The Daily Commute

● **Movement** Commuters patiently wait for their train in Newark, New Jersey. Commuter trains enable people to work in major industrial centers and still make their homes away from the bustle of the city. *What other form of transportation has allowed individuals greater mobility?*

of the United States on page 117, the Rocky Mountains and the Sierra Nevada Ranges formed huge geographical barriers. Thousands of Chinese and European immigrant workers performed the dangerous and difficult work of laying the tracks. By 1869, the continent's first transcontinental railroad was complete.

After the end of the Civil War in 1865, railroads became the country's most important form of transportation. Cities along the railroads grew rapidly. Chicago, located centrally between the coasts, had the best location on the railroad network, so it became the largest city in the Midwest. New York City acquired so many people, businesses, and activities that it developed into the foremost metropolitan area in the United States.

Automobiles Until the invention of the automobile, efficient travel was limited to waterways and railroads. The automobile gave Americans a new freedom; they could go anyplace where there were roads at any time they wished. To meet the increasing demand for automobiles, auto manufacturers produced as many as 8 million new cars each year during the 1950s. The 1956 Interstate Highway Act provided $26 billion to build an interstate highway system more than 4,000 miles (6,436 km) long.

The increased availability of automobiles and public transportation, such as trolleys and subways, made it possible for people to travel longer distances to work. After World War II many businesses and people moved from the cities to the **suburbs**—the mostly residential areas on the outer edges of a city. Suburbs grew at the end of rail lines because land there was available and less expensive. A 1952 advertisement for Park Forest, a town about 40 miles (64 km) outside of Chicago, attracted newcomers with these words: "Come out to Park Forest where small-town friendships grow— and you can still live so close to a big city." The scope of cities widened as suburbs grew.

The Impact of Popular Preferences

All of these advances in transportation allowed people more freedom to select where their businesses would operate and where they would

Air Pollution

In response to consumer demands for more environmentally sound automobiles, several oil companies have developed reformulated gasolines. One type of gasoline cuts some pollutants by more than one third. In addition, several automobile companies are redesigning their engines to run on fuels other than gasoline.

United States Occupational Groups: Projection for 2005

At the beginning of the 20th century 41 percent of the labor force was engaged in farming. *According to this graph, what will be the leading occupation at the start of the 21st century?*

2.5% 3.8%
17.5% 10.3%
10.4%
17.2% 10.6%
15.5% 12.1%

- Administrative support
- Agriculture, forestry, fishing
- Executive
- Marketing and sales
- Operators, fabricators, laborers
- Precision production, craft, and repair
- Professional specialty
- Service occupations
- Technicians and related support

Source: *The World Almanac and Book of Facts*

live. Today many people choose locations that they feel offer the best possible surroundings. As a result, cities in the South and West, where winters are less severe than in the Northeast, have flourished. Because of new industries along the Gulf coast as well as its cultural attractions, New Orleans has regained the importance it had lost when railroads replaced steamboat traffic. At the same time, New York, Chicago, and other large centers have maintained their positions because they offer many jobs and varied activities.

Urban Areas

Although today nearly 80 percent of all people in the United States live in metropolitan areas teeming with business and industry, about 20 percent continue to live in small towns and villages. Regardless of how small or large each of these places is, they all play a specific role in the nation's economy.

Interconnections The next time you are in a grocery store, find a can of peas or sweet corn. Where did these vegetables come from? Your can of vegetables may list the name of a major city. Obviously, the vegetables were not grown in a city, but the headquarters of the company that distributes the vegetables are most likely to be located in a large city. The corporate executives have their

offices there. The advertising campaigns and research also originate there.

The canned vegetables were likely grown on a farm in Mississippi, California, or some other agricultural region. Once they were ripe, they were harvested and trucked directly to a processing plant. Cleaned, tested, cooked, and canned within hours, they were then trucked to distant towns and cities.

One hundred years ago, the peas or corn in that can would probably not have gone farther than the dinner table on the farm where they were grown. Because of advances in technology, canned vegetables, as well as farm-fresh produce, can be found in cities many miles from the nearest field.

Function and Size Geographers often talk about the nation's urban places in terms of a **hierarchy,** or rank, according to their function. Smaller places serve a limited area in limited ways, while larger cities provide other, wider-ranging functions.

Different terms describe urban places in each size category. Large cities are called metropolises, and their **hinterlands**—the areas that they serve—are quite large. For some activities, the hinterland may be the entire United States and much of the rest of the world. For example, New York is the most important financial center in the Western Hemisphere. Chicago is the nation's leading agricultural market, where orders for millions of farm animals and billions of bushels of grain are made. Los Angeles, California, is the world's leading film-production center.

Cities like Atlanta, Denver, Seattle, and Minneapolis–St. Paul are regional metropolises and have much smaller hinterlands. But like larger metropolises they support advanced medical care facilities, art galleries, major-league sports teams, and stores that sell expensive clothing and accessories.

Smaller cities like Des Moines, Albany, Nashville, and Tucson have a more limited range of activities and smaller hinterlands. These are places that usually have large shopping centers, daily newspapers, and computer software stores.

Some towns are small, and their service areas are quite limited. Few people outside the immediate area are familiar with these places. Such towns are home to automobile dealers, fast-food restaurants, and medium-sized supermarkets. Villages often have only small grocery stores. Post offices and video-rental stores may be present in some villages, but a general store often is the only business in the smallest hamlets.

Cities of similar size are not alike in all parts of the United States. They have distinct characteristics based in part on regional differences within the United States. In the next chapter you will read about the nation's four distinct regions.

Urban Hierarchy

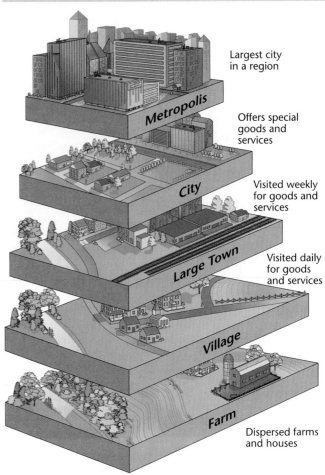

Largest city in a region

Metropolis
Offers special goods and services

City
Visited weekly for goods and services

Large Town
Visited daily for goods and services

Village

Farm
Dispersed farms and houses

DIAGRAM STUDY

● The metropolis tops the urban hierarchy pyramid because it offers the most services and serves an extensive area. *Which place serves the most limited area?*

● Critical Thinking *What services does a large metropolis provide that cannot be found in a town?*

Section 2 Review

Vocabulary and Main Ideas

1. **Define: a. suburb b. hierarchy c. hinterland**

2. **How did railroads affect the growth of some United States cities?**

3. **Why have cities in the South and West flourished in recent decades?**

4. **Critical Thinking:** *Drawing Conclusions* **How does the urban hierarchy in the United States contribute to interdependence among people?**

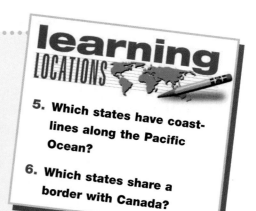

learning LOCATIONS

5. **Which states have coastlines along the Pacific Ocean?**

6. **Which states share a border with Canada?**

Focus on Skills

☑ Social Studies

☐ Map and Globe

☐ Critical Thinking and Problem Solving

Reading Urban Diagrams

Geographers have noticed that many cities in the world have similar structures. Geographers use several models to illustrate these structures, three of which are shown below.

One model shows cities organized in concentric circles. The center of the city is the Central Business District, or CBD. The CBD is surrounded by a transition zone where skyscrapers are gradually replaced by deteriorating housing. Industries are located in both the CBD and in the transition zone. The third ring is made up of low-income housing, and high-income housing makes up the outer ring. Beyond are the suburbs where commuters live.

Some geographers argue that industry does not encircle a city, but instead is located along transportation routes, which run outward from the CBD. In this, the sector model, regions of the city are like pieces of pie. Sections are determined by major transportation routes such as highways and commuter rail lines and topographical features, such as hills or valleys.

A third model, called the multiple nuclei model, is based on the argument that cities do not have just one single core, but instead have several outlying business districts that duplicate the function of the CBD. Acting as independent mini-cities, they reduce the interaction people have with the city's CBD.

1. Analyze the three models. Carefully review the models below. Then answer the following questions: (a) In all three models, what is the relationship between industrial areas and low-income housing? (b) Where would highways fit into the sector and the multiple nuclei models? (c) How do you think a river would affect the sector and the multiple nuclei models?

2. Apply the models to actual places.
(a) Think of a city. Which model does it resemble the most, if any, and why? (b) How do transportation routes and terrain affect the structure of the city?

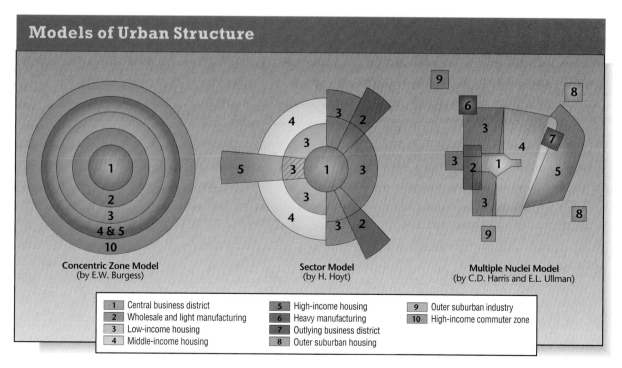

Models of Urban Structure

Concentric Zone Model
(by E.W. Burgess)

Sector Model
(by H. Hoyt)

Multiple Nuclei Model
(by C.D. Harris and E.L. Ullman)

1	Central business district	5	High-income housing	9	Outer suburban industry
2	Wholesale and light manufacturing	6	Heavy manufacturing	10	High-income commuter zone
3	Low-income housing	7	Outlying business district		
4	Middle-income housing	8	Outer suburban housing		

Source: Kingston, John. *Longman Geography Book*, 1988

Review and Activities

Summarizing Main Ideas

Section 1 A Resource-Rich Nation

- Abundant resources, new technology, hard-working individuals, and a government supportive of a free enterprise system all helped to make the United States a wealthy nation.
- Transportation and communication systems that link the industries to both raw materials and consumers are vital to the nation's economic success.

Section 2 A Nation of Cities

- The United States has become a nation of city dwellers.
- Changes in transportation, economic activities, and popular preferences affected the growth of cities.
- Cities of different sizes are related to one another in an urban hierarchy. Small places function in limited ways for a limited area, while successively larger cities provide major services for an extensive surrounding area.

Reviewing Vocabulary

Use each of the following terms in a sentence that shows their meaning.

1. hinterlands
2. hierarchy
3. telecommunications
4. free enterprise
5. suburb
6. gross national product
7. rugged individualism

Applying the Geographic Themes

1. **Region** What is the most important natural resource that the Midwest and Great Plains offer?
2. **Movement** Why are transportation links important to the economic success of a country?
3. **Human-Environment Interaction** Describe two types of technology that were developed to harvest or gain access to the nation's natural resources.
4. **Movement** How did transportation affect the growth of New York and Chicago?
5. **Location** Why do some cities grow and others decline in population over time?

Critical Thinking and Applying Skills

1. **Recognizing Ideologies** How did belief in individual worth influence the American political system?
2. **Drawing Conclusions** How do you think the free enterprise system contributed to the economic development of the United States?
3. **Reading Urban Diagrams** Refer to the diagram on page 137 to answer the following questions.

   a. Where would high-income housing tend to be located?

   b. Where would low-income housing tend to be located?

Writing Across Cultures

▶ 1. The notion that any hardworking individual—regardless of wealth, cultural background, or religion—can find opportunity and success in the United States has drawn many immigrants to the country. Write two paragraphs describing the kinds of opportunities you think draw immigrants to the United States today.

▶ 2. Write a few paragraphs exploring the advantages and disadvantages of living in a nation in which many cultures are represented.

INTERNET link

Economic development in the United States came at some cost to the environment. Read about people who are working to improve the quality of our waters. Visit the heroes room at the Smithsonian Institution's Ocean Planet Exhibit. Link to this site from:

• www.phschool.com

Read about a few people, and write about the accomplishment that impresses you most.

The United States

Number from 1 to 12 on your paper. Next to each number, write the letter of the place on the map that corresponds to the states listed below.

1. Idaho
2. Wyoming
3. Washington
4. California

5. New Mexico
6. Arkansas
7. Louisiana
8. New York

9. Illinois
10. Massachusetts
11. Pennsylvania
12. North Dakota

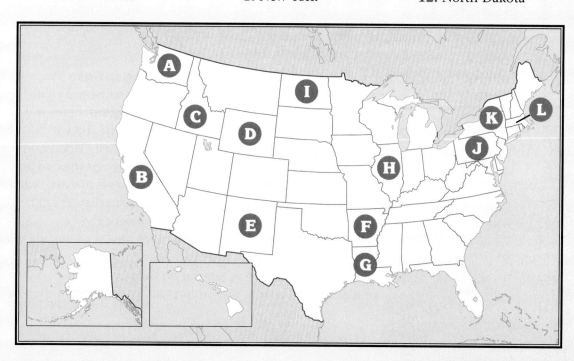

Map Skills for Life

Andre Lafontaine and his family, whose home is in Seattle, Washington, are visiting the eastern United States. They look forward to seeing as much of the Southeast as they can, by following the network of interstate highways.

During their vacation, the Lafontaines want to visit these historic cities:

★ Washington, D.C., the nation's capital.

★ Richmond, Virginia, the Confederate capital during the Civil War.

★ Charlotte, North Carolina.

★ Charleston, South Carolina, and Savannah, Georgia, both famous for their colonial mansions.

★ St. Augustine, Florida, the oldest permanent European settlement in the United States, settled by the Spanish in 1565.

★ Atlanta, Georgia, site of the 1996 Olympics.

Reading the Map

Follow the steps to understand how the Lafontaines can use the interstate highway map for their trip around the eastern United States. Notice that this map does not include all of the roads of the interstate highway system, just some major routes of the network.

Interstate highways are usually referred to by the letter I and their number, for example, I-95.

1. Locate the cities they want to visit on the map. Many of the cities that the Lafontaines want to visit are in a line going southward along the east coast of the United States. Traveling south from Washington, D.C., which of the other cities would they reach first?

2. Find the highways that connect their destinations. Using a photocopy of the road map, Andre circles their destinations with a marker and highlights the roads that connect them to find the best route. **(a)** If the Lafontaines decide to drive directly from Washington to Charlotte and then on to Atlanta, which interstate highways will they take? **(b)** How will their route be different if they travel from Washington directly to Savannah and St. Augustine?

3. Use the map scale to estimate distances and driving times between different points. With this information, figure out about how long each part of the trip will take. Remember to measure the actual distance on the map, not a straight line between the two points. If Andre's family wants to drive only about 250 miles each day, can they go from Atlanta to Savannah in one day?

Road maps on a smaller scale often note the distances between two points. These usually appear on the map as a small numeral in color beside a marked segment of the road.

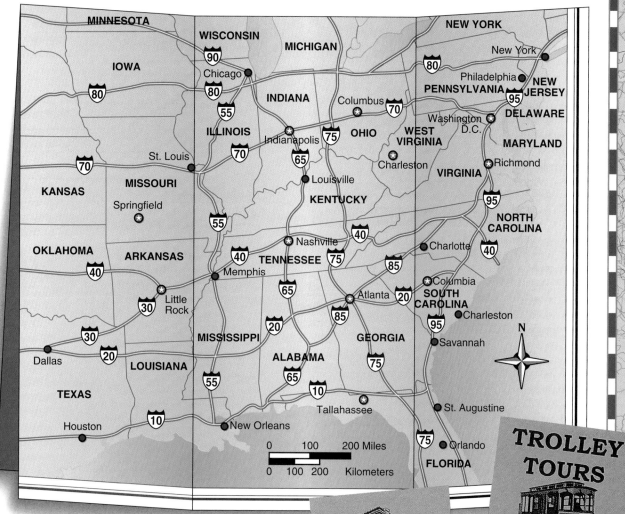

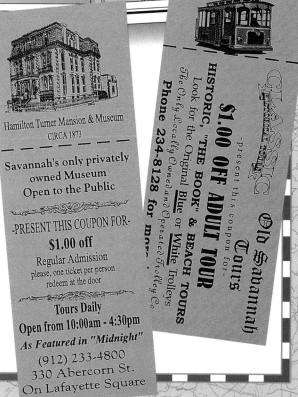

Test Yourself

1. **(a)** If the Lafontaines want to make a side trip to visit friends in Dallas, Texas, which of their target cities would be the best starting point?
(b) Can they travel directly to Dallas on an interstate highway? Which one?

2. Charleston, South Carolina, is not on any of the interstate highways on this map. Which route will bring the Lafontaines closest to this city?

Regions of the United States

The United States: POLITICAL

200   400 mi
200 400 km

Seattle

Superior

L. Ontario

Boston

NORTHEAST

Minneapolis

L. Michigan

L. Huron

L. Erie

New York

MIDWEST

Chicago

Washington, D.C.

Sacramento

St. Louis

San Francisco

WEST

ATLANTIC OCEAN

Los Angeles

Phoenix

Atlanta

PACIFIC OCEAN

Dallas

SOUTH

Miami

Gulf of Mexico

WEST

Anchorage

Arctic Circle

Gulf of Alaska

PACIFIC OCEAN

0   400 mi
0   400 km

KEY

• City

✪ State capital

⊛ National capital

Lambert Azimuthal Equal-Area Projection

Honolulu

WEST

0   100   200 mi
0   100 200 km

learning LOCATIONS

Mapping the Region in Detail
Create a map like the one above, lightly
shading each region in a different color.
Then add the labels for each major city.

1 The Northeast

Section Preview

Main Ideas

- The Northeast's water bodies have been valuable resources throughout the region's history.

- The Northeast was one of the early sites of industry.

- The Northeast has become one of the most highly urbanized and densely populated regions of the world.

Vocabulary

megalopolis

APPEARED IN *NATIONAL GEOGRAPHIC*

A Maine lobsterman tends his traps.

People define regions in order to identify places that have similar characteristics or close connections. As you read in Chapter 1, there are many ways to define the regions of the United States: historically; by the ways people live, work, and play in them; or by their political orientation. As the maps in Chapter 5 show, landforms, climate, and vegetation all suggest different boundaries for North America's physical regions. The economic activity and population density maps suggest other divisions, based on human characteristics.

In this textbook, we look to the United States government for regional classifications. The government, for the purpose of collecting statistics, divides the country into four major regions: the Northeast, South, Midwest, and West. Look at the map on page 142 to identify these regions. The government's definition of these regions is based on a combination of physical, economic, cultural, and historical factors, many of which you will read about in this chapter.

The Northeast at a Glance

Ogden Tanner, a writer whose ancestors settled in New England—a region that includes six states in the Northeast—once wrote:

> *I think if I had to show someone New England only at one instant, in one time and place, it would have to be this: from a canoe suspended on a silver river, surrounded by the great, silent autumnal explosion of the trees. On the hills the evergreens stand unchanging.... Scattered in abstract patterns through their ranks, the deciduous trees ... produce the glorious golds, oranges, reds, and purples ... a New England autumn.*

This brilliance is a result of the geography and climate of the region. The unique combination of precipitation, type of soil, and varieties of trees that thrive in the region give New England

◀ **Autumn in New England** (photo left)

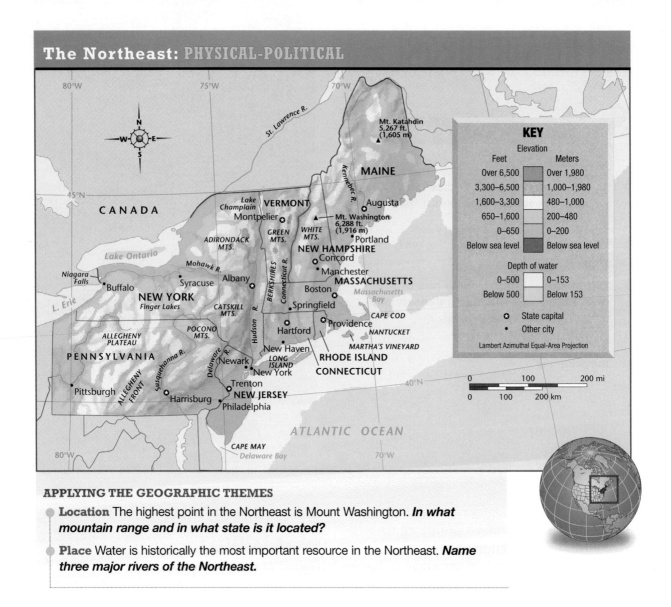

KEY

Elevation

Feet		Meters
Over 6,500		Over 1,980
3,300–6,500		1,000–1,980
1,600–3,300		480–1,000
650–1,600		200–480
0–650		0–200
Below sea level		Below sea level

Depth of water

0–500		0–153
Below 500		Below 153

◎ State capital
• Other city

Lambert Azimuthal Equal-Area Projection

APPLYING THE GEOGRAPHIC THEMES

● **Location** The highest point in the Northeast is Mount Washington. *In what mountain range and in what state is it located?*

● **Place** Water is historically the most important resource in the Northeast. *Name three major rivers of the Northeast.*

its breathtaking fall colors. But the Northeast has far more to offer than magnificent forests.

A visitor wanting a broad view of the Northeast might head for the craggy coast of Maine, New York's spectacular Niagara Falls, or the rolling farmlands of Pennsylvania. Still another distinctive feature of this region is its cities. Every year millions of tourists flock to the Northeast just to explore its world-famous cities. New York is considered by many to be the cultural center of the nation, while Boston and Philadelphia offer visitors a view into the nation's history.

Natural Resources of the Northeast

Compared with other regions of the United States, the Northeast has few natural resources.

The region's thin, rocky soils and steep hills are a challenge to the area's farmers. The northern reaches of the Appalachian Mountains make some parts of the Northeast quite rugged. Apart from the coal-rich area of Pennsylvania, the region has few mineral resources. But the Northeast has one resource that has turned it into a center of trade, commerce, and industry—its waters.

Since Colonial times, the rich Grand Banks in the North Atlantic Ocean have yielded large and abundant harvests of fish. The growth of the fishing industry and trade was aided by the region's rocky and jagged shoreline, which provides many excellent harbors. Throughout the 1700s and 1800s, these natural harbors helped the Northeast grow into a major commercial center.

A Leader in Industry

The Northeast's many rivers, including the Connecticut and the Hudson, have been vital to its history. The same steep hills that hindered farming aided industrialists in the nineteenth century. The abundant precipitation, about 40 to 60 inches (102 to 152 cm) annually, combined with the hilly terrain, keeps the rivers of the region flowing swiftly. Industrialists harnessed the power of these rivers by building water wheels, which converted water power into machine power.

Throughout the 1800s—especially in Massachusetts, Rhode Island, and New Hampshire—factories were built at waterfalls along the region's many rivers. The factories produced shoes, cotton cloth, and other goods that were sold across the United States and shipped to markets around the world. The region's river valleys served as trade routes, railroad routes, and later as modern highway routes for the Northeast. By the early 1900s, the Northeast was the most productive manufacturing region in the world.

The Megalopolis

Cities along the Atlantic coast first grew in importance as harbors of international trade and as centers of shipbuilding. As manufacturing grew, those cities attracted industries that needed a large supply of workers. Decade after decade, new industries developed—and the Northeast's cities grew in population. Young people from the Northeastern countryside flocked to the factory towns to take industrial jobs.

By the mid-1800s, European immigrants were streaming across the Atlantic to the Northeast. In 1840, about 84,000 Europeans immigrated to the United States; by 1850, the number skyrocketed to 370,000. Throughout the 1800s and early 1900s, some of the nation's most populous cities—New York, Boston, and Philadelphia—were located in the Northeast.

Over time coastal cities began to spread and run together. The far suburbs of one city in some cases stretched to the suburbs of the next. By the 1960s, the area from Boston to Washington, D.C., had earned a new name: **megalopolis** (mehg uh LAH puh luhs), a word based on Greek roots meaning "a very large city." About 42 million people now live in this megalopolis—one sixth of the entire United States population. The map on

GLOBAL issues

Air Pollution

States in the Northeast are hit hard by acid rain. Twenty-five percent of the lakes in the Adirondack Mountains of New York are too acidic to support fish. Forests throughout the Northeast show signs of decline. In response, Massachusetts and New Hampshire have started programs to reduce activities that lead to the creation of acid rain.

APPEARED IN *NATIONAL GEOGRAPHIC*

Skating in Central Park

Place New York City is the business center of the United States and a world leader in industry, trade, and finance. It is also the cultural heart of the nation, supporting theater, music, dance, visual and literary arts, museums, and the largest public library in the country. It also boasts more parks than any other U.S. city. Central Park, its most famous, provides residents and visitors with a variety of recreational activities. *What factors contributed to the growth of cities in the Northeast?*

A Mounting Concern

Place New York City is running out of places to dump the 12,000 tons of garbage it produces each day. Many cities in the Northeast are solving their landfill problems by exporting their trash to other states. Many people, however, are concerned that garbage export will cause a rise in disposal costs and that the fleet of garbage trucks will congest the region's already busy highways. *Critical Thinking How else might cities handle their garbage problems?*

page 119 shows the population density of this crowded part of the east coast.

While the east coast megalopolis remains one of the dominant centers of American business and industry, it faces serious problems, too. After decades of steady expansion, its inhabitants now have serious concerns that the area might run short of water or of facilities for waste disposal.

Another problem facing some cities in the Northeast is the decline in population. Between 1970 and 1990, for example, the population of Philadelphia decreased by about 364,000, and it continues to decline. As a result, the government of Philadelphia collects fewer taxes from residents and businesses. Thus the city has less money to pay for basic services, such as street repairs, police protection, or garbage collection.

Yet the Northeast remains a vital area. New York City is the business capital of the world. New businesses and industry continue to locate in the Northeast. During the 1980s, many highly technical and computer-related businesses opened their doors in the area. And less populous areas in Maine, New Hampshire, Vermont, upstate New York, and parts of Pennsylvania offer residents very agreeable natural environments in which to live.

Section 1 Review

Vocabulary and Main Ideas

1. **Define: megalopolis**

2. **Describe three physical characteristics of the Northeast.**

3. **How have the Northeast's waters been important in its history?**

4. **What geographic factors make farming difficult in the Northeast?**

5. **Critical Thinking:** *Drawing Conclusions* **Overall, do you think the growth of the Boston-Washington megalopolis has had a mostly positive or mostly negative effect on the major cities of the Northeast? Support your answer with evidence.**

learning LOCATIONS

6. **Which states are included in the Northeast region of the United States?**

7. **Name the three major cities of the Northeast megalopolis.**

2 The South

Section Preview

Main Ideas

- Warm climates and rich soils produce dense vegetation in many parts of the South.

- The South's climate and natural resources have shaped its economic development.

- Migration to the Sunbelt has led to the rapid growth of Southern cities.

Vocabulary

mangrove, bayou, Sunbelt

APPEARED IN *NATIONAL GEOGRAPHIC*

The Southern climate produced the Okefenokee Swamp.

Many Americans think of the South as the old Confederacy. In 1860 and 1861 eleven states ranging from Texas to Virginia withdrew from the United States because of conflicts over economic and moral issues, including tariffs and, especially, slavery. These states formed the Confederate States of America. Between 1861 and 1865, however, United States military forces from the Northeast and Midwest fought a bloody war with the Confederacy—the Civil War, also known as the War Between the States. At the war's end, slavery was abolished and the South was drawn back into the Union.

As you can see from the map on page 142, the South, as we define it, does include the states of the old Confederacy, plus five others—Oklahoma, Kentucky, West Virginia, Maryland, and Delaware—as well as the District of Columbia. Together they make up a region rich in resources and culture that has become an increasingly popular place in which to live and work.

As a region, the South stands out from the rest of the country because of its humid, subtropical climate and the lush, mixed forests that are common to most of its areas.

American naturalist, explorer, and writer John Muir captured the essence of the climate and vegetation of the South in a diary he kept while on a trek through the region in 1867. Along the Savannah River in Georgia he saw magnificent, plumed grasses and "rich, dense, vine-clad forests." Commenting on a mysterious cypress swamp, he wrote:

> *This remarkable tree, called cypress, grows large and high. . . . The groves and thickets of smaller trees are full of blooming evergreen vines. These vines are arranged . . . in bossy walls and heavy, mound-like heaps and banks. Am made to feel that I am now in a strange land.*

Linking Climate to Vegetation

The South's location closer to the Equator makes it warmer than other regions in the United States farther north. In addition, weather systems moving north from the Gulf of Mexico and the Caribbean Sea bring ample precipitation to most

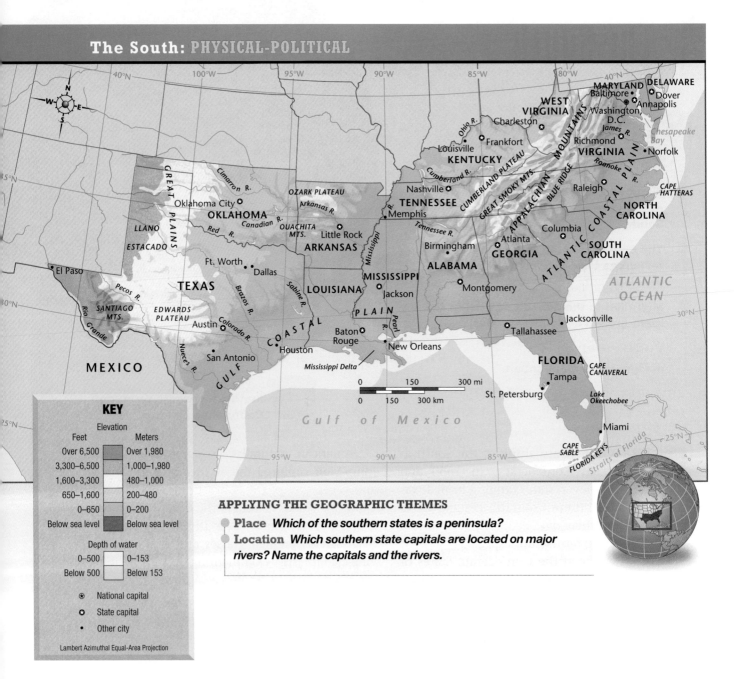

KEY

Elevation

Feet	Meters
Over 6,500	Over 1,980
3,300–6,500	1,000–1,980
1,600–3,300	480–1,000
650–1,600	200–480
0–650	0–200
Below sea level	Below sea level

Depth of water

0–500	0–153
Below 500	Below 153

⊛ National capital

✪ State capital

• Other city

Lambert Azimuthal Equal-Area Projection

APPLYING THE GEOGRAPHIC THEMES

● **Place** *Which of the southern states is a peninsula?*
● **Location** *Which southern state capitals are located on major rivers? Name the capitals and the rivers.*

of the region. The coastal areas of Louisiana and Mississippi receive well over 60 inches (152 cm) of precipitation annually. Parts of Florida receive an average of 55 inches (140 cm) of rain per year.

The warm, wet climate produces thick, mixed forests of pine and other trees, or marshy stands of mangrove trees. **Mangroves** are tropical trees that grow in swampy ground along coastal areas. Other vegetation regions unique to the South include the marshy inlets of lakes and rivers of Louisiana called **bayous** (BY oos). In Florida, the Everglades—a large area of swampland covered in places with tall grass—provide a refuge for a wide variety of birds and animals.

In general, the farther west one moves within the South, the less the average annual precipitation. Oklahoma and western Texas have a warm, semiarid climate. Parts of Oklahoma average 30 inches (76 cm) of rain per year; El Paso, Texas, only 8 inches (20 cm). Such a climate supports the temperate grasslands known as prairies.

Linking Climate, History, and Agriculture

The South's wide variety of plant and animal life is due not only to the subtropical climate of most of the region, but also to the rich soils of the wide coastal plains. People have taken advantage of these fertile soils for hundreds of years. Native American groups, such as the Natchez, Creek, and Cherokee, grew maize, melons, squash, beans, tobacco, and other crops. Later, by the mid-1500s, Europeans also began to settle in the South. The first permanent European settlements in the present-day United States were located in the South.

As word spread about the South's rich soils and long growing season, more and more Europeans migrated to the region. Some built huge plantations and used enslaved people from Africa and the West Indies to do the work of raising tobacco, rice, or cotton. Today, farming remains important to the South's economy.

Despite its mostly fertile soil and mild climate, parts of the South have large areas where people live in bleak poverty. For example, a rural area in the Appalachian Mountains, called Appalachia, is one of the poorest areas in the United States. Its rocky soil and steep slopes make it an unproductive site for farming. Little industry has located in the area.

Linking Resources to Industry

The traditional image of the South has been of a rural region, largely dependent on agriculture. But the South has long had a number of important industries, too.

In the 1840s, entrepreneurs built textile mills powered by the fast-moving streams of the Piedmont section of the Carolinas. These mills were built on the fall line. The fall line is an imaginary line between the Appalachian Mountains and the Atlantic coastal plain. It is the place where rivers and streams form waterfalls and rapids as they descend from plateau to coastal plain. Many cities sprang up along the waterfalls on the fall line in both the Northeast and the South. Textile mills were built close to farms that grew cotton. Even today, textile mills in the Carolinas produce a variety of fabrics.

The oil industry in the South began in eastern Texas in 1901. Some of the United States' largest oil reserves are located in this region. By

Oil Drill

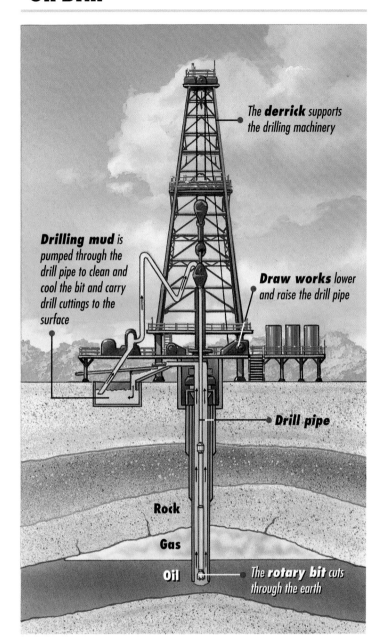

The **derrick** supports the drilling machinery

Drilling mud is pumped through the drill pipe to clean and cool the bit and carry drill cuttings to the surface

Draw works lower and raise the drill pipe

Drill pipe

Rock

Gas

Oil

The **rotary bit** cuts through the earth

DIAGRAM STUDY

Drilling for oil is an enormous undertaking. The first step is to locate a suitable well and obtain the proper leases and permits to drill. The chosen site then has to be made clear and level in order to support the drilling rigs. Roads to the site must be built, and the rigs erected before drilling can begin. *Explain in your own words how an oil drill works.*

the 1960s and 1970s, that industry was bringing great wealth to the region. In the 1980s however, oil prices dropped sharply. This decline brought economic hardship to the oil-producing states of Texas, Oklahoma, and Louisiana.

Net Profits

● **Human-Environment Interaction** Both the Atlantic and Gulf coast waters are rich in many kinds of fish. The southern fishing industry earns over a billion dollars annually. *What other industries are important to the South's economy?*

GLOBAL issues

Development

Many Floridians are searching for ways to preserve Florida's wetlands while still encouraging agriculture and development. The Florida Everglades supply water for crops and for drinking and are home to many endangered species.

A Changing Region

Until only recently, people often thought of the South as a slow-moving, slow-changing region. In the last few decades, that image has been shattered. As newspaper editor Joel Garreau said in 1981, "Change has become [the South's] most identifiable characteristic."

Continued Growth of Industry Not all industry was related to agriculture or the landscape. In the 1950s, both large and small industries began taking root in the South. Some were brand new, like the space industry that developed in the 1960s in Florida, Alabama, and Texas. But many industries were not new; they simply moved south from northern cities. Within several years, this migration of business became a steady wave.

The South attracted businesses for a number of reasons. Southern industrial plants often were newer, in better condition, and more efficient than those in the Northeast.

New factories could be built on land that was cheaper than land in the megalopolis of the Northeast. Because labor unions were much less common in the South, labor costs were usually lower.

The Sunbelt Looking for job opportunities, thousands of people moved to the South. But business growth is not the only reason why the region has thrived. Thanks to the South's mild climate, it has grown enormously as a retirement and tourism center. Beaches along the Gulf of Mexico and the southern Atlantic provide welcome relief from northern winters. In fact, the band of southern states from the Carolinas to southern California became known as the **Sunbelt.** The Sunbelt region actually overlaps two regions—the South and the West.

Southern Population

During the 1970s the South's population increased in number more than that of any other region of the country—an increase of 7 million, or 20 percent. By 1990 three of the largest cities in the nation were located in the South—Houston, Dallas, and San Antonio. By 1995, Texas had replaced New York as the second most populous state in the United states.

Latin Flavor

● **Movement** Immigration accounts for much of the South's diversity. Nine percent of southern residents are of Hispanic origin. In Miami, 40 percent of the population hails from Cuba. As this storefront window shows, the city has a distinctly Latin flavor. *How has movement of people within the United States contributed to the diversity of southern population?*

A Varied Population Today, the South has a diverse population. Over half of the nation's African American population lives in the South. The direction of African American migration is away from the industrial Northeast to southern cities. This reverses a century-long trend begun after the Civil War, during which thousands of African Americans migrated to the Northeast from the South in search of jobs.

Another large segment of the southern population is the hundreds of thousands of Hispanics who have moved there from Mexico and other Latin American countries. San Antonio, Texas, is one of the nation's largest cities, and one of the first major cities in the United States to have a Hispanic majority in its population.

Another large Hispanic group lives in southern Florida—the Cubans. Many Cubans have settled in the Miami area since 1960, after the communist takeover of their homeland. One area of Miami is populated by a Cuban majority. Called Little Havana, it is the part of the city where Cuban restaurants and Spanish-language television and radio stations reflect Cuban heritage.

Many white Southerners have ancestors who came from England, Scotland, or Ireland. In Louisiana, many boast of French ancestry. The French settled the area in Colonial times and have made a lasting imprint on the region's culture. New Orleans, for example, is famous for its French cuisine.

Major Cities The South is home to many important cities. New Orleans is a major trading center near the mouth of the Mississippi River. Miami is the United States gateway to the Caribbean and South America. Atlanta, Georgia, once a major railroad center, is now a major airline hub, and its cable televisions stations are watched by people around the world.

Houston, Texas, is a large industrial and trading center. Much of the nation's new space exploration is monitored at the National Aeronautics and Space Administration (NASA), which is located there. Houston is also a center for the oil and banking industries. Fort Worth, about a four-hour drive north from Houston, is the heart of the Texas cattle industry, while Dallas is a business and electronics center.

Capital City

● **Place** The South's most famous city is Washington, D.C., the nation's capital. The seat of the federal government and home of the Supreme Court, the capital also contains some of the nation's most important museums and monuments. Examine this aerial photograph of Washington, D.C. *How does it differ from many other cities in the nation?*

The city of Washington is not located in any state, but rather in the District of Columbia. This district was carved from the states of Maryland and Virginia when it was chosen as the site for the nation's capital in 1790. Located on the shore of the Potomac River, Washington, D.C., was the first planned city in the nation. Because of its wide avenues, public buildings, and dramatic monuments, many people consider Washington to be one of the most beautiful cities in the world. As the nation's capital, it is home to the nation's leaders and to hundreds of foreign diplomats.

Section 2 Review

Vocabulary and Main Ideas

1. **Define: a. mangrove b. bayou c. Sunbelt**

2. **How does the climate of the South affect its vegetation?**

3. **Why has the South's population increased so much in recent years?**

4. **How has the South's economy changed since the 1950s?**

5. **Critical Thinking:** *Making Comparisons* **How does the recent industrial growth in the South compare to the industrial growth of the Northeast in the 1800s?**

learning LOCATIONS

6. **Which states are included in the South?**

7. **Name a major city located in southern Florida.**

③ The Midwest

Section Preview

Main Ideas

- Agriculture is one distinctive characteristic of the Midwest.

- Because of variations in climate and soil, the Midwest produces a variety of crops and livestock.

- Industries grew up in the Midwest because resources and transportation were available.

Vocabulary

silo, growing season, grain elevator, grain exchange

APPEARED IN *NATIONAL GEOGRAPHIC*

The alternating patterns of strip cropping help prevent erosion.

What do you think of when you hear the term *Midwest*? The lush, wooded hills of the Ozarks in Missouri? The barren, eroded Badlands of South Dakota? The vast, blue-green Great Lakes? Or the acres of steel mills in the industrialized area around Gary, Indiana?

The Midwest is all of these and more, but a drive along any of the numerous highways crisscrossing the Midwest reveals that farms unite this region. Mile upon mile of fields and pastures stretch as far as the eye can see, interrupted only by scattered farmhouses and **silos**—the tall, round, airtight buildings used for storing grain.

The Agricultural Heartland

Most of the Midwest is relatively flat, and its soil is especially fertile. During the last ice age, ancient glaciers deposited mineral-rich materials that promote plant growth throughout the region. Temperate grasslands that once covered much of the area gave other nutrients to the soil.

The Midwestern climate, too, favors farming. Although winters can be bitterly cold, summers are generally long and hot. Most places receive at least 20 inches (51 cm) of precipitation annually.

Regional Variations Within the broad expanse of the Midwest are variations in climate and soil that affect farming. For example, eastern Ohio gets twice as much precipitation annually as central South Dakota. In southern Kansas, the **growing season**—the average number of days between the last frost of spring and the first frost of fall—is more than 200 days long. Near the Canadian border, the growing season is less than 120 days long.

In the warmer, wetter parts of Illinois, Indiana, and Iowa, corn and soybeans are the major crops. These states are also among the nation's leading producers of livestock, especially hogs. In the drier Great Plains states to the west, farmers are more likely to grow grains such as wheat or oats or sunflowers, which are a source of cooking oil. Along the northern margins of the region in states such as Wisconsin, cooler conditions and poorer soils favor the growth of hay and the raising of dairy cattle.

The Nation's Breadbasket Thanks to favorable natural conditions, Midwestern farms are among the most productive in the world. In recent years, for example, Iowa produced more corn, soybeans, and hogs than any other state in the nation. This output has earned the Midwest the nickname of "the nation's breadbasket."

Midwestern productivity is one factor responsible for the average American's being well fed. This remarkable productivity also allows the United States to export sizable amounts of its produce to other countries around the world. Without the agricultural output of the farms of the Midwest region, the United States would be far less affluent.

The Changing Face of American Farms

In years past, American farms were mostly modest family enterprises, run by single families working through long days of hard physical labor. Few such farms remain. Today, farming is big business.

Farming Technology By the 1800s, farmers had the ability to grow huge crops of grain, but had no way to harvest it quickly. In 1831 Cyrus McCormick revolutionized farming by inventing a mechanical reaper. McCormick's reaper allowed farmers to harvest vast amounts of wheat in much less time than it took by hand. As more and more farm tasks were mechanized, farmers could produce more crops than

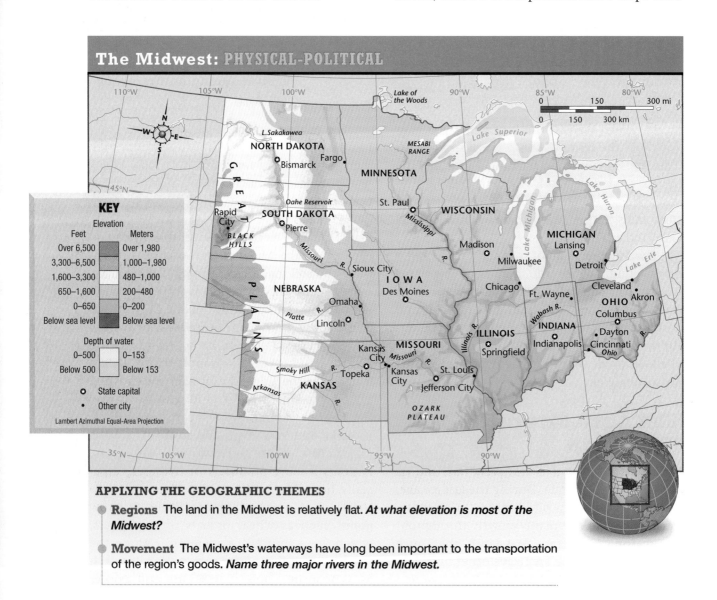

The Midwest: PHYSICAL-POLITICAL

KEY

Elevation

Feet	Meters
Over 6,500	Over 1,980
3,300–6,500	1,000–1,980
1,600–3,300	480–1,000
650–1,600	200–480
0–650	0–200
Below sea level	Below sea level

Depth of water

0–500	0–153
Below 500	Below 153

✪ State capital
• Other city

Lambert Azimuthal Equal-Area Projection

APPLYING THE GEOGRAPHIC THEMES

● **Regions** The land in the Midwest is relatively flat. *At what elevation is most of the Midwest?*

● **Movement** The Midwest's waterways have long been important to the transportation of the region's goods. *Name three major rivers in the Midwest.*

Combine Harvester

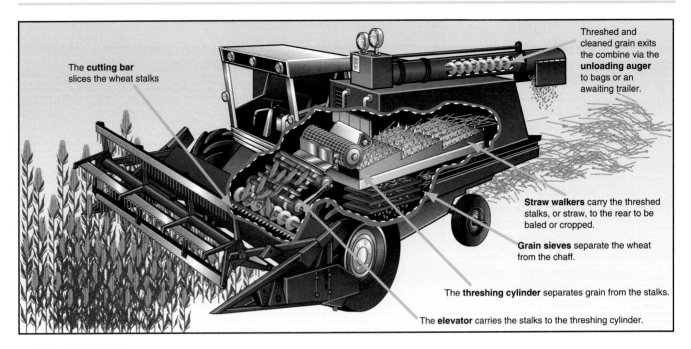

The **cutting bar** slices the wheat stalks

Threshed and cleaned grain exits the combine via the **unloading auger** to bags or an awaiting trailer.

Straw walkers carry the threshed stalks, or straw, to the rear to be baled or cropped.

Grain sieves separate the wheat from the chaff.

The **threshing cylinder** separates grain from the stalks.

The **elevator** carries the stalks to the threshing cylinder.

DIAGRAM STUDY

Farm machines such as the combine harvester have revolutionized farming.
How many different tasks does a combine perform?
Critical Thinking **How have improved farming techniques both helped and harmed farmers?**

ever before and with fewer workers. There are now fewer farms and farm workers than ever before, but farm size and output has increased dramatically.

Farmers who hope to stay abreast of their competition invest heavily in new technology. Many mortgage their farms in order to buy not only more equipment, but more land to cultivate, too. Some farmers have expanded, but thousands have been unable to afford such investments and have "gone under."

Linking Farms to Cities Agriculture dominates the economy even in many Midwestern towns and cities. Business activities center on dairies or **grain elevators**—tall buildings equipped with machinery for loading, cleaning, mixing, and storing grain.

Large Midwestern cities, too, are closely linked to the countryside. Some of the tallest office buildings in Minneapolis, Kansas City, and Omaha are homes to companies whose names appear on flour bags and feed sacks. Radio stations broadcast frequent reports from the Chicago Mercantile Exchange and the Chicago Board of Trade. The Mercantile Exchange is the world's busiest market for eggs, hogs, cattle, and other farm products; the Board of Trade is the largest **grain exchange**—a place where buyers and sellers deal for grain.

Linking Industries to Resources

Partly because of its rich supply of natural resources, the Midwest's cities are also home to much heavy manufacturing. Minnesota leads the states in iron ore production. Sizable coal deposits are found in Indiana and Illinois. Availability of these minerals spurred the development of steel mills in northwestern Indiana

GLOBAL issues

Water

A vast reservoir of groundwater lies below 170,000 square miles (440,300 sq km) of the Great Plains. The Ogallala aquifer, as it is called, supplies most of the water that transforms the drier parts of the Midwest into abundant cropland. Scientists estimate that 25 percent of Ogallala's water will be used up by the year 2020.

The Mighty Mississippi

● **Region** The Mississippi River flows 2,348 miles (3,787 km) from Minnesota to the Gulf of Mexico. In this photograph you can see where the Ohio River (right) empties into the Mississippi. Look at the physical map on page 117. *What other rivers flow into the Mississippi?*

● **Movement** *Why have rivers been important to the development of industry?*

and in Ohio. The automobile industry grew up in the Detroit area in part because of the city's location near these steel-making centers.

Linking Transportation and Industry

Many Midwestern cities, such as Cleveland, Chicago, Minneapolis, St. Louis, Detroit, and Omaha, are located on the shores of the Great Lakes or along major rivers. Water transportation aided the growth of heavy industries, such

as the manufacture of automobiles and machinery. Over 600 million tons (544 metric tons) of goods travel through the Mississippi River system each year.

With the growth of the United States' railway system, thousands of railroad cars were pulling into Chicago every year. Freight cars brought millions of bushels of grain and head of livestock from farms farther west. In Chicago, the grain was processed and the livestock slaughtered. The meat and grain were then shipped eastward by railroad.

Section 3 Review

Vocabulary and Main Ideas

1. Define: **a.** silo **b.** growing season **c.** grain elevator **d.** grain exchange

2. How are large Midwestern cities linked to agriculture?

3. What physical characteristics make the Midwest a productive farming region?

4. How were natural resources important in shaping the Midwest's industries?

5. Critical Thinking: *Synthesizing Information* Explain the relationship between the development of new farm machinery and the declining number of American farms.

learning LOCATIONS

6. Which states are included in the Midwest?

7. What major U.S. city is located on the shore of Lake Michigan?

Focus on Skills

- ☐ Social Studies
- ☑ Map and Globe
- ☐ Critical Thinking and Problem Solving

Interpreting a Weather Map

The weather report on the television news gives you information about temperature, precipitation, and the movement of air masses. The map below uses graphics and color to show the weather patterns and temperatures in the continental United States on one day. Look over the map below. Then use the following steps to analyze the information.

1. Evaluate the information pertaining to temperature. The map legend uses seven colors to show temperature ranges for the country. Examine the key and then answer the following questions: (a) What region of the country is the coldest? (b) Which cities are coldest? (c) Name two cities that have temperatures in the 60°s.

2. Evaluate the information pertaining to precipitation. Study the symbols used to show showers, rain, and snow. Then answer the following questions: (a) Name two states that are experiencing showers. (b) Name two states that are experiencing rain.

3. Evaluate the information pertaining to weather fronts. A weather front is the boundary between two air masses of different temperature and humidity. There are three basic types of fronts: cold, warm, and stationary. The arrows and half-circles on this map indicate the direction in which the fronts and air masses are moving. Fronts often bring to an area sudden and dramatic changes in weather. A warm front is followed by warmer weather and a cold front by colder weather. Answer the following questions: (a) What two cities can expect colder weather in the days ahead? (b) Is Salt Lake City's weather likely to change in the next few days? (c) Will Dallas be affected by the cold front?

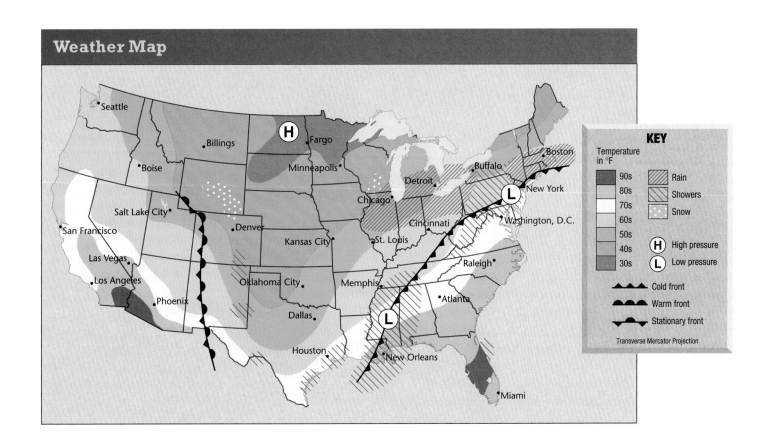

Weather Map

KEY

Temperature in °F
- 90s
- 80s
- 70s
- 60s
- 50s
- 40s
- 30s

- Rain
- Showers
- Snow

H High pressure
L Low pressure

Cold front
Warm front
Stationary front

Transverse Mercator Projection

4 The West

Section Preview

Main Ideas

- The West's natural landscape is its most outstanding feature.

- Abundance or scarcity of water affects natural vegetation, economic activity, and population patterns in the West.

Vocabulary

aqueduct

APPEARED IN *NATIONAL GEOGRAPHIC*

Kauai Island is one of Hawaii's main islands.

Breathtaking natural landscape—this is the most memorable feature of much of the West. Towering snow-capped peaks rise throughout the Rocky Mountains. Rivers have carved spectacular canyons. Broad plains sweep on for hundreds of miles. Massive glaciers loom over icy Alaskan waters, while smoking volcanoes frequently spill red-hot lava over the Hawaiian land. The landscape of the West is varied and magnificent, but the physical characteristic that most affects the region is water.

Available Water

The abundance or scarcity of water is the major factor shaping the West's natural vegetation, economic activity, and population density. Looking again at the climate map on page 120, you will notice that most of the West has a semiarid or arid climate. San Diego, California, averages 9 inches (23 cm) of rain per year; Reno, Nevada, gets only 7 inches (18 cm). In dry areas such as these, the natural vegetation consists of short grasses, hardy shrubs, sagebrush, and cactus.

In contrast, the western side of the cordillera generally receives adequate rainfall and contains rich deciduous and coniferous forests at lower elevations. Along the northwest coast—in Seattle, Washington, for example, where rainfall averages 39 inches (99 cm) per year—lofty Douglas fir trees and giant redwoods thrive.

Hawaii and Alaska, the nation's two remote states, offer another contrast. Much of Hawaii has a wet tropical climate and dense tropical rain forest vegetation. A world apart is northern Alaska's tundra—a dry, treeless plain that sprouts grasses and mosses only in summer, when the top layer of soil thaws.

Resources and the Economy

Beneath the jagged peaks of the Rocky Mountains and the Sierra Nevada lies an immense storehouse of minerals—gold, silver, uranium, and other metals. When gold and silver deposits were discovered in the mid-1800s, fortune-seeking prospectors and settlers swarmed into the area. Few individuals struck it rich in these gold rushes. Most of the region's wealth was deep underground, out of reach to the average prospector. More successful were the huge mining companies that had the equipment and resources to reach deep

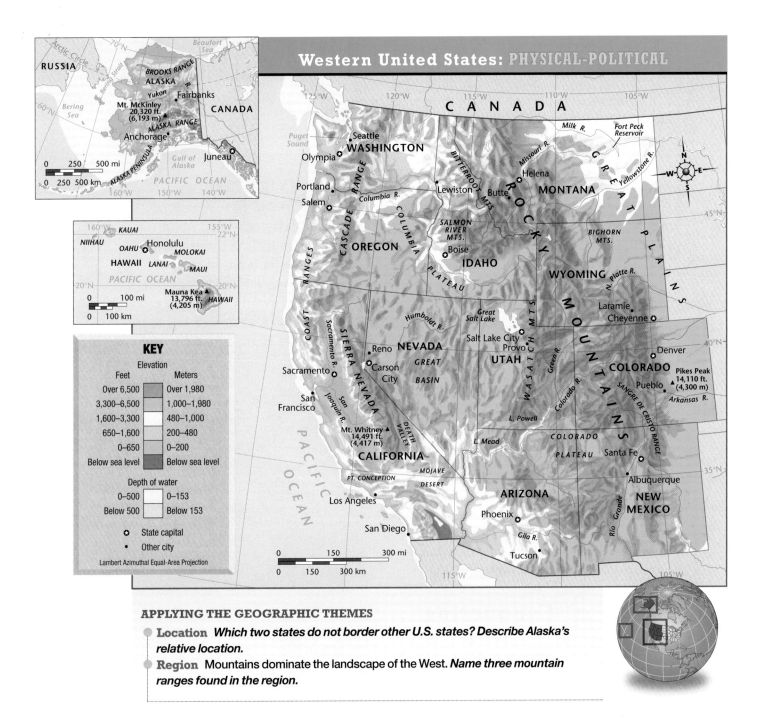

APPLYING THE GEOGRAPHIC THEMES

Location *Which two states do not border other U.S. states? Describe Alaska's relative location.*

Region Mountains dominate the landscape of the West. *Name three mountain ranges found in the region.*

---

into the earth for not only gold and silver, but minerals such as copper and tin, as well.

Still, rumors of great strikes and dreams of wealth kept people pouring into the region. Along with the prospectors came enterprising people who set up business to provide goods and services to the miners. The population of the West grew rapidly.

Deeper still within their rugged surface, Western lands also contain valuable deposits of natural gas and oil. The discovery of a major oil field near Prudhoe Bay, Alaska, in the 1960s led to the transformation of that state's economy. The Trans-Alaska Pipeline, built in the 1970s, carries crude oil across the tundra south to Alaska's Prince William Sound.

The West's natural resources support two other important economic activities—forestry and commercial fishing. Nearly half of the nation's lumber is taken from the forests of the Pacific Northwest. The billions of tons of fish caught in the waters off Alaska, Hawaii, and other Pacific Coast states bring in nearly 2 billion dollars annually.

The Growth of Western Cities

The completion of the first transcontinental railroad in 1869 spurred the growth of towns and cities along the ribbon of silvery track. In the 1880s the railroads lowered the fare between the Midwest and Los Angeles to only one dollar. Thousands jumped at the opportunity to move out West. Because of the harsh landscape and climate, relatively few people settled in the region's countryside. Even today, a higher percentage of the West's population prefer to live in cities.

Anchoring the southwest corner of the continental United States is the nation's second-largest city, Los Angeles, California. It began as a cattle town, providing beef for prospectors in San Francisco during the Gold Rush. By the 1920s the city was attracting new residents with the development of the military and civil aircraft industry and the motion picture industry.

To support its growing population, Los Angeles has to obtain huge amounts of water via **aqueducts**—large pipes that carry water over long distances. The California Aqueduct, completed in 1973, brings water from California's Sacramento Valley 685 miles (1,102 km) to the north. A drought that began in California in 1987 and lasted until 1993 forced Los Angeles to reduce drastically its water consumption.

GLOBAL issues

Population

Early in the next century, California will have no racial majority. The percentage of whites in California is decreasing, while the percentage of Hispanics and Asians is growing. Even now Los Angeles is one of the few urban areas in the world to have no racial majority.

Conquering Western Distances

The two outlying states of the western region, Alaska and Hawaii, face challenges in surmounting distances.

Alaska Alaska is the largest state, but it is one of the least populated. Only 550,000 people live in an area that is more than three times larger than all of the Northeast. Very few roads pass through the rugged mountains, the

A WORLD OF eXtremes

Death Valley

EXTREMELY LOW
At 282 feet (86 meters) below sea level, Death Valley is the lowest point in the western hemisphere. It lies mainly in east-central California and was formed by faulting of the earth's crust.

EXTREMELY HOT
Death Valley holds the record for the highest temperature ever recorded in the United States—a scorching 134° F (57° C).

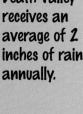

EXTREMELY DRY
The parched landscape of Death Valley receives an average of 2 inches of rain annually.

Traveling the Tundra

Movement The Trans-Alaska Pipeline snakes across the fragile Arctic tundra. Millions of barrels of oil pass through the pipeline system each year. *To which location does the pipeline bring the oil?*

Human-Environment Interaction The pipes are elevated in order to prevent thawing of the permafrost. *Critical Thinking Why do you think oil is sent through the pipeline, instead of being trucked across Alaska?*

Alaska Range and the Brooks Range, which cover much of Alaska. Juneau, the state capital, can be reached only by boat or airplane. Even Anchorage, a city with more than 200,000 residents, has only two roads leading out of town.

Hawaii The state of Hawaii is made up of eight main islands and more than 100 smaller ones in the central Pacific Ocean. It is located more than 2,000 miles (3,218 km) from the United States mainland. It was Hawaii's location, however, that first drew the attention of the United states.

In the late nineteenth century, when the United States established trading relationships with China and Japan, it sought to control islands that it could use as refueling stations for its naval vessels. In 1898, the United States annexed Hawaii, and in 1959 Hawaii became the 50th state.

Today, technological improvements have shortened the distance between Hawaii and the rest of the nation. Jet travel has made Hawaii popular with tourists from North America and Asia. With the recent development of communications satellites, Hawaiians no longer have to rely on radios for news from the mainland.

Section 4 Review

Vocabulary and Main Ideas

1. **Define: aqueduct**

2. **How have people made dry areas of the West productive?**

3. **What is one way in which Los Angeles has provided enough water for its residents?**

4. **Critical Thinking** *Predicting Consequences*
   More and more tourists visit the West's national parks every year. What might be the consequences if this trend continues?

learning LOCATIONS

5. **Which states are included in the West?**

6. **What major U.S. city is located on Puget Sound in Washington?**

Summarizing Main Ideas

SECTION 1 The Northeast

- As one of the earliest sites of industry, the Northeast became a world leader in commerce and industry, a position it still holds today.
- The area from Boston to Washington, D.C., is a region of high population density that is sometimes called a megalopolis.

SECTION 2 The South

- Because of its warm climate and rich soil, most of the South has dense vegetation.
- Farming is the major economic activity, but recently the region, part of the Sunbelt, has seen growth in business, industry, and population.
- The South has a diverse population and many large cities.

SECTION 3 The Midwest

- Highly productive agriculture results from a moist climate, fertile soil, and a relatively long growing season, and is the distinguishing characteristic of this region.
- Many industries have developed in the Midwest because of available resources and a sound transportation system.

SECTION 4 The West

- A beautiful, varied landscape is the distinguishing feature of the West.
- Water is the key factor in area development. Farmers use special techniques to raise crops in an arid climate.
- Industries are based on the region's natural resources.

Reviewing Vocabulary

Use each of the following terms in a sentence that shows their meaning.

1. megalopolis
2. mangrove
3. bayou
4. silo
5. growing season
6. grain elevator
7. grain exchange

Applying the Geographic Themes

1. **Movement** How did population migration help industry grow in the Northeast in the 1800s?
2. **Regions** How did the Northeast's coastal cities become a megalopolis?
3. **Regions** Why has the South grown so much in recent years?
4. **Location** How are the Midwest's cities linked to the surrounding farmlands?
5. **Place** How have various physical features of the West shaped its development?

Critical Thinking and Applying Skills

1. **Identifying Alternatives** Choose one basis—either physical, economic, human, or historical—on which to divide the United States into regions different from the ones presented in this chapter. Give reasons that explain your choices.
2. **Interpreting a Weather Map** Use the map on page 157 to answer these questions.
   a. What is the temperature in Boise on this particular day?
   b. What is the likely forecast for Atlanta, Georgia, for the next few days?

Writing Across Cultures

▶ 1. Use the five themes of geography to write five questions you would like to ask someone living in a different region than you.

▶ 2. Write two postcards from Miami's Little Havana to the folks back home—one from the perspective of a tourist and the other from the perspective of a Cuban immigrant.

INTERNET link

Find out more about the place you live by visiting the Census Bureau. Link to this site from:

• www.phschool.com

Enter your zip code. Make note of your latitude, longitude, and the population of your town or city. Now click on your location to see a map of the area. See if you can find your street or neighborhood and zoom in on it.

Cities and Capitals

Number from 1 to 12 on your paper. Next to each number, write the letter of the place on the map that corresponds to the cities listed below.

1. Seattle
2. San Francisco
3. Honolulu
4. Los Angeles
5. Dallas
6. St. Louis
7. Chicago
8. Miami
9. New York
10. Phoenix
11. Boston
12. Atlanta

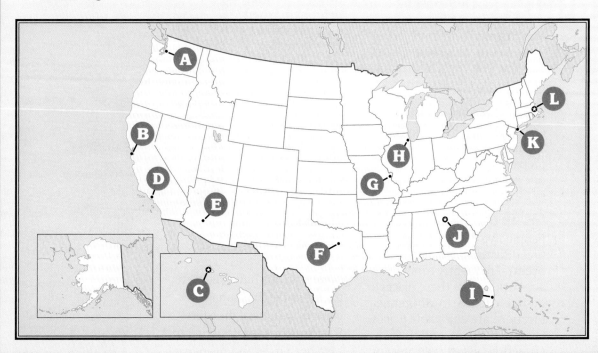

Natural Disasters

The Issue

Around the world people live in places where natural disasters are likely to cause destruction and loss of life.

No Place Is Safe Natural disasters strike everywhere in the world, including the United States. The buildings demolished along our southeastern coast by hurricanes and the havoc wrought on Midwestern farms by massive spring flooding are reminders of the overwhelming forces of nature.

Assessing the Hazards

Some kinds of natural hazards pose dangers infrequently. Others occur repeatedly. Some hazards threaten only small areas, while others cause widespread damage. The worst kind of natural hazards are those that occur suddenly with no forewarning. Winter blizzards can be predicted days in advance. People have time to prepare for their arrival. But no one knows when an earthquake or tornado will arrive.

Life on the Edge Why do people live in places where natural disasters are likely to occur? Frequently other characteristics make these places desirable to live in. Shoreline locations are enjoyable places to visit or live in, and their attractions offset the threat of occasional hurricanes. And even repeated earthquakes have not kept millions of people from moving to California in search of good jobs, wonderful scenery, and pleasant weather.

Global Impact If natural disasters are extensive enough, like the earthquake that hit the port city of Kobe, Japan, in 1995, they can temporarily cripple a country's economy and upset the flow of world trade. In addition, some countries must turn to the world community for help when disasters strike. They may lack the financial resources, the technology, and the volunteer organizations to provide fast and effective aid to people affected by natural disasters.

Some Solutions

Public and private organizations have taken steps to minimize the damage caused by natural disasters. Some actions are designed to save both lives and property.

Improved Engineering

Considerable research has been conducted to learn how structures can be designed to resist the forces of nature. This knowledge is used to revise building and construction codes so that new and renovated buildings and roads can withstand earthquakes and other types of natural hazards. Engineers have also designed levees and other flood-control structures that

Rough Seas

Human-Environment Interaction The strong winds of a hurricane can cause severe damage. These boats were picked up and piled together when Hurricane Andrew swept through Florida in 1994.

Tornado Alley

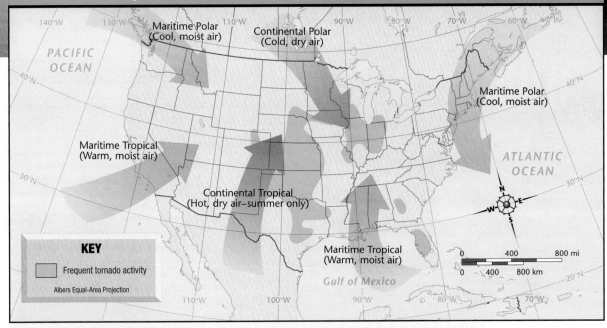

KEY

Frequent tornado activity

Albers Equal-Area Projection

APPLYING THE GEOGRAPHIC THEMES

● **Regions** This map shows the four major types of air masses that affect weather in the United States. More tornados occur in the United States than in any other place in the world. Tornados form when cool, dry air collides with moist, warm air from the Gulf of Mexico. *Which air masses affect weather where you live?*

more effectively keep rivers in their channels.

Planning for Disaster In cases where it is impossible to protect property, the emphasis is placed on saving lives. Towns and cities throughout California educate their residents about how to prepare for and survive an earthquake. Populated areas along the Gulf of Mexico and the Atlantic coastlines have clearly marked evacuation routes that people use to move to safer locations when hurricanes are predicted. Despite the risks, people continue to live and work in potentially dangerous areas. Good planning and education can help keep people safe when disaster strikes.

YOU DECIDE

1. Which natural hazards are the hardest to prepare for?

2. Why don't people avoid living in areas with natural hazards?

3. **Problem Solving** You are appointed to a committee to write procedures for responding to a natural hazard in your area, such as a blizzard, flood, tornado, or earthquake. Brainstorm a list of all the factors that should be considered.

4. **What You Can Do** Learn more about the National Weather Service and the systems they have in place for informing the public in the event of an emergency.

5. **Internet Activity** Severe flooding in North Korea in 1995 spurred the creation of an Internet campaign of assistance. Read about the campaign to help North Korea. Then write a paragraph summarizing the situation. Link to this site from:
• www.phschool.com

8

Canada

SECTIONS

1 Regions of Canada

2 The Search for a National Identity

3 Canada Today

Canada: POLITICAL

Lambert Azimuthal Equal-Area Projection

KEY

⊛ National capital

⊗ Provincial capital

• Other city

ARCTIC OCEAN

GREENLAND (DEN.)

Bering Sea

Beaufort Sea

Baffin Bay

ALASKA (U.S.)

YUKON

NORTHWEST TERRITORIES

NUNAVUT

Iqaluit

Whitehorse

Yellowknife

CANADA

Labrador Sea

NEWFOUNDLAND

St. John's

BRITISH COLUMBIA

ALBERTA

Edmonton

SASKATCHEWAN

MANITOBA

Hudson Bay

QUEBEC

PRINCE EDWARD ISLAND

Charlottetown

Vancouver

Calgary

Saskatoon

Regina

Winnipeg

ONTARIO

NEW BRUNSWICK

Quebec

Fredericton

Halifax

PACIFIC OCEAN

Victoria

Hull

Ottawa

Montreal

NOVA SCOTIA

ATLANTIC OCEAN

Toronto

UNITED STATES

Great Lakes

0   400   800 mi

0   400   800 km

learning LOCATIONS

Mapping the Region in Detail
Create a map like the one above, lightly shading each province and territory a different color. Then add labels for the provinces, territories, and capitals that are shown on this map.

1 Regions of Canada

Section Preview

Main Ideas

● Canada can be divided into five distinct regions based on physical features, culture, and economy.

● Rugged landscapes and a cold climate have limited human interaction with the environment in many parts of Canada.

● Location has played a key role in the development of Quebec and Ontario as Canada's heartland.

Vocabulary

province, maritime, lock, bedrock

APPEARED IN *NATIONAL GEOGRAPHIC*

Nova Scotia leads Canada's fishing industry.

Canada is a vast land that covers most of the northern half of North America. Canada shares many physical characteristics with the United States, yet it is a distinct nation with its own unique character, opportunities, and challenges.

Canada's ten **provinces**, or political divisions, and two territories can be divided into five regions based on physical features, culture, and economy. As you read in Chapter 7, the regions of the United States overlap one another. The regions of Canada, however, are more distinct than those of the United States. Two reasons for this clear separation are the country's relatively small population and the structure of its government, which gives a great deal of power to the provinces.

The Atlantic Provinces

Tucked into the southeastern corner of Canada are the four Atlantic provinces of Newfoundland, Prince Edward Island, Nova Scotia, and New Brunswick. Locate these provinces on the map on page 166. As the name of the region implies, all four provinces border on the Atlantic Ocean. The land in this region forms part of the Appalachian Mountains, which extend south-

ward into the eastern United States. Hills covered with thick mixed deciduous forest and rugged mountaintops highlight the landscape in most of the region. Thousands of lakes and small ponds dot the rugged terrain. As in New England, glaciers once moved across the area, leaving the soil thin and strewn with rocks and boulders.

Links to the Sea The Atlantic provinces are often called the Maritimes because of their close ties with the sea. The word **maritime** means "bordering on or related to the sea." The coastlines of these provinces are marked by hundreds of bays and inlets, providing excellent harbors for fishing fleets. Most residents of this region live along the coast.

The Atlantic provinces are the smallest of Canada's regions, including only about 5 percent of Canada's land and only about 10 percent of its people. Although small in area, the Atlantic provinces have been fundamental to Canada's settlement and development.

Economic Activities The Grand Banks area off the coasts of Newfoundland and Nova Scotia remain among the world's richest fishing areas. People here catch large quantities of lobsters, herring, scallops, and other fish and shellfish. Nova Scotia earns more income from fishing than does any other Canadian province. Overfishing in the region, however, has led to heavy layoffs in the fishing and fish-processing industries.

Forestry and farming are also important in the Maritimes. Some fruit, vegetable, and dairy farming takes place where the soil and local climate permit. The gentle, rolling plains and fertile soil of Prince Edward Island are particularly well suited to farming. Because it is a small island, and more of its land is close to the moderating influences of water, Prince Edward Island has a milder climate and a longer growing season than the mainland provinces.

In recent years, many Maritime residents have found work in tourism and military or defense industries. Rugged coastlines and scenic hills make the region a popular vacation spot for many visitors. Despite the beauty that draws visitors, few natural resources other than the sea abound in the provinces. As a result, the Atlantic provinces are Canada's poorest income-producing region.

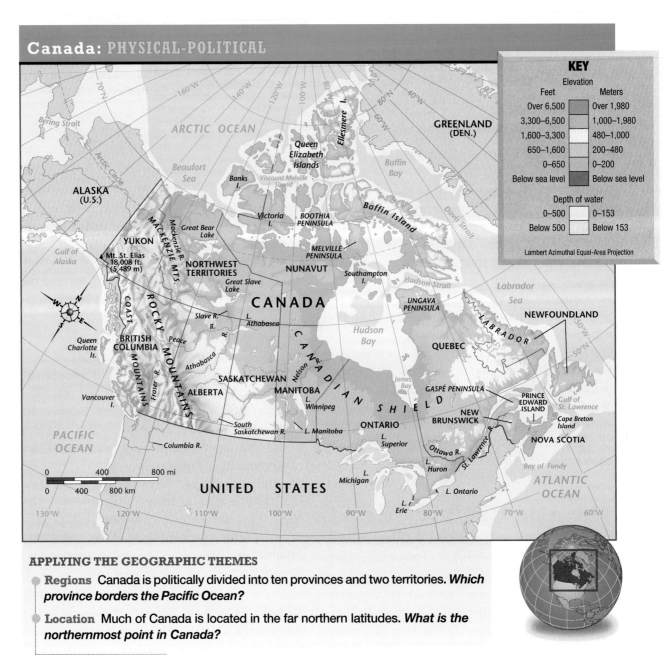

Canada: PHYSICAL-POLITICAL

KEY

Elevation

Feet		Meters
Over 6,500		Over 1,980
3,300–6,500		1,000–1,980
1,600–3,300		480–1,000
650–1,600		200–480
0–650		0–200
Below sea level		Below sea level

Depth of water

0–500	0–153
Below 500	Below 153

Lambert Azimuthal Equal-Area Projection

APPLYING THE GEOGRAPHIC THEMES

● **Regions** Canada is politically divided into ten provinces and two territories. *Which province borders the Pacific Ocean?*

● **Location** Much of Canada is located in the far northern latitudes. *What is the northernmost point in Canada?*

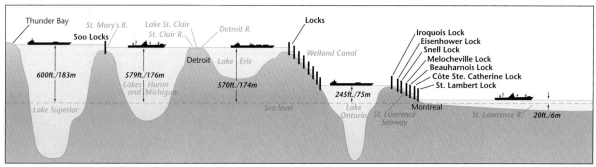

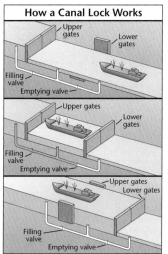

DIAGRAM STUDY

● **Movement** The cross-sectional diagram shows how a series of canals and locks have connected the Great Lakes and the St. Lawrence River in a way that is usable to ships. *What is the purpose of the canals?*

The Great Lakes and St. Lawrence Provinces

In sharp contrast to the Atlantic provinces, the two provinces surrounding the Great Lakes and the St. Lawrence River are the core of Canada's population and its economic activity. The large provinces of Quebec and Ontario are the heartland of Canada. These provinces are distinguished by three distinct landscapes. The first is the Canadian Shield. It has poor soil and a cold climate but contains rich mineral deposits. The Canadian Shield covers most of Quebec and Ontario. The second landscape is the Hudson Bay Lowlands—a flat, sparsely populated, swampy region between the Canadian Shield and Hudson Bay. The St. Lawrence Lowlands—third of the landscapes—have rich soil and a relatively mild climate. Sixty percent of Canada's population lives in this region around the Great Lakes and the St. Lawrence River valley.

Characteristics of Ontario One of Ontario's most important features is its system of waterways. The St. Lawrence Seaway, which connects the Great Lakes to the St. Lawrence River, has been called Canada's highway to the sea because of the volume of goods that travels its length.

The Great Lakes differ greatly in elevation. Lake Superior is the highest at 600 feet (183 m) above sea level, while Lake Ontario is the lowest, at 245 feet (75 m) above sea level. To make up for the differences in water levels, the Great Lakes–St. Lawrence waterway system has a series of locks. A **lock** is an enclosed

Northern Exposure

● **Regions** To the northeast of the Interior Plains lies an area of exposed bedrock called the Canadian Shield. During the Ice Age, which ended about 10,000 years ago, glaciers scraped the ancient bedrock clear of overlying materials.
Critical Thinking Why do you think this region is so sparsely populated?

area on a canal that raises or lowers ships from one water level to another. (See the diagram on page 169.) Canada and the United States have taken advantage of the difference in height between the Great Lakes and sea level by jointly constructing a hydroelectric plant along the seaway.

In addition to a central location and excellent waterways, Ontario has rich soil and abundant mineral resources. Much of the land in the southeastern part of the province is used for farming, and it is here that most of the province's people live. A network of cities has evolved in which a wide range of products—cars, food products, clothing, and building materials—are manufactured and distributed. Because of the province's location, industries based on processing minerals or manufacturing goods can easily ship their products to other parts of Canada and to the United States.

Toronto, Ontario's capital, is the largest metropolitan area in Canada. More than one third of Canada's largest companies now have their main offices in Toronto. This city also contains Canada's banking and financial center, as important to Canada as New York's Wall Street is to the United States.

Ottawa, the national capital of Canada, is located on the Ottawa River in southeastern Ontario. Together, Ottawa and its neighbor across the river, Hull, Quebec, make up Canada's fourth-largest metropolitan area.

Characteristics of Quebec Although Quebec is Canada's largest province in terms of area, its population is not equally distributed. Most residents live in the cities in and around the St. Lawrence River valley. Few people live on the Canadian Shield, an area of exposed bedrock which covers the northern four fifths of the province. **Bedrock** is solid rock that is usually covered by soil, gravel, and sand. Most of this region has remained a wilderness of forests, rivers, lakes, and streams. Treeless tundra with lichens and mosses covers the northernmost parts of Quebec.

The Appalachian Mountains rise gently along the southeastern border of the province. Both of these regions, the southeast and the Canadian Shield, are centers of mining and forestry. Farming remains an important activity in the fertile plains of the St. Lawrence Valley. In recent decades, however, increasing numbers of

Quebec's residents have been attracted to manufacturing and service jobs.

Quebec's largest city is Montreal, a beautiful metropolis at the Lachine Rapids of the St. Lawrence. Development that began when Montreal hosted Expo '67 transformed it from a provincial city into a dynamic urban center.

The capital of the province, also called Quebec, is the oldest city in Canada. It was founded in 1608 by Samuel de Champlain, who was sent by France to establish a colony. The historic sites and European charm of Quebec make it a popular tourist attraction. Section 2 describes the province of Quebec's unique culture as the center of Canada's French-Canadian population.

The Prairie Provinces

The provinces of Alberta, Manitoba, and Saskatchewan lie in southwestern Canada between the Rocky Mountains and the Canadian Shield. Known as the Prairie Provinces, they have long been associated with rolling fields of wheat. One writer described the landscape as looking "as if someone had taken a colossal pencil to the countryside and erased anything taller than a bush." The prairies are more than crop-covered flatlands, however. For the traveler who leaves the main highways, the prairies also offer clear, cool lakes; lazy rivers; and mysterious badlands filled with strange, eroded sand and rock formations. Huge tracts of sand dunes are also found stretching across these broad, semiarid plains.

The Location of Cities Half or more of the people in each of the three Prairie Provinces live in cities. The largest cities in the region are located at strategic points along the railroads that were built in the late 1800s. Winnipeg was established at an important river crossing as railroad tracks were laid from the east through the Canadian Shield. From Winnipeg, two rail lines were built to the west, each taking a different set of passes through the Rocky Mountains. The cities of Edmonton and Calgary in Alberta were established at points where each rail line headed into the mountains. Roughly midway between those cities and Winnipeg, the Saskatchewan cities of

Energy

Tides, which are caused by the gravitational pull of the moon on the earth, have enormous energy potential. The Bay of Fundy is considered an ideal location for a tide-powered hydroelectric plant. There, tides rise as high as 70 feet (21 m)—higher than any other place on earth. One small power plant is already in operation there.

Grains and Trains

● **Regions** The Prairie Provinces are Canada's agricultural heartland. Canada is one of the world's major producers of grain, particularly wheat and barley. *Critical Thinking* **How are the Prairie Provinces similar to the United States Midwest?**

● **Movement** *Canada is threaded with 48,452 miles (78,148 km) of railroad tracks. What role does Canada's freight train system play in agriculture?*

Wheat is the major agricultural crop. Most grain is exported and is transported by rail to ports on the Pacific Ocean, the Great Lakes, or Hudson Bay.

Tourism is an important economic activity in many of the region's magnificent parks. The snowcapped Rocky Mountains of western Alberta have some of North America's most spectacular scenery. The discovery of oil and natural gas in Alberta provided a new source of wealth for the region. The oil industry also had a major effect on the growth of cities like Calgary and Edmonton.

British Columbia

The natural beauty of the Rockies stretches farther west into British Columbia. Canada's westernmost province is unlike any other region in Canada. The Inside Passage, a waterway between the long string of off-shore islands and the Coast Ranges of British Columbia, provides travelers with many scenic wonders:

> *Always the ultimate backdrop is rank on rank of mountains, some velvety green, some topped with snow, some populated with giant trees on the lower slopes but turning to sheer rock decorated with sheets of ageless ice. Here and there, like a silver thread in the mountain distance, is a glimpse of plunging river, disappearing into the green as if into a deep sponge.*

Notice on the map on page 168 that mountains of several ranges cover nearly all of British Columbia. As a result, more than four fifths of the province's residents live in or near the city of Vancouver.

Plentiful natural resources, including salmon, forests, and minerals, have helped British Columbia become one of Canada's wealthiest provinces. But for many residents and visitors, its cities are its most memorable attractions. Victoria, the capital, is located at the southeastern tip of Vancouver Island. It has the relaxed charm of a small British city, with manicured gardens that bloom year-round in the mild, wet, marine west coast climate.

Vancouver Merchants

● **Place** The Chinese-Canadian community forms the largest minority group in Canada, and more than one quarter of Chinese-Canadians live in Vancouver. In fact, most of Canada's minorities live in urban areas, such as Toronto, Vancouver, and Montreal. *How has Vancouver's location affected immigration from Asia?*

Saskatoon and Regina were founded as major service centers along the rail lines. Lacking both an inland river system and frequent precipitation, the Prairie Provinces have been described as a region where "grains and trains dominate life."

A Changing Economy The Prairie Provinces provide most of Canada's grain and cattle.

Vancouver, the province's largest city, occupies a site by an excellent harbor. It is Canada's major port on the Pacific Ocean, and has grown rapidly during recent decades as trade with Asia increased. Immigration from Asia has increased Vancouver's population. Vancouver's population has also swelled due to the many Canadians from other provinces who are moving to Vancouver when they retire because of its desirable climate and scenic beauty.

The Northern Territories

The northern 40 percent of Canada consists of the Yukon Territory and the Northwest Territories. These cold, largely treeless lands are sparsely settled; together they are home to fewer than 1 percent of Canada's population. (See the population density map on page 119.) Nearly all the population lives in small settlements along the Mackenzie River and the arctic coastline. Still, these lands have a stark and distinctive beauty that is awe inspiring to those who are drawn to the far northern reaches of the continent.

A Changing Culture Many residents of the northern territories are native people who call themselves Inuit, a term that means "the people." Inuit, rather than Eskimo, is the name by which these people prefer to be known. The Inuit generally live north of the forests, while other Native Canadian groups live farther south. Recently, a writer who traveled from one end of Canada to the other told of the Inuit's attitude toward the land.

> *Of all Canadians . . . [the Inuit] have developed . . . [and] maintained perhaps the closest relationship with the geography. They have a saying: "Our land is our life." Recognizing they are but one of the land's many elements—and certainly not the most important—the Inuit use the harsh geography to survive, as an astute judo student turns the momentum of an onrushing attacker to his own advantage.*

Contact with persons of European ancestry has changed the ways in which the Inuit live. Although seal hunting is still an important economic activity, modern Inuit hunters now use snowmobiles instead of dog sleds to cross the frozen lands. Modern technology is used to overcome vast distances in other ways as well. Inuit children remain at home, taking classes transmitted by satellite over radio and television systems, and their teachers may be thousands of miles away.

A Difficult Environment The northern territories contain rich deposits of minerals.

Electronic Education

● **Location** Schools in Canada's remote northern areas are using modern technology, such as video-conferencing and the Internet, to reduce their isolation. *Critical Thinking How does technology change a place's relative location?*

Tapping Resources

● **Human-Environment Interaction** Beneath the fragile tundra lie deposits of valuable minerals, such as petroleum. *Why is Canada having difficulty developing these northern resources?*

A wealth of gold, silver, copper, zinc, lead, iron ore, and uranium can be found in the region. So can large reserves of petroleum and natural gas. Most of this wealth remains buried within the earth. Because the harsh climate and rugged terrain make it difficult to mine and transport these materials, many deposits have not been developed.

In spite of the difficulties of life in the north, the people who reside there live with a knowledge of the hardships and a deep appreciation for the beauty and bounty that the land offers.

Section 1 Review

Vocabulary and Main Ideas

1. **Define: a. maritime b. lock c. bedrock**

2. **Why are the Atlantic provinces often called the Maritimes?**

3. **How has the economy of the Prairie Provinces changed in recent decades?**

4. **Name two characteristics of British Columbia that make it a desirable place in which to live.**

5. **Critical Thinking:** *Making Comparisons* **Besides the harsh climate, what factors do you think have limited the human impact on the lands of northern Canada?**

learning LOCATIONS

6. **What is Canada's westernmost region?**

7. **Which provinces are east of Manitoba?**

The Search for a National Identity

Section Preview

Main Ideas

- Canada's history reflects conflict between two major cultures: English and French.

- Many Canadians continue to have strong ethnic and regional ties.

- The Canadian government supports the cultural diversity of its people while attempting to maintain a strong national unity.

Vocabulary

separatism, secede

Like these modern Inuit, some of Canada's earliest inhabitants lived in the arctic north.

Like Canada's landscapes, the nation's population is extremely varied. Canada has come to define itself as a multicultural country—a mosaic of many pieces with varying colors. Unity is difficult to achieve because the country is so vast and there are such great differences among the provinces and territories as well as among the people. This lack of unity is partly explained by Canada's history.

Historical Roots

Canada has had to struggle to develop a single national identity. One reason is that many of its people identify more strongly with regional and ethnic groups than with the nation as a whole. Most of the population are of British and French ancestry. About 40 percent of all Canadians have British ancestors; another 27 percent are of French descent.

The First Canadians The first people to live in what is now Canada were the Inuit and Native Americans whose ancestors migrated to North America thousands of years ago. These first Canadians developed stable societies and

adapted to a wide range of environments. Many lived in villages along the Pacific coast, enjoying the abundance of resources in the forests, bays, and rivers. Others were nomadic, gathering food and hunting game, such as walruses and seals in the arctic north, moose and caribou along the Canadian Shield, and buffalo in the plains. Many in the Great Lakes–St. Lawrence lowlands lived in permanent settlements and raised maize, squash, and other crops.

Beginning in the 1500s, the rival European empires of England and France began colonizing the region, devastating the native population with European diseases and warfare. Soon England and France were battling each other for control of the land.

Colonial Rivalries French and English colonists competed with each other for the prosperous North American fur trade and clashed over land claims. Between 1689 and 1763, British and French colonists fought four wars in North America. Finally, British troops defeated the French in the Battle of Quebec in 1759, and by 1763 France surrendered all of its empire in what is now Canada. Britain then assumed control over the entire region.

Separatist Protest

● **Place** Canada's attempt at fostering a bilingual, multicultural society has not been enough for many Quebecois. Despite impassioned efforts of the separatists, Quebec remains part of Canada. *Why do so many Quebecois want Quebec to secede?*

Ties to Britain Canada remained under direct British rule until 1867 when the British created the Dominion of Canada. This act gave Canada its own government, but foreign policy and military decisions were still made by the British. Canada became a completely independent country in 1931, when the last British controls ended. Even today, however, Canada's symbolic ruler is the British monarch.

GLOBAL issues

Indigenous People

Canada has agreed to a land claim settlement with the Inuit of Canada's central and eastern Northwest Territories. Related to the land claim, a new territory, called Nunavut, was carved out of the Northwest Territories and established in 1999.

Conflict Between Two Cultures

When France lost its empire in what is now Canada to Britain, about 70,000 French colonists lived there. Since then Canada's French-Canadian population has grown to over one quarter of the country's total population. The great majority of French-speaking Canadians live in the province of Quebec.

In 1774 the British government passed laws to ensure that French Canadians, many of whom also lived in Ontario, would be able to maintain their own language, laws, and culture. When Canada became an independent country, the government continued to protect the rights of French-speaking citizens. Both English and French are official languages in Canada. However, only about 15 percent of Canadians speak both languages.

Many French Canadians today feel discriminated against by the English-speaking majority. They claim that they are denied jobs in government or industry because they are of French descent.

The Quebecois (kay-beh-KWAH), Quebec's French-speaking citizens, consider themselves the guardians of French culture in Canada. Starting in the 1960s, many Quebecois began to press for changes that would assure the preservation of French culture. Some people favored **separatism**, that is, making Quebec an independent country.

In 1974 the government of Quebec made French the official language of the province.

As a result, many English-speaking residents and businesses left Quebec, and the province suffered economically. Since 1976, political leaders dedicated to separation often have controlled the government of Quebec. In 1995, a referendum allowing residents to decide whether Quebec should **secede**, or withdraw from the rest of Canada, failed by a narrow margin.

Welcoming Diversity, Promoting Unity

The multicultural nature of Canada's population is one of its most distinctive characteristics. Although most Canadians have British or French ancestors, many other groups are represented in the population.

A Multicultural Society Inuit and Native Americans had been living in what is now Canada for thousands of years before Europeans arrived. Today, most of Canada's 27,000 Inuit live in the territories and in northern areas of Newfoundland, Ontario, and Quebec. Canada has nearly 370,000 Native Canadians, the majority of whom live on reserves.

Canada has welcomed immigrants from central and eastern Europe as well as other parts of the world. During the late 1970s, Canada accepted about 60,000 refugees from Cambodia, Laos, and Vietnam. Recently, people from other parts of South Asia and East Asia have settled in Canada, particularly in British Columbia.

Ethnic Composition of Canada

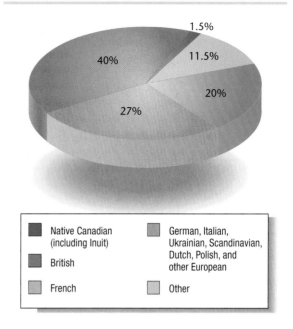

Legend:
- Native Canadian (including Inuit)
- British
- French
- German, Italian, Ukrainian, Scandinavian, Dutch, Polish, and other European
- Other

GRAPH STUDY

Canada's historical ties to Europe can be seen in its ethnic composition. *To which European country do most Canadians owe their heritage?*

Uniting Canada's Regions Canada has been successful in uniting its regions and its people through transportation and communication links. Canada's modern leadership in telecommunications largely results from efforts to communicate with residents in its remote, northern regions. Yet, establishing a truly national identity is proving difficult to achieve.

Section 2 Review

Vocabulary and Main Ideas

1. **Define: a.** separatism **b.** secede

2. **What are the historical roots of the conflict between French-speaking and English-speaking Canadians?**

3. **Why is a Canadian national identity difficult to achieve?**

4. **Critical Thinking:** *Making Comparisons* **The multicultural characteristic of the United States is sometimes called a "melting pot." In Canada, it is often called a "mosaic." What do you think is the difference between these terms?**

learning LOCATIONS

5. **Name the national capital of Canada.**

6. **Which province shares a name with a major city?**

Focus on Skills

□ Social Studies

□ Map and Globe

☑ Critical Thinking and Problem Solving

Identifying Central Issues

Identifying central issues means finding the main ideas in an article or passage. Sometimes the issue is clearly stated in the language of the text. In other cases it may be implied and not explicit.

Use the following steps to identify the central issues in the passage below.

1. Find the topic of the passage. Quickly scan the passage below. Watch for topic sentences or other key phrases that may summarize the content of the passage in question. (a) How would you state the topic addressed in this paragraph? (b) What two aspects of this topic are considered?

2. Determine the point of view. The point of view may contribute bias to the passage. Be alert for strong language that seems to distort an argument in favor of one side or another. Also watch for statements lacking evidence to support them. (a) What is the point of view expressed in this paragraph? (b) How did you determine the point of view?

3. Look for evidence supporting the key statements in the passage. Answer these questions: (a) What evidence is given of cooperation between Canada and the United States during war? (b) What evidence is given of their peacetime cooperation?

4. Identify the central issue. By thinking back over what you have read, you should be able to identify the central issue in the passage. (a) How would you express the central issue here? (b) Which part of the central issue receives more attention in the passage?

Canada and the United States share the longest undefended border in the world. No fences separate these two countries. They also share the Great Lakes and the St. Lawrence Seaway, which the two countries developed as partners. During World War II, Canada and the United States formed a permanent joint defense board to protect the Atlantic and Pacific coasts. This joint effort resulted in a radar network called the Distant Early Warning (DEW) Line, which stretches across northern Canada and detects hostile planes. In the late

St. Lawrence Seaway

1980s, the system was upgraded and renamed the North Warning System. Because they are neighbors, it is essential for the two countries to work together in the event of war.

3 Canada Today

Section Preview

Main Ideas

- Canada's future, like its past, depends on overcoming the challenges of geography.

- Links between Canada and the United States have resulted in a peaceful but uneven relationship.

- Its location, size, and population make Canada well suited to international cooperation.

Vocabulary

customs

Arctic wildlife are at the mercy of Canada's resource development.

The history of Canada has centered on the struggle to overcome a harsh environment. Canada has emerged from that struggle to become a prosperous nation. Its gross national product is among the top twenty in the world. Its stable government and high standard of living attracted millions of immigrants in recent decades. Canada has developed a blend of cultures while becoming a leader in worldwide organizations.

Challenges and Opportunities

In its continuing progress, Canada faces challenges as well as opportunities. Canada's future, like its past, largely depends on its geography. The themes of human-environment interaction and movement are of basic importance in understanding Canada's future development.

Movement of Resources Canada must balance the opportunities of developing its northern resources with the challenges of protecting the fragile environment of the tundra. The use of heavy machinery to recover oil and minerals in

the Arctic causes permanent damage to the landscape. Construction of a pipeline above ground avoids the problem of disrupting the permafrost, but it creates barriers to the migration of caribou and other arctic animals.

Movement of People In 1900 only about one third of Canada's people lived in urban areas. Today, 77 percent of the nation's people live in cities. Canada has more than twenty metropolitan areas with a population of 100,000 or more. Urbanization has created many challenges: providing housing and services, controlling pollution, and preventing overcrowding.

Links with the United States

The border between Canada and the United States is the longest undefended border in the world—more than 5,000 miles (8,045 km) long. Travelers between the two countries pay **customs**—tariffs or fees charged by one country's government on goods people bring in from the other country. But no fence exists along the Canadian–United States border.

The Water is Wide

● **Region** On the border between Canada and the United States is a pair of waterfalls known as Niagara Falls. Though both are less than 170 feet high, together they are over half a mile wide. People on both sides of the border enjoy the spectacular sight of water thundering over the falls at a rate of 195,000 cubic feet (5,525 cubic meters) per second. *What other kinds of links does Canada share with the United States?*

Wildlife

To survive the Arctic's long, cold winters, animals such as polar bears and muskoxen must conserve their energy. Therefore, these animals spend much of their time in an inactive state. Scientists are concerned that human activity will disturb the animals' dormant periods, forcing them to flee. This exertion could be fatal to the animals.

Cultural Links Some of Canada's links with the United States are cultural. People living close to the border can enjoy radio and television programs from stations in both countries. Professional baseball and hockey leagues include teams from both nations.

Economic Links Canada and the United States have important economic links. Canada buys nearly 25 percent of all United States exports, and the United States buys about 75 percent of Canadian exports.

In recent years Canada and the United States negotiated two important trade agreements. The first, the Free Trade Agreement (FTA), was signed in 1988. It called for an end to export barriers, including the elimination of all tariffs by the year 1999. Before the agreement, tariffs had made buying and selling between the two countries very expensive.

The FTA produced mixed reactions. On the one hand, Canadians were able to take advantage of lower prices by shopping across the border. On the other hand, many Canadians blamed the FTA for plant closings and rising unemployment, as major firms relocated south of the border where costs were lower.

Canada and the United States extended the FTA in 1992 to include Mexico. This new pact, the North American Free Trade Agreement (NAFTA), was designed to establish a free trade zone across all of North America. The agreement marked a giant step toward creating the world's largest trading bloc, with about 376 million consumers.

An Uneven Relationship Although there are many positive links between Canada and the United States, some Canadians are uncomfortable because the relationship between the two nations is so uneven.

Canada's location relative to the United States provides its people with great opportunities. At the same time, Canada still struggles to prevent its identity from being overshadowed by the United States. Canadians are generally aware of what's happening in the United States, while Americans tend to give little thought to their northern neighbors. Mordecai Richler, a well-known Canadian writer, spoke for many Canadians when he declared that he wanted his country to be "something more than this continent's attic."

Facts in BRIEF

Country	Population	Life Expectancy (years)	Per Capita GNP (in U.S. $)
Canada	29,600,000	78	$20,670
United States	263,200,000	76	24,750

Source: Population Reference Bureau

CHART SKILLS

● *Which country has the higher per capita GNP?*

● *Critical Thinking Which country has the larger population? What factors contribute to population growth?*

Links with the World

In contrast to the United States, a so-called superpower, Canada plays the role of a middle power in the global community. Middle powers often join together to achieve their common goals. Because of its location, size, and multicultural population, Canada is very well suited to working with other nations.

The Importance of Location
Canada has a unique position with regard to other nations because of its location. With major ports on both the Atlantic and Pacific coasts, Canada has access to trade with Japan and other Asian countries as well as with Europe.

Member of the Commonwealth
Canada maintains links with many nations through its membership in the Commonwealth of Nations. This is a group of countries, mostly former British colonies, that now have independence under the symbolic protection of the British crown. Commonwealth nations often work together to promote better trade, health, and education in their countries.

As a member of the Commonwealth of Nations, Canada has links with developing countries. Membership also puts Canada in a favorable position with regard to trade with the European Community, a group of Western European countries that have united their economic resources.

The Role of Peacekeeper Lester Pearson, Canada's prime minister from 1963 to 1968, once said:

> *The best defense of peace is not power, but the removal of the causes of war, and international agreements which will put peace on a stronger foundation than the terror of destruction.*

Much of Canada's international policy has been based on Pearson's ideas. Canada has taken an active part in promoting arms control and disarmament among other nations of the world.

Section 3 Review

Vocabulary and Main Ideas

1. **Define: customs**

2. **Why is the relationship between Canada and the United States uneven?**

3. **How does Canada's location influence its role in international trade?**

4. **Critical Thinking:** *Synthesizing Information* **Why might Canada have advantages over the United States in attempting to mediate peaceful relations in the world?**

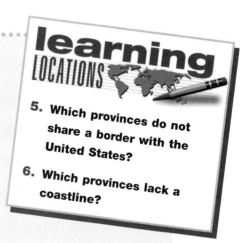

learning LOCATIONS

5. Which provinces do not share a border with the United States?

6. Which provinces lack a coastline?

Section Summaries

Section 1 Regions of Canada

- Canada is a vast land made up of ten provinces and two territories.
- Based on its physical features, culture, and economy, Canada can be divided into five distinct regions.
- Location has helped the development of some regions but has limited human interaction with the environment in other parts of the country.

Section 2 The Search for a National Identity

- Colonial conflicts between Britain and France are reflected in the cultural conflicts between English-speaking and French-speaking Canadians today.
- Canada's multicultural people have strong ethnic and regional ties which make it difficult to achieve a national identity. The Canadian government supports multiculturalism but encourages unity among its people.

Section 3 Canada Today

- Canada is a prosperous nation, but still faces the challenge of developing its northern resources while protecting the environment.
- Canada maintains a peaceful but uneven relationship with the United States.
- Canada has become a leader in international cooperation by active involvement in world organizations.

Reviewing Vocabulary

Use each of the following terms in a sentence that shows their meaning.

1. separatism
2. customs
3. maritime
4. secede
5. lock
6. bedrock

Applying the Geographic Themes

1. **Regions** How did the Atlantic provinces play important roles in Canada's settlement and development?
2. **Human-Environment Interaction** What are the major economic activities in the area known as the Great Lakes–St. Lawrence provinces?
3. **Place** Why have the major cities of Alberta grown rapidly in recent decades?
4. **Regions** Why do some people favor making Quebec an independent country?
5. **Human-Environment Interaction** What challenges does Canada face in developing its northern resources?

Critical Thinking and Applying Skills

1. **Predicting Consequences** What do you think would result if the Canadian government passed a law making English the only official language? Give reasons for your answer.
2. **Identifying Central Issues** Use what you have learned in the skill lesson on page 178 to identify and describe the central issue in the following passage:

According to many Canadians, the United States has invested too heavily in Canada. Canadians want to work toward more control of their own economy, rather then depending on the United States. Presently, Canada's economy is vulnerable to conditions in the United States. Furthermore, the United States receives much of the profit from Canadian industries because it has controlling interests in many of them. These facts have led to disagreements among Canadians.

Journal Activity

Writing Across Cultures

▶ 1. Write a paragraph identifying several ways the development of the northern region of Canada would affect Canada's Inuit population.

▶ 2. Imagine that you are a resident of Quebec. Write a letter to the editor of your local newspaper arguing for or against secession.

▶ 3. Imagine you are a Canadian of Asian descent. Write a letter to a relative in Asia telling what you do to maintain your Asian heritage.

INTERNET link

Explore Canada's diverse cultures by visiting the Royal Ontario Museum. Link to this site from:

• www·phschool·com

Read through the list of exhibit subjects. Choose one of interest and write a paragraph describing what you saw.

learning LOCATIONS

Canada

Number from 1 to 9 on your paper. Next to each number, write the letter of the place on the map that corresponds to the places listed below.

1. Toronto

2. Nova Scotia

3. Saskatchewan

4. Alberta

5. Yukon

6. British Columbia

7. Newfoundland

8. Edmonton

9. Prince Edward Island

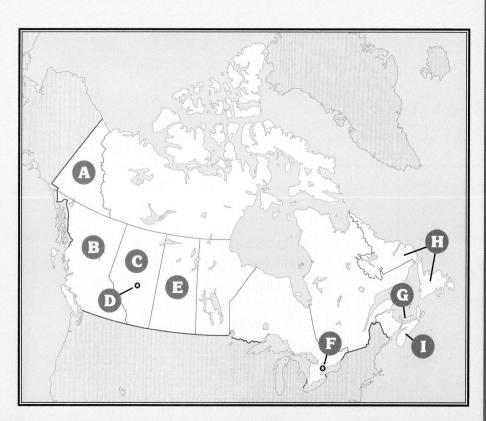

OIL SPILL CLEANUP

Imagine that you are a volunteer helping to clean up a huge oil spill. What methods would you use? What obstacles would you face? Think about these questions as you perform the experiment.

MATERIALS:

Shallow pan

Sand

Water

Olive oil

Feather

Medicine dropper

Wooden sticks

Paper towels

Cotton ball

Plastic bag

PROCEDURES:

Step 2

1. On a flat surface, fill one end of a shallow pan with sand to create a small beach as shown in the illustration.

2. Fill the remaining portion of the pan with water as shown.

Step 3

3. Carefully pour 20 mL of olive oil into the water at the opposite end from the sand. Observe how the oil behaves.

4. Dip a feather and your finger into the oil. Observe how they are affected by the oil. Try to wipe the oil off of the feather using a paper towel.

5. Using the wooden sticks, try to prevent the oil spill from reaching the beach.

6. Use the cotton ball, paper towels, and medicine dropper to recover as much oil as possible. Dispose of oil-soaked items in the plastic bag.

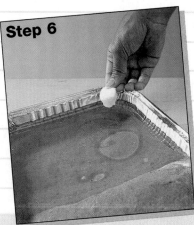
Step 6

OBSERVATIONS AND ANALYSIS:

1. How successful were you in cleaning up the oil spill? How difficult was the chore? Are the water and sand as free of oil now as they were before the spill?

2. List at least four factors that would make cleaning up an actual oil spill more difficult than the task you just performed.

3. What happened to the feather and your finger when they were dipped in oil? Were you able to clean them? Explain the significance for fish, birds, and other sea animals.

4. Look at the used cleanup materials in the plastic bag. What additional problems for cleanup crews does this suggest?

5. Imagine that your volunteer efforts cleaning up the oil have been going on for a week. You have made some progress, but much work still remains. Write a letter to a friend describing your work and your feelings.

100,000 BARRELS OF OIL
SPILL INTO THE BAY

An oil tanker hit a reef yesterday, causing one of the worst oil spills in history. The reef cut through the hull of the ship, spilling thousands of barrels of crude oil into the waters. Cleanup efforts will begin immediately. Volunteers will race against time to save nearby fisheries, birds, and other sea life. But with predicted high winds and strong currents, environmentalists expect considerable damage.

taking *Action*

Although you cannot prevent oil spills, you can be informed about how they impact the environment. Consider doing one of the following:

✔ Write to a major oil company to learn more about safety measures being taken to prevent oil spills.

✔ Research the latest technologies and techniques used for cleaning up after an oil spill.

Oil-covered bird

Cleaning Newport Beach, CA after a spill

Latin America

CHAPTERS

A Global Perspective

Latin America begins at the southern border of the United States and stretches southward to the tip of stormy Cape Horn, almost to Antarctica. The countries of this large region are located in North, South, and Central America and on many islands in the Caribbean Sea.

Robinson Projection

Amazon River

KEYS TO UNDERSTANDING THIS REGION

1 Countries and Cities *(pp.188–189)*
The countries of Latin America are varied in climate, landforms, and resources, but all share a common history as former colonies of European nations.

2 Physical Features *(pp. 190–191)*
The Andes and other mountain ranges run the length of Mexico and Central and South America, defining regions on the mainland. Great river systems, especially the Amazon, provide a way into the interior.

3 People and Cultures *(pp. 192–193)*
While the cultures of Spain and Portugal have been major influences in the region, the heritage of Indian cultures remains strong in many countries.

4 Climate and Vegetation *(pp. 194–195)*
Mountains and proximity to water influence climate and vegetation in the region. The tropical rain forests of the Caribbean islands and the Amazon Basin are home to millions of species of plants and animals.

5 Economy and Resources *(pp. 196–197)*
Many Latin American countries have rich mineral and agricultural resources and are developing rapidly economically. A large gap still exists between rich and poor in many places.

VISUAL PREVIEW ACTIVITY

Each of the five keys above corresponds to a section of the Regional Atlas that follows. Number from 1 to 5 on a piece of paper. Use information from the maps, graphs, and photographs in the Regional Atlas to write one additional fact for each of the first five keys.

Chapter 9

LATIN AMERICA

Use the Map, Graph, and Photo Studies in the Regional Atlas to gain a better understanding of Latin America's physical and cultural geography.

ATLAS VOCABULARY

cay	savanna	hurricane
coral	mestizo	El Niño
basin	tropical storm	canopy

1 COUNTRIES AND CITIES

LARGEST METROPOLITAN AREAS

Mexico City, Mexico
15,525,000

Buenos Aires, Argentina
10,686,000

Rio de Janeiro, Brazil
9,817,000

São Paulo, Brazil
9,480,000

Lima, Peru
6,415,000

Santiago, Chile
4,386,000

Bogota, Colombia
3,975,000

Havana, Cuba
2,119,000

Salvador, Brazil
2,056,000

Belo Horizonte, Brazil
2,049,000

= 2,000,000 people

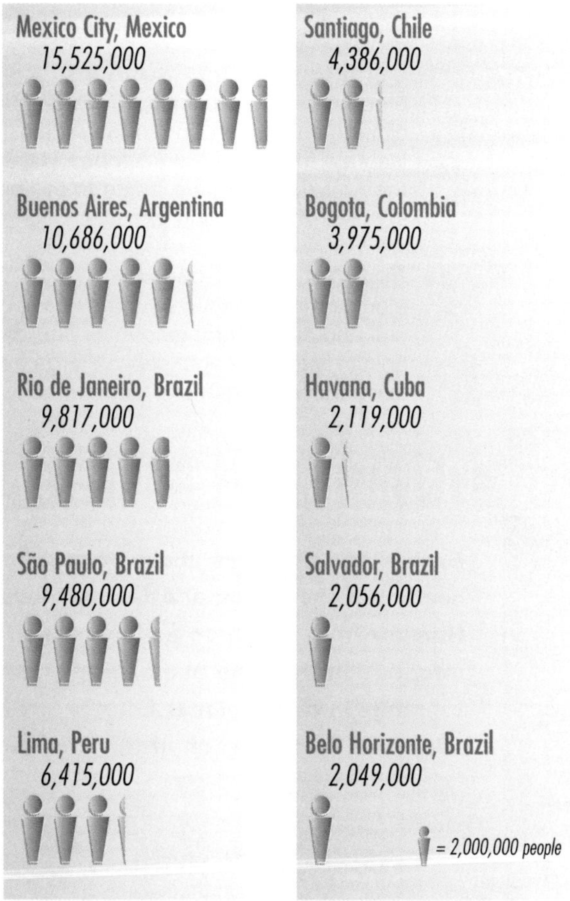

Source: Population Reference Bureau

GRAPH STUDY

1 **Largest Cities** Well over half of all Latin Americans today live in cities. Many of the world's largest metropolitan areas are in Latin America. In Central America and the Caribbean, especially, many rural people have moved to fast-growing cities in the hope of finding factory jobs. *Which country in the region has the largest number of large metropolitan areas?*

MAP STUDY
Applying the Geographic Themes

2 **Location** Although Mexico and the Caribbean islands are located generally due south of the United States, most of South America lies farther to the east. *Across which countries in South America does the Equator pass?*

3 **Movement** The Americas were home to several great Indian civilizations. Long before A.D. 1000 the Maya had built cities in the Yucatán Peninsula and nearby areas. Tenochtitlán, capital of the even larger Aztec empire, stood on the site of modern Mexico City. *In what modern country is the Yucatán Peninsula located?*

LATIN AMERICA

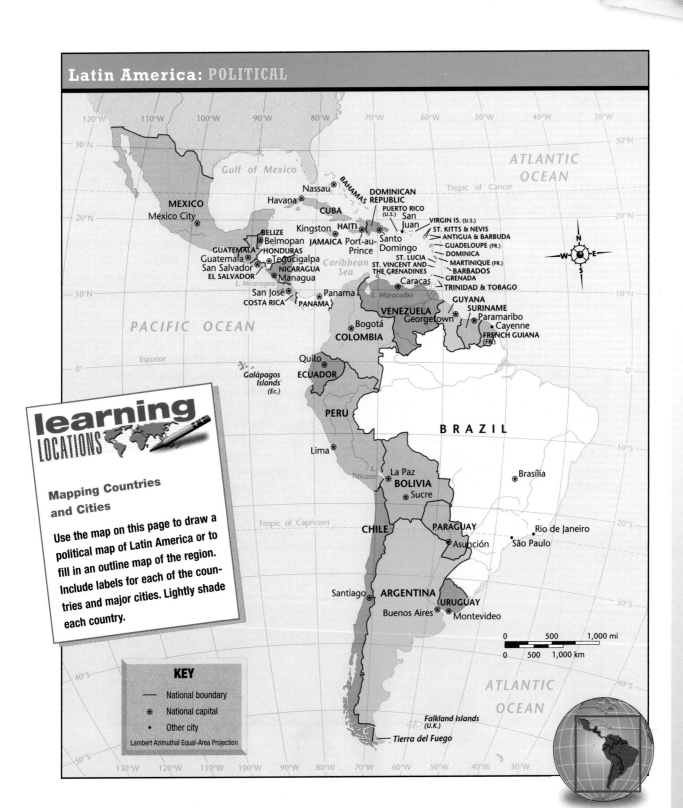

Latin America: POLITICAL

learning LOCATIONS

Mapping Countries and Cities

Use the map on this page to draw a political map of Latin America or to fill in an outline map of the region. Include labels for each of the countries and major cities. Lightly shade each country.

KEY

— National boundary

⊛ National capital

• Other city

Lambert Azimuthal Equal-Area Projection

4 Human-Environment Interaction
Latin Americans tend to live near the coast rather than in the interior regions. One reason is that the coastal plains are good for agriculture. *Name two national capitals in Central America that are located on or near the seacoast.*

LATIN AMERICA

MAP STUDY
Applying the Geographic Themes

1 **Location** Mountain ranges dominate the landscape of Mexico, defining the country's regions. The central plateau, a huge, bumpy highland region that ranges in altitude from 6,000 to 8,000 feet (1,800 to 2,400 m), lies between two great mountain ranges. Continuing south, mountains, including active volcanoes, form the highlands of Central America. *Name the two mountain ranges that lie on either side of Mexico's central plateau.*

2 **Place** Some of the islands in the Caribbean Sea are the jagged tops of a vast underwater mountain chain. Flatter islands of the Caribbean are **cays** (keez), low-lying islands, formed over thousands of years from the accumulation of **coral**, the rock-like skeletons of tiny sea animals. The islands are divided into three main groups: the Bahamas, the Greater Antilles (an TIHL eez), and the Lesser Antilles. *What are the four largest islands in the Caribbean Sea?*

3 **Regions** South America's largest lowland is the **basin** of the Amazon River, the area drained by this huge river and its tributaries. The Amazon Basin covers 2.7 million square miles (7 million sq km), a region two thirds the size of the United States. It carries a larger volume of water than any other river on earth. *Name two other major river systems in South America and the countries through which they flow.*

4 **Place** Between the Andes and the highlands of the east, wide plains fill the center of the continent of South America. In the north is a lowland region of tropical grasslands, or **savanna**, called the Llanos (YAH nohs). Savannas have long dry seasons and short, warm rainy seasons. In the south are the pampas, a large region of temperate grasslands in Argentina and Uruguay. *Between which two countries does the Llanos lie?*

Cross Section: Latin America

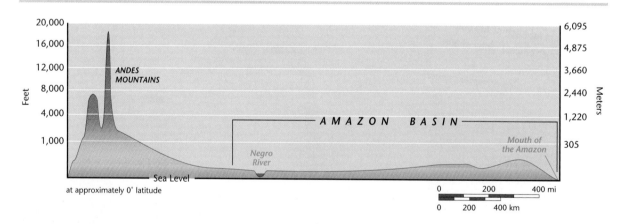

DIAGRAM STUDY

5 **Physical Profile** The towering Andes, the world's second highest mountain range, line the western edge of Latin America, dropping to level plains in the interior. The east has lower, less rugged highland areas.

The relatively small Guiana Highlands curve across the northeast, while the Brazilian Highlands sprawl over one fourth of the continent's land area. *Which highlands area is shown on the east in this cross section?*

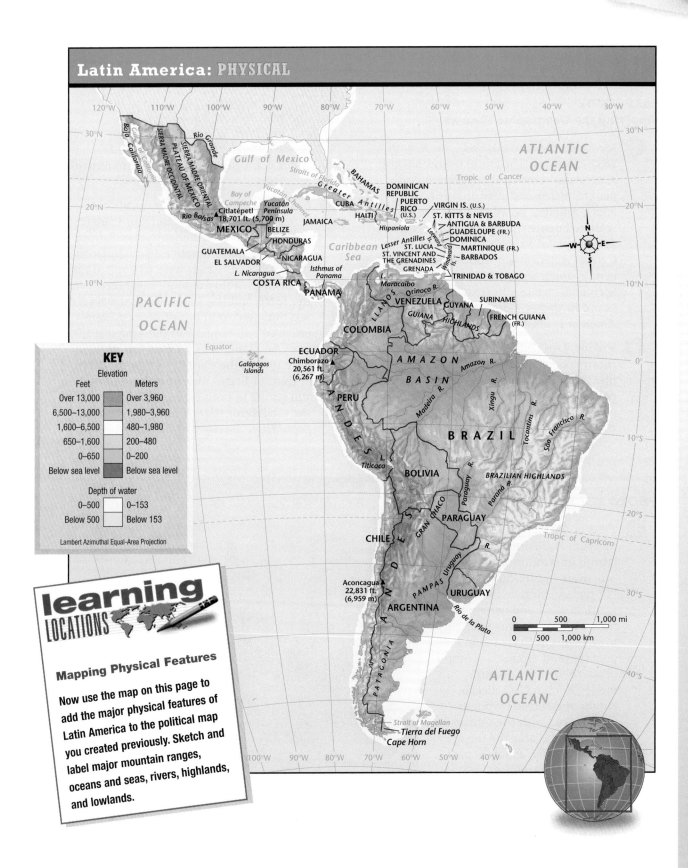

Latin America: PHYSICAL

KEY

Elevation

Feet	Meters
Over 13,000	Over 3,960
6,500–13,000	1,980–3,960
1,600–6,500	480–1,980
650–1,600	200–480
0–650	0–200
Below sea level	Below sea level

Depth of water

0–500	0–153
Below 500	Below 153

Lambert Azimuthal Equal-Area Projection

learning LOCATIONS

Mapping Physical Features

Now use the map on this page to add the major physical features of Latin America to the political map you created previously. Sketch and label major mountain ranges, oceans and seas, rivers, highlands, and lowlands.

ATLANTIC OCEAN

Tropic of Cancer

Gulf of Mexico

BAHAMAS

DOMINICAN REPUBLIC

PUERTO RICO (U.S.)

VIRGIN IS. (U.S.)

ST. KITTS & NEVIS

ANTIGUA & BARBUDA

GUADELOUPE (FR.)

DOMINICA

MARTINIQUE (FR.)

BARBADOS

GRENADA

TRINIDAD & TOBAGO

CUBA

HAITI

JAMAICA

Hispaniola

Greater Antilles

Lesser Antilles

ST. LUCIA

ST. VINCENT AND THE GRENADINES

Caribbean Sea

Straits of Florida

Yucatán Channel

Bay of Campeche

Yucatán Peninsula

Citlaltépetl 18,701 ft. (5,700 m)

Rio Balsas

MEXICO

BELIZE

HONDURAS

GUATEMALA

EL SALVADOR

NICARAGUA

L. Nicaragua

COSTA RICA

Isthmus of Panama

PANAMA

Baja California

Gulf of California

SIERRA MADRE OCCIDENTAL

PLATEAU OF MEXICO

SIERRA MADRE ORIENTAL

Rio Grande

PACIFIC OCEAN

Equator

Galápagos Islands

ECUADOR

Chimborazo 20,561 ft. (6,267 m)

PERU

ANDES

COLOMBIA

VENEZUELA

L. Maracaibo

Orinoco R.

LLANOS

GUIANA HIGHLANDS

GUYANA

SURINAME

FRENCH GUIANA (FR.)

AMAZON BASIN

Amazon R.

Madeira R.

Xingu R.

Tocantins R.

São Francisco R.

BRAZIL

BRAZILIAN HIGHLANDS

BOLIVIA

L. Titicaca

Paraguay R.

Paraná R.

GRAN CHACO

PARAGUAY

CHILE

Uruguay R.

PAMPAS

URUGUAY

Aconcagua 22,831 ft. (6,959 m)

ARGENTINA

Rio de la Plata

Tropic of Capricorn

PATAGONIA

ATLANTIC OCEAN

Strait of Magellan

Tierra del Fuego

Cape Horn

0	500	1,000 mi
0	500	1,000 km

MAP STUDY
Applying the Geographic Themes

1 Human-Environment Interaction The entire region of Latin America is home to about 460 million people, distributed very unevenly. In South America, people tend to live in scattered dense clusters near the coast. The people of Mesoamerica—Mexico and Central America—are also concentrated in certain areas. Some live in cool, interior highlands, while others are in coastal and island lowlands. *What part of South America is most sparsely populated?*

2 Place Descendants of the Aztec and Incan peoples as well as other Indian peoples make up a large percentage of the population in several Latin American countries. Many other Latin Americans are **mestizos** (meh STEE zohs)—people of mixed European and Indian ancestry. *What is the population density in central Mexico?*

3 Movement Spain and Portugal colonized most of the mainland, but France, Britain, and the Netherlands also claimed colonies in Latin America. Plantations on the Caribbean islands were well suited for producing a valuable crop: sugar. Between the 1500s and the 1800s, when slavery was outlawed, millions of Africans were enslaved and brought to the Americas to work on plantations. About half of them were sold in the Caribbean islands, another third in Brazil. African influences are still strong in both places. *What areas of the Caribbean islands have the greatest population density?*

PHOTO STUDY

4 Town Plaza Colonization by Spain and Portugal made a lasting imprint on Latin American culture. Spanish and Portuguese, both derived from Latin, became and remain the region's major languages. Many towns built in the colonial period were built around a central plaza, following a Spanish model. Roman Catholicism, taught and spread by priests who arrived with the soldiers in the 1500s, became the major religion. Today, about 90 percent of Latin America's people are Roman Catholic. *Critical Thinking: What Spanish influences are shown in this photo of the Mexican city of Guadalajara?*

LATIN AMERICA

Latin America: POPULATION DENSITY

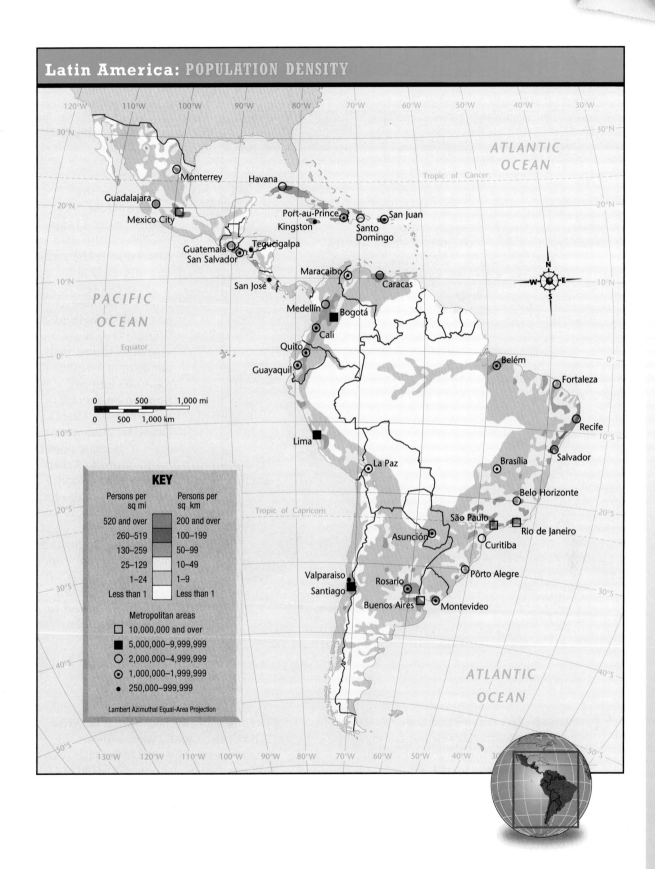

PACIFIC
OCEAN

ATLANTIC
OCEAN

ATLANTIC
OCEAN

Tropic of Cancer

Equator

Tropic of Capricorn

Monterrey
Guadalajara
Mexico City
Guatemala
San Salvador
Tegucigalpa
San José
Havana
Port-au-Prince
Kingston
Santo Domingo
San Juan
Maracaibo
Caracas
Medellín
Bogotá
Cali
Quito
Guayaquil
Belém
Fortaleza
Recife
Salvador
Lima
La Paz
Brasília
Belo Horizonte
São Paulo
Rio de Janeiro
Curitiba
Asunción
Pôrto Alegre
Valparaiso
Santiago
Rosario
Buenos Aires
Montevideo

0   500   1,000 mi
0   500   1,000 km

KEY

Persons per sq mi	Persons per sq km
520 and over	200 and over
260–519	100–199
130–259	50–99
25–129	10–49
1–24	1–9
Less than 1	Less than 1

Metropolitan areas

☐ 10,000,000 and over
■ 5,000,000–9,999,999
○ 2,000,000–4,999,999
◉ 1,000,000–1,999,999
• 250,000–999,999

Lambert Azimuthal Equal-Area Projection

LATIN AMERICA

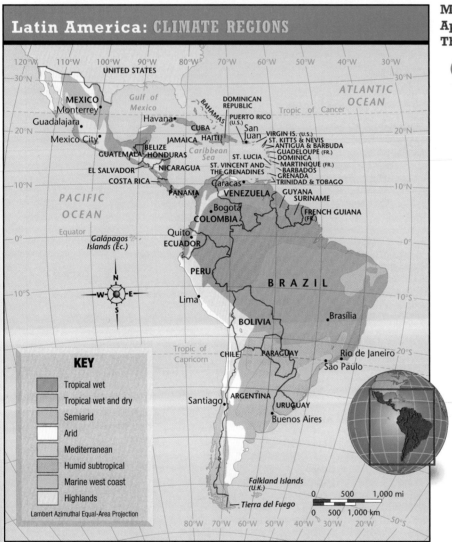

Latin America: CLIMATE REGIONS

KEY

- Tropical wet
- Tropical wet and dry
- Semiarid
- Arid
- Mediterranean
- Humid subtropical
- Marine west coast
- Highlands

Lambert Azimuthal Equal-Area Projection

MAP STUDY
Applying the Geographic Themes

1 **Human-Environment Interaction** Most Atlantic storms begin to form off the coast of Africa during the summer and early fall, when ocean temperatures are warmest. A few gain strength to become **tropical storms**—storms with winds of at least 39 miles (63 km) per hour. In an average year, only six Atlantic Ocean tropical storms grow to become powerful hurricanes. A **hurricane** is a tropical storm with winds of at least 74 miles (119 km) per hour. These destructive storms can devastate island homes and businesses. *What group of Caribbean islands are closest to where hurricanes form?*

2 **Human-Environment Interaction** One of South America's richest fishing regions is where two cold-water currents, the Peru (Humboldt) and California currents, meet off the coast of Peru and Ecuador. Winds blowing across this cold surface water lose their moisture at sea and are dry when they reach the land. About every three years, around December, a current known as **El Niño** ("The Christ Child") warms these cold surface waters. The change in water temperature disrupts fishing. Birds and animals that usually feed on the fish die. El Niño also alters world weather patterns, causing both droughts and floods. *What kind of climate and vegetation are found on the coast of Peru and northern Chile?*

LATIN AMERICA

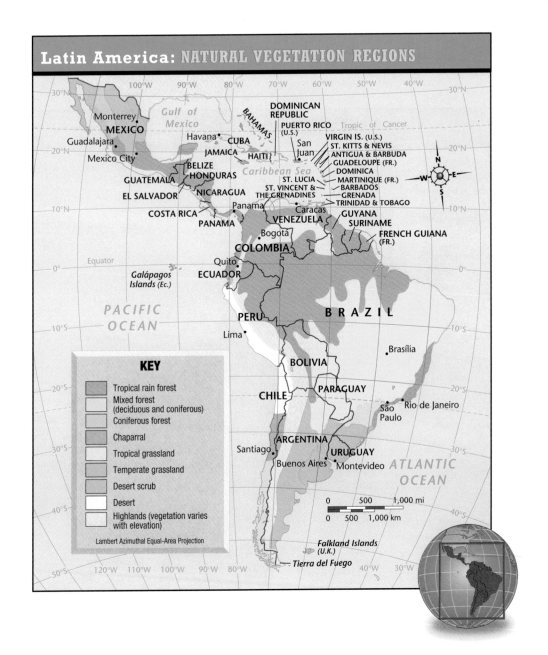

Latin America: NATURAL VEGETATION REGIONS

KEY

- Tropical rain forest
- Mixed forest (deciduous and coniferous)
- Coniferous forest
- Chaparral
- Tropical grassland
- Temperate grassland
- Desert scrub
- Desert
- Highlands (vegetation varies with elevation)

Lambert Azimuthal Equal-Area Projection

3 **Place** Scant rainfall in much of northern Mexico supports only desert scrub including cacti and patches of coarse grass. Only the hillsides of the Sierras are forested. From the southern border of Mexico through Central America, however, the vegetation is broad leafed and luxurious because of steamy tropical climates and heavy rainfall. *What kinds of vegetation are found on the Yucatán Peninsula?*

4 **Region** The Amazon rain forest is the single largest mass of vegetation anywhere on earth, home to millions of species. Tangles of vines line the banks of the rain forest's rivers. The forest is dimly lit, for little sunlight can filter through the **canopy**—the topmost forest layer, where branches of tall trees meet. Only small, low-growing plants grow on the brown forest floor. *Where are tropical rain forests found in Latin America outside the Amazon Basin?*

LATIN AMERICA

5 ECONOMY AND RESOURCES

Latin America: ECONOMIC ACTIVITY AND RESOURCES

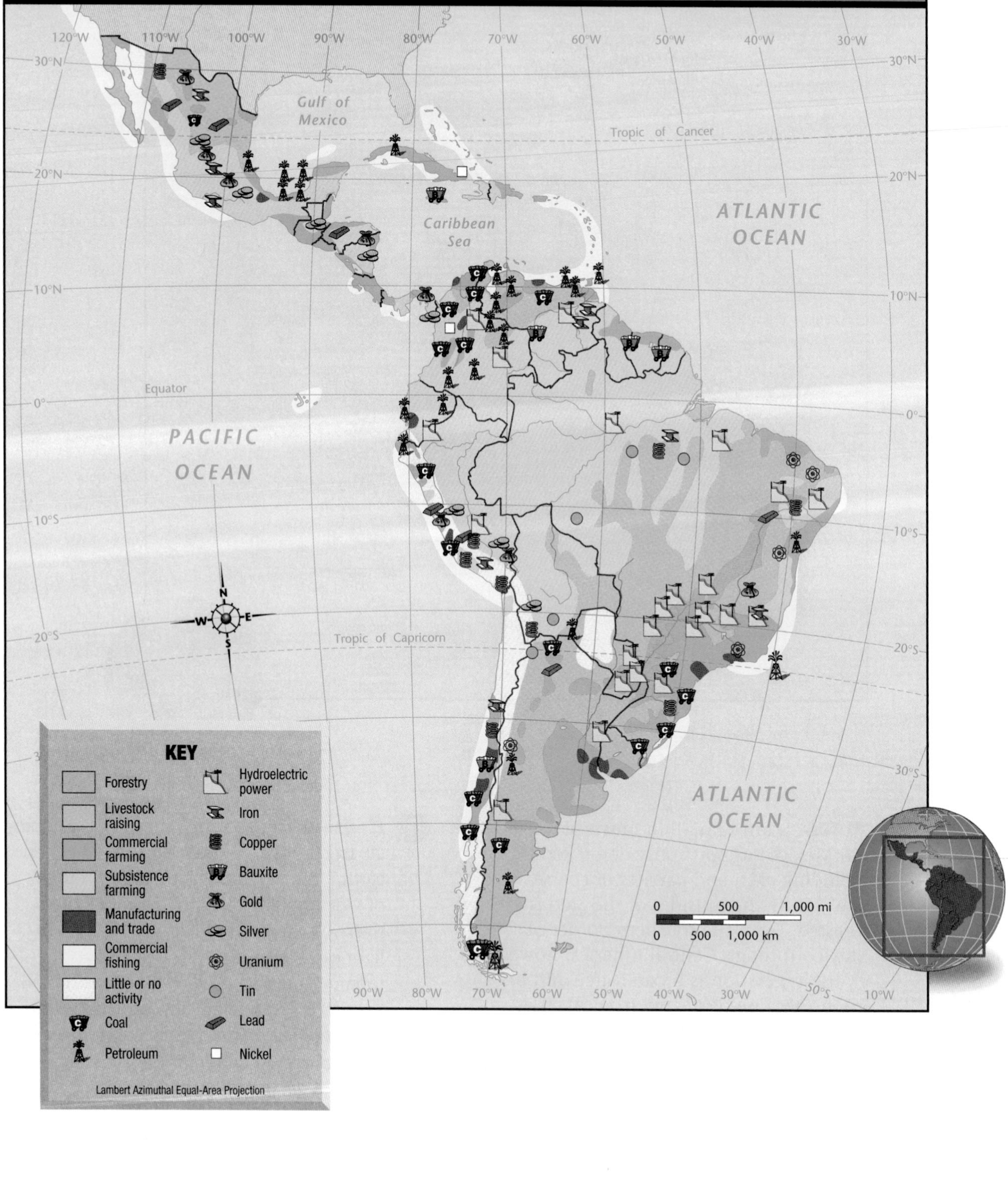

120°W
110°W
100°W
90°W
80°W
70°W
60°W
50°W
40°W
30°W
30°N
20°N
10°N
0°
10°S
20°S
30°S
Gulf of Mexico
Tropic of Cancer
Caribbean Sea
ATLANTIC OCEAN
Equator
PACIFIC OCEAN
Tropic of Capricorn
N
S
E
W
ATLANTIC OCEAN
0
500
1,000 mi
0
500
1,000 km
90°W
80°W
70°W
60°W
50°W
40°W
30°W
50°S
10°W
KEY
Forestry
Livestock raising
Commercial farming
Subsistence farming
Manufacturing and trade
Commercial fishing
Little or no activity
Coal
Petroleum
Hydroelectric power
Iron
Copper
Bauxite
Gold
Silver
Uranium
Tin
Lead
Nickel
Lambert Azimuthal Equal-Area Projection

MAP STUDY
Applying the Geographic Themes

1 Place Wide disparities exist between rich and poor in much of Latin America today. Even before Europeans arrived, cultures such as the Aztec and Inca empires had strict class differences. Spanish colonial governments changed the social structure but made the differences between people even greater. A few landowning families of European descent became a wealthy upper class. Artisans and business people, many of them mestizos, filled the middle class. Most people, though, were poor peasant farmers of mestizo, Indian, or African ancestry. *In what countries of South America do many people still live by live-stock raising?*

2 Regions Many parts of Latin America are too mountainous for farming but are rich in minerals. The search for silver and gold was one factor that drew European colonists to the Americas. *Name three countries that have deposits of silver or gold.*

3 Place Cash crops such as coffee, bananas, and cotton, are grown commercially on large plantations. They account for well over half of Central America's income from exports. *In what areas of Latin America is commercial farming an important economic activity?*

4 Human-Environment Interaction Most of the Caribbean islands have a warm tropical climate all year, making tourism an important economic activity. Summer temperatures average 80°F (27°C), but the northeast trade winds blowing over the ocean keep the days comfortable. Rainfall on the islands varies dramatically. Sudden rains may fall daily on the northeast, or windward side of an island, while mountains protect the leeward side. *Besides tourism, what other economic activities take place in the Caribbean islands? What islands have mineral resources?*

5 Regions In a number of places, such as the Andes and Central America, Latin Americans of Indian ancestry follow older, traditional lifestyles. Many Indians continue to dress, speak, farm, and trade much as their ancestors did. *What economic activities take place in the areas settled by people of Indian ancestry?*

atlas REVIEW

Vocabulary and Main Ideas

1. Define: a. cay b. coral c. basin d. savanna e. mestizo f. tropical storm g. hurricane h. El Niño i. canopy

2. Identify and name the landforms that dominate western Latin America.

3. What are the three groups of islands in the Caribbean region?

4. Critical Thinking: *Making Comparisons* Why do you think population patterns in Mesoamerica and in South America are different?

learning LOCATIONS

5. What is the largest country in Latin America?

6. What countries are at the border where Central America meets South America?

LATIN AMERICA

The Columbian Exchange

*W*hat's so unusual about tomatoes on Italian pasta or hamburger in a Mexican taco? Today, nothing. But tomatoes are not native to Italy. Neither are cattle native to Mexico. How did they get there?

The Columbian Exchange

For most of human history, the Americas have been cut off from the rest of the world by great expanses of ocean. That isolation ended abruptly in 1492, when Christopher Columbus reached what Europeans called the "New World." Soon other Europeans arrived, bringing their customs—and foods—with them. They took back to Europe some foods from the Americas. This two-way trade is known as the **Columbian Exchange**. As the chart on the facing page shows, the exchange included food plants, animals—and, unfortunately, diseases. These diseases killed millions of Native Americans. Weakened as a result, Native American societies found it hard to resist European invaders.

Foods Taken from the Americas

Corn Corn, or maize, was one of the first plants domesticated in the Western Hemisphere. Native Americans began growing it about 5,000 years ago. Along with squash and tomatoes, corn was a staple food. It was so important that it was included in Indian creation stories as one of the most treasured gifts from the gods to humans. In one such story, the creator of the earth gave people corn before giving them water, sun, or wind.

With the growth of transatlantic travel, corn soon became an important food crop in western Africa. It also thrived in parts of southern and central Europe.

Potatoes Not only corn, but also potatoes soon fed a rapidly growing world population. People of the Andes not only domesticated the potato but also found ways to preserve it. At night, they froze potatoes in the cold mountain air. The next day, after the potatoes had thawed, people squeezed out the water and set the potatoes out to freeze again. After a few days of this, the potatoes were "freeze dried" and could last for years without spoiling.

Potatoes were well suited to the cool, rainy parts of northern Europe, such as Ireland and Germany. They soon became a staple food, especially for poorer people. When disease ruined the Irish potato crop in the mid-1840s, famine resulted, causing many Irish to emigrate to the United States.

Tomatoes Tomatoes were another American food. While it is hard to imagine Italian pasta without them, tomatoes were one of the most exotic imports from the Americas. For many years, they were thought to be dangerous and even poisonous. Once the tomato became popular, it was widely grown and eaten throughout Europe.

Foods Brought to the Americas

Sugar Cane This tall tropical grass from the islands of Southeast Asia thrived in the Caribbean islands, but with terrible consequences. Harvesting sugar cane was hard and painful work, needing the labor of many people. At first, European plantation owners forced the native islanders to do this work. But as the islanders died off, plantation owners turned to African slaves to do the work.

Livestock Animals were one import that improved life for people in the Americas. Spanish soldiers brought horses, which soon

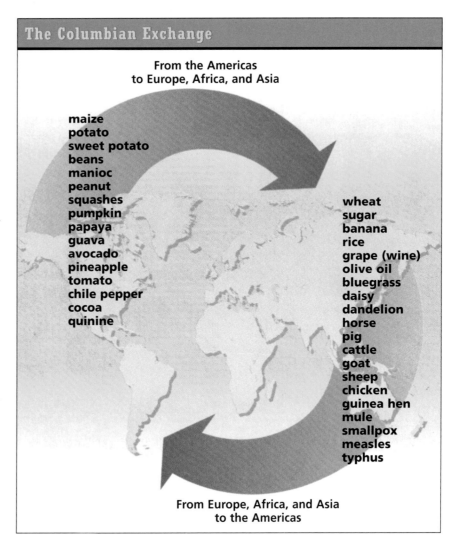

The Columbian Exchange

From the Americas to Europe, Africa, and Asia

maize
potato
sweet potato
beans
manioc
peanut
squashes
pumpkin
papaya
guava
avocado
pineapple
tomato
chile pepper
cocoa
quinine

wheat
sugar
banana
rice
grape (wine)
olive oil
bluegrass
daisy
dandelion
horse
pig
cattle
goat
sheep
chicken
guinea hen
mule
smallpox
measles
typhus

From Europe, Africa, and Asia to the Americas

became important in many Native American cultures for hunting and war. Sheep and goats from Spain flourished in mountainous regions like Chile and northern Mexico. Cattle did well in both North and South America. Pigs also adapted to the Western Hemisphere. Two dozen pigs brought to Cuba in 1498 were estimated to have increased in number to 30,000 only sixteen years later.

connecting TO TODAY

1. What was the Columbian Exchange?

2. a) Name two foods that "migrated" from the Americas to Europe.
   b) Name two foods that "migrated" to the Americas.

3. **Critical Thinking** Give an example that shows how the introduction of new foods can have negative consequences.

4. **Hands-On Activity** Create a poster called "Transatlantic Gourmet." (*Transatlantic* means "across the Atlantic Ocean.") Draw a map of the world on the poster and label the Americas, Europe, and Africa. Next to the Americas, paste pictures from newspapers and magazines of foods brought across the Atlantic. Next to Europe and Africa, place pictures of foods taken there from the Americas.

SECTIONS

1	**A Land Defined by Mountains**

2	**A Place of Three Cultures**

Mexico: POLITICAL

KEY

— State boundary
⊗ National capital
• Other city

Lambert Azimuthal Equal-Area Projection

| 0 | 200 | 400 mi |
| 0 | 200 | 400 km |

UNITED STATES

Tijuana

BAJA CALIFORNIA

SONORA

Ciudad Juárez

CHIHUAHUA

COAHUILA

Gulf of California

BAJA CALIFORNIA SUR

DURANGO

SINALOA

NUEVO LEÓN

Monterrey • Matamoros

MEXICO

Gulf of Mexico

Tropic of Cancer

Mazatlán

ZACATECAS

TAMAULIPAS

AGUASCALIENTES

SAN LUIS POTOSÍ

PACIFIC OCEAN

NAYARIT

Puerto Vallarta

GUANAJUATO

QUERÉTARO

HIDALGO

Guadalajara

JALISCO

DISTRITO FEDERAL

México City

TLAXCALA

Bay of Campeche

YUCATÁN

QUINTANA ROO

Manzanillo

MICHOACÁN

MÉXICO

MORELOS

PUEBLA

Veracruz

VERACRUZ

TABASCO

CAMPECHE

COLIMA

GUERRERO

Acapulco

OAXACA

CHIAPAS

CENTRAL AMERICA

Mapping the Region

Create a map like the one above. Then add labels for cities and bodies of water that are shown on the map.

A Land Defined by Mountains

Section Preview

Main Ideas

- Mountains dominate the landscape of Mexico.

- Mexico's central plateau region is the heartland of the country.

- Mexico's coastal regions are very different in landforms and other physical characteristics.

Vocabulary

peninsula, irrigation, sinkhole

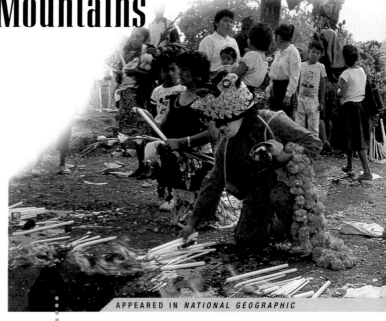

APPEARED IN *NATIONAL GEOGRAPHIC*

Festivalgoers pray for rain in the mountains of Guerro, Mexico.

According to an old story, Charles V, the ruler of Spain, asked Hernan Cortés, the Spanish explorer who conquered Mexico, to describe the country's physical features. Cortés answered by crumpling a piece of paper and throwing it on the table. The wrinkled paper represented what Cortés could not describe in words: Mexico's rugged terrain.

Mountains dominate Mexico's physical setting. The largest mountain range, the Sierra Madre (see EHR uh MAH dray) Occidental, extends along the western coast. Mexico's second great mountain range, the Sierra Madre Oriental, runs parallel to the eastern coast, along the Gulf of Mexico. Between the Sierra Madres—which means "mother ranges"—lies Mexico's largest region, the central plateau.

Between the mountains and the ocean are Mexico's different coastal plains regions. The northern Pacific coast includes Baja (BAH hah) California, a **peninsula**, or strip of land that juts out into the Pacific Ocean. In spite of its name, which means "Lower California," it is part of Mexico. The southern Pacific coast, south of the central plateau, is a narrow strip of tropical coastline. The resort city of Acapulco is located at the midpoint of the southern Pacific coast.

On the east, the Gulf coastal plain curves around the Gulf of Mexico into the Yucatán Peninsula. The Yucatán, set apart from the rest of Mexico, sticks out into the Gulf like a thumb.

Mexico's Heartland

The central plateau is Mexico's most important and populous region, with several large cities. The southern part of the plateau, nourished by rich soil and plenty of rainfall, has Mexico's best farmland. About four fifths of the country's people live here.

Geological Dangers Mexico's central plateau is geologically unstable, however. The reason, as the plate tectonics map on page 43 shows, is that Mexico is located at the intersection of four tectonic plates—the North American Plate, the Caribbean Plate, the Pacific Plate, and the Cocos Plate. As the plates move, slide, or collide, they have pushed up jagged mountain ranges. Some of the mountains on the southern edge of the plateau are active volcanoes. In addition, earthquakes often shake the land. In 1985, a strong earthquake struck Mexico City, killing an estimated 7,000 people and causing $4.1 billion in damage.

Climate Factors In spite of these dangers, other factors make Mexico's central plateau an attractive place to live. Climate is a major reason. In much of northern Mexico, the towering Sierra Madres block rainfall coming from the ocean. Some arid sections receive less than 4 inches (10 cm) of precipitation each year. Farther south, though, moist ocean winds find their way through the mountains to bring rain to the lower end of the plateau. Compare the annual precipitation and population maps on page 203, noticing where population is densest.

Elevation is a key factor in the climate of the central plateau. Although the southern part of the plateau is in the tropics, its climate is not tropical. The high elevation, averaging about 7,000 feet (2,100 m), keeps temperatures mild and makes the climate pleasant year round. Mexico City, at about 7,340 feet (2,240 m) above sea level, enjoys moderate temperatures. The average high temperature is 74°F (23°C) in July, 66°F (19°C) in January.

Drawn partly by Mexico City's attractive climate, scores of people have flocked to the city in search of a better life. The city is now encircled by *ciudadas peridas* or "lost cities." Many of the city's arrivals are underemployed—working, but earning little money. Families live on about four dollars a day.

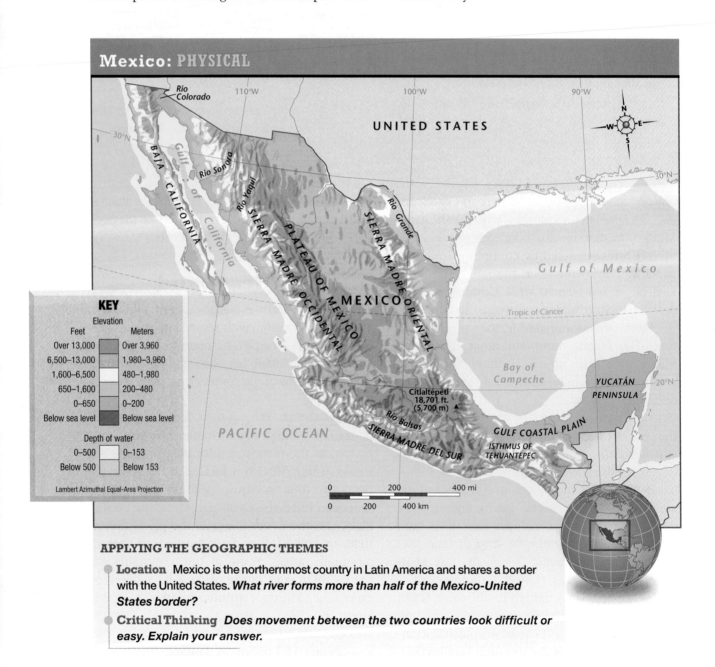

Mexico: PHYSICAL

KEY

Elevation

Feet		Meters
Over 13,000		Over 3,960
6,500–13,000		1,980–3,960
1,600–6,500		480–1,980
650–1,600		200–480
0–650		0–200
Below sea level		Below sea level

Depth of water

0–500		0–153
Below 500		Below 153

Lambert Azimuthal Equal-Area Projection

Citlaltépeti 18,701 ft. (5,700 m) ▲

0   200   400 mi

0   200   400 km

APPLYING THE GEOGRAPHIC THEMES

● **Location** Mexico is the northernmost country in Latin America and shares a border with the United States. *What river forms more than half of the Mexico-United States border?*

● **Critical Thinking** *Does movement between the two countries look difficult or easy. Explain your answer.*

In the past such newcomers were treated as illegal squatters. Today they are legally allowed to own small parcels of land after having lived on them for five years. Schools have improved and electrical services are now provided.

The Coastal Regions

Mexico's coastal plains regions are a study in contrasts. As the map on page 202 shows, the rugged mountains dictate the width of the plains. The plains are widest along the Gulf coast and the northern Pacific coast, stretching inland as much as 80 miles (130 km) before rising up to meet the mountains. On the southern Pacific coast, mountains crowd close to the ocean, leaving a coastal plain that is often only 15 miles (24 km) wide.

Northern Pacific Coast Dry, hot, and for the most part thinly populated describes Mexico's northern Pacific coast. The city of Tijuana (tee WAH nuh), just across the border from the state of California, is one of Mexico's fastest-growing cities. Despite its arid climate, this region has some of the best farmland in the country. The reason is **irrigation**, the artificial watering of farmland by storing and distributing water drawn from reservoirs or rivers. Dams have been built on three widely spaced rivers— the Colorado, the Sonora, and the Yaquí [yah KEE]—making it possible for farmers to raise wheat, cotton, and other crops.

By contrast, the Baja California peninsula is a long, thin arm—760 miles (1,223 km) in length—of mostly mountainous desert. An American who visited Baja California described an overnight trip into Baja's desert in August in this way:

As we drove south . . . we passed the canteen back and forth in a kind of trance, lulled by heat waves rising off the pavement. I wiped dust from the little plastic thermometer I'd clipped to my bag; it read 110 degrees. The scene out our window was a no-man's-land of reddish volcanic mountains and scorched vegetation. Mars with cactus.

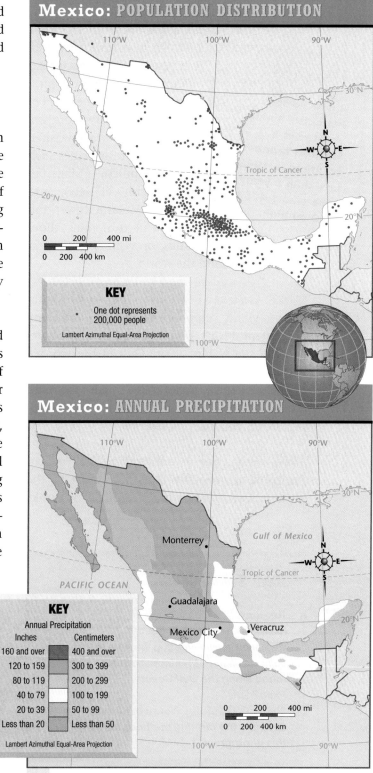

Mexico: POPULATION DISTRIBUTION

KEY

One dot represents 200,000 people

Lambert Azimuthal Equal-Area Projection

Mexico: ANNUAL PRECIPITATION

Monterrey

PACIFIC OCEAN

Gulf of Mexico

Tropic of Cancer

Guadalajara

Mexico City Veracruz

KEY

Annual Precipitation

Inches	Centimeters
160 and over	400 and over
120 to 159	300 to 399
80 to 119	200 to 299
40 to 79	100 to 199
20 to 39	50 to 99
Less than 20	Less than 50

Lambert Azimuthal Equal-Area Projection

APPLYING THE GEOGRAPHIC THEMES

- **Location** Compare the two maps above. *How is the amount of annual rainfall related to the distribution of Mexico's population?*
- **Critical Thinking** *What might account for this relationship between rainfall and population?*

Southern Pacific Coast A smaller mountain range, the steep-sided Sierra Madre del Sur, edges the narrow southern Pacific coast. There is little farmland, but the region's spectacular natural setting and tropical climate favor another kind of economic activity—tourism. The sunny, wave-washed beaches of resort cities such as Acapulco, Mazatlán (mah suh TLAHN), and Puerto Vallarta (pwer toh vah YAR tuh) draw thousands of visitors each year from around the world.

Gulf Coastal Plain The Gulf coastal plain is vitally important to Mexico's economy in a different way. Along the plain and offshore, beneath the waters of the Gulf of Mexico, are vast deposits of petroleum and natural gas. These geological riches have made the Gulf coastal plain one of the world's major oil-producing regions.

The Yucatán Peninsula The Yucatán Peninsula is generally flat, in contrast to the mountains that cover much of Mexico. Unlike the volcanic soil that covers the land in other regions, the bedrock that underlies the Yucatán is porous limestone. When rain falls here, it seeps through the surface of the land, working its way into the rock. The limestone is gradually dissolved, creating underground caverns. Periodically the roof of a cavern collapses, and a **sinkhole** is formed. The landscape of the Yucatán is dotted with sinkholes, which the ancient Maya used as wells.

Facts in **BRIEF**

Country	Population	Life Expectancy *(years)*	Per Capita GNP *(in US $)*
Mexico	93,700,000	72	3,750
United States	263,200,000	76	24,750

Source: Population Reference Bureau

CHART SKILLS

● *Which country has the higher per capita GNP?*

● **Critical Thinking** *Which country has the larger population? What factors contribute to population growth?*

How Sweet It Is!

● **Regions** Sugar cane is one of Mexico's chief crops. The sugar plantation shown here is in the state of Veracruz. *What other industries are found along the Gulf Coastal Plain?*

● **Critical Thinking** *How would you describe the farming methods in this photograph?*

Baja California

● **Place** Stark, dry, and largely uninhabited, Baja California has few resources. However, interest in its harsh beauty, miles and miles of coastline, and rich sport-fishing grounds—along with the development of a peninsular highway—have created a growing tourist industry.

● **Critical Thinking** *What are the benefits of tourism in a place like Baja California? What are the potential drawbacks?*

Despite its level terrain, the population is fairly sparse in the Yucatán. Mérida, with a population of 400,000 people, is the largest city in the region. Tourism along the Caribbean coastline has greatly influenced development in cities such as Cancún and San Miguel. Ancient Mayan ruins attract both tourists and archaeologists seeking to learn more about the ancient empires and people that once populated the Yucatán. You can learn more about the ancient Mayan city of Chichén Itzá on pages 214–215.

Section 1 Review

Vocabulary and Main Ideas

1. Define: a. peninsula b. irrigation c. sinkhole

2. How does geography help explain why most Mexicans live in the central plateau?

3. What is the chief economic activity along Mexico's southern Pacific coast? Why?

4. Critical Thinking: *Analyzing Evidence* Why would sinkholes have been important as a water source in the Yucatán?

5. What mountain ranges define Mexico's central plateau on the east and the west?

6. The Colorado, Sonora, and Yaquí rivers, used for irrigation, empty into the same body of water. What is it? Which of the three rivers originates in the United States?

Focus on Skills

☑ Social Studies

☐ Map and Globe

☐ Critical Thinking and Problem Solving

Interpreting Population Pyramids

A population pyramid is a type of bar graph that shows the percentages of males and females by age group in a given country. By its shape, a population pyramid also shows whether a population is growing or declining. If the pyramid is wide at its base, the population is growing. If the pyramid is narrow at its base, the population is declining. A graph with a nearly rectangular shape indicates a population that is neither growing nor declining.

Use the following steps to read and interpret the population pyramid at the right.

1. Study the graph to become familiar with how information is presented. Population pyramids present information in a certain way. The vertical axis shows age. The horizontal axis shows percentage of population. One side of the pyramid shows the male population. The other side shows the female population. (a) Which side of the population pyramid for Mexico shows the male population? (b) How many age groups are represented on the vertical axis?

2. Practice reading the information shown in the population pyramid. Each bar in the pyramid represents a percentage of people in a certain age range. For example, the bar at the bottom of the pyramid represents people age 4 and under. The horizontal axis shows that 14 percent of the males are in this age group and about 13 percent of the females are in this age group. Add the two numbers together and divide by 2 to see that 13.5 percent of the total population is age 4 and under. Each full square represents 1 percent of the total population, so you could count the number of squares and get the same answer. (a) What percentage of Mexico's population is between the ages of 5 and 9? (b) What percentage of Mexico's population is between the ages of 25 and 29?

3. Look for relationships among data. A population pyramid is helpful in detecting characteristics of a population. For instance, the shape of the pyramid can tell you if a population is evenly divided among young and old or males and females. Answer the following questions: (a) Are the majority of people in Mexico under age 40? (b) Is the population of Mexico equally divided between males and females?

4. Use the graphs to draw conclusions. Population pyramids can provide clues that help you draw conclusions about a country's population. Answer the following questions: (a) Is the population of Mexico growing or declining? (b) How might demands for housing, food, and health care be affected by Mexico's population?

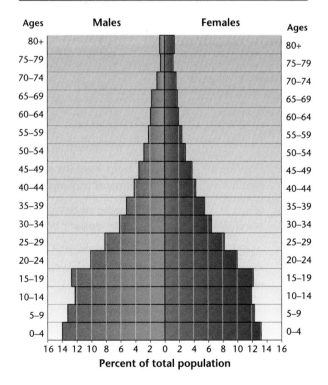

Mexico: Population Pyramid

Source: United Nations

2 A Place of Three Cultures

Section Preview

Main Ideas

- Mexico is composed of three cultures—ancient Indian, colonial Spanish, and modern Mexican.

- Spain overthrew the Aztec rulers in 1521 and ruled Mexico as a colony for three hundred years.

- Since gaining independence, Mexico has become a democratic republic but is still working to improve social justice and economic opportunities.

- Most Mexicans live in urban areas, while poverty and poor land are problems for rural farmers.

Vocabulary

hacienda, land redistribution, *ejido*, subsistence farming, *latifundio*, cash crop, migrant worker

Unearthed during subway construction, an Aztec temple gives testimony to Mexico's past.

A broad square in Mexico City stands as a symbol of the complexity of Mexican culture. The Plaza de las Tres Culturas—the Three Cultures—is located on the site of an Aztec center that fell to the Spanish in a 1521 battle. In the center are the restored ruins of an Aztec temple pyramid. On one side of the square is a church built by the Spanish conquerors in 1609. On another side, twin office buildings of glass and concrete represent Mexico's modern culture. A busy eight-lane highway runs past the plaza.

Together, these three cultures—Indian, Spanish, and modern—make up modern Mexico. The result is a nation aware of the traditions of the past and the possibilities of the future.

From Empire to Colony

Drawing on elements from earlier cultures, the Aztecs built the most powerful empire in early Mexico. By the early 1400s, their capital city of Tenochtitlán (teh noch tee TLAHN) was the center of an empire that spread over much of south-central Mexico. Tenochtitlán, built on an island in a lake, occupied the site of modern Mexico City. On its main square were great temples and the palaces of Aztec royalty. The city had open plazas and huge marketplaces. In the 1400s, it was one of the largest cities in the world. An estimated 60,000 Aztecs gathered each day to trade goods.

The Spanish Conquest Spanish adventurer Hernan Cortés, with six hundred Spanish soldiers, marched into Tenochtitlán in 1519. The Spaniards had come inland from Mexico's Gulf coast, making allies of the Aztecs' enemies along the way. Within two years, the conquistadors, or conquerors, destroyed the Aztec empire. Tenochtitlán and other Aztec towns lay in ruins. The Spanish then went on to conquer the remaining Indian groups in Mexico. The territory won by Cortés became the colony of New Spain.

Tenochtitlán

DIAGRAM STUDY

● Shown above is the central plaza of the ancient Aztecs' bustling capital, Tenochtitlán, as it might have appeared before the Spanish conquest. Tenochtitlán contained temples, administrative buildings, sports arenas, and marketplaces. **Critical Thinking** *How was Tenochtitlán similar to modern capital cities?*

New Spain Four social classes emerged as the Spanish settled New Spain. At the top were the *peninsulares* (peh nin suh LAHR es). This group, those born in Spain, held high official positions. The next highest group were the *criollos* (cree OHL yos), people of Spanish ancestry born in the Americas. Mestizos, people of mixed ancestry, ranked third, and the Indians ranked lowest. Over the next three hundred years, life in New Spain followed these strict social lines.

As in other Spanish colonies in the Americas, Indians provided the labor on **haciendas** (hah see EN duhs). These were large, Spanish-owned estates of land, usually run as farms or cattle ranches. Both the haciendas and the Indians who worked on them were granted to the conquistadors as rewards by the Spanish king. Under this system, known as the *encomienda*, landowners were supposed to care for their workers' welfare. But in fact low wages and constant debt forced most Indians to live a slave-like existence.

Road to Democracy

Spanish colonial rule continued into the early 1800s. Then the resentment the *criollos* felt for the privileged *peninsulares* erupted into conflict. In 1810 a *criollos* priest named Miguel Hidalgo called for a rebellion against Spanish rule. His cry sparked a war of independence. By 1821, the independent nation of Mexico was established.

But while Mexico had finally achieved independence, the new nation was not democratic. The search for democracy took about another hundred years. During that time, the country went through a series of political struggles and even a civil war. Strong military leaders ruled as dictators, while the people wanted democracy.

By the end of the 1800s, Mexico was stable enough to attract large amounts of foreign capital and industry. Railroads were built, ranches were expanded, and Mexico's valuable oil reserves were developed. Such efforts to modernize the country, however, mainly helped wealthy Mexicans become even wealthier. The gap between rich and poor, established in colonial times, continued unchanged.

The Mexican Revolution In 1910, peasants and middle-class Mexicans rebelled. In the Mexican Revolution, they stood up to the military dictator and the landlords who together controlled the country. By the time the fighting ended in 1920, Mexico had a new president and a new constitution. The new government promised "land, bread, and justice for all."

The democratic republic established by the Mexican Revolution remains in place today. Mexico, like the United States, is a federal republic headed by an elected president and congress. Unlike the United States, however, one political party, the Institutional Revolutionary Party (PRI), has held power continuously. In the late 1990s, it was clear that government and politics in Mexico were troubled by corruption. A political clean-up seemed vital for economic success.

Mexico Today

Mexico has worked to preserve both its Indian and Spanish heritages. Nearly all Mexicans use Spanish as their official language. People of Indian descent, however, often speak their ancestral languages at home. The constitution grants freedom of religion, but most Mexicans are Roman Catholics.

Although Mexico has made great economic strides in modern times, a minority still holds much of the country's wealth. The country is still working to achieve social justice and create economic opportunities for more people.

Rural Life Most people in the Mexican countryside work in agriculture. In 1910 nearly all Mexican land that could be used for farming was part of about 8,000 haciendas. After the revolution, the government began a program of buying out landowners and breaking up their large haciendas. The estates were divided among landless peasants. The government still follows this policy of **land redistribution**. About half of the haciendas have been broken up in this way.

The government awarded most of the reclaimed land in the form of *ejidos* (ay HEE doz), farmland owned collectively by members of a rural community. Many *ejido* farmers practice **subsistence farming**. They grow only enough crops to meet their family's needs.

Approximately one third of Mexican farms, however, are huge commercial farms owned by individuals or by farming companies. These commercial farms are called *latifundios.* Mexico's commercial farms and some *ejidos* raise **cash crops**, farm crops grown for sale and profit, such

Modern Cowboys

Regions Mexican cowboys today still ride in the harsh lands of the north. They work on ranches that raise beef cattle. Many ranchers face competition from imported U.S. beef. Many hope to improve business by buying United States cattle breeds that give more meat of a higher quality. *How did the ranches of New Spain, the haciendas, operate?*

Air Pollution

As one way to reduce Mexico City's choking, eye-stinging air pollution, access by automobiles is restricted. Depending on its license number, every car is banned from the city streets at least one day a week.

as corn, sugar cane, coffee, and fruit.

An estimated 3 to 4 million rural Mexican families have neither the land nor opportunities for work. Some try to coax crops from land unsuitable for farming. Many landless, jobless peasants become **migrant workers**. That is, they travel from place to place where extra workers are needed to cultivate or harvest crops. At harvest time many migrant workers also cross the Rio Grande into the United States. While some have permits to cross the border, others cross illegally.

Urban Life The heart of modern Mexican culture is its urban areas, where more than two thirds of Mexico's population lives. Mexico City is one of the largest urban areas in the world and is still growing. For many Mexicans, city life means better economic opportunities than those found in the countryside. Cities also offer chances for education and excitement.

Although there is a small, wealthy, educated upper class in the cities, most urban dwellers in Mexico are the very poor and must struggle to survive. A growing middle class includes government workers, professionals, and business owners. Mexico's working-class citizens are generally skilled workers who maintain strong ties to traditional Mexican culture. They may live in adobe-block houses in older neighborhoods or in new worker apartment complexes.

Mexico's Economy

With the passage of the North American Free Trade Agreement (NAFTA) in 1993, many Mexicans hoped their struggling economy would improve. NAFTA was designed to compete with the European Union. It phased out trade barriers between the United States, Canada, and Mexico. Mexicans hoped that it would help them lower unemployment, increase manufacturing, and raise the standard of living. Results in the first few years were disappointing, however.

Major Industries Two of Mexico's most important economic activities are petroleum extraction and tourism. Great reserves of petroleum were first discovered in 1901 off Mexico's Gulf coast near the city of Tampico. Pemex (Petroleos Mexicanos) is the state-owned oil company.

Climate, scenery, tropical beaches, and a rich cultural history make tourism a major source of

APPEARED IN *NATIONAL GEOGRAPHIC*

Tourism in Mexico

● **Place** Every year hundreds of thousands of tourists from around the world flock to the resort city of Cancún. One look at Cancún helps explain why tourism is a multi-billion dollar industry in Mexico. *For what reason is Mexico popular with tourists?*

income for Mexico. Since Acapulco became a popular international tourist destination in the 1950s, national and foreign investment in tourism has exploded. Another resort area grew up around the planned city of Cancún.

Tourism is important for another reason. Manufacturing has long contributed to Mexico's economy, with Mexico City as the country's leading industrial center. But factories create a heavy load of pollution. In Mexico City, particularly, polluted air from factories and cars collects over the city because mountains trap the air on three sides. Tourism is a cleaner economic alternative. In fact, Mexicans call it the "smokeless industry."

Border Industries Clustered along the United States-Mexico border are more than two thousand *maquiladoras*. These are factories that assemble products almost exclusively for consumers in the United States. Together, these factories employ more than 450,000 people and bring more than $3.5 billion into Mexico each year. *Maquiladoras* have profoundly changed the appearance of cities in northern Mexico.

Despite the benefits that *maquiladoras* have brought to Mexico, many people have expressed concerns about the rapid expansion of the factories. Although many new jobs have been created, critics argue that most of them provide tedious work for low pay. Concerns have also been expressed regarding the impact of *maquiladoras* on health and the environment. Many factories have been accused of air and water pollution and

Borderline Business

● **Location** Eleven percent of Mexican workers have jobs in industry. The people in this photograph work in a *maquiladora*. *Why are* maquiladoras *located along the United States-Mexico border?*

improper disposal of waste products. The Mexican government continues to encourage job growth while monitoring the impact of industry on the environment.

Section 2 Review

Vocabulary and Main Ideas

1. **Define: a. hacienda b. land redistribution c. *ejido* d. subsistence farming e. *latifundio* f. cash crop g. migrant worker**

2. **What three cultural strands contributed to Mexico's culture?**

3. **Name two of Mexico's most important economic activities.**

4. **Critical Thinking:** *Identifying Central Issues* **What major problems do many rural Mexicans face? How do these relate to the country's history and geography?**

learning LOCATIONS

5. **Name the river that runs between Mexico and the United States.**

6. **Cancún, Puerto Vallarta, and Acapulco are all popular beach vacation spots. Where in Mexico are they located?**

Summarizing Main Ideas

Section 1 A Land Defined by Mountains

- Two mountain ranges, the Sierra Madre Oriental and the Sierra Madre Occidental, dominate Mexico's landscape and divide the country into regions.
- Mexico's central plateau is the largest and most populous region, where the country's major cities are located. The region has a generally moderate, pleasant climate, although earthquakes are a threat.
- Mexico's three coastal regions—northern Pacific, southern Pacific, and Gulf coastal plain—are very different in landforms and other physical characteristics. The flat Yucatán Peninsula is a separate region.

Section 2 A Place of Three Cultures

- Mexican culture draws on three sources— ancient Indian, colonial Spanish, and modern Mexican.
- Spanish culture was introduced in the early 1500s, when Spanish conquistadors overthrew the Aztec empire and ruled Mexico for 300 years as the colony of New Spain.
- Mexico gained independence in the early 1800s but did not become a democracy until the Mexican Revolution of 1912.
- More than 70 percent of Mexicans live in urban areas. Poverty and a lack of land are problems for farmers in rural areas.
- Petroleum extraction, tourism, and manufacturing are important in the Mexican economy. The country is working to improve its economy and its people's lives.

Reviewing Vocabulary

Use each of the following terms in a sentence that shows its meaning. You may use two terms in one sentence.

1. **peninsula**
2. **irrigation**
3. **sinkhole**
4. **hacienda**
5. *ejido*
6. **land redistribution**
7. *latifundio*
8. **subsistence farming**
9. **cash crop**
10. **migrant worker**

Applying the Geographic Themes

1. **Place** What three strands make up the culture of modern Mexico?
2. **Location** Describe the physical location of Mexico's central plateau and the landforms that define it.
3. **Human-Environment Interaction** What factors encourage and discourage people from settling in Mexico's central plateau? Which group of factors have proved stronger?
4. **Movement** Why do most of Mexico's people live in cities?
5. **Regions** How is the Yucatán Peninsula different from Mexico's other regions?

Critical Thinking and Applying Skills

1. **Identifying Central Issues** Mexicans sometimes say that the Mexican Revolution is still going on. In what respect might this be true?
2. **Interpreting a Population Pyramid** Refer to the population pyramid on page 206 to answer the following questions.

   a. Developing nations have young populations. How does the pyramid show that Mexico has a young population?

   b. If Mexico's population had an equal number of young and old people, what shape would the pyramid be?

Journal Activity

Writing Across Cultures

▶ 1. Look at the photograph on page 207. What symbols can you see that illustrate the cultures that make up Mexico's heritage? Write a short poem describing your reactions to this photograph.

▶ 2. People in both Mexico and parts of the Caribbean frequently face the threat of volcanic eruptions and earthquakes. Research one of these disasters—recent or historic—and write a short "on the scene" news story that gives your readers or listeners a vivid mental picture of what is happening.

Find out more about the Aztec language. Link to this site from:

- www.phschool.com

After reading the information offered, list the Nahuatl words that are most similar to their English counterparts.

Mexico

Number from 1 to 6 on a piece of paper. Next to each number, write the letter of the place on the map that corresponds to each of the places listed below.

1. Guadalajara
2. Acapulco
3. Gulf of Mexico
4. Yucatán Peninsula
5. Mexico City
6. Baja California

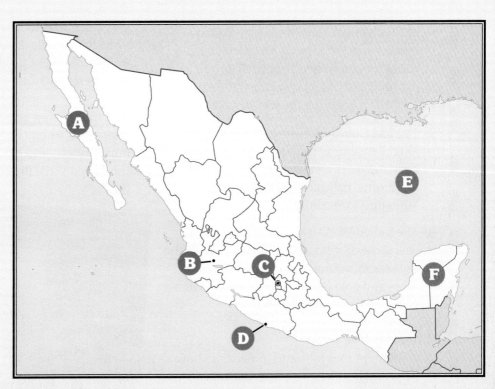

Map Skills *for Life*

Skill: Reading an Archaeological Site Map
Setting: Touring Chichén Itzá, Mexico

Concha Gisbert and her classmates from a school in Merida, Mexico, are on a school trip to Chichén Itzá (chee CHEN eet SAH) in Mexico's Yucatán peninsula. On this site are many remarkable stone buildings from the culture of the ancient Maya. The most famous were built during the 11th to 13th centuries A.D.

During their visit, Concha and her friends especially want to see these famous structures:

★ El Castillo, or "the Castle," the huge, square central pyramid that has become the symbol of Chichén Itzá. The Maya were skilled astronomers, who created a complicated calendar. Researchers believe that the pyramid and other buildings at the site were related to observing the sun and stars.

★ The Ball Court, a long field flanked by two long platforms with terraces for spectators. Carvings on the walls show scenes from the ceremonial ball game played in several Mesoamerican cultures.

★ The Sacred Well, or cenote, a large natural well some 65 yards (60 meters) across. In the dry season, young people, dressed in fine robes and gold jewelry, were sacrificed in its waters to Chac, the rain god.

Reading the Map

Read the steps that follow to understand how Concha and her classmates can use a site map to find the buildings they most want to see.

1. Find the starting location on the map. Notice where the Parking and Tourist Center are located. This is where visitors enter the site. If Concha and her friends follow the marked path, what structure will they see directly ahead of them as they come through the entrance gate into the archaeological site?

2. Locate the specific places to see. A site map draws outlines of buildings to show their shape and size, as if one were looking at them from above. Chichén Itzá has several ball courts, but the main one is much larger than the others. **(a)** How can Concha use the map to find the right Ball Court? **(b)** Where is it?

3. Plan a route that includes the selected sites, and keep the map handy to find the way from one to another. (a) What is the best route for Concha and her friends? **(b)** As Concha walks around El Castillo, what other structures can she see? **(c)** Can she fit them in on her route?

4. Use the map scale to determine the distances between sites. (a) What route must Concha and her group take in order to see the Sacred Well? **(b)** About how far must they walk?

Chichén Itzá • Mexico

Chichén Itzá Site Map

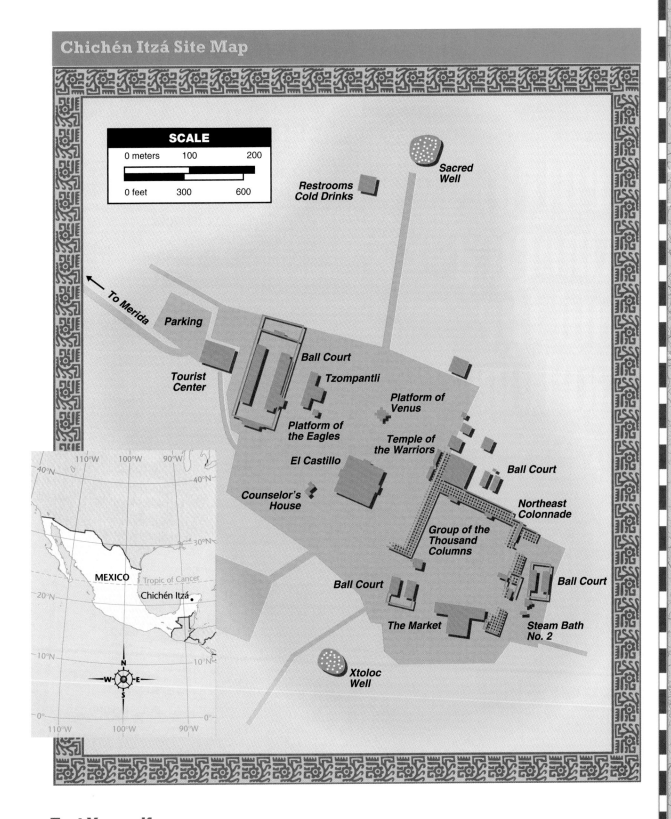

SCALE

0 meters	100	200

0 feet	300	600

Restrooms
Cold Drinks

Sacred Well

To Merida

Parking

Tourist Center

Ball Court

Tzompantli

Platform of Venus

Platform of the Eagles

Temple of the Warriors

El Castillo

Ball Court

Northeast Colonnade

Counselor's House

Group of the Thousand Columns

Ball Court

Ball Court

The Market

Steam Bath No. 2

Xtoloc Well

MEXICO

Tropic of Cancer

Chichén Itzá

Test Yourself

1. The weather in the Yucatán is often hot and dry. Can Concha and her friends stop for a cold drink on the way to the Sacred Well, or must they go back to the Tourist Center?

2. When Concha climbs to the top of El Castillo, she can see an open plaza and an L-shaped platform dotted with hundreds of broken columns. Looking at the map, she identifies this building. What is it?

Central America and the Caribbean

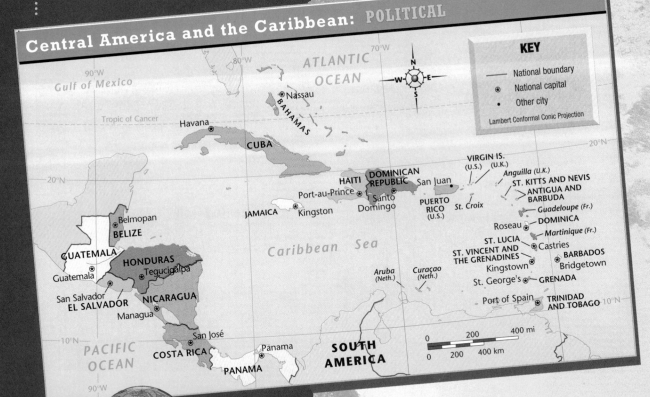

Central America and the Caribbean: POLITICAL

KEY

— National boundary

⊛ National capital

• Other city

Lambert Conformal Conic Projection

ATLANTIC OCEAN

Gulf of Mexico

Tropic of Cancer

Nassau

BAHAMAS

Havana ⊛

CUBA

VIRGIN IS. (U.S.)

Anguilla (U.K.)

ST. KITTS AND NEVIS

ANTIGUA AND BARBUDA

HAITI

DOMINICAN REPUBLIC

San Juan

Port-au-Prince ⊛

⊛ Santo Domingo

PUERTO RICO (U.S.)

St. Croix

Guadeloupe (Fr.)

DOMINICA

JAMAICA

Kingston

Roseau ⊛

Martinique (Fr.)

Belmopan

BELIZE

Caribbean Sea

ST. LUCIA

ST. VINCENT AND THE GRENADINES

Castries

BARBADOS

GUATEMALA

HONDURAS

Tegucigalpa ⊛

Kingstown

Bridgetown

Guatemala ⊛

Aruba (Neth.)

Curaçao (Neth.)

St. George's ⊛ GRENADA

San Salvador ⊛

EL SALVADOR

NICARAGUA

Managua ⊛

Port of Spain ⊛ TRINIDAD AND TOBAGO

San José ⊛

PACIFIC OCEAN

Panama ⊛

COSTA RICA

PANAMA

SOUTH AMERICA

0   200   400 mi

0   200   400 km

learning LOCATIONS

Mapping the Region

Create a map like the one above, shading each country a different color. Then add labels for countries and bodies of water that are shown on the map.

① Central America

Section Preview

Main Ideas

Central America is an area with diverse physical landscapes and climates.

Agriculture dominates the economy, and the vast majority of people are subsistence farmers.

Large gaps between rich and poor have given power to a few people and led to violent political conflicts.

Vocabulary

isthmus, guerrilla, caudillo

APPEARED IN *NATIONAL GEOGRAPHIC*

This Guatemalan woman is weaving a blanket with a colorful design. Weaving is an ancient Indian art.

The small region of Central America curves between the giant land masses of North America and South America. Central America is an **isthmus**—a narrow strip of land, with water on both sides, that connects two larger bodies of land. Central America thus forms a land bridge between the two continents.

Until 1914, Central America greatly hindered movement of people and goods between the Atlantic and Pacific oceans. In that year, the opening of the Panama Canal made it possible for ships to cross the isthmus and sail between the two oceans. Many days were saved because ships did not have to travel thousands of extra miles around the tip of South America.

Seven countries occupy this narrow, curving strip of land between Mexico and Colombia. Beginning in the north, they are Belize, Guatemala, Honduras, El Salvador, Nicaragua, Costa Rica, and Panama. As the map on page 218 shows, these countries are small in area, with a combined land area only about one fourth the size of Mexico. However, packed into this small region is a diverse physical and human landscape as complex as the designs in traditional Indian clothing. This great complexity explains many of the challenges that Central America faces today.

Landforms and Climate

Naturalist Jonathan Evan Maslow captured the physical diversity of Central America in this description of Guatemala:

> *Up and down, round and round, the countryside never stayed the same more than a few miles at a stretch. . . . Granite heights that looked clawed by blind and angry titans [giants] pitched into patches of lowland rain forest . . . it was like an entire continent stuffed as in an expertly packed suitcase into a country the size of Massachusetts.*

This narrative could be used to describe many of the countries in this region. While the landscape of most of Central America is widely

◀ **Half Moon Bay, Antigua Island** (photo left)

varied, even this diverse landscape can be divided into regions. Three major landform regions make up Central America—the mountainous core, the Caribbean lowlands, and the Pacific coastal plain. Each landform region has its own climate.

The Mountainous Core As in Mexico, mountains run the length of Central America, some towering more than 13,000 feet (4,000 m) above sea level. These rugged mountains are difficult to cross, causing serious problems for transportation in the region. Many of these mountains are active volcanoes.

Two climate zones exist in the high elevations of Central America's mountainous core. Elevations between 3,000 and 6,000 feet (900 and 1,800 m) have a year-round, springlike climate, free of frosts but cool enough to grow corn, wheat, and coffee. Above 6,000 feet (1,800 m) the climate is cold. Because of frequent frosts, few crops besides potatoes and barley can grow at these elevations.

Caribbean Lowlands On the eastern side of Central America, the mountainous core gives way to lowlands that edge the Caribbean Sea. The Caribbean lowlands have a tropical wet climate—hot and humid with year-round high temperatures and heavy rainfall. Northeast trade winds may bring as much as 100 inches (250 cm) of rain in a year. Dense rain forest vegetation covers much of the land. The rain forest soil is not very fertile, limiting the crops that can be grown there.

Pacific Coastal Plain Unlike the Caribbean coast, the Pacific coast has a tropical wet and dry climate with savanna, or grassland, vegetation. The difference in climate on the two coasts is due to the moist winds that sweep from the northeast across the Caribbean

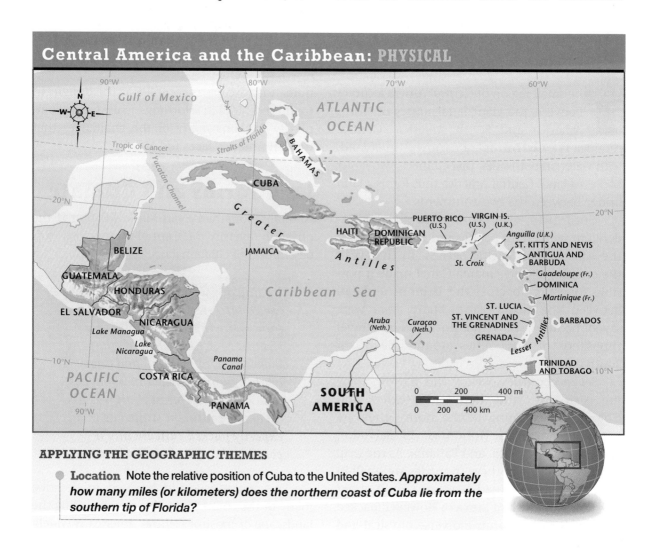

Central America and the Caribbean: PHYSICAL

APPLYING THE GEOGRAPHIC THEMES

● **Location** Note the relative position of Cuba to the United States. *Approximately how many miles (or kilometers) does the northern coast of Cuba lie from the southern tip of Florida?*

toward Central America. These winds drop rain on the Caribbean coast and the eastern mountain slopes throughout the year. In contrast, the Pacific coast can depend on rain only in the summer. Volcanoes high in the mountains above the Pacific coastal plain affect the land. Lava flows and deposits of volcanic ash make Pacific coast soils extremely fertile. During the rainy season, the land is lush and green.

Nicaragua's Pacific coastal plain has several freshwater lakes. The largest is Lago de Nicaragua, or Lake Nicaragua, a large oval lake scattered with small islands. It is more than 100 miles (160 km) long. Scientists believe that it was once a bay, cut off from the Pacific Ocean when a volcanic eruption created a ridge of mountains. Although the lake is freshwater, ocean creatures such as sharks and swordfish swim in its deep blue waters.

The Region's People

As the map on page 225 shows, Central America is home to several ethnic groups. Each group tends to be concentrated in a specific location. One reason for this is that throughout the region's history, the mountains have made it difficult for people to travel between areas and mingle with other groups.

Indians The people who have lived longest in Central America are the Indians. Each Indian group has a traditional home, as well as its own distinct history, culture, and language. The largest number of Central American Indians live in Guatemala. There they make up more than half the population.

Europeans and Mestizos Europeans arrived in Central America in the 1500s, when Spaniards conquered and colonized the region. Because of this history, Spanish is the official language in almost all of Central America. The exception is Belize, a former British colony, where the primary language is English.

The largest European settlement today is in Costa Rica, where 90 percent of the people are of European—mostly Spanish—descent. Another large group in Central America's population consists of people of mixed European and Indian

Ethnic Diversity

- **Regions** Central America is home to many ethnic groups. In general, each group is concentrated in a specific region. The Belizan boy shown above is of African descent. *When and how did Africans migrate to the region?*
- **Place** *Which ethnic group has lived in Central America for the longest time?*

background called mestizos. Both El Salvador and Nicaragua have large mestizo populations.

African Descent People of African descent are an important population group on Central America's Caribbean coast. Some are descendants of African slaves, who were brought to Central America as early as the 1500s. Most, however, are descended from people who migrated to the region from the Caribbean islands in the early 1900s. They came to work on banana plantations or to help build the Panama Canal.

Cutting Cane

Place Forty percent of El Salvador's labor force are agricultural workers. They often work long hours for little pay, like the sugar cane cutter shown here. El Salvador is facing a shortage of skilled workers, but has a large pool of unskilled labor. **Critical Thinking** *How might the size of the unskilled labor pool affect the wages of farm laborers?*

Wealth and Poverty

Most of the people of Central America are very poor. The wealthy constitute only a tiny percentage of the total population. Most of them are plantation owners and are European or mestizo. The rich dominate government and politics in the region.

At least two thirds of all Central Americans are poor, with little political power. They include millions of farmers who have little or no land, and laborers who earn low wages on plantations or in factories. Most are people of Indian and African descent.

The middle class is a small but very important third category in Central America's social structure. This group includes farmers who own small, non-commercial farmland and some employees of urban industries and services. Central America's middle class is a growing population, but it remains small in comparison with the millions of poor people.

GEOfacts

Belize has the longest coral reef in the Western Hemisphere. More than 250 miles (400 km) of atolls and lagoons are home to several species of dolphins and turtles.

A Farming Economy

The majority of Central America's people earn their living by some kind of farming. In Guatemala and Honduras, farming employs more than 50 percent of the people. Most of the rural population of Central America lives by subsistence farming. On small farms, using only their hands and a few basic tools, families labor to grow enough corn, beans, and squash to stay alive.

In sharp contrast are the large plantations owned by wealthy families and corporations. Plantation owners hire workers at very low wages and bring in the newest machines, fertilizers, and pesticides to produce cash crops of coffee, bananas, or cotton. Most of these crops are shipped to the United States or Europe. These cash crops account for well over half of Central America's income from exports.

Political Unrest

Picture deep-red coffee beans ripening in the warm sun and workers on ladders reaching to cut clumps of bananas from the trees. Now imagine the crack of gunfire and the sound of soldiers scrambling through mountain forests.

For years, these two images have contributed to the nature of Central America.

Armed conflicts have troubled Central America for much of its history. Each nation has specific problems, but some causes for conflict apply to the region as a whole. One important problem is the shortage of available farmland to meet the needs of a growing population, made worse by the unequal distribution of usable land.

In addition, recent governments in Central America have mainly served the interests of the wealthy. Opponents of those governments have sometimes organized **guerrilla** movements, armed forces outside the regular army, who often fight in small bands.

Nicaragua In 1979, a group called the Sandinistas (Sandinista Front for National Liberation) led a movement that overthrew Nicaragua's government. For 40 years the country had been controlled by the wealthy Somoza family. The Sandinistas governed the country under a socialist system, taking property from landowners and giving it to their supporters. Government control of agriculture and industry caused lower production and a drop in exports.

Soon other Nicaraguans, dissatisfied with these moves, tried to overthrow the Sandinista government, claiming it was turning the country toward communism. These guerrilla fighters were known as the *contras*, from the Spanish word for "against." Fighting between the two factions raged in Nicaragua and the borders of neighboring countries throughout the 1980s, causing thousands of deaths.

A cease-fire brought a measure of peace to Nicaragua in 1990. A new president, Violeta Chamorro (vee oh LEH tah chah MOH roh), took office in April 1990. For the first time in the country's history, power passed peacefully to a democratically elected government. Problems of poverty and unemployment grew worse during the 1990s, however.

El Salvador Political instability and violence have troubled other countries in Central America. In El Salvador, as landlessness among ordinary people increased, wealthy landowners feared a popular revolution. They hired "death squads" to eliminate political opponents who wanted reform. Between 1979 and 1992, El Salvador was the scene of a bloody civil war that involved the army, the death squads, and anti-government guerrillas. More than 70,000 people, many of them civilians, died. In 1992 a peace agreement mediated by the United Nations ended the war. With the

Nicaragua Today

Place A young man buys his lunch from a city sidewalk food vendor. Sixty-two percent of Nicaraguans are city dwellers. *Why has Nicaragua's economy suffered in the past two decades?*

peace agreement, the people of El Salvador looked forward to tackling the many challenges their nation faced.

Guatemala The most populous country in Central America, Guatemala has a political history similar to that of El Salvador and Nicaragua. After gaining independence from Spain in 1821, Guatemala was ruled by a series of **caudillos**, or military dictators. Following World War II, a liberal government was elected, ending the long-term dictatorship of Jorge Ubico.

In the decades that followed, the military gained power. Civil war erupted in the 1960s as leftist guerrilla movements challenged the harsh military regime. During the civil war, the government ruled through the heavy hand of "death squads" who routinely tortured and murdered critics, including student and labor leaders. More than 100,000 people were killed and another 40,000 "disappeared."

Guatemala returned to civilian rule in the mid-1980s, although the military remained a powerful force behind the scenes. The crisis-ridden government of President Jorge Serrano Elías was ousted by the military in 1993. Congress then elected Ramiro de León Carpio to complete the term. De León, who was re-elected in 1995, is respected internationally as a champion of human rights.

As the 30-year civil war tapered off in the 1990s, the United Nations worked to negotiate

Facts in BRIEF

Country	Population	Life Expectancy (years)	Per Capita GNP (in US $)
Belize	200,000	68	2,440
Costa Rica	3,300,000	76	2,160
El Salvador	5,900,000	68	1,320
Guatemala	10,600,000	65	1,110
Honduras	5,500,000	68	580
Nicaragua	4,400,000	65	360
Panama	2,600,000	72	2,580
United States	263,200,000	76	24,750

Source: Population Reference Bureau

CHART SKILLS

● *Which country, aside from the United States, has the highest GNP?*

● *Which country, aside from the United States, has the highest population?*

a settlement between the government and the guerrillas. A 1995 UN report blamed state authorities for the majority of human rights violations in Guatemala. For the first time, a number of police and military personnel were arrested for their "death squad" activities.

Section 1 Review

Vocabulary and Main Ideas

1. Define: a. isthmus b. guerrilla c. caudillo

2. Describe Central America's location relative to the United States.

3. What are Central America's three landform regions?

4. Critical Thinking: *Cause and Effect* How has Central America's history affected the four main ethnic groups and their positions in society?

learning LOCATIONS

5. Which Central American country or countries borders South America? Mexico?

6. Name the Central American country that does not have a Pacific coastline.

Focus on Skills

☑ Social Studies

☐ Map and Globe

☐ Critical Thinking and Problem Solving

Reading Tables and Analyzing Statistics

Tables are often used to present large amounts of data or statistics. Use the following steps to read and interpret the table shown below.

1. Determine what type of information is presented in the table. This table presents statistics from five different categories for three Latin American countries: population, urban population, per capita GNP, infant mortality, and life expectancy. GNP stands for *gross national product*, which means the total value of goods and services produced in a country in a year. Per capita GNP is the number you get when you divide the GNP by the country's population. The per capita GNP shows what each person's income would be if the country's income were divided equally among all of its people. Because this is not often the case, per capita GNP figures can be misleading. A country's infant mortality rate is the number of children who die before their first birthday, for every 1,000 live births. Life expectancy refers to the average number of years a person is likely to live. (a) What is the population of the Dominican Republic? (b) What is the infant mortality rate for El Salvador? (c) What is the life expectancy for people in Panama?

2. Find relationships among the figures. Tables help you to compare data. (a) How do the three countries rank in terms of per capita GNP? (b) How do the countries rank in terms of infant mortality? (c) What is the relationship between infant mortality and per capita GNP in the three countries?

3. Use the data to draw conclusions. Use the table to draw conclusions about the levels of population, wealth, and health care in these countries. For example, what is the relationship between a nation's wealth and its health services?

Population, Wealth, and Health Care for Three Latin American Countries

	El Salvador	Dominican Republic	Panama
1995 Population (in millions)	5.9	7.8	2.6
Urban population (percent)	46	61	54
Per capita GNP (in U.S. dollars)	1,320	1,080	2,580
Infant mortality rate (per 1,000 live births)	41	42	28
Life expectancy at birth (in years, at current mortality rates)	68	70	72

Source: Population Reference Bureau

2 The Caribbean Islands

Section Preview

Main Ideas

The Caribbean islands are located in the tropics and consist of three major island groups.

The people of the Caribbean are descendants of African, European, Native American, and Asian peoples.

Caribbean islanders have a tradition of migration, both within the islands and outside the region.

Vocabulary

archipelago, windward, leeward

Bananas and plantains are a vital part of Dominica's market economy.

A large billboard looms over the highway that connects the city of Santo Domingo with its airport. The billboard often features baseball players from the Dominican Republic endorsing soft drinks and other products. These players, though, have gained fame by playing baseball in the United States and Canada, not in their native land. The billboard symbolizes the predicament of many people who live on the Caribbean islands. Like those athletes, islanders from the Caribbean have had to travel to wealthier countries in search of opportunity.

The Caribbean is a beautiful region of forest-covered mountains, warm temperatures, and clear, blue waters. However, many Caribbean nations are struggling to develop their economies. That is one reason why some of its people have left the islands to find opportunities their homelands cannot yet offer.

A Tropical Location

As you learned in the Regional Atlas (Chapter 9), the Caribbean islands consist of three island groups: the Greater Antilles, the Lesser Antilles, and the Bahamas. Except for some of the islands in the Bahamas, all of the islands are located in the tropics.

The Greater Antilles include the four largest islands of the region—Cuba, Jamaica, Hispaniola (divided into the countries of Haiti and the Dominican Republic), and Puerto Rico. The Bahama **archipelago** (ar kih PEHL ih goh), or group of islands, includes nearly 700 islands northeast of Cuba. Most of the Lesser Antilles form another archipelago, a curving arc that separates the Caribbean Sea from the Atlantic Ocean. The rest, including Aruba, Trinidad and Tobago, and the Netherlands Antilles, hug the coast of South America.

Island Formations If you were to fly over the Caribbean islands, you would notice mountainous islands as well as islands with fairly level land. The varying landforms are the result of differing physical forces that shaped the islands. The Greater Antilles and some of the Lesser Antilles, including those just off the coast of South America, are the tops of volcanic mountains that have been pushed up from the ocean floor. These rugged islands generally slope from a central mountain to coastal plains. The western arc of islands in the Lesser Antilles were formed by more recent volcanoes, some of which are still active. Violent eruptions have taken place on islands such as Martinique and St. Vincent in the last 100 years. The volcanic islands have rich soil, but their slopes are quickly drained of nutrients and easily eroded.

The islands with flatter terrain are coral islands. They were created by the remains of colonies of tiny, soft-bodied sea animals called coral polyps. Coral polyps take in water and nutrients and release calcium carbonate, or limestone, to form a hard outer skeleton. As the corals die, the limestone skeletons form a coral reef. Sand and sediment begin to pile on top of it. Eventually soil forms, plants take root, and an island is formed. The sandy soil, however, cannot support much agriculture. All of the Bahamas are coral islands.

Marine Climate The climate of the Caribbean islands is affected more by sea and wind than by elevation. As you know, nearness to water affects the climate of coastal areas. As light breezes blow over the Caribbean Sea, they take on the temperature of the cooler water beneath them. When the winds blow onshore, they moderate the land temperature. Even though most of the Caribbean islands lie in the tropics, where the sun's rays are most direct, year-round temperatures reach only an average high of 80° F (27° C). However, the humidity can be high.

Prevailing winds also affect the amount of rainfall in the Caribbean. On the **windward** northern and eastern sides of the islands—facing the wind—rain can fall in torrents, reaching as much as 200 inches (500 cm) a year. On the **leeward** sides—facing away from the wind— rainfall may be only 30 inches (75 cm) a year.

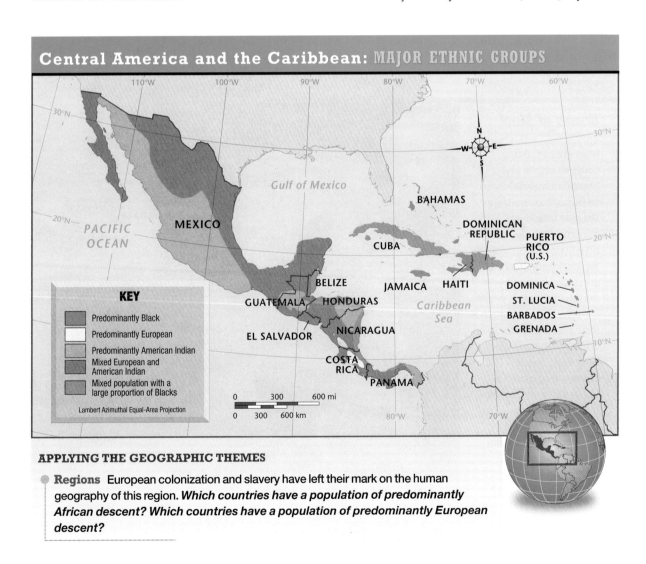

Central America and the Caribbean: MAJOR ETHNIC GROUPS

KEY
- Predominantly Black
- Predominantly European
- Predominantly American Indian
- Mixed European and American Indian
- Mixed population with a large proportion of Blacks

Lambert Azimuthal Equal-Area Projection

0   300   600 mi
0   300   600 km

APPLYING THE GEOGRAPHIC THEMES

● **Regions** European colonization and slavery have left their mark on the human geography of this region. *Which countries have a population of predominantly African descent? Which countries have a population of predominantly European descent?*

Ethnic Roots

Visitors to the Caribbean islands today find little evidence of the original inhabitants. European colonists arrived with Columbus in 1492, and within a century, most of the Indians had vanished. Many died from diseases brought by the foreigners, others from their cruel treatment.

African Descent European colonists in what were then called the West Indies needed laborers to do the hard work on their plantations, growing and harvesting sugar cane. They brought millions of Africans to work as slaves. Most of the region's present population is descended from those enslaved Africans or from Europeans and native Indians.

Caribbean culture has been greatly influenced by its African roots. One example is calypso music, a form of folk music that spread from Trinidad throughout the Caribbean. Calypso features witty lyrics and clever satire, set to a rhythmic beat and accompanied by a band of steel drums. The music traces its roots to the songs of enslaved Africans who worked on the plantations of Trinidad.

Asian Immigrants The Caribbean islands today also have a sizable Asian population. Most are descendants of immigrants from East Asia and South Asia who came voluntarily to work in the Caribbean islands in the nineteenth century. When slavery was abolished, plantation owners searched halfway around the world for replacement laborers.

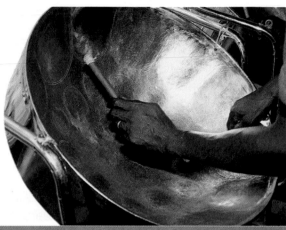

Drums of Steel

Movement Many Calypso artists are hoping to make Calypso as popular overseas as Reggae music has become. Calypso songs owe their vitality to timely topics, improvisation, and their constant updating for each year's Carnival. Their strength is their connection to tradition and culture. However, these characteristics are a barrier to marketing the music overseas.

Critical Thinking *How might a Calypso artist make songs more appealing to an American audience?*

A Nation of Farmers

Place Agriculture is the chief economic activity in Haiti. Most Haitian workers are farmers, though few own enough land to grow more than the food they need to feed their families. Others work on plantations that raise cash crops. Some crops, such as the rice shown here, face competition from cheap imports. *What is Haiti's economic standing?*

Caribbean Nations Today

Today the Caribbean reflects its past. About 90 percent of the Caribbean's population live in independent countries. They include Cuba, Haiti, the Dominican Republic, Barbados, Jamaica, the Bahamas, and Trinidad and Tobago (one country made up of two islands).

Many other Caribbean islands are still politically linked to European countries or the United States. The British Virgin Islands, the Cayman Islands, Montserrat, and several others remain colonies of the United Kingdom. Others, such as Jamaica and the Bahamas, are independent members of the British Commonwealth. The U.S. Virgin Islands is United States territory. Puerto Rico is a United States commonwealth. Residents of both Puerto Rico and the U.S. Virgin Islands are American citizens. The islands of Guadeloupe and Martinique are overseas departments of France. The Netherlands Antilles and Aruba are associated with the Netherlands but govern themselves.

Living from the Land

The economies of many Caribbean islands depend on agriculture. Because of the extremely fertile soil in the volcanic islands, much of the world's sugar, bananas, coconuts, cocoa, rice, and cotton are produced in the region. Besides farm laborers, many others work in industries related to agriculture—refining sugar, packaging coconut and rice products, and making textiles. Still others work on the docks, loading and shipping exports to North America, Europe, or Northern Eurasia.

Because of their natural beauty, the islands draw tourists from all over the world. Visitors flock there to enjoy the tropical climate, relax on white sandy beaches, and sail, snorkel, and scuba dive in the warm turquoise water.

Yet, while tourism thrives, the islanders themselves reap few benefits. Most of the hotels, airlines, and cruise ships are owned by foreign corporations, not by people of the Caribbean islands. Most of the profits end up overseas. Local people hired for unskilled

Health

There's only one doctor for every 6,856 Haitians. (In the United States there are 416 people per doctor.) Haitians are also one of only a few Latin American peoples who get less than 100% of the necessary number of calories a day: 89%. The others are in Honduras, Bolivia, and Peru.

service jobs in the tourist industry are poorly paid and face layoffs in the summer off-season. But since jobs are scarce, even these jobs are better than none.

Migration

Since the first European colonization, Caribbean islanders have been ready to move. Most often, they have migrated in search of jobs. Traditionally, sugar plantations have been the major employers, but the plantation's busy season lasts only four months. The other eight months are called the *tiempo muerto*—the dead season. During the dead season, idle workers pack up and head to other islands, to Central America, or to the United States to find work. When they receive a paycheck, they send money to their families back home.

At the start of the twentieth century, many islanders found work in Panama, helping to build the Panama Canal for the United States government. Once the canal opened, most migrants returned to their homes, although many remained in Panama.

Starting in the 1940s, large numbers of Puerto Ricans began moving to cities in the United States. A large percentage of these migrants have settled in New York City, where they have built a large and vibrant Hispanic community.

Political Unrest Political changes have also prompted movement away from the Caribbean. For example, in 1959 Fidel Castro led a successful revolution to topple Cuba's dictatorial government. In its place, Castro set up a Communist government. Since then, about one million Cubans, unhappy with the new order, have emigrated to the United States. Many have settled in Florida.

Between 1957 and 1986, Haiti was ruled by a military dictatorship. Thousands of people fled to the United States to escape the cruelty. In 1986 Haitians ousted their dictator, but the military regained control of the government. Finally in 1994, with backing from the United States, the democratically elected president, Jean-Bertrand Aristide, was restored to office. In 1995 Haiti held another free election. Despite some instances of violence, the young democracy seemed to be in place with the transition of presidential power to Rene Preval.

Country	Population	Life Expectancy (years)	Per Capita GNP (in US $)
Antigua and Barbuda	100,000	73	6,390
Bahamas	300,000	73	11,500
Barbados	300,000	76	6,240
Cuba	11,200,000	75	NA
Dominica	100,000	77	2,680
Dominican Republic	7,800,000	70	1,080
Grenada	100,000	71	2,410
Guadeloupe (Fr.)	400,000	75	NA
Haiti	7,200,000	57	NA
Jamaica	2,400,000	74	1,390
Martinique (Fr.)	400,000	76	NA
Netherlands Antilles	200,000	76	NA
Puerto Rico (U.S.)	3,700,000	74	7,020
St. Christopher-Nevis	40,000	69	4,470
Saint Lucia	100,000	72	3,040
St. Vincent & the Grenadines	100,000	73	2,130
Trinidad and Tobago	1,300,000	71	3,730
United States	263,200,000	76	24,750

Source: Population Reference Bureau   NA indicates data not available.

CHART SKILLS

● *Which country, aside from the United States, has the highest population?*

● **Critical Thinking** *Which countries do not have data available for per capita GNP? Give one possible reason why this data might be unavailable.*

Economic Benefits The Caribbean islands have lost many people to emigration, but they have also benefited from it. The hundreds of millions of dollars that emigrants have

Star 51?

Place Whether to become the 51st U.S. state is an ongoing argument in Puerto Rico. Referendums have been held in 1967, 1993, and 1998. Each time, Puerto Rican voters rejected statehood. Although citizens of the United States, Puerto Ricans cannot vote in federal elections and do not pay federal income tax.

Critical Thinking *What are the advantages and disadvantages of becoming a state for Puerto Rico?*

sent home—not all of it from the United States—have helped reduce the burden of poverty throughout the Caribbean. With that money, the people at home have bought consumer goods such as radios and televisions. The resulting changes are so great that returning migrants are often amazed to find their island home has been transformed. Their feelings of bewilderment are captured by Puerto Rican poet Tato Laviera, who wrote:

> *I fight for you, Puerto Rico, do you know that?*
> *I defend your name, do you know that?*
> *When I come to the island, I feel like a stranger, do you know that?*

Section 2 Review

Vocabulary and Main Ideas

1. Define: a. archipelago b. windward c. leeward

2. Physically, what are the two types of Caribbean islands? How was each formed?

3. What links with European colonial powers still remain in the Caribbean?

4. Why do the Caribbean islands have moderate temperatures?

5. Critical Thinking: *Drawing Conclusions* What factors brought different ethnic groups—Africans, East Asians, and South Asians—to the Caribbean? Do these same factors affect migration today?

learning LOCATIONS

6. Which island group in the Caribbean region is the farthest north? In what climate zone is it located?

7. Name the two Caribbean nations that occupy the same island. What is the island called?

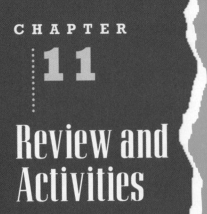

CHAPTER 11

Review and Activities

Summarizing Main Ideas

Section 1 Central America

- The seven countries of the Central American isthmus are made up of rugged mountains with cool climates, temperate middle-level elevations, and tropical lowlands.
- The region's population includes four main groups—Indians, Europeans, mestizos, and Africans.
- Farming is the basis of the economy, but most rural families are poor subsistence farmers. A few wealthy plantations employ others.
- A sharp division between rich and poor has been one cause of intense political conflict throughout Central America.

Section 2 The Caribbean Islands

- The Caribbean islands include three island groups: the Greater Antilles, the Bahamas, and the Lesser Antilles.
- The islands are either volcanic or formed of coral. Most have a tropical climate.
- Most people of the Caribbean are descended from African slaves or from European, Asian, and Indian ancestors.
- The Caribbean region relies on agriculture and tourism, but widespread unemployment has led thousands of people to emigrate to other countries in search of work.

Reviewing Vocabulary

Use each of the following terms in a sentence that shows its meaning.

1. archipelago
2. caudillo
3. guerrilla
4. isthmus
5. leeward
6. windward

Applying the Geographic Themes

1. **Place** What are the major ethnic groups in the Caribbean today? How did each group come to this region?
2. **Location** Name the three groups of islands in the Caribbean and describe their relative locations.
3. **Human-Environment Interaction** Which crops account for most of Central America's profits from exports?
4. **Movement** Where is the Panama Canal? What was the significance of its opening?
5. **Regions** What two different kinds of physical processes created islands in different parts of the Caribbean?

Critical Thinking and Applying Skills

1. **Analyzing Evidence** What influences of European colonization can still be seen in the Caribbean?
2. **Reading Tables and Analyzing Statistics** Refer to the table on page 223 to answer the following questions about three Central American countries.
   a. Which country has the smallest population?
   b. Which country has the largest percentage of urban population?
   c. How does the relative wealth of these countries relate to their infant mortality rates?
   d. Explain the probable relationship between infant mortality and per capita GNP.

Journal Activity

Writing Across Cultures

▶ 1. Write two paragraphs describing the Caribbean, one from a tourist's point of view and one from the point of view of a person who lives and works in the region. How are the two points of view similar? How are they different?

▶ 2. The Mexican poet Octavio Paz expressed the feelings of many Latin Americans when he wrote, "North Americans are always among us, even when they ignore us or turn their back on us. Their shadow covers the whole hemisphere. It is the shadow of a giant." Write a paragraph explaining why Latin Americans might see the United States as a giant shadow over them.

INTERNET link

Explore the Visit Trinidad and Tobago site. Link to this site from:

• www.phschool.com

Examine the information presented in this site. Create a five-day tour of the islands, and write a paragraph explaining how your tour will give a greater understanding of geography.

learning LOCATIONS

Central America and the Caribbean

Number from 1 to 8 on a piece of paper. Next to each number, write the letter of the place on the map that corresponds to each of the places listed below.

1. Belize
2. Honduras
3. Costa Rica
4. Isthmus of Panama
5. Cuba
6. Bahamas
7. Haiti
8. Dominican Republic

*B*razil

SECTIONS

1 **The Land and Its Regions**

2 **Brazil's Quest for Economic Growth**

Brazil: POLITICAL

VENEZUELA
SURINAME
GUYANA
FRENCH GUIANA (FR.)
COLOMBIA
ECUADOR
Manaus
Amazon R.
Tapajós R.
BRAZIL
Tocantins R.
Fortaleza
Recife
Equator
PERU
Salvador
BOLIVIA
Brasília
Belo Horizonte
Paraná R.
PACIFIC OCEAN
PARAGUAY
São Paulo
Rio de Janeiro
Tropic of Capricorn
ATLANTIC OCEAN
ARGENTINA
Pôrto Alegre
URUGUAY

80°W, 70°W, 60°W, 50°W, 40°W
0°, 10°S, 20°S, 30°S

KEY

— National boundary
⊛ National capital
• Other city

Lambert Azimuthal Equal Area Projection

0   300   600 mi
0   300   600 km

learning LOCATIONS

Mapping the Region

Create a map like the one above. Then add labels for cities and bodies of water that are shown on the map.

1 The Land and Its Regions

Section Preview

Main Ideas

- Brazil's northeast is a region of great poverty.

- The southeast has many resources and two major cities.

- Brazil's new capital city was built in the barren Brazilian Highlands.

- The Amazon River Basin is a huge interior plain rich in tropical vegetation and animal life.

Vocabulary

escarpment, *favela*

Rio de Janeiro's Carnival inspires the creation of splendid costumes.

Brazil is the giant of South America. Nearly half the continent's people and land lie within its borders. Despite its huge land area, Brazil has just two major types of landforms—plains and plateaus. A fertile ribbon of lowlands, 10 to 30 miles (16 to 48 km) wide, winds along the curving Atlantic coastline. The immense Amazon River basin is also a plains region.

Behind the coastal plains is a huge interior plateau. As it drops sharply to the plains, it forms an **escarpment**—a steep cliff between two level areas at different heights. In earlier centuries, the escarpment was a natural barrier to the interior. As a result, much of the interior of Brazil was undeveloped and sparsely populated.

Northeast Region

Brazil's northeast region bulges out into the Atlantic Ocean. Portuguese colonists, who landed on its shores in 1500, built large sugar plantations along the fertile coastal plain. They established port cities from which to ship the valuable crop to Europe. Brazil became the world's major producer of sugar.

Over the next 300 years, Brazil's colonists brought in more than 3 million enslaved Africans to do the hard work on the plantations. The folktales, food, and religion of the northeast still reflect this African heritage.

Inland from the northeast's coastal plains lies the *sertao* (ser TY oh), or interior plateau. With a tropical wet and dry climate, the *sertao* often bakes through a year or more of drought. When the rains eventually come, the land is devastated because the hard soil can not absorb the heavy rainfall.

Poverty is severe in the northeast. Because of their impoverished lives and chronic malnutrition, the people of this region have an average life expectancy at birth of only 49 years—well below the rest of Brazil. Here, a

◀ **Rio de Janeiro, Brazil** *(photo left)*

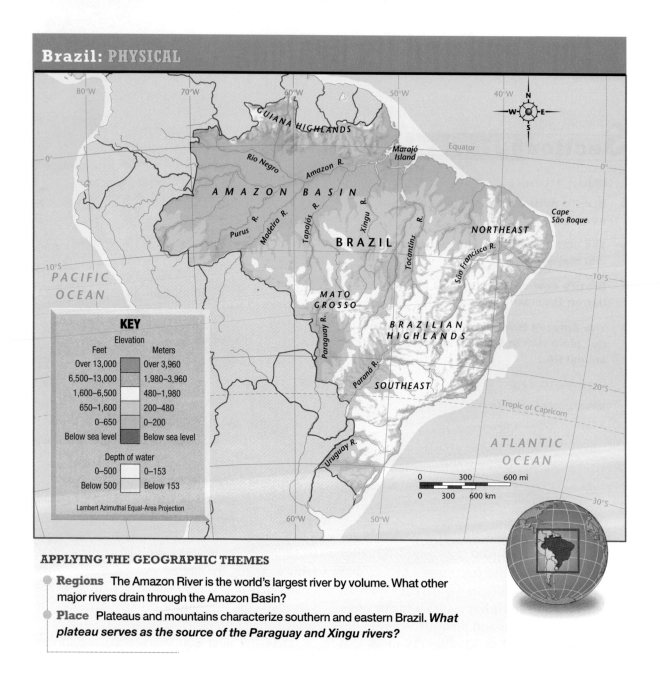

APPLYING THE GEOGRAPHIC THEMES

● **Regions** The Amazon River is the world's largest river by volume. What other major rivers drain through the Amazon Basin?

● **Place** Plateaus and mountains characterize southern and eastern Brazil. *What plateau serves as the source of the Paraguay and Xingu rivers?*

family's average yearly income may be only one third the income of a similar family living in the southeast.

Southeast Region

The southeast, Brazil's smallest region, is its economic heartland. With only 17 percent of the country's area, it is home to 40 percent of the population. Because of the region's mostly humid subtropical climate and fertile soil, farmers can easily grow great quantities of cash crops such as cotton, sugar cane, rice, and cacao, the base of chocolate.

The southeast's biggest and most important crop, however, is coffee. In the 1800s, thousands of people migrated from various parts of the world to this region in Brazil to work on coffee plantations. Today, Brazil is often referred to as the world's "coffeepot," growing one fourth of the world's supply.

Despite the southeast's healthy agriculture, most people live in or near the cities of São Paulo and Rio de Janeiro. The beauty, excitement, and economic health of Rio and São Paulo draw rural Brazilians looking for a better life. Undereducated and without much experience, many find no jobs or settle for low-paying ones. Most end up in slum communities called *favelas*. A journalist who visited Rio de Janeiro described its *favelas*:

> The houses [of the favelas], built illegally on hillsides or swampland, generally consist of wood planks, mud, tin cans, corrugated iron and anything that comes to hand. Some cling to slopes so [steep] that the dwellings are in constant danger of being swept away in the heavy tropical rain storms that burst over the city.

Every Brazilian city has *favelas*, although the government has tried to improve the situation.

Urbanization of Brazil

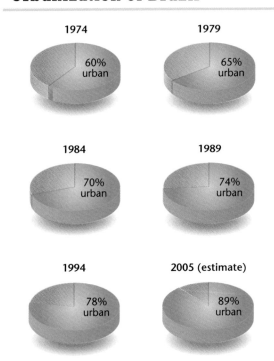

1974 — 60% urban
1979 — 65% urban
1984 — 70% urban
1989 — 74% urban
1994 — 78% urban
2005 (estimate) — 89% urban

GRAPH STUDY

● For the past twenty years there has been steady movement of people from the rural to the urban areas of Brazil. *What percent of the population was urban in 1974? What percent is expected to be urban in 2005?*

● **Critical Thinking** Nearly one third of Brazil's urban population lives in slums called favelas. *Why do you think this is so?*

Some *favelas* have been torn down and replaced by affordable public housing.

Despite its poverty, most people around the world associate Rio de Janeiro with its famous festival known as Carnival. Carnival takes place during the four days preceding Lent—a period of 40 days of fasting and penitence before the Christian celebration of Easter. A year of planning, rehearsing dance steps, sewing costumes, and designing floats culminates in four days and nights of music and dancing. During Carnival, Brazilians take part in dance competitions and perform the samba—Brazil's national dance.

Brazilian Highlands

North of the southeast region lie the Brazilian Highlands, the geographic heart of Brazil on the country's central plateau. Brazil's capital, Brasília, is located in the Highlands, far from the country's other large cities. For years, overcrowded Rio de Janeiro was the capital of Brazil. In 1956, hoping to boost development of the interior and to draw people away from the coastal cities, the national government decided to build a new capital city 600 miles (960 km) inland. Officially "inaugurated" in 1960, Brasília in the mid-1990s had a population of about 1.8 million.

Amazon River Basin

Of Brazil's major regions, the largest and least explored is the Amazon River basin, which spreads across more than half of the country. Moist trade winds that blow from the Atlantic Ocean drop more than 80 inches (200 cm) of rain on the region each year. With heavy rainfall and constant temperatures of about 80°F (27°C), the growing season never ends. As a result, the Amazon rain forest is home to thousands of

Life on the Amazon

Regions This Amazonian Indian boy managed to land a fish bigger than himself. *In what ways has the development of Brazil affected the lives of the Amazon Indians?*

The Amazon Indians Only about 10 percent of Brazilians live in the Amazon Basin, including about 200,000 Indians from 180 different tribes. Brazil's original Indian population was much larger. When the Portuguese arrived in the 1500s, between 2 and 5 million Indians were living in what is now Brazil. Over the years, many were killed by settlers or by diseases that Europeans brought with them.

Even in modern times, Indians are being exposed to new diseases. In spite of modern medicines, thousands of Indians died from diseases against which they had no resistance. One tribe for example—the Parakana—had 700 to 1,000 members in 1970. Ten years later, when the region had been developed, only 300 of them had survived. As observers remarked: "There didn't seem to be anything you could call murder. Yet, the Indians were dying just the same."

Today, the Indians' traditional ways of life are subject to dramatic changes. These have been caused by government regulations designed to preserve the environment, and the arrival of people from outside the area.

The government set up reservations for several Indian groups. But when Indians live in such reservations, they often lose their own culture. Slowly they lose their language, customs, religion, and way of life. Such change often marks the beginning of a tribe's disappearance, as Indians become assimilated into the country's majority culture.

species of plants and animals, including orchids, palms, monkeys, jaguars, and toucans. Piranha and dolphins live in the river.

Section 1 Review

Vocabulary and Main Ideas

1. **Define: a.** escarpment **b.** *favela*

2. **What are the two main types of landforms in Brazil?**

3. **What is Brazil's main agricultural area? What are some of its most important crops?**

4. **Critical Thinking:** *Expressing Problems Clearly* **Why do** *favelas* **develop in cities even when agriculture in the same region is flourishing?**

learning LOCATIONS

5. What is unusual about the location of Brazil's capital city, Brasília?

6. Name three rivers along Brazil's southeast border.

Focus on Skills

☐ Social Studies

☑ Map and Globe

☐ Critical Thinking and Problem Solving

Using Latitude and Longitude to Estimate Distance

One of the most remote places in the world—a spot in Brazil's tropical rain forest—can be located by using a global grid. As you have read, the grid is made up of lines of latitude, called parallels, and lines of longitude, called meridians. Parallels of latitude can be used to estimate the distance north or south of the Equator. Meridians can be used to estimate the distance east or west of the Prime Meridian, which is 0°.

A circle contains 360 degrees. From the Equator to either pole, there are one fourth of 360, or 90, degrees of latitude.

A place can be found by identifying the intersection of parallels and meridians at its location. For example, Brasilia's location may be expressed as 16°S, 48°W. However, if degrees of latitude and longitude were not further broken down into smaller units of measure, the absolute location of a place could be in error by as much as 69 miles (111 km).

Fortunately geographers, pilots, and engineers have more precise measurements available to them. To pinpoint further the location of a place, each degree of latitude and longitude is divided into 60 minutes ('). Each minute is divided into 60 seconds ("). By measuring to the nearest second, a place can be found to within 100 feet of its absolute location on earth.

Use the steps below to approximate distances using latitude and longitude.

1. Approximate Distances Using Latitude.
Each degree of latitude is equal to about 69 miles (111 km). (a) Use the grid below to estimate the distance north to south from the southern tip of Africa to the Arctic Circle. (b) Use the map on page 232 to estimate the distance from Pôrto Alegre to Belo Horizonte, Brazil, using latitude instead of the map scale. (c) Now compare the distance that you estimated to the distance you find by using the map scale.

2. Approximate Distances Using Longitude.
The distance between two whole degrees of longitude depends on where they are measured. One degree of longitude equals about 69 miles (111 km) at the Equator, about 49 miles (79 km) at 45°, and 0 miles (0 km) at either pole. (a) Use the map on page 232 to approximate the distance between Manaus and Fortaleza, Brazil, using longitude instead of the map scale. (b) Compare the distance that you estimated to the distance you find by using the map scale.

Global Grid

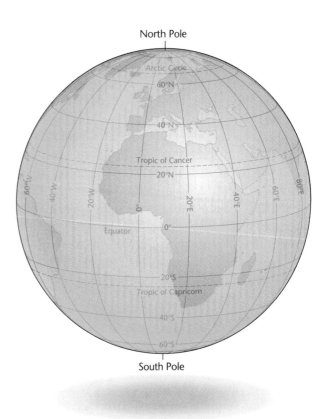

North Pole

South Pole

2 Brazil's Quest for Economic Growth

Section Preview

Main Ideas

To help reduce poverty, Brazil has developed new industries and encouraged settlement in the country's interior.

Industries and development have improved the lives of some Brazilians and led to the growth of a middle class.

Development also has had some harmful effects on the environment.

Vocabulary

sertao, gasohol, service industry

Brazil struggles to improve life in the *favelas*.

Brazil is a country of extremes. It is a huge country rich in natural resources, but it is also a country with much poverty. In the past few decades, Brazil has begun to realize its potential. The government has taken steps to modernize the economy and improve the lives of its people. Many have benefited, but some have not.

Brazil today, like much of Latin America, is no longer a society of only rich and poor. The growth of industry and manufacturing has helped to create a middle class, as people have been needed to manage and work in factories and offices. Likewise, as cities have grown, doctors, teachers, government workers, and others have moved in to fill the needs of a growing urban population.

Brazil's Poor

Most of Brazil's poorest people live in the urban *favelas* or the rural northeast. Many parents in the *favelas* cannot feed or house their children, much less provide them with schooling. Hungry, homeless children live dangerously on the streets, seeking menial jobs or begging for coins with which to buy food.

Conditions in agriculture contribute to poverty. Although the Brazilian agriculture industry is very profitable, only a handful of wealthy families own the large plantations. Most of the rural population are subsistence farmers working tiny plots of land barely large enough to support a family. Those without land work for low wages on the plantations.

Many of Brazil's small farmers live in the inhospitable region of the *sertao*. This "backwoods" region suffers from poor soil, scarce grazing lands, and uncertain rainfall. Few farmers in the *sertao* can afford the farm machines that could help boost productivity.

Policies for Growth

Since the mid-1940s, the Brazilian government has undertaken several massive programs to ease the burden of poverty for its people. These programs have had two major aims: to boost the growth of industry and to encourage settlement and development in the country's interior.

An Industrial Base During the 1940s and early 1950s, the Brazilian government built the country's first steel mill and oil refinery. It also began to build a series of huge hydroelectric dams to produce power for the planned industrial expansion. The dams were built where rivers dropped over the steep escarpment. To further encourage the growth of industry, the government established a bank that loaned money to people who wanted to start new businesses.

Manufacturing began to thrive in the 1950s with tremendous growth in the automobile, chemical, and steel industries. Within ten years, millions of Brazilians began to move from rural to urban areas, seeking jobs in the new factories. Brazil's coastal cities, especially São Paulo, became crowded industrial centers.

Developing the Interior With São Paulo and Rio de Janeiro rapidly becoming overcrowded, Brazil's leaders recognized the need to develop the country's vast interior. In the late 1950s the new capital city, Brasília, was "planted" in the Brazilian Highlands, 600 miles (960 km) inland from the Atlantic Coast. The city was to be a showplace of shiny glass and gleaming steel architecture. When viewed from the air, the city has the shape of a bow and arrow or, some say,

an airplane. Either way, Brasília's shape symbolizes movement—the readiness of the country to take off.

Brasília represented movement in another way. Because the country as a whole had few roads except along the coast, the government began a massive road-building project with Brasília at its center. By the 1970s the country boasted thousands of miles of new roads, including one that stretched across the Amazon Basin for 2,700 miles (4,300 km).

To promote settlement in the north, the government gave away thousands of plots of land in the Amazon region, as well as thousands of mining or prospecting permits. New roads and free land grants drew many settlers to the Brazilian Highlands and Amazon regions. Between 1970 and 1985, more than 1 million people migrated to the Amazon region.

Development Successes

Brazil's development programs have had remarkable success. Manufacturing now accounts for one third of Brazil's gross national product. The country ranks among the world's leading industrial nations.

Industry Takes Off

Movement Manufacturing accounts for 23 percent of Brazil's gross domestic product and employs 15 percent of its workers. The workers in this photograph are assembling commuter aircraft. Manufacture of airplanes, automobiles, and other transportation equipment are leading industries in Brazil. *How did the development of industry affect Brazil's cities?*

Biodiversity

Brazil has more species of primates, parrots, land vertebrate animals, freshwater fish, amphibians, flowering plants, and, probably, insects than any other country on earth. It contains 30 percent of the world's tropical forests.

One major step was the successful development of a new alcohol-based fuel called **gasohol**, a mix of gasoline and ethanol, in response to the high cost of imported oil in the 1970s. Ethanol, a type of alcohol, is made from Brazil's own sugar cane. In a sense, Brazilian farmers are *growing* fuel. Brazil no longer has to import expensive foreign oil.

These and other industrial developments have changed the way Brazilians earn a living. In 1940, two thirds of the work force was employed in agriculture. By 1980, nearly one third worked in manufacturing, construction, or mining. More than one fourth of the labor force now works in **service industries**, such as hotels and restaurants, retail stores, and government, that have sprung up as offshoots of the nation's industrial growth.

The new jobs usually pay more than agricultural work. They have given Brazil a skilled, educated, growing middle class, something that scarcely existed before the 1940s. Yet much poverty still remains, mainly in the cities and in the agricultural northeast.

Negative Effects

While economic development has brought many positive changes to Brazil, it has had some unintended effects. In the nation's big industrial cities, poverty has actually increased. As thousands of rural Brazilians have flocked to cities to look for well-paying industrial jobs, there have been more migrants than jobs. As a result, the *favelas* have become an ever larger part of these cities. In São Paulo, for example, population doubled between 1970 and 1985, but the population of its *favelas* increased fifteen times.

Environmental Impact Along the Amazon, the challenges have been different. Many settlers moved to the region to farm or ranch. But after clearing the forest to plant crops, they found that it was the thick rain forest vegetation that had kept the soil and nutrients from washing away during the heavy rains. Despite the lush vegetation, the soil was thin and not very fertile. After a few years of farming and erosion, the soil was no longer usable.

Artistic Tradition

Place Brazil has a strong artistic tradition that ranges from traditional aboriginal art to colonial architecture to modern murals depicting Brazilian history. It also boasts a strong literary tradition and unique musical styles. **Critical Thinking** *How can a country's arts contribute to our understanding of its development?*

Fighting for Their Lives

● **Location** Brazil's Yanomami Indians are protesting the severe threats their population faces from gold miners. The Yanomami reserve is rich in gold and diamonds. Prospectors illegally mining on Yanomami land have killed dozens of Yanomami in retaliation for government enforcement of Yanomami territorial borders. *What other threats do Amazonian Indians face from outsiders?*

Rain forest soil that has been exhausted by both the rains and planting does not recover. Rather, it becomes barren red clay, hard as brick. This gradual destruction of the rain forest has damaged the delicate ecology of the Amazon region and threatens to harm the ecology of the entire world. Moreover, the loss of forest can destroy species of plants and animals that scientists have never studied. You can read more about the destruction of the rain forest and its global impact on pages 244 and 245.

Brazil's Future

The last half-century brought Brazil much progress—and some serious new challenges. Yet there are reasons to expect the country's future to be brighter. The nation still has millions of acres of fertile land outside the Amazon region that could produce more food and a better living for its people. It has a rich culture and fine climate that can draw increasing numbers of tourists. Brazil has the potential to become a major world power.

Section 2 Review

Vocabulary and Main Ideas

1. Define: a. *sertao* b. gasohol c. service industry

2. Describe the growth and makeup of Brazil's growing middle class.

3. What were the two main goals of Brazil's program to develop the country?

4. **Critical Thinking:** *Predicting Consequences* What is the likely future of the rain forest in the Amazon region?

learning LOCATIONS

5. Name the city located south of Rio de Janeiro in southeastern Brazil.

6. Only two countries in South America do not share a border with huge Brazil. What are they?

Review and Activities

Summarizing Main Ideas

Section 1   The Land and Its Regions

- Brazil is the largest country in Latin America. Geographical barriers limited early settlements and development to coastal areas.
- Brazil's northeast, the region that bulges into the Atlantic, is a place of great poverty. Most of Brazil's poor live in the *favelas* of the coastal cities, or in the dry interior *sertao*.
- The southeast region, the country's heartland, has both rich agriculture and the major cities of Rio de Janeiro and São Paulo.
- As part of its plan to develop the interior, Brazil built a new capital city, Brasília, in the barren Brazilian Highlands.
- The Amazon River Basin is a huge interior plain rich in tropical vegetation and animal life.

Section 2   Brazil's Quest for Economic Growth

- To help reduce poverty, Brazil has had a two-part program: to develop new industries and to encourage settlement and development in the country's vast interior.
- Brazil has become a major industrial nation with a growing middle class and people working in government and service industries.
- Development has drawn many people to the cities and increased *favelas*, or slum areas. It has also harmed the environment of the rain forest.

Reviewing Vocabulary

Match the definitions with the correct terms.

1. area of shanties and slums in Brazilian cities
2. a mix of gasoline and ethanol
3. steep cliff between two level areas at different heights
4. area drained by a river and its tributaries
5. business that provides a service instead of manufacturing a product
6. barren interior region of Brazil's northeast

   a. **basin**
   b. **escarpment**
   c. **gasohol**
   d. *favela*
   e. *sertao*
   f. **service industry**

Applying the Geographic Themes

1. **Place** Which landform in Brazil discouraged people from settling the region's vast interior?
2. **Location** What factors make agriculture in the southeast so prosperous? What is the most important crop there?
3. **Human-Environment Interaction** Why is farming difficult in Brazil's *sertao*?
4. **Movement** How did the northeast region come to have many African influences?
5. **Regions** Why is the future of the Amazon Basin important to people outside Brazil?

Critical Thinking and Applying Skills

1. **Recognizing Ideologies** In their attempts to reduce poverty, Brazil's leaders did little to change conditions in agriculture. Why do you suppose they took this approach?
2. **Using Latitude and Longitude** Review the information on page 237 and answer the following questions.
   a. Why is it that one degree of latitude measures approximately 69 miles (111 km) anywhere in the world, but a degree of longitude ranges between 0 and 69 miles (0 and 111 km)?
   b. Why is it important to subdivide degrees of latitude and longitude into minutes and seconds?

Journal Activity

Most Brazilians know a poem about their country called the "Song of Exile," written by Antonio Gonçalves Dias. Read this excerpt from the poem and respond with your own short poem or song lyric. (The sabiá is a bird.)

There are palm trees in my country,
And the singing Sabiá;
The birds warbling here
Don't sing as they do there.
Our heavens have more stars,
Our meadows far more blooms,
Our forests have more life. . . .
My country has a loveliness
That I don't find here;
When I dream—alone, at night—
I find more pleasure there. . . .

INTERNET link

Find out about the food of Brazil at Maria-Brazil. Link to this site from:

• www.phschool.com

Select Maria's Cookbook. Browse through the recipes. What sounds good? Are any of the recipes familiar? Can you see the influence of any particular culture? Make up a menu for a meal you'd like to try.

learning LOCATIONS

Brazil

Number from 1 to 6 on a piece of paper. Next to each number, write the letter of the place on the map that corresponds to each of the places listed below.

1. Brasília
2. Fortaleza
3. São Paulo
4. Rio de Janeiro
5. Recife
6. Belo Horizonte

Tropical Rain Forests

The Issue

Rain forests throughout the world are being destroyed at a rapid rate. Here are a few of the reasons why this is causing international concern.

Improving Their Standard of Living

Governments, hoping to improve the economic well-being of their countries, encouraged people to develop the resources of the rain forests. Beginning in the 1960s, for example, the Brazilian government began carving roads into the forests to give people better access to valuable hardwoods and farmland.

Putting Economic Needs First

People in need of land to farm or wood to sell burn and cut down thousands of acres of rain forests. They sometimes clear whole sections of forest to get a few prized trees. Unfortunately, the soils of the forests have few nutrients so crops grow well for only a few years. Settlers must then move on, cutting and burning still more rain forest.

Global Impact

About one half to two thirds of all of the plant and animal species on earth are found in tropical rain forests. Rain forest plants provide ingredients for at least one quarter of the world's medicines. Scientists fear that the destruction of the rain forests will lead to the extinction of more plants and animals. Valuable medical resources will be lost forever. In addition, dense forest vegetation absorbs a large share of carbon dioxide in the earth's atmosphere. If more forests are cleared, global warming may accelerate.

Some Solutions

Governments and nonprofit environmental groups have made some progress in slowing down the rate of rain forest destruction. Here are some of the solutions they are working on.

Balancing Economic and Environmental Concerns

Economic development can take place without further excessive destruction of forests. Researchers are trying

Up in Flames

Human-Environment Interaction Burning rain forests exposes the fragile soils to heavy rains and erosion. Some people are trying to build a market for rain forest products, such as these Brazil nuts, to generate income without destroying the forests.

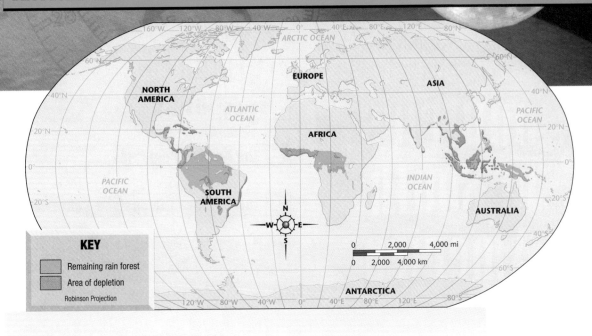

APPLYING THE GEOGRAPHIC THEMES

● **Regions** The map above compares the land area covered by rain forests 20 years ago with the area covered by rain forests today. *What part of the world has suffered the greatest loss of rain forest?*

to determine which parts of the rain forest regenerate quickly and naturally after they have been cleared. If settlers are directed into these areas and taught soil-conserving techniques, long-term damage may be minimized.

Debt-For-Nature Swaps Governments have experimented with debt-for-nature swaps. Swaps involve payment of parts of a nation's debt in exchange for its agreement to protect rain forests.

Create New Markets Companies are trying to change the economic forces that lead to the destruction of rain forests. They are working to increase demand for the nuts, fruits, and oils that can be harvested from rain forests without destroying them.

YOU DECIDE

1. What are some of the threats to the tropical rain forests?

2. What do you think is the best solution to rain forest deforestation?

3. **Problem Solving** You are appointed to a panel of experts designing a rain forest development policy for Brazil. Draft a one-page public policy statement with three to five proposals for how to balance the needs of Indian groups living in the rain forests, the country's poor, and environmentalists.

4. **What You Can Do** Learn more about a nonprofit environmental group that works to preserve rain forests.

5. **Internet Activity** Read about some successes in reversing the tide of extinction on the U.S. Fish and Wildlife Service's Endangered Species page. Then make a list of ten of the species mentioned. Include the name, location, and change in status for each species. Link to this site from:

• www.phschool.com

CHAPTER

13

Countries of South America

SECTIONS

1 The Northern Tropics

2 The Andean Countries

3 The Southern Grassland Countries

South America: POLITICAL

Caribbean Sea
Maracaibo
Barranquilla
Caracas
VENEZUELA
Georgetown
Paramaribo
GUYANA
SURINAME
Cayenne
FRENCH GUIANA (FR.)
Medellín
Bogotá
COLOMBIA
Cali
Equator
Quito
Galápagos Is. (Ec.)
ECUADOR
Guayaquil
Belém
BRAZIL
Recife
Trujillo
PERU
Salvador
Lima
Brasília
La Paz
BOLIVIA
PACIFIC OCEAN
Arequipa
Sucre
Belo Horizonte
Campinas
Rio de Janeiro
PARAGUAY
São Paulo
Curitiba
Tropic of Capricorn
Asunción
ATLANTIC OCEAN
San Ambrosio I.
San Félix I. (Chile)
(Chile)
Pôrto Alegre
Córdoba
Rosario
URUGUAY
Valparaíso
Santiago
Montevideo
Buenos Aires
Juan Fernández Is. (Chile)
CHILE
ARGENTINA
KEY
National boundary
National capital
Other city
Lambert Azimuthal Equal-Area Projection
Falkland Is. (U.K.)
South Georgia (U.K.)
Tierra del Fuego
0 500 1,000 mi
0 500 1,000 km
N
S
E
W
10°N
0°
10°S
20°S
30°S
50°S
100°W
90°W
80°W
70°W
60°W
50°W
40°W
30°W
20°W

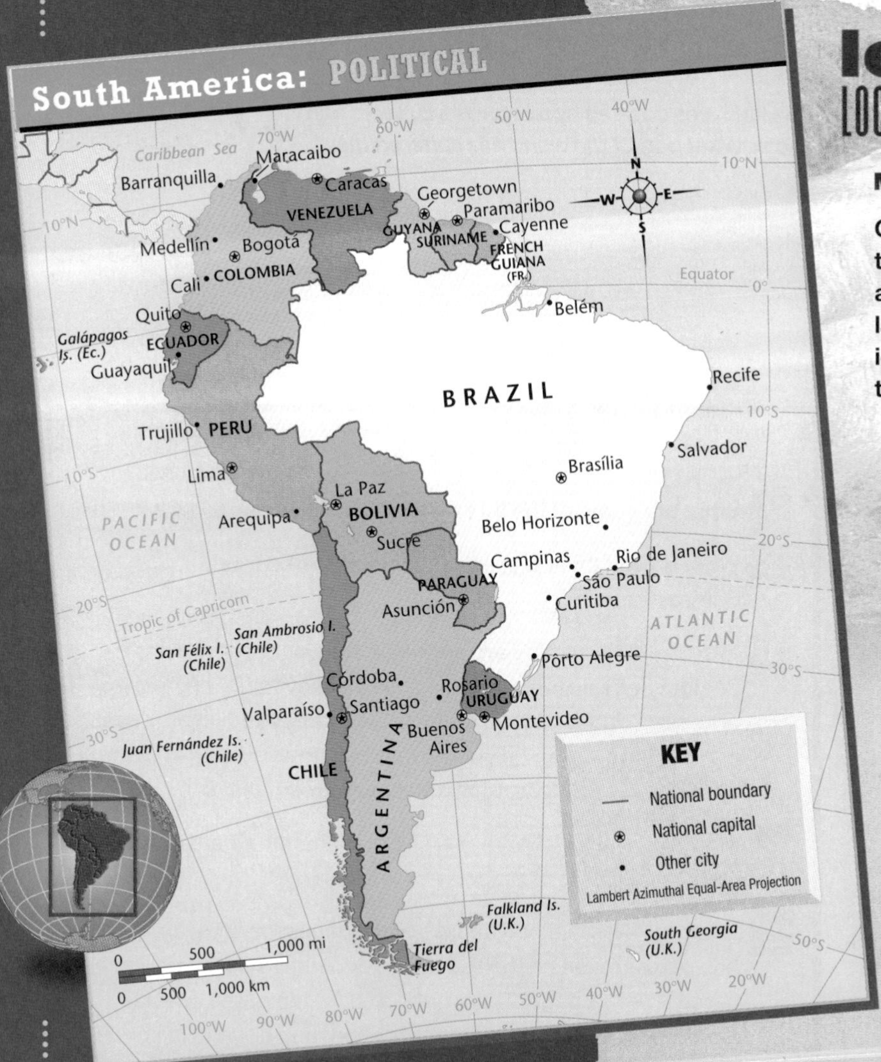

learning LOCATIONS

Mapping the Region

Create a map like the one to the left, shading each country a different color. Then add labels for countries and bodies of water that are shown on the map.

1 The Northern Tropics

Main Ideas

The human geography of each of the Guianas reflects its history as a European colony.

Venezuela has a rich, oil-based economy that is rapidly diversifying.

Colombia's economy depends heavily on coffee and illegal drugs.

Vocabulary

mulatto, bauxite, Llanos, cordillera, campesino

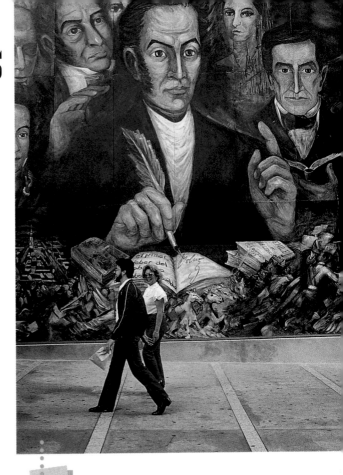

Historical figures in this mural watch over the streets of Caracas, Venezuela.

Grouped around Brazil, like smaller paintings around a larger canvas, are the twelve other countries of South America. These countries shown on the map on the facing page can be separated into the three regions. The northern tropics, the countries on the northern coast of South America, share some characteristics, but they differ in their ethnic makeup, their economies, and their physical geography.

The Guianas

Guyana, Suriname (SUR ih nahm), and French Guiana together are known as the Guianas (gee AHN ahs). They share a tropical wet climate, vast stretches of rain forest, and a narrow coastal plain on the Atlantic Ocean. But, their human geography gives each a distinct personality. These differences are a reflection of each country's history and pattern of colonization. They also set the Guianas apart culturally from most of the rest of South America, where Spanish or Portugese are spoken and Roman Catholicism is the main religion.

Guyana's official language, for example, is English because it was once the English colony of British Guiana. Dutch is spoken in Suriname, a colony of the Netherlands until 1975. Many people in both countries are Muslim or Hindu. French is the official language of French Guiana, which is not an independent nation but an overseas department of France.

Ethnic Differences Ethnic composition varies in the three Guianas. After colonization, Africans were brought there by Europeans to work as slaves on sugar plantations. Asians from China, India, and Southeast Asia began arriving as workers in the mid-1800s, after slavery was abolished. Today most people in Guyana belong to those two major ethnic groups. People of Asian descent make up about half the population, many speaking Hindi and Urdu,

◄ **Mt. Fitzroy in the Andes, Argentina** (photo left)

Major Ethnic Groups in Selected Latin American Countries

● Latin American countries vary in ethnic composition. *Which country has the most diverse population? Which country has the least diverse population?*

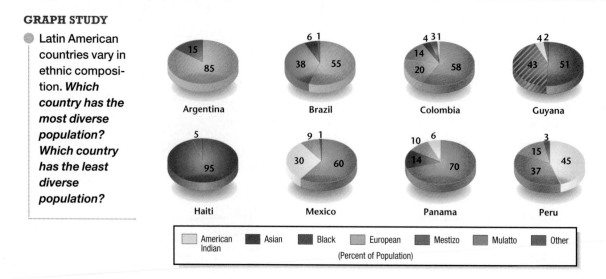

| Argentina | Brazil | Colombia | Guyana |
| Haiti | Mexico | Panama | Peru |

American Indian | Asian | Black | European | Mestizo | Mulatto | Other
(Percent of Population)

languages of India. Another 43 percent are of African ancestry.

Suriname's population has greater variety. Just over 50 percent are descended from the Asian workers who came in the 1800s, but only about 10 percent are of African descent. About 30 percent are **mulattoes**, people of mixed African and other ancestry. Most of the rest are indigenous Indians. The ethnic makeup of French Guiana is similar to that of Suriname, except that mulattoes are the largest group. People of European descent also live in French Guiana.

Economies Although their populations are different, the three Guianas have similar economies because of their shared natural resources. Fishing boats harvest large quantities of fish and shrimp from the sea. In the low-lands, farmers grow sugar cane and rice. From the hills of Guyana and Suriname, miners extract **bauxite**, a mineral used in making aluminum. Guyana is one of the world's largest bauxite exporters.

Venezuela

Guyana's larger western neighbor, Venezuela, is a striking contrast. While fewer than 1 million people live in Guyana, Venezuela's population is 21.8 million. Guyana's annual per capita GNP of about $350 makes it the poorest nation in South America. Venezuela has an annual per capita GNP of over $2,840.

Venezuela's culture is more typical of the rest of South America than are those of the Guianas. Its official language is Spanish, and its people are mainly mestizos or of European descent. Nearly all are Roman Catholics.

The Andean Highlands Venezuela's landscapes are varied. In the northwest corner, the Andes tower over a narrow Caribbean coastal plain. A lower range of mountains, hills, and plateaus, the Andean Highlands, stretch across the rest of northern Venezuela. Most of Venezuela's people live in fertile mountain valleys. The capital city, Caracas, is located in this region.

Side by side with the sidewalk cafes, universities, and busy department stores of Caracas are scenes of poverty. As Brazil's cities have their *favelas*, Caracas has its *ranchos*, or small shacks, where almost one third of the people live. In the last thirty years the government has used its oil wealth to launch massive programs to improve living conditions for the country's poor.

Waterfalls and Grasslands In south-eastern Venezuela, another mountain system, the Guiana Highlands, covers nearly half of the country. Near the border with Brazil are dense tropical forests.

The world's highest waterfall, Angel Falls, is located in Canaima National Park in the Guiana Highlands. This thundering ribbon of water drops more than 3,200 feet (980 m) into the Churun River, a tributary of the Orinoco.

Between the two highland regions, the great Orinoco River flows through central Venezuela. Along both sides of the river stretches a wide tropical grassland, or savanna, region called the **Llanos** (YAH nohs), which means "plains" in Spanish. The Llanos flood during the rainy season, from April to December. For the rest of the year, the hot sun of the dry season quickly burns the vegetation, and the soil becomes parched and cracked. Still, the region is important for grazing cattle.

Elevation and Climate Venezuela lies within the tropics, but its varied climates depend more on elevation than on distance from the Equator. As in many mountainous areas of Latin America, Spanish terms are commonly used for the different climate zones that occur as elevation increases. The diagram on page 250 describes these vertical climate zones.

Venezuelan farmers grow different crops at different elevations. Coffee trees, for example, are ideally suited for growing in the *tierra templada*—"temperate country"—climate zone. At that middle elevation, temperatures are relatively mild.

An Oil-Rich Region Venezuela's wealth can be described in one word: oil. Four large beds of "liquid gold" lie in the eastern Llanos, the Orinoco delta, the lowlands near Lake Maracaibo, and offshore. Each year the Venezuelans pump some 700 million barrels of oil out of the ground, placing the country among the top ten oil producers in the world.

Experts have suggested that Venezuela could become the Western Hemisphere's biggest oil and gas producer in the 21st century. While it has huge oil reserves, they are finite. Venezuela therefore has reinvested a large share of its oil profits in other industries. It is developing bauxite and iron mines, building power plants, and setting up factories that will provide jobs when the oil wells run dry.

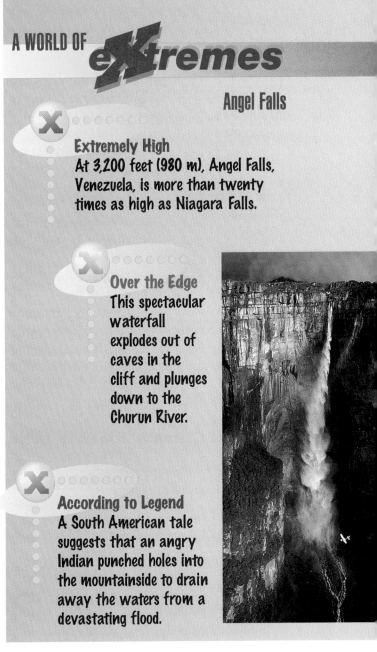

A WORLD OF eXtremes

Angel Falls

Extremely High
At 3,200 feet (980 m), Angel Falls, Venezuela, is more than twenty times as high as Niagara Falls.

Over the Edge
This spectacular waterfall explodes out of caves in the cliff and plunges down to the Churun River.

According to Legend
A South American tale suggests that an angry Indian punched holes into the mountainside to drain away the waters from a devastating flood.

Colombia

Colombia—named after Christopher Columbus—is the only country in South America that borders both the Caribbean Sea and the Pacific Ocean. Its population of more than 37 million makes it the second most populous country on the continent.

Land and Climate Like neighboring Venezuela, Colombia has three distinct physical regions—lowlands, mountains, and the Llanos, or grassy plains. About 75 percent of the country's people live in fertile valleys

GLOBALissues

Volcanoes!

Many peaks in the Andes are active or dormant volcanoes. In 1985 an eruption of the Nevado del Ruiz in Colombia sent floods of mud and water down the mountains, killing more than 22,000 people.

between three **cordilleras**, or parallel mountain ranges, of the Andes. Bogotà (bo guh TAH), Colombia's capital and largest city, lies on a high plateau of the Andes.

A Single Crop Although many different crops can grow in mountain climates, Colombia's farmers depend heavily on one crop. Surpassed only by Brazil, Colombia is famous for coffee, which is grown on more than 300,000 small farms. Most of the country's farmland is owned by a few wealthy families who rent small amounts of land to tenant farmers at high prices. Small farmers, or **campesinos**, are often barely able to grow enough food for their

families because they focus their efforts on producing a cash crop of coffee.

A country that depends on one crop, such as coffee, is at risk if world demand for coffee drops, or if the coffee trees are destroyed. Officials are trying to reduce Colombia's dependence on a single cash crop by encouraging the export of other farm products.

The Drug Trade While coffee is Colombia's major legal crop, two other products have proved to be extremely profitable for a small minority of Colombians. Huge quantities of marijuana and cocaine, a dangerous addictive drug made from the leaves of the coca plant, are illegally exported from Colombia. Authorities estimate that smuggling illegal drugs brings twice as much money into Colombia as coffee does. Those who control the illegal drug trade also hold considerable power. The governments of Colombia and the United States are working

Vertical Climate Zones in Latin America

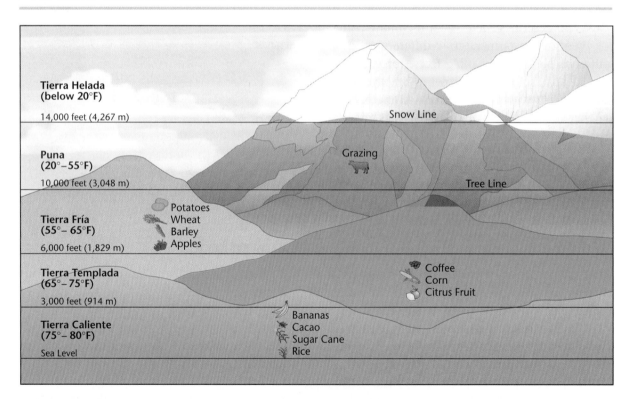

DIAGRAM STUDY

In mountainous areas, climate varies greatly with elevation. *What do Latin Americans call the region between 6,000 and 10,000 feet? Which crops are commonly grown in the tierra templada?*

250 Chapter 13 ▪ Section 1

Mountain Grown

Regions The Andes offer soil and climate perfect for growing coffee. Colombia is a world leader in coffee production, and coffee makes up half of all Colombian agricultural exports. **Critical Thinking** *What is the danger of a country depending on a single cash crop for income?*

together to stop the drug trade and the violence associated with it.

Social Challenges Colombia has had a stormy political history since it gained independence from Spain in 1824. Continuing disputes between the country's two major political parties reached a violent climax in the 1950s, when about 200,000 people were killed in a bloody civil war. In 1958, however, the two parties agreed to work together. Since that time, they have shared political offices and have tried to develop Colombia's economy.

Like many South American countries, Colombia struggles with the challenges that result from social inequality. A few people hold a majority of the country's wealth and power, while many suffer from extreme poverty. At times, antigovernment violence erupts among Colombia's least fortunate and angriest people.

Section 1 Review

Vocabulary and Main Ideas

1. Define: a. mulatto b. bauxite c. Llanos d. cordillera e. campesino

2. In what ways are the Guianas unlike other countries in South America?

3. How does elevation affect agriculture in mountainous parts of South America? How are higher elevations used?

4. Critical Thinking: *Defining Problems* What are the advantages and the disadvantages of an economy based on one crop or one product?

learning LOCATIONS

5. Name the river that flows through the Llanos in Venezuela.

6. In which country of South America can you go to a beach on either the Caribbean Sea or the Pacific Ocean?

2 The Andean Countries

Section Preview

Main Ideas

The Andes have shaped the economies of Ecuador, Peru, Bolivia, and Chile.

Ethnic background influences the way in which most people in the Andean nations earn a living.

Vocabulary

altiplano, *parámos*, timber line, *selva*

Traditional and modern boats ply the waters of Lake Titicaca.

The Andes form the backbone of Ecuador, Peru, Bolivia, and Chile. It is the longest unbroken mountain chain in the world, soaring higher than any range except the Himalayas in South Asia. Some of the Andes' snow-capped peaks tower more than 20,000 feet (6,000 m) above sea level. The Andes have shaped not only the physical geography of the Andean nations, but also the economies and lifestyles of the people who make their homes in this region.

A Mountainous Land

The Andes stretch 4,500 miles (7,200 km) all the way from the Caribbean Sea to the southern-most tip of South America. At places in Peru and Bolivia the mountain range is nearly 500 miles (800 km) wide. Its rocky walls divide the Andean nations into three distinct environments: coastal plain, highlands, and forest.

Coastal Plain Between the mountains and the sea, a narrow plain stretches along the entire Pacific coast from Colombia to the southern end of Chile. At some points it is no more than a sandy beach at the foot of the mountains; in other places it reaches inland for 100 miles (160 km).

The Atacama Desert, the driest and one of the most lifeless places on earth, occupies the coastal plain in northern Chile. Because ocean winds lose their moisture blowing across the cold waters of the Peru Current, only dry air ever reaches the land, creating a desolate wasteland. The Atacama is so dry that archaeologists have found perfectly preserved relics from ancient times. These include colored textiles woven hundreds of years ago, ancient mud-brick dwellings, and even human mummies. The desert is rich in minerals, however.

Coastal plains north and south of the Atacama get more rainfall. To the north, along the coast of Ecuador, lie oppressively hot and humid rain forests. To the south lies an area with a Mediterranean climate of hot, dry summers and mild, rainy winters.

Highlands Inland from the coastal plain, the peaks of the Andes rise skyward to incredible heights. Between the cordilleras lie highland valleys and plateaus. The high plateaus range from

6,500 to 16,000 feet (1,980 to 4,900 m) above sea level. Plateau regions are known by different names in different countries: the *altiplano,* or "high plains," in Peru and Bolivia, and the *páramos* in Ecuador.

The climate in the Andes varies with elevation. At very high elevations, the vegetation is known as alpine tundra. Alpine tundra usually grows above the **timber line**, the boundary above which continuous forest vegetation cannot grow. Only plants that can survive cold temperatures, gusting winds, spotty precipitation, and short growing seasons grow in the alpine tundra.

The highest altitudes of the Andes are in the midsection of the mountain chain. Mountaintop areas here are snow-covered and cold all year long. Further north, however, the picture changes. Mountain temperatures there are warmer, rains more frequent, and rain forest growth thick and lush.

Tropical Forests Inland, the eastern slopes of the Andes descend to forested tropical lowlands. A dramatic contrast exists between the cold, dry mountains and the steamy lowlands. In Ecuador, Peru, and Bolivia, these forested regions are called the *selva.* The rain forests of the Amazon River basin begin in the *selva.* Jaguars, hummingbirds, monkeys, and toucans inhabit this region, but not many people.

Rich Resources

People have always been drawn to the Andes because of the area's natural resources. The soil is mostly rich and suited for growing a variety of crops, depending on the elevation. The mountains contain a wealth of gold, silver, tin, copper, and other minerals. At the same time, the mountains have often served as barriers to trade among the Andean countries and with the outside world.

Vertical Trade One way in which the people of the Andes have adapted to mountain living is by "vertical trade." In a typical Andean market town, people from villages at different elevations meet to trade their crops. Because people grow crops suited to their own climate

Frozen in Time

- **Place** The 500-year-old mummified remains of a young Inca boy, along with a cache of figurines, were found in Chile at an altitude of more than 20,000 feet. **Critical Thinking** *Why do researchers study mummies and ancient artifacts?*
- **Regions** *What importance have the Andes historically had to the people who live in the region?*

zone, here they trade "up" and "down." Tropical foods such as bananas and sugar cane, grown in the *tierra caliente,* may be traded for the potatoes and cabbages that grow in the *tierra fría.* Village farmers, highland cheesemakers, coastal fishermen, and peddlers all meet in the Andean market town.

Physical Effects The original inhabitants of the highlands, before the Spanish arrived in the 1500s, were groups of Native Americans. Indians still make up between 25 and 55 percent of the populations of Bolivia, Ecuador, and Peru. Andean Indians, who have lived for centuries at altitudes up to 17,000 feet (5,200 m) have developed unusual physical characteristics, such as larger hearts and lungs, that let them live and work in the thin, oxygen-poor air.

Ecuador

Ecuador takes its name from the Equator which cuts across the country. About one fourth of the 11.5 million Ecuadorians are of Indian descent. They speak Quechua (KECH wah), the language of the Incas. They follow a traditional lifestyle in the highlands, making their living as subsistence farmers. People of European background make up only about 10 percent of Ecuador's population. But because they own the largest farms and factories, they have the most political influence.

Roughly half of its population are mestizos, who speak Spanish and live mainly in highland cities and towns. Some work in urban factories, while others have moved to the coastal plain and work as tenant farmers on plantations that grow bananas, cacao, and coffee for export.

Only a few decades ago, Ecuador's population was concentrated in the mountainous central highland. Today, due to internal migration, the population is about evenly divided between the highlands and the coastal lowlands. East of the mountains, the tropical forest region remains sparsely populated.

In the 1960s, Ecuadorians discovered oil in the *selva* lowlands. In spite of the challenges of transporting oil by pipeline from the *selva* to the coast, petroleum became Ecuador's chief export. About three quarters of production is controlled by the state-owned oil company, Petroecuador. The country's economy grew steadily for most of the 1990s.

Peru

Peru was the heart of the vast Inca Empire, which fell to the Spaniards in the early 1500s. The conquistadors destroyed the empire but the Incas remain. About 45 percent of Peru's population are Indians who speak Quechua or Aymara (EYE muh RAH). Most live by subsistence farming or herding llamas and alpacas in the highlands. Magnificent ruins, such as the

Facts in BRIEF

Country	Population	Life Expectancy (years)	Per Capita GNP (in US $)
Argentina	34,600,000	71	7,290
Bolivia	7,400,000	60	770
Brazil	157,800,000	66	3,020
Chile	14,300,000	72	3,070
Colombia	37,700,000	69	1,400
Ecuador	11,500,000	69	1,170
Guyana	800,000	65	350
Paraguay	5,000,000	70	1,500
Peru	24,000,000	66	1,490
Suriname	400,000	70	1,210
Uruguay	3,200,000	73	3,910
Venezuela	21,800,000	72	2,840
United States	263,200,000	76	24,750

Source: Population Reference Bureau

CHART SKILLS

- *Which country, aside from the United States, has the longest life expectancy?*

- **Critical Thinking** *What country has the lowest GNP? What problems can be associated with a low GNP?*

fortress of Machu Picchu and the buildings of the Inca capital city of Cuzco, are fine examples of Incan architectural design.

Most other Peruvians are mestizos who live in urban areas in or near the coastal plain. For the most part, they work for low wages in factories that produce fish meal for animal feed, or on plantations that export cotton, sugar cane, and rice. Poverty and unemployment are widespread.

In Peru, as in Ecuador, a minority of people of European descent control most of the country's wealth and are leaders in the government and in the army. More recently, many Asians have immigrated to Peru. In 1995, Alberto Fujimori, a Peruvian of Japanese ancestry, was elected to a second term as Peru's president. Fujimori made economic reforms and suppressed a terrorist movement, the Shining Path. In 2000, following a series of corruption scandals, Fujimori called for new elections and announced that he would not be a candidate.

Bolivia

Because Bolivia is landlocked, it lacks the profitable coastal ports and factories of Ecuador and Peru. Lake Titicaca, the world's highest navigable lake, straddles the border between Bolivia and Peru. Bolivia does have many minerals, including the Western Hemisphere's largest reserves of tin. Unfortunately the best ores have already been removed. As in Peru and Ecuador, the majority of Bolivia's people are Indians—mostly subsistence farmers who live in the highlands. Bolivian farm families grow potatoes, wheat, and barley. At higher elevations they herd alpacas and llamas. Children contribute to the family economy by helping herd the animals.

Bolivia's climate varies with the altitude—from humid and tropical to cold and semi-arid. The cold, thin air of the high plateau makes physical activity difficult for non-native born people.

Chile: Land of Contrasts

Chile, meaning "end of the land," was appropriately named by the Indians who once lived on this strip of land. Chile edges the west coast of South America like a long, narrow ribbon. The country is about 2,700 miles (4,300 km) long but only averages 100 miles (160 km) wide. About two thirds of the more than 14 million people in Chile are mestizos. Another quarter are of

GLOBAL issues

Epidemics

The 20th century's first outbreak of cholera—an often-fatal disease caused by contaminated water—started in Peru in 1991. That year, 500,000 cases of cholera were reported in South America.

Expanding Services

Place Peruvian president Alberto Fujimori is shown here celebrating the arrival of electricity to a remote village. Modernization has been a slow and difficult process in some areas because of the rugged terrain of the Andes. **Critical Thinking** *In what ways does the terrain impact efforts to extend basic services to isolated villages in Peru?*

Going Out to Sea

Human-Environment Interaction
The 7 million tons (6.5 million metric tons) of fish caught off the coast of Chile each year makes Chile a world leader in the fishing industry. Most of this catch is processed into fish meal and fish oil and sold to other countries. *How does Chile's shape and location aid the fishing industry?*

European descent—mostly Spanish, British, and German. Unlike the other Andean nations, Chile has relatively few Indians.

The barren Atacama Desert in the north is uninhabited. In contrast, about three fourths of the Chilean people live in the thickly populated Central Valley. It is a region of fertile river basins between the Andes and the coastal ranges. Fruit, vegetables, and wine grapes grow there in abundance. Because Chile's productive summer season comes during the Northern Hemisphere's winter, its products find good markets in the United States and Europe.

Most of Chile's cities and factories are also in the Central Valley. Santiago, the capital, is home to about one third of the country's population. Many people are newcomers from the countryside, unskilled and illiterate. As a result, Santiago has high unemployment and many poor, crowded communities. Although Chile's economy has grown rapidly, about 4 million of its people still live below the poverty line.

Section 2 Review

Vocabulary and Main Ideas

1. Define: a. *altiplano* b. *parámos* c. timber line d. *selva*

2. What ethnic group makes up the majority of population in the northern Andean nations?

3. Where do most of the Chilean people live? Why?

4. Critical Thinking: *Cause and Effect* What are some of the ways in which the people of Ecuador, Peru, and Bolivia have adapted to life in a high, mountainous region?

learning LOCATIONS

5. Why does its location make Bolivia's economy different from those of Peru and Ecuador?

6. Where is the Atacama Desert? What is unusual about this area?

Focus on Skills

☐ Social Studies
☐ Map and Globe
☑ Critical Thinking and Problem Solving

Determining Relevance

The study of geography often involves being able to see connections between the physical characteristics of a place and its human geography, or people's lives. When thoughts or ideas are connected or related to each other, we say that the thoughts and ideas are relevant to each other. Determining relevance means finding a logical connection between two pieces of information. If a relevant connection can be made, you can use one item to learn about the other.

For example, the dizziness felt by tourists traveling in the Andes is related to the high elevation there. On the other hand, the fact that some places in the Andes are located at the Equator is *not* relevant when we discuss altitude-related dizziness. Learning to identify what is relevant and what is not when answering a question or solving a problem is an important skill in critical thinking.

Use the following steps to analyze the passages below and to practice determining the relevance of different pieces of information.

1. Identify the main ideas in the passage. Read each passage to determine what the main ideas are. Answer the following questions: (a) What are the two main ideas expressed in Passage A? (b) How would you describe the main idea of Passage B?

2. Look for connections between the ideas. Ask yourself if the ideas are related to each other. Answer the following questions: (a) What connection is suggested in Passage A between the physical features of South America and human settlement, movement, and communication on that continent? (b) How are military rule and contemporary problems in Brazil linked in Passage B?

Passage A

In extreme contrast to the tropical rain forests of the Amazon, other parts of South America have cold deserts and dry, rugged mountains. The Atacama Desert of southern Peru and northern Chile is mostly barren and unable to support life. The Andes Mountains run more than 5,000 miles (8,000 km) north to south along the western coast of South America. The Andes are a formidable barrier to transportation and communication. The southernmost parts of South America are close to Antarctica and are thus very cold.

Passage B

Between 1956 and 1964, Brazil was a democracy. Then a military dictatorship ruled the nation from 1964 to 1985. Injustice in the form of censorship and political oppression marked those years. At the same time, Brazil became one of the most highly industrialized countries in Latin America. In 1985, the military rulers agreed to free elections and a return to civilian rule. The elected rulers faced a massive foreign debt of over $100 billion. Overpopulation and poverty also present major problems for Brazil.

The Southern Grassland Countries

Section Preview

Main Ideas

- Southern South America is a region of great physical diversity bound together by a river system.

- Uruguay and Argentina are two of the wealthiest and most urbanized nations of South America.

Vocabulary

estuary, piedmont, pampas, gauchos

Rosario, Argentina, on the Paraná River, is a major commercial center.

The three nations of southern South America—Uruguay, Paraguay, and Argentina—contrast sharply with the rest of the continent. Although they face economic problems, they are among the most prosperous South American nations. Ethnically, they have more in common with Europe than with their neighbors.

Rivers and Regions

Southern South America consists of several physical regions with varying landforms, climates, and vegetation. These regions are bound together by a great river system.

Great Rivers As the map on page 191 shows, several large rivers flow from the interior into the Río de la Plata. Although its name means "River of Silver," the Plata is an **estuary**, a broad river mouth formed where a flooded river valley meets the sea.

Four rivers in the Plata estuary system form national boundaries: the Uruguay, the Pilcomayo,

the Paraguay, and the Paraná. The capitals of Argentina and Uruguay—Buenos Aires and Montevideo—are both located on the Río de la Plata. This vast river system provides an inexpensive and efficient way for people to ship goods.

Andean Region The highest peaks of the Andes are in western Argentina. They include the four highest mountains in the Western Hemisphere, including Mount Aconcagua (ah kuhn KAH gwah), which towers 22,831 feet (6,959 m) above sea level. From this great height, the Andes gradually give way to a gently rolling **piedmont**, or foothills, region.

Tropical Lowlands The Gran Chaco, meaning "great swamp," is a hot, interior lowland region of savanna and dense shrub that spreads over parts of Paraguay, Argentina, Bolivia, and Brazil. Temperatures in the Gran Chaco are mild and change little during the year. Rainfall, however, is seasonal. Summer rains turn the area into mud. In winter the soil is dry and windblown.

Grasslands The **pampas** of Argentina and Uruguay are one of South America's best-known features. These temperate grasslands, which stretch for hundreds of miles, were formerly home to hundreds of **gauchos** (GOW chohs), the cowboys who herded cattle there. Fewer gauchos now work on Argentina's interior ranches. Today the pampas are Argentina's breadbasket, producing about 80 percent of the nation's grain and about 70 percent of its meat. The pampas have warm summers and cold winters. Occasional violent winter thunderstorms are known as "pamperos."

Patagonia South of the pampas lies the windswept plateau of Patagonia. This desolate, dry, cold, and sometimes foggy plain is well suited for raising sheep. It also has rich deposits of oil and bauxite.

Paraguay

Although Paraguay is landlocked, the Plata river system provides an outlet to the sea. Almost all Paraguayans live in the highlands of the eastern part of their country, rather than the swampy Chaco. About half the people live in urban areas, especially the capital city of Asunción, on the Paraguay River. Most Paraguayans are mestizos, who speak Guarani, the local Indian language, as well as Spanish.

The Paraguayan economy is based on agriculture, mostly cotton, grains, and livestock. Paraguay and Brazil have cooperated in building the huge Itaipú Dam on the Paraná River, one of the world's largest hydroelectric projects. It began generating electricity in 1984. Paraguayans hope that inexpensive hydroelectric power will make up for the country's lack of minerals and other resources.

For 35 years, Paraguay was ruled by a military dictator, General Alfredo Stroessner. During the period, political freedoms were severely limited and critics of the regime were harassed and persecuted. In 1989, however, discontented military officers replaced him with another general. The new leader, General Andres Rodriguez, surprised them by making the government more responsive to people's needs. In May 1993, Paraguay held its first democratic election and chose a civilian president.

Uruguay

Uruguay takes its name from the Indian word meaning "river of the painted bird." The name probably comes from the brightly colored

A Mighty Dam

Human-Environment Interaction The waters of the Paraná River power the Itaipú Dam's hydroelectric plant. The world's second-largest capacity hydroelectric plant, the Itaipú has the potential to generate 13,320 megawatts of electricity. (A megawatt is one million watts, the basic unit for measuring electric power.) *Why has Paraguay invested in hydro-electricity?*

tropical birds found along the Rió de la Plata. Because much of Uruguay is rolling grasslands, the country's economy is based on raising livestock, processing meat, and making products such as wool and leather. About 75 percent of the land is devoted to livestock grazing and another 10 percent to raising grains to feed cattle and sheep. Uruguay produces no fuel and few consumer goods, so it must import these expensive products.

Most Uruguayans are of European descent, mainly Italian and Spanish. The country has a large middle class, who live comfortably in urban areas with few slums. They enjoy the country's beautiful beaches. Politically, however, Uruguay has an unstable history. In 1973, the military took power, ruling for 12 years. Repression was widespread, and many people were imprisoned. Since 1985, Uruguay has held free elections. People have often held demonstrations to show their desire for freedom of the press and other democratic rights.

Argentina

Like their neighbors in Uruguay, most of Argentina's 34.6 million people have European ancestors, mostly Spanish and Italian. Eighty-six percent of them live in cities. More than 10 million live in sprawling Buenos Aires. Argentina is Latin America's wealthiest nation in terms of per capita GNP, although wealth is unevenly distributed.

A Bustling City Buenos Aires is a vibrant capital city that looks to Europe for its fashions, art, food, and style. Busy factories produce goods for export, and the harbor is filled with freighters from all over the world. One result of all this activity is the heavy air pollution that blankets Buenos Aires. Like many of Latin America's cities, Buenos Aires is a magnet for poor, rural people seeking jobs and a better way of life.

Political History From the mid-1940s until 1983, Argentina was ruled by a series of military dictators. The best known was Juan Domingo Perón, who was president from 1946 to 1955. Perón wanted to develop Argentina's industry and to distribute wealth more evenly

Wool for Export

Human-Environment Interaction This gaucho is vaccinating sheep. Wool is one of Uruguay's major exports. In fact, most of Uruguay's export income is generated by agriculture. *Why is Uruguay well-suited to raising livestock?*

among the people. His first wife, Eva, became a heroine to Argentina's poor. Other dictators used government power to help the wealthy, ignoring the problems of the poor. But all of them censored newspapers, closed down universities, and imprisoned political opponents. They tried to give the appearance of progress by borrowing money from foreign banks to build dams, roads, and factories.

Conditions under military rule in the 1970s were particularly bad. So many people were kidnapped by the military and never seen again that the period became known as the "dirty wars." Every Thursday afternoon a group of women marched in front of the presidential palace. They carried pictures of missing family members and demanded to know what had happened to them.

In 1981 Argentina lost a war with Great Britain over the Falkland Islands off the country's southern Atlantic coast. Facing disgrace, the military agreed to allow open elections. Carlos Menem, elected in 1989 and reelected in 1995, cut government spending and tried to improve Argentina's international standing. Menem has also tried to set up a regional market, called Mercosur, with other nations of southern South America.

Sea of Green

Human-Environment Interaction Moderate rainfall creates large areas of grassland. In Argentina, the temperate grasslands are called pampas. *Estancias*, or cattle ranches, like the one shown here, and farms of the vast, fertile pampas make Argentina a leading exporter of food. *How much of Argentina's food is produced on the pampas?*

Section 3 Review

Vocabulary and Main Ideas

1. **Define: a. estuary b. piedmont c. pampas d. gaucho**

2. **Name the four types of land environments of the southern South American countries.**

3. **Why are the pampas so valuable to Argentina and Uruguay?**

4. **Critical Thinking: *Determining Relevance* What changes or factors will help the future of democracy in southern South America?**

learning LOCATIONS

5. **What capital cities are located on the Rió de la Plata or other rivers in the Plata system?**

6. **What countries are Uruguay's neighbors?**

Summarizing Main Ideas

Section 1   The Northern Tropics

- The Guianas—French Guiana, Suriname, and Guyana—share many physical characteristics, but their languages, cultures, and ethnic mix derive from their history as colonies of European nations.
- Venezuela is one of the world's main oil-producing nations, using its wealth to improve people's living standards.
- Colombia's economy depends on the export of coffee and battling the illegal drug trade.

Section 2   The Andean Countries

- The Andes divide the Andean countries—Ecuador, Peru, Bolivia, and Chile—into three geographical environments: coastal plains, highlands, and tropical forests, or *selva*.
- People have adapted to mountain life by growing crops adapted to each climate zone and developing a system of vertical trade.
- Indians are a large population group in Ecuador, Peru, and Bolivia.
- The Andes have rich natural resources, but Indians and mestizos are mostly subsistence farmers or low-paid city workers.

Section 3   The Southern Grassland Countries

- Much of Argentina and Uruguay is a fertile grassland plains, the pampas.
- Uruguay and Argentina are two of the wealthiest nations of South America. Most of their people are of European descent.
- All these nations have had many years of military rule but have recently elected civilian governments.

Reviewing Vocabulary

Match the definitions with the correct terms.

1. Andean highlands in Ecuador
2. rural farmer in Latin America
3. Andean highlands in Bolivia and Peru
4. Argentinian cowboy
5. forested regions
6. parallel mountain ranges
7. foothills region
8. temperate grasslands of Argentina and Uruguay

a. *altiplano*
b. piedmont
c. pampas
d. gaucho

e. *parámos*
f. *selva*
g. cordillera
h. campesino

Applying the Geographic Themes

1. **Place** How are the languages and cultures of the Guianas different from those of the Andean countries?
2. **Location** How does elevation influence agriculture and lifestyles in the Andean nations?
3. **Human-Environment Interaction** Why are the pampas important to the economies of Uruguay and Argentina?
4. **Movement** What countries depend on the Río de la Plata system for trade and transportation?
5. **Regions** What characteristics do the nations of northern South America share?

Critical Thinking and Applying Skills

1. **Identifying Central Issues** Why do you think military dictatorships have been so common throughout South America?
2. **Determining Relevance** Using the steps you have learned on page 257, examine an editorial in your local newspaper. What is the main idea of the editorial? Is the evidence provided relevant? Can you extend the editorial's argument into related areas? Present your findings to the class.

Journal Activity

Writing Across Cultures

▶ 1. Imagine that you are managing the political campaign of a civilian candidate for president of a South American country that has been under military rule for 15 years. Write a brief (three paragraph) speech for your candidate, explaining to voters what he or she will do to restore democracy and improve people's lives.

▶ 2. Like the American West, the pampas of Argentina and Uruguay have inspired books and songs about the free, outdoor life of the gauchos. After looking at photographs and other sources, write your own short "South American Western" song or story.

INTERNET link

Find out more about Colombia at a site at Colorado State University. Link to this site from:

• www.phschool.com

Visit links of interest, then write a paragraph explaining why you would or would not like to visit Colombia.

learning LOCATIONS

South America

Number from 1 to 6 on a piece of paper. Next to each number write the letter of the place on the map that corresponds to the places listed below.

1. Peru
2. Argentina
3. Colombia
4. Bolivia
5. Venezuela
6. Ecuador

GLOBAL WARMING

Each year, the United States releases 2.6 trillion pounds of carbon dioxide (CO_2) emissions by burning fossil fuels. Although these gases are invisible, they could be greatly affecting our climate by increasing the temperature of our atmosphere. This process is referred to as Global Warming. The following activity will help you understand how CO_2 gas can affect the temperature of the air.

MATERIALS:

Double-sided tape

2 plastic containers
with plastic lids

Masking Tape

Marker

2 Thermometers

2 Bright lights
(same
wattage)

Vinegar

Baking soda

1/4 cup
measurer

Safety goggles

PROCEDURE:

1. Put on your safety goggles. Use the double-sided tape to attach a thermometer to the inside of each plastic container. Label one container A and the other B.

2. Fill the bottom of each plastic container with a half inch of vinegar. Record the temperature of the air in container A, then cover it with a lid.

3. Carefully, add 1/4 cup of baking soda to container B. Observe what happens. Wait about 20 seconds, then record the temperature of the air in container B and cover it with a lid.

Step 3

Step 2

Step 4

4. Place each container under a light, leaving about three inches between the container and the light.

5. Record the temperature of the air in each container after 10 minutes.

OBSERVATIONS AND ANALYSIS:

1. Describe your results. Explain what you think is happening in each container. Explain any differences in the temperature of each container.

2. What activities in our society produce CO_2? What activities do you participate in that produce CO_2?

3. How do the results of this lab support the theory of global warming? What activities counteract global warming or reduce the amount of CO_2 in our atmosphere?

4. What are some of the possible consequences of rising water levels to deserts, coastlines, and available food supply?

5. The presence of water vapor can also increase the average temperature of our atmosphere. If our atmospheric temperatures rise, how will that affect the amount of water vapor in the air? Would that increase or decrease global warming?

Scientists Question STABILITY OF ICE SHEETS

At a meeting of experts this week, the stability of the southern polar ice cap was debated. The consequences of the melting of this cap and the impact of global warming due to increased carbon dioxide (CO_2) in the atmosphere were also discussed. Scientists in the fields of geology, meteorology, and marine biology concluded that sea levels could rise 150 feet with the melting of just 30% of one of the ice sheets.

taking Action

We can slow the process of global warming. Here are some ways you can help by reducing activities that produce CO_2:

✔ Drive less, turn down thermostats, and use less hot water.

✔ Plant trees to help increase CO_2 absorption.

✔ Learn more about solar power sources.

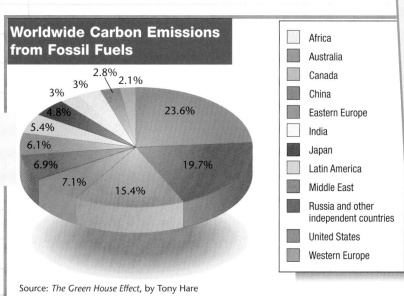

Worldwide Carbon Emissions from Fossil Fuels

23.6%
19.7%
15.4%
7.1%
6.9%
6.1%
5.4%
4.8%
3%
3%
2.8%
2.1%

- Africa
- Australia
- Canada
- China
- Eastern Europe
- India
- Japan
- Latin America
- Middle East
- Russia and other independent countries
- United States
- Western Europe

Source: *The Green House Effect,* by Tony Hare

UNIT four

Western Europe

CHAPTERS

14 Regional Atlas: Western Europe

15 The British Isles and Nordic Nations

16 Central Western Europe

17 Mediterranean Europe

A Global Perspective

The continent of Europe is sometimes called "a peninsula of peninsulas" because a number of smaller peninsulas jut out to the north, west, and south. In the north is the Scandinavian Peninsula. On the southwest is the Iberian Peninsula, made up of Spain and Portugal. Stretching into the Mediterranean Sea is the Italian peninsula. It takes the shape of a boot with a "heel" pointing to Greece—which forms yet another peninsula.

Robinson Projection

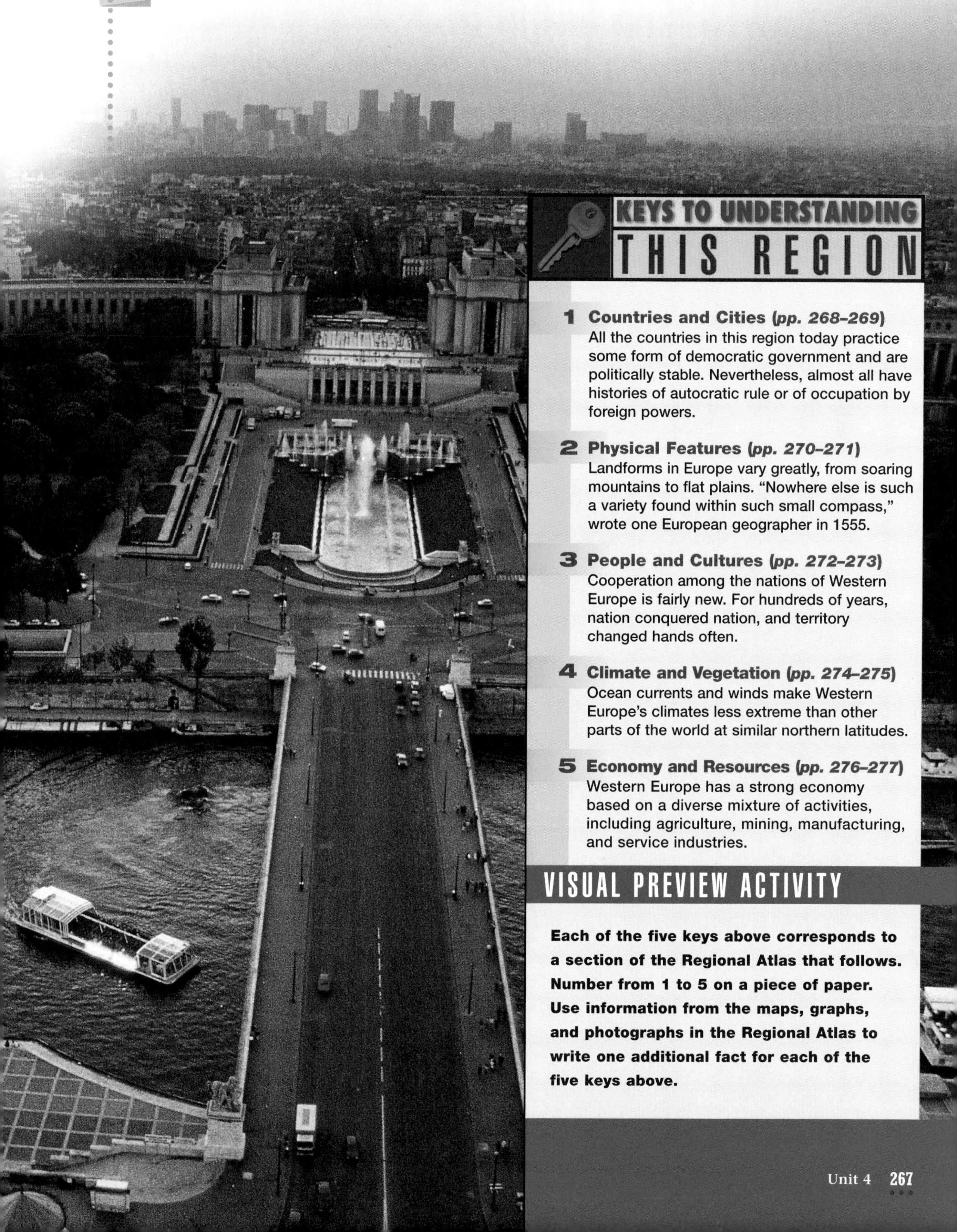

Paris, France

THIS REGION

1 Countries and Cities (*pp. 268–269*)
All the countries in this region today practice some form of democratic government and are politically stable. Nevertheless, almost all have histories of autocratic rule or of occupation by foreign powers.

2 Physical Features (*pp. 270–271*)
Landforms in Europe vary greatly, from soaring mountains to flat plains. "Nowhere else is such a variety found within such small compass," wrote one European geographer in 1555.

3 People and Cultures (*pp. 272–273*)
Cooperation among the nations of Western Europe is fairly new. For hundreds of years, nation conquered nation, and territory changed hands often.

4 Climate and Vegetation (*pp. 274–275*)
Ocean currents and winds make Western Europe's climates less extreme than other parts of the world at similar northern latitudes.

5 Economy and Resources (*pp. 276–277*)
Western Europe has a strong economy based on a diverse mixture of activities, including agriculture, mining, manufacturing, and service industries.

VISUAL PREVIEW ACTIVITY

Each of the five keys above corresponds to a section of the Regional Atlas that follows. Number from 1 to 5 on a piece of paper. Use information from the maps, graphs, and photographs in the Regional Atlas to write one additional fact for each of the five keys above.

Chapter 14

WESTERN EUROPE

Use the Map, Graph, and Photo Studies in this Regional Atlas to gain a better understanding of the region's physical and cultural geography.

ATLAS VOCABULARY

summit	multilingual	prevailing westerlies

1 COUNTRIES AND CITIES

LARGEST CITIES

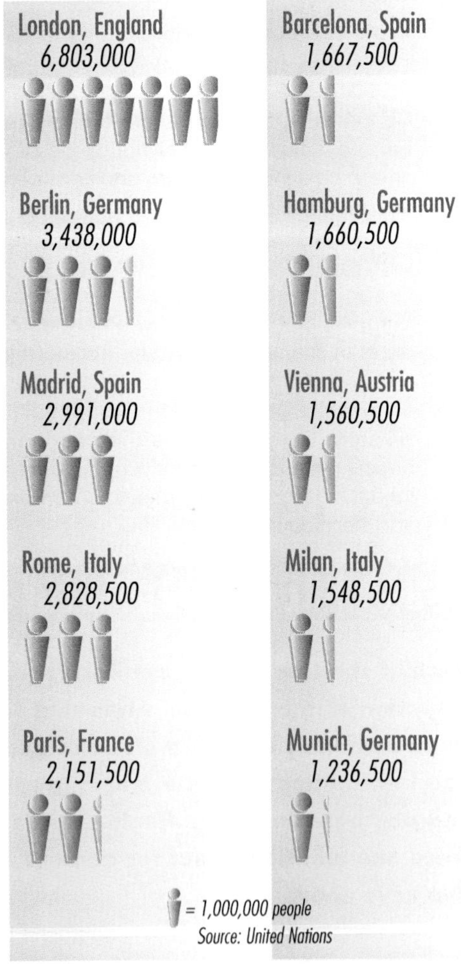

London, England
6,803,000

Berlin, Germany
3,438,000

Madrid, Spain
2,991,000

Rome, Italy
2,828,500

Paris, France
2,151,500

Barcelona, Spain
1,667,500

Hamburg, Germany
1,660,500

Vienna, Austria
1,560,500

Milan, Italy
1,548,500

Munich, Germany
1,236,500

= 1,000,000 people
Source: United Nations

MAP STUDY
Applying the Geographic Themes

1 **Location** Western Europe stretches from the Scandinavian Peninsula in the north to the Iberian Peninsula in the south. Reykjavik and Helsinki are the northernmost capitals of Western Europe. *Which are the two southern-most capitals?*

2 **Location** Almost every Western European country has a coastline. *Which countries are entirely surrounded by land?*

3 **Movement** Shipping and trade have traditionally been an important part of Western Europe's economy. Cities with access to the coast, such as London and Lisbon, have grown into the great ports of this region. *On which bodies of water are these ports located?*

GRAPH STUDY

4 **Largest Cities** Two thirds of Western Europe's people live in four nations: the United Kingdom, France, Germany, and Italy. In these countries people are concentrated in large metropolitan areas. *Name the five largest cities in Western Europe.*

WESTERN EUROPE

REGIONAL *atlas*

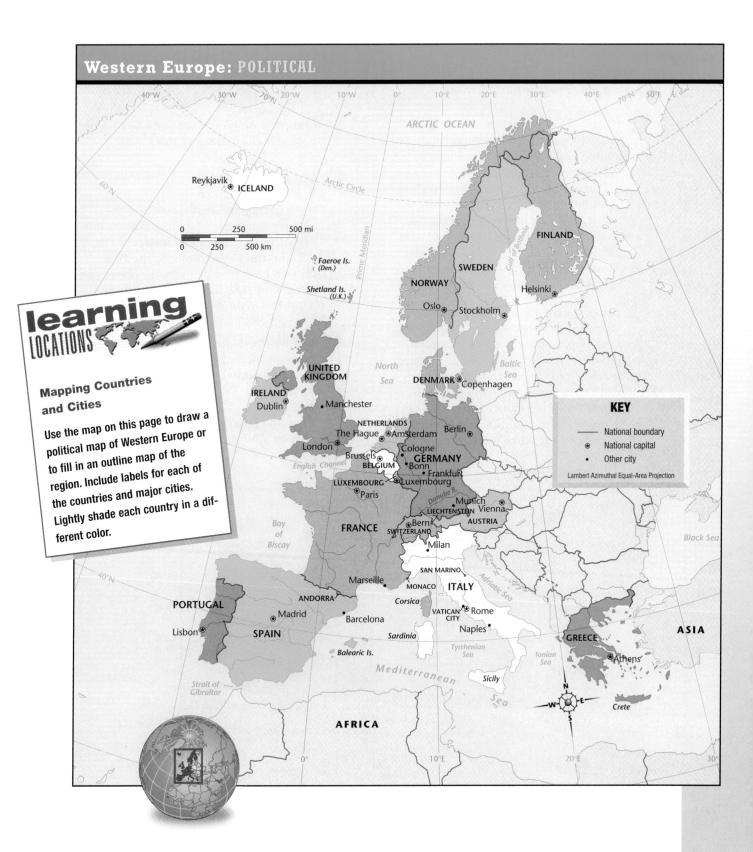

Western Europe: POLITICAL

Learning LOCATIONS

Mapping Countries and Cities

Use the map on this page to draw a political map of Western Europe or to fill in an outline map of the region. Include labels for each of the countries and major cities. Lightly shade each country in a different color.

KEY

— National boundary
⊛ National capital
• Other city

Lambert Azimuthal Equal-Area Projection

ARCTIC OCEAN

Reykjavik ⊛ ICELAND

Arctic Circle

0   250   500 mi
0   250   500 km

Faeroe Is. (Den.)

Shetland Is. (U.K.)

FINLAND

SWEDEN

NORWAY

Helsinki

Oslo ⊛   ⊛ Stockholm

UNITED KINGDOM

North Sea

Baltic Sea

Gulf of Bothnia

IRELAND
Dublin ⊛   • Manchester

DENMARK ⊛ Copenhagen

NETHERLANDS   Berlin •
The Hague ⊛ Amsterdam

London ⊛

Brussels   Cologne •
English Channel   ⊛ BELGIUM   GERMANY
LUXEMBOURG   Bonn ⊛   Frankfurt •
⊛ Luxembourg

• Paris   Munich •   ⊛ Vienna
LIECHTENSTEIN   AUSTRIA
Bern ⊛

Bay of Biscay   FRANCE   SWITZERLAND

Milan •

PORTUGAL   Marseille •   SAN MARINO   Adriatic Sea
ANDORRA   MONACO   ITALY
Corsica   VATICAN CITY ⊛ Rome

⊛ Madrid   • Barcelona
Lisbon ⊛   SPAIN   Sardinia   Naples •

Balearic Is.   Tyrrhenian Sea   GREECE

Strait of Gibraltar   Mediterranean   Sicily   Ionian Sea   ⊛ Athens

Crete

AFRICA   AFRICA

Black Sea

ASIA

Danube R.

Prime Meridian

2 PHYSICAL FEATURES

MAP STUDY
Applying the Geographic Themes

1 Place The mountains in northern Scandinavia formed more than 400 million years ago. The mountains in the southern part of Europe, the Alps, are higher and younger. They formed about 25 million years ago. Mont Blanc is the tallest mountain in the Alps mountain range. Its **summit**, or highest point, is 15,771 feet (4,807 m) above sea level. *Name at least three other mountain ranges in Europe besides the Alps.*

2 Cause and Effect: Elevation and Vegetation The North European Plain is an important source of agricultural products. Its flat, fertile land is irrigated by some of Europe's great rivers. The plain stretches more than 1,200 miles (1,931 km) from France through Germany and into Eastern Europe and Northern Eurasia. *What other Western European countries, besides France and Germany, have broad expanses of flat lands?*

3 Movement Many rivers crisscross Western Europe. Throughout history, these rivers have carried much of the region's commerce. Two major rivers flow east or south. The Rhône in France empties into the Mediterranean. The Po in Italy empties into the Adriatic. *Name two rivers that flow west or north into the Atlantic Ocean or North Sea.*

4 Location Many Western European cities are located on the banks of rivers. Paris, the capital of France, was founded more than 2,000 years ago on an island in the Seine (SEHN) River. *Critical Thinking Describe the advantages of such a location.*

Cross Section: Western Europe

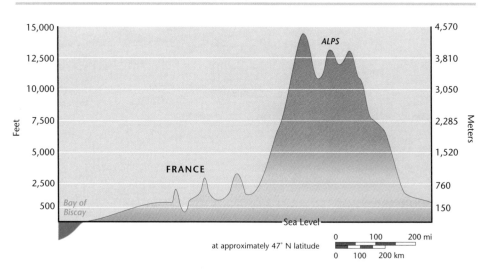

at approximately 47° N latitude

DIAGRAM STUDY

5 Physical Profile The Alps run through Italy, France, Austria, and Switzerland, making an almost solid barrier between Italy and lands to the north. *What is the highest elevation of the portion of the Alps shown in the cross-section?*

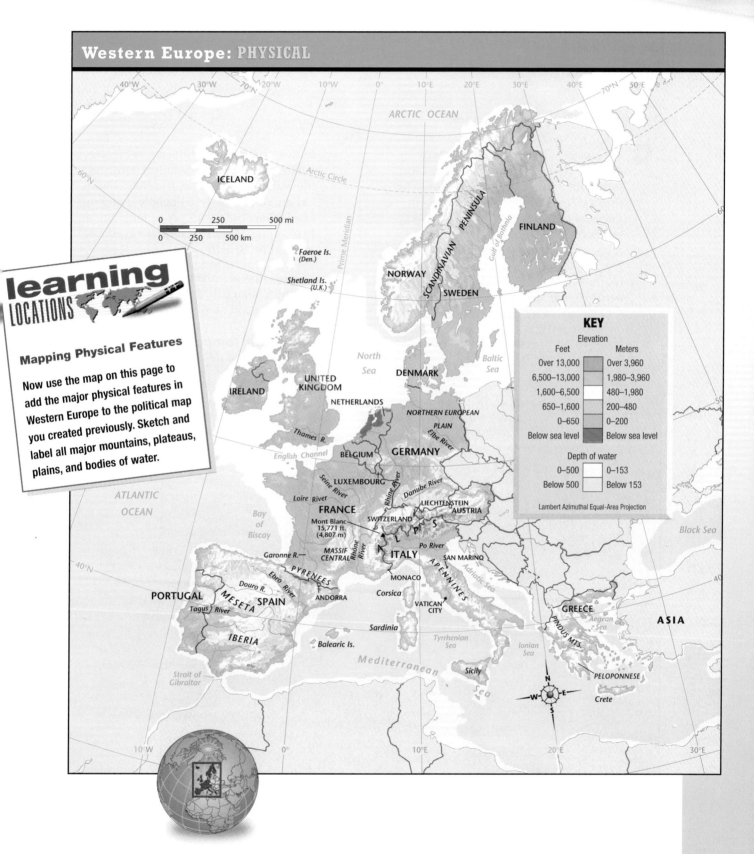

Western Europe: PHYSICAL

learning LOCATIONS

Mapping Physical Features

Now use the map on this page to add the major physical features in Western Europe to the political map you created previously. Sketch and label all major mountains, plateaus, plains, and bodies of water.

KEY

Elevation

Feet		Meters
Over 13,000		Over 3,960
6,500–13,000		1,980–3,960
1,600–6,500		480–1,980
650–1,600		200–480
0–650		0–200
Below sea level		Below sea level

Depth of water

0–500		0–153
Below 500		Below 153

Lambert Azimuthal Equal-Area Projection

ARCTIC OCEAN

Arctic Circle

ICELAND

Faeroe Is. (Den.)

Shetland Is. (U.K.)

NORWAY

SCANDINAVIAN PENINSULA

Gulf of Bothnia

FINLAND

SWEDEN

North Sea

Baltic Sea

DENMARK

IRELAND

UNITED KINGDOM

NETHERLANDS

NORTHERN EUROPEAN PLAIN

Elbe River

Thames R.

English Channel

BELGIUM

GERMANY

ATLANTIC OCEAN

LUXEMBOURG

Rhine River

Danube River

LIECHTENSTEIN

AUSTRIA

Seine River

Loire River

FRANCE

Mont Blanc 15,771 ft. (4,807 m)

SWITZERLAND

A L P S

Po River

ITALY

Bay of Biscay

MASSIF CENTRAL

Rhône River

Garonne R.

APENNINES

SAN MARINO

Adriatic Sea

Black Sea

PYRENEES

MONACO

Ebro River

Douro R.

ANDORRA

Corsica

VATICAN CITY

GREECE

ASIA

PORTUGAL

MESETA

SPAIN

Tagus River

IBERIA

Balearic Is.

Sardinia

Tyrrhenian Sea

PINDUS MTS.

Aegean Sea

Ionian Sea

PELOPONNESE

Strait of Gibraltar

Mediterranean Sea

Sicily

Crete

Prime Meridian

3 PEOPLE AND CULTURES

MAP STUDY
Applying the Geographic Themes

1 Regions Centuries of movement among groups in Western Europe have produced a **multilingual** region, where many different languages are spoken. Many of the languages spoken in Western Europe fall into two major groups. Romance languages, such as Spanish and French, evolved from Latin. Most other nations in Western Europe speak Germanic languages. *Name the countries in which Germanic languages are spoken.*

2 Human-Environment Interaction Western Europe occupies less than 3 per-

cent of the world's landmass, yet it has one of the highest population densities in the world. For example, the Netherlands has an average of 1,164 people living in each square mile (449 per sq km). *Name two countries that include areas of low population density.*

3 Place The population of Western Europe is unevenly distributed. Compare the population density map on page 273 with the physical map on page 271. *Name two physical features that explain the low population density in some areas.*

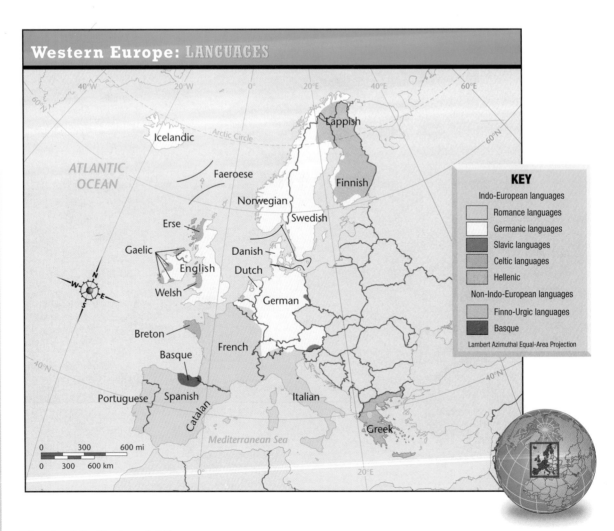

Western Europe: LANGUAGES

KEY

Indo-European languages
- Romance languages
- Germanic languages
- Slavic languages
- Celtic languages
- Hellenic

Non-Indo-European languages
- Finno-Urgic languages
- Basque

Lambert Azimuthal Equal-Area Projection

Western Europe: POPULATION DENSITY

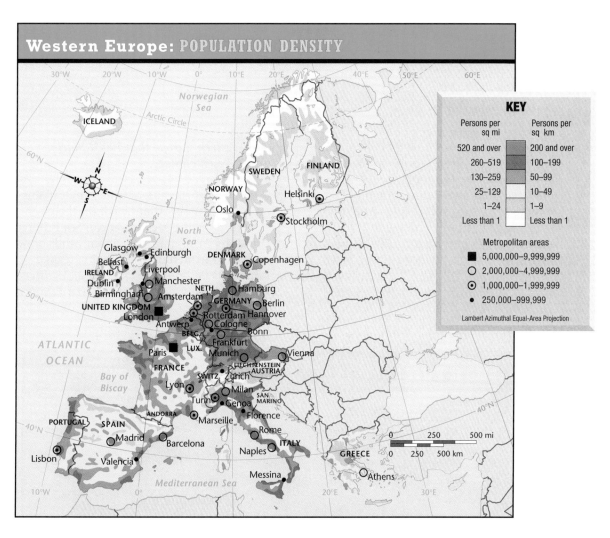

KEY

Persons per sq mi		Persons per sq km
520 and over		200 and over
260–519		100–199
130–259		50–99
25–129		10–49
1–24		1–9
Less than 1		Less than 1

Metropolitan areas
- 5,000,000–9,999,999
- 2,000,000–4,999,999
- 1,000,000–1,999,999
- 250,000–999,999

Lambert Azimuthal Equal-Area Projection

PHOTO STUDY

4 **Catholic Cathedral** The Roman Catholic Church is prominent in many countries of Europe. Some of the most impressive Catholic churches and cathedrals, such as the one shown here at Chartres, France, were constructed during the twelfth, thirteenth, and four-teenth centuries. For hundreds of years, they have been the reli-gious, social, and cultural centers of towns and cities. *Connections: Art Think of three adjectives that describe the style of archi-tecture pictured here.*

WESTERN EUROPE

MAP STUDY
Applying the Geographic Themes

1 **Regions** The North Atlantic Drift, a powerful ocean current, carries tropical waters toward the coast of Europe. The winds that blow across this warm current are the **prevailing westerlies**—the constant flow of air from west to east in the temperate zones of the earth. The ocean currents and winds produce a warm, moist climate in most of Western Europe. *Connections: Math Estimate the percentage* *of Western Europe that has a marine west coast climate.*

2 **Location** Because southern mountains block the moist Atlantic winds, the climate along the Mediterranean Sea is hot and dry in summer. In winter, winds blow off the Mediterranean, bringing regular rainfall. *Describe the location of Mediterranean climate areas in Western Europe.*

Western Europe: CLIMATE REGIONS

KEY
- Semiarid
- Mediterranean
- Humid subtropical
- Marine west coast
- Humid continental
- Subarctic
- Tundra
- Highlands

Lambert Azimuthal Equal-Area Projection

WESTERN EUROPE

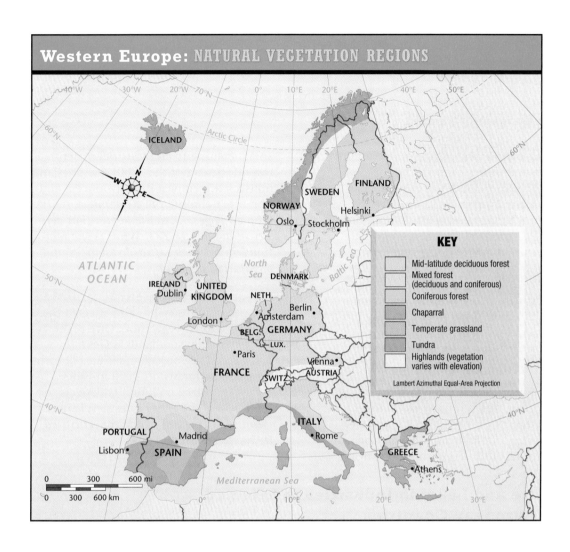

Western Europe: NATURAL VEGETATION REGIONS

KEY

Mid-latitude deciduous forest

Mixed forest
(deciduous and coniferous)

Coniferous forest

Chaparral

Temperate grassland

Tundra

Highlands (vegetation
varies with elevation)

Lambert Azimuthal Equal-Area Projection

③ Place On the Scandinavian Peninsula, northern mountains block warm Atlantic winds creating a very dry, cold, subarctic climate. *What other climate regions are found on the Scandinavian Peninsula?*

④ Regions Forests once blanketed the marine west coast climate area. Most of the Mediterranean climate area was also once covered with the broadleaf and mixed forests that grow well in hot, dry summers. *What types of vegetation are found in the semiarid regions of Spain?*

⑤ Human-Environment Interaction Over the years, people cut down most of the natural forests in Western Europe,

using the timber for fuel and building materials. Today, most land in Europe is used for farming and grazing. *Where are the largest remaining areas of coniferous forests in Western Europe?*

⑥ Cause and Effect: Elevation and Vegetation Elevation greatly influences climate and vegetation. The lower slopes of a mountain may be warm enough to farm. Cooler, higher slopes may be covered with forests. Compare the natural vegetation map above with the physical map on page 271. *What accounts for the highlands vegetation region in Switzerland and Austria?*

WESTERN EUROPE

MAP STUDY
Applying the Geographic Themes

1 **Movement** In the 1950s some Western European countries formed a "common market" for their mutual economic benefit. Common Market countries have agreed not to tax goods passing from one country to another. They also coordinate transportation and banking systems in an organization called the European Union (EU). Western Europeans hope that these measures will increase productivity and strengthen their position as a trading bloc in the world economy. *Critical Thinking Describe the barriers to trade movement within Western Europe.*

2 **Human-Environment Interaction** A belt of coal fields runs across Europe from Britain to France, Belgium, and Germany. When the Industrial Revolution began to transform Western Europe from an agricultural to an industrial society toward the end of the 1700s, factories and mills sprang up near deposits of coal and iron ore. *Compare the economic activity map on page 277 to the population density map on page 273. What is the relationship between natural resources and population density?*

3 **Human-Environment Interaction** The rise of industry has also affected the region's natural vegetation. One of the few remaining woodlands is Germany's Black Forest region, a famous area known for its dense forests on steep hillsides. Today, industrial pollution endangers the Black Forest and other forests. *Where is manufacturing and trade concentrated in Western Europe?*

Agriculture and Leading Industries in Selected Western European Countries

DIAGRAM STUDY

4 **Agriculture** Modern farmers use sophisticated farming methods to produce high crop yields. Moderate temperatures, fertile soils, and plentiful rains make the North European Plain an especially bountiful agricultural region. *Which three Western European countries depend most heavily on farming?*

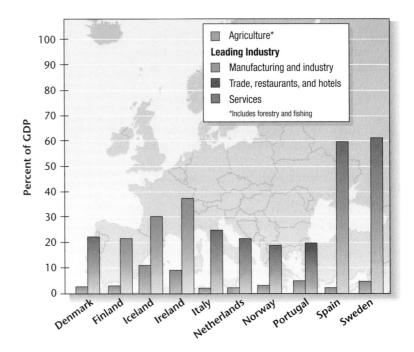

REGIONAL *atlas*

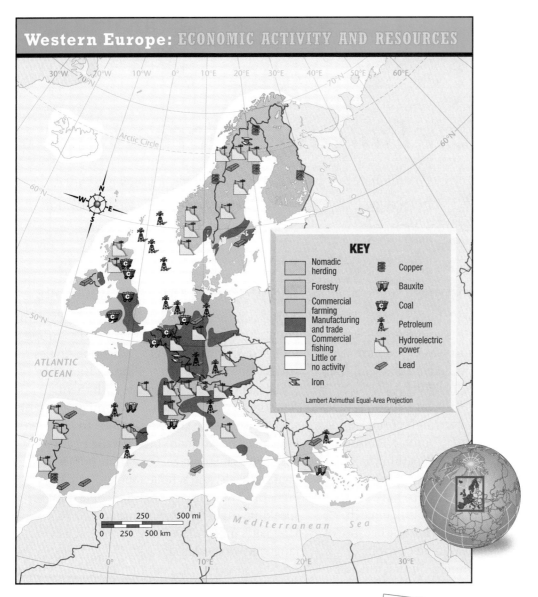

Western Europe: ECONOMIC ACTIVITY AND RESOURCES

KEY

- Nomadic herding
- Forestry
- Commercial farming
- Manufacturing and trade
- Commercial fishing
- Little or no activity
- Iron
- Copper
- Bauxite
- Coal
- Petroleum
- Hydroelectric power
- Lead

Lambert Azimuthal Equal-Area Projection

ATLANTIC OCEAN

Mediterranean Sea

0   250   500 mi
0   250   500 km

atlas REVIEW

Vocabulary and Main Ideas

1. Define: **a. summit b. multilingual
c. prevailing westerlies**

2. Describe the two main types of climate in Western Europe.

3. How have Western European nations cooperated in recent years?

4. Critical Thinking: *Drawing Conclusions* **How did human settlement of Western Europe change the region's physical geography?**

learning LOCATIONS

5. Which country is located southeast of Italy?

6. What country borders Belgium, Germany, and France?

How Languages Spread

*W*hy do millions of people around the world speak languages that come from Western Europe? Over centuries of history, European colonial powers took their cultures and languages to other parts of the world.

The Language of Rome

Europe is a small continent, but its nations have built great empires that influenced people in all parts of the world. The first was the Roman Empire, which reached its height about A.D. 120. Along with Roman laws, its soldiers took Latin, the language of Rome, to western and central Europe.

The Roman Empire itself fell apart in the fifth century A.D., but Latin continued to have an important influence in Western Europe because of the Roman Catholic Church. Church officials and all educated people spoke and wrote Latin.

Centuries of Roman rule also influenced people's everyday language. At one time, various groups in Europe had their own languages—Celtic, Iberian, Germanic. By the Middle Ages, most people in Western Europe were speaking rough versions of Latin called the *vernacular*. These developed into modern languages such as Italian, French, Spanish, and Romanian.

Illustrated Latin manuscript

The English Language Develops

A later conquest led to modern English. Even in Roman times, most people in northern Europe spoke Germanic languages. When the Angles and Saxons migrated to the British Isles, they took their Germanic language with them.

Then, in 1066, William of Normandy, led his soldiers across the English Channel to conquer England. The Normans brought their Latin-based French language. For a time, nobles, law court officials, and scholars spoke Norman French. Most ordinary English people went on speaking Anglo-Saxon. Gradually the two languages mixed. They created the English language we speak today.

Languages of Colonialism

Beginning in the 1500s, western European nations competed to build colonial empires around the world. Spain and England in particular took their national cultures and languages to their colonies.

Spanish and Portuguese Spain's colonies included Mexico and most of Central and South America. Spanish was the official language; Roman Catholicism the only religion. Spanish conquistadors, friars, and officials did all they could to eliminate native languages and religions. Today, while Spain's population is

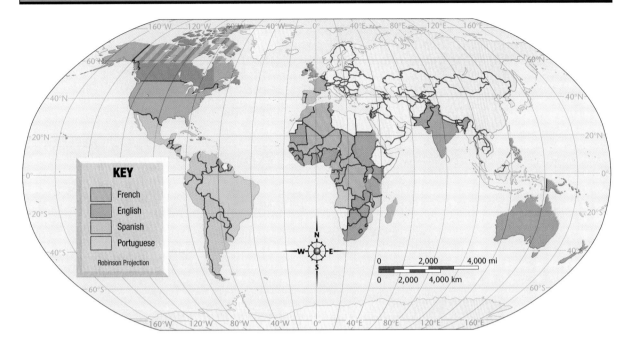

about 40 million, the Spanish language is spoken by about 300 million people worldwide.

Portugal's empire lay mainly in Asia. The Portuguese language and its Catholic religion took hold in its one American colony, Brazil.

English and French England and France were rivals in several places. In North America, they fought over territory and colonies. The English language, along with English law, became dominant in the original American colonies and in most of Canada. French language and customs, however, persisted in Quebec and in some Caribbean islands.

France and England also competed in India and Africa. India was Britain's most prized colony until it gained independence in 1947. English is still an official language in both India and Pakistan. English is also spoken in many former British colonies in Africa and the Caribbean, while people in France's former colonies in northern and western Africa speak French.

connecting TO TODAY

1. Name two modern languages that are based on the language of the Roman Empire.

2. In what parts of the Americas did Spain establish colonies?

3. Critical Thinking Why would a colonial power want to impose its language on the people of a distant colony?

4. Hands-On Activity Draw or trace a map showing the borders of present-day nations in South and Southeast Asia. Use colored markers or pencils to show those countries where English, French, Spanish, or other European languages are spoken as official languages, in addition to local languages. Make a key to show which language each color represents.

The British Isles and Nordic Nations

SECTIONS

learning LOCATIONS

Mapping the Region

Create a map like the one below, lightly shading each country a different color. Then add the labels for countries and bodies of water that are shown on this map.

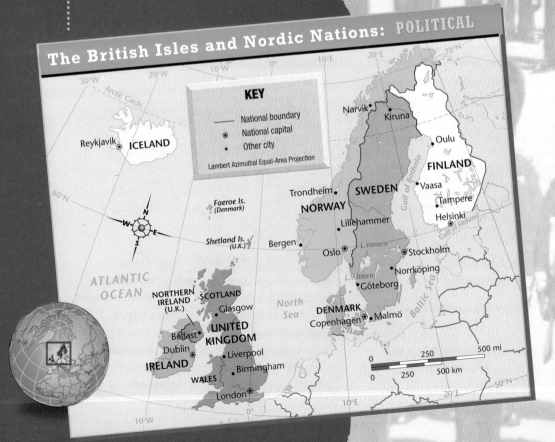

The British Isles and Nordic Nations: POLITICAL

KEY

— National boundary
⊛ National capital
• Other city

Lambert Azimuthal Equal-Area Projection

Arctic Circle

Reykjavik ICELAND

Narvik
Kiruna
Oulu
FINLAND
Vaasa
Tampere
Helsinki

Faeroe Is. (Denmark)

Trondheim SWEDEN
NORWAY
Lillehammer

Shetland Is. (U.K.)

Bergen
Oslo ⊛ L. Vänern
Stockholm ⊛
L. Vättern Norrköping
Göteborg

ATLANTIC OCEAN

NORTHERN IRELAND (U.K.)
SCOTLAND
Glasgow

North Sea

DENMARK
Copenhagen ⊛ • Malmö

Baltic Sea

Belfast
Dublin ⊛
UNITED KINGDOM
Liverpool

IRELAND
Birmingham

WALES

London

Gulf of Bothnia

Gulf of Finland

0   250   500 mi
0   250   500 km

1 England

Section Preview

Main Ideas

- The United Kingdom includes England, Scotland, Wales, and Northern Ireland.

- Britain's location made it a center of Atlantic exploration and trade.

- Britain possessed the financial and natural resources to fuel the Industrial Revolution.

Vocabulary

fertile, estuary, ore

This lush garden reflects the moderate climate and rich soils of southwestern Great Britain.

The many islands clustered off the northwest coast of Europe are called the British Isles. The largest island in the British Isles—and in all of Europe—is Great Britain.

The island of Great Britain comprises three formerly independent countries: England, Scotland, and Wales. Together with Northern Ireland, they form the United Kingdom of Great Britain and Northern Ireland, or simply the United Kingdom.

The core of the United Kingdom is England. Notice from the population map on page 273 that England is the most densely populated area in the British Isles. Nearly 80 percent of the region's population live here.

England's Rural Landscape

"Our England is a garden," declared English poet Rudyard Kipling in the late 1800s. Kipling was describing rural England with its green, rolling meadows, peaceful rivers, and neat farms. The English landscape is actually made up of three very different areas: the Highlands, Midlands, and Lowlands.

The Highlands are a band of hills running the length of England's west coast. Older and harder rock formations in this region have been worn down by centuries of weathering. Even so, some peaks rise to 3,000 feet (900 m), and the land is difficult to farm.

A short distance to the southeast are the Midlands. Here lie the thick veins of coal that fueled the country's Industrial Revolution. Factory towns such as Birmingham, Manchester, and Stoke-on-Trent still darken the air with fumes from their mills. Heavy industrial development means that some of England's highest population densities are in the Midlands.

To the south and east are the rolling Lowlands. The land slopes gently toward the English Channel, and elevations rarely top 1,000 feet (300 m). Younger, softer rocks lie beneath the land's surface. Because these rocks break up easily, soil in the Lowlands tends to be **fertile**—able to produce abundant crops.

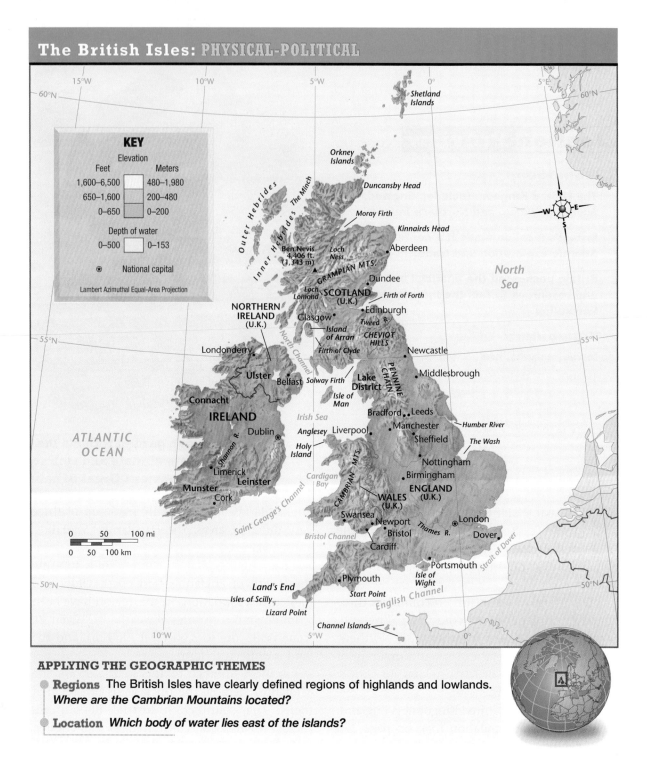

KEY

Elevation

Feet		Meters
1,600–6,500		480–1,980
650–1,600		200–480
0–650		0–200

Depth of water

| 0–500 | | 0–153 |

⊛ National capital

Lambert Azimuthal Equal-Area Projection

Shetland Islands

Orkney Islands

Duncansby Head

Moray Firth

Kinnairds Head

Ben Nevis 4,406 ft. (1,343 m)

Loch Ness

Aberdeen

GRAMPIAN MTS.

Dundee

Loch Lomond

SCOTLAND (U.K.)

Firth of Forth

Outer Hebrides

The Minch

Inner Hebrides

NORTHERN IRELAND (U.K.)

Glasgow

Edinburgh

Tweed R.

CHEVIOT HILLS

Londonderry

North Channel

Ulster

Belfast

Solway Firth

Newcastle

Middlesbrough

Connacht

IRELAND

Lake District

PENNINE CHAIN

Isle of Man

Irish Sea

Bradford

Leeds

Firth of Clyde

Island of Arran

Anglesey

Liverpool

Manchester

Humber River

Dublin

Holy Island

Sheffield

The Wash

ATLANTIC OCEAN

Shannon R.

Limerick

Leinster

Nottingham

Birmingham

Munster

Cork

Cardigan Bay

CAMBRIAN MTS.

WALES (U.K.)

ENGLAND (U.K.)

Swansea

Newport

Thames R.

London

Saint George's Channel

Bristol Channel

Bristol

Dover

Cardiff

Portsmouth

Strait of Dover

Land's End

Plymouth

Isle of Wight

Isles of Scilly

Start Point

English Channel

Lizard Point

Channel Islands

North Sea

0   50   100 mi

0   50   100 km

APPLYING THE GEOGRAPHIC THEMES

● **Regions** The British Isles have clearly defined regions of highlands and lowlands. *Where are the Cambrian Mountains located?*

● **Location** *Which body of water lies east of the islands?*

The Lowlands provide England with some of its most productive farms. Farmers grow wheat, vegetables, and other crops on small plots of land. They set aside larger parcels of land for pasture. The cool, moist weather of England's marine west coast climate is perfect for raising sheep and dairy and beef cattle. British goods are sold both in the United Kingdom and other European Union nations.

England's Urban Landscape

Even before industrialization, England's farms produced surplus goods for export. Trade within England and with other European nations fostered the growth of cities along rivers and the coast. Of these, London was the most important. Why did London, with its inland location, become one of the greatest commercial and shipping cities in the world? The answer can be found in one of the five geographic themes—location.

London's Relative Location The map on page 282 shows that although London is only about 70 miles (110 km) from the continent of Europe, the city of Dover is even closer to the mainland. So why isn't Dover the English capital of trade? London has a big advantage over Dover and other southern coastal ports. The hills along the English Channel drop sharply, forming steep cliffs that plunge straight down to the water. In contrast, London is located on the Thames (TEHMZ) River. Since the Thames Valley was formed, the level of the Atlantic Ocean has risen. The result is an **estuary**—a flooded valley at the wide mouth of a river. Thus ships could sail directly up to the port of London.

As early as the 1500s, London was a bustling port. One writer described the waterfront in this way:

> *A forest of masts. . . . Huge square-rigged ships lay side by side, surrounded by barges and small craft . . . . The . . . boats had to fight . . . to their landing places.*

Changes in Relative Location The port of London grew rapidly in the 1500s because of changes in patterns of world settlement and trade. The influence of the Roman Empire meant that the Mediterranean Sea traditionally had been the center of trade. London remained on the far edge of European trade. In the late 1400s, however, improved ships and navigation devices allowed Europeans to push westward across the Atlantic Ocean. Great Britain's strategic, central location on the Atlantic was ideal for trade. So, as trade across the Atlantic increased, Britain's relative location improved.

Workshop of the World

In the 1500s, Britain shipped mostly the products of its farms. But within its small area, the

Source: Population Reference Bureau

Country	Population	Life Expectancy (years)	Per Capita GNP (in US $)
Denmark	5,200,000	75	26,510
Finland	5,100,000	76	18,970
Iceland	300,000	79	23,620
Ireland	3,600,000	75	12,580
Norway	4,300,000	77	26,340
Sweden	8,900,000	78	24,830
United Kingdom	58,600,000	76	17,970
United States	*263,200,000*	*76*	*24,750*

CHART SKILLS

● *What is the life expectancy in Sweden?*

● *Critical Thinking* *Which country has the lowest population? What might account for its small population?*

island nation had the resources to fuel the start of the Industrial Revolution.

As shipowners and merchants earned profits from trade, they looked for new ways to invest their money. Wealthy business owners built factories to produce manufactured goods to sell to Britain's colonies. As ships plied the oceans loaded with British goods, Britain became known as the "workshop of the world."

The Rise of Heavy Industry Some of the earliest technological advances of the Industrial Revolution were used in factories that produced textiles, or cloth. British manufacturers first used water power to run spinning machines, but later switched to coal as a source of power.

Major coal fields lay along the edges of the

Water Pollution

The Thames River was once so polluted that Britain's capitol building, the Parliament, had to be equipped with chemical-soaked curtains to keep out the odor. Now anti-pollution efforts have resulted in a river so clean it is again a home to salmon.

Pennine Mountain range, as well as in the northeast, near the city of Newcastle. Britain also possessed large reserves of iron **ore**, or rocky material containing a valuable mineral. Inventors improved methods of melting iron ore and using it in the production of steel. New manufacturing centers such as Birmingham, Sheffield, and Newcastle sprang up near deposits of coal and iron.

The Industrial Revolution brought wealth to Britain, but the factories and mines also changed the English landscape. English poet William Blake condemned the "dark, Satanic mills" for destroying "England's green and pleasant land." A visitor to Birmingham in the early 1800s reported that the noise there was "beyond description," and the filth was "sickening."

Challenges to British Industry

Britain's plentiful supply of raw materials and its position on major sea routes made it the world's industrial leader for years. But in the late 1800s, Britain was challenged by two new industrial powers—Germany and the United States. By 1900, both the United States and Germany were making as much steel as the United Kingdom.

In recent years, British industry has fallen upon hard times. Much of the area's coal supply was used up during the Industrial Revolution. Since the 1970s, Britain has turned to oil and

An Industrial Giant

● **Movement** Birmingham became one of the world's leading industrial cities during the 1800s. With workers flooding into Birmingham, the city's population grew from 70,000 in 1801 to nearly 700,000 at the end of the century. *How did this movement of people into cities change the landscape of Great Britain?*

The English Channel Tunnel

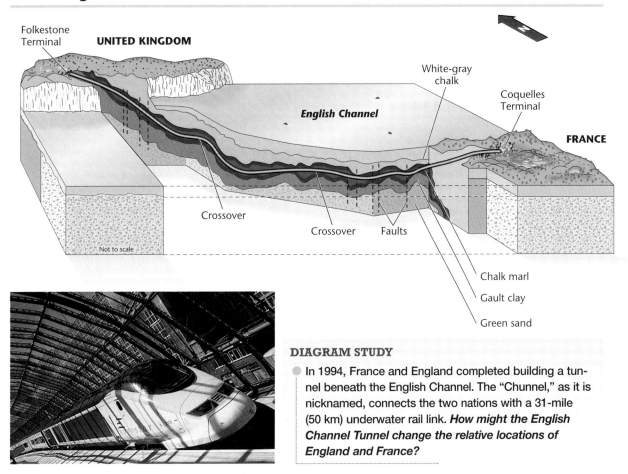

Folkestone Terminal

UNITED KINGDOM

White-gray chalk

Coquelles Terminal

English Channel

FRANCE

Crossover

Crossover

Faults

Not to scale

Chalk marl

Gault clay

Green sand

DIAGRAM STUDY

● In 1994, France and England completed building a tunnel beneath the English Channel. The "Chunnel," as it is nicknamed, connects the two nations with a 31-mile (50 km) underwater rail link. *How might the English Channel Tunnel change the relative locations of England and France?*

gas deposits beneath the floor of the North Sea as a source for fuel.

To offset the loss of heavy industry, the British government has encouraged the development of service industries, such as tourism, finance, and data processing. Despite its problems, however, Britain's overall economy has been growing steadily in recent years. Inflation has been low, and unemployment has been decreasing. It remains to be seen whether the twenty-first century will bring continued growth.

Section 1 Review

Vocabulary and Main Ideas

1. Define: a. fertile b. estuary c. ore

2. Which countries make up the United Kingdom?

3. Why was Britain a center of Atlantic exploration and trade?

4. What resources fueled Britain's Industrial Revolution?

5. Critical Thinking: *Cause and Effect* How did Britain's relative position in the world change in the 1500s? How would you describe its relative location today?

learning LOCATIONS

6. Where is London located on the island of Great Britain?

7. Which body of water lies directly south of Great Britain?

2 Scotland and Wales

Section Preview

Main Ideas

● Scotland and Wales have kept cultural identities separate from that of England.

● Scotland and Wales are each divided physically into highlands and lowlands.

● Older industries in Scotland and Wales have fared poorly.

Vocabulary

moor, bog, glen

Bagpipes are a unique feature in Scotland's cultural landscape.

An English writer once remarked, "[A Scot] is British, yes, and he will sing 'There will always be an England,' but he murmurs to himself, 'As long as Scotland is there.'" This story reveals something about how the Scots view England. The two nations have been tied together politically for almost three hundred years. Still, Scotland has always kept its own identity. The same can be said of Wales, which has been united with England since the late 1200s.

The Scottish Landscape

Scotland occupies nearly one third of the land area in the United Kingdom, but less than 10 percent of the nation's population live there. The landscape is rugged. It bears the marks of heavy glaciers that moved across the northern part of Great Britain during the last ice age.

The map on page 282 shows that the Cheviot Hills and the Tweed River are the physical features that separate Scotland from England. Scotland itself is divided into three regions—the northern Highlands, the central Lowlands, and the southern Uplands.

The Highlands The Highland region is a large, high plateau with many lakes, called lochs (LAHKHS), which were carved by retreating glaciers. The Grampian Mountains cut across the region with peaks reaching past 4,000 feet (1,200 m). Both coasts are etched deeply by the sea with inlets called firths.

Much of the Highlands are covered with **moors**—broad, treeless rolling plains. The moors, in turn, are dotted with **bogs**—areas of wet, spongy ground. Steady winds off the Atlantic Ocean bring abundant rainfall to the moors. The dampness of the soil limits plant growth to grasses and low shrubs such as purple heather.

The land, water, and climate of the Highlands are well suited to the region's economies of fishing and sheep herding. A few people produce a type of handwoven, woolen cloth known as tweed. This Scottish home industry has continued over hundreds of years, in sharp contrast to the factory production of textiles in England.

The Central Lowlands South of the Highlands runs a long lowland region. Nearly 75 percent of Scotland's people live in this region, stretching between Glasgow and Edinburgh (EHD ihn BUHR oh).

Industry came to the central Lowlands in the early 1800s. The Clyde River near Glasgow grew into a huge shipbuilding center. The Clyde shipbuilders played a major role in establishing the United Kingdom as the world's leading naval power. Explained one observer:

> *Through all the transitions—wood to iron, iron to steel, paddle to . . . turbine engines—Clyde shipbuilders have been to the front with ships.*

Since the mid-1900s, however, heavy industries in Scotland have fallen on hard times. Old factory centers such as Glasgow have declined. The loss of jobs has caused more than one third of Glasgow's residents to leave since 1960.

The Southern Uplands Closest to the English border, the Southern Uplands is primarily a sheep-raising region. The Tweed River valley woolen mills are kept well supplied with wool by area farmers. Medieval abbeys and low, hilly landscapes draw many visitors to the region.

Scotland Today

New industries are slowly taking the place of mining, steel making, and shipbuilding. Oil discoveries in the North Sea, off the northeastern shore of Scotland, have helped the economies of some cities such as Aberdeen. Computer and electronic businesses have also developed along the Clyde and Tweed rivers. Some people call the Clyde Valley "Silicon Glen," after the area in California known as "Silicon Valley." A **glen** is a narrow valley.

Although politically united with England, Scotland has retained its own culture. When the Scottish and English parliaments were united through the Act of Union in 1707, Scotland kept important trading and political rights. Scotland

Heather on a Scottish Moor

Regions Scotland's climate supports vegetation quite different from England's lush meadows and dense forests. On these moors, heather and tough grasses stretch for miles. **Critical Thinking** *What other factors might determine a region's vegetation?*

still has its own system of laws and its own system of education. Many Scots also remained members of the Presbyterian Church, rather than joining the Church of England. A small minority of Scottish people even talk of once again becoming a separate country. As Scottish patriot Gordon Wilson explained:

> *You can tell me that Scotland is a part of the United Kingdom, and I will tell you that that is the truth but not the whole truth. . . . You see, national boundaries are not simply a matter of geographical frontiers. It's culture we're talking about, a set of national characteristics. These Scotland has retained.*

Wales

A similar spirit of pride and independence burns in Wales, which also has a culture distinct from that of England. It has its own capital city, postage stamps, national flag, and language.

However, Wales is strongly influenced by its powerful neighbor, England, which conquered it in 1284. Since that time, the seat of Welsh government and law has been in London.

The Welsh Landscape Wales is really a peninsula of the island of Great Britain. About the size of Massachusetts, it has a landscape similar to that of Scotland. On the map on page 282 you can find a highland area in northern Wales, lowlands running along the southern coast near Cardiff, and the Cambrian Mountains in central Wales.

Wales enjoys a marine west coast climate like the rest of Great Britain. However, the rain-carrying winds from the Atlantic pass over Wales before reaching England. So Wales usually receives even more rain than southern England.

A Separate Language Since the 1500s, Welsh representatives have sat in Parliament. Some have risen to high office in the British government, including that of Prime Minister. Even so, the Welsh have fought for cultural independence.

One of the keys to preserving Welsh culture is language. Most of its 2.9 million people speak English, but nearly 20 percent still speak Welsh as their first language. Handed down from the Celtic peoples who lived in Wales for thousands of years, Welsh is spoken mainly in the mountains of northern Wales. In the 1980s, Welsh

APPEARED IN *NATIONAL GEOGRAPHIC*

A Living Fence

Human-Environment Interaction With the right conditions, bushes planted in a row can grow so tightly together that livestock cannot pass through. Here, a dense double hedge separates two flocks of sheep. **Critical Thinking** *Could hedges this dense be grown in less fertile land? Explain your answer.*

A History of Mining

Location The Welsh have a long history of mining: the Romans mined gold in the Welsh mountains as early as A.D. 250. Since then the Welsh have mined coal, lead, and zinc, and have quarried both limestone and slate. *What products do you use that are mined from the ground?*

patriots fought for and won the right to broadcast television programs entirely in Welsh.

The New Welsh Economy

The economic history of Wales is similar to that of England and Scotland. In the late 1800s and early 1900s, industry and coal mining changed the landscape and economy of southern Wales. Mines in the Rhondda Valley, just north of the capital city of Cardiff, became some of Britain's biggest coal producers.

By the mid-1900s, however, heavy industries in Wales had fallen behind in technology. A writer described the Welsh economy in 1945:

[Miners] still picked coal by hand from two-foot seams. . . . In many places things like bread, milk and coal were still being delivered by horse and cart.

By the 1980s, most of the coal mines in the Rhondda Valley had closed. Unemployment rates soared, and many students leaving high school could not find jobs despite the arrival of new petroleum refineries.

In the 1990s the situation improved as foreign investment in Wales, as in Scotland, provided new jobs in high-tech industries. Some people in Wales also promoted tourism for those interested in seeing the traditional Welsh way of life.

Section 2 Review

Vocabulary and Main Ideas

1. Define: a. moor b. bog c. glen

2. How are the cultural identities of Scotland and Wales related to that of England?

3. What physical landscape features exist in both Scotland and Wales?

4. Critical Thinking: *Drawing Inferences* Why do you think survival of the Welsh language goes hand in hand with a spirit of nationalism in Wales?

learning LOCATIONS

5. Where is Scotland located in relation to England?

6. Where is Wales located in relation to London?

Focus on Skills

☑ Social Studies

☐ Map and Globe

☐ Critical Thinking and Problem Solving

Using Time Lines

A time line helps you place events in chronological order. Seeing events set out in the order they took place can help you understand the events and their relationship to each other. Study the time line below, then practice using a time line by following these steps.

1. Identify the time period covered by the time line. Study the entire time line to learn the span of history that it covers. (a) What is the earliest date shown on the time line? (b) What is the latest date shown? (c) How many years are covered in the time line?

2. Determine how the time line has been divided. Most time lines are divided into equal intervals, or units, of time, such as 10, 25, or 100 years. Into what intervals is this time line divided?

3. Study the time line to see whether events might be related. A time line helps you to see relationships between events. (a) What events in the 1700s help explain how the Industrial Revolution started in Britain? (b) What events on the time line help show the effect of industry on children and other workers?

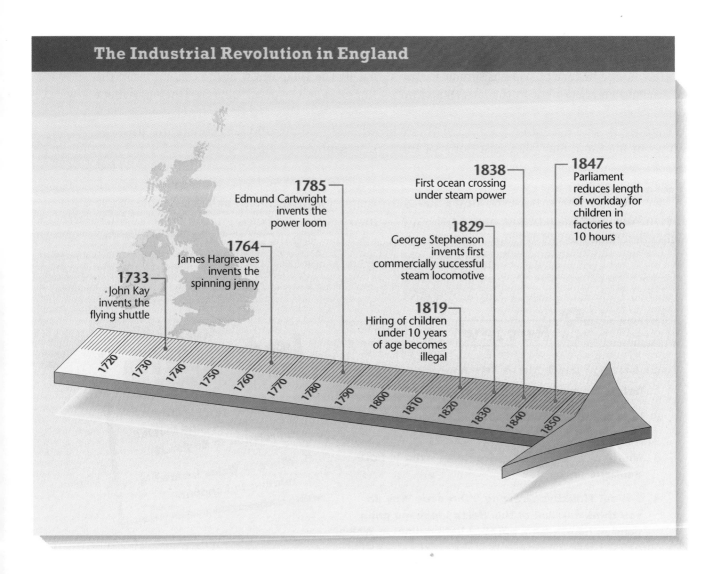

The Industrial Revolution in England

1733 — John Kay invents the flying shuttle

1764 — James Hargreaves invents the spinning jenny

1785 — Edmund Cartwright invents the power loom

1819 — Hiring of children under 10 years of age becomes illegal

1829 — George Stephenson invents first commercially successful steam locomotive

1838 — First ocean crossing under steam power

1847 — Parliament reduces length of workday for children in factories to 10 hours

1720 1730 1740 1750 1760 1770 1780 1790 1800 1810 1820 1830 1840 1850

3 The Two Irelands

Section Preview

Main Ideas

- The island of Ireland is divided into two political regions: Northern Ireland, which is part of the United Kingdom, and the independent Republic of Ireland.

- The two Irelands share a long history of religious and political conflicts.

- Ireland has experienced great poverty because of religious turmoil, political struggles, and natural disasters.

Vocabulary

peat, annex, blight

APPEARED IN *NATIONAL GEOGRAPHIC*

Young Catholics mourn a death in Northern Ireland.

Ireland is divided politically into two parts: Northern Ireland and the Republic of Ireland. Ireland is also divided in religion between Protestants and Catholics. Finally, Ireland is divided culturally between the descendants of native Celtic peoples and the descendants of English and Scottish immigrants.

The Emerald Isle

The divisions in Ireland are not visible immediately. The island itself looks like a huge bowl. Hills ring most of the coastline, while the middle of the island is a plain that drains into the River Shannon. Ireland's moist marine west coast climate keeps vegetation a brilliant green for most of the year. To the eye, Ireland lives up to its nickname, "The Emerald Isle."

About one sixth of the island is covered by **peat**, a spongy material containing waterlogged mosses and plants. Because Ireland has few forests, farmers cut and dry blocks of peat as fuel for cooking and heating. The Republic of Ireland recently developed a method for using peat in power plants, which now produce nearly one quarter of the nation's electricity.

A Region of Conflict

Ireland's history has been shaped by invasions and wars. Celtic tribes from Europe first settled Ireland around 300 B.C. They repeatedly defended themselves against Viking raids, which lasted roughly from A.D. 800 to 1016.

In 1066, Norman invaders from France conquered England. Some of the Normans also seized large tracts of land in Ireland, built castles to protect themselves, and tried to control the Celts. They forbade marriage between Normans and Celts, banned use of the Celtic language, known as Gaelic (GAY lik), and even outlawed Celtic harp music.

King Henry II of England declared himself Lord of Ireland in 1171 and tried unsuccessfully to force Norman lords to obey him. But English rulers who followed Henry held on to the title and began thinking of Ireland as a possession.

Religious Conflicts Until the 1500s, the Roman Catholic Church had directed religious affairs in much of Western Europe. In the early 1500s, groups in Europe tried to change some of the Church's practices and started a reform movement known as the Reformation. A split soon developed between the Roman Catholics and the Protestants, the name given to those Christians who protested the policies of the Roman Catholic Church.

In 1534, Henry VIII of England broke away from the Roman Catholic Church and founded the Church of England. He made himself head of the church and moved to strengthen his power. He changed his title from Lord of Ireland to King of Ireland.

Henry did not try to force the Irish to give up the Roman Catholic religion. But some of his descendants did. Most of the Irish remained strongly Roman Catholic, however, and fought bitterly against the English. When the English eventually won, they imposed harsh laws on the Irish and gave away large parcels of Irish land to Protestant settlers from Great Britain.

The divisions in Ireland soon became economic as well as religious. The Protestant minority controlled much of the wealth, while the defeated Irish Catholics fell into poverty.

The British policy toward Ireland left a legacy of bitterness and hatred. In 1798, the French supported a rebellion in Ireland. The United Kingdom responded in 1801 by **annexing** Ireland, or formally adding it to its territory.

Movement for Independence Many Irish continued to press for independence throughout the nineteenth century. Rebellions between 1916 and 1921 led officials in the United Kingdom and Ireland to divide the island into two parts. The six northeastern counties remained part of the United Kingdom, but the rest of Ireland became a free state under British supervision. This free state declared its total independence as the Republic of Ireland in 1949. Independence did not end political turmoil on the island.

Roughly two thirds of the 1.6 million people who live in Northern Ireland today are Protestant. Most of the rest are Catholic. Most Catholics support the reunification of Ireland, while most Protestants oppose it.

Both Protestant and Catholic extremists have used violence to try to win control of Northern Ireland. Tensions rose in the late 1960s when British troops were sent to Northern Ireland. Bombings, hunger strikes, and gun battles kept antagonism high. Steps toward peace talks began in 1994, and hopes increased that problems that began in the 1500s might finally be resolved. Talks proceeded slowly, however, as both sides worked to build trust between groups with different goals.

The Emerald Isle

Regions Ireland is known for its lush, green landscape. Farmland and sheep paddocks on the Dingle Peninsula show why Ireland is called the Emerald Isle. *What climate conditions make this lush landscape possible?*

The Feel of the Irish Countryside

Place Ireland has one of the least urbanized populations in Western Europe. Many young Irish still have plenty of contact with ponies and other livestock. **Critical Thinking** *What role do you think horses and ponies had on Ireland's traditional farms?*

Changing Economic Patterns

The poverty of Ireland's early years still troubles it today. The Republic of Ireland ranks low in national wealth.

The Potato Famine Ireland never industrialized as did most of Great Britain. Instead, it depended heavily on the harvesting of potatoes, which thrived in Ireland's moist climate and crumbly soil. However, in the 1840s, a severe **blight**, or plant disease, wiped out Ireland's potato crop and created massive famine. The island's population dropped when millions of people left the island, many coming to the United States. During the 1900s, Ireland sought to rebuild. Today farmers rely more on beef and dairy cattle.

Putting Location to Work As the world map on pages 12-13 shows, the Republic of Ireland is located between mainland Europe and North America. The Irish have taken advantage of this location by upgrading Shannon Airport near Limerick in the west. Many transatlantic flights now refuel there. This activity in turn attracts other industries, such as tourism.

Section 3 Review

Vocabulary and Main Ideas

1. **Define:** a. peat b. annex c. blight

2. **What are the two political regions of Ireland?**

3. **How did religious conflicts emerge in Ireland between 1500 and 1700?**

4. **Critical Thinking:** *Analyzing Information* **Tell whether you agree or disagree with the following statement: "Protestants and Catholics in Northern Ireland both feel threatened by the past and are reluctant to negotiate." Support your answer with evidence from the text.**

learning LOCATIONS

5. Where is Dublin located?

6. What body of water lies to the west of Ireland?

4 The Nordic Nations

Section Preview

Main Ideas

● Northern Europe includes the Nordic nations of Norway, Sweden, Finland, Denmark, and Iceland.

● Location and cultural similarities define northern Europe as a region.

● The Nordic nations enjoy strong, varied economies.

Vocabulary

fjord, geothermal energy, mixed economy, politically neutral

APPEARED IN *NATIONAL GEOGRAPHIC*

Scenic Skogelflaa Fjord is one of many glacial valleys that cut sharply into Norway's Atlantic coast.

The people of northern Europe call their land *Norden*, from an ancient word meaning "Northlands." Norden includes five independent nations: Norway, Sweden, Finland, Denmark, and Iceland. These nations, called the Nordic nations in English, are unified as a region by location and strong cultural bonds.

A Northern Location

Norden is identified as a region in part by its location in the northern latitudes. Parts of some Nordic nations reach past the Arctic Circle into the polar zone.

A Varied Landscape The region is a collection of peninsulas and islands separated by seas, gulfs, and oceans. The most continuous land masses are the Scandinavian and Jutland peninsulas. The terrain varies dramatically throughout the Nordic nations. Denmark is so flat that its highest point is less than 600 feet (183 m) high, while Norway is one of the most mountainous nations in Europe.

The Effect of Glaciers Much of the landscape on the Scandinavian Peninsula is the product of the last Ice Age. Glaciers carved out thousands of lakes across the peninsula. They also removed topsoil and other materials and deposited them in Denmark and other parts of Western Europe. As a result, much of the soil in Scandinavia today remains rocky and difficult to farm.

Notice the jagged coastlines along the Scandinavian Peninsula on the map on page 295. When the glaciers advanced, they carved out deep valleys along the coasts. When the glaciers melted, water filled the valleys, creating flooded glacial valleys known as **fjords** (fee YAWRDZ). Some fjords are so deep that ocean-going ships can sail into them. Most have such steep walls that even mountain climbers find them difficult to scale.

Iceland, Fire Land In Iceland, volcanoes and glaciers exist side by side. Icelanders call their island "a land of fire and ice." They have learned to take advantage of the island's geology to produce **geothermal energy**, or

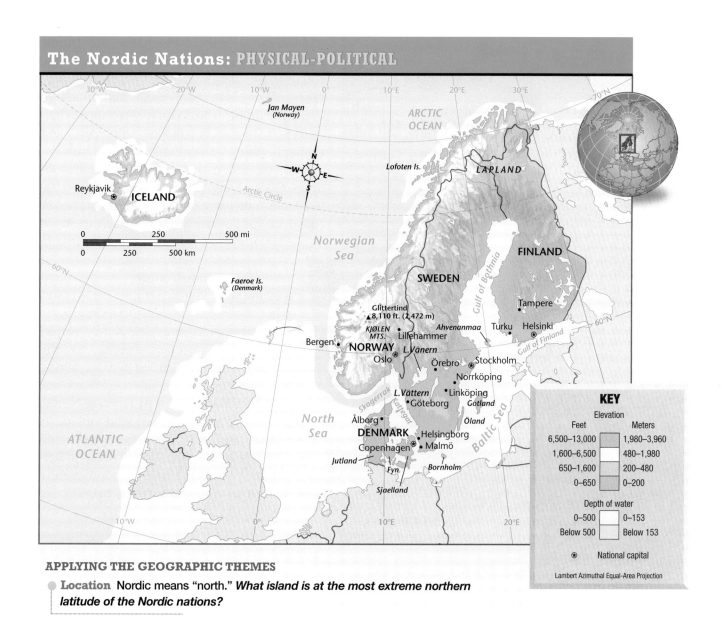

The Nordic Nations: PHYSICAL-POLITICAL

APPLYING THE GEOGRAPHIC THEMES

● **Location** Nordic means "north." *What island is at the most extreme northern latitude of the Nordic nations?*

energy produced from the heat of the earth's interior. Today, geothermal energy accounts for a large share of the power used for heat and electricity in Iceland.

Long Winters, Short Summers

"Winter is the element for which we are born," declared a Finnish historian in the 1800s. Norden's location to the far north results in long winters and short summers. At midwinter the sun may shine only two or three hours a day. In midsummer, it shines for more than twenty hours.

Winter is when the greenish white and red lights of the aurora borealis, or northern lights, shine most brightly in the Nordic nations.

These lights appear when atomic particles from the sun, attracted by the magnetic fields of the North Pole, break through the northern atmosphere.

The start of summer is a public holiday in most Nordic nations, when people celebrate the return of the "midnight sun." In the northernmost territories, the sun never really sets for several weeks in midsummer. People call the long twilight hours of evening the "white nights."

The Ocean and the Climate

Despite the length of winter, the climate in much of Norden can be surprisingly mild. As is evident from the climate map on page 274, half of Iceland, all of Denmark, the west coast of

A WORLD OF eXtremes

Iceland's Hot Springs

X EXTREMELY HOT
The hot spring called Strokkur spurts burning hot water and steam 20 meters into the air every three minutes.

X FORMER GLORY
In the past Iceland's most famous hot spring, Geysir, spouted nearly 80 meters. It ceased erupting when tourists threw tons of rocks and dirt into the spring.

X TOO HOT TO HANDLE
People enjoy soaking in many of Iceland's hot springs. However, rising temperatures can make some unsafe for bathing. The temperature of the hot spring Grjótagjá has risen to a scalding 140° F (60° C) in recent years.

Norway, and southern Sweden have mild marine west coast climates. The warm currents of the North Atlantic Drift moderate the weather and keep the coast free of ice.

The coldest areas in Norden lie just east of a mountain chain that runs northeast to southwest through Norway. This range prevents the warm, moist ocean winds from reaching the rest of the Scandinavian Peninsula. The result is a cold, dry subarctic climate.

Shared Cultural Bonds

More than climate and location bind the Nordic nations into a region. They also have strong cultural ties.

Similar Historic Roots The Nordic nations have similar histories. From around A.D. 800 to 1050, Vikings sailed out of the fjords and inlets of southern Norden to raid much of Western Europe. The Vikings were more than warriors. They were traders, colonizers, and explorers who left their mark on world history.

The Nordic nations were also united at times. Queen Margrethe of Denmark joined the five lands under one crown in 1397. The union ended in 1523 when Sweden (which included Finland) withdrew. But Denmark, Norway, and Iceland remained united for several centuries more. Sweden and Finland were united until the early 1800s, when Sweden ceded Finland to Russia.

Religion, too, unites the Nordic people. Most Nordic peoples belong to the Lutheran Church, first established during the Reformation.

With the exception of Finnish, Nordic languages have common roots. Finland is bilingual, and most Finns have a working knowledge of Swedish, Finland's second language. In addition, Nordic schools require students to learn English, which helps bridge any linguistic differences.

Governments and Economies Nordic countries share certain political and economic beliefs. All five of the Nordic nations are democracies, and their economic systems are **mixed economies**, or systems combining different degrees of government regulation. They practice a mixture of free enterprise and socialism.

Most businesses in the Nordic countries operate much as they do in the United States. But the Nordic governments guarantee certain goods and services to everyone and operate some industries that are run privately in the United States. For example, Denmark and Sweden have state-run day-care centers and state-supported medical care.

As a rule, the Nordic nations are **politically neutral** in foreign affairs. That is, they do not take sides in international disputes. Currently, Norway refuses to open its excellent harbors for military use. It also forbids the storage of nuclear weapons on its territory. Denmark and

Open to the Baltic

Human-Environment Interaction Stockholm, Sweden's capital since 1523, is tied closely to the Baltic Sea. The city is built on a group of islands along Sweden's eastern shore. In the 1600s the city became the center of a thriving empire that dominated many parts of Europe. **Critical Thinking** *How can you tell from this photograph that Stockholm has a long, prosperous history?*

Sweden actively promote peaceful solutions to international crises.

Sound Economies

Compared with other regions of the world, the Nordic nations have sound economies. They derive their wealth from varied sources. Denmark and southern Sweden have flat land and a mild climate suitable for agriculture.

Denmark uses 60 percent of its land for farming, and in recent years produced more than three times the amount of food needed to feed its people. Fishing is also an important economic activity. The Norwegians, in particular, look to the sea. They compare it to farmland and call their offshore waters "The Blue Meadow." The region also profits from oil and gas production, high-grade ores, and vast expanses of forest.

Section 4 Review

Vocabulary and Main Ideas

1. **Define: a. fjord b. geothermal energy c. mixed economy d. politically neutral**

2. **What are the five Nordic nations?**

3. **Name at least three cultural bonds that help link the nations of northern Europe.**

4. **Describe the relationship between the government and the economy in the Nordic nations.**

5. **Critical Thinking:** *Demonstrating Reasoned Judgment* **Give evidence that would support this statement: "Because of their physical geography, the Nordic nations rely more heavily on shipping than any other region in Europe."**

learning LOCATIONS

6. **Which Nordic nations border Finland?**

7. **Where is Helsinki located in relation to Oslo?**

Summarizing Main Ideas

Section 1 England

- England comprises three different regions: the Highlands to the north and west, the central Midlands, and the Lowlands to the south.
- The wealth Britain earned from its export trade combined with the country's abundant reserves of coal and iron to fuel the Industrial Revolution.

Section 2 Scotland and Wales

- Although part of the United Kingdom, Scotland and Wales retain their cultural identities.
- In both Scotland and Wales, the rugged highlands remain rural while the lowlands are urban and industrial.

Section 3 The Two Irelands

- Religious conflicts begun in the 1500s continue to divide the Republic of Ireland and Northern Ireland, which is part of the United Kingdom.
- The Republic of Ireland hopes that its location between North America and Europe will attract industry and tourists.

Section 4 The Nordic Nations

- Denmark, Norway, Sweden, Finland, and Iceland share a northern location, a common religion, related languages, and similar political beliefs.
- Because of its northern location, Norden experiences long winters with little daily sun, and short summers with many hours of sunlight each day.

Reviewing Vocabulary

Match the definitions with the terms.

1. a flooded glacial valley
2. rocky material that contains a mineral
3. wet, spongy ground
4. not to take sides in international disputes
5. a narrow valley
6. able to produce abundant crops
7. a flooded valley near the mouth of a river
8. a broad, treeless plain

a. ore	e. bog
b. fjord	f. glen
c. estuary	g. fertile
d. moor	h. politically neutral

Applying the Geographic Themes

1. **Place** Describe how glaciers and volcanoes have affected the Nordic countries.
2. **Human-Environment Interaction** How do the people of Ireland use the landscape to provide a basic need?
3. **Location** Describe how the prevailing winds and ocean currents affect climates of the British Isles and the Nordic countries.
4. **Movement** What forms of transportation have been especially important to the peoples of the British Isles and the Nordic countries?
5. **Regions** How are the landscapes of the United Kingdom and the Nordic countries similar? How are they different?

Critical Thinking and Applying Skills

1. **Predicting Consequences** Some demographers estimate that Catholics will outnumber Protestants in Northern Ireland by the early twenty-first century. What might be the political results of such a trend?
2. **Using Time Lines** Look again at the time line on page 290. Then answer the following question. How many years passed between the invention of the steam locomotive and the first steam-powered ocean crossing?

Journal Activity

Writing Across Cultures

▶ 1. Write two paragraphs describing what it would be like to live in one of the Nordic nations during the winter and during the summer. How would it affect your life if the sun shone only three or four hours a day during the winter months? What would you do differently during the summer if it was light outside for twenty hours a day?

▶ 2. In the 1860s, an underwater telegraph cable linked Britain and the United States. Write a paragraph explaining some benefits of improved communication with Europe during the Industrial Revolution.

INTERNET link

Only a handful of women have won the Nobel Peace Prize. Two of them are Mairead Corrigan and Betty Williams, peace activists in Northern Ireland. Read about the history of women and the Nobel Peace Prize at the Nobel Prize Internet Archive. Link to this site from:

- www.phschool.com

Then follow the links to Mairead Corrigan and Betty Williams. What made them decide to step forward and make a change? What makes you take action? Write a short explanation.

learning LOCATIONS

The British Isles and the Nordic Nations

Number from 1 to 10 on a piece of paper . Next to each number, write the letter of the place on the map that corresponds to the place listed below.

1. Iceland
2. Dublin
3. Wales
4. Oslo
5. Finland
6. London
7. Stockholm
8. Northern Ireland
9. Scotland
10. Denmark

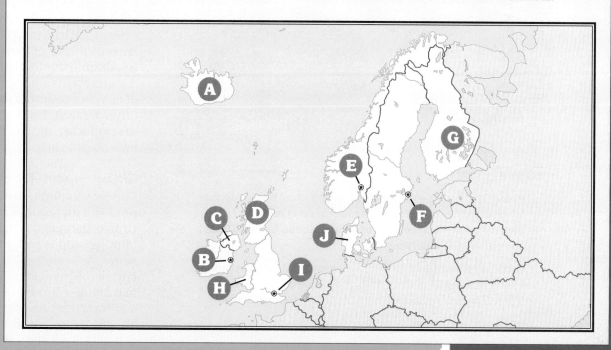

The European Union

The Issue

The European Union (EU) is the world's largest trading block—and it is still growing. Here are some of the challenges success has created for this economic giant.

Attracting a Crowd Fifteen western European countries currently belong to the EU. Member countries pay no tariffs when trading with one another. As a result, trade among member countries has increased and the standard of living of citizens living in EU countries has risen. Several eastern European countries, including Poland, Hungary, and Romania, are eager to join their European cousins and enjoy the economic benefits of EU membership. Some EU members, particularly Great Britain, are opposed to expanding the EU.

The Eurodollar In 1992 representatives of the EU countries agreed to create a common currency called the *euro*. They planned to begin using the *euro* by 1999, but now there are some concerns that the launch of the *euro* will be delayed. Before adopting the *euro*, each country must meet strict criteria to ensure that its economy is strong. Few countries seem able to meet these requirements.

A United States of Europe? In addition to working together for economic growth, EU members also cooperate politically. Citizens of EU countries enjoy a single European citizenship that allows them to live and work anywhere in the Union. They can also vote in local elections in the country where they live, even if they are not citizens of that country. Despite this level of unity, disagreements among leaders of member countries sometimes weaken the EU's ability to act quickly and forcibly on important issues.

Global Impact The EU is a leading economic power. It produces more goods than the United States and is the largest importer and exporter in the world. As a result, it plays a crucial role in negotiating and managing world-trade rules. In addition, its economic power has given it responsibilities for

U.S. Trade with the European Union

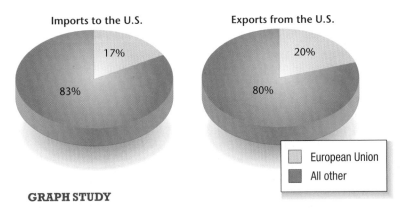

Imports to the U.S.
17%
83%

Exports from the U.S.
20%
80%

European Union
All other

GRAPH STUDY

- **Place** The European Union plays an important role in regulating world trade rules. It is also a major trading partner of the United States. *What percent of imports to the United States does the EU account for?*

- **Critical Thinking** Compare the percent of EU imports to the United States with percent of United States exports to the EU. *Is this a favorable balance of trade for the United States?*

providing financial help to poor, nonmember countries and negotiating peace treaties between warring nations.

Some Solutions

Leaders of EU member states are meeting the challenges the EU faces so that their union can remain strong. Here are some of the solutions they are working on.

Expanding the Union

Formal talks concerning the admission of new members are planned to begin before the end of 1997. Germany is particularly eager that modern eastern European countries, such as Poland, be admitted into the Union. It is concerned that denying nations entry into the EU could condemn them to poverty and create two classes of European nations—the haves and the have-nots.

Valuing the Euro

EU representatives are meeting to talk about ways to bring monetary union to Europe. Some leaders suggest relaxing the strict criteria that countries must meet in order to adopt the *euro*. Others have suggested extending the 1999 deadline so that countries that are temporarily experiencing slow growth can recover.

YOU DECIDE

1. Why would European countries that do not belong to the EU be at a disadvantage?

2. What challenges does the European Union pose to the United States?

3. Problem Solving You are an EU leader who is a member of a committee formed to draw up guidelines for countries that want to join the EU. Draft a one-page policy for admission to the Union. Include at least five criteria that countries must meet.

4. What You Can Do Find out more about trade between the United States and the EU.

5. Internet Activity Visit the European Union's Web site. Choose a link to follow, perhaps *THE EUROPEAN UNION—An Historical Achievement*, and read about something of interest. Write a paragraph about what you read. Link to this site from:

• www.phschool.com

Central Western Europe

Central Western Europe: POLITICAL

KEY

— National boundary
⊛ National capital
• Other city

Lambert Azimuthal Equal-Area Projection

North Sea

Hamburg
Berlin
Leipzig

NETHERLANDS
Amsterdam
The Hague ⊛
Antwerp
Essen
GERMANY
Brussels
BELGIUM
Frankfurt
LUXEMBOURG

50°N

English Channel

Le Havre
Seine
Luxembourg ⊛
Paris
River
Stuttgart Munich
Danube River
Vienna ⊛

ATLANTIC OCEAN

Nantes

FRANCE

⊛Bern
SWITZERLAND
Zurich
LIECHTENSTEIN
Innsbruck
AUSTRIA
Graz

50°N

Bay of Biscay

Bordeaux
Lyon
Geneva

Rhone River

Adriatic

45°N

Toulouse
Nice
Ligurian Sea

Marseille
MONACO
Corsica

0   150   300 mi
0   150   300 km

ANDORRA

5°W   0°   5°E   10°E   15°E

learning LOCATIONS

Mapping the Region

Create a map like the one above, lightly shading each country a different color. Then add labels for the countries and bodies of water that are shown on this map.

1 France

Section Preview

Main Ideas

- France has a great variety of physical and economic regions.

- History, language, and culture combined have created a distinct French identity.

- France faces economic and social uncertainties in the years ahead.

Vocabulary

dialect, Impressionism, nationalize, recession

APPEARED IN *NATIONAL GEOGRAPHIC*

The Eiffel Tower graces the skyline of Paris, France.

The map of France on page 305 shows why the French sometimes call their country "The Hexagon." If you smooth out the zigs and zags of France's borders, you will see that the country is roughly six-sided. Water borders three of the sides. Mountains form forbidding barriers on two other sides. Only in the northeast do low hills and flat, wide plains provide easy passage from France into neighboring countries.

Over the centuries, the French have established a strong national identity. As journalist Flora Lewis observed, "The French have no problems of identity. They know who they are and can't imagine wanting to be like anybody else."

A Country of Varied Regions

Even while France maintains a strong national identity, historic cultural and economic regions exist within the nation. The people of each of France's regions proudly continue their own traditions and way of life. From rich farming areas to huge, urban manufacturing and commercial centers, the different regions of France contribute to the country's varied economy.

Northern France In the interior of northern France lies the Paris Basin, a part of the North European Plain that stretches across northern Europe. The Paris Basin is a large, flat, circular area drained by the Seine (SEHN) and other rivers.

In the center of the Paris Basin, on the banks of the Seine River, lies Paris, the economic, political, and cultural capital of France. Paris and its surrounding area form France's chief manufacturing center. Raw materials shipped here from other parts of France and from other countries are turned into finished products.

The city of Lille (LEEL), north of Paris, is another important industrial center. Since the the late 1800s, the availability of coal for fuel in nearby Belgium has attracted many industries to this area. Steel mills, textile factories, and chemical plants in and around Lille have provided jobs for many people. Lille's location near northern European Union countries has helped it recover in recent years from economic problems and high unemployment.

Vineyards of the Southwest In the southern parts of France, the air is warmer and the soil drier. The grapes used to make French wines thrive in these conditions. Wine grapes are grown in many parts of France. However, the region around the busy seaport of Bordeaux (bor DOH) in southwestern France has a reputation for producing the best wines. The town of Bordeaux has given its name to the whole wine crop of the region. How the region's physical geography helps wine production is explained by Baron Geoffroy de Luze, who owns vineyards near Bordeaux.

> *It's a combination of the sun, . . . just the right amount of rainfall and no frost, and . . . the miserable soil. . . . It's true. You'll notice how stony and poor the soil is here. . . . When the soil is rich, the production of grapes is large. So the individual grapes draw less concentration of the good things in the earth and from the sun. You'll find that the most refined wines come from the poorest soil. With fewer fruits and more sun, one arrives at unbelievably good grapes.*

Life in Southern France East of Bordeaux lie two mountainous areas—the Massif Central (ma SEEF sahn TRAHL) and the Alps. Dividing these two rugged regions is the Rhône River. The Massif Central lies to the west of the Rhône, and forms one sixth of France's land area. The landscape is a mixture of older peaks worn flat by time and newer, sharper peaks that are not yet eroded. Though much of the soil is poor, various crops are grown and there is some industry.

East of the Rhône are the Alps, a rugged barrier of mountains that provide spectacular scenery. Unlike the Massif Central, the Alps are a long range of towering, snowcapped mountains. Mont Blanc, the tallest peak in the Alps, rises 15,771 feet (4,807 meters) above sea level.

For centuries, the Alps hindered movement between France and Italy. In 1787, Horace de Saussure, a naturalist and physicist, climbed to the top of Mont Blanc. He wrote, "Someday, a carriage road will be built under Mont Blanc, uniting the two valleys." His vision took 178 years to become reality. In 1965 engineers dug a highway tunnel through Mont Blanc, which straddles the border between France and Italy.

The Alps are known worldwide for their fashionable ski resorts and challenging skiing. During the summer, a magnificent array of alpine wildflowers covers the mountain slopes. Hikers come from around the world to enjoy the scenery.

The Vineyards of the Rhône Valley

● **Regions** The Romans first recognized that the Rhône Valley was well suited for raising grapes over 2000 years ago. Today, the Rhône Valley is still one of France's most important wine regions. *What geographic factors make a region valuable for growing grapes?*

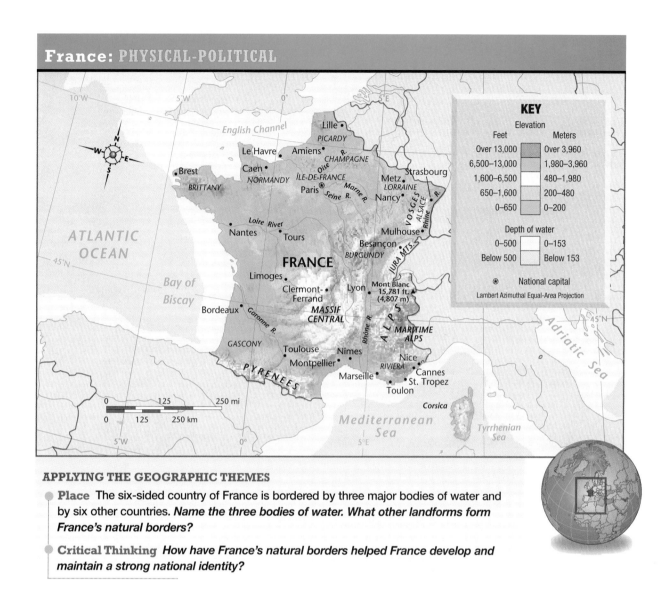

KEY

Elevation

Feet	Meters
Over 13,000	Over 3,960
6,500–13,000	1,980–3,960
1,600–6,500	480–1,980
650–1,600	200–480
0–650	0–200

Depth of water

0–500	0–153
Below 500	Below 153

⊛ National capital

Lambert Azimuthal Equal-Area Projection

APPLYING THE GEOGRAPHIC THEMES

● **Place** The six-sided country of France is bordered by three major bodies of water and by six other countries. *Name the three bodies of water. What other landforms form France's natural borders?*

● **Critical Thinking** *How have France's natural borders helped France develop and maintain a strong national identity?*

Along the Mediterranean Nestled between the Alps and the Mediterranean Sea in southeastern France is a thin strip of low-lying coastal land. This area, known as the Riviera, attracts millions of tourists each year. The warm climate is ideal for sunbathing on the region's famous beaches and swimming in the sea. The French Riviera is also known as the Côte d'Azur—the Azure Coast—for the magnificent scenery formed by the sky, the sea, and the local flower, lavender. Many people like to visit the lively resort cities of Cannes (KAHN), Nice (NEES), and Saint-Tropez (SAN troh PAY). The city of Cannes is also famous for its annual international film festival.

The port of Marseille (mar SAY) is the busiest seaport in France and the second most active in all of Western Europe. Tanker ships bring petroleum from Southwest Asia and North Africa to be unloaded at Marseille and processed at large oil refineries along the coast. Many French exports, including wine, electronic goods, and chemicals, are shipped from Marseille to other countries.

Industry in the East In the east of France lies the Rhine Valley. Here the Rhine River, Europe's busiest waterway, forms part of France's border with Germany. Two resource-rich provinces in the Rhine Valley, Alsace (al ZAS) and Lorraine, have changed hands many times during conflict between France and Germany. Lorraine has France's largest deposits of iron ore. Nearby, coal is mined. Strasbourg, France's major port on the Rhine, is located in Alsace.

The Artist and the City

- **Place** Artists have shaped the look and culture of Paris, France, for centuries. Here, a painter focuses on the Cathedral of Notre Dame. The cathedral was begun in 1163. **Critical Thinking** *What are some ways in which the city's artistic heritage have influenced the way Paris looks?*

France's History

Referring to France's great diversity, former French President Charles de Gaulle once said, "How can you govern a country that has 246 varieties of cheese?" Despite having the kinds of cultural and economic differences that have often caused other countries to break apart, France is a highly unified country.

A Long History of Unity France was known as Gaul when the Romans conquered it in the first century B.C. For more than five hundred years, the area prospered under the Romans. The Gauls, the native people of the area, were strongly influenced by the Romans, adopting the Latin language and Christian religion.

As the Roman Empire declined, the Franks, who came from the area that is now Germany, conquered the region. The Franks gave France its name. One of the most famous conquerors of all time, Charlemagne (SHAR luh mayn), became king of the Franks in A.D. 768. By the time Charlemagne died in 814, he controlled a huge empire, known as the Holy Roman Empire, that included much of Western Europe.

Charlemagne set up an efficient government in his realm. He sent out missionaries to spread the teachings of Christianity throughout northern Europe. He also encouraged the arts and a revival of learning. Charlemagne's empire

GLOBAL issues

Immigration

Nearly 2 million North Africans have arrived in France since the end of World War II. Islam has replaced Protestantism as France's second-largest religion, after Roman Catholicism.

fell apart after his death. By the tenth century, most of the power lay in the hands of the nobles who controlled land in the kingdom. In 987, these nobles chose Hugh Capet (HUE ka PAY), the ruler of Paris and the lands around it, as their new king.

Under Hugh Capet and his heirs, the monarchy grew strong. The lands ruled by the various nobles were united under one leader. Gradually the ruling monarchs of France expanded the kingdom's boundaries until, by 1589, they were almost the same as those of modern France. For the next two hundred years, French kings exercised absolute control over their lands. Then, in 1789, the monarchy came to a violent and bloody end during the French Revolution.

Since then, France has had several different forms of government, including a republic of the people, a constitutional monarchy, and empires under Napoleon Bonaparte and his nephew, Louis-Napoleon. Three times since 1870, German armies have swept across the flat northeastern plains and overrun northern France. The last two invasions, during World War I and World War II, were repelled with help from other countries, including the United States.

Language and Culture

Throughout their turbulent history, the people of France have maintained a strong sense of national identity. One reason for this is their belief in the historical unity of France. Language and culture have also played important roles in creating the French identity.

One Country, One Language Before the 1500s, the language that is now called French was spoken only in and around Paris. As the French kings expanded their control, they decreed that the language of Paris become the language of all the lands they ruled.

Several other languages, for example, Alsatian, German, Basque, and Breton, are still spoken in various parts of France. So are several **dialects**—variations of a language that are unique to a region or community. French, however, is the national language. New French words are published in official dictionaries only if they are approved by the French Academy. This body was established in 1634 to preserve

Facts in BRIEF

Country	Population	Life Expectancy (years)	Per Capita GNP (in US $)
Austria	8,100,000	77	23,120
Belgium	10,200,000	77	21,210
France	58,100,000	78	22,360
Germany	81,700,000	76	23,560
Liechtenstein	30,000	NA	NA
Luxembourg	400,000	76	35,850
Netherlands	15,500,000	77	20,710
Switzerland	7,000,000	78	36,410
United States	263,200,000	76	24,750

Source: Population Reference Bureau   NA indicates data not available.

CHART SKILLS

● *Which country in Western Europe has the highest per capita GNP?*

● **Critical Thinking** *What is the average life expectancy in Western Europe? What would account for a long life expectancy?*

the purity of the French language. It is a symbol of French cultural pride.

Cultural Identity The French also take enormous pride in their intellectual and artistic achievements. Among their greatest heroes are philosophers René Descartes (ruh NAY day CART), Jean-Paul Sartre, (ZHAHN PAUL SART ruh) and Voltaire. Many of the world's most famous painters have been French, including Claude Monet (mo NAY) and Pierre Auguste Renoir (PYER aw GOOST ruhn WAHR). These artists were leaders in a style of painting known as **Impressionism**. This school of art sought to capture fleeting visual "impressions" made by color, light, and shadows. The French also take a lead role in setting clothing styles. Famous French designers create clothes that influence fashion all over the world.

For centuries Paris has been the cultural center of France. The city's atmosphere of freedom has attracted artists and intellectuals from many nations. Countless developments in the arts and literature can be traced to the studios of artists and writers living in Paris. Today the city's art galleries and museums, including the famous Louvre (LOOV ruh), celebrate the achievements of these artists. Paris is also known for its theaters, ballets, operas, orchestras, and cinemas.

France Today

Following World War II, the French government established national planning programs to modernize the economy and encourage more balanced growth among France's regions. It also reached out to its Western European neighbors to form new trade agreements. Because of these changes, France enjoyed a period of great prosperity and is today one of the leading exporters of goods in the world.

In recent decades, the French government has taken different approaches to stimulating its economy. It has **nationalized**, or brought under state control, some businesses considered vital to national interests. And it has privatized some government-owned companies to promote economic growth. Under pressure to meet standards set by the European Union, officials have enacted strict economic measures.

France is a wealthy nation, but it faces social and economic uncertainty. In the 1990s France has struggled to recover from a deep economic **recession**—an extended decline in general business activity. Unemployment continues to be high, workers and students have waged strikes against government reforms, and foreign

Unemployment in France: 1990–1994

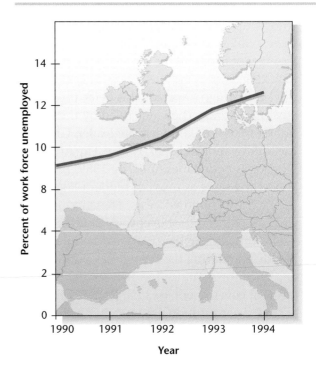

GRAPH STUDY

⬤ France's economic woes of the 1990s included a rise in unemployment. France began the 1990's with an already unhealthy unemployment rate of 9.1 percent. *What percentage of France's work force was unemployed by 1994?*

⬤ **Critical Thinking** *How is a high unemployment rate a symptom of economic recession?*

residents have become the focus of racial tensions. As the new century begins, it is unclear if the future of France will be as bright as its past.

Section 1 Review

Vocabulary and Main Ideas

1. **Define: a. dialect b. Impressionism
   c. nationalize d. recession**

2. **Where is France's manufacturing center?**

3. **How has language helped to unite France?**

4. **Give evidence that the French have challenges to overcome in the years ahead.**

5. **Critical Thinking:** *Determining Relevance* **How do you think France's diverse regions have contributed to its economic prosperity?**

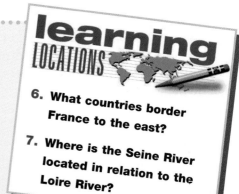

learning LOCATIONS

6. **What countries border France to the east?**

7. **Where is the Seine River located in relation to the Loire River?**

2 Germany

Section Preview

Main Ideas

● Germany was reunited in October 1990.

● Germany is Europe's leading industrial country.

● Germany is one of the world's mightiest economic powers.

Vocabulary

reparations, inflation, lignite

After separating Berlin for nearly thirty years, the Berlin Wall came down late in 1989.

On Thursday night, November 9, 1989, thousands of East and West Berliners gathered along the Berlin Wall. Just hours earlier, the East German government had announced that the borders between East and West Germany would be opened. As reporter Serge Schmemann wrote:

> *They seemed to be drawn by the sense that . . . the barrier of concrete and steel that had figured so prominently in the history of this city and the world, might soon be relegated to history. Some came with hammers and chisels, others with guitars, most with cameras.*

People all over the world were moved to tears of joy. The wall that had separated east from west was finally torn down.

Germany's Struggle for Unity

The 103-mile-long wall was built in 1961 by the Communist East German government to keep its citizens from escaping to West Germany. The Berlin Wall created a physical boundary between two different political regions. Even before this century, Germany's history as a nation has been one of divisions and unifications.

Divided German States The area that is now Germany was once part of Charlemagne's great Holy Roman Empire. After Charlemagne's death, Germany broke up into many small, independent political units. Princes, dukes, counts, and bishops all ruled their own domains. Many cities were free states. Often there was bitter rivalry and fighting among these states.

During the 1500s, a movement called the Protestant Reformation divided the German states even further. The Protestants objected to many of the practices and teachings of the Roman Catholic Church. In the early 1600s, the Reformation sparked thirty years of warfare between Protestants and Catholics throughout Germany and other parts of Central Europe.

Starting in the late 1700s, the state of Prussia, in what is now eastern Germany, led a movement to merge many German states into a single confederation. After Germany defeated

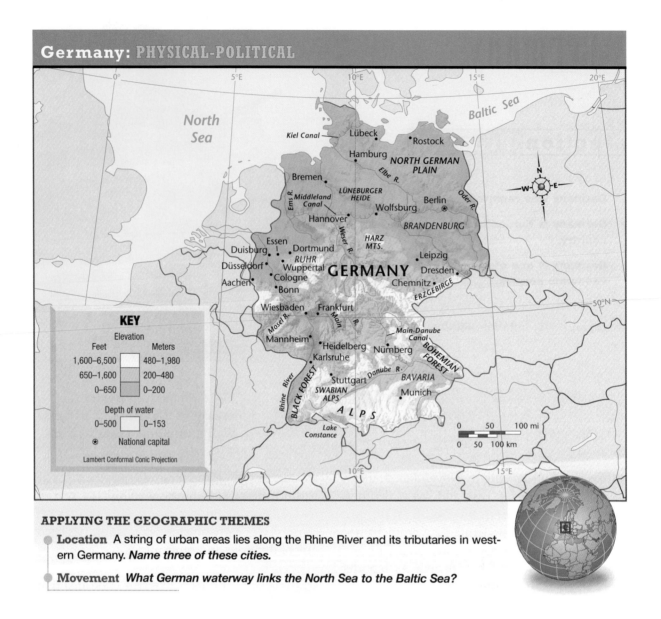

APPLYING THE GEOGRAPHIC THEMES

● **Location** A string of urban areas lies along the Rhine River and its tributaries in western Germany. *Name three of these cities.*

● **Movement** *What German waterway links the North Sea to the Baltic Sea?*

France in the Franco-Prussian War of 1870–71, German states that until then had remained independent agreed to join the new German Empire.

United Germany's Defeats In 1882 Germany joined with Austria-Hungary and Italy to form a military alliance known as the Triple Alliance. Between 1914 and 1918, Germany, Austria-Hungary, and other countries fought against France, Russia, the United Kingdom, the United States, and other allies in World War I.

According to the terms of the treaty following the war, a defeated Germany had to pay the victors **reparations**—money for war damages. As a result, Germany suffered economically. The economy collapsed in the early 1920s when **inflation**, or sharply rising prices, ruined the value of Germany's currency. In 1929, a worldwide economic depression left millions of Germans without jobs.

In the early 1930s, Adolf Hitler and his Nazi party came to power in Germany. Hitler promised to restore Germany's past glory and to improve the economy. He blamed the Jews and other people whom he considered to be racially inferior for all of Germany's problems.

In 1939 Germany invaded Poland and World War II began. During the war Hitler had millions of Jews, Poles, Gypsies, Slavs, and other people killed in concentration camps. Finally, in 1945 Germany was defeated by the allied countries—the United States, the United Kingdom, France, and the Soviet Union.

One People, Two Countries Following the war, tensions grew between the Western Allies and the Soviet Union concerning Germany's future. In 1949, Western leaders established the democratic country of the Federal Republic of Germany—West Germany. The Soviet Union set up the Communist German Democratic Republic—East Germany. Although Berlin, the former German capital, was located within East Germany, American, British, and French forces remained in the western half of the city, which became part of West Germany.

For forty years Germany remained divided between East and West. Then in late 1989 a wave of demonstrations calling for democracy swept through Eastern Europe and overturned East Germany's Communist government. Soon the new East German government announced that it would open the country's borders. Celebrations in East and West Berlin were especially joyous. Within weeks large sections of the Berlin Wall, symbol of a divided Germany, were destroyed. On October 3, 1990, East and West Germany were officially reunited.

A Mosaic of Regions

The physical regions of Germany are varied, but the differences between regions are not as dramatic as they are in France. As journalist Flora Lewis observed:

> *It is a [mild] land, brisk but bright along the North Sea coast, heaving gently above green valleys to the majestic Bavarian Alps. The mighty Rhine, one of Europe's oldest, most traveled highways, is still a great commercial lifeline.*

Germany's land can be divided into three bands that extend across the country. The high, craggy mountains of the south turn into hills, low peaks, and tall plateaus in central Germany before leveling off into the flat lands of the north.

Germany's generally mild climate is due largely to the influence of the North Sea. Away from the sea, in southern areas of the country, a humid continental climate prevails, causing colder winters and warmer summers. But even in January, temperatures are usually above freezing. However, cold winds from the east may bring sharp drops in temperatures for short periods.

Plains, Rivers, and Cities Northern Germany is covered by the North German Plain, which is a part of the North European Plain. For

Castles and German History

- **Regions** For many German villages, the castle was the center of political, economic, and social life. It was also a place of refuge during times of war. Here, the Hartenfels Castle rises above Torgau, Germany. **Critical Thinking** *Why did Germany's history of disunion produce a large number of castles?*

hundreds of miles flat, sandy plains spread out until they reach the North and Baltic seas. Wide rivers flow north out of the southern highlands across the plains to the sea.

Although much of the land in the plains is farmed, manufacturing and trade are also important economic activities. Hamburg, Germany's largest port and second-largest city, is built around a harbor where the Elbe River flows into the North Sea. Since the end of the Middle Ages, Hamburg has been a leading center of trade. Most of Hamburg's old structures were destroyed in bombing raids during World War II and were rebuilt after the war.

Another German port, Rostock, is also a tribute to German achievement after World War II. When East Germany cut its connections with West Germany, it lost access to West German ports. Needing an outlet to the sea for shipping, the East Germans dug a new harbor at Rostock, creating a major port on the Baltic Sea.

Berlin, Germany's capital and its largest city, was badly damaged during World War II. Both East and West Germany spent a great deal of money to rebuild the parts of Berlin that they controlled. Today, Berlin is once again the prosperous capital of a united Germany.

Rich Resources and Industry Two major rivers, the Rhine and the Elbe, flow through the central parts of Germany. This region of Germany is one of the most important industrial centers in the world. In the 1800s huge coal deposits were found near the Ruhr (ROOR) River. With plenty of available fuel, the Ruhr Valley became Germany's first industrial center.

Today, the Ruhr Valley produces most of Germany's iron and steel. It also has important chemical and textile industries. Over eight million people live in the large cities of Duisburg (DOOS boorg), Essen, Bochum (BO khuhm), and Dortmund and the smaller cities and towns in the area that form one huge metropolis.

In the eastern part of central Germany is another large industrial region. Steel, machinery, automobiles, and textiles are produced in cities such as Leipzig and Dresden and in the surrounding area. Power for the factories comes

GEO facts

There are 345 citizens per physician in Germany. (U.S.=416)

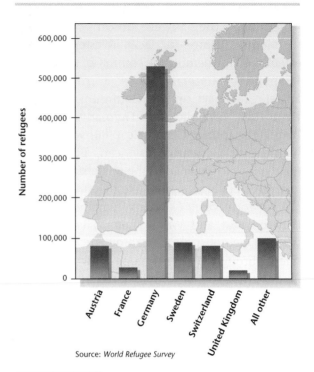

Refugees to Western Europe

Number of refugees

600,000
500,000
400,000
300,000
200,000
100,000
0

Austria · France · Germany · Sweden · Switzerland · United Kingdom · All other

Source: *World Refugee Survey*

GRAPH STUDY

● In recent years refugees have been pouring into Western Europe to escape war, poverty, and oppression. Most come from Eastern Europe, North Africa, Turkey, and the republics of the former Soviet Union. *According to the graph above, which country received the most refugees in 1992?*

● **Critical Thinking** *What problems might such a sudden rise in population cause a host country?*

mostly from **lignite**, a soft, brown coal. Lignite is easy to mine, but it pollutes the air heavily.

Not everyone in central Germany lives in a big, industrial city. Many people live in cities such as Frankfurt, Germany's banking center, and Heidelberg (HY duhl berg), the site of a world-famous university. Others live on fertile farmland located in the southern part of central Germany.

Scenic Southern Germany Along Germany's southern border lie the Bavarian Alps. North of the Alps, the land is less mountainous. The Rhine and Danube rivers flow through this hilly land. Skiers and hikers enjoy the spectacular scenery of these mountains, rivers, hills, and thick evergreen forests.

Shaping a High-Tech Future

Human-Environment Interaction
Germany has been an industrial leader for decades. Two Germans named Daimler and Benz were pioneers of the automobile industry in the 1880s. Today Germany is the third largest producer of cars in the world. *What natural resources have helped make Germany a leading industrial nation?*

The largest city in southern Germany is Munich (MYOO nikh). After World War II, Munich became Germany's cultural center. Theaters and museums that were destroyed during the war have been renovated. Damaged paintings and sculptures have been restored and are once again exhibited.

Germany in the World Today

After World War II the Germans worked hard to rebuild their shattered economies. In 1994 Germany was the leading industrial country in Western Europe, and it ranked second in the world after the United States in the amount of goods it exported. It is one of the strongest economic powers in the world. Germany maintains strong economic ties with Northern Eurasia and with other Eastern European countries, and it is a leading member of the European Union. Germany, therefore, has access to increasing markets in which to sell its valuable products.

Despite its strengths, reunified Germany faces a number of major problems. Among the challenges to be met are unemployment, rising violence against foreign workers, environmental degradation, and housing shortages.

Section 2 Review

Vocabulary and Main Ideas

1. Define: **a.** reparations **b.** inflation **c.** lignite

2. How has the process of unification played a role in Germany's history?

3. Why is the Ruhr Valley important to Germany's economy?

4. Why is Germany likely to have good markets in which to sell its goods in future years?

5. Critical Thinking: *Drawing Inferences* Why do you think some European countries, such as France, might be uneasy now that Germany is united?

learning LOCATIONS

6. Name the countries that border Germany to the west.

7. Where in Germany is the Rhine River located?

Focus on Skills

- [ ] Social Studies
- [ ] Map and Globe
- [x] Critical Thinking and Problem Solving

Distinguishing Fact from Opinion

To determine the soundness of an author's ideas, you need to be able to distinguish between fact and opinion. This ability allows you to reach your own conclusions about issues and events. Use the following steps to practice this skill.

1. Determine which statements are based on facts. A fact can be proven by checking other sources. It does not include someone's own values or opinions. Read statements A through G below. Answer the following questions: (a) Which statements are based solely on facts? (b) List two sources you could use to check that these statements are true.

2. Determine which of the statements are opinions. An opinion states a person's belief or feeling about a subject. It usually cannot be proven even if it is a widely held opinion. Study statements A through G again. Answer the following questions: (a) Which of the statements obviously include someone's opinion of Otto von Bismarck? (b) Which words in each of the opinion statements indicate that the statement is an opinion?

Statements About Von Bismarck

A. Otto von Bismarck was born in 1815.

B. Bismarck was truly an extraordinary human being.

C. As leader of Prussia, he won a series of wars, including the Danish War of 1864 and the Austro-Prussian War of 1866.

D. He was a very capable general.

E. Few people have ever exercised power more ruthlessly than Bismarck.

F. Bismarck once said, "Not by speeches and resolutions of majorities are the great questions of time decided upon . . . but by blood and iron."

G. Bismarck, tall and handsome, was a leader in the move for German unification in the nineteenth century.

3 The Benelux Countries

Windmills have shaped
the Netherland's land-
scape for centuries.

Section Preview

Main Ideas

The Dutch have reclaimed one fifth of the Netherlands from the sea.

Two distinct ethnic groups make up Belgium's population.

Luxembourg is a small country with a high standard of living.

Vocabulary

dike, polder, decentralize

Crowded together in northwestern Europe are three small countries—Belgium, the Netherlands, and Luxembourg. From the first letters of their names, together these countries are known as the Benelux countries. The Benelux countries are also called the Low Countries because so much of their land is low and flat. Their combined land area is small, but their combined population of 26.1 million people is almost as large as Canada's. After Monaco, Belgium and the Netherlands are the most densely populated countries in Europe.

Land from the Sea

"God made the world, but the Dutch made [the Netherlands]," commented French philosopher René Descartes. In few places is the result of human interaction with the environment more evident than in the Netherlands. The map on page 316 shows that the entire western side of the country is bordered by the North Sea. The Dutch have created one fifth of their country's land by reclaiming it from sea, lakes, and swamps. A Netherlander stated the national goal of his country in one sentence: "It is to possess land where water wants to be."

Technology Creates Land Over two thousand years ago, people living in the area that is now the Netherlands began to build low mounds and surrounded them with stone walls to make dry islands on which to live and farm. When the Romans conquered the area, they constructed sophisticated **dikes**, or embankments of earth and rock to hold back the water.

The Dutch became even more skillful at creating new land. They encircled a piece of land with dikes and then pumped the water out into canals. The Dutch call land reclaimed from the sea in this way a **polder**. Beginning in the 1200s, the Dutch used windmills to power the pumps that removed water from the land. Much of this new land is used for farming, but cities have also been built on some of the land.

Almost one third of the country is below sea level. Standing in a polder field, one often looks up to see ships passing by in canals that run alongside the land.

Making Good Use of Land The table beginning on page 702 shows that the Netherlands has an extremely high population density. With so many people living in such a small area, the Dutch have learned to make the best possible use of their land.

Dutch farmers cannot afford to waste any of the Netherlands' farmland. Over half of the land is used for agriculture, either to grow crops or as pasture. Throughout the Netherlands, farmers fertilize heavily and use modern agricultural methods.

Government leaders are devoting special attention to preserving the country's farmlands. The cities of The Hague (HAYG), Rotterdam, Amsterdam, and Utrecht (YOO trekht) form one huge arc-shaped metropolis that the Dutch call *Randstad*, or ring city. The government is trying to prevent this densely populated area from expanding into nearby rural areas.

Advantages of Location The Dutch have also learned to make good use of their location on the North Sea. Rotterdam and Amsterdam are both important ports. Because it is situated near the mouth of Europe's largest inland waterway, Rotterdam serves as a link between much of Europe and the rest of the world.

Two Peoples, One Place

The people who inhabit the modern country of Belgium are an uneasy mix. About 30 percent of all Belgians speak French and call themselves Walloons. About 55 percent speak Flemish, a dialect of Dutch.

After Belgium gained independence from the Netherlands in 1830, relations between the Walloons and the Flemings grew tense. French was the country's only official language. Most government leaders spoke French, and all Belgian universities used French. As a result the Flemings, who spoke Dutch, could not hold government positions or enter professions in which a university education was needed.

Yet the Flemings made up a large part of the population. They wanted the same cultural and economic rights that the Walloons enjoyed. To help resolve the conflict, the Belgian

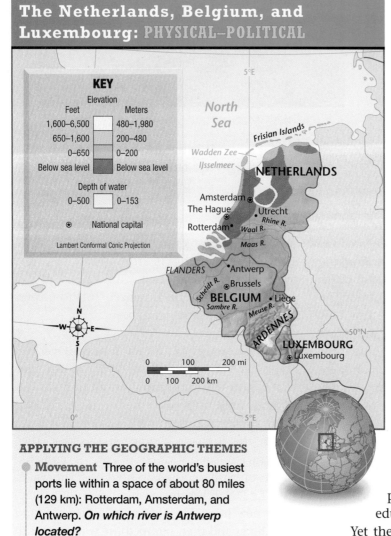

The Netherlands, Belgium, and Luxembourg: PHYSICAL–POLITICAL

KEY

Elevation

Feet	Meters
1,600–6,500	480–1,980
650–1,600	200–480
0–650	0–200
Below sea level	Below sea level

Depth of water

0–500	0–153

⊛ National capital

Lambert Conformal Conic Projection

North Sea
Frisian Islands
Wadden Zee
Ijsselmeer
NETHERLANDS
Amsterdam ⊛
The Hague •
Utrecht •
Rotterdam •
Rhine R.
Waal R.
Maas R.
FLANDERS • Antwerp
Scheldt R.
⊛ Brussels
BELGIUM • Liège
Sambre R.
Meuse R.
ARDENNES
LUXEMBOURG
• Luxembourg

5°E
50°N
0°
5°E

| 0 | 100 | 200 mi |
| 0 | 100 | 200 km |

APPLYING THE GEOGRAPHIC THEMES

● **Movement** Three of the world's busiest ports lie within a space of about 80 miles (129 km): Rotterdam, Amsterdam, and Antwerp. *On which river is Antwerp located?*

● **Regions** *Where is the wooded plateau region of Ardennes located?*

Crossroads at Luxembourg

● **Location** Luxembourg shares borders with France, Germany, and Belgium. The nation's languages reflect these close ties. French and German are two of the major languages in the country. A third language, Luxembourgish, is unique to the nation. *How does Luxembourg's economy benefit from these ties?*

government made Flemish an official language in 1898. More recently, the Belgian Parliament passed laws to **decentralize** its government—that is, transfer power to smaller regions. These regions are Wallonia, Flanders, and Brussels.

Luxembourg

Luxembourg covers only 990 square miles (2,564 sq km), an area smaller than the state of Rhode Island. Despite its small size, Luxembourg has managed to endure for more than one thousand years. Although Luxembourg has close cultural ties to Germany, France, and Belgium, it has maintained an independent spirit. In

Luxembourg three languages are spoken: French, German, and a German dialect called Luxembourgish.

Luxembourg has one of the highest standards of living in Europe. Economic activity, once dominated by the manufacture of steel, has become increasingly diversified. High-tech firms and service industries fill the gap left by reduced steel production. Luxembourg is a member of the European Union, and trades most of its goods and services with other EU members.

GEO facts

With a per capital GNP of $35,850, Luxembourg ranks second in the world.

Section 3 Review

Vocabulary and Main Ideas

1. **Define: a. dike b. polder c. decentralize**

2. **What use do the Dutch make of the land they reclaim from the sea?**

3. **Which two ethnic groups make up most of Belgium's population?**

4. **What are Luxembourg's most important economic activities?**

5. **Critical Thinking:** *Cause and Effect* **How did technological advances help the Netherlands to develop as a country?**

learning LOCATIONS

6. **Locate and name the capital of Belgium.**

7. **Name the countries that border Luxembourg.**

4 Switzerland and Austria

Switzerland, in the heart of the Alps, is Europe's most mountainous country.

The Alps tower above the two small, land-locked countries of Switzerland and Austria. They cover more than half of each country's land area. Both countries are politically neutral. Neither is a member of NATO. Despite these similarities, Switzerland and Austria are strikingly different.

Switzerland

Switzerland has three official languages—French, German, and Italian—and some of its people speak a dialect called Romansch. About 64 percent of the population speak German, and 19 percent speak French. Each Swiss ethnic group has its own name for Switzerland. The German-speaking Swiss call it Schweiz (SHVYTS). Suisse (SWEES) is the name used by those who speak French. Italian-speaking citizens call their country Svizzera (SVEE tay rah). Switzerland's official name is Confederation Helvetica. We know it as the Swiss Confederation. A **confederation** is a loose organization of states united for their common good.

For over seven hundred years, the Swiss have absorbed people from different cultural traditions to become a proud, prosperous, independent country. Yet these various cultural groups have maintained their distinctive identities as well as much of their political autonomy.

Uniting for Defense

Switzerland was formed in 1291 when leaders of three **cantons**, or states, formed the Swiss Confederation to fight an Austrian emperor. They fought several wars against the Austrians. Attracted by the growing strength of the confederation, other cantons began to join. By 1513 thirteen cantons belonged to the confederation.

Switzerland fought Italy in 1515 and was defeated. It never again fought in a foreign war. In 1798 Napoleon's armies occupied Switzerland. When Napoleon's forces were finally defeated, the countries of Europe formally recognized Switzerland as a neutral country. Since that time, Switzerland has not taken sides in conflicts between other countries, and no other European country has invaded its borders.

Strong Identities Today, twenty-six cantons make up Switzerland. These cantons differ from one another greatly in language, religion, customs, and the ways in which people make a living. The people of each canton work hard to preserve their particular way of life.

The cantons have a great deal of control over their own affairs. In the early history of the Swiss Confederation, each canton governed itself as a separate country. Even today, any law passed by the national government must be ratified by popular vote if enough Swiss citizens so request. This practice gives Swiss citizens more direct control of their government.

A Prosperous Economy The independent spirit of the cantons exists alongside strong feelings of national unity. This, together with Switzerland's neutrality, has helped the country thrive. The Swiss enjoy one of the highest standards of living in the world. Although Switzerland has few natural resources within its borders, it has developed specialized economic activities that are highly profitable.

Dairy farming is the most important form of agriculture, because there is little flat land on which to grow crops. Cattle are driven to high mountain pastures in the spring. In the fall they are brought down to the valleys to protect them from the harsh winter temperatures in the Alps. Since milk is a **perishable good**, meaning it does not stay fresh for long, most of it is turned into processed products like chocolate and cheese for export. Switzerland is famous throughout the world for its high-quality chocolates.

Manufacturing and Service Industries Switzerland has none of the mineral resources, such as iron ore, coal, or petroleum, needed for heavy industry. So the Swiss specialize in making products that require skilled labor, instead of many materials or costly transportation. For hundreds of years Swiss jewelers have produced watches known the world

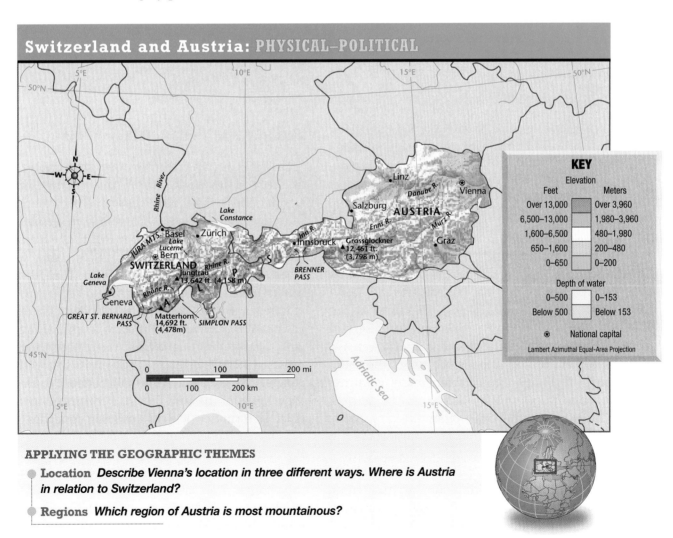

Switzerland and Austria: PHYSICAL-POLITICAL

KEY

Elevation

Feet	Meters
Over 13,000	Over 3,960
6,500–13,000	1,980–3,960
1,600–6,500	480–1,980
650–1,600	200–480
0–650	0–200

Depth of water

0–500	0–153
Below 500	Below 153

⊛ National capital

Lambert Azimuthal Equal-Area Projection

APPLYING THE GEOGRAPHIC THEMES

● **Location** *Describe Vienna's location in three different ways. Where is Austria in relation to Switzerland?*

● **Regions** *Which region of Austria is most mountainous?*

Austria's Iron Belt

● **Location** Iron ore is an important natural resource in the eastern Alps. Austria has used this resource to build its steel industry, a mainstay of the nation's economy. **Critical Thinking** *How does iron mining help Austria maintain a balanced economy?*

ssues

Acid Rain

Austria has passed a variety of laws concerning acid rain and the protection of trees. They include a law in Vienna requiring anyone who cuts down a tree to replace it, as well as laws limiting auto and industrial emissions.

over for their accuracy. Switzerland produces very high-quality tools, including microscopes and measuring and cutting tools. Today, the Swiss are also world leaders in the development of new medicines.

Banking is an important service industry in Switzerland. Switzerland is seen as a safe place to keep money because of the country's neutrality. People from many countries deposit their money in banks in Zurich, Geneva, and other Swiss cities.

Tourism is also very important to Switzerland's economy. Many people come to ski at resorts such as Zermatt and Saint-Moritz in the snowy Alps. Others come to hike, climb mountains, or simply to enjoy Switzerland's spectacular scenery.

Austria: New and Old

Although Austria's present borders were created at the end of World War I, this country of German speakers has roots that reach back more than one thousand years. It grew from a small region with its own ruler in A.D. 976 to the large Austrian Empire by the early 1800s. After a defeat in 1866, Austria became part of the Austro-Hungarian Empire. In the late 1800s, this empire controlled parts of Italy and much of Eastern Europe. Austria-Hungary fought along with Germany during World War I. With their defeat in 1918 the empire collapsed. Austria and Hungary were separated into independent countries. Much of the land they had controlled was taken to form new Eastern European countries.

One of modern Austria's biggest challenges has been to rebuild itself within its new, smaller boundaries. Because mountains cover much of the country, Austria's population is concentrated in the eastern lowlands, where the terrain is mostly flat or gently sloping.

The Music of Austria

● **Place** Many great composers, including Haydn, Mozart, and Schubert, lived in Vienna. Vienna still has a musical heart, as seen in its lively street-side entertainment. **Critical Thinking** *What does it mean for a city to be a "cultural center"?*

Austria has used Switzerland as a model for its economic renewal. Like Switzerland, Austria has created specialized industries. Much of its economic activity centers on manufacturing machine tools, chemicals, and textiles. Cattle breeding and dairy farming are important agricultural activities. However, unlike Switzerland, Austria has the added benefit of some mineral resources. Deposits of iron ore are mined in the eastern Alps, and then processed into iron and steel products. Other mined resources include magnesite, aluminum, copper, and lead.

Vienna, the country's capital, has also had to adapt to its changing role in history. The political and cultural center of the Austrian Empire, Vienna had two million residents in 1910 and was one of the world's largest cities. It was home to many great composers, including Haydn (HY duhn), Mozart (MOH tsart), and Schubert (SHOO burt). The city even lent its name to a popular dance in the late 1800s— the Viennese Waltz. Today its population is only 1.5 million, but modern industries that find Vienna too congested prefer to locate in smaller cities like Graz, Linz, or Innsbruck.

Section 4 Review

Vocabulary and Main Ideas

1. **Define: a. confederation b. canton c. perishable good**

2. **Why does Switzerland have three official languages?**

3. **Which war brought an end to the Austro-Hungarian Empire?**

4. **Critical Thinking:** *Identifying Central Issues* **What factors have helped Switzerland become a prosperous country?**

learning LOCATIONS

5. **Which countries border Switzerland?**

6. **Name the capital of Austria.**

Review and Activities

Summarizing Main Ideas

Section 1 France

- France is a country of varied regions, from the industrialized northern cities of Paris and Lille to the wine-growing areas of Bordeaux and the mountainous Massif Central.
- A shared history and culture have given the French a deep sense of national unity.

Section 2 Germany

- The physical regions of Germany can be divided into three wide bands—rugged highlands, gentle hills, and flat lowlands.
- As a result of World War II, Germany was divided into two separate countries—East Germany and West Germany. In 1990 East and West Germany were officially reunified.
- The country is heavily industrialized and has major shipping outlets on the North and Baltic Seas.

Section 3 The Benelux Countries

- Belgium, the Netherlands, and Luxembourg are called the Benelux countries. They make up the most densely populated region of Europe.
- The Dutch have increased the size of their country by reclaiming land from the sea.

Section 4 Switzerland and Austria

- A neutral country, Switzerland is a confederation representing peoples from many different ethnic groups. Today three languages and one dialect are spoken in Switzerland.
- Austria's history dates back more than one thousand years. Since the breakup of the Austro-Hungarian Empire, Austria has had to redefine itself as a nation.

Reviewing Vocabulary

Use each of the following terms in a sentence that shows its meaning.

1. confederation
2. recession
3. decentralize
4. perishable good
5. dialect
6. canton
7. nationalize
8. reparations
9. inflation
10. lignite
11. dike
12. polder

Applying the Geographic Themes

1. **Location** What effect do the Alps have on France and Switzerland?
2. **Human-Environment Interaction** How did East Germany change its environment in order to secure a shipping outlet to the Baltic Sea?
3. **Place** Describe the conditions that are favorable for growing grapes for wine.
4. **Regions** What landscape feature defines northern France and Germany?
5. **Movement** What is one way to cross the Alps between France and Italy?

Critical Thinking and Applying Skills

1. **Making Comparisons** How do France and Switzerland differ in the role that language plays in their identities?
2. **Distinguishing Fact from Opinion** The following is a statement that might have been made by Otto von Bismarck. Which sentences in the statement express an opinion? *I can't wait to go to war with France. History has shown that wars often lead to a more unified nation. And a more unified nation will be well worth the deaths of our citizens.*

▶ 1. Imagine the United States Congress has proposed a law making it illegal to include any word in an American English dictionary that has not been approved by a special government official. Write a paragraph in your journal expressing your opinion of this proposal. Describe at least one positive and one negative effect of the law.

▶ 2. Write two paragraphs describing life in Berlin when the Berlin Wall still existed. In one paragraph, imagine life as a West Berliner. In the other paragraph, write from the perspective of an East Berliner.

INTERNET link

Take a tour of Paris from WebMuseum. Link to this site from:

• www.phschool.com

Wander around this site. Then write a diary entry detailing what you saw on your trip.

learning LOCATIONS

Central Western Europe

Number from 1 to 11 on a piece of paper. Next to each number, write the letter of the place on the map that corresponds to the place listed below.

1. Paris
2. Austria
3. Belgium
4. Berlin
5. Vienna
6. France
7. Germany
8. Luxembourg
9. Amsterdam
10. The Netherlands
11. Switzerland

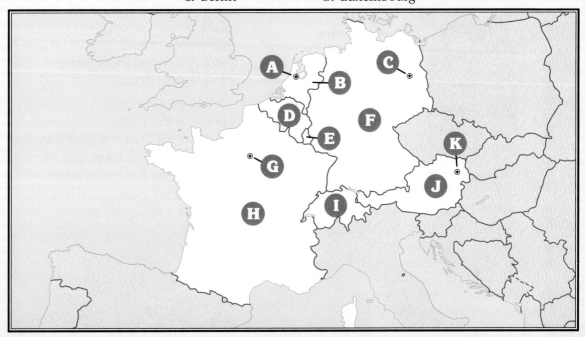

Map Skills
for Life

Sven Ohlsson, who lives in Sweden, is visiting Vienna, Austria. The city is famous for its museums, palaces, churches, and beautiful streets.

Sven knows that there are several attractions he wants to see, but they are in different parts of the city. He decides to take the Vienna subway, which has five lines crossing the city. These are the things that Sven wants to see:

★ Schönbrunn Palace, famous for its beautiful gardens, one corner of which now houses the Vienna Zoo.

★ The Museum of Art History, which contains many masterpieces by artists such as Rembrandt, Brueghel, and Titian.

★ The famous trained Lippizaner horses at the Spanish Riding School, which is part of the Hofburg, the Imperial Palace of the Hapsburgs.

★ The huge Ferris wheel in the Prater, a public amusement park near the Danube River. Emperor Joseph II turned this area of imperial parklands over to the public in 1766.

Reading the Map

Follow the steps below to understand how Sven can use the subway map to find his way around Vienna. Because this map is intended for visitors, it lists the subway stops for a number of popular sites. From his guidebook, Sven knows that subway stations are marked with blue "U" signs. (The U stands for *U-bahn*, German for "subway.")

1. Skim the map to get a general idea of where each subway line goes. Vienna's subway lines are numbered, for example "U4." Notice where the different lines cross, for Sven will probably have to change from one line to another. For instance, several lines cross at Karlsplatz. **(a)** Which are they?

Sven is beginning his trip from Stephansplatz, the square where the famous St. Stephen's Cathedral stands. **(b)** What subway lines serve this landmark?

2. Check the key to find the sights and the subway line and stop for each of them.
(a) Since Sven is already at Stephansplatz, which would be easier for him to visit first—the Spanish Riding School at the Hofburg or the Museum of Art History? **(b)** Which subway line will he take?

3. Figure out the best ways to go from one place to the next. With the map, Sven is trying to figure out where he must change subway lines as he goes from Schönbrunn Palace to the Prater. To do this, he has to find where lines U4 and U1 cross. **(a)** Where will Sven change trains?
(b) Where should he get off the U1 train to ride the Ferris wheel in the Prater?

Vienna Subway System Map

Vienna

See Vienna by U-Bahn!
Belvedere Palace: U1, U2, U4, Karlsplatz
Hofburg (Imperial Palace): U3, Herrengasse
Museum of Art History: U2, Babenbergerstrasse
Museum of Natural History: U2, U3, Volkstheater
Prater: U1, Praterstern
Schönbrunn Palace: U4, Schönbrunn
St. Stephens Cathedral: U1, U3, Stephansplatz
Stadtpark (public city park): U4, Stadtpark
Football (Soccer) Museum: U1, Praterstern
Westbahnhof (train station): U3, U6, Westbahnhof

U6 U4 Heiligenstadt
Friedensbrücke
Volksoper
U1 Kagran
Alte Donau
U3 Johnstrasse
Schottentor
U2 Schottenring
Praterstern
Westbahnhof
Herrengasse
Stephansplatz
Landstrasse
Babenbergerstrasse
U2
U4 Hütteldorf
Schönbrunn
Längenfeldgasse
Karlsplatz
Erdberg
U3
Meidling Philadelpia-brücke
U6 Siebenhirten
Reumannplatz
U1

AUSTRIA
Linz
Vienna
Innsbruck
Graz
10°E 14°E 16°E
48°N
46°N
10°E 12°E 14°E 16°E

N

Test Yourself

1. After all that sightseeing, Sven is ready for some Austrian pastry. He remembers that the famous Cafe Demel is near the Imperial Palace, the Hofburg. **(a)** How can Sven get there from the Prater? **(b)** What subway stop should he look for?

2. Sven's vacation is over, and he must catch the train back to Sweden. Most trains going north leave Vienna from the West Station—the Westbahnhof. Which subway line can Sven take to the train station?

17

Mediter-ranean Europe

SECTIONS

1 Spain and Portugal

2 Italy

3 Greece

Mediterranean Europe: POLITICAL

KEY

— National boundary
⊛ National capital
• Other city

Lambert Azimuthal Equal-Area Projection

learning LOCATIONS

Mapping the Region

Create a map like the one above, lightly shading each country a different color. Then add labels for the countries and bodies of water that are shown on this map.

Spain and Portugal

Section Preview

Main Ideas

- The physical characteristics of the Iberian Peninsula isolate it from the rest of Europe.

- Spain's economy depends on both agriculture and industry.

- Minority groups in Spain are striving for greater independence.

- Portugal is a small country with a history of overseas trade.

Vocabulary

navigable, sirocco, hub

APPEARED IN *NATIONAL GEOGRAPHIC*

The Alcazar Castle sits on top of a high cliff in Segovia, Spain.

As the map on page 328 shows, the Iberian Peninsula dangles off the southwestern edge of Europe, separating the waters of the Mediterranean Sea from the Atlantic Ocean. Two countries dominate the peninsula, Spain and Portugal. Spain covers most of the peninsula; Portugal occupies about one sixth of the land.

Spain and Portugal seem closely tied to the rest of Europe. But location can be deceptive. The French emperor Napoleon once said, "Europe ends at the Pyrenees (PIHR uh neez)"—the mountains that divide the Iberian Peninsula from the rest of Europe. The reason people think of Spain and Portugal as isolated from the rest of Europe is revealed in the histories and in the distinct characteristics of the two countries.

Spain: Unique in Europe

A castle appears on Spain's coat of arms. The castle is a symbol both of Spain's history and of its physical setting. Historically, the castle represents Castile (cas TEEL) and the hundreds of years of war that are part of Spain's history. Castile was one of the Christian kingdoms of Spain that fought the Muslim Moors and finally expelled them in 1492, after being under their rule for more than 700 years.

Geographically, Spain is like a well-guarded castle. The Pyrenees Mountains block easy passage across the nation's only land border with the rest of Europe. Approaches by water are no easier. Steep cliffs rise directly from the water along large stretches of the coastline. Elsewhere coastal plains are very narrow.

Rising from the slender coastal plains are the high plateaus that form most of Spain. The plateau of central Spain is known as the *Meseta* (me SAY tuh), the Spanish word for "plateau." Several large rivers flow across the Meseta and between the few mountain ranges that divide the plateau. Of these rivers, only the Guadalquivir is **navigable**; that is, deep and wide enough to allow ships to pass. Dangerous rapids make all other rivers unnavigable.

Climate and Elevation Almost all of Spain has a Mediterranean climate of mild, rainy winters and hot, dry summers. Spain's elevation has a strong influence on its climate. Moist, Atlantic winds rising over the Cantabrian (can TAH bree uhn) Mountains along the northern coast drop ample rain for farmers to raise corn

and cattle there. The Meseta in the interior, however, is in the rain shadow of the mountains, and is much drier. Farmers in the Meseta grow wheat or barley, using dry-land farming methods that leave land unplanted every one or two years in order to gather moisture. Sheep and goats graze on slopes too steep or dry for growing crops.

Parts of southeastern Spain are much drier than the rest of the country, making them semi-arid. **Siroccos**, or hot, dry winds from northern Africa, blow over this area. Irrigation provides water for growing citrus fruits and olive trees on the eastern coastal plains near cities such as Valencia and Barcelona.

Spain's Economy Although 18 percent of its exports are agricultural, in recent years Spain's economy has shifted toward new

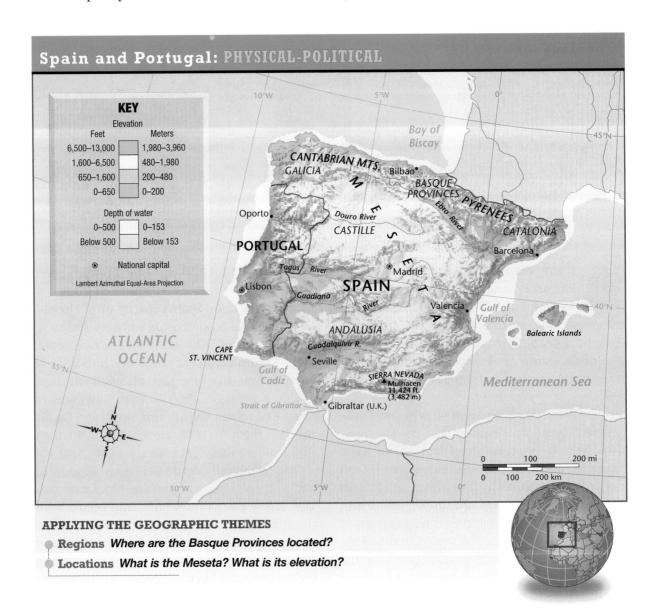

Spain and Portugal: PHYSICAL-POLITICAL

KEY

Elevation

Feet		Meters
6,500–13,000		1,980–3,960
1,600–6,500		480–1,980
650–1,600		200–480
0–650		0–200

Depth of water

0–500		0–153
Below 500		Below 153

⊛ National capital

Lambert Azimuthal Equal-Area Projection

APPLYING THE GEOGRAPHIC THEMES

● **Regions** *Where are the Basque Provinces located?*

● **Locations** *What is the Meseta? What is its elevation?*

Bounty from the Sea

Human-Environment Interaction
The northern region of Spain is dominated by the Basques, who have struggled to maintain their identity and independence. Their region is rich in resources, including seafood. *How has the geography of northern Spain helped the Basques retain their cultural identity?*

industries based on the country's natural resources. Its major export is transportation equipment. One major industrial center is in the north, around the city of Bilbao. Local iron ore provides material for producing steel and other products. Barcelona, the nation's largest port, is a center for the manufacture of textiles and plastics.

Madrid's Central Location Spain's largest city is its capital, Madrid. King Philip II made this city his capital in 1561. One story suggests that the king selected this site on the Meseta because its dry climate eased the pain of his gout, a disease that causes painful joints. Historical geographers give another reason for the capital's status: its central location. This factor allowed Philip and later rulers to control people and resources in all parts of the nation.

Over the years such central control grew easier as Madrid became the **hub**—a center point of concentrated activity and influence—of new transportation routes. The city prospered by tapping the wealth of other Spanish regions. An old Spanish saying suggested, "Everyone works for Madrid, and Madrid works for no one."

In recent decades, the Spanish have built newer industries in the area around Madrid. Migrants from poor farming areas have moved to the city and surrounding area. The metropolis now has more than 3 million residents. It also has problems associated with a large population, including heavy traffic and air pollution.

The Regions of Spain Despite nearly five hundred years of central control, Spain's regions hold on to their strong independent identities. Writer V. S. Pritchett said this about the Spanish people's strong regional ties:

> *They are rooted in their region, even nowadays. . . . They are Basques, Catalans, Galicians, Castilians . . . and so on, before they are Spaniards.*

The most striking example of an independent identity may be the Basque (BASK) people of northern Spain. The Basques number fewer than 1 million people, yet they inhabit one of Spain's richest areas.

The Basque language is not related to any other European language and is difficult to learn. A Spanish story tells of a person who "spent seven years learning it and in the end knew only three words."

The Basques have always wanted to maintain their cultural identity apart from the rest of Spain. As a result they have been persecuted by many Spanish leaders throughout history. Some Basques demand total independence. A few of these separatists have engaged in violent acts against the central Spanish government.

Political tensions are less severe in Catalonia, the region surrounding Barcelona. However, pressures for greater use of the Catalan language—a mixture of French and Spanish— are evident in this region, too. Other parts of Spain are also asking for greater local control.

Portugal

English professor and novelist Frank Tuohy explained the differences he saw between Spain and Portugal this way:

> *Spain is like a novel with half a dozen chapters; Portugal is a short story. A compact country, with variety in a limited space, one small village church will commemorate six centuries of history and three golden ages of architecture.*

Portugal is about the size of the state of Indiana but has twice as many residents. The northeastern corner of the country is mountainous, but the land slopes gently toward the Atlantic. At least 20 inches (50 cm) of rain fall each year in much of the country.

The abundant rainfall favors farming. Grains such as wheat, corn, and barley grow on flat lands. Olive oil from the south is a major export, as is the port wine produced in northern valleys near the city of Oporto. Cork and cork products that are made from the bark of oak trees that grow in central Portugal are also major exports.

GLOBAL issues

Water Pollution

Oil spills and industrial and human waste are polluting the Mediterranean Sea. It takes nearly 100 years for the sea to renew its waters through the Strait of Gibraltar, so pollutants that enter the Mediterranean stay there. Countries bordering the Mediterranean have been working together for change since 1975, but progress is slow.

Facts in BRIEF

Country	Population	Life Expectancy (years)	Per Capita GNP (in US $)
Greece	10,500,000	77	7,390
Italy	57,700,000	77	19,620
Malta	400,000	75	NA
Portugal	9,900,000	75	7,890
San Marino	30,000	76	NA
Spain	39,100,000	77	13,650
United States	263,200,000	76	24,750

Source: Population Reference Bureau   NA indicates data not available.

CHART SKILLS

- *Which country, aside from the United States, has the highest per capita GNP?*
- *Which country, aside from the United States, has the largest population?*

A History of Exploration Portugal has had a large impact on world affairs. It emerged as an independent nation in 1143 when rulers of the area around Oporto defeated the Moors. Portugal quickly became a trading nation. Portugal's capital, Lisbon, became the leading port of the new nation.

In the fifteenth century Portugal explored new sea routes to East Asia around Africa and established many trading colonies. When both Spain and Portugal expanded their colonial empires into South America, conflicts arose over the division of land. In 1494 the two countries signed a treaty and Portugal gained control of large parts of Africa and Brazil. Spain claimed most of the rest of Latin America.

Independence in Africa The empires of Portugal and Spain shrank in the early 1800s as many colonies gained their independence. Not until 1975 did the Portuguese grant independence to their largest African colonies. Since

A Heritage of Exploration

● **Regions** The Monument to the Discoveries in Lisbon celebrates Portugal's long history of exploration by sea. The best known of Portugal's great explorers was Vasco da Gama, who opened the sea route around Africa and into the Indian Ocean. Portuguese colonists settled in South America, Africa, and Asia. *For how long did Portugal maintain its colonies?*

that time, nearly 1 million people from the former African colonies have immigrated to Portugal, seeking greater opportunities.

Banker Antonio Vasco de Mello observed about the old Portugal, "We didn't know if we were a small European country with big African holdings or a big African country with a foothold in Europe." When Portugal gave its colonies their freedom, the country turned back toward Europe. Like Spain, Portugal joined the European Union in 1986.

Portugal in the Future Portugal's economy, once based heavily on agriculture, is currently heading in new directions. As in Spain, industry now plays a major role in Portugal's economy. Most factories in Portugal are small; their products include clothing, paper, and cork. The nation is working to increase its literacy rate of about 87 percent. Industrial pollution is a growing problem, and Portugal faces economic, environmental, and human challenges as it moves into the future.

Section 1 Review

Vocabulary and Main Ideas

1. **Define: a. navigable b. sirocco c. hub**

2. **How do Spain's mountains affect its climate?**

3. **What is the meaning of "everyone works for Madrid, and Madrid works for no one"?**

4. **How did a small country like Portugal come to have a great influence on the world from the 1400s to the 1800s?**

5. **Critical Thinking: *Predicting Consequences* Why might the Spanish government be reluctant to grant the Basques their independence?**

6. **Where is Lisbon located in relation to Barcelona?**

7. **Where are the Basque Provinces located in relation to Madrid?**

2 Italy

Section Preview

Main Ideas

Italy has a mountainous terrain, but agriculture is still important to the economy.

Many Italians have migrated to the industrial north to find employment in factories.

Italy's three larger regions are made up of many smaller, distinctive regions.

Vocabulary

seismically active, subsidence, Renaissance

The vineyards at San Gimignano help give northern Italy its characteristic landscape.

Italy has perhaps the best-known outline of any country in the world. Most people suggest that Italy looks like a giant boot ready to kick the triangular "rock" of Sicily across the Mediterranean Sea.

Farms and Factories

Italy's boot is formed around the Apennine Mountains. This mountain range begins in the northwest and arcs all the way down the Italian Peninsula. No peak in the Apennines is higher than 10,000 feet (3,000 m) above sea level. But they and other highlands cover much of the Italian peninsula, leaving the narrow coastal plains as the country's only flat land. This young range is **seismically active**—that is, it has many earthquakes and volcanic eruptions. The southern toe of Italy and the island of Sicily have been sites of historic and recent volcanic eruptions. Sicily's Mount Etna violently erupted most recently in 1985.

Climate and Vegetation The Alps run from east to west along the entire northern boundary of Italy. Their tall peaks block much of the moisture that the prevailing westerlies carry from the North Atlantic into Western Europe. As a result, Italy's climate south of the Alps is Mediterranean—hot and dry in summer and mild and wet in winter.

Trees that once covered many hillsides have been cleared for space and fuel over the centuries. Only scrub vegetation remains. In addition, large volumes of soil have eroded through overgrazing by goats and sheep.

In spite of the dry climate and the scarcity of flat land, until recently Italy relied heavily on agriculture. As late as 1960, more than one third of the population lived and worked on farms. Today, however, only 10 percent of Italy's work force is agricultural.

Overpopulation Italy has a population of about fifty-eight million people. Because people cannot easily make their homes on the mountains that dominate much of Italy's landscape, the populated areas are very crowded.

In the early 1900s, many Italians were forced to move because the small amount of farmland could not support the population. Unemployment in rural areas is still high, especially in southern Italy. Since World War II, many workers have migrated from the poor southern regions to the northern provinces of Lombardy and Piedmont to find jobs in factories.

A Growing Economy The Italian government has encouraged the development of new factories and services in recent years. Automobiles, home appliances, and other metal goods have been the most successful products. These industries have boosted Italy's steel industry and helped the growth of many smaller factories that supply parts and machines.

Italy has turned its geographic disadvantages into opportunities. Before the 1950s, Italy was largely agricultural and relatively poor, but worked hard to help form the European Union. Once the EU began to operate, Italy could reach a much larger and richer market. Because Italy was poor, its workers were willing to work for low wages. Italian goods could be sold at lower prices, and Italian industries boomed.

Creativity also played a role in the industrial boom. Italian businesses developed new styles, designs, and methods for making their products. These improvements made Italian products, such as sleek home furnishings and high-fashion clothes, more attractive to foreign markets.

One Nation from Many Parts

After the Roman Empire collapsed in the fifth century, the Italian peninsula became a changing patchwork of separate political units. Over the next thirteen hundred years, many Italian cities operated as independent states. Kingdoms grew and declined. As the influence of Christianity spread, the Roman Catholic Church gained control over large amounts of land.

It was not until 1861 that states in the northern part of the peninsula joined together to form the country of Italy. Within a decade, the entire peninsula was united. During the twentieth century, a united Italy has survived two world wars and changes in national government.

Italy: PHYSICAL-POLITICAL

APPLYING THE GEOGRAPHIC THEMES

● **Movement** *What landform separates Italy from its northern neighbors?*

Place *Name two islands that are part of Italy.*

Italy's survival as a unified nation is impressive because of the striking differences that exist among its many regions. Although each of its smaller regions has a distinct local character, Italy may be roughly divided into three large regions: northern, central, and southern Italy.

Northern Italy

The country's northern region is often called European Italy. The provinces in this region are located close to the rest of Europe, and they resemble central European countries more than other Italian provinces do.

The heart of northern Italy is the lush Po River valley, a broad plain between the Alps and the Apennines. Since drainage was improved in the Middle Ages, the valley has been Italy's most productive agricultural area. Wheat and rice are important crops.

The Po Valley is now an important industrial center. About two thirds of Italy's factory products are made there. Early industrial development focused on the cities of Milan and Turin, which are located near sources of raw materials. Today hydroelectricity from rivers in the Alps powers many factories. The industrial growth of the Po Valley has made Genoa a thriving port city.

Other parts of the northern region also are prosperous. Ski resorts in the Alps and the area's splendid lakes attract visitors all year round. Dairy farms are very productive and profitable.

Frequent flooding in the area around Venice has stunted its agricultural and industrial growth. Venice itself faces problems of pollution and **subsidence**, a geological phenomenon in which the ground in an area sinks. But it remains popular with tourists for its intricate network of canals that serve as streets, and the ornate palaces built by Venetian traders in the late Middle Ages.

APPEARED IN *NATIONAL GEOGRAPHIC*

The Canals of Venice

● **Location** The city of Venice has uniquely close ties to the sea. It is built on a series of small islands two miles off the Italian mainland. The city is cut by 180 canals which are used as streets. Boats called gondolas carry people and goods through the city. *What problems does Venice face because of its location?*

Central Italy Central Italy consists of Rome and the surrounding regions, which were once controlled by the Roman Catholic Church. Rome was chosen as the capital in the late 1800s for two reasons. First, its location was central. Second, it had been the capital of the Roman Empire, and its history symbolized the glory that the Italians hoped to restore to their new nation. Still standing there are the ruins of the Colosseum—ancient Rome's largest stadium—and the Forum, a public meeting place.

American novelist Michael Mewshaw described the flurry of activity one sees in Rome:

> *Many streets are as narrow as hallways, as steep as staircases, as dim and cool as cellars. Yet even where these cramped passages open into broad avenues and roomlike piazzas [open squares] full of people, Romans maintain their inalienable right to do outdoors anything they might do at home. . . . Romans simply like to do things together; they enjoy sharing with the world the endless wonder they take in themselves and in one another.*

Within the city of Rome is an area measuring less than one square mile (2.6 sq km) known as Vatican City. This small tract serves as the world headquarters of the Roman Catholic Church. Fewer than one thousand people live in Vatican City, but the district swells daily with visitors to its two main structures, St. Peter's Basilica and the Vatican Museums.

Rome is not the only major city in central Italy. Bologna is a leading agricultural center known for its wonderful variety of foods. Florence is a cultural center made famous by Michelangelo and other Italian painters during the **Renaissance**. This was a great period of art and learning that started in Italy in the 1300s and spread throughout Europe.

The Glory that Was Rome

Movement Caesar Augustus (right) was Emperor of Rome when it was at its greatest power. At the time of his death the Empire stretched from the British Isles to the Middle East. It was said that all roads lead to Rome. Rome still attracts millions of visitors each year to see its famous sights, including the Colosseum (below). *What are some reasons for people to come to Rome today?*

APPEARED IN *NATIONAL GEOGRAPHIC*

The Sicilian Landscape

Regions Caltabellota and the surrounding land are typical of Sicily's landscape. The island is hilly, with rough, rocky outcroppings in many places. The soil is often thin and poor for farming. Still, Sicilian culture has survived for thousands of years. *Does Sicily's land make it suitable for large-scale agriculture?*

Southern Italy The southern region of Italy is known as the Mezzogiorno (MET soh ZHOR noh) and includes the islands of Sicily and Sardinia. The name means "midday" and points out one of the region's most noted features: its intense noontime sun. Poor roads used to make travel difficult in this area. New freeways now bring this region closer to the rest of the nation. Agriculture is not highly profitable here because of poor soil and outdated farming techniques. Some heavy industries located here after World War II, but have suffered in recent decades. As a result, many southerners have migrated to northern Italy.

Other southern Italians have moved to Naples, the largest city in the region. This port city suffers from some of the worst poverty in Europe. The number of available jobs cannot keep pace with the number of people who wish to work. The people hope that as Italy's economy develops within the European Union, more jobs will become available.

Section 2 Review

Vocabulary and Main Ideas

1. **Define: a. seismically active b. subsidence c. Renaissance**

2. **How do Italy's landforms affect the density of its population?**

3. **How has Italy developed as an industrial nation?**

4. **Why have many southern Italians migrated to northern Italy?**

5. **Critical Thinking:** *Analyzing Information* **What are some of the advantages to Italy of having such diverse regions? What are some disadvantages?**

6. **Why does Rome's location make it a good choice for Italy's capital?**

7. **Where are the Apennine Mountains in relation to the Alps?**

Focus on Skills

☑ Social Studies

☐ Map and Globe

☐ Critical Thinking
and Problem Solving

Analyzing Line and Bar Graphs

Line and bar graphs are useful ways to present information visually and condense large amounts of data. Graphs allow us to see the relationships between two or more sets of data, and to discern trends.

Use the following steps to read and analyze the line and bar graphs shown.

1. Identify the kind of information presented in the graph. Line and bar graphs are useful for showing different types of information. Answer the following questions: (a) What subject does the line graph portray? (b) What do the numbers on the vertical axis (the left side) of the line graph represent? (c) What do the numbers on the horizontal axis (along the bottom) of the line graph represent? (d) What does the bar graph portray? (e) What does the key for the bar graph tell you?

2. Practice reading the information shown in the graphs. Line graphs often show changes or trends over time, whereas bar graphs allow you to compare data. Answer the following questions: (a) Which of the countries shown on the line graph had the greatest population growth between 1965 and 1975? (b) Which country experienced a population decline during these same years? (c) Which country shown on the bar graph imported the most goods?

3. Look for relationships among the data. In addition to reading individual pieces of data on the graphs, you can also study trends and compare data. Answer the following questions: (a) How did Italy's imports compare to Spain's in 1993? (b) During what ten-year period were the rates of population growth of Portugal, Spain, and Mexico roughly the same?

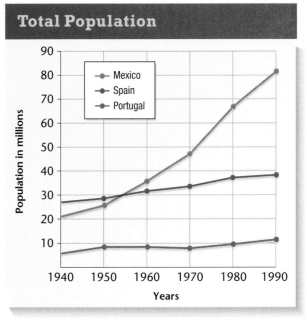

Total Population

Source: *The Statesman's Year-Book*

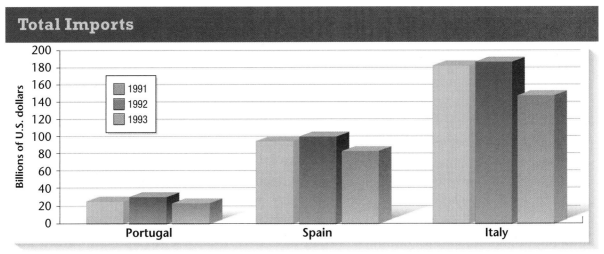

Total Imports

Source: *The Statesman's Year-Book* and *The World Factbook*

3 Greece

Section Preview

Main Ideas

- Greece has felt the influence of both Western and Eastern cultures.

- Greece is a mountainous land with a largely agricultural economy.

- Greece has relied on the sea for trade and contact with its many islands throughout its history.

Vocabulary

graben, inhabitable, tsunami

APPEARED IN *NATIONAL GEOGRAPHIC*

Visitors to this Greek island ride donkeys up the steep path to a village.

Greece does not fit neatly into any single regional group. There are several reasons to consider Greece to be part of Mediterranean Europe. First, Greece has strong geographical and historical ties to the Mediterranean. Second, Greece is now a member of both the EU and NATO. Third, Greece is the birthplace of a culture that reached full expression in Western Europe.

Greece bears the imprint of other regions, too. As the map on the next page shows, Greece shares its northern border with the region of Eastern Europe occupied by Albania, Bulgaria, and the former Yugoslav republic of Macedonia. On the east it meets the Southwest Asian nation of Turkey.

Place: A Rugged Land

The land area of Greece includes about 1,450 islands. Its northern mountains are extensions of the Dinaric Alps, which form the mountainous backbone of the Balkan nations. Southern Greece is the product of tectonic forces—it is where the Eurasian tectonic plate meets the African Plate. Major faults here thrust some lands higher and caused others to sink. **Grabens**, areas of land that have dropped down between faults, were flooded. The Aegean Sea to the east of the Greek mainland occupies one such graben.

Another graben was flooded to form the Gulf of Corinth. As shown on the map on the next page, this thin inlet separates most of Greece from the Peloponnese (pel uh puh NEES), a large peninsula of rugged mountains.

Agriculture Amid Mountains

Greece is a country covered by mountains and rocky soil. Its tallest peak, Mount Olympus, rises 9,570 feet (2,900 m), and many areas have elevations over 3,000 feet (900 m). Parallel ranges make travel difficult in many parts of the country. Narrow coastal plains, however, provide flat areas on which wheat and other grains are grown. Here, olive and citrus groves also abound. Agriculture is important to Greece despite problems such as poor soil, sparse rainfall, and outdated farming methods. With financial assistance from their government and from the European Union, Greek farmers are growing new products for export.

On the more rugged slopes, farmers graze sheep and goats. As in other Mediterranean nations, however, these animals have destroyed natural forests, leaving a scrubby vegetation that does little to prevent soil erosion.

Athens Greece's capital, Athens, is located in a part of Greece known as Sterea Hellas. Modern Athens has matured mainly within the last hundred years. It is one of the youngest capital cities in Europe. But the monuments of Athens have stood on the hill known as the Acropolis for thousands of years.

Over one third of Greece's 10.5 million inhabitants live in and around this crowded city. Modern apartments and houses line crowded city streets, as do new office buildings and an array of stores, taverns, and restaurants. One hallmark of this modern city is its daily traffic jams. The downtown streets are so choked by traffic that walking is faster than driving. As one visitor noted, "There is only one proven solution to Athens' traffic problems: live television coverage of an important international soccer match.

Whenever that happens, the streets are deserted."

Focus on the Sea
Just 5 miles (8 km) to the south, Athens merges with Greece's largest port, Piraeus (py REE us). The harbor there has grown steadily in importance during the twentieth century. As one might expect in a nation where no point is more than 85 miles (137 km) from the sea, Greece relies heavily on trade over water. It has one of the world's largest commercial shipping fleets, and shipbuilding is an important industry. Other industries also have located near the docks of Piraeus, taking advantage of low transportation

Pollution

Greece is finding solutions to its severe pollution problems. To combat air pollution in Athens, car and truck traffic is restricted. Greece has more solar collectors than any other country in Europe, and power stations run by wind as well as photovoltaics (electricity generated by sunlight) now provide some of Greece's electricity.

Greece: PHYSICAL-POLITICAL

KEY

Elevation

Feet		Meters
6,500–13,000		1,980–3,960
1,600–6,500		480–1,980
650–1,600		200–480
0–650		0–200

Depth of water

0–500		0–153
Below 500		Below 153

⊛ National capital

Lambert Azimuthal Equal-Area Projection

Ionian Sea

Gulf of Corinth

Ionian Is.

Peloponnese

PINDUS MTS.

Mt. Olympus 9,570 ft. (2,917 m) ▲

Thessaloníki ●

GREECE

Aegean Sea

Euboea

Athens ⊛

Piraeus

Cyclades Is.

Rhodes

Crete

Mediterranean Sea

0	100	200 mi
0	100	200 km

APPLYING THE GEOGRAPHIC THEMES

● **Place** Greece is composed of many island groups and peninsulas. *Name the largest island.*

● **Location** *Where is Greece located relative to the Ionian Sea?*

The Mystery of Crete

Part of Greece's appeal to visitors lies in its rich history. One historical mystery surrounding the island of Crete puzzles archaeologists to this day.

About thirty-five hundred years ago, the Mediterranean island of Crete was the center of Greece's flourishing Bronze Age culture. This culture is called Minoan after Minos, a legendary king of Crete. Expert shipbuilders, the Minoans traveled and traded throughout the Aegean and Mediterranean seas.

Then, around 1500 B.C., Minoan culture fell into a rapid decline. Some scholars believed that people from the Greek mainland attacked and destroyed Crete. Others thought that an earthquake demolished the island. But Greek archaeologist Spyridon Marinatos believed these explanations were incomplete.

Excavating near an ancient port in Crete, Marinatos discovered a piece of pumice from Thera, an island located 70 miles (113 km) from Crete. From that rock and others, he proposed a theory. He described destruction caused by a blanket of ash from a volcanic eruption, giant sea waves called **tsunamis** (TSOO nah meez), and earthquakes that caused oil lamps to overturn and set fires.

Investigations by other scientists appear to show that Marinatos' theory was incorrect. Evidence gathered elsewhere from ice core samples and tree rings of ancient trees date the eruption on Thera to more than one hundred years before the collapse of the Minoan civilization. The fate of the Minoan civilization has once again been cast into doubt. Archaeologists must reconsider the evidence to determine what happened to this once vital civilization.

A History of Influences

Discussing the in-between cultural area to which some say Greece belongs, geographer T.R.B. Dicks observed:

> *Many would argue that the Greeks are a curious mixture of eastern and western. . . . It is in the towns and cities that western influence is most marked, but even in Athens the colors of the Orient are strongly represented.*

A Mediterranean Resource

● **Location** Olive trees thrive in the Mediterranean climate and are grown in many countries around the sea. Olives and especially olive oil were considered great resources by the ancient Greeks, and have been cultivated there ever since. *What factors might make Greece a good place to grow olive trees?*

costs for imported raw materials and exported manufactured goods.

The sea also enables Greece to maintain contact with its many islands. Many of these are in the Aegean Sea, although the largest, Crete, is south of the mainland in the Mediterranean Sea. Fewer than two hundred of these islands are **inhabitable**—that is, able to support permanent residents. Many people make a living from fishing, but tourism continues to grow as a major economic activity. Visitors from around the world seek the sun, sparkling water, and gleaming beaches of the Greek islands.

Like Jewels in the Water

Regions The Cyclades, the Greek islands in the Aegean Sea, are marked by their stark landscape. The vegetation is brushy, the climate clear and dry, and the land itself cut in sharp relief. **Critical Thinking** *What are some economic activities that this landscape might encourage?*

Greece as a Western Nation Greece may be considered a Western nation in part because Western culture has so many of its roots in ancient Greece. One rich example is found in Homer's great epic poems, the *Iliad* and the *Odyssey*, composed during the eighth century B.C. The inspiring stories of these poems were based on the Trojan War and the fall of Troy. To the ancient Greeks they also provided a guide for moral behavior and were the cornerstone of a classical Greek education.

Foreign Influences While the influence of ancient Greek culture spread through Western Europe, other cultures put their stamp on Greece, usually through military conquest. From the second century B.C. to the fifth century A.D., Greece was part of the Roman Empire. As the Roman Empire declined, Greece became an important part of the Byzantine Empire. For the next thousand years, Greece was invaded from all directions, over land and water. Slavs, Albanians, and Bulgarians came from the north. Arabs swept in from the south. Normans and Venetians attacked from the west. In 1453, Turks conquered Constantinople, now the city of Istanbul, and ruled Greece for almost four centuries. Finally, after a ten-year rebellion, the modern state of Greece gained its independence from Turkey in 1830.

Section 3 Review

Vocabulary and Main Ideas

1. Define: a. graben b. inhabitable c. tsunami

2. Describe Greece's relationship to Western and Eastern cultures.

3. Describe the major landforms that are found throughout Greece.

4. Critical Thinking: *Synthesizing Information* Do you think that centuries of foreign rule weakened or strengthened the Greek national identity? Give reasons for your answer.

learning LOCATIONS

5. What is the capital of Greece and where is it located?

6. What body of water lies to the east of Greece?

Review and Activities

Summarizing Main Ideas

Section 1   Spain and Portugal

- The location and geography of the Iberian Peninsula have historically kept Spain and Portugal remote from the rest of Europe.
- Spain's regions have strong individual identities. Many Basques in northern Spain want independence for their region. Catalans, who live in the region near Barcelona, are demanding greater use of their own language.
- Portugal has used the sea as its trading passport to the world. Its rainy climate supports farming.

Section 2   Italy

- Italy's mountainous terrain makes farming difficult. Industry, supported by the government and strengthened by membership in the EU, has become important in recent years.
- Northern Italy is quite European and has the heaviest concentration of industry. Central Italy contains Rome, the nation's capital.
- Southern Italy is deprived economically, and unemployment has led many southerners to move north to find work in factories.

Section 3   Greece

- Greece has evolved into a mixture of Eastern and Western cultures. Athens, Greece's capital, has ancient ruins alongside modern buildings.
- Farming remains important to Greece's economy despite the rugged terrain. Financial support from the EU and the Greek government are encouraging new exports.
- The sea has always been important for Greek trade and cultural exchange but has made the country vulnerable to invasion.

Reviewing Vocabulary

Match the definitions with the terms.

1. areas of land that have dropped down between faults
2. having many earthquakes and volcanic eruptions.
3. able to support permanent residents
4. deep and wide enough to allow ships to pass
5. a hot, dry wind from northern Africa
6. a central point of concentrated activity and influence
7. a rebirth of art and learning beginning in the 1300s
8. giant sea waves

a. **hub**
b. **Renaissance**
c. **seismically active**
d. **sirocco**
e. **grabens**
f. **tsunamis**
g. **navigable**
h. **inhabitable**

Applying the Geographic Themes

1. **Human-Environment Interaction** How does the environment continue to affect life in Greece?
2. **Regions** Describe the similarities between Greece and Italy.
3. **Place** Describe two groups of people living in Spain today.
4. **Movement** How have Spain and Portugal had an impact on world history?
5. **Location** How has Portugal's relative location changed in the last five hundred years?

Critical Thinking and Applying Skills

1. **Drawing Conclusions** The Greek philosopher Plato mentioned a "lost continent" of Atlantis, thought to lie beneath the sea. What events in Greek history might support such a theory?
2. **Analyzing Line and Bar Graphs** Look again at the line graph on page 337. **(a)** In approximately what year did the population of Mexico equal that of Spain? **(b)** How did Spain's population compare to Mexico's by 1990?

Journal Activity

Writing Across Cultures

▶ 1. Imagine that you are a fifteenth-century Spanish or Portuguese explorer. What would your motivations be? What would it be like to discover a "new" world, such as North America or South America? What would your impressions be of the people and the landscape that you encountered?

▶ 2. The poet Percy Shelley once called Italy a "paradise of exiles." Write two paragraphs that describe life in Italy, one from the view of a tourist there, the second from the view of a worker. What are the similarities and differences between these two views?

INTERNET link

Visit the Sistine Chapel at the Vatican in Rome. Link to this site from:

• www.phschool.com

Look at some of the paintings. Consider the difficulties involved in painting on a ceiling. Describe the paintings you looked at and your reaction to them.

learning LOCATIONS

Mediterranean Europe

Number from 1 to 8 on a piece of paper. Next to each number, write the letter of the place on the map that corresponds to the place listed below.

1. Athens
2. Greece
3. Italy
4. Lisbon
5. Madrid
6. Portugal
7. Rome
8. Spain

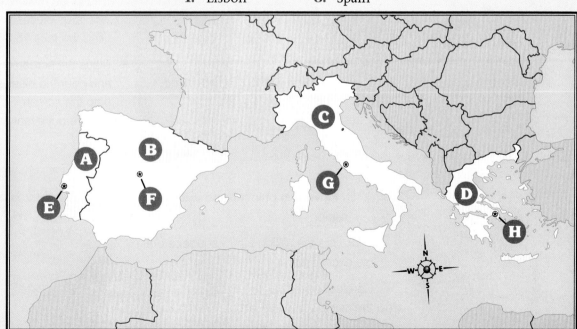

RECYCLING PAPER

The amount of waste generated in our country has more than doubled in the last thirty years. Finding better ways to reduce, reuse, and recycle waste is becoming necessary as landfill space continues to shrink. Think about the amount of paper you use each day as you learn what is involved in the process of paper recycling.

MATERIALS:

Old newspaper

Large pan

Water

Stirrer

Rolling pin

Electric blender

1/8 and 1/4
 measuring cups

Flat, wire
 screening

Cornstarch

Wax paper

PROCEDURE:

1. Tear the newspaper into small pieces, place it in the pan, and cover it with water. Let the paper soak overnight.

Step 1

2. Place a small handful of the soaked paper in the blender with 1/4 cup of water and 1/8 cup of cornstarch. This will make one 8 1/2" x 11" sheet of paper.

3. Blend the mixture until most of the large pieces are gone. This will take 15-30 seconds.

Step 2

4. Place the screen over the pan and pour the blended mixture onto the screen. Spread the mixture out evenly over the screen.

5. Cover the pulp mixture with wax paper.

6. Use the rolling pin to squeeze out the excess water.

7. Carefully peel away the wax paper and allow the new paper to dry for one to two days.

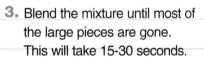
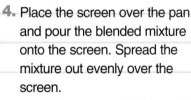

Step 4

OBSERVATIONS AND ANALYSIS:

1. How easy or difficult did you think it was to recycle paper? How could you improve this recycling technique?

2. What is the quality of the paper that you made? What kind of market do you think there would be for recycled paper?

3. How much used paper was needed to make one 8 1/2" x 11" sheet? What would the cost be for you to make recycled paper? Were the energy, time, and resources used worth the outcome for you? Why or why not?

4. How much paper do you use in one day? Make an estimate and then keep track of your paper usage for a few days. How close were you to your estimate?

Investing in Trash TURNS A PROFIT

Stock prices have risen for the third week in a row for The Crown Paper Company. Industry officials report that the rise is due to Crown's investment in a new paper recycling division. Technological advances, government legislation, and consumer demand have led to the increased sales of recycled paper goods. The Forest and Paper Association reports that in less than ten years, the percentage of newspapers that are recycled has increased from 35 to 58 percent.

Shredded waste paper ready for recycling

Planting saplings on a cleared area

taking *Action*

Paper recycling is one way to conserve the earth's resources. Here are some additional things you can do to reduce, reuse, and recycle.

✔ Ask your family to reduce the amount of unwanted junk mail sent to your house by writing or calling the companies that send it. Ask them to take your family off their mailing list.

✔ Reuse paper that only has writing on one side.

Eastern Europe

CHAPTERS

A Global Perspective

Eastern Europe is not so much a distinct physical region as it is a political one. For decades after World War II it formed a buffer between the West and the Communist superpower, the Soviet Union. Today the region is made up of a number of countries seeking to find a new identity and a new place in the world.

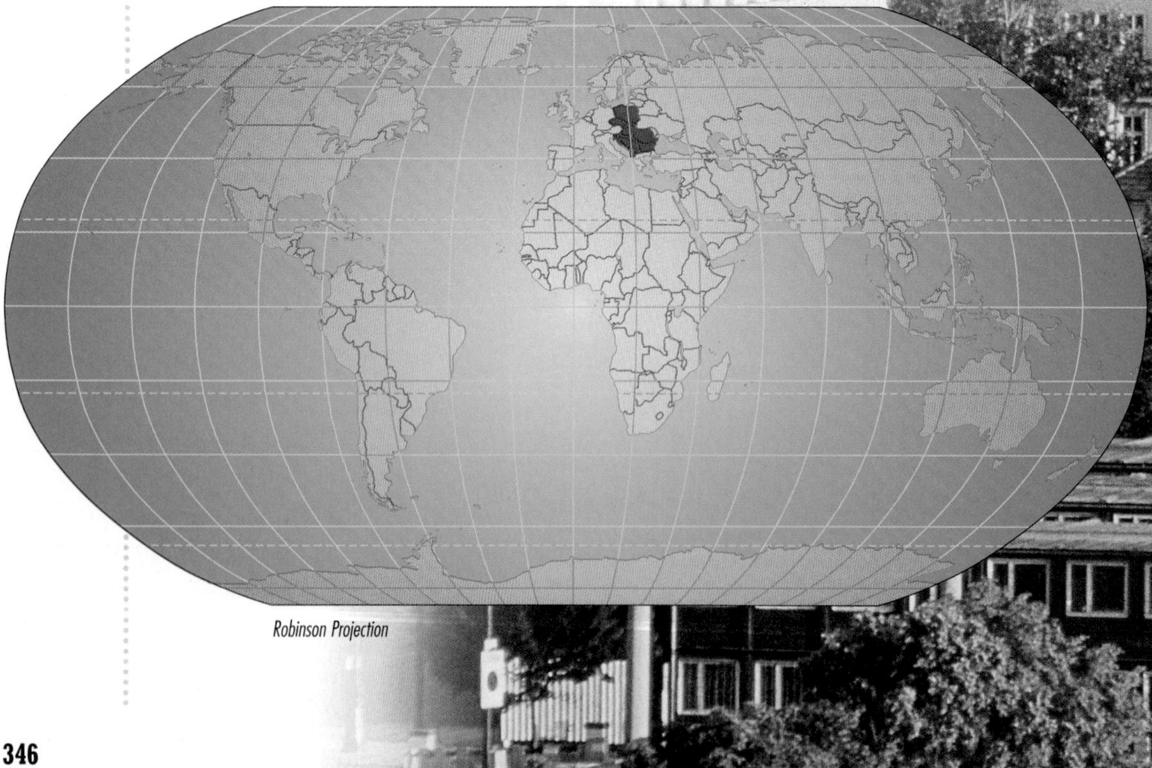

Robinson Projection

Prague, Czech Republic

KEYS TO UNDERSTANDING

THIS REGION

1 Countries and Cities *(pp. 348–349)*
Eastern European nations were all Communist until the late 1980s and early 1990s. Now they have more democratic governments. But the political situation is not settled. In the Balkans, in particular, some borders are still shifting.

2 Physical Features *(pp. 350–351)*
The Danube River, which wends through Eastern Europe, is a major trade route among Eastern European countries.

3 People and Cultures *(pp. 352–353)*
Although roughly two thirds of the region's people are Slavs, Eastern Europe has a complex mix of ethnic groups.

4 Climate and Vegetation *(pp. 354–355)*
Climate across Eastern Europe shows a gradual shift from the moderate climates of Western Europe to the harsh, continental climate of Northern Eurasia.

5 Economy and Resources *(pp. 356–357)*
Some of the countries of Eastern Europe have rich mineral resources that will help economies struggling with the changeover from Communist to capitalist systems.

VISUAL PREVIEW ACTIVITY

Each of the five keys above corresponds to a section of the Regional Atlas that follows. Number from 1 to 5 on a piece of paper. Use information from the maps, graphs, and photographs in the Regional Atlas to write one additional fact for each of the five keys above.

EASTERN EUROPE

Use the Map, Graph, and Photo Studies in the Regional Atlas to gain a better understanding of the region's physical and cultural geography.

ATLAS VOCABULARY

karst	multiethnic	pustza

EASTERN EUROPE

1 COUNTRIES AND CITIES

LARGEST CITIES

Budapest, Hungary
2,017,000

Bucharest, Romania
1,807,000

Warsaw, Poland
1,654,500

Prague, Czech Republic
1,212,000

Sofia, Bulgaria
1,141,000

Belgrade, Serbia
1,137,000

Łódź, Poland
846,500

Kraków, Poland
750, 500

Source: United Nations

= 1,000,000 people

GRAPH STUDY

1 Largest Cities Following World War II, a move from agriculture to industry changed the population distribution in Eastern Europe. *Use the graph above and the political map on the next page to locate the eight largest cities.*

MAP STUDY
Applying the Geographic Themes

2 Regions In 1989, Eastern Europe included eight nations: Albania, Bulgaria, Czechoslovakia, East Germany, Hungary, Poland, Romania, and Yugoslavia. *List the nations of the region today.*

3 Place Political changes have dramatically altered boundaries in Eastern Europe. For example, what was once East Germany has merged with West Germany to form Germany. *What nations do you think took the place of the united country of Czechoslovakia?*

4 Location Many of the nations of Eastern Europe have no seacoast. It is no surprise, then, that none of the capital cities of Eastern Europe are located on seacoasts. *What three Eastern European nations have capitals on rivers, and what are the capitals of each?*

5 Movement Rivers are valuable shipping routes in Eastern Europe. *How many Eastern European countries do major rivers pass through?*

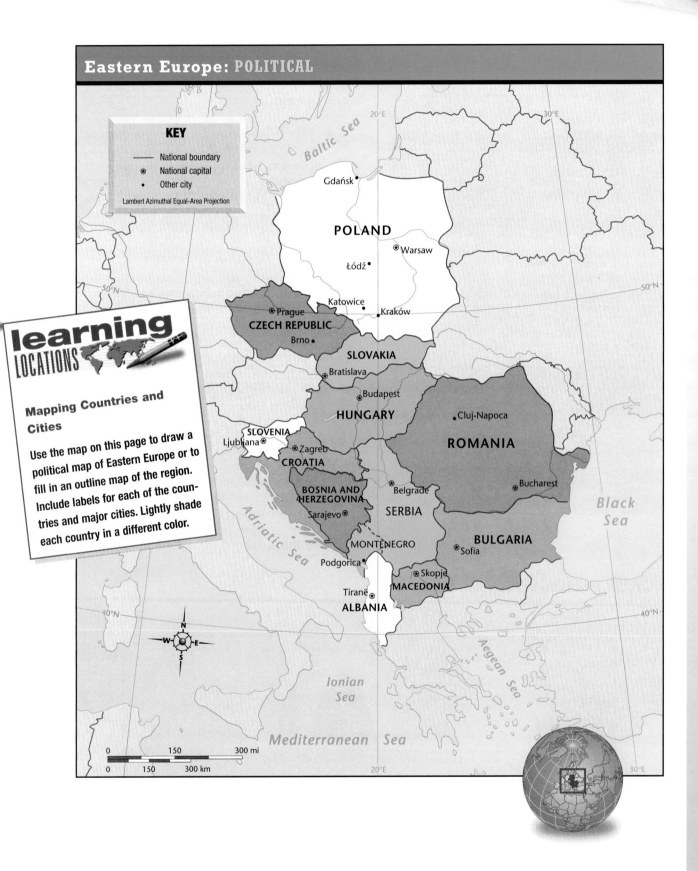

Eastern Europe: POLITICAL

KEY

— National boundary
⊛ National capital
• Other city

Lambert Azimuthal Equal-Area Projection

Baltic Sea

Gdańsk•

POLAND

⊛ Warsaw

Łódź•

⊛ Prague
CZECH REPUBLIC
Katowice•
Kraków•

Brno•
SLOVAKIA
Bratislava ⊛

Budapest ⊛

HUNGARY
•Cluj-Napoca

SLOVENIA
Ljubljana⊛ ⊛Zagreb
ROMANIA
CROATIA

⊛Bucharest

BOSNIA AND
HERZEGOVINA
Belgrade•

Sarajevo ⊛
SERBIA

Black Sea

MONTENEGRO
BULGARIA
Podgorica⊛
⊛ Sofia

Adriatic Sea

⊛ Skopje

Tiranë⊛
MACEDONIA

ALBANIA

Ionian Sea

Aegean Sea

Mediterranean Sea

0   150   300 mi
0   150   300 km

Learning LOCATIONS

Mapping Countries and Cities

Use the map on this page to draw a political map of Eastern Europe or to fill in an outline map of the region. Include labels for each of the countries and major cities. Lightly shade each country in a different color.

EASTERN EUROPE

2 PHYSICAL FEATURES

PHOTO STUDY

1 **The Dinaric Alps** These mountains run along much of the Adriatic seacoast. The dominant landform in this region is **karst**, an area made up of soft limestone. *Critical Thinking* **What force carved the Dinaric Alps into their current shapes?**

MAP STUDY
Applying the Geographic Themes

2 **Place** Eastern Europe has four broad bands of distinct landforms. The North European Plain forms the northernmost landform region. It stretches from the Atlantic Ocean in the west to the Ural Mountains in the east. *What nation covers most of the North European Plain in Eastern Europe?*

3 **Movement** The southernmost landform region in Eastern Europe is the Balkan Peninsula. It is the tangled web of mountain ranges and valleys south of the Danube River. *What mountains prevent easy movement from the Wallachian Plain of Romania to the southern part of Bulgaria?*

Cross Section: Eastern Europe

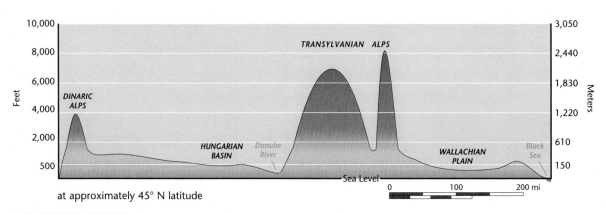

at approximately 45° N latitude

DIAGRAM STUDY

4 **Physical Profile** The Danube River dominates the region below the Carpathians. It has been called "a lifeline" in the region. *What is the elevation of the Hungarian Basin, part of the Danube River valley?*

Eastern Europe: PHYSICAL

KEY

Elevation

Feet	Meters
Over 13,000	Over 3,960
6,500–13,000	1,980–3,960
1,600–6,500	480–1,980
650–1,600	200–480
0–650	0–200
Below sea level	Below sea level

Depth of water

0–500	0–153
Below 500	Below 153

Lambert Azimuthal Equal-Area Projection

Baltic Sea

10°E   20°E   30°E

0   150   300 mi
0   150   300 km

BALTIC LAKE PLAINS

Vistula R.

Neisse R.

Oder R.

SILESIAN PLAIN

MAZOVIAN PLAIN

POLAND

50°N

SUDETIC MTS.

BOHEMIAN FOREST

CZECH REPUBLIC

CARPATHIAN

SLOVAKIA

MOUNTAINS

MOLDOVAN PLATEAU

Lake Balaton

HUNGARY

Prut R.

SLOVENIA

HUNGARIAN BASIN

ROMANIA

CROATIA

Sava R.

TRANSYLVANIAN ALPS

DINARIC ALPS

BOSNIA AND HERZEGOVINA

WALLACHIAN PLAIN

SERBIA

Danube R.

Black Sea

Adriatic Sea

MONTENEGRO

BALKAN MTS.

BULGARIA

RHODOPE MTS.

PINDUS MTS.

MACEDONIA

ALBANIA

40°N   40°N

Aegean Sea

Ionian Sea

Mediterranean Sea

20°E

learning LOCATIONS

Mapping Physical Features

Now use the map on this page to add the major physical features in Eastern Europe to the political map you created previously. Sketch and label all major mountain ranges, plains, basins, and bodies of water.

Chapter 18 ▪ Regional Atlas

EASTERN EUROPE

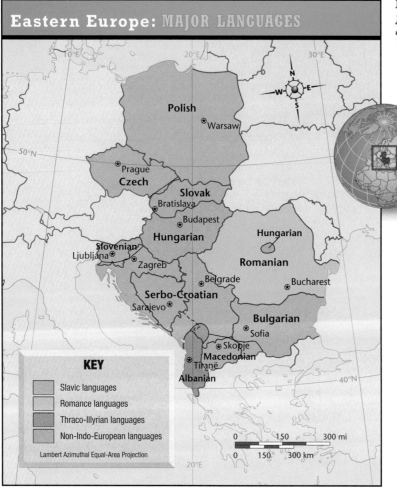

Eastern Europe: MAJOR LANGUAGES

Polish
⊛Warsaw

50°N

⊛Prague
Czech

Slovak
Bratislava⊛

⊛Budapest

Hungarian

Hungarian

Slovenian
Ljubljana⊛ ⊛Zagreb

Romanian

⊛Belgrade   ⊛Bucharest

Serbo-Croatian
Sarajevo⊛

Bulgarian
⊛Sofia

⊛Skopje
Macedonian
⊛Tiranë
Albanian

40°N

KEY

- Slavic languages
- Romance languages
- Thraco-Illyrian languages
- Non-Indo-European languages

Lambert Azimuthal Equal-Area Projection

0 — 150 — 300 mi
0 — 150 — 300 km

20°E

MAP STUDY
Applying the Geographic Themes

1 Regions Most Eastern European nations are **multiethnic**, or composed of many ethnic groups. The many languages spoken in Eastern Europe are the best indication of the region's great cultural diversity. Polish, Czech, Slovak, Hungarian—these are just some of the languages that can be heard between the Baltic and Black seas. *What family of languages is the most common in the region?*

2 Movement The Magyars moved into Eastern Europe centuries ago. They probably came from Asia. Many of the people of Hungary proudly trace their origin to the Magyars. *What is the population density of Hungary now?*

PHOTO STUDY

3 Ethnic Clashes Most Eastern European nations have at least one large minority group. The Macedonian women shown here are Roma, or Gypsies. Romania is home to 1.8 million Magyars. Romania's treatment of this minority group has sometimes caused clashes with neighboring Hungary, which is mostly Magyar. *Critical Thinking* **Propose a solution to the problem of ethnic clashes.**

EASTERN EUROPE

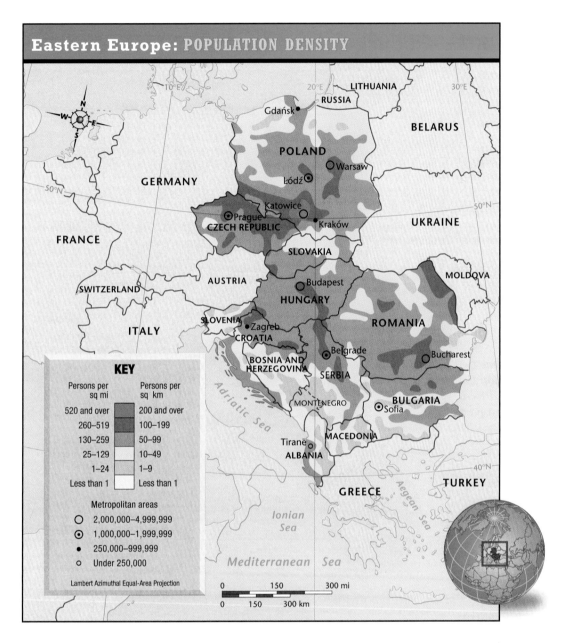

Eastern Europe: POPULATION DENSITY

KEY

Persons per sq mi		Persons per sq km
520 and over		200 and over
260–519		100–199
130–259		50–99
25–129		10–49
1–24		1–9
Less than 1		Less than 1

Metropolitan areas

○ 2,000,000–4,999,999
◉ 1,000,000–1,999,999
● 250,000–999,999
○ Under 250,000

Lambert Azimuthal Equal-Area Projection

0   150   300 mi
0   150   300 km

MAP STUDY
Applying the Geographic Themes

4 Movement Roughly two thirds of the people of Eastern Europe are descended from the Slavs. The Slavs arrived in the Carpathian Mountains about 2,000 years ago. They then moved north to the Baltic Sea, south toward Greece, west toward Germany, and east into Russia. *Which areas inhabited by the Slavs have the highest population density now?*

5 Place Dozens of other ethnic groups live in the region. They include the Bulgars, the Romanians (linked to the ancient Romans), Albanians (linked to a very ancient people on the Adriatic Sea), Germans, Turks, Roma (once called Gypsies), and Jews. *Connections: History Why would the Romans have been involved in Eastern Europe, hundreds of miles from Rome?*

EASTERN EUROPE

MAP STUDY
Applying the Geographic Themes

1 Place The climate of Eastern Europe reflects its position between Western Europe, Northern Eurasia, and the Mediterranean Sea. *What are the four climate regions of Eastern Europe?*

2 Location Lands in the northeast part of the region are cooler and drier than lands on the Balkan Peninsula, which generally has a Mediterranean climate. *Name the countries in the region that have a Mediterranean climate in at least part of their territory.*

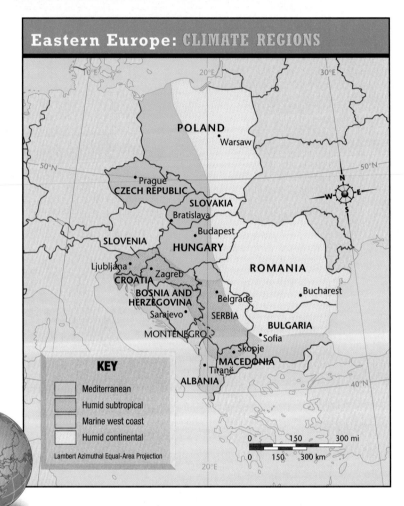

Eastern Europe: CLIMATE REGIONS

POLAND
• Warsaw
• Prague
CZECH REPUBLIC
SLOVAKIA
• Bratislava
• Budapest
SLOVENIA
HUNGARY
Ljubljana •
• Zagreb
ROMANIA
CROATIA
BOSNIA AND
HERZEGOVINA
• Belgrade
• Bucharest
Sarajevo •
SERBIA
BULGARIA
MONTENEGRO
• Sofia
• Skopje
MACEDONIA
• Tiranë
ALBANIA

KEY
- Mediterranean
- Humid subtropical
- Marine west coast
- Humid continental

0   150   300 mi
0   150   300 km
Lambert Azimuthal Equal-Area Projection

PHOTO STUDY

3 Plains of Poland The North European Plain stretches from the Atlantic Ocean in the west to the Ural Mountains in the east. The eastern part of the plain in Poland has a harsh continental climate. *Critical Thinking How would the climate affect the movement of invading armies through Poland?*

EASTERN EUROPE

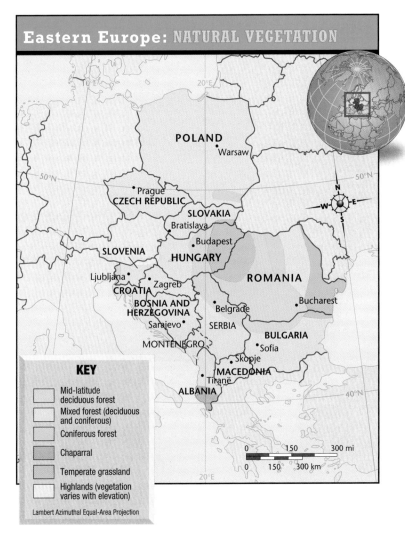

Eastern Europe: NATURAL VEGETATION

POLAND
• Warsaw

• Prague
CZECH REPUBLIC
SLOVAKIA
Bratislava
• Budapest
SLOVENIA
HUNGARY
Ljubljana
• Zagreb
CROATIA
ROMANIA
BOSNIA AND
HERZEGOVINA
• Belgrade
• Bucharest
Sarajevo
SERBIA
MONTENEGRO
BULGARIA
• Sofia
• Skopje
MACEDONIA
Tiranë
ALBANIA

KEY

Mid-latitude deciduous forest

Mixed forest (deciduous and coniferous)

Coniferous forest

Chaparral

Temperate grassland

Highlands (vegetation varies with elevation)

Lambert Azimuthal Equal-Area Projection

0   150   300 mi
0 150   300 km

4 **Human-Environment Interaction** Thousands of years ago, thick forests blanketed the plains of Eastern Europe. Now nearly half the land has been cleared for farming or grazing. *Critical Thinking **What are the advantages to having widely varied vegetation in a region rather than just a few types of vegetation?***

5 **Cause and Effect: Climate and Vegetation** The natural vegetation that still remains in Eastern Europe ranges from deciduous forest to temperate grassland. ***What is the dominant type of vegetation in Eastern Europe?***

PHOTO STUDY

6 **The Hungarian Basin** The Danube River wends its way from northwest to southeast across a large plain. The western part of the plain covers much of Hungary and is known as the Hungarian Basin. Hungarians call this area the **pustza** (POOSH tsa). It is now covered with farmlands rather than wild grasslands. *Critical Thinking **What makes this region suitable for farming?***

5 ECONOMY AND RESOURCES

MAP STUDY
Applying the Geographic Themes

1 Regions At the end of World War II, the Soviet Union installed Communist governments in the nations of Eastern Europe. These governments totally controlled the lives of the people, including the economic activities they pursued. *What is the most common economic activity in the region today?*

2 Place Under the Communist regimes, the people of Eastern Europe suffered severe shortages of basic goods

such as food, soap, and clothing. *In what countries is manufacturing and trade common?*

3 Place In the late 1980s and early 1990s, the people of Eastern Europe cast off their Communist systems. But new governments and economic systems often brought increased hardship. During the transition period, nations with their own energy resources had a significant advantage. *In what countries is coal found?*

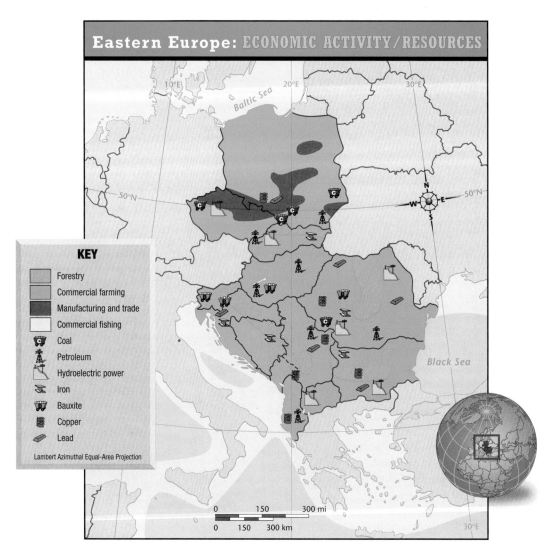

Eastern Europe: ECONOMIC ACTIVITY/RESOURCES

KEY

- Forestry
- Commercial farming
- Manufacturing and trade
- Commercial fishing
- Coal
- Petroleum
- Hydroelectric power
- Iron
- Bauxite
- Copper
- Lead

Lambert Azimuthal Equal-Area Projection

Baltic Sea
Black Sea

0   150   300 mi
0   150   300 km

EASTERN EUROPE

Economic Growth in Eastern Europe, 1991–1994

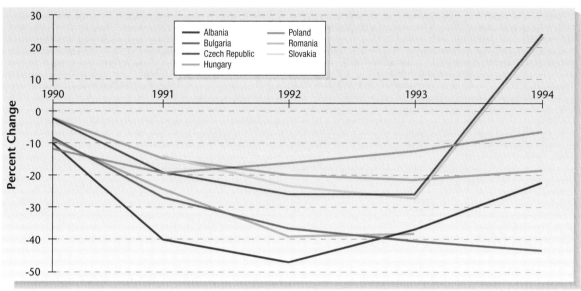

Albania	Poland
Bulgaria	Romania
Czech Republic	Slovakia
Hungary	

Source: *Central and Eastern Europe,* by John Dornberg

GRAPH STUDY

4 **GNP of Eastern European Countries** In the confusion that followed the change to economies free of Communist control, all the Eastern European nations experienced a change in their ability to produce goods. *Describe the overall trend in production in the Eastern European countries. Which nations experienced the highest rate of economic growth between 1993 and 1994?*

atlas REVIEW

Vocabulary and Main Ideas

1. **Define: a. karst b. multiethnic c. pustza**

2. **What is the major river highway of Eastern Europe?**

3. **What is one cause of the ethnic clashes common in Eastern Europe?**

4. **How does the climate of Eastern Europe change as one travels from east to west across the northern part of the region?**

5. **Critical Thinking:** *Making Comparisons* **Compare the population density map on page 353 with the economic activity map on page 356. Make a general statement about the population density in areas in which manufacturing and trade is common.**

learning LOCATIONS

6. **Which is the northernmost nation in Eastern Europe?**

7. **Identify the nations where Budapest and Bucharest are located.**

The Balkan "Powder Keg"

Why have conflicts so often erupted in the small nations of southeastern Europe? The answers lie in the region's central location, which has given it a long and troubled history.

A Region of Divided Loyalties

For thousands of years southeastern Europe, between the Black Sea and the Adriatic, has been the scene of conflicts. Forces from east and west have pulled at the people of the northern Balkan peninsula. Invaders and groups on the move have added to the ethnic mix. The region has been split by religion, by ethnic differences, by politics, and by language. Although great empires have ruled the Balkans, its people never really became part of a larger national identity. Each group's ethnic and religious loyalties remained strong, ready to resurface.

The East-West Tug-of-War

The ancient Roman Empire unified much of Europe. But as the Empire weakened, its eastern provinces in the Balkans were the first to fall. Goths and other Germanic invaders moved across the countryside. Huns from Asia settled on the broad Danube Plain.

Before the Roman Empire finally fell, it split into eastern and western halves. The split cut across the Balkans. Part of the region was in the Eastern Empire, later the Byzantine Empire. The Adriatic coast was in what remained of the Western Empire. Attila and the Huns ruled the north.

Other influences had an impact on the region. The Roman Empire became officially Christian in the 4th century, but Christianity itself was divided into the Greek-speaking Orthodox Church in the east and the Latin-speaking Roman Catholic Church in the west.

An Ethnic Patchwork

For the next several centuries, an assortment of ethnic groups, mostly from central Asia, moved through eastern Europe. Those who stayed

Balkan Peninsula, 998

included Slavs, Bulgars, and Magyars. After the rise of Islam in the 600s, different Muslim groups also moved into eastern Europe. The map to the left shows the Balkan peoples at that time, about A.D. 998.

By the late 1400s, the Muslim Turkish sultans of the Ottoman Empire ruled the entire Balkan peninsula. To the north was the Austrian Empire. For hundreds of years the border between those two empires shifted back and forth in the Balkans.

Divisions between ethnic groups increased. The South Slavs, for instance, had converted to Christianity but split over religion. Croats became Roman Catholic; Serbs were Orthodox. Their spoken languages were almost alike, but Croats wrote in the Roman alphabet, Serbs in the Cyrillic. Croatia was part of Hungary for centuries; for most of that time, Serbs lived within the Ottoman Empire.

Many Nations Emerge in the Balkans

Early in the 1800s the Ottoman Empire was weakening. Serbs, Greeks, Romanians, and Bulgars all saw a chance to gain independence.

By the 1870s, other European rulers wanted to help Balkan peoples escape from Muslim rule. The actual task was left up to the czar of Russia. When Russian troops finished their mission, the northern Balkans were a patchwork of small nations, some in the Austro-Hungarian Empire, some with their own rulers. The map below is a snapshot of the region at that time, 1885.

World War I brought the end of both the Austro-Hungarian and Ottoman empires. Nationalist groups demanded and got their own countries. Yugoslavia, for example, was supposed to bring together all the South Slavs. Many people, however, simply found themselves minorities in the new nations. Along with centuries of history, this set the stage for still more conflicts to erupt in the Balkans in the 1990s.

Hungarians battle invaders from the East.

Balkan Peninsula, 1885

GERMAN EMPIRE

RUSSIAN EMPIRE

AUSTRO-HUNGARIAN EMPIRE

Adriatic Sea

BOSNIA   K. OF SERBIA

MONTENEGRO

KINGDOM OF ROMANIA

PRINCIPALITY OF BULGARIA

Black Sea

KINGDOM OF ITALY

OTTOMAN EMPIRE

KINGDOM OF GREECE

| 0 | 150 | 300 mi |
| 0 | 150 | 300 km |

connecting TO TODAY

1. **According to the maps, what different groups held territory in the Balkans in the year 998? In the year 1885?**

2. **What two empires dominated the Balkans for most of the past 500 years?**

3. **Critical Thinking** How did domination by outside empires affect the peoples of the Balkans? Could such domination have had a different effect? Why?

4. **Hands-On Activity** Choose one of the major ethnic groups of the Balkans and find out more about its culture, including its food, music, language, religion, folktales, and national dress. Set up a display of objects and pictures to give your classmates an overview of that culture.

CHAPTER

19

The Countries of Eastern Europe

SECTIONS

1 Poland

2 The Czech and Slovak Republics, and Hungary

3 The Balkan Peninsula

Eastern Europe: POLITICAL
Baltic Sea
N
S
E
W
Gdańsk
POLAND
Warsaw
Łódź
50°N
Prague
Katowice
Kraków
CZECH REPUBLIC
Brno
SLOVAKIA
Bratislava
Budapest
HUNGARY
Cluj-Napoca
ROMANIA
SLOVENIA
Ljubljana
Zagreb
CROATIA
Belgrade
Bucharest
Black Sea
BOSNIA AND HERZEGOVINA
SERBIA
Danube R.
Sarajevo
Adriatic Sea
BULGARIA
MONTENEGRO
Sofia
Podgorica
Skopje
MACEDONIA
Tiranë
ALBANIA
40°N
KEY
National boundary
National capital
Other city
Lambert Azimuthal Equal-Area Projection
Aegean Sea
Ionian Sea
Mediterranean Sea
30°E
0
150
300 mi
0
150
300 km

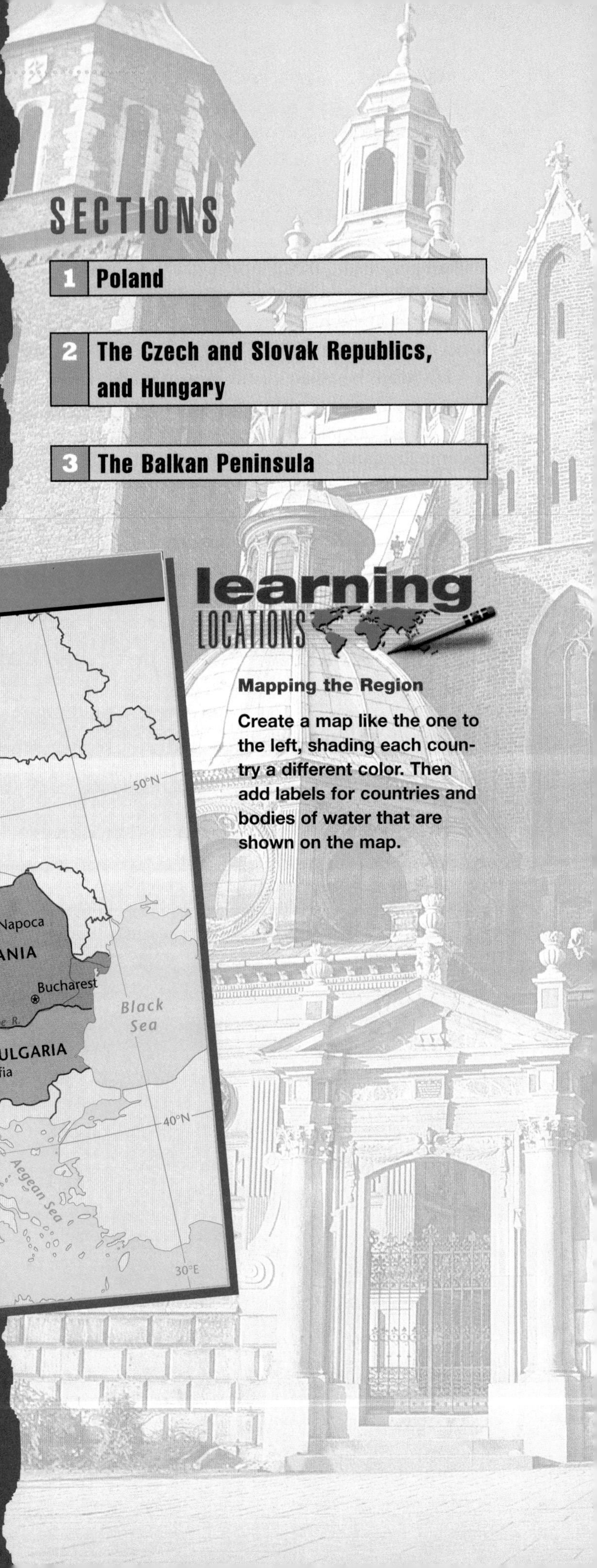

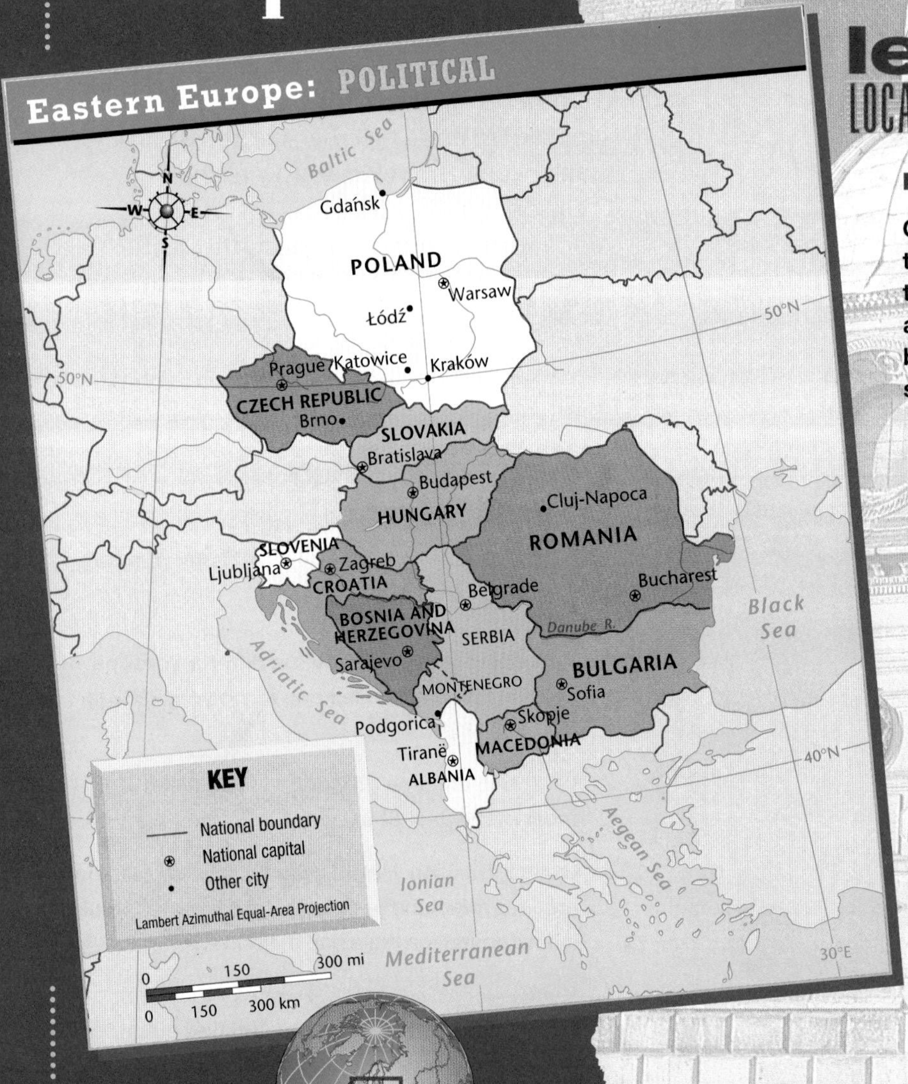

learning LOCATIONS

Mapping the Region

Create a map like the one to the left, shading each country a different color. Then add labels for countries and bodies of water that are shown on the map.

1 Poland

Section Preview

Main Ideas

- The Poles have clung to their culture through nearly two centuries of foreign domination.

- Attachment to the land and belief in the Roman Catholic religion have helped shape the Polish character.

- Today Poles are working slowly toward economic reform.

Vocabulary

national identity, ghetto, Holocaust

APPEARED IN *NATIONAL GEOGRAPHIC*

A Polish family pitches hay on their farm in the Carpathian Mountains.

"If you cannot prevent your enemies from swallowing you, at least prevent them from digesting you." This was the advice that French philosopher Jean-Jacques Rousseau offered to the Poles in the late 1700s.

For more than two centuries, Poles have followed Rousseau's advice. Although they have seen their nation "swallowed" many times, the Poles have refused to allow foreign nations to "digest" the Polish **national identity**, or sense of what makes the Polish people a nation. For example, even though the former Soviet Union controlled Poland in the years following World War II, the Polish people never forgot their cultural heritage or gave up hope for reclaiming independence. During the 1980s they launched an independence movement to reclaim their national identity.

The Field Country

One factor that has helped the Poles and many other nationalities retain their identity as a people is their attachment to the land. Most of Poland is covered by the North European Plain. Thick forests once covered the flat lands, but most of the trees were cut down long ago to create farmland. Today more than three quarters of Poland is open field.

Although much of Poland's soil is fertile, it tends to become poor and sandy and thus less suited for farming in the east and northeast. In the northeast, around the Baltic Sea, thousands of lakes break up the landscape.

Poland has valuable industrial resources, too. In the Carpathian Mountain region of the south, large deposits of coal, sulfur, and copper have been found. However, Poland must depend upon other countries for two vital minerals—iron ore and petroleum.

A Polish Nation

Nearly ninety-five out of every one hundred people who live in Poland are Roman Catholic. But this was not always the case. Before World War II, Poland was a multiethnic nation. However, Nazi occupation and Soviet control changed this ethnic diversity.

The Holocaust Today no more than 9,000 Jews live in all of Poland—a nation once

Poland: PHYSICAL-POLITICAL

KEY

Elevation

Feet		Meters
Over 13,000		Over 3,960
6,500–13,000		1,980–3,960
1,600–6,500		480–1,980
650–1,600		200–480
0–650		0–200
Below sea level		Below sea level

Depth of water

0–500		0–153
Below 500		Below 153

Lambert Azimuthal Equal-Area Projection

0   100   200 mi
0   100   200 km

APPLYING THE GEOGRAPHIC THEMES

● **Movement** *Judging from its location, why do you think Gdańsk is an important Polish city?*

● **Location** *Describe the relative location of Warsaw.*

had been killed in concentration camps, about half of them Jews. In all, the Nazis massacred more than 6 million Jews from across Europe. This destruction of human life is known as the **Holocaust**. The word derives from a Greek word that means "a fire that burns something completely."

Fleeing Soviet Control

After the war, the former Soviet Union took over lands in eastern Poland. The Soviets then expanded Poland's western border into what had once been Germany. Millions of Poles fled from lands seized by the former Soviet Union. Germans living in lands given to Poland also fled. As a result, nearly everyone living in Poland today is Polish.

Communist No More

A Communist government backed by the former Soviet Union took control in Poland in the late 1940s. The Communists never enjoyed widespread support of the Polish people despite their efforts to develop industry within the nation.

The Catholic Church

Although the government tried to stamp out religion, the Roman Catholic Church continued to play an important role in the everyday lives of most people. It unified the Poles as it always had, even when there was no Polish nation. Catholic leaders worked out an uneasy compromise with the Communist government leaders that allowed churches to remain open.

Solidarity

Solidarity is an independent Polish workers' labor union. It gained worldwide recognition in 1980 when its members staged a strike by shipyard workers in the Baltic port of Gdańsk. Led by Lech Walesa (LEK vah LEN sah), Solidarity pressed for economic and democratic reform.

home to more than 3 million Jews. Almost all of Poland's Jews were killed by the Nazis during World War II. The Nazis sealed off Jewish **ghettos** in Polish cities such as Warsaw. A ghetto is an area of a city where a minority is forced to live. When Jews in the Warsaw ghetto rebelled, the Nazis retaliated and slaughtered all the people remaining in the ghetto, then burned it to the ground.

The Nazis also built six of their infamous concentration camps, or prison camps, in Poland. Here people from many nations suffered horribly or were brutally murdered, but the majority of those who lost their lives were Poles. By the war's end, roughly 6 million Poles

GLOBAL issues

Pollution

Poland, one of the most polluted industrialized countries in the world, has devised a unique approach to the problem. Instead of repaying its foreign debt, an arrangement with lending countries allows Poland to spend the money on environmental cleanup.

Ongoing Struggle

Place In this photograph, Lech Walesa (right) is appealing to an audience of prospective West German investors. Poland's economy suffered under communism, and its problems have been further complicated by the transition to private enterprise. Within a year following communism's collapse, inflation rose 600 percent.

Critical Thinking *How did Poland's faltering economy affect Walesa's career as president?*

Solidarity was outlawed by the government in 1981, but the movement did not die. In 1989, public opinion forced the first free elections in Poland in more than 40 years, and Solidarity candidates won a large majority of the votes. By the end of 1990, Walesa had been elected the nation's president.

A Troubled Economy The end of communism did not bring instant prosperity to Poland. Converting state-controlled industries into private enterprises was difficult. It was also difficult to attract much-needed capital from foreign investors. With diminished government control, prices for food and consumer products rose rapidly at first, and many people became unemployed. By the mid-1990s, however, economic growth was up, and the rise in unemployment had slowed.

All the same, lingering economic problems had a curious result. In 1995, Walesa was voted out of office, and a former Communist, Aleksander Kwasniewski (kvash NYEF skee), became president. All across Poland, voters wanted economic reform to take place—but not to take place so quickly that it hurt.

Section 1 Review

Vocabulary and Main Ideas

1. **Define: a. national identity b. ghetto c. Holocaust**

2. **What cultural traits have helped define the Polish people as a nation?**

3. **What seems to be the current attitude of most Poles toward economic reform?**

4. **Critical Thinking:** *Identifying Central Issues* **What key part of their national identity have the Poles lost in the twentieth century?**

learning LOCATIONS

5. **Explain the probable reason that Warsaw is located where it is.**

6. **What landforms mark Poland's southern border?**

Focus on Skills

☑ Social Studies

☐ Map and Globe

☐ Critical Thinking
and Problem Solving

Making a Decision

Every day you have to make decisions—such as deciding what time to get up; how to dress for school; and what to eat for lunch. Although most of your decisions are as routine as these, you sometimes must face harder ones. Difficult decisions require much thought because they can make important differences in your life.

Do you sometimes avoid tough choices because they make you feel anxious? Do you ever rush headlong into decisions without really thinking them through? A six-step process called DECIDE makes decision making easier. This process is simple to remember because each letter in the word *DECIDE* stands for a step in the decision-making process. After looking over the steps, read the statement and consider what you would do in the same situation.

1. Define the problem. Look carefully at the decision you are facing, and state the problem clearly.

2. Explore the alternatives. Make a list of all possible alternatives you can think of for solving your problem.

3. Consider the consequences. Think about what might happen for each alternative you listed. Include both the positive and negative results that could occur.

4. Identify your values. Your values—the principles that you believe in strongly—affect how you make decisions. What values are important to you? Which alternative is most in line with your values?

5. Decide and act. Use the information you have collected to compare each of the alternatives. Decide which one is best for you. Remember, sometimes there is more than one right choice.

6. Evaluate the results. After you have put your decision into effect and seen some results, take time to review it. How did your decision work out? How has it affected your life? How has it affected others? If you could make your decision over again, would you do anything differently?

DECIDE

D efine the problem.
E xplore the alternatives.
C onsider the consequences.
I dentify your values.
D ecide and act.
E valuate the results.

Carlos works as a waiter in the neighborhood's most popular cafeteria. He noticed that the cafeteria used polystyrene trays for customers' use. He asked the manager to replace these plastic-foam trays with paper trays. The manager told him to mind his own business, pointing out that paper trays would cost a nickel more per tray. Carlos believed that customers might be willing to pay a little bit extra for a material that was biodegradable, and therefore less damaging to the environment. But he also wanted to keep his job.

The Czech and Slovak Republics and Hungary

Section Preview

Main Ideas

● Although the Czech Republic has done well in shifting to a free-market economy, it still faces problems, such as severe pollution.

● Slovakia has been struggling with a repressive government and a difficult transition to a free market.

● Hungary has a new, stable government that is using privatization to make the economy grow.

Vocabulary

velvet revolution, privatization, collective farm

APPEARED IN *NATIONAL GEOGRAPHIC*

Street performers in Prague celebrate the breakup of Czechoslovakia into separate republics.

If you asked residents of the Czech Republic, Slovakia, and Hungary what region they live in, they would answer that they were part of Europe. But for more than forty years after the end of World War II, they were controlled by the former Soviet Union. As Communist control ended in the late 1980s, Czechs, Slovaks, and Hungarians reaffirmed their historical links with the West.

Although they share Western outlooks and ways, the three countries have crucial differences. Those differences will require them to use distinct approaches to address the problems they face as former Communist nations.

The Czech Republic

More than 10 million people live in the Czech Republic, a land about the size of South Carolina. It has few flat areas, except the plains that lie beside the Elbe and Danube rivers. The landscape is dominated by plateaus and mountains, and high ridges define its boundaries.

Although the Czech people in this rugged and mountainous land have been recognized as a separate ethnic group for almost a century, the Czech Republic did not exist as an independent nation until 1993.

Path to Nationhood The Czech kings ruled an independent kingdom within the Holy Roman Empire into the 14th century. Then came nearly 400 years of rule by the Austrian Hapsburg monarchs. In 1918, during the final weeks of World War I, the victorious allies approved plans to create a new nation— Czechoslovakia. Brought together were Czech lands and Slovakia, which had been controlled by Hungary. Despite the multiethnic character of the new nation, over the next two decades it developed one of the most stable, democratic governments in the region.

Hitler used the fact that many Germans lived in northwestern Czechoslovakia as an excuse to invade the republic in the late 1930s. After Soviet forces expelled the Germans in

1945, they directed a Communist takeover. From 1948 to 1989, Communists controlled the nation.

The declining influence of the Soviet Union in the late 1980s spurred a *"velvet revolution"*—a revolution without bloodshed. It resulted in the election of a democratic parliament. Under the leadership of President Vaclav Havel (VAH tsluhv HAH vuhl), Czechoslovakia began a transition to a free society and a market-based economy.

Despite the new government's attempts at fairness and equality, Slovaks increasingly felt that the Czech-dominated government did not serve their interests adequately. As a result, Czech and Slovak leaders worked together on a "velvet divorce," creating two separate countries in 1993—the Czech and Slovak republics.

The Other Vaclav The Czechs pursued their strategies for economic reforms under the direction of their prime minister, Vaclav Klaus. A tough economist, Klaus brought about the **privatization** of the Czech economy by the mid-1990s. Privatization is the process of selling government-owned industries and businesses to private owners who can run them more efficiently. Under Klaus's management, unemployment remained very low. Despite his success, Klaus left office in November 1997 after his party was accused of corruption. The Czechs hope to join NATO and the European Union, but a recent slowdown in the economy has raised questions about the high cost.

Two Regions

The western half of the Czech Republic is a region known as Bohemia. This region contains many of the nation's mines and industries. Coal, iron ore, copper, and lead are mined in the mountains of the north. Bohemia also has deposits of quartz, a substance used to make glass. The Czech capital city of Prague lies in

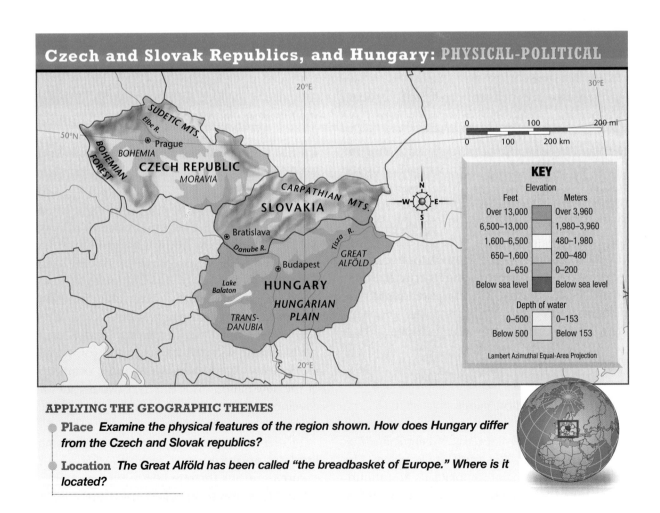

Czech and Slovak Republics, and Hungary: PHYSICAL-POLITICAL

KEY

Elevation

Feet	Meters
Over 13,000	Over 3,960
6,500–13,000	1,980–3,960
1,600–6,500	480–1,980
650–1,600	200–480
0–650	0–200
Below sea level	Below sea level

Depth of water

0–500	0–153
Below 500	Below 153

Lambert Azimuthal Equal-Area Projection

APPLYING THE GEOGRAPHIC THEMES

● **Place** *Examine the physical features of the region shown. How does Hungary differ from the Czech and Slovak republics?*

● **Location** *The Great Alföld has been called "the breadbasket of Europe." Where is it located?*

Slovakian Slopes

Regions The southwest corner of Slovakia boasts a resort region in a part of the Carpathians known as the High Tatras. Much of the land is under the protection of national park status, but the region offers world-class skiing and other mountain recreations. It was even under consideration as the site for the 2002 Winter Olympics. **Critical Thinking** *How might hosting the Olympics help Slovakia's economy?*

central Bohemia. More than 100 church steeples rise above the rooftops—a visual reminder of the region's Roman Catholic heritage.

The eastern region of the Czech Republic is known as Moravia. Its industry dates back to the Industrial Revolution. Moravia's old coal and steel industries now face an uncertain future, because they are too inefficient to compete in the world market.

Among the gravest challenges facing Moravian industries, as well as those in Bohemia, is ending air and water pollution. Experts estimate that 56 percent of the nation's forests had been destroyed by acid rain and industrial pollution by 1993. And trees were not the only victims. One scientist observed: "If you go to the doctor with a sore throat, cough, or a headache, the [doctor] . . . will tell you, 'You must have opened a window last night.'"

Slovakia

Slovakia, also called the Slovak Republic, became an independent nation in 1993 when Czechoslovakia was peacefully divided. More than 5 million people live cradled within the arch formed by the Carpathian Mountains. Slovakia unfolds from rugged peaks in the north

to the plains of the Danube in the south. Unlike the Czech Republic, Slovakia has a mixed economy of farming and manufacturing.

Farms Slovakia traditionally was an agricultural region. Fruits, vegetables, and grains are still grown near the Danube. Oats and potatoes are raised farther north in higher elevations.

The Communists ended private ownership of farms in 1948 and set up government-owned **collective farms**. On collective farms, workers were paid by the government and they shared the profits from their products. In Slovakia, as elsewhere in Eastern Europe, a major task of the present-day government is to find ways of returning land to private ownership.

Factories Manufacturing did not become important until the Communists assumed power after World War II. They built many new plants in the region. Because wages in factories were better than they were in rural areas, many Slovaks left the farms and moved into cities like the capital, Bratislava.

Since the breakup of Czechoslovakia, Slovaks have not been as successful as their for-

A River Runs Through It

● **Place** Straddling the Danube River is Hungary's capital city, Budapest. Budapest was once three separate cities: Obuda and Buda on the west bank and Pest on the east bank. Merged in the late 19th century, Budapest is now the largest city of Hungary and its industrial and commercial center. About one fifth of Hungary's people live there. *To which ethnic group do most Hungarians belong?*

mer partners, the Czechs. They have had to endure political problems created by a prime minister who has been accused of being repressive and corrupt. "We are becoming an authoritarian country run by people with no ideology, just an insatiable hunger for power," said one Slovak opposition leader. Furthermore, unemployment had climbed to over 14 percent by the mid-1990s, and inflation was high.

Hungary

Like Poland, Hungary's population is dominated by one ethnic group. About 95 percent of Hungarians are descended from the Magyars who settled the area in the late 800s.

The Roman Catholic faith and fierce patriotism have guided Hungarians throughout their history. They date the birth of their nation from the year 1000, the year the Pope crowned King Stephen. Several times since then the Hungarians have had to throw off foreign rulers. They even tried to oust a Soviet-backed Communist government in 1956, but their revolt was crushed. Not until 1990 were Hungarian voters able to freely elect their first non-Communist government in over forty years. But they considered this just one more step in their long history. A member of the new parliament declared, "The Magyar nation has been preserved!"

Hungary's Landscape Today Hungary is about the size of the state of Indiana. The Danube River divides it into two parts. The eastern half consists of a broad plain known as the Great Alföld. This region's fertile soil has given Hungary the nickname "the breadbasket of Europe."

The western half of Hungary has more hills. Because this region lies west of the Danube, it is known as Transdanubia, or "land across the Danube." The region is an area of plateaus, hills, and valleys. It contains large deposits of bauxite, coal, and iron ore that support Hungary's aluminum and steel industries.

GLOBAL issues

Reforestation

Hundreds of Hungarians responded when an international tree-planting organization known as Global ReLeaf called for proposals to plant trees in Hungary. Grants were awarded for trees to be planted near a contested dam on the Danube River, at an apartment complex, in a children's park, and in and around a number of other places.

Flocking to Free Enterprise

● **Place** Rather than raising his flock on a collective farm, this Hungarian goose farmer rents his barn and land and buys his geese from a cooperative. He raises the geese at his own expense, with the help of workers he pays, and then sells the meat and feathers back to the cooperative. **Critical Thinking** *How is this arrangement an example of free enterprise?*

Free Enterprise Like other nations in Eastern Europe, Hungary faced many difficulties in converting from Communist control to an economic system based on a free market. As old, inefficient industries that had been supported by the government struggled or failed outright, production dropped sharply. Unemployment was high, the government was badly in debt, and most people were getting poorer, not richer. Hoping for an upturn, the government began an ambitious program of privatization as the 1990s drew to a close. Although industrial production was rising again by the late-1990s, experts predicted it would take until 2004 for Hungary's economy to return to the level of 1989.

As in Poland, former Communists have taken a hand in the new government. But Hungary's new government system appears to be stable and long-lasting. It should be well able to guide the nation of the Magyars into the twenty-first century.

Section 2 Review

Vocabulary and Main Ideas

1. Define: a. velvet revolution b. privatization c. collective farm

2. Give evidence that the Czech Republic has been successful in changing to a free-market economy.

3. What is the Hungarian government doing to bring about an economic upturn?

4. Critical Thinking: *Making Comparisons* How do the economies of the Czech Republic and Slovakia differ?

learning LOCATIONS

5. What mountains are located along Slovakia's northern border?

6. Name Hungary's capital city, located on the banks of the Danube River.

Map Skills
for Life

The end of the Soviet Union and the coming of democracy made it much easier for people in eastern and central Europe to travel. Jana Frintova, who lives in Prague, Czech Republic, is looking forward to visiting several neighboring countries. Traveling with a railroad pass, Jana is planning a trip that will include these places:

★ the historic cities of Budapest, Hungary; Vienna, Austria; Bratislava, Slovakia; and Krakow, Poland.

★ the Carpathian Mountains, which run in an arc from northern Slovakia into Romania.

★ the resort area around beautiful Lake Balaton in Hungary, central Europe's largest lake.

Reading the Map

Follow the steps to understand how Jana can use the railroad map to plan her trip. One thing she must consider in reading the railroad map is whether there is a direct line between destinations or whether she has to change trains along the way.

1. Locate all the cities on the map where she will travel. Then notice their locations relative to one another and to the starting point. Of the cities that Jana wants to visit, the closest to Prague is Vienna, Austria. Another of the cities on her list is only about 56 miles (90 km) east of Vienna. **(a)** What is that city? **(b)** Can Jana take a direct train from Prague to Vienna? **(c)** From Prague to the other city?

2. Plan a route that includes the destinations in a logical order. Use the map to look for direct rail connections as well as destinations that are close together. Direct lines may be harder to find between cities in different countries than within one country. For example, there is a direct line from Warsaw, Poland, to Kraków, Poland, but Jana will have to take a roundabout route to get to Kraków from any of the other cities. Assuming that train connections are best between large cities, what route should Jana follow to go from Prague to Kraków?

3. Use the map scale to estimate distances between different points. To make her final plans, Jana will also have to look at a railroad schedule as well as the map, in order to see at what time trains leave and how long they take to travel between places. Knowing approximate distances is still important. Jana will probably decide to make her trip to Lake Balaton after she has seen Budapest. About how far is it from the city to the nearest part of the lake?

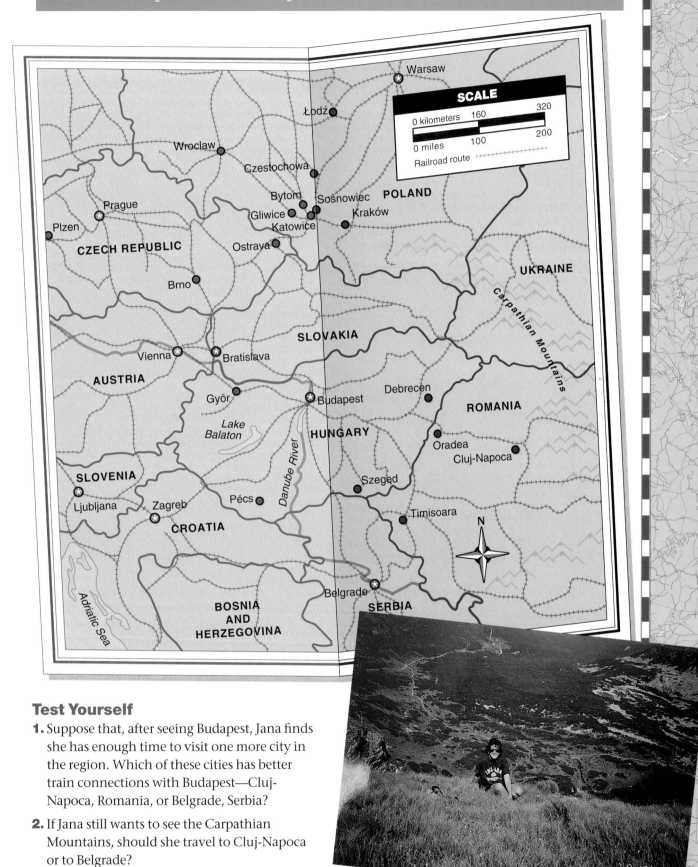

SCALE

0 kilometers   160   320

0 miles   100   200

Railroad route

Warsaw

Łódź

Wrocław

Czestochowa

Bytom   Sosnowiec   POLAND

Gliwice

Prague   Katowice   Kraków

Plzen

CZECH REPUBLIC   Ostrava

UKRAINE

Brno

Carpathian Mountains

SLOVAKIA

Vienna   Bratislava

AUSTRIA   Debrecen

Györ   Budapest   ROMANIA

Lake   HUNGARY

Balaton   Oradea

Cluj-Napoca

SLOVENIA   Szeged

Ljubljana   Zagreb   Pécs   Timisoara

CROATIA   N

Danube River

Belgrade

Adriatic Sea   BOSNIA   SERBIA

AND

HERZEGOVINA

Test Yourself

1. Suppose that, after seeing Budapest, Jana finds she has enough time to visit one more city in the region. Which of these cities has better train connections with Budapest—Cluj-Napoca, Romania, or Belgrade, Serbia?

2. If Jana still wants to see the Carpathian Mountains, should she travel to Cluj-Napoca or to Belgrade?

3 The Balkan Peninsula

Section Preview

Main Ideas

● Nations in the Balkan Peninsula share histories of internal division and foreign domination.

● Many different ethnic groups live in the Balkan Peninsula.

● Great turmoil has characterized Balkan nations since the end of Communist rule there, but most economies seem to be recovering.

Vocabulary

balkanize, entrepreneur, multiplier effect

Romanians feast their eyes on their first free press newspaper.

In 1918, a new term crept into the English language: **balkanize.** The word *balkanize* means "to break up into small, mutually hostile political units." It is what took place in the Balkans after World War I. The term grew out of the complex cultural and political geography of the Balkan Peninsula.

Perhaps the one thing that the Balkan nations share is their historical experience. The peoples of this region have all known the ordeal of foreign domination. For five hundred years they were ruled by the Turks, whose influence can be seen there to this day.

Today the Balkan Peninsula is divided into many small nations. Most of them fell under Communist control after 1948, but anticommunist revolutions overturned the governments of those states in the late 1980s and early 1990s. Internal strife and conflict between nations have nevertheless continued to affect the region.

Romania

Nearly 23 million people live in Romania. Most belong to the Romanian ethnic group. They speak a language derived from Latin, and most people practice the Eastern Orthodox faith.

Romania possesses broad plains with fertile soils along the Danube River. Farther north, the foothills of the Carpathian Mountains hold many minerals. Despite these natural resources, the Romanian people have been impoverished in recent decades.

Romania's first Communist leader oversaw a Soviet-style industrialization. The second leader, Nicolae Ceausescu (NIH kah lie chow CHESS koo), gradually led the nation to economic chaos. Energy was so scarce that television aired only two hours each night. In 1989 Ceausescu was forced from office and executed. The next leader, Ion Iliescu (ee AHN ill ee CHESS koo) promised to bring democracy and economic reform in the early 1990s. But under his leadership the economy grew even worse. Experts predicted that it would be 2025 before Romania could again see an economy even as good as the terrible economy of 1989.

One ray of hope shone in Romania's economic nightmare, however. An American soft drink maker spent $150 million in Romania to build up its operations there. Its investment helped about 25,000 small shops start or stay in business, selling soft drinks. Some **entrepreneurs**—go-getter individuals who start and build businesses—have made small fortunes selling soft drinks in Romania. Through the **multiplier effect**, eleven new jobs have been added to Romania's economy for each job that the soft drink company created. The multiplier effect is the effect an investment has in multiplying related jobs throughout an economy. For instance, Romanian plastics makers have added jobs to handle the new demand for soft drink bottles, and printers have added jobs to print labels. Observers hope that Western investment, and the multiplier effect, will bring dramatic changes not just to Romania, but to all of Eastern Europe.

Bulgaria

Bulgaria is located south of the Danube from Romania. It enjoys the fertile soils of the Danube Plains and the plains south of the Balkan Mountains. Summers are warm, and winters along the Black Sea coast are mild. Because of these physical features, Bulgaria is known as the garden of Eastern Europe.

The Bulgarians are a Slavic people. The Russians, also largely a Slavic people, have long been strong supporters of native Bulgarians. Because of this fact, many Bulgarians welcomed Soviet control after World War II.

Bulgaria turned away from strict communism in the early 1990s. It now has a democratic government, though Communists still play a large role in the country. Like other nations in the region, Bulgaria saw its economy go into a tailspin in the first years of freedom. But by the

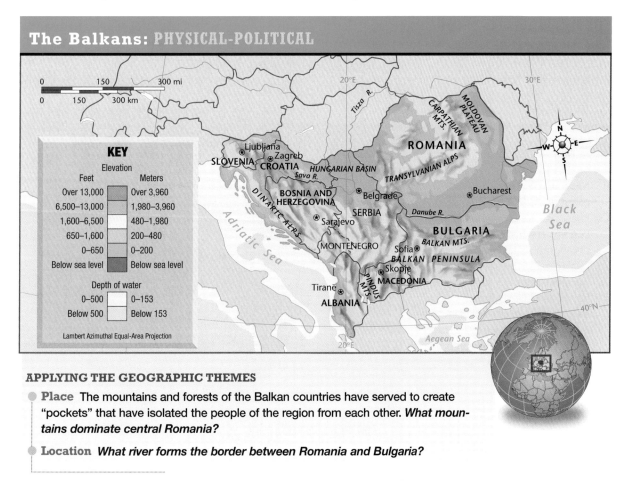

The Balkans: PHYSICAL-POLITICAL

APPLYING THE GEOGRAPHIC THEMES

● **Place** The mountains and forests of the Balkan countries have served to create "pockets" that have isolated the people of the region from each other. *What mountains dominate central Romania?*

● **Location** *What river forms the border between Romania and Bulgaria?*

mid-1990s, it was beginning to find new markets for its goods in Western countries. American, German, Dutch, British, and Swedish companies were beginning to make investments. Millions of new tourists were coming to Bulgaria's Black Sea resorts, bringing with them desperately needed foreign currency.

Albania

Tucked beside the Adriatic Sea in the southwestern part of the Balkan Peninsula is Albania. About 3.5 million people live in this mountainous nation. Known for decades as "Europe's hermit," Albania is now rebuilding links with other nations.

As a people living in a small nation with a distinctive culture, Albanians have often felt threatened by their neighbors. This fear continued after World War II, when its Communist leaders turned away from both the former Soviet Union and China. This isolation left Albania one of the poorest nations in Europe.

Since the coming of democracy in the early 1990s, Albania's economy has received billions of dollars in aid from foreign nations and from Albanians living overseas. Since most Albanians make only about $60 a month, Italian and Greek manufacturers have expressed interest in build-

ing factories there to take advantage of the low wages. Albania is expected to have a thriving economy in place by the turn of the century.

Other Balkan Nations

The most complex new nation created at the end of World War I was Yugoslavia. The name meant "the land of the southern Slavs." But a common Slavic heritage did not produce unity. Six separate republics made up the unsteady nation, which after World War II was held together only by strict Communist rule. Within these republics, some two dozen independent ethnic groups lived, either intermixed or in jigsaw-puzzle ethnic regions.

After Communist control ended in the late 1980s, internal tensions increased. First Slovenia grew restless. It was the most wealthy republic and was afraid the other Yugoslavian republics would drag it down into poverty. Soon Croatia, too, grew nervous about its future, fearing that the wealth it gained from the tourist business on its long Mediterranean coastline would be eaten up by other regions. Both Slovenia and Croatia declared themselves independent in 1991. They were quickly followed by Macedonia, and then, in 1992, by Bosnia-Herzegovina (sometimes called simply

Daily Bread

Movement The collapse of communism in Albania created near-chaos in Europe's poorest country. The bread in this photograph is distributed from behind bars in an attempt to maintain order. Some Albanians have been killed in bread riots that erupt as hungry crowds clamor for food. **Critical Thinking** *How might an end to isolation help Albania's economy?*

Dayton Discord

Place In November 1995 the presidents of Croatia, Bosnia, and Serbia began UN-sponsored peace talks in Dayton, Ohio. Despite the protests, such as the Serbian protest shown here, the peace plan was signed in December. The plan gave 51 percent of Bosnia to the Muslim-Croat Federation and 49 percent to the Serbs. Despite the accord, peace still eludes the region. *How many people have been killed or displaced by the war in Bosnia?*

Bosnia). All that was left of Yugoslavia were the republics of Serbia and Montenegro.

Conflicts flared within and between the new nations. Worst hit was Bosnia-Herzegovina, in which three main groups—Muslims, ethnic Croats, and ethnic Serbians—battled for power for four years. As a result of the Bosnian conflict alone, an estimated 250,000 people lost their lives and 2 million were driven from their homes. During this war, the term "ethnic cleansing" first entered the world's vocabulary. Serbs used it to describe the process of driving other ethnic groups out of regions the Serbs had captured. In practice it meant mass murder and terror.

Until 1995, international efforts to stop the bloodshed were feeble at best. Finally, in November 1995, the leaders of Serbia, Bosnia-Herzegovina, and Croatia agreed to sign a peace agreement that divided Bosnia along ethnic lines. NATO forces entered the region in 1996 to enforce the treaty.

Serbia and Montenegro After the other republics broke away and formed independent nations, Serbia and Montenegro kept the name Yugoslavia for their own union. About 6.5 million of the 10 million people in these republics are Serbs. Another 2 million Serbs live in neighboring republics.

The physical geography of this area includes both the rugged peaks of Montenegro and the fertile plains of the Danube valley in Serbia, where extensive farming takes place. Industries are poorly developed in these two republics.

The breakup of Yugoslavia, and the wars and political problems that followed, resulted in economic disaster for Serbia and Montenegro. Production of industrial goods plummeted. Unemployment soared to more than 50 percent.

By the mid-1990s, Serbia and Montenegro reversed their economic slide. Production and wages began to climb again, and economists predicted that recovery would continue through the decade.

Refugees

By the mid-1990s, civil war and other disasters had driven some 1.5 million refugees from one part of Eastern Europe to another. Croatia alone had 530,000 refugees from the fighting in Bosnia-Herzegovina and another 35,000 people who were escaping from ethnic cleansing in Serbia.

Facts in BRIEF

Country	Population	Life Expectancy (years)	Per Capita GNP (in US $)
Albania	3,500,000	72	340
Bosnia-Herzegovina	3,500,000	72	NA
Bulgaria	8,500,000	71	1,160
Croatia	4,500,000	70	NA
Czech Republic	10,400,000	73	2,730
Macedonia	2,100,000	72	780
Poland	38,600,000	72	2,270
Romania	22,700,000	70	1,120
Slovakia	5,400,000	71	1,900
Slovenia	2,000,000	73	6,310
Yugoslavia	10,800,000	72	NA
United States	263,200,000	76	24,750

Source: Population Reference Bureau   NA indicates data not available.

CHART SKILLS

● **Which country, aside from the United States, has the highest per capita GNP?**

● **Critical Thinking** *What would account for the lack of per capita GNP data for Bosnia-Herzegovina, Croatia, and Yugoslavia?*

Croatia More than three quarters of the nearly 5 million people who live in Croatia are ethnic Croats. Croats descended from the same early Slavic people as the Serbs, and the spoken languages of the two groups are nearly identical. Serbs practice Eastern Orthodoxy and use the Cyrillic alphabet, while most Croats are Roman Catholics and use the Latin alphabet. These differences have been heightened by frequent conflicts between Serbs and Croats.

After Croatia declared its independence, Serbs within its borders fought to gain their own independence or to link themselves with Serbia. Although fighting has tapered off, political and economic uncertainty continues.

Slovenia Most of the 2 million residents of Slovenia are Slovenes, one of the Slavic peoples. This nation in the Julian Alps has long maintained close ties with Western European nations. Industrial development took place earlier in Slovenia than in other parts of the Balkan Peninsula. Because of its solid industrial base, Slovenia was expected to recover quickly from the problems brought by war and independence.

Bosnia-Herzegovina Although the former Yugoslav republic of Bosnia-Herzegovina declared itself independent in 1991, its long-term prospects were not promising. Its population was a complex ethnic mix; of every ten residents, three were Serbs and two were Croats. Most of the other Bosnians were Muslims.

Long-standing hostility between different groups in Bosnia-Herzegovina erupted into war when Communist control ended. After many efforts to end the fighting failed, a peace treaty in 1995 subdivided the nation into two parts.

Civil war has made the desperately poor region of Bosnia-Herzegovina even poorer. Only foreign aid kept its people alive. In 1994 alone, for example, the United Nations and NATO peacekeepers trucked in nearly 1 million tons of food and medicine.

If a peace agreement could be made to work, Bosnia-Herzegovina has many natural resources that could be exported. Before the civil war, it mined and sold iron ore, lead, zinc, manganese, and bauxite. Rebuilding these industries will take time and investment.

Macedonia While other former Yugoslav republics were erupting into conflict, Macedonia remained relatively quiet. However, even before independence it was the poorest of the Yugoslav republics. During the 1990s, its economic growth was hampered by challenges from its southern neighbor, Greece. The Greeks were worried that Macedonia was planning to take over part of Greece's northern province, which is also called Macedonia. Furthermore, nearby Albania is concerned about the status of Albanian Muslims, who comprise about one fifth of Macedonia's population. Thus Macedonia's exports to Western Europe travel by a long, costly, overland route through Bulgaria, Romania, and Hungary. These products include iron ore, nickel, gold, tobacco, fruit, cotton, textiles, and clothing.

Keeping the Peace

Movement In 1993 the United Nations sent a peace-keeping force to Macedonia in order to shield it from its warring neighbors. *Critical Thinking Which Balkan nations might be a threat to Macedonian independence?*

Kosovo In the late 1990s, the key point of conflict turned out to be not Macedonia, but Kosovo. Tensions heightened as the Serbian government ended self-rule in the region. As protests by the ethnic Albanian majority led to repression, the Kosovo Liberation Army waged guerrilla war against the Serbs.

In 1999, after pushing unsuccessfully for peace talks, NATO launched air strikes against Serbian targets. After the Yugoslav forces withdrew, NATO peacekeepers moved in. Still, the region's economy was devastated. Massive aid efforts were needed, and large numbers of refugees continued to live in temporary shelters.

Section 3 Review

Vocabulary and Main Ideas

1. Define: a. balkanize b. entrepreneur c. multiplier effect

2. What historical experiences have the Balkan nations shared?

3. What are the causes of conflict in the Balkan Peninsula?

4. What was the general outlook for economies in the Balkan region in the late 1990s?

5. Critical Thinking: *Drawing Inferences* How do you think people in the Balkan nations feel about the change from Communist rule? List three facts to support your answer.

learning LOCATIONS

6. Describe Bulgaria's location.

7. How does Macedonia's location hamper its economy?

Human Rights

The Issue

Many people around the world are deprived of their human rights. Here are a few of the issues that have caused international concern.

An Abuse of Power

Governments or groups in control in many countries routinely deny people their basic human rights. They subject their citizens to arbitrary police searches and seizures, imprisonment, torture, and execution without public trial.

Two Roots of Evil

Abuses sometimes have ethnic or religious roots. For example, in the former Yugoslavia, hundreds of thousands of people were driven from their homes, tortured, or even murdered during campaigns of "ethnic cleansing."

Afraid of Losing Control

Still other human rights violations grow out of political tensions. In countries where pro-democracy movements threaten authoritarian governments, citizens are imprisoned, tortured, and beaten to discourage any challenge to the government's authority. For example, Chinese forces cracked down on its citizens after the 1989 pro-democracy student demonstration in Tiananmen Square.

Global Impact

We all belong to a common humanity. Recognizing this, nations and cultures throughout the world agree that there are certain fundamental human rights that no government or law should deny. These rights include freedom of speech, freedom from arbitrary arrest, basic health and education, and dignity. When these and other rights outlined in the UN's Universal Declaration of Human Rights are threatened anywhere, it affects people everywhere.

Some Solutions

The international community is attempting to stop human rights violations. Here are some actions that have proven effective.

Pressure from Other Governments

Members of the United Nations Human Rights Commission meet yearly to pass resolutions condemning countries that abuse their citizens' human rights. In addition to political pressure, economic measures such as boycotts, that isolate abusive countries, have also proven effective.

Nongovernmental Organizations

Private groups have also met with some success in reducing human rights

Fighting for Freedom

Place Aung San Suu Kyi led an opposition movement against the military government in Myanmar. Placed under house arrest for six years, she was finally released in 1995. She is shown here meeting with journalists after her release.

Excerpts from the Universal Declaration of Human Rights

Article 1

All human beings are born free and equal in dignity and rights. They are endowed with reason and conscience and should act toward one another in a spirit of brotherhood.

Article 3

Everyone has the right to life, liberty, and security of person.

Article 5

No one shall be subjected to torture or to cruel, inhuman, or degrading treatment or punishment.

Article 6

Everyone has the right to recognition everywhere as a person before the law.

Article 9

No one shall be subjected to arbitrary arrest, detention, or exile.

Article 10

Everyone is entitled in full equality to a fair and public hearing by an independent and impartial tribunal, in the determination of his rights and obligations and of any criminal charge against him.

Article 12

No one shall be subjected to arbitrary interference with his privacy, family, home, or correspondence, nor to attacks upon his honour and reputation. Everyone has the right to the protection of the law against such interference or attacks.

Article 25

Everyone has the right to a standard of living adequate for the health and well-being of himself and of his family, including food, clothing, housing, and medical care and necessary social services.

Source: Brownlie, Ian, Editor, *Basic Documents on Human Rights*, 1971

violations. Such organizations offer support for victims and publicize human rights violations. In this way they bring the pressure of world opinion to bear on governments that do not protect and respect human rights.

Conflict Resolution The lasting solution to human rights abuses, however, lies in defusing the types of situations that lead to them: ethnic, religious, and political conflicts. In other words, conflict resolution, more than declarations and boycotts, provides the ultimate key to ensuring that all of the world's people enjoy the human rights to which they are entitled.

YOU DECIDE

1. Why are human rights important?

2. Which solutions for protecting human rights do you think are the most effective? Explain.

3. **Problem Solving** Choose a country in the Americas, Europe, Africa, or Asia and research its human rights record. Draft a list of three to five possible ways to stop abuses in this country.

4. **What You Can Do** Research organizations that work to prevent human rights abuses. Contact one to see what you can do. Choose an action and follow through on it.

5. **Internet Activity** Read what other young people are saying about war at UNICEF's Voices of Youth home page. Follow the link to *The Meeting Place*, then read messages in the *Children and War* section. Write your own statement on the subject or respond to a previously posted message.

• www.phschool.com

Vocabulary Development

Use each term in a sentence that shows the meaning of the term.

1. national identity
2. ghetto
3. Holocaust
4. velvet revolution
5. privatization
6. collective farm
7. balkanize
8. entrepreneur
9. multiplier effect

Summarizing Main Ideas

Section 1 Poland

- The Polish people clung to their culture through nearly 200 years of foreign domination.
- Two keys to the Polish national identity are attachment to the land and belief in the Roman Catholic religion.
- During the 1980s, Solidarity pressed for economic reform and personal freedom.
- In the 1990s, Poles slowed their rush to economic reform by voting a former Communist into office as president.

Section 2 The Czech and Slovak Republics, and Hungary

- The Czech Republic and Slovakia became two separate countries in 1993.
- The Czech Republic has a strong industrial base and has privatized many of its industries without too much economic upheaval.
- Slovakia has a mixed economy. Its growth since independence has been hampered by a repressive and corrupt government.
- An ambitious privatization program and a stable government promise hope for Hungary's struggling economy.

Section 3 The Balkan Peninsula

- Internal ethnic divisions and long periods of foreign domination have troubled the people of the Balkan Peninsula for centuries.
- Turmoil has characterized the region since the removal of its Communist governments.
- The Balkan nations face challenges in seeking peace and making the transition to free-market economies.

Applying the Geographic Themes

1. **Place** Give one example of how the Polish people have struggled to maintain their national identity.
2. **Location** How does the location of Poland explain why its government was closely tied to that of the former Soviet Union?
3. **Regions** What was the reason for the Czech Republic and Slovakia's "velvet divorce"?
4. **Place** How did Communist rule change agriculture in Czechoslovakia?
5. **Regions** Why did Yugoslavia fall apart after the end of Communist control?

Critical Thinking and Applying Skills

1. **Recognizing Bias** Many people in Eastern Europe believe that use of the term *Eastern* reflects a bias on the part of the United States and the rest of Europe. Do you agree? Why or why not?
2. **Making a Decision** Using the steps you learned on page 364, write a paragraph about a situation in which a person faces a complicated decision on a recent issue in your school or community. Include enough information about the problem to show that it involves a tough choice. Then, use DECIDE to reach a decision. Finally, exchange your writing with another class member and analyze each other's paragraphs for coherence and effectiveness.

Journal Activity

Writing Across Cultures

▶ Suppose you are an official in an Eastern European nation. Write a letter to a major manufacturer in the United States. In the letter, explain why the manufacturer might want to set up a factory in your nation. Choose a specific nation and a specific manufacturer. Use knowledge about Eastern Europe you have gained from the text and your own general knowledge about the kinds of products the manufacturer makes in order to write the letter.

INTERNET link

Read what travellers are saying about Romania. Link to this site from:

- www.phschool.com

Click on *Postcards*, then browse through the entries. Write a paragraph sharing information that was new to you.

learning LOCATIONS

Eastern Europe

Number from 1 to 12 on a piece of paper. Next to each number, write the letter of the place that corresponds to the places listed below.

1. Serbia and Montenegro
2. Albania
3. Bosnia-Herzegovina
4. Bulgaria
5. Slovakia
6. Croatia
7. Czech Republic
8. Hungary
9. Macedonia
10. Poland
11. Romania
12. Slovenia

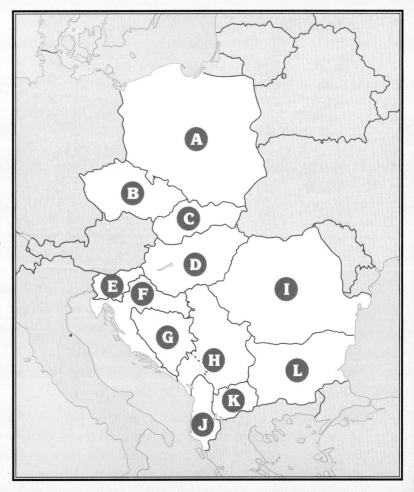

EFFECTS OF ACID RAIN

You read about some of the effects of acid rain on page 367. Imagine that you are a scientist assigned to study these effects. How does acid rain affect the natural and human-made elements of our world? The following experiment will help you draw your conclusions.

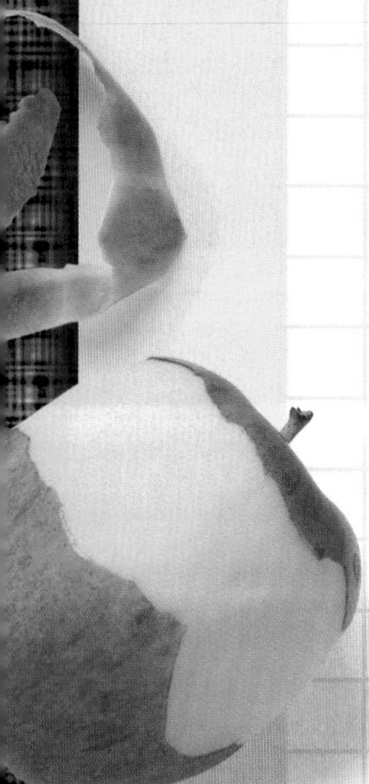

MATERIALS:

1/2 Liter of vinegar

Distilled water

pH paper

Apple

Iron nails (not
   galvanized)

Marble chips

6 Glass jars

Eye protection

Knife

Marker

Masking Tape

Small Plate

PROCEDURE:

Step 2

1. Pour small amounts of vinegar into 3 of the jars and label them as having vinegar in them.

2. Test the pH by dipping the pH paper into one of the jars.

3. Pour equal amounts of distilled water into the remaining 3 jars and label them.

4. Test the pH of the water.

5. Peel 2 small pieces of skin off the apple. Make sure that the 2 pieces look fairly similar in size. Observe their appearance.

6. Place one apple peel in a jar with vinegar and one in a jar that has distilled water. Set both jars aside.

Step 6

7. Choose 2 marble chips and observe their appearance. Place one marble chip in a jar with vinegar and one in a jar with distilled water. Set aside.

8. Choose 2 identical pieces of metal and observe their appearance. Place one in a jar with vinegar and one in a jar with distilled water. Set aside.

Step 9

9. Let the objects soak overnight. Remove all objects from their jars and place them on small plates. Observe and compare the appearances of the objects placed in vinegar to the objects in water at different time intervals (10 minutes, 1 hour, 1 day, 1 week).

OBSERVATIONS AND ANALYSIS:

1. The pH of acid rain varies from 3.5 to 4.5. What was the pH of your vinegar? What was the pH of the distilled water?

2. Describe any differences in the appearances of the objects that were placed in the vinegar.

3. If a solution with the same pH as the vinegar you used in this activity was raining down on buildings, statues, and plants, what could the effects be?

4. If you were a scientist reporting to the government on this issue, what would your conclusions be? What would your recommendations be for dealing with this problem?

Cleaning Up THE PAST

"I believe that the first [requirement] for really solving our ecological problems is true democracy," states an environmental official of the Czech Republic. "Without an educated and engaged public you cannot change anything." Among the environmental problems he is referring to is the problem of acid rain, which has damaged 70% of the area's forests. The damage is the result of more than 35 years of burning brown coal, which contains large amounts of sulphur.

Czech factories spew pollution

Czech forest destroyed by acid rain

taking Action

Reducing air pollution can help slow the effects of acid rain. You can help by being more informed about the problem.

✔ Research the effects of acid rain and then draw posters to illustrate the before and after effects of acid rain on buildings, monuments, or statues.

✔ Survey your community to see if you find any effects of acid rain. Photograph any problems you note and create a collage illustrating the problem.

*N*orthern Eurasia

CHAPTERS

A Global Perspective

Northern Eurasia sprawls across two continents, from the Baltic Sea to the Pacific Ocean, and covers nearly half the Northern Hemisphere. Climates range from the marshy tundra of Siberia, near the Arctic Sea, to subtropical vineyards and orange groves near the Black Sea. Russia has long dominated most of Northern Eurasia, but the region is home to many peoples with different languages, religions, and ways of life.

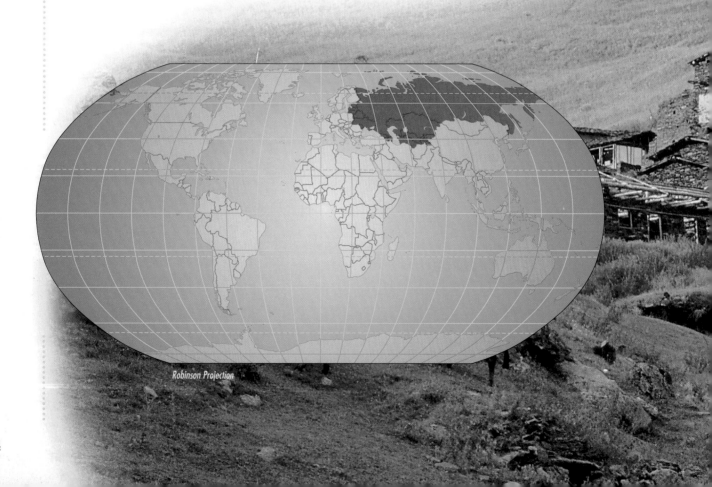

Robinson Projection

Caucasus Mountains, Georgia

KEYS TO UNDERSTANDING
THIS REGION

1 Countries and Cities *(pp. 386–387)*
Most of Northern Eurasia was once part of the Russian Empire. Following the Russian Revolution of 1917, the region's varied peoples came under the new Soviet Union. With the breakup of the Soviet Union in 1991, its former republics became independent nations.

2 Physical Features *(pp. 388–389)*
Despite its vast expanse, the landforms of Northern Eurasia follow one overall pattern. Flat plains dominate the west and center, rising to highlands in the east. Along the southern border lie great lakes, inland seas, and rugged mountain ranges.

3 People and Cultures *(pp. 390–391)*
While Russia dominates the region, more than 100 ethnic groups speaking more than 200 different languages live in Northern Eurasia. Cultures differ widely from one nation to another.

4 Climate and Vegetation *(pp. 392–393)*
Most of Northern Eurasia is far from the moderating effects of ocean water, giving the interior of Russia and its neighbors a continental climate. The major influence on climate is not landforms but the region's high-latitude location.

5 Economy and Resources *(pp. 394–395)*
Russia has more natural resources than any country on earth. Yet it has struggled to utilize this natural wealth to create a higher standard of living for its people. The end of the Soviet Union and its planned economy brought drastic economic and political changes and challenges.

VISUAL PREVIEW ACTIVITY

Each of the five keys above corresponds to a section of the Regional Atlas that follows. Number from 1 to 5 on a piece of paper. Use information from maps, graphs, and photographs in the Regional Atlas to write one additional fact for each of the five keys above.

NORTHERN EURASIA

Use the Map, Graph, and Photo Studies in this Regional Atlas to gain a better understanding of Northern Eurasia's physical and cultural geography.

ATLAS VOCABULARY

Eurasia	steppe	taiga
czar	tundra	chernozem

1 COUNTRIES AND CITIES

GRAPH STUDY

1 **Largest Cities** Urbanization varies greatly from country to country in Northern Eurasia. In the European-influenced countries, such as Estonia, Belarus, and Ukraine, two thirds or more of the population live in cities. In Russia, nearly three fourths live in cities of over a million in population, from Moscow and St. Petersburg in the west to Omsk and Novosibirsk in the east. *Aside from Russia, what is the largest city in Northern Eurasia?*

LARGEST CITIES

Moscow, Russia
8,746,500

St. Petersburg, Russia
4,436,500

Kiev, Ukraine
2,643,000

Tashkent, Uzbekistan
2,094,000

Kharkov, Ukraine
1,622,000

Minsk, Belarus
1,613,000

Novosibirsk, Russia
1,442,000

= 1,000,000 people
Source: United Nations

MAP STUDY
Applying the Geographic Themes

2 **Location** Some geographers suggest that the huge connected landmass of Europe and Asia should be seen as one continent—**Eurasia**. The region known as Northern Eurasia sprawls across nearly half of the Northern Hemisphere. More than three quarters of the region is occupied by Russia, the largest country on earth. The other nations of the region are former republics of the Soviet Union. *From west to east, what are the eight southernmost countries in the region?*

Northern Eurasia: POLITICAL

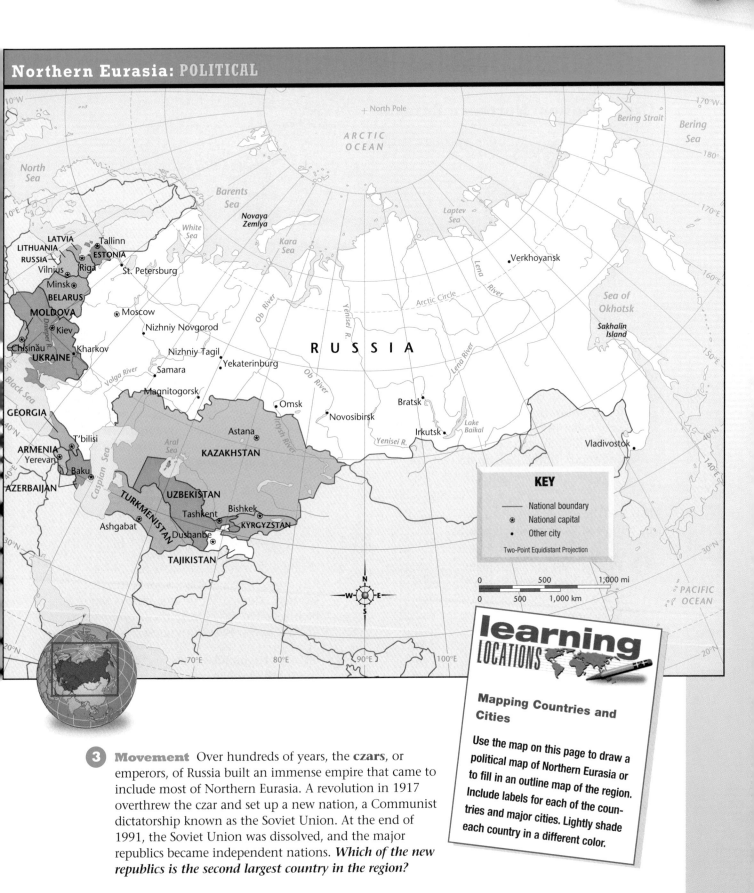

KEY

— National boundary
⊛ National capital
• Other city

Two-Point Equidistant Projection

| 0 | 500 | 1,000 mi |
| 0 | 500 | 1,000 km |

learning LOCATIONS

Mapping Countries and Cities

Use the map on this page to draw a political map of Northern Eurasia or to fill in an outline map of the region. Include labels for each of the countries and major cities. Lightly shade each country in a different color.

3 **Movement** Over hundreds of years, the **czars**, or emperors, of Russia built an immense empire that came to include most of Northern Eurasia. A revolution in 1917 overthrew the czar and set up a new nation, a Communist dictatorship known as the Soviet Union. At the end of 1991, the Soviet Union was dissolved, and the major republics became independent nations. *Which of the new republics is the second largest country in the region?*

Chapter 20 ▪ Regional Atlas

Cross Section: Northern Eurasia

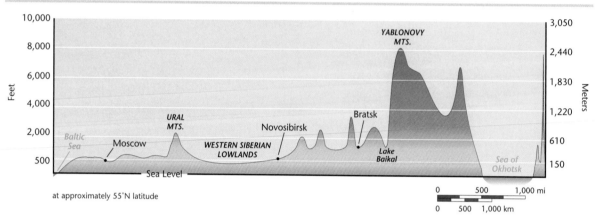

at approximately 55°N latitude

DIAGRAM STUDY

1 **Physical Profile** Even though Northern Eurasia is huge, its basic landforms follow one overall pattern. The land is flat in the west and becomes increasingly mountainous toward the east and south. In the Russian far east, the East Siberian Highlands are a jumble of ridges, steep valleys, and volcanic peaks. Along the southern border of the region lie great lakes and high mountains. *What is the approximate difference in elevation between Moscow and Bratsk?*

MAP STUDY
Applying the Geographic Themes

2 **Place** Vast grassland plains, the **steppes**, sweep across central Russia, divided by a low-lying mountain range, the Ural Mountains. The Urals are usually considered the boundary between Europe and Asia. They average only 3,000 to 4,000 feet (900 to 1,200 m) in elevation. The fertile, rolling western plain is the continuation of the European Plain, a huge lowland that stretches from the Atlantic Ocean across Europe. *What steppe region lies just south of the Ural Mountains?*

3 **Regions** Siberia is the Asian part of Russia, the land from the Ural Mountains eastward to the Pacific Ocean. The Western Siberian Lowland covers more than 1 million square miles (2.6 million sq km) and is the largest area of unbroken lowland in the world. Much of this land is swampy or remains partly frozen all year. Although Siberia is famous for its harsh subarctic climate, its short summers can be hot. *What rivers form the boundaries of the Central Siberian Plateau?*

4 **Place** Highlands, lakes, and seas line the southern edge of Northern Eurasia. Between the Black Sea and the Caspian Sea stand the rugged, forested peaks of the Caucasus Mountains. They form Russia's border with Georgia and Azerbaijan. Farther east are other steep, forbidding mountain ranges. The highest peaks in the region reach 25,000 feet (7,600 m) above sea level and are found in the Pamirs, where the borders of Tajikistan, China, and Afghanistan meet. *What countries in this region have coastlines on the Black Sea?*

REGIONAL atlas

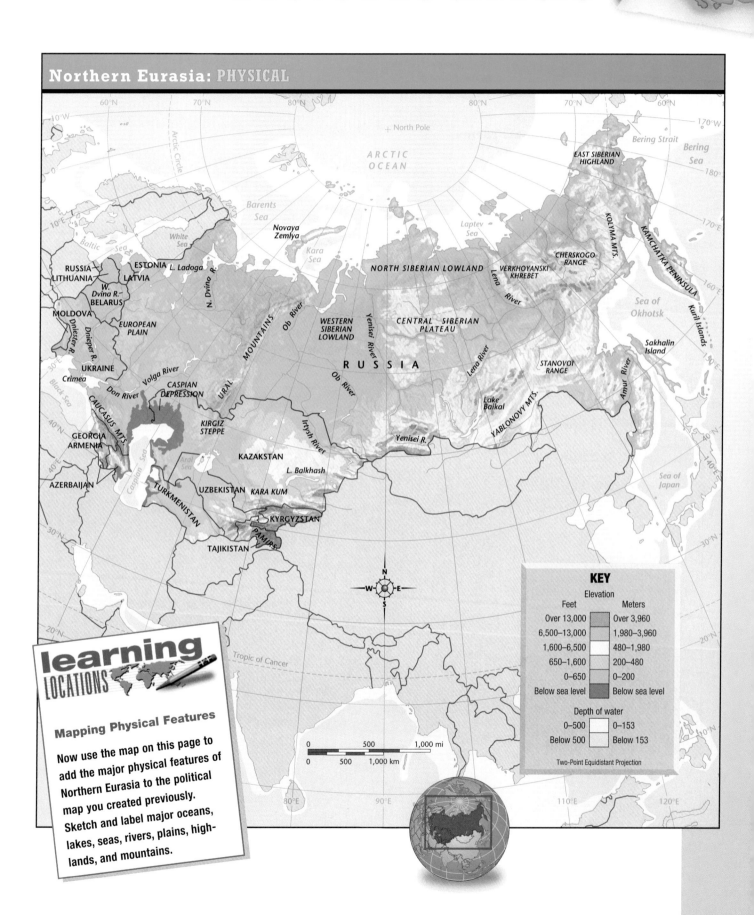

Northern Eurasia: PHYSICAL

ARCTIC OCEAN

North Pole

Bering Strait

Bering Sea

EAST SIBERIAN HIGHLAND

Barents Sea

Novaya Zemlya

Kara Sea

Laptev Sea

KOLYMA MTS.

CHERSKOGO RANGE

VERKHOYANSKI KHREBET

NORTH SIBERIAN LOWLAND

KAMCHATKA PENINSULA

White Sea

Baltic Sea

RUSSIA
LITHUANIA
ESTONIA
LATVIA
L. Ladoga
N. Dvina R.

W. Dvina R.
BELARUS

MOLDOVA

EUROPEAN PLAIN

Dniester R.

Dnieper R.

UKRAINE

Crimea

Black Sea

CAUCASUS MTS.

GEORGIA
ARMENIA

AZERBAIJAN

Don River

Volga River

Caspian Sea

CASPIAN DEPRESSION

KIRGIZ STEPPE

Aral Sea

TURKMENISTAN

UZBEKISTAN

KARA KUM

KAZAKSTAN

L. Balkhash

URAL MOUNTAINS

Ob River

WESTERN SIBERIAN LOWLAND

Irtysh River

Yenisei River

Ob River

CENTRAL SIBERIAN PLATEAU

R U S S I A

Lena River

Yenisei R.

Lake Baikal

YABLONOVY MTS.

STANOVOI RANGE

Lena River

Amur River

Sea of Okhotsk

Sakhalin Island

Kuril Islands

Sea of Japan

KYRGYZSTAN

PAMIRS

TAJIKISTAN

Tropic of Cancer

KEY

Elevation

Feet		Meters
Over 13,000		Over 3,960
6,500–13,000		1,980–3,960
1,600–6,500		480–1,980
650–1,600		200–480
0–650		0–200
Below sea level		Below sea level

Depth of water

0–500		0–153
Below 500		Below 153

Two-Point Equidistant Projection

Scale: 0 500 1,000 mi / 0 500 1,000 km

learning LOCATIONS

Mapping Physical Features

Now use the map on this page to add the major physical features of Northern Eurasia to the political map you created previously. Sketch and label major oceans, lakes, seas, rivers, plains, highlands, and mountains.

MAP STUDY
Applying the Geographic Themes

1 **Human-Environment Interaction**
Although Northern Eurasia has a population of nearly 300 million, the average population density is low. The most densely settled area is in the west, which has fertile soil and industry. The intensely cold climate of Siberia discourages settlement, except along rivers or in planned industrial cities. People have settled the deserts only in places where a canal, a river, or a moisture-catching mountain range makes farming possible. Compare the population density map with the physical map on page 389. *What is the population density along the Yenisei and Lena rivers?*

2 **Movement** Almost three fourths of the people of Northern Eurasia live in the European Plain. Three large historic cities are population centers: Moscow and St. Petersburg in Russia, and Kiev in Ukraine. Other areas of high population are near rivers, canals, railways, and mines. *Where is the largest area of very high population density in Northern Eurasia?*

Northern Eurasia: POPULATION DENSITY

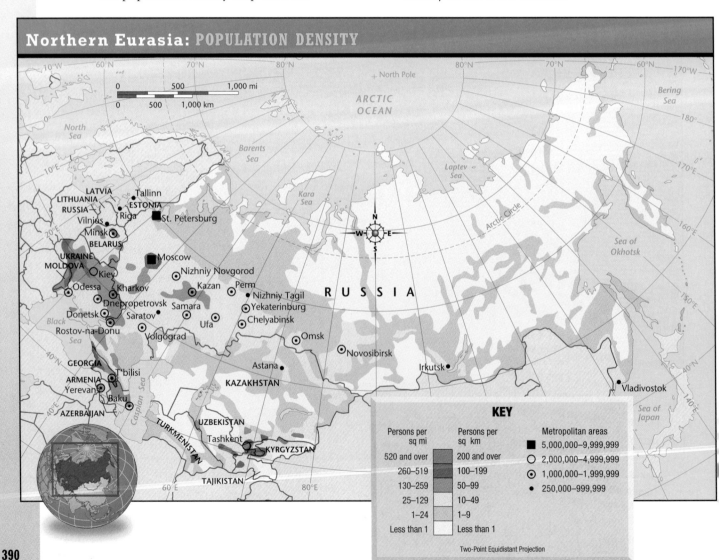

KEY

Persons per sq mi	Persons per sq km
520 and over	200 and over
260–519	100–199
130–259	50–99
25–129	10–49
1–24	1–9
Less than 1	Less than 1

Metropolitan areas
■ 5,000,000–9,999,999
○ 2,000,000–4,999,999
◉ 1,000,000–1,999,999
• 250,000–999,999

Two-Point Equidistant Projection

3 Place The people of Northern Eurasia belong to more than 100 ethnic groups and speak more than 200 different languages. The Slavs are the largest ethnic group in Russia and the European republics. Most people in central Asia are of Turkic background. Georgians and Armenians are Caucasian peoples who speak non-Slavic languages. In the Soviet era, Russian was the official language and is still widely spoken. Today each republic has its own official language. *Besides Russian, what other Slavic languages are spoken in Northern Eurasia?*

Northern Eurasia: MAJOR LANGUAGES

KEY

Indo-European

Slavic
- Russian
- Ukrainian
- Byelorussian

Baltic
- Lithuanian
- Latvian

Other
- Armenian
- Romanian
- Tajik

Turkic
- Uzbek
- Chuvash
- Tatar
- Kazakh
- Kirghiz
- Azerbaijani (Azeri) and Turkmen
- Other Turkic

Other
- Georgian
- Other Finnic
- Mongolian
- Paleosiberian
- Eskimo-Aleut
- Tungus

Two-Point Equidistant Projection

PHOTO STUDY

4 Shaping Culture Cultures and ways of life differ widely from one nation to another across Northern Eurasia. In the Baltic republics and Ukraine, for example, city dwellers live in much the same way as their neighbors in Poland. In more distant parts of Russia, dozens of native groups maintain their own cultures. Many people in central Asia share the religion of Islam with their neighbors across the border in Iran. *Critical Thinking What types of local cultures and cultural influences would you be likely to find in the Russian far east?*

MAP STUDY
Applying the Geographic Themes

1 **Cause and Effect: Climate and Vegetation** Northern Eurasia has four broad east-west bands of vegetation: tundra, forest, steppe, and desert. Only **tundra** vegetation—tough grasses, mosses, and lichens—can grow in the polar conditions near the Arctic Ocean. Vegetation grows rapidly during the short summer, when the surface of the permafrost thaws and becomes marshy. *At about what latitude is the tundra region located?*

2 **Place** The largest forest region in the world covers nearly half of Northern Eurasia, south of the tundra. The northern part of this region is scattered with coniferous trees. This type of forest is called the **taiga** (TY guh), the Russian word for "little sticks." Farther south, with decreasing rainfall, come the vast, grassy steppes. East of the Caspian Sea lie dry lands, where the natural vegetation is desert scrub. *What three kinds of forest grow in Northern Eurasia?*

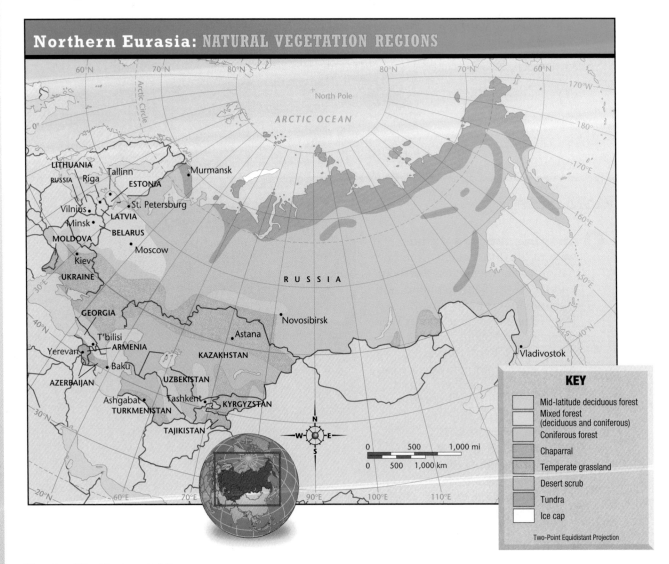

Northern Eurasia: NATURAL VEGETATION REGIONS

North Pole
ARCTIC OCEAN

LITHUANIA
RUSSIA Riga Tallinn
 Vilnius ESTONIA
  •St. Petersburg •Murmansk
 •Minsk LATVIA
MOLDOVA BELARUS
 •Kiev • Moscow
UKRAINE

R U S S I A

GEORGIA
 •T'bilisi •Novosibirsk
Yerevan• ARMENIA •Astana
 •Baku KAZAKHSTAN •Vladivostok
AZERBAIJAN UZBEKISTAN
 Ashgabat• •Tashkent KYRGYZSTAN
 TURKMENISTAN
 TAJIKISTAN

N
W—E
S

0   500   1,000 mi
0   500 1,000 km

KEY

	Mid-latitude deciduous forest
	Mixed forest (deciduous and coniferous)
	Coniferous forest
	Chaparral
	Temperate grassland
	Desert scrub
	Tundra
	Ice cap

Two-Point Equidistant Projection

NORTHERN EURASIA

Northern Eurasia: CLIMATE REGIONS

KEY

- Semiarid
- Arid
- Mediterranean
- Humid subtropical
- Humid continental
- Subarctic
- Tundra
- Highlands

Two-Point Equidistant Projection

3 **Place** Outside the interior, Northern Eurasia has a variety of climates. In the north, chilling winds from the Arctic Ocean create a tundra climate, while a subarctic climate extends from northeastern Russia across most of Siberia. The southern part of the European Plain has a humid continental climate with warm summers. South of that, from Ukraine to Kazakstan, is a semiarid climate zone, with warm winters and hot summers. *Around what body of water is the climate the driest?*

4 **Place** Winds from the Atlantic Ocean and the Baltic Sea bring moisture to coastal European parts of Northern Eurasia. Autumn in the European Plain is often cool, gray, and rainy. In northwestern Russia, heavy precipitation means frequent, heavy snowfalls. Snow often stays on the ground in Moscow for six months of the year. *Considering its location, what kind of climate would you expect in St. Petersburg, Russia? Why?*

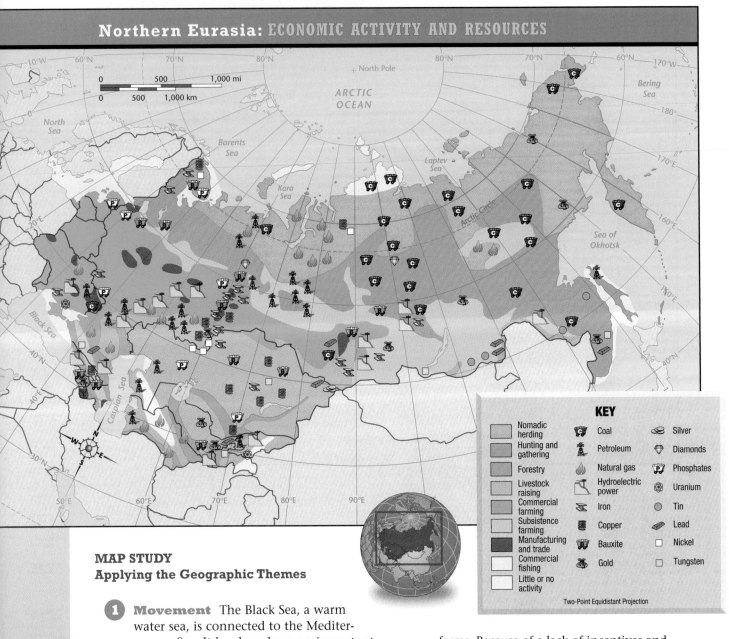

Northern Eurasia: ECONOMIC ACTIVITY AND RESOURCES

KEY

Nomadic herding	Coal	Silver	
Hunting and gathering	Petroleum	Diamonds	
Forestry	Natural gas	Phosphates	
Livestock raising	Hydroelectric power	Uranium	
Commercial farming	Iron	Tin	
Subsistence farming	Copper	Lead	
Manufacturing and trade	Bauxite	Nickel	
Commercial fishing	Gold	Tungsten	
Little or no activity			

Two-Point Equidistant Projection

MAP STUDY
Applying the Geographic Themes

1 **Movement** The Black Sea, a warm water sea, is connected to the Mediterranean Sea. It has long been an important trade route for the countries of Northern Eurasia. *Critical Thinking* *What factors make the Black Sea so important for trade in this region?*

2 **Place** Under Soviet rule, the government controlled agriculture, forcing farmers to work together on state farms and collective farms. Because of a lack of incentives and state planning, Soviet agricultural production and distribution were poor. Russian diets depended on potatoes and grains and were low in meats, fruits, and fresh vegetables. Private gardens were and still are important sources for fruits and vegetables. *What countries of the region have large areas devoted to commercial farming?*

3 **Human-Environment Interaction**
Most Russian rivers are frozen in winter, but for centuries they have been highways for trade and communication. The Ob, Yenisei, and Lena rivers transport ships carrying lumber cut from the Siberian forests through otherwise almost unpopulated territory. During the long winter, trucks use the frozen rivers as highways. *Name four minerals found in Siberia.*

4 **Movement** Many of Russia's resources are in remote locations. Huge deposits of coal, oil, natural gas, and even gold and diamonds lie beneath the permafrost in Siberia. The former Soviet government concentrated on making the country an industrial giant. Industrial factories were built near the natural resources. *In what part of the region are most manufacturing activities concentrated?*

PHOTO STUDY

5 **The Steppes** These temperate grasslands of the European Plain stretch from Ukraine across Russia into Kazakstan. The fertile topsoil beneath the grasses is called **chernozem** (CHER nuh zem), or "black earth." The steppes are so well suited for growing crops like the wheat shown here that the area has been populated continuously for about 4,000 years. *Besides farming, what other economic activities take place in the steppes?*

atlas REVIEW

Vocabulary and Main Ideas

1. **Define: a. Eurasia b. czar c. steppe d. tundra e. taiga f. chernozem**

2. **Name the two lowlands that dominate the interior of Northern Eurasia.**

3. **What are the four major vegetation zones of Northern Eurasia?**

4. **Critical Thinking: *Cause and Effect* What factors explain the much greater population density in the western half of this region?**

learning LOCATIONS

5. **What countries lie between the Black Sea and Caspian Sea?**

6. **What mountain range separates Europe from Asia?**

NORTHERN EURASIA

Russian Expansion

The huge country of Russia dominates the northern parts of two continents—Europe and Asia. How did one nation acquire so much territory?

Russian doll

Small Beginnings

The Russian state began in the 800s in a city that is no longer in Russia: Kiev (a city in Ukraine). There, on a forested bluff above the wide Dnieper River, Viking traders built a fort. Another fort, Novgorod, was farther north. The traders came from Scandinavia, bringing furs, honey, and beeswax for candles, along with amber from the Baltic Sea area. They followed a river route from the Baltic Sea to the Black Sea and Constantinople, center of the Byzantine Empire.

Viking leaders organized the local Slavic peoples under their rule and became Grand Princes of Kiev. The two ways of life blended. Traders also brought Byzantine culture to

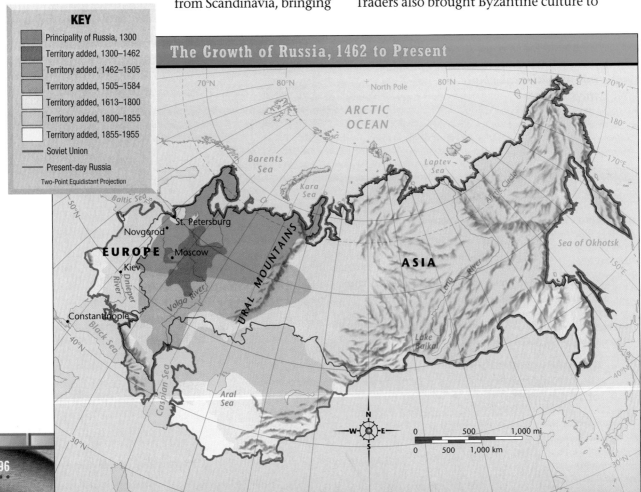

KEY

- Principality of Russia, 1300
- Territory added, 1300–1462
- Territory added, 1462–1505
- Territory added, 1505–1584
- Territory added, 1613–1800
- Territory added, 1800–1855
- Territory added, 1855-1955
- Soviet Union
- Present-day Russia

Two-Point Equidistant Projection

The Growth of Russia, 1462 to Present

Russia. Kiev's rulers adopted Orthodox Christianity in about A.D. 988.

Power Shifts to Moscow

Around 1240, nomadic Mongols from central Asia invaded and conquered Kievan Russia. During more than 200 years of Mongol rule, Russia was an isolated agricultural country, cut off from trade and contact with Europe.

Power shifted from Kiev to Moscow. In 1480 Ivan III, prince of Moscow, stopped paying tribute to the Mongol rulers and unified the other Russian towns. Since the Byzantine Empire had collapsed, Ivan declared himself the successor to the emperors of both Rome and Constantinople. He took the title czar—the Russian equivalent of "Caesar."

Russia Builds an Empire

Czar Ivan "the Great" quickly moved to expand Russia in all directions. His armies retook land from the Mongols and gained new territory across the Ural Mountains, the traditional dividing line between Europe and Asia.

Later rulers were equally ambitious. They fought neighboring rulers in Poland and Sweden for land. Cossacks, peasant groups organized in military units, led the conquest of the vast eastern lands of Siberia.

Under Peter the Great, who ruled from 1682 to 1725, and Catherine the Great, who ruled from 1762 to 1796, the Russian Empire expanded greatly. Peter went to war for land on the Baltic Sea. He brought in technology from western

Europe and built a new capital city, St. Petersburg, as Russia's "window to the West." Catherine also took many ideas from western Europe. She acquired territory on the Black Sea and annexed rich farmlands in Ukraine and Poland. The map on the previous page shows how much the country grew between the reigns of Ivan the Great and Catherine the Great.

The Soviet Union—and Afterward

Czars during the 1800s made Russia still larger, adding territory around the Caspian Sea. In 1891 construction began on the great Trans-Siberian Railroad, which runs some 5,700 miles (9,300 km) from Moscow to Vladivostok on the Sea of Japan. By 1914, on the eve of World War I, the huge Russian Empire included Poland, Finland, and much of central Asia.

The Bolshevik Revolution in 1917 destroyed the empire and created the Soviet Union. Many ethnic groups had separate republics within the Soviet Union. When the Soviet Union broke apart in 1991, the republics became independent nations. Even without the rest of its empire, Russia is still the largest country in the world in land area.

Soviet magazine

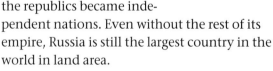

connecting TO TODAY

1. What two cities were the center of the earliest Russian state?

2. What region accounts for the largest land area in Russia? About when did it become part of the Russian Empire?

3. **Critical Thinking** What do you think were the results of building the railroad from Moscow across Siberia to Vladivostok?

4. **Hands-On Activity** Choose one region of historic or present-day Russia and make a poster to draw tourists there. Think of a slogan for your poster that refers to the region's history. Include photos or drawings of scenic attractions.

Russia and the Independent Republics

learning LOCATIONS

Mapping the Region

Create a map like the one below, lightly shading each country a different color. Then add the labels for countries, cities, and bodies of water that are shown on this map.

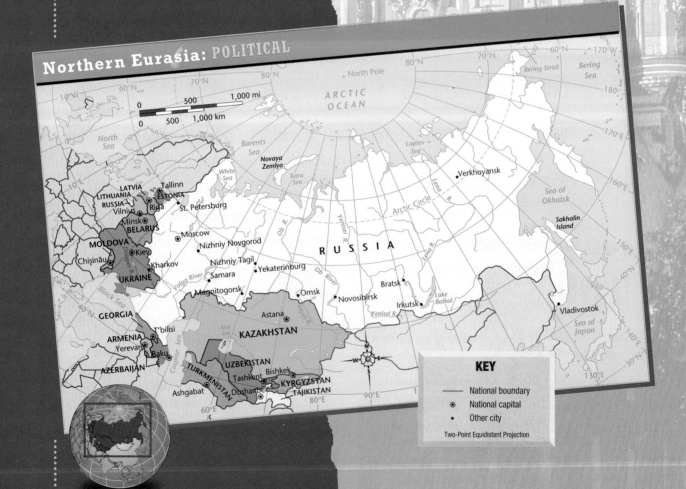

Northern Eurasia: POLITICAL

0 500 1,000 mi
0 500 1,000 km

ARCTIC OCEAN

North Pole

Bering Strait

Bering Sea

North Sea

Barents Sea

Novaya Zemlya

White Sea

Kara Sea

Laptev Sea

Verkhoyansk

Sea of Okhotsk

LATVIA
LITHUANIA
ESTONIA Tallinn
RUSSIA
Vilnius Riga St. Petersburg
Minsk
BELARUS
Moscow Nizhniy Novgorod
MOLDOVA
Kiev
Chişinău
Kharkov Nizhniy Tagil Yekaterinburg
UKRAINE Samara
Magnitogorsk Omsk Novosibirsk
GEORGIA Astana
T'bilisi KAZAKHSTAN
ARMENIA Aral Sea
Yerevan
Baku
AZERBAIJAN UZBEKISTAN Bishkek
TURKMENISTAN Tashkent KYRGYZSTAN
Ashgabat Dushanbe TAJIKISTAN

RUSSIA

Ob R.
Yenisei R.
Lena R.
Arctic Circle
Ob River
Yenisei R.
Bratsk
Irkutsk
Lake Baikal
Vladivostok

Sakhalin Island

Sea of Japan

Volga River
Black Sea
Caspian Sea

Syr Darya

KEY

— National boundary
⊛ National capital
• Other city

Two-Point Equidistant Projection

1 Russia

Section Preview

Main Ideas

- Russia is the largest country on earth, with mainly cool climates and huge areas of forest and grassland.

- Russia possesses rich natural resources, but its climate and size present challenges to developing them.

- Under the Soviet Union, heavy industry was developed and agriculture was reorganized.

- Sweeping political and economic changes in the 1990s improved life for many Russians, but left others insecure.

Vocabulary

permafrost, soviet, command economy, heavy industry, *glasnost, perestroika*

APPEARED IN *NATIONAL GEOGRAPHIC*

Residents look out on Red Square in Moscow.

There are many ways to get an idea of Russia's huge size. On a globe, it occupies more than three quarters of Northern Eurasia, with a land area nearly twice the size of any other large nation, such as Brazil or Canada. Its easternmost cities are closer to the United States than to Moscow, Russia's capital. From west to east, Russia stretches across ten time zones. Before people in St. Petersburg have gone to bed on Tuesday evening, it is Wednesday morning on the Kamchatka Peninsula.

Land and Resources

Thick forests and broad grasslands dominate the Russian landscape. Western Russia's interior has a continental climate—warm summers and cold, snowy winters. Siberia, the Asian part of Russia, has a mainly subarctic climate. Much of Siberia is cool and swampy, with a layer of permanently frozen soil, or **permafrost**. In some places, permafrost extends 5,000 feet (1,500 m) below the ground.

Modern high-rise buildings in Siberia stand 6 feet (1.8 m) off the ground on special pilings, or posts. This allows the frigid air to circulate beneath them and diffuse the heat that buildings generate. Engineers learned this tactic after the first tall buildings erected on permafrost collapsed when their heat thawed the soil around their foundations.

Forest and Steppe The largest forest region in the world sprawls across central and eastern Russia. It extends more than 4 million square miles (10 million sq km). The colder northern part of this forest, the taiga, is scattered with coniferous trees. Few people live in the taiga, where forest fires can rage unnoticed for weeks. Farther south grow broad stands of mixed coniferous and deciduous trees, such as birches and poplar.

The steppes are the rolling, temperate grasslands of Russia, Ukraine, and Kazakstan. Their rich "black earth," or chernozem, is good for growing grain and grazing livestock.

Siberia's Frozen Highways

Location Far from the moderating effects of the oceans, winters are severe in Russia's interior. Ice grows thick enough on rivers to support even heavy trucks. *How does this temporary highway system help the Russian economy?*

Rich Resources Russia's great size is matched by its economic potential. It has more natural resources—timber, oil, gold, silver, diamonds—than any other country on earth. Many resources, however, are in hard-to-reach parts of Siberia. Extracting and using them is difficult.

As part of their drive to make Russia an industrial giant, its leaders sometimes built entire new industrial cities near resources. For example, the city of Magnitogorsk (mag NEET uh gorsk) in the Ural Mountains was built in 1929 after a rich iron ore deposit was found nearby. More than 441,000 people now live in Magnitogorsk, the site of one of the world's largest metal refineries.

Transportation

Russia's great size and harsh climates make it hard to establish good transportation routes. In many places, travel by road is often not practical. More than three quarters of all raw materials come from Siberia, where winter frosts buckle concrete and summer thaws turn roadways into mushy swamps. Siberian roads often are covered only with gravel. Although there is no speed limit, the roads themselves often limit how fast one can travel. Air travel is expensive and unsuitable for transporting many raw materials, such as oil and natural gas. These resources are brought to the western areas where they are needed through a maze of pipelines that crisscross the frozen wilderness.

Rivers Rivers have historically been important trade routes even though most Russian rivers are frozen for many months of the year. One journalist described how even frozen rivers can be useful transportation:

> *Throughout Siberia, boats ply rivers only in the summer; winter turns artery into bone. On the frozen surface, transportation is far easier. Trucks drive along the part-time pavement of the rivers and on the zimniki, as Siberians call their icy winter roads, a system far more reliable than the same quagmire routes during the brief summertime.*

One danger of this part-time road system comes in the spring as the ice begins to thaw and shift. Truckers must be careful to gauge the thickness of the ice, or they risk losing their cargos in the rivers.

Railroads With more than 90,000 miles (145,000 km) of track in the system, railroads are the greatest movers of people and goods in Russia. They are a practical alternative to pipelines for shipping oil. Because rail transport is inexpensive, Russian rail lines carry nearly half of all the railroad freight in the world. The great Trans-Siberian Railway, completed in 1905, runs across the country some 5,700 miles (9,300 km) from Moscow to Vladivostok on the Sea of Japan. (See the map below.)

Another major rail line runs about 1,900 miles (3,100 km) between Lake Baikal and the Amur River, near the Pacific coast. The Baikal-Amur Mainline opened in 1984. Its route crosses some 3,700 bodies of water and seven mountain ranges, passing through tunnels as much as 9 miles (14 km) long. An eighteenth-century Russian scientist said "Siberia will make Russia strong." A wealth of resources, however, has not automatically made Russia a wealthy nation.

Politics and the Economy

Russia grew to its great size over hundreds of years. A series of Russian czars, or emperors, conquered and annexed the homelands of more than one hundred different ethnic groups. By the beginning of the twentieth century, Russia controlled nearly all of Northern Eurasia.

The Russian Revolution in 1917 overthrew the czar and established a government that was based on the ideas of Karl Marx, a German economist. Marx and his followers believed that to achieve social equality, land and businesses should be owned by people in common, hence the word *communism*. When the Union of Soviet Socialist Republics was established, it comprised Russia and the homelands of the largest ethnic groups. Each republic had its own **soviet**, or governing council. The Supreme Soviet in Moscow made national laws.

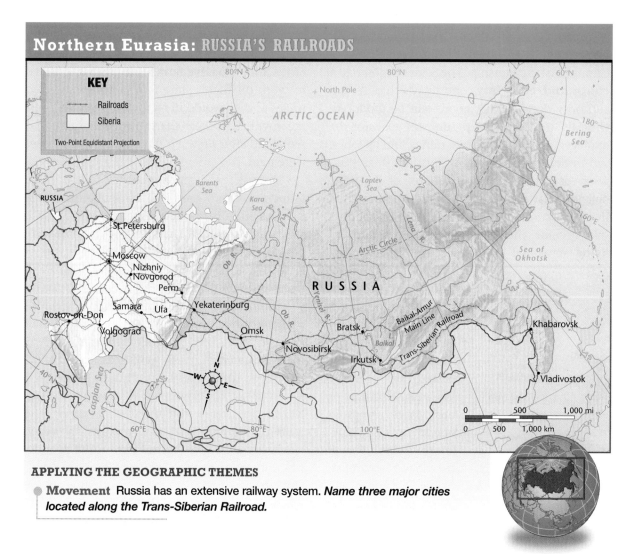

Northern Eurasia: RUSSIA'S RAILROADS

APPLYING THE GEOGRAPHIC THEMES

● **Movement** Russia has an extensive railway system. *Name three major cities located along the Trans-Siberian Railroad.*

Rise of Industry

Human-Environment Interaction Before the Communists came to power, most Russians were peasant farmers. Once in power, the Soviet government pushed the development of heavy industry, including the production of steel. **Critical Thinking** *Why do you think the Soviets favored industrial development in Russia?*

The Soviet System Leaders such as V.I. Lenin and, later, Joseph Stalin, established a Communist dictatorship. The Soviet Union had a **command economy**, one in which a central authority decides what goods will be produced. Officials in Moscow set production goals for the managers of state-run farms, mines, and factories.

Under the czars, most Russians had been poor peasant farmers. Millions of Russians believed that communism would improve their lives. They found instead that the Communists had become their new masters. Standards of living remained poor. Moreover, people had no freedom to make personal decisions or express their opinions. The state controlled their lives as well as the economy. Millions who resisted or objected were sent to prisons or forced-labor camps in Siberia or elsewhere. Enormous numbers of people were executed. Terror became a key part of life under communism.

Health

Average life expectancy for Russian men fell during the transition period, from 62 years in 1992 to 57 years in 1995. The average life expectancy for American men is about 72 years.

Industry and Agriculture Under Soviet rule, farmland was reorganized into state farms and collective farms. Farmers were forced to work on them. State farm workers received wages as they would in factories. On collectives, meanwhile, workers shared any surpluses that remained after products were sold and expenses were paid.

Because few incentives existed to encourage farmers to work hard, Soviet agricultural production and distribution remained low. Despite strict central control, many Soviet farmers were permitted to cultivate gardens on small plots of land. These gardens became major sources of fruits and vegetables.

Stalin's policies also emphasized the development of **heavy industry**—the production of goods that are used in other industries, such as machines or steel. Workers were assigned to factory work, sometimes far from their homes.

By 1940, the Soviet Union was the second-largest producer of iron and steel in Europe. The costs of industrialization were high, however. Heavy industry grew at the expense of producing consumer goods. Everyday items such as clothing, soap, vegetables, and shoes were scarce. People grew used to waiting in long lines to buy anything they could use or trade.

Environmental Impact Many decisions made by Soviet central planners were wasteful and inefficient. The intense effort to industrialize depleted resources and hurt the environment. Siberia, with its rich storehouse of natural resources, has been particularly hard hit. Many Siberian cities rank among Russia's 70 most polluted urban centers. In some areas, lung cancer levels and respiratory infections among children occur at an alarming rate. Oil spills and industrial pollution threaten to pollute rivers and lakes beyond repair.

Change and Challenge

In the late 1980s, a new leader, Mikhail Gorbachev (gor buh CHAWF), began a series of radical reforms. The policy of *glasnost* (GLAHZ nost), or "openness," allowed Soviet citizens to say what they wished without fear of government persecution. The government eased censorship. Newspapers and television news programs began to report openly on issues such as crime.

Russian Population: Access to Clean Air

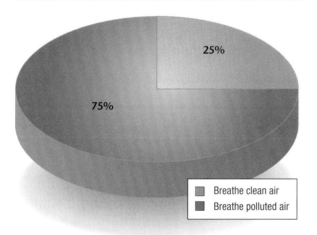

25%

75%

- Breathe clean air
- Breathe polluted air

Source: World Press Review

CHART STUDY

● Air quality is an ongoing problem in Russia. *What percent of Russians breathe unpolluted air?*

● *What role did Soviet leaders play in the creation of pollution?*

A WORLD OF eXtremes

Lake Baikal

X Extremely Deep
More than a mile (1.6 km) deep, Lake Baikal, Russia, is the deepest lake in the world.

X Ancient Waters
This deep water lake is over 25 million years old, making it also the oldest lake in the world.

X EcoDiversity
Lake Baikal's waters are home to more than 2,400 plant and animal species, two thirds of which exist nowhere else on earth.

X Plenty of Water
Containing about one fifth of the world's fresh water, Lake Baikal holds more water than the Great Lakes of North America combined.

X Fill It Up
It would take all the major rivers of the world, including the Amazon, Thames, Seine, and Ganges, nearly one year to fill Baikal's basin.

Economic Reorganization Gorbachev also offered a plan for economic restructuring, or *perestroika* (per uh STROY kuh). It called for a gradual change from a command system to private ownership. Under *perestroika*, the government began to allow factory managers rather than central planners to decide what to produce and how much to charge for goods. The government also converted several factories from the production of military goods to the production of consumer goods. Many factories set goals to improve the quality of goods produced.

Farmers were granted long-term leases on land. By making farmers "masters of the land," Gorbachev hoped to increase food production. For the first time in decades, people were allowed to set up independent businesses. Given such freedom, many people called for an end to communism and the domination of the central government.

A New World Once started, changes came quickly. In mid-1991 Russians voted in their first democratic election, choosing Boris Yeltsin as president of the Russian Republic. A few months later, some officials and army officers tried unsuccessfully to restore old-style communism, but the attempt backfired. The Soviet republics one by one declared themselves independent nations. People tore down statues of Communist leaders. At the end of the year, Gorbachev resigned, announcing the end of the Soviet Union. "We live in a new world," he said. Some of the republics joined with Russia in a loose association, the Commonwealth of Independent States (CIS). As they established their own governments, however, these new nations placed greater emphasis on their own independence than on cooperation with other states.

Building the Future With no experience in democracy, Russia faced many challenges. Although many leaders were committed to democratic reforms, the constitution allowed the president to rule by decree and ignore the elected parliament. Except for the Communist party, there were no real political organizations.

Russians were divided and sometimes confused about the changes in their country. They now had freedom and opportunity, but many had lost secure government jobs, benefits, and pensions. Consumer goods were no longer as scarce, but many people could not afford them. Many people, especially the elderly, were devastated financially. But other Russians quickly began to make the new system work for them, starting their own businesses. Many prospered.

Russia's second democratic presidential election, in 1996, tested people's support for the new Russia. Voter turnout was high. Many people voted for the Communist candidate, who promised a return to security, but a decisive majority reelected President Boris Yeltsin.

In 1999, Yeltsin resigned, and Vladimir Putin became acting president. Putin was elected in his own right in 2000.

Changes in Russia

● **Regions** After the breakup of the Soviet Union, economic troubles plagued the Russian military. As president, Vladimir Putin [center] worked to improve conditions and support for soldiers. *Why might the military have been negatively affected by the fall of the Soviet Union?*

Russia's Capital of High Culture

Location The Mariinsky Theater in St. Petersburg is a jeweled reminder of the city's past. St. Petersburg was built in the 1700s to be the capital of a new, westernized Russia. Since then the city has been one of Russia's great cultural centers. **Critical Thinking** *How does St. Petersburg's location make it open to the West?*

Life in Russia Today

Within such a vast country, ways of life vary greatly. Almost three fourths of Russia's people live in large cities, while traditional ways of life continue in villages and rural areas. During Soviet rule, housing shortages in cities became common. The government built huge apartment blocks, but several families often had to share an apartment. To escape crowded conditions, people look forward to spending weekends and vacations in the country.

Russians love the beauty of their countryside and enjoy hiking or camping in the mountains and forests. The Black Sea coast is a favorite vacation spot. Soccer and other sports are popular, as are movies and television. With the end of Soviet censorship, young Russians are free to enjoy and play rock, pop, and jazz.

Russia has a long, rich tradition of artistic creativity, although in the past, writers and composers were persecuted and silenced by Soviet authorities. Despite economic problems, many Russians enjoy concert, opera, and ballet performances. They fill famous theaters such as the Bolshoi in Moscow and the Mariinsky (Kirov) in St. Petersburg.

Section 1 Review

Vocabulary and Main Ideas

1. **Define: a.** permafrost **b.** command economy **c.** heavy industry **d.** *glasnost* **e.** *perestroika*

2. **What are the two major vegetation regions in Russia? Where are they?**

3. **Why are trains more useful than trucks for transporting resources out of Siberia?**

4. **Critical Thinking:** *Making Predictions* **Why might many Russian voters vote for more political and economic change despite the hardships that rapid change has caused?**

learning LOCATIONS

5. **Near what body of water is the city of Irkutsk located?**

6. **What is considered the dividing line between Europe and Asia in Russia?**

Map Skills
for Life

People from all over the world flock to the Hermitage, a huge museum and art gallery in St. Petersburg, Russia. One of them is Ivan Cherenkov, a student from Moscow, who is studying Russian history.

The Hermitage is housed in three connected palaces along the Neva River: the Winter Palace, Small Hermitage, and Large Hermitage. Ivan starts by studying a map of the ground floor along with a guide that tells him the floor and room numbers of major collections. He decides to begin with these attractions:

★ the galleries devoted to Primitive Art and Culture.

★ the collection of Egyptian Antiquities.

★ the Special Collection featuring the world's largest collection of artifacts from tribes that roamed the Caucasus, Siberia, and the Ukraine between 700 and 200 B.C.

Reading the Map
Follow the steps below to understand how Ivan can use this map of the rooms in the Hermitage to find what he wants to see.

1. Find the starting location on the map.
Look over the map to get a general idea of how the museum is laid out. Notice that what would be the "first floor" in the United States is called the "ground floor." If Ivan comes in by the main entrance, which palace is he in?

2. Use the map and key to locate the places Ivan wants to see.
With a large museum such as this one, notice especially which collections or features are in each building. **(a)** According to the key, what is the number of the Egyptian Antiquities room? On what floor is it located? **(b)** In which palace is the collection located? **(c)** If Ivan is at the main entrance, which way should he go to reach the Egyptian collection?

3. Plan a route that will include the selected sights. Use the map to find the way from one to another.
(a) After Ivan has seen the Egyptian Antiquities, which of his goals is closer: the galleries of Primitive Art and Culture or the Special Collection? **(b)** Where is each collection located? **(c)** How can he get to the one that is farther away?

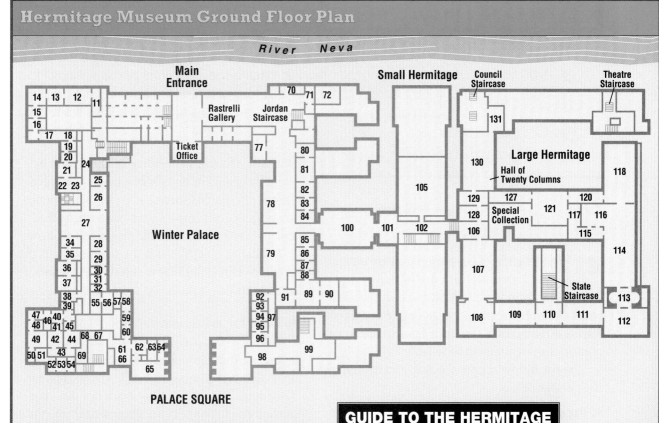

Hermitage Museum Ground Floor Plan

River Neva

Main Entrance

14 13 12 11

15

16

17 18

19

20

24

21

22 23 25

26

27

Winter Palace

34 28

35 29

36 30

37 31 32

38

39

55 56 57 58

47 40

48 46 41 59

45

49 42 44 68 67 60

50 51 43 69 61 62 63 64

52 53 54 66

65

PALACE SQUARE

Rastrelli Gallery

Ticket Office

Jordan Staircase

77

70 71 72

80

81

82

83

84

78

100 101 102

85

86

87

88

79

89 90

91

92

93

94 97

95

96

98

99

Small Hermitage

105

Council Staircase

131

130

129 127

128 **Special Collection** 121

106

107

108 109 110 111 112

Hall of Twenty Columns

Large Hermitage

118

120

117 116

115

114

State Staircase

113

Theatre Staircase

GUIDE TO THE HERMITAGE

Classical Antiquities	Ground Floor 101–130
Dutch & Flemish Art: 15th–18th century	First Floor 244–258
Egyptian Antiquities	Ground Floor 100
English Art: 17th–19th century	First Floor 298–301
French Art: 15th–18th century	First Floor 272–289
Italian Art: 13th–16th century	First Floor 207–230
Modern European Art	Second Floor 314–350
Numismatic Collection	Second Floor 398–400
Primitive Art & Culture	Ground Floor 11–33
Russian Art & Culture	First Floor 157–167
Special Collection	Ground Floor, Large Hermitage
Spanish Art: 16th–18th century	First Floor 239 & 240
State Rooms	First Floor 189–198

St. Petersburg

Moscow

RUSSIA

Arctic Circle

Test Yourself

1. According to Ivan's guidebook, you must have a special ticket to join a guided tour of the Special Collection. If Ivan is in the Large Hermitage, which palace must he pass through to get to the ticket office?

2. While in the Special Collection, Ivan decides to go up to the first floor to see the elaborate State Rooms, known for their gold and marble decorations. What is the closest staircase he could use to get to the first floor?

Focus on Skills

- ☐ Social Studies
- ☐ Map and Globe
- ☑ Critical Thinking and Problem Solving

Distinguishing False from Accurate Images

We all believe some things that are not true. Often a false image or stereotype can gain force and extend its influence widely. It is critical, therefore, to make a habit of testing our images of the truth against new information that we judge to be reliable.

Use the following steps to read and to analyze the passage below.

1. Identify the main point of the passage.
New information allows you to examine a widely held belief about a person, place, or thing and determine whether or not this belief is based in fact. In order to judge the significance of any new information, you must first identify its central message. Answer the following questions: (a) What is the main point of the passage? (b) How does this main idea point out problems with the relationship between Boris Yeltsin and the Russian Mafia?

2. Evaluate the reliability of the source.
Popular beliefs or images of a person or place arise from many sources, and not all of them are reliable. It is important to determine if a source is reliable or biased. Answer the following questions: (a) What is the source of this passage? (b) How would you describe the reliability of the source?

3. Look for evidence.
A point of view presented without evidence to support it may be just opinion. Many false images of people or places are based on opinion, not fact. Answer the following questions: (a) What evidence does the author cite to support his statements? (b) What other sources could you consult to check the accuracy of his references?

Mr. Yeltsin has long relied on the Mafia-linked clans that influence many decisions in politics and especially the economy. Most clan leaders of industry, agriculture, and banking, with their corrupt allies in government, do not want democracy or serious economic reform. They want Mr. Yeltsin to continue to make Russia safe for them. In particular, they want security for the assets they acquired in the furtive carving up of the old Soviet economy. This requires tough rule to suppress political opposition, control the media, and intimidate workers, the poor and the

pensioners. It also requires an end to anything but a facade of democracy.

—Peter Reddaway,
The New York Times,
July 2, 1996

2 Other Independent Republics

Section Preview

Main Ideas

- The Baltic nations have close historic ties to Europe, as does Moldova.

- Europe and Russia both have influenced Ukraine and Belarus, whose people are mainly Slavic.

- The Caucasus region is home to a variety of peoples who speak unrelated languages and have different cultures.

- Most of the people of Azerbaijan and the central Asian nations are Muslims who belong to Turkic ethnic groups.

Vocabulary

ethnic minority, genocide, nationalism, yurt

APPEARED IN *NATIONAL GEOGRAPHIC*

A couple dances to the folk music of Estonia.

The Soviet Union seemed indivisible after World War II. The strong central authority of the Soviet Union, dominated by Russia, hid the diversity of the individual republics. This same diversity ultimately caused the Soviet Union to break apart in 1991. Although Russia remains the largest and most powerful nation to emerge from the former Soviet Union, about 145 million people live in the smaller nations of Northern Eurasia, slightly less than Russia's population of 147.5 million.

During the Soviet regime, many people moved or were sent from place to place within the Soviet Union. Today they constitute cultural subgroups, or **ethnic minorities**, in the republics, outnumbered by members of the dominant culture. For instance, 42 percent of the people of Kazakstan are Kazaks, while 37 percent are Russians. Clashes between ethnic groups have caused violence in some of the new nations.

The Baltic States

The small nations of Lithuania, Latvia, and Estonia are tucked along the eastern edge of the Baltic Sea. Their combined populations total about 7.7 million. Historically, the Baltic states have been closer in culture to Europe than to Russia. All three nations have benefited from their location along major trade routes. But they have also been subject to frequent conquests by other powers. Over the years they have been ruled by larger neighboring states such as Poland, Denmark, and Russia.

The Baltic states share a similar flat terrain, covered with marshy lowlands and fertile low plains. In Estonia the average elevation is only 164 feet (50 m). Lithuania is scattered with many small lakes. The region's humid continental climate is influenced by the air coming off the Baltic Sea. Generally, the region experiences wet, moderate winters and summers.

Lithuanians and Latvians speak similar languages. Estonians speak a distinctive non-Indo-European tongue closely related to Finnish. Most Estonians and Latvians are Lutheran, while Lithuania is largely Roman Catholic.

All three Baltic countries were established as independent nations after World War I, but the Soviet Union forcibly annexed them in 1940. Because of their strategic location on the Baltic Sea, the Soviet Union established naval bases in all three Baltic nations.

Estonia, Lithuania, and Latvia were the first Soviet republics to seek independence in the late 1980s. Their more advanced economies, based on exports of food products, textiles, and machinery, gave them a promising future. Still, they face many challenges, including the cleanup of chemicals and petroleum products used and dumped on the military bases of the former Soviet Union.

European Border Nations

Ukraine, Belarus, and Moldova are the other nations along the border between Northern Eurasia and Eastern Europe. Notice their location on the map below.

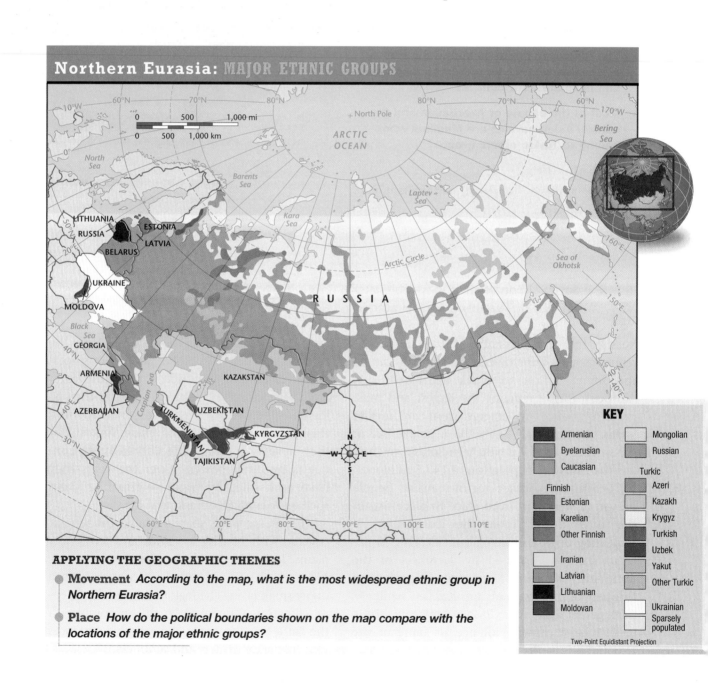

Northern Eurasia: MAJOR ETHNIC GROUPS

KEY

Armenian	Mongolian
Byelarusian	Russian
Caucasian	**Turkic**
Finnish	Azeri
Estonian	Kazakh
Karelian	Krygyz
Other Finnish	Turkish
Iranian	Uzbek
Latvian	Yakut
Lithuanian	Other Turkic
Moldovan	Ukrainian
	Sparsely populated

Two-Point Equidistant Projection

APPLYING THE GEOGRAPHIC THEMES

● **Movement** *According to the map, what is the most widespread ethnic group in Northern Eurasia?*

● **Place** *How do the political boundaries shown on the map compare with the locations of the major ethnic groups?*

Fallout from a Nuclear Disaster

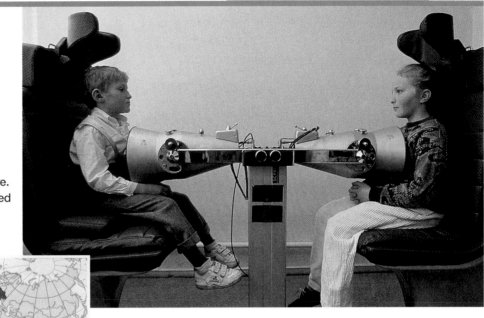

Human-Environment Interaction Radioactive material released from the nuclear reactor at Chernobyl settled onto the region's land and crops. It can also be detected in many people there. These children are being tested for radioactivity. **Critical Thinking** *How might the Chernobyl accident have affected Ukraine's animal population?*

Ukraine According to an old proverb, "Moscow is the heart of Russia, St. Petersburg its head; but Kiev, its mother." The first Russian state began in Kiev, now the capital of Ukraine (yoo KRAYN), more than 1,000 years ago. Kievan traders carried fur, honey, and farm products to the busy markets of Constantinople, the capital of the Byzantine Empire.

Despite its rich history, Ukraine has usually been controlled by one of its neighbors—Lithuania, then Poland, then Russia. The Polish tried to establish Roman Catholicism, causing a religious split with Ukrainians who remained Orthodox. Russian czars tried to replace the Ukrainian language with Russian.

Ukraine, slightly smaller than the state of Texas, was once the "breadbasket" of the Soviet Union. Now its 52 million residents help produce about one fifth of all of the food and industrial products of Northern Eurasia. Farmers in the region grow wheat, rye, barley, and potatoes. Ukraine's agriculture is productive because the country lies in the part of the "black earth" belt with warm weather and adequate precipitation.

Parts of Ukraine suffered serious damage in 1986 when an accidental explosion destroyed a nuclear reactor at Chernobyl (CHAYR noh bul), sending a cloud of radiation into the air. At least 26 people were killed, hundreds more injured, and millions exposed to radiation. Some 12.3 million acres (5 million hectares) of land were polluted by radiation from the damaged plant. Ukrainians still must deal with the long-term effects of Chernobyl, including water pollution, birth defects, and various kinds of cancer. The town of Chernobyl no longer exists. Its people were evacuated and its buildings bulldozed underground. The nuclear reactor was encased in steel and concrete to prevent further radiation from escaping and causing harm. The land surrounding Chernobyl is not likely to be fit for human occupation for a long time.

Belarus Belarus (byel ah ROOS), north of Ukraine, is a nation of over 10 million people in an area about the size of Kansas. Like Russians and Ukrainians, its people are mainly Slavic and traditionally Orthodox Christians. Unlike most of the other new nations, many people in Belarus were in favor of reestablishing close political and economic ties with Russia.

Belarus suffered severely from the Chernobyl disaster, as winds blew the radioactive cloud northward from Ukraine. More than one fifth of the country's farmland was contaminated by radioactivity. People were forced to stop using this land to produce food. Belarus's

Facts in BRIEF

Country	Population	Life Expectancy (years)	Per Capita GNP (in US $)
Armenia	3,700,000	71	660
Azerbaijan	7,300,000	71	730
Belarus	10,300,000	69	2,840
Estonia	1,500,000	70	3,040
Georgia	5,400,000	73	560
Kazakhstan	16,900,000	69	1,540
Kyrgyzstan	4,400,000	68	830
Latvia	2,500,000	68	2,030
Lithuania	3,700,000	71	1,310
Moldova	4,300,000	68	1,180
Russia	147,500,000	65	2,350
Tajikistan	5,800,000	70	470
Turkmenistan	4,500,000	66	1,380
Ukraine	52,000,000	69	1,910
Uzbekistan	22,700,000	69	960
United States	263,200,000	76	24,750

Source: Population Reference Bureau

CHART SKILLS

● *Which Northern Eurasian country has the highest per capita GNP?*

● **Critical Thinking** *What factors contribute to a nation's economy?*

GEOfacts

The Silk Road, the trade route between the Roman Empire and China, crossed central Asia. Cities such as Tashkent, Bukhara, and Samarkand were important stops.

economy now depends mainly on industry. However, it must import most of the raw materials needed to produce the finished goods. Belarus has oil reserves and refineries as well as large deposits of potash, which is used to make fertilizer.

Moldova Landlocked between the states of Ukraine and Romania, Moldova is the second smallest of the former Soviet republics and the most densely populated. Moldova's hilly terrain slopes gradually in a southerly direction toward the Black Sea. Its location and inviting terrain have made it a historic route between Asia and Southern Europe. It has also been subject to frequent invasions.

Moldova was once a Romanian principality. Most of its over four million residents are of Romanian descent. With the end of the Soviet Union, Romanian again became the language used in schools. Soviet planners had built up Moldova's factories, but the economy depends on exports of wine, sugar beets, and seed oils.

The Caucasus

Georgia, Armenia, and Azerbaijan (ah zur by ZHAHN) lie in the Caucasus Mountains between the Black and Caspian seas. Since ancient times, the Caucasus region has been home to a wide diversity of ethnic groups, who speak different languages and follow different religions. Many Russians and Ukrainians also live here. Ethnic and religious differences have led to frequent conflicts.

Georgia Nestled on the southern slopes of the Caucasus, the nation of Georgia is slightly larger than the state of West Virginia. Georgia is mainly mountainous. Good, fertile soil can be found in the river valley flood plains of the Mtkvari River basin in eastern Georgia.

The warmest winters and heaviest rainfall in Northern Eurasia occur along the Black Sea coastline. Georgia thus enjoys a warm subtropical climate that attracts vacationers. The country produces wine, tobacco, tea, silk, peaches, and citrus fruit. The 5.4 million Georgians generally follow Eastern Orthodox Christianity, like the Russians, with whom they have traditionally had close ties.

Armenia Landlocked Armenia is the smallest nation in Northern Eurasia. Most of the land is extremely rocky, although farmers grow a variety of crops in southern valleys. Rugmaking is a traditional craft both here and in neighboring Azerbaijan. Small factories also manufacture goods, especially in the capital of Yerevan. Armenia's people, an ancient Indo-European

Surviving on Marginal Lands

Regions Sheep can thrive where other livestock fail. This chilly plateau in Azerbaijan is too dry to support rich pastures or intensively farmed crops. Still, sheep survive here and produce valuable wool and meat. **Critical Thinking** *What environmental danger is posed when livestock graze in a dry, fragile ecosystem?*

group, have been Christians since about A.D. 300, with their own national Orthodox church.

Pinched between the Turkish and Russian empires, the Armenians have suffered a painful history. At the outbreak of World War I, the Turks attempted to deport the entire Armenian population of 1,750,000. About one third died en route or were massacred by the Turks in an act of **genocide**, the intentional destruction of a people. Many fled into Russia.

Azerbaijan Azerbaijan, located on the western shore of the Caspian Sea, has rich deposits of petroleum, the country's main source of wealth. Almost half of the people live in rural areas. Some herd goats, sheep, and cattle on the mountain slopes. Farmers in the irrigated lowlands, meanwhile, produce fruit, cotton, tea, and silk in the mild climate.

About 83 percent of Azerbaijan's 7.3 million residents are ethnic Azerbaijanis who follow Islam. Ethnic Armenians, mainly Orthodox, are a large ethnic minority, with ties to people in neighboring Armenia. Feelings of **nationalism**—the desire of a cultural group to rule themselves as a separate nation—are strong in both groups. Since gaining independence from the former Soviet Union, Azerbaijan

has experienced violent conflicts between Armenians and Azerbaijanis.

Central Asia

East of the Caspian Sea are lowlands of dusty deserts and grasslands, edged with a fringe of high mountains on the border with China. Precipitation falls mainly as summer rains, amounting to less than 10 inches (25 cm) a year. Some locations in the Kara Kum, or the "black sands," of Turkmenistan get less than 3 inches (8 cm) of rain each year. To the north, the steppes of southern Russia continue eastward across Kazakhstan. In the southeast, the rugged Tian Shan and Altai mountains, with huge glaciers and snow-covered peaks, dominate the landscapes of Tajikistan and Kyrgyzstan. Parts of the region have large reserves of oil and natural gas, as well as other valuable minerals.

Muslims make up about one sixth of Northern Eurasia's population. Most live in Azerbaijan or in the five central Asian countries. Those countries are Kazakhstan (kah zak STAN), Turkmenistan (turk MEN ih STAN), Uzbekistan (ooz BEK ih STAN), Kyrgyzstan (kihr geez STAN), and Tajikistan (tah jihk ih STAN). Their combined area is roughly half the size of the mainland United States. As new nations, they are

A Legacy of Soviet Rule

● **Movement** Kazakhs like these have returned to their homeland after fleeing Communist rule in the 1920s. During the Communist era thousands of Ukrainians, Latvians, and others were deported to Kazakhstan as a political punishment. Today Kazakhstan has people from over 100 ethnic backgrounds. **Critical Thinking** *What kinds of language problems do you think Kazakhstan might face today?*

trying to establish stable governments, develop their economies, and keep peace between ethnic groups.

The central Asian republics were created by the Soviet Union in the 1920s and 1930s from an area known as western Turkestan. Four major groups—Kazakhs, Turkmen, Uzbeks, and Kyrgyz—spoke related Turkic languages. The Tajiks speak an Iranian language. Many people also speak Russian, once the official language.

Ethnic Traditions Though each country is named after a single Turkic group, they are home to a mixture of peoples. For instance, Uzbeks are about 23 percent of the population of Tajikistan. In addition, as long ago as the mid-1800s, the czar's government encouraged Russian and Ukrainian peasants to settle here and turn grazing lands into wheat fields. Russians now are a large ethnic minority in several of these five countries.

Traditionally many people in central Asia, especially in Kazakhstan and Kyrgyzstan, were nomadic herders. Herds of sheep, goats, and yaks grazed in mountain valleys. Herders lived in huge, portable tents called **yurts**, round tents made of wooden frameworks covered with felt or skins. People in other areas were farmers. Most groups have ancient traditions of epic poetry and folk songs.

Changes in the Economy When the region was brought into the Soviet Union, people's lives changed dramatically. While most people here were herders, Soviet planners wanted to develop industry and agriculture. They forced nomadic peoples to settle in villages and work on government farms. With intensive irrigation, people successfully grew cotton, wheat, and grain for animal feed.

Today, more than half the people of Kazakhstan live in cities. In the other republics most people are still rural villagers, herders, and farmers. Livestock raising and agricultural products such as wool, fruits, and grains are a major part of their economies. Kazakhstan grows about one third of Northern Eurasia's wheat, despite its dry climate. Industries include mining, hydroelectric power, chemicals, and food processing.

Irrigation: Promise and Costs

● **Human-Environment Interaction** Irrigation allowed farmers in Central Asia to double their cotton production between 1960 and 1990. However, heavy irrigation has left many fields poisoned with salts and agricultural chemicals. *What two rivers supply the water for irrigation in the Aral Sea region?*

Environmental Impact Eager to increase production, Soviet planners often ignored the ecological effects of development. One extreme example is the salty Aral Sea, on the border between Kazakhstan and Uzbekistan. Because most of this region is semiarid, irrigation was the only way to grow cotton and rice. Fresh water from the Amu Darya and Syr Darya rivers, which flow into the Aral Sea, was diverted to irrigate cotton fields nearby.

While the Soviet Union became a leading cotton producer, the irrigation project devastated the Aral Sea region. With less fresh water flowing in, the sea shrank steadily and grew saltier, losing about two thirds of its volume. The local fishing industry died out. Clouds of sand and chemicals blew from the dry exposed seabed, further contributing to the desertification of the surrounding area. Heavy doses of chemical fertilizers and pesticides used in the production of cotton created serious health risks for workers. In 1994, efforts began to protect and restore the Aral Sea.

Other parts of Central Asia have been equally devastated by pollution. Some scientists consider the Apsheron Peninsula in Azerbaijan to be one of the most ecologically damaged regions in the world. The soil and water in this area is extremely polluted. This is due mainly to the use of the pesticide DDT and toxic defoliants used in the production of cotton. The entire region faces many difficult challenges as people work to clean up the ecological disasters caused by overuse of chemical pesticides and fertilizers.

Section 2 Review

Vocabulary and Main Ideas

1. Define: a. ethnic minority b. genocide c. nationalism d. yurt

2. Which nations of Northern Eurasia have been closest to Europe in history and culture?

3. What characteristics make the countries of central Asia a distinct region?

4. Critical Thinking: *Making Generalizations* Now that the different nations of Northern Eurasia have become independent, what similar challenges do they face?

learning LOCATIONS

5. What countries are located in the Caucasus region?

6. What is the capital of Ukraine?

Nuclear Waste Disposal

The Issue

The end of the arms race between the United States and the former Soviet Union reduced the possibility of a large-scale nuclear war. Now the global community has a new issue. It must deal with the disposal of the radioactive waste created when nuclear weapons are dismantled.

Creating the Toxic Mess

Over the course of the Cold War, the United States and the former Soviet Union manufactured nearly 50,000 nuclear warheads. In the process, tons of radioactive materials were produced. Little thought was given to the future and how these materials could be disposed of safely.

A Difficult Cleanup Now the United States and Russia are left with a massive cleanup. But a number of experts say "cleanup" is the wrong word. Many nuclear wastes will take hundreds of centuries to break down so that they are no longer toxic. The most that can be hoped for is to stabilize, or contain, the wastes safely. And this, according to the U.S. Department of Energy, will cost between $230 and $500 billion and take 75 years to accomplish in the United States alone.

An Environmental Disaster

Some experts have great concerns about the long-term impact of nuclear wastes on the environment. Much of the stored wastes are in old containers that could leak toxins into the environment at any time. Nuclear wastes in some locations have already seeped into the soil and ground water.

Global Impact Radioactive wastes are highly toxic to humans and the environment. Studies link higher rates of

Pathways of Contamination

DIAGRAM STUDY

● **Human-Environment Interaction** Radioactivity from leaking nuclear waste containers is spread through the environment into living organisms via several pathways. *How does nuclear waste get into the water cycle?*

Critical Thinking How is it possible for a person to be exposed to nuclear waste even if he or she has not had direct contact with it?

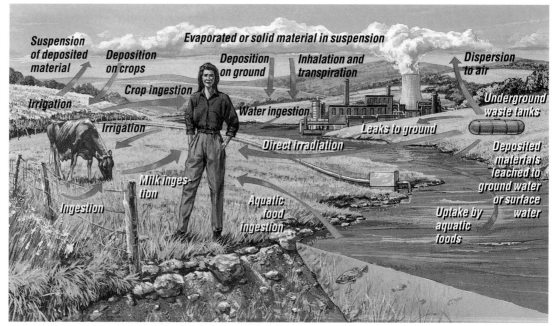

Suspension of deposited material

Deposition on crops

Evaporated or solid material in suspension

Deposition on ground

Inhalation and transpiration

Dispersion to air

Crop ingestion

Irrigation

Water ingestion

Irrigation

Leaks to ground

Underground waste tanks

Direct irradiation

Deposited materials leached to ground water or surface water

Milk ingestion

Ingestion

Aquatic food ingestion

Uptake by aquatic foods

illness and cancer to exposure to radioactivity. When these wastes leak into the air or water supply, they can be spread over huge distances and affect large populations.

Some Solutions

Scientists and other experts have made some progress in finding ways to safely contain the waste from nuclear weapons production.

Improving Storage The United States plans to store the most highly radioactive materials deep underground in special metal containers. But until an appropriate site is established, the materials must be stored above ground. New and stronger tanks are being built. Others are being repaired to stop leakage.

Changing Its Form Experts are also working on ways to change liquid nuclear wastes into solid forms, which are more stable and easier to store. Radioactive wastes can also be reprocessed into powder and glass, and then placed in storage containers.

Recycling Scientists are discussing what should be done with the supply of plutonium, one of the main components of nuclear warheads. As the warheads are dismantled, the supply of plutonium is increasing. Because it costs billions of dollars to produce, some argue that it should be used to fuel nuclear power plants. Others say that plutonium should be disposed of as permanently and quickly as possible. One suggestion is to dispose of it beneath the ocean floor. However, many environmentalists are opposed to this plan.

YOU DECIDE

1. Why do you think so little thought was given to the environment and the future health of humankind when nuclear weapons were being produced?

2. Why is it a priority to clean up nuclear wastes?

3. **Problem Solving** You are a citizen in a town located just ten miles from a nuclear waste disposal site. Draft a letter to the U.S. Department of Energy requesting information in order to decide if the disposal facility poses a potential hazard to your community.

4. **What You Can Do** Find out more about government efforts to clean up waste from the production of nuclear weapons by requesting information from the U.S. Energy Department's Office of Environmental Management.

5. **Internet Activity** Visit the *CISAC Ongoing Research Projects* page of the Center for International Security and Arms Control. Choose one project related to arms control and write a brief summary of it. Link to this site from:

• www.phschool.com

Summarizing Main Ideas

Section 1   Russia

- Russia is the largest country on earth, with a variety of landscapes, mainly forest and steppe. Most of European Russia has a continental climate; Siberia is mainly subarctic.
- Russia possesses rich natural resources such as timber and oil, but its climate and great size present challenges to developing them.
- The Soviet Union was a Communist dictatorship with a centrally planned economy. Planners emphasized the development of heavy industry and agriculture, leading to shortages of consumer goods.
- Sweeping political and economic changes in the 1990s led to the collapse of the Soviet Union. As Russia builds a new political and economic structure, life has improved for some Russians but not others.

Section 2   Other Independent Republics

- The Baltic nations and Moldova have closer historic ties to Europe than to Russia.
- Europe and Russia both have influenced Ukraine and Belarus, where most people are Slavic and Eastern Orthodox.
- The Caucasus region is mountainous. It has long been home to a variety of peoples who speak unrelated languages and have different cultures.
- Most of the people of Azerbaijan and the central Asian nations are Muslims. They belong to different Turkic ethnic groups.
- Independence has brought challenges to these new nations as they try to establish new governments and economies. Ethnic and national tensions have led to violence in some places.

Reviewing Vocabulary

Select the correct term for each definition.

1. economic "restructuring" and reform (*perestroika*/*glasnost*)
2. production of goods such as steel and machinery, which are used by other industries (command economy/heavy industry)
3. deliberate destruction of an ethnic group (nationalism/genocide)
4. coniferous forest area of Northern Eurasia (taiga/yurt)
5. economic system in which a central authority decides what goods will be produced (*glasnost*/command economy)

Applying the Geographic Themes

1. **Place** How do the languages and cultures of the Baltic states set them apart from Russia?
2. **Location** How does nearness to the Black Sea affect the economies of Ukraine, Georgia, and southern Russia?
3. **Human-Environment Interaction** How did the Soviet emphasis on industrial and agricultural production affect the environment? Give a specific example.
4. **Movement** What are the special problems involved in transporting resources in Siberia?
5. **Regions** What characteristics do the nations of central Asia share?

Critical Thinking and Applying Skills

1. **Identifying Central Issues** What are the main problems Russians face in shifting from the command economy of the Soviet Union to a free-enterprise market economy? Which people are likely to make the transition most easily?
2. **Distinguishing False from Accurate Images** Many people's image of Northern Eurasia consists of a frozen landscape and Russian people bundled in fur hats and coats trying to keep warm. Explain why this image is not accurate for all of Northern Eurasia.

Journal Activity

Writing Across Cultures

▶ A culture's proverbs and sayings often reveal people's attitudes and values. Read these Russian proverbs and then explain them in your own words. Can you think of any American sayings that express the same ideas or an opposite point of view?

- At home one can even eat straw.
- Do not judge a watermelon by its rind or a man by his clothes.
- Do not buy a cat in a sack.
- Do not make an elephant out of a fly.

Find out what young people living near Chernobyl had to say about the nuclear disaster ten years after it occurred. Link to this site from:

- www.phschool.com

Read the entries, then write a paragraph telling how the accident affected these young people and their families.

Northern Eurasia

Number from 1 to 12 on a piece of paper. Next to each number write the letter of the place on the map that corresponds to the places listed below.

1. Kazakhstan
2. Azerbaijan
3. Kiev
4. Belarus
5. Moscow
6. St. Petersburg
7. Latvia
8. Uzbekistan
9. Georgia
10. Vilnius
11. Vladivostok
12. Yerevan

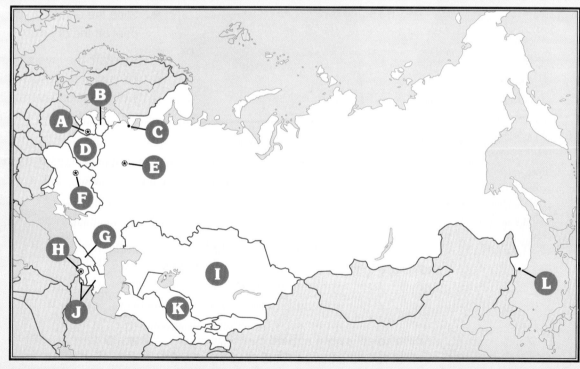

THE EFFECTS OF SALINIZATION

As you read on page 415, the Aral Sea is shrinking, causing the concentration of salt in the water to rise. The following experiment shows how changes in the concentration of salt can affect plant cells.

MATERIALS:

Measuring cup

Measuring spoons

Onion

Water

Table salt

3 Glass jars

Knife

Labels

Pen

PROCEDURE:

1. Add 4 teaspoons of salt to 8 oz (1 cup) of water in one of the jars and label the jar "high salt."

2. Add 1 teaspoon of salt to 1 cup of water in another jar and label the jar "low salt."

Steps 1 & 2

3. Add 1 cup of water to the third jar and label it "no salt."

Step 6

4. Slice the onion into quarters and peel off the dry skin.

5. Separate the layers from one of the quarters. Observe the flexibility of the onion layers. Choose 3 pieces that are similar in size and thickness.

6. Put one segment in each of the marked jars.

7. After 30 minutes, remove the piece of onion from the jar marked "no salt" and observe its flexibility. Do the same for the onions in the other jars. Return the onions to the jars.

8. After 1 hour, examine the onion pieces again and compare the flexibility of each.

9. After the pieces have soaked overnight, examine them for the final time and compare the flexibility of each.

Step 9

OBSERVATIONS AND ANALYSIS:

1. How did the flexibility of each onion layer compare after 30 minutes? 1 hour? overnight? How did the higher concentration of salt affect the flexibility of each?

2. According to your observations, how could an increased salt concentration affect the plant life in a body of water?

3. Living cells can respond to their surroundings by either absorbing or releasing water. Explain what happened to the onion cells in regard to this phenomenon.

4. How can the concentration of salt increase in a body of water? What could be done to decrease the concentration of salt in the Aral Sea?

The Death of the ARAL SEA

The Aral Sea region has been officially declared a disaster area. Thirty years of growing water-intensive crops in the desert has led to the present crisis. Water from the Syr Darya and Amu Darya rivers that is needed to replenish the Aral Sea has been diverted to irrigate cotton and rice crops. The sea has lost 60 percent of its volume, increasing the salt content to four times its natural level. The shoreline has retreated to 40 miles from where it once was. Saving the sea would require an immediate halt to all irrigation upstream, which would end cotton production.

Fishing boats left dry by the retreating Aral Sea

Satellite image showing the shrinking Aral Sea

taking *Action*

Here's how you can help conserve water:

✔ *Call your local water utility and see what devices, services, and information they offer for conserving water.*

✔ *Ask your family to buy produce from growers that employ ecologically responsible farming techniques.*

UNIT

seven

Southwest Asia

CHAPTERS

22 Regional Atlas: Southwest Asia

23 The Countries of Southwest Asia

A Global Perspective

Southwest Asia, also called the Middle East, is often described as a global intersection where three continents—Europe, Africa, and Asia—meet. For centuries, global "traffic" has passed through this intersection both picking up and leaving behind goods and ideas that have spread to the far corners of the world. The traffic continues today. This intersection has also been the site of numerous accidents, however, as empires or ideas collided. As you read this unit, watch for evidence of movement and conflict in this Southwest Asian intersection.

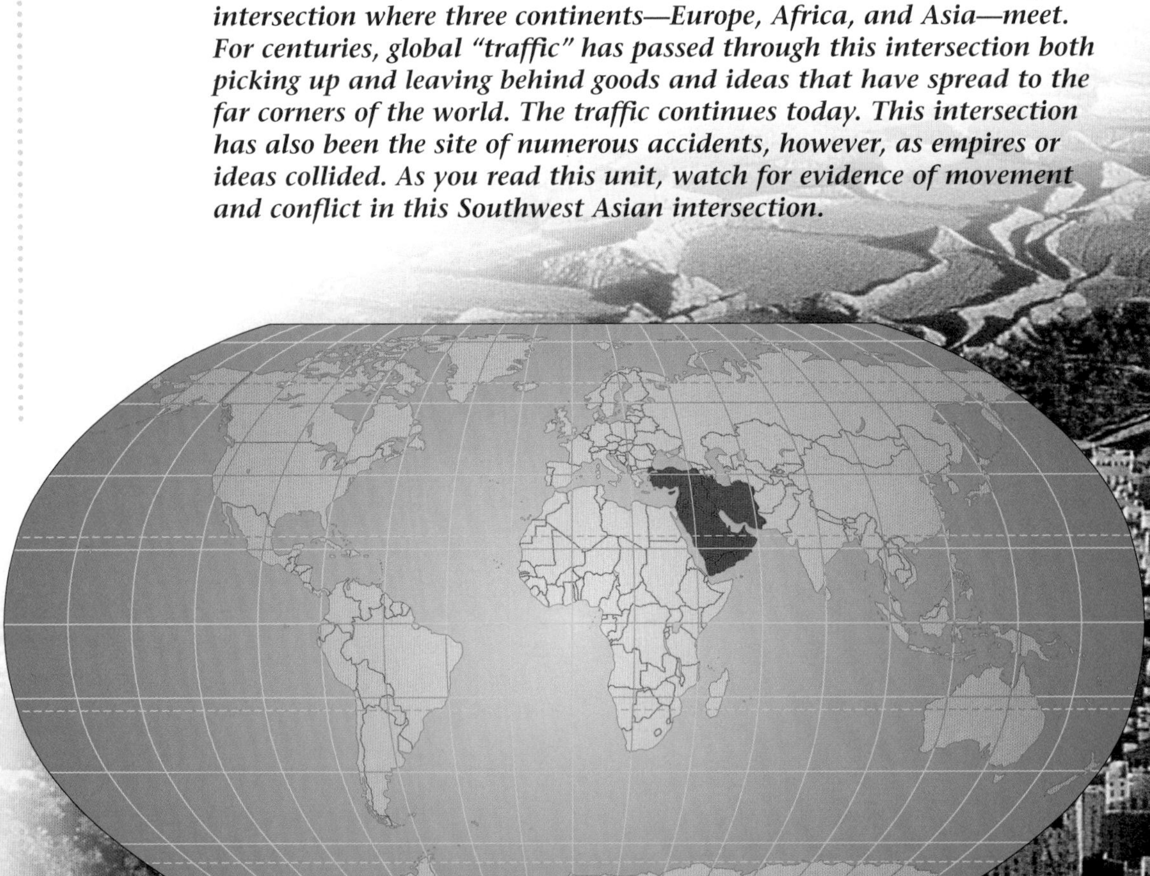

Shibam, Yemen

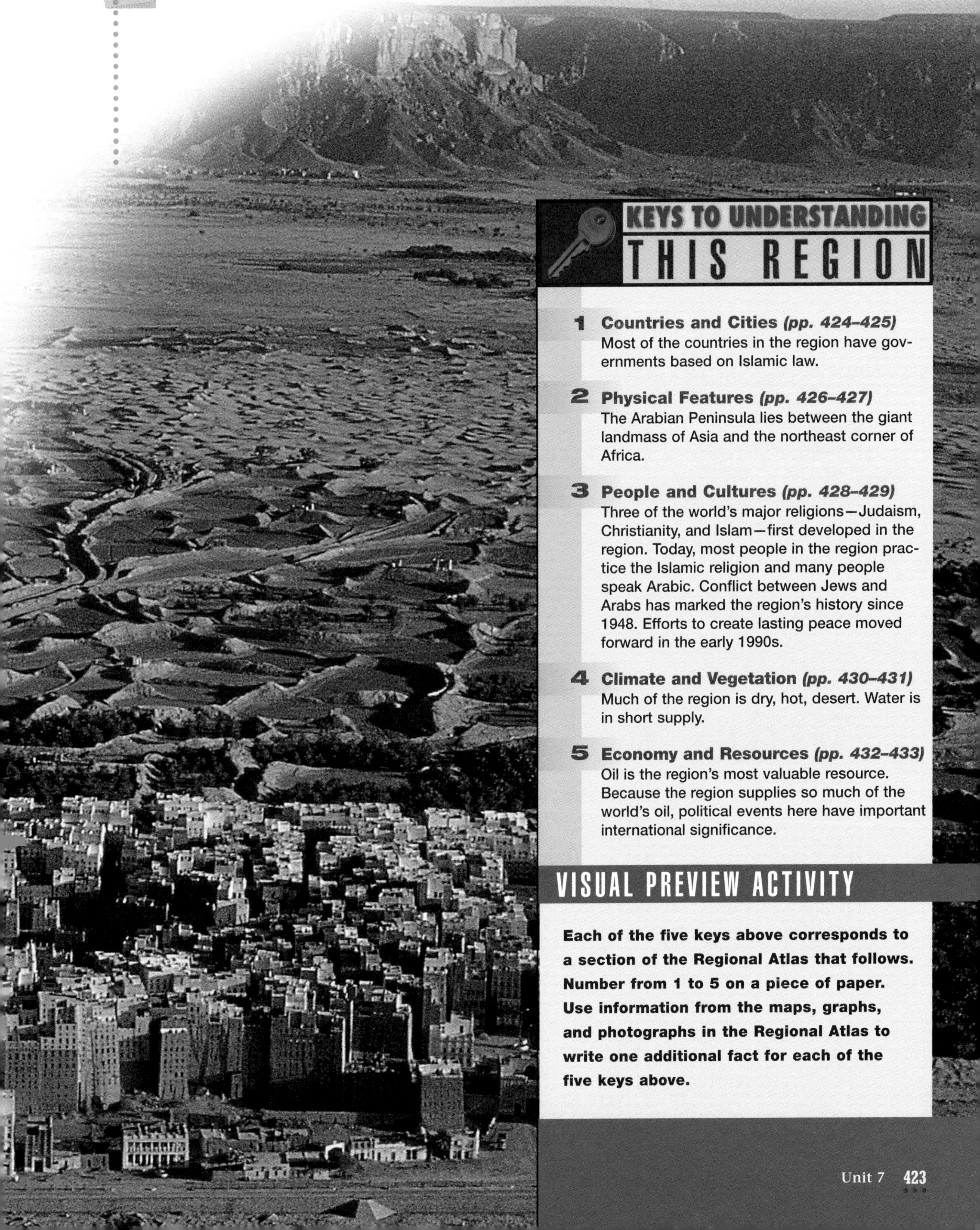

KEYS TO UNDERSTANDING
THIS REGION

1 Countries and Cities *(pp. 424–425)*
Most of the countries in the region have governments based on Islamic law.

2 Physical Features *(pp. 426–427)*
The Arabian Peninsula lies between the giant landmass of Asia and the northeast corner of Africa.

3 People and Cultures *(pp. 428–429)*
Three of the world's major religions—Judaism, Christianity, and Islam—first developed in the region. Today, most people in the region practice the Islamic religion and many people speak Arabic. Conflict between Jews and Arabs has marked the region's history since 1948. Efforts to create lasting peace moved forward in the early 1990s.

4 Climate and Vegetation *(pp. 430–431)*
Much of the region is dry, hot, desert. Water is in short supply.

5 Economy and Resources *(pp. 432–433)*
Oil is the region's most valuable resource. Because the region supplies so much of the world's oil, political events here have important international significance.

VISUAL PREVIEW ACTIVITY

Each of the five keys above corresponds to a section of the Regional Atlas that follows. Number from 1 to 5 on a piece of paper. Use information from the maps, graphs, and photographs in the Regional Atlas to write one additional fact for each of the five keys above.

Chapter 22

SOUTHWEST ASIA

Use the Map, Graph, and Photo Studies in the Regional Atlas to gain a better understanding of the region's physical and cultural geography.

ATLAS VOCABULARY

prophet	Muslim	minaret
Hajj	mosque	oasis
monotheism	muezzin	arable

1 COUNTRIES AND CITIES

LARGEST METROPOLITAN AREAS

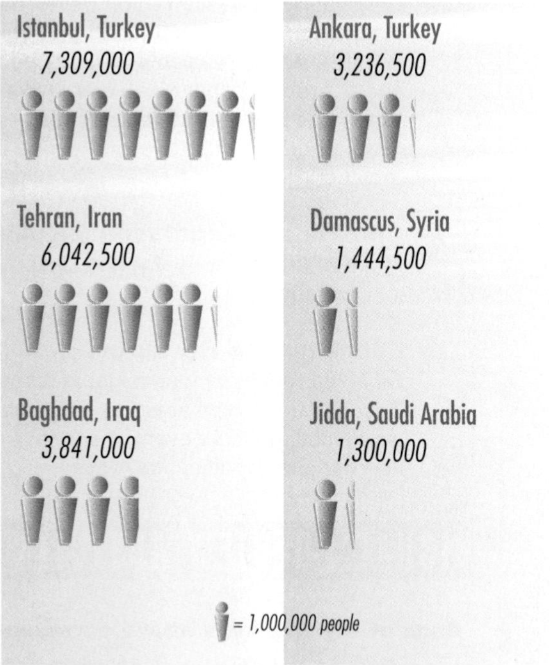

Istanbul, Turkey
7,309,000

Ankara, Turkey
3,236,500

Tehran, Iran
6,042,500

Damascus, Syria
1,444,500

Baghdad, Iraq
3,841,000

Jidda, Saudi Arabia
1,300,000

= 1,000,000 people

Source: United Nations

MAP STUDY
Applying the Geographic Themes

1 **Location** Southwest Asia, often referred to as the Middle East, is located at the far western and southern edge of the Asian continent. *Which country in the region lies farthest to the north?*

2 **Location** The first letters of the four countries that lie on the eastern end of the Mediterranean Sea are in alphabetical order from south to north. *Name the four countries.*

3 **Place** Tehran, the capital of Iran, is the second largest city in the region. *What body of water is located just north of Tehran?*

GRAPH STUDY

4 **City Living** Some of the oldest cities in the world are located in Southwest Asia. Because farmland is scarce, urban populations are growing rapidly. *Name the three largest cities in this region.*

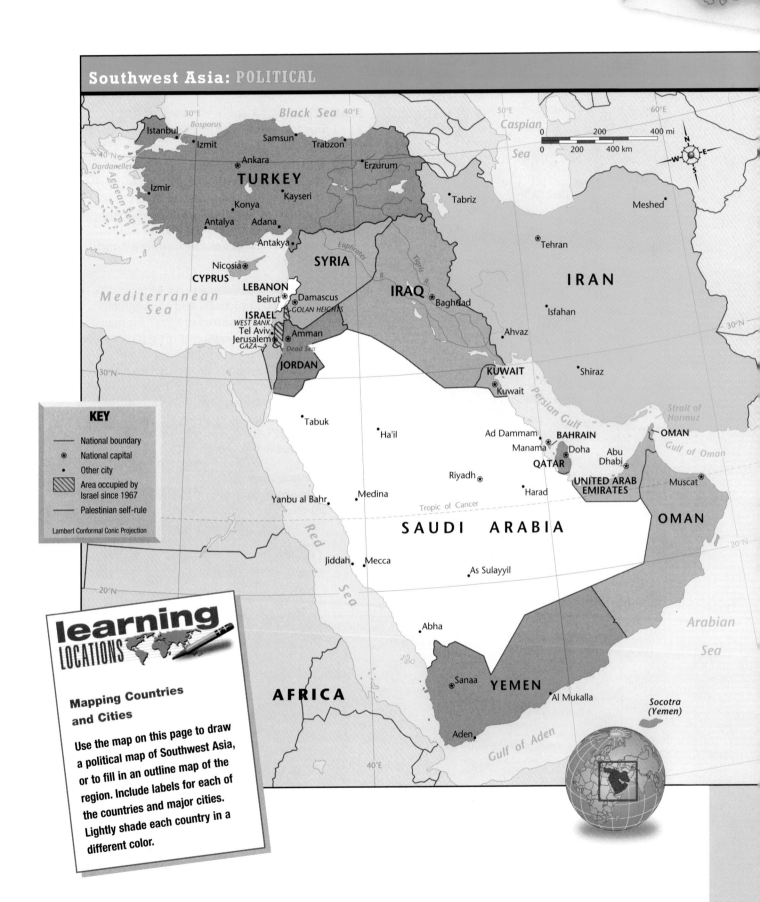

Southwest Asia: POLITICAL

KEY

— National boundary
⊛ National capital
• Other city
▨ Area occupied by Israel since 1967
— Palestinian self-rule

Lambert Conformal Conic Projection

learning LOCATIONS

Mapping Countries and Cities

Use the map on this page to draw a political map of Southwest Asia, or to fill in an outline map of the region. Include labels for each of the countries and major cities. Lightly shade each country in a different color.

Map labels:

Black Sea, Bosporus, Istanbul, Izmit, Samsun, Trabzon, Ankara, Erzurum, TURKEY, Dardanelles, Aegean Sea, Izmir, Kayseri, Konya, Antalya, Adana, Antakya, Euphrates R., Tigris R., Tabriz, Meshed, Tehran, IRAN, Nicosia, CYPRUS, SYRIA, Mediterranean Sea, LEBANON, Beirut, Damascus, GOLAN HEIGHTS, IRAQ, Baghdad, Isfahan, Ahvaz, ISRAEL, WEST BANK, Tel Aviv, Jerusalem, GAZA, Amman, Dead Sea, JORDAN, KUWAIT, Kuwait, Shiraz, Caspian Sea, Tabuk, Ha'il, Ad Dammam, BAHRAIN, Manama, OMAN, Strait of Hormuz, Doha, Abu Dhabi, Gulf of Oman, QATAR, UNITED ARAB EMIRATES, Muscat, Riyadh, Harad, Medina, Yanbu al Bahr, Tropic of Cancer, SAUDI ARABIA, OMAN, As Sulayyil, Red Sea, Jiddah, Mecca, Abha, Arabian Sea, AFRICA, Sanaa, YEMEN, Al Mukalla, Socotra (Yemen), Aden, Gulf of Aden

PHOTO STUDY

1 **The Tigris River in Iraq** Some of the world's first complex cultures and cities began along the Tigris and Euphrates rivers. *Critical Thinking Name five ways that people use rivers.*

MAP STUDY
Applying the Geographic Themes

2 **Place** Much of the land of Southwest Asia is desert. Wind shapes the landscape into great expanses of sand dunes. *Use the map on page 427 and the natural vegetation map on page 431 to name the major desert located in southern Saudi Arabia.*

3 **Human-Environment Interaction** The Tigris, Euphrates, and Jordan rivers are important sources of water for many countries in the region. Rising populations, agriculture, and industry have increased demands on limited water supplies. Countries that share these rivers compete for their water. Dams built by one country can create political conflict. *Through which countries does the Euphrates River flow?*

4 **Cause and Effect: Elevation and Climate** Mountains in the region have an effect on climate. Compare the mountainous areas on the physical map to the same areas on the climate map on page 430. *What types of climate are found in these mountainous areas?*

Cross Section: Southwest Asia

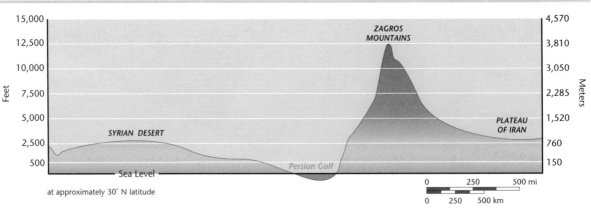

at approximately 30° N latitude

DIAGRAM STUDY

5 **Physical Profile** The highest elevations in the region are found in the Zagros Mountains of Iran. *How high are these mountains?*

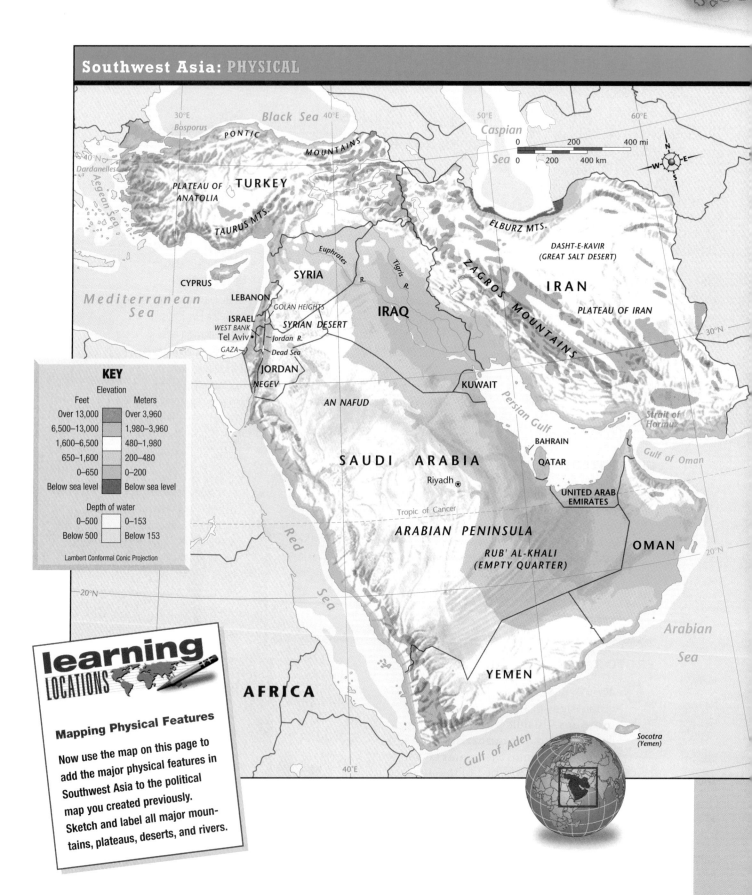

REGIONAL *atlas*

Southwest Asia: PHYSICAL

Black Sea

Caspian Sea

PONTIC MOUNTAINS

Bosporus

30°E   40°E   50°E   60°E

40°N

Dardanelles

Aegean Sea

PLATEAU OF ANATOLIA

TURKEY

TAURUS MTS.

ELBURZ MTS.

DASHT-E-KAVIR
(GREAT SALT DESERT)

IRAN

CYPRUS

Euphrates R.

SYRIA

Tigris R.

ZAGROS MOUNTAINS

PLATEAU OF IRAN

Mediterranean Sea

LEBANON

GOLAN HEIGHTS

IRAQ

ISRAEL

WEST BANK

Tel Aviv

SYRIAN DESERT

Jordan R.

GAZA

Dead Sea

JORDAN

NEGEV

30°N

KUWAIT

Persian Gulf

Strait of Hormuz

AN NAFUD

BAHRAIN

Gulf of Oman

KEY

Elevation

Feet	Meters
Over 13,000	Over 3,960
6,500–13,000	1,980–3,960
1,600–6,500	480–1,980
650–1,600	200–480
0–650	0–200
Below sea level	Below sea level

Depth of water

0–500	0–153
Below 500	Below 153

Lambert Conformal Conic Projection

SAUDI ARABIA

QATAR

Riyadh

UNITED ARAB EMIRATES

Tropic of Cancer

ARABIAN PENINSULA

OMAN

20°N

Red Sea

RUB' AL-KHALI
(EMPTY QUARTER)

Arabian Sea

20°N

YEMEN

Socotra
(Yemen)

AFRICA

Gulf of Aden

40°E

0   200   400 mi
0   200   400 km

learning LOCATIONS

Mapping Physical Features

Now use the map on this page to add the major physical features in Southwest Asia to the political map you created previously. Sketch and label all major mountains, plateaus, deserts, and rivers.

THE BIRTHPLACE OF THREE MAJOR RELIGIONS

Judaism

- Judaism first developed around 1000 B.C. along the eastern shore of the Mediterranean Sea. It was the religion of the Hebrews.

  - Five holy books, together known as the Torah, record the early history of the Hebrews and their religion.

  - A large temple located in the city of Jerusalem served as a religious center. The site of this temple is sacred to Jews.

Christianity

- Christianity first developed around A.D. 30 along the eastern shore of the Mediterranean. It is based on the teachings of Jesus, who Christians believe to be the son of God. Jesus was tried and crucified—put to death on a cross—in Jerusalem.

- The Christian Bible consists of the Old Testament (the Torah of Judaism) and the New Testament, which includes four gospels, or accounts, of Jesus' life.

Islam

- Islam first developed around A.D. 600 in Arabia. It is based on the teachings of the **prophet** Muhammad. A prophet is a person whose teachings are believed to be revealed by God.

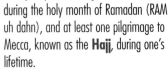

- The Five Pillars of Islam are described in the Koran, the Muslim holy book. The Five Pillars include stating a belief in one God, performing daily prayers, giving to charity, daytime fasting during the holy month of Ramadan (RAM uh dahn), and at least one pilgrimage to Mecca, known as the **Hajj**, during one's lifetime.

CHART STUDY

1 **Regions** Judaism, Christianity, and Islam are all monotheistic religions. **Monotheism** is a belief in one God. Most people in Southwest Asia today are **Muslims**—followers of Islam—and many speak Arabic. *In which part of the region did each religion develop?*

PHOTO STUDY

2 **Muslim Mosque** Some of the most visible signs of Islamic culture are the **mosques**—Islamic places of worship. Five times a day, a **muezzin** (MYU ez in), or crier, climbs the **minaret**, the tall, thin tower attached to the mosque, to call the people to prayer. *Connections: Art Think of three adjectives that describe the Islamic style of architecture pictured here.*

SOUTHWEST ASIA

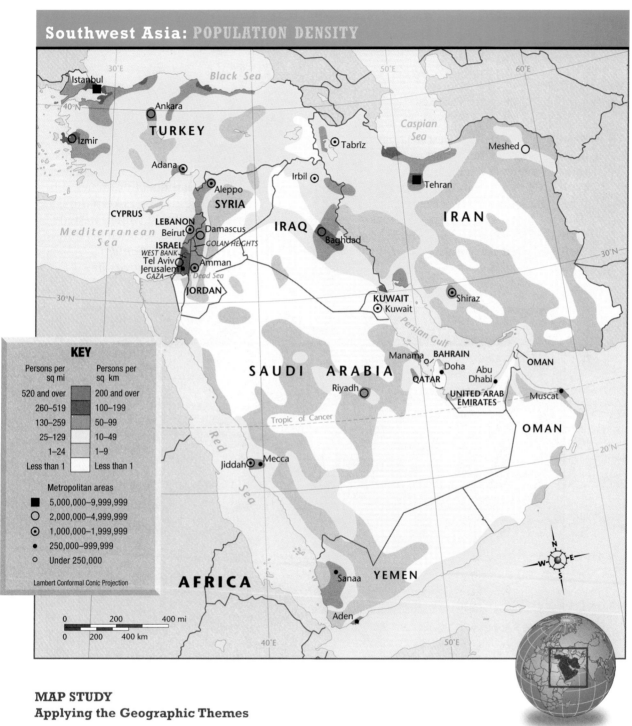

Southwest Asia: POPULATION DENSITY

KEY

Persons per sq mi	Persons per sq km
520 and over	200 and over
260–519	100–199
130–259	50–99
25–129	10–49
1–24	1–9
Less than 1	Less than 1

Metropolitan areas

■ 5,000,000–9,999,999
○ 2,000,000–4,999,999
◉ 1,000,000–1,999,999
● 250,000–999,999
○ Under 250,000

Lambert Conformal Conic Projection

0   200   400 mi
0   200   400 km

MAP STUDY
Applying the Geographic Themes

3 **Regions** Most of the people in Southwest Asia live near rivers, along coasts, in the mountains and plateaus, and at oases. *Which part of the region is largely uninhabited?*

4 **Place** People in Southwest Asia also tend to live in areas where the climate is relatively cool. Compare the climate map on page 430 with the map above. *Which area is most densely populated?*

S O U T H W E S T   A S I A

MAP STUDY
Applying the Geographic Themes

1 **Place** Much of Southwest Asia has an arid or semiarid climate and receives less than 10 inches (25 cm) of rain per year. With little moisture in the air, few clouds form. The sun's hot rays beat directly onto the land, raising temperatures as high as 125°F (52°C). *Connections: Math Estimate what percentage of Southwest Asia has an arid climate.*

2 **Location** Mediterranean climates are located on the west coast of continents and along the Mediterranean Sea between 30°N and 40°N latitude. In summer, subtropical high pressure areas keep the sky clear with little rain. In winter, westerly winds bring rain and keep temperatures mild. *Describe the location of Mediterranean climate areas in Southwest Asia.*

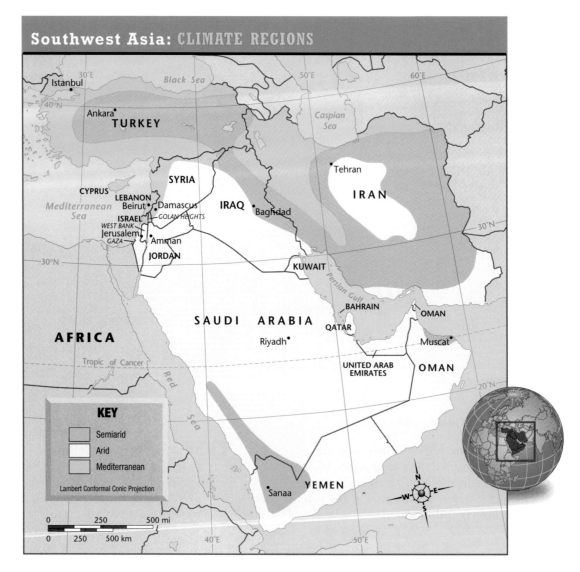

Southwest Asia: CLIMATE REGIONS

KEY
- Semiarid
- Arid
- Mediterranean

Lambert Conformal Conic Projection

0   250   500 mi
0   250   500 km

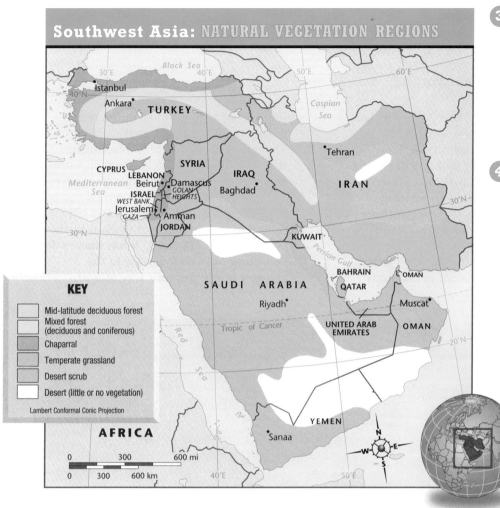

Southwest Asia: NATURAL VEGETATION REGIONS

KEY

- Mid-latitude deciduous forest
- Mixed forest (deciduous and coniferous)
- Chaparral
- Temperate grassland
- Desert scrub
- Desert (little or no vegetation)

Lambert Conformal Conic Projection

Black Sea
Istanbul
Ankara
TURKEY
Caspian Sea
CYPRUS
LEBANON
SYRIA
Beirut
Damascus
GOLAN HEIGHTS
IRAQ
Baghdad
Tehran
IRAN
Mediterranean Sea
ISRAEL
WEST BANK
Jerusalem
GAZA
Amman
JORDAN
KUWAIT
Persian Gulf
BAHRAIN
QATAR
OMAN
SAUDI ARABIA
Riyadh
Muscat
Red Sea
Tropic of Cancer
UNITED ARAB EMIRATES
OMAN
AFRICA
YEMEN
Sanaa

0   300   600 mi
0   300   600 km

③ Regions This region is dominated by desert. Most of the land sustains only sparse vegetation. *Which countries have large areas of desert and desert scrub vegetation?*

④ Cause and Effect: Climate and Vegetation Limited precipitation and high temperatures make it difficult for plants to survive in much of this region. *What is the predominant vegetation in arid and semiarid regions on the climate map?*

APPEARED IN *NATIONAL GEOGRAPHIC*

PHOTO STUDY

⑤ A Desert Oasis in Saudi Arabia In a few places, deep underground springs force their way up to the surface creating **oases** or places where a supply of fresh water makes it possible to support life in a dry region. In some places, people have created their own oases by digging deep wells. *Critical Thinking* **What do oases offer in addition to water?**

MAP STUDY
Applying the Geographic Themes

1 **Human-Environment Interaction**
Only a small percentage of the region is made up of **arable** land, that is, land that can be farmed. By building dams and irrigation systems, farmers have created additional farmland. *Besides farming, name three economic activities that are common throughout Southwest Asia.*

2 **Movement** For centuries, small groups of nomadic herders known as Bedouins

(BED uh wins) have lived in the region's deserts herding camels, goats, and sheep. They moved from place to place using their knowledge of the location of water and seasonal weather changes to survive. Today many Bedouins have settled on the outskirts of villages and cities and sell their livestock products at markets in the cities. *Critical Thinking What factors do you think have contributed to the changes in the Bedouin way of life?*

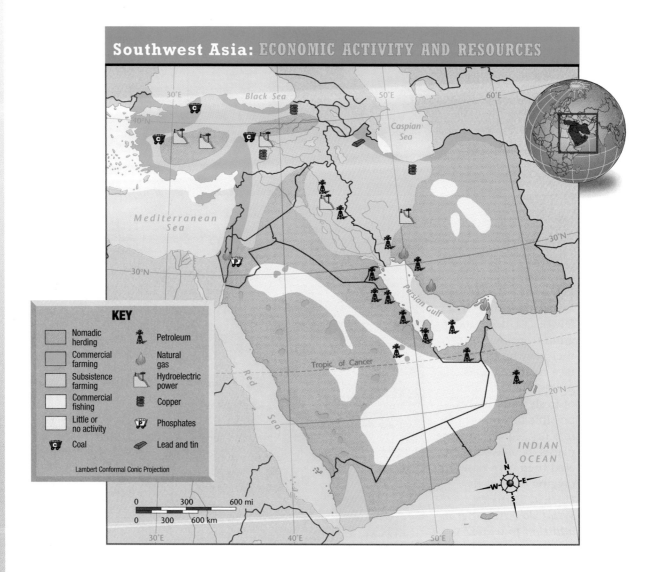

Southwest Asia: ECONOMIC ACTIVITY AND RESOURCES

KEY

- Nomadic herding
- Commercial farming
- Subsistence farming
- Commercial fishing
- Little or no activity
- **C** Coal
- Petroleum
- Natural gas
- Hydroelectric power
- Copper
- Phosphates
- Lead and tin

Lambert Conformal Conic Projection

0   300   600 mi
0   300   600 km

SOUTHWEST ASIA

Oil from the Persian Gulf

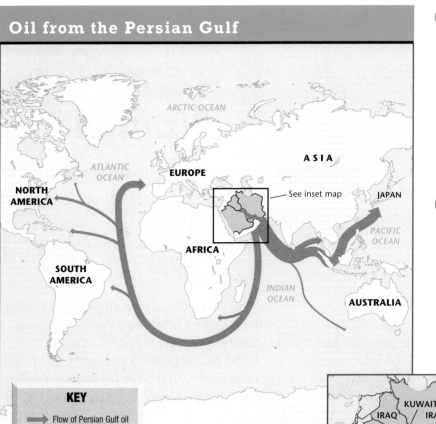

KEY

→ Flow of Persian Gulf oil

Width of arrow denotes volume of oil

Miller Cylindrical Projection

ARCTIC OCEAN

ATLANTIC OCEAN

NORTH AMERICA

EUROPE

ASIA

See inset map

JAPAN

PACIFIC OCEAN

AFRICA

SOUTH AMERICA

INDIAN OCEAN

AUSTRALIA

ANTARCTICA

KUWAIT
IRAQ IRAN
Persian Gulf
SAUDI ARABIA
BAHRAIN
QATAR
Strait of Hormuz
UNITED ARAB EMIRATES

③ Movement Much of the world's oil passes through the Persian Gulf and the Strait of Hormuz via tanker ship. *Find these strategic waterways on the map and name the countries that border them.*

④ Regions A great percentage of the world's oil comes from Southwest Asia. *Which two areas of the world import large amounts of oil from Southwest Asia?*

atlas REVIEW

Vocabulary and Main Ideas

1. Define: a. prophet b. Hajj c. monotheism d. Muslim e. mosque f. muezzin g. minaret h. oasis i. arable

2. Name three sources of water in Southwest Asia.

3. What is the predominant religion practiced in Southwest Asia?

4. Critical Thinking: *Cause and Effect* Why do temperatures get so high in Southwest Asia?

learning LOCATIONS

5. What country is located east of Iraq?

6. Name the island country south of Turkey.

SOUTHWEST ASIA

The Birth of Civilization

When people in ancient times began to build permanent settlements, they chose places with special characteristics. How did the locations of the first cities help early civilizations grow?

Cities and Civilization

For much of early human history, people were nomads. They wandered, hunting animals and gathering wild foods. About 10,000 years ago, some groups settled in villages. They tamed, or domesticated, wild plants and animals for their own use. They planted farm crops. These changes set the stage for a huge step forward for humankind: the growth of cities and civilization.

Cities and civilization go together. As cities began to grow, so did other human accomplishments. Artisans in the cities learned specialized

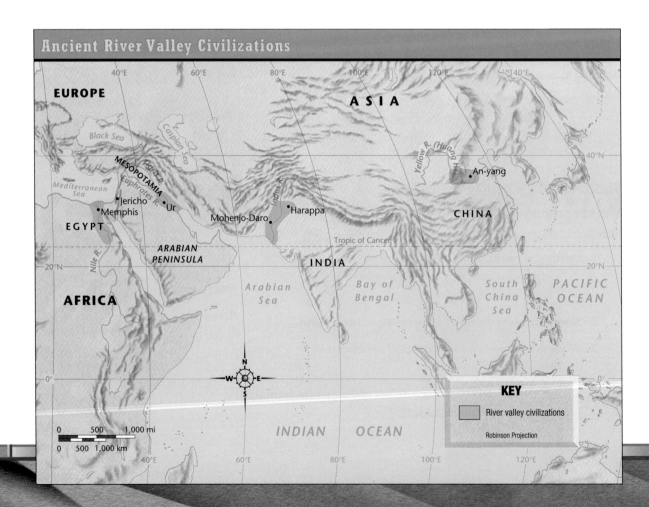

Ancient River Valley Civilizations

KEY

River valley civilizations

Robinson Projection

trades and crafts and developed new technologies. Some invented symbols for writing and keeping records. Trade increased. Systems of government and religions developed. Many early rulers were also the chief priests and were thought of as gods.

River Valley Civilizations

As the map shows, the first four great ancient civilizations began in Asia and northern Africa. Their cultures differed, but they were alike in one vital way: they were all in river valleys.

The earliest civilization grew up about 5,000 years ago in Southwest Asia, between the Tigris and Euphrates rivers (modern Iraq). This area was called Mesopotamia, which means "land between the rivers." Two other early civilizations were also in Asia. A city civilization developed about 4,500 years ago near the Indus River in South Asia, in what is now Pakistan. About 500 years later, another grew up along the Huang He (Yellow River) in northeastern China. The Nile River in Egypt was the site of the fourth great ancient culture.

Chinese jar, c. 3000 B.C.

Living by the River

Rivers were important in several ways to the growth of cities. Practically speaking, a river provided fresh water for humans, their domestic animals, and their crops. People could store river water for use in dry seasons. Some rivers flooded regularly, leaving behind silt that enriched the land. Travel by boat was quicker and easier than travel overland, encouraging trade.

Historians have suggested other ways in which a riverside location helped civilization grow. As people worked together to control floods and build irrigation systems, some people emerged as strong leaders. They knew how to organize others and get them to work on major public projects. People developed systems of government and religion, too. With many people living close together, they needed laws and belief systems that outlined rules for behavior.

Modern Cities Follow the Pattern

In later centuries, people continued to build cities near rivers. As trade and commerce became more important, river transportation was essential. Many of the historic cities of Europe and Asia, including London, Paris, Rome, Calcutta, and Bangkok, are located on major rivers.

European settlers in the Americas also depended on rivers. Rivers were the highways that let them travel into the thickly forested interior of North America. Philadelphia, Montreal, and St. Louis are just a few of the cities that grew up at strategic locations on rivers.

connecting
TO TODAY

1. **Where were the four earliest civilizations?**

2. **What were some of the changes that marked the development of civilization in the first cities?**

3. **Critical Thinking** Explain this statement: "Cities and civilization go together."

4. **Hands-On Activity** Imagine that you are the public relations director of an ancient city (real or imaginary). Write and illustrate a short pamphlet explaining the advantages your city has for new residents and businesses.

23

The Countries of Southwest Asia

Southwest Asia: POLITICAL

KEY

— National boundary

⊛ National capital

• Other city

▨ Area occupied by Israel since 1967

— Palestinian self-rule

Lambert Conformal Conic Projection

0   300   600 mi
0   300   600 km

TURKEY — Ankara, Istanbul
CYPRUS
Mediterranean Sea
SYRIA — Damascus
LEBANON — Beirut
ISRAEL — Tel Aviv, Jerusalem
JORDAN — Amman
IRAQ — Baghdad
IRAN — Tehran
KUWAIT — Kuwait
Persian Gulf
BAHRAIN — Manama
QATAR — Doha
Riyadh
SAUDI ARABIA
UNITED ARAB EMIRATES — Abu Dhabi
OMAN — Muscat
Strait of Hormuz
Gulf of Oman
Arabian Sea
Tropic of Cancer
INDIAN OCEAN
Caspian Sea
Mecca
Red Sea
AFRICA
YEMEN — Sanaa
Aden
Gulf of Aden
Socotra (Yemen)

learning LOCATIONS

Mapping the Region

Create a map like the one above, lightly shading each country a different color. Then add the labels for countries and bodies of water that are shown on this map.

Creating the Modern Middle East

The city of Jerusalem is sacred to Muslims, Christians, and Jews.

Section Preview

Main Ideas

- Many ethnic and religious groups in the Middle East demanded political independence when the Ottoman Empire fell.

- World War I greatly influenced the modern history of the Middle East.

- The 1948 war between Israel and the Arab countries left the Palestinians without a homeland.

Vocabulary

mandate, Zionist, self-determination

The Middle East has a long and turbulent history. More than three thousand years ago, the region's great wealth and location at the center of trading routes between Europe, Africa, and Asia made it an important source of power. This area was repeatedly conquered by groups from within and without. The movement of conquering peoples across the Middle East gave the region a unique character. It became a tangle of diverse ethnic groups and religious beliefs.

Uniting Peoples

When the followers of Muhammad swept out of the Arabian Peninsula into the ancient lands of Mesopotamia, Palestine, and Persia in the mid-600s, they encountered a mosaic of cultures. Most of the conquered people adopted the Islamic religion and the Arabic language. Others, mainly Christians and Jews, continued to practice their religions. The Persians, Kurds, and Armenians maintained their own strong cultural identities.

For over 150 years Islam was successful in governing these different peoples as one political region. But beginning in the tenth century, the Arabs could no longer control their huge empire in the Middle East. Within a short time, large numbers of Turks, led by the Seljuks (SEL jooks), conquered almost all of the Middle East. They adopted the Islamic religion and ruled the Middle East for more than four hundred years before losing control to the region's last great empire builders—the Ottoman Turks.

Under the Ottomans, the people of the region continued to practice their religions. The Ottomans did not impose Islamic law on non-Muslims. Christians and Jews were allowed to govern important aspects of their lives, such as marriage and death, according to their beliefs.

Beginning in the late 1700s, discontent and rivalry developed among the different ethnic and religious groups under Ottoman control. Many of these groups were eager to establish independent homelands. The Ottoman

◄ **Muslims at prayer in Mecca** *(photo left)*

A Mighty Islamic Empire

● **Movement** The map at right shows the Islamic Empire at its height around A.D. 750. Arabs brought their technological achievements to the lands they conquered. Pictured above is an elaborate, water-powered clock described in *The Book of Knowledge of Ingenious Mechanical Devices*, written in 1206. *What other aspects of their culture did the Arabs bring to their empire?*

leadership was no longer powerful enough to hold its empire together.

At the same time, European nations were eager to exert political influence in the Middle East and gain new markets for their products. By the mid-1800s, the Ottoman Empire was being called "the sick man of Europe." And Great Britain, France, and Russia were waiting for it to die.

World War I

In 1914 World War I broke out. Great Britain, France, and Russia, known as the Allies, were on one side. On the other side were Germany and Austria-Hungary, known as the Central Powers. The Ottoman Empire joined in alliance with the Central Powers. Although World War I was fought mainly in Europe, it greatly affected the course of modern Middle Eastern history.

Secret Negotiations Soon after the war started, the Allies began secret negotiations to decide how to divide the Ottoman Empire when it was defeated. They agreed that, except for the Arabian Peninsula, each of them would control different parts of the empire. The Arabs on the Arabian Peninsula would be given their independence when the war ended. Great Britain, eager to exert its power in the area, entered into other, separate agreements as well.

In 1915, Sir Henry McMahon, a representative of the British government, began to correspond with Husayn ibn 'Ali. Husayn was the Arab ruler of the sacred cities of Mecca and Medina on the Arabian Peninsula. He was an important leader among the Muslim Arabs who wanted to break away from the Ottoman Empire and establish an independent Arab homeland. In his letters, McMahon hoped to convince the Arabs to support Great Britain in its fight against the Ottomans. Letters discussing possible arrangements went back and forth between the two men for almost a year.

Finally, Husayn agreed to revolt against the Ottomans in exchange for British support of a homeland for all Arabs, including Christians. From the letters that had passed between him and McMahon, Husayn believed that almost all of the area from southern Turkey to southern Arabia, and from the Mediterranean Sea east to the borders of Iran would be one vast Arab country.

A Broken Promise Unknown to Husayn, however, Great Britain and France were secretly working out another agreement for dividing the Ottoman Empire. This agreement, known as the Sykes-Picot Agreement, limited the independent Arab state to the area that is now Saudi Arabia and Yemen. It gave the French control of Syria and allotted Palestine and Iraq to Great Britain. When the Arabs discovered this, they felt Great Britain had broken its promise to them.

At the peace conference following the Allies' victory, the once-great empire of the Ottomans was reduced to a single independent country—Turkey. The Arab state the British promised to Husayn was limited to the area that is now Saudi Arabia and Yemen. France and Great Britain divided the rest of the Ottoman Empire between them. France took Syria—including the area that would become the country of Lebanon—as a mandate. A **mandate** referred to land to be governed on behalf of the League of Nations until it was ready for independence. Great Britain was given Palestine, Trans-Jordan, and Iraq as mandates.

Arabs and Jews

By the mid-1940s, Iraq, Jordan, Syria, and Lebanon had been established as independent countries. The political future of what remained of Palestine after the creation of Jordan was still to be decided, however.

The issue of independence for Palestine created a dilemma for Great Britain. Two groups claimed Palestine as their homeland—the Arabs and the Jews. The Arabs had lived for centuries in Palestine. Many of them traced their ancestry back to the area's earliest settlers. But the Jews also had ancient historical ties to Palestine. Their ancestors had migrated to this region beginning around 1900 B.C. to 1700 B.C. By 1000 B.C. these people were known as the Hebrews. The Hebrews established a kingdom, which later split into two kingdoms and then was defeated in a succession of military conquests. After their

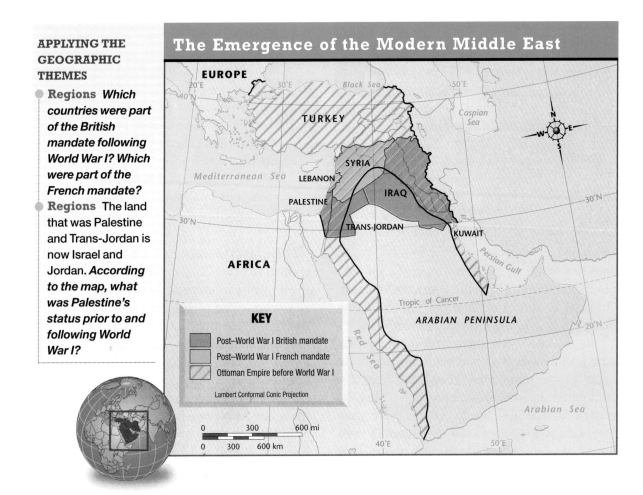

APPLYING THE GEOGRAPHIC THEMES

- **Regions** *Which countries were part of the British mandate following World War I? Which were part of the French mandate?*
- **Regions** The land that was Palestine and Trans-Jordan is now Israel and Jordan. *According to the map, what was Palestine's status prior to and following World War I?*

The Emergence of the Modern Middle East

KEY

- Post–World War I British mandate
- Post–World War I French mandate
- Ottoman Empire before World War I

Lambert Conformal Conic Projection

0   300   600 mi

0   300   600 km

began to emigrate. Some called themselves **Zionists**, after the hill in Jerusalem to which Jews had always prayed to return. They believed that the only way to solve the problem of oppression was by returning to the place they considered their homeland—Palestine—and creating their own country.

In 1882 the first group of Zionists immigrated to Palestine. Their numbers had reached almost 85,000 by 1914. As Jewish immigration increased, the Arabs who were living in Palestine under Ottoman rule grew more and more fearful of losing their land.

Two Peoples, One Homeland The Zionists put increasing pressure on Great Britain and other European nations to support their plan for an independent homeland. In 1917, in the midst of World War I, the British government issued the Balfour Declaration. It stated Britain's support for the creation of a Jewish national home in Palestine without violating the rights of Arabs living there:

> *His Majesty's Government view with favour the establishment in Palestine of a national home for the Jewish people, and will use their best endeavours to facilitate the achievement of this object, it being clearly understood that nothing shall be done which may prejudice the civil and religious rights of existing non-Jewish communities in Palestine, or the rights and political status enjoyed by Jews in any other country.*

The Arabs were shocked and dismayed by the content of the declaration. They had been led by the British to believe that all Arabs would be granted the right of **self-determination**, or the right to decide their own political future. They believed that Palestine would become part of a larger, independent Arab country. The British sent representatives to Arab leaders to assure them that Great Britain's goal was still self-determination for the Arabs. As both groups pressured Great Britain to fulfill its promises to them, it became clear that the goals of Jews and Arabs were at odds.

Independence Day

Place The creation of Israel was a joyous moment for many people. *How did the creation of a Jewish national homeland in Palestine conflict with Arab self-determination?*

defeat and exile by the Babylonians in 586 B.C., however, the Jews began to move to other lands. Over the centuries most Jews settled in other places, although some remained in Palestine.

By the late 1800s, there were about ten million Jews scattered throughout the world. In many of the places they lived, they were discriminated against and cruelly persecuted. In eastern Europe and Russia, where more than half of the world's Jews lived, they faced increasing oppression. Afraid of what lay ahead, Jews

Arab-Israeli Conflict

Movement Troops from Jordan, shown here patrolling the Palestinian border, and other Arab Legion nations attacked the newly created nation of Israel in 1948. *What was the outcome of this Arab-Israeli war?*

While Britain searched for a way to solve the problem, the struggle between Jews and Arabs in Palestine became increasingly violent. As Jewish immigration grew, so did Arab feelings that their political future as an independent Arab country was threatened. Finally, the Arabs revolted by boycotting Jewish businesses and burning bridges and crops. The Jews retaliated. People on both sides were killed.

Meanwhile, Hitler came to power in Germany in 1933. As Nazi Germany began to persecute Jews, thousands fled to Palestine. By 1939, the number of Jews living in Palestine had increased from 85,000 to 445,000.

Tensions between Great Britain, the Palestinians, and the Jews mounted. Great Britain decided to limit Jewish immigration to the area, leaving Jews stranded in Germany and other parts of Europe. The Jews in Palestine began a campaign of guerrilla warfare against the British.

The Creation of Israel Nearly six million Jews had perished in Nazi concentration camps by the time World War II ended in 1945. Thousands of survivors had no place to go. When the world learned of the Holocaust, there was an outpouring of support for a Jewish homeland in Palestine.

However, the Arabs made up 70 percent of Palestine's population. They were bitterly opposed to the creation of a Jewish state in Palestine. Why, they wondered, should they give up their land because of what the Nazis had done?

In 1947, realizing it had no hope of finding an acceptable solution, the British government announced that it was withdrawing from Palestine and turning the problem over to the United Nations. Immediately the United Nations formed a special committee to find a solution to the problem. After months of debate, the committee recommended that Palestine be partitioned into two states—one Arab and one Jewish. The city of Jerusalem, sacred to Jews, Christians, and Muslims would be designated an international city.

The Jews accepted the United Nations plan. However, the Arabs were furious. According to the plan, the

GLOBAL issues

Conflict

Many of the world's regional conflicts are related to geographic boundaries and disputes over territory. The Golan Heights, the West Bank, and Gaza, shown on the map on page 444, are all examples of such disputed territories.

Road to Recovery

Movement These Palestinian refugees, left homeless in 1948, are building a road through their settlement in Jordan. **Critical Thinking** *What is the importance of having a road?*

Jewish state would include more than half the total land of Palestine, though less than one third of the population was Jewish.

Arab leaders warned that dividing Palestine would result in war. One Arab leader stated, "We Arabs shall not be losers. We shall be fighting on our ground and shall be supported . . . by 70 million Arabs around us."

Nevertheless, the United Nations voted to approve the partition of Palestine. In May 1948, David Ben-Gurion, leader of the Palestinian Jews, announced the independent, new state of Israel. In a matter of hours, neighboring Arab countries attacked Israel. By the end of the 1948 war, Israel controlled almost three fourths of Palestine, including land in the Negev Desert and half of Jerusalem. Jordan and Egypt divided the rest of Palestine between them. The Palestinians were left with no country at all.

Section 1 Review

Vocabulary and Main Ideas

1. Define: a. mandate b. Zionist c. self-determination

2. What effect did World War I have on the Middle East?

3. What was the Balfour Declaration?

4. Critical Thinking: *Demonstrating Reasoned Judgment* Why do you think the Arab nations were opposed to the creation of the nation of Israel?

learning LOCATIONS

5. Name five countries in Southwest Asia that border the Mediterranean Sea.

6. Name six Southwest Asian countries that share a border with Iraq.

2 Israel: A Determined Country

Section Preview

Main Ideas

- Israel has turned swamps and desert into productive land.

- Israel is a leader in high technology.

- Many different cultural, ethnic, and religious groups give Israel diversity.

- Israel has taken steps to achieve peace with its Arab neighbors.

Vocabulary

drip irrigation, Knesset

In a kibbutz, or collective community, all property is shared.

There was nothing but desert and swamp; they had to clear it and build. . . . They never stopped to say, "Should we clear a potato patch here, . . . or raise sheep over there?" . . . No, our founders said with breathtaking simplicity: "Let there be a potato patch. . . . Anywhere, everywhere, and right away." We do not say, "Let there be a potato patch, and scratch it into the nearest soil." We must say, "Should there be a potato patch? And, if so, where is the best place to put it? . . . How much irrigation will it need? . . . Or do we need more cotton, more tools, or is there a more nutrient, efficient food than potatoes?"

Gideon Samet, a young Israeli journalist, used these words to describe the changing character of Israel. Today Israel is a very different place from when its founders first cleared, irrigated, and farmed the land. Its landscape is different. Its diverse economy is different. Even the character of its people has changed. Since gaining independence, Israel has raced along a path of urgent development to become one of the most technologically advanced countries in the world.

Changing the Land

When the first Zionist settlers arrived in Palestine, people were already living along the fertile coastal plains and in the rich valleys of the highland regions. Much of the land available to the immigrants was either mosquito-infested swamp or barren stretches of desert. In the 1880s settlers began the long, slow process of reclaiming the land. Acre by acre they drained the swamps. Patiently they coaxed water into the desert.

Since 1948, when Israel became independent, the Israeli government has viewed the desert as one of the main challenges to its existence. David Ben-Gurion, Israel's first prime minister, said, "If the state does not put an end to the desert, the desert is likely to put an end to the state." Then and now, an important part of Israel's national policy has been directed at turning the unwelcoming desert into productive land that can be used for agriculture, industry, and settlement.

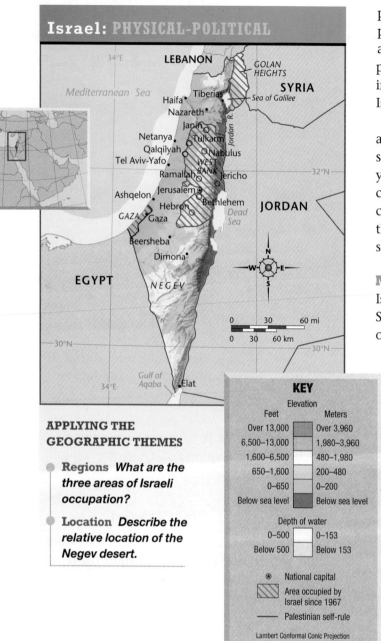

Israel: PHYSICAL-POLITICAL

APPLYING THE GEOGRAPHIC THEMES

- **Regions** *What are the three areas of Israeli occupation?*

- **Location** *Describe the relative location of the Negev desert.*

KEY

Elevation		
Feet		Meters
Over 13,000		Over 3,960
6,500–13,000		1,980–3,960
1,600–6,500		480–1,980
650–1,600		200–480
0–650		0–200
Below sea level		Below sea level

Depth of water		
0–500		0–153
Below 500		Below 153

⊛ National capital

▨ Area occupied by Israel since 1967

— Palestinian self-rule

Lambert Conformal Conic Projection

---

process called **drip irrigation** preserves precious water resources by letting precise amounts of water drip onto plants from pipes. Agricultural production in Israel has increased greatly in the last forty years. Today Israel produces almost all of its own food.

However, Israel's agricultural success has a price. Increased demands for water have severely taxed limited supplies. In recent years, the government has been forced to cut the use of water for irrigation by 30 percent in some places. Like other countries in the region, Israel could face a serious water shortage in the near future.

Mining the Dead Sea Between Israel and Jordan lies the Dead Sea. The Dead Sea is actually a huge saltwater lake. Because of the quantity of minerals in the sea, fish or other animals cannot live in it. Even the surrounding land is a dry, lifeless wilderness. The Israelis have built processing plants to extract potash—which is used in explosives and fertilizer—table salt, bromine, and other minerals from the Dead Sea. Israel exports these minerals worldwide.

Encouraging Movement to the Desert Despite the Israeli government's drive to develop the Negev and other desert areas, it was difficult to attract people to these places to work. Few people wanted to live and raise families away from the conveniences of modern life and in such an isolated area. New towns, such as Arad, had to be built. Workers had to be offered high pay and extra time off.

Still, feelings about living in the desert are mixed. One Israeli couple, Zvi and Rebecca Rubin, had differing views about their life in Arad.

> *I [Zvi] came to Arad because I was offered a high salary, a good flat, and low taxes. . . . This is a good place to live, work, and put money aside. . . . For him [Zvi] it is a good place to work and live. For me [Rebecca] it is the desert. . . . I wish he could find a job back in Haifa.*

Technology Transforms the Desert

The Negev Desert is Israel's driest region. It covers over half of the country. Here the Israelis have built a system of pipelines, canals, and tunnels almost 100 miles (160 km) long called the National Water Carrier. Water from the Sea of Galilee is pumped southward through the system to irrigate parts of the Negev. A region that was once barren stretches of sand is now striped with huge tracts of fertile green land.

The Israelis have also invented other scientific methods for growing crops in desert soil. A

Rich Human Resources Israel has successfully developed its few natural resources. However, its agricultural and chemical industries alone could not produce enough employment opportunities to support the nation's rapidly growing population. It had to develop new industries.

Israel looked in part to high technology to help its struggling economy. With the help of grants and loans from other countries, Israel's well-educated and highly-trained scientists and engineers applied their skills to make Israel a world leader in medical laser technology, sophisticated weaponry, aerospace equipment, and electronics.

Israel also developed service industries to support its growing population. Today almost three quarters of all Israelis work in areas such as education, housing, and tourism.

Diverse Citizens

Israel's citizens come from a great variety of backgrounds. About eighty percent are Jewish. But at any public gathering you will recognize that great differences exist even among the Jews of Israel. To strengthen the nation, the Israeli government has encouraged Jews to immigrate from around the world. If you listen, you will hear Hebrew spoken with a variety of accents—Russian, American, Turkish, and German.

Israel's Jews Until recently, two groups of Jews—European Jews and Oriental, or Sephardic, Jews—formed a sharp division in Israeli society. Almost all the Jews who immigrated to Israel before 1948 came from Europe. As a result, when Israel was established it had a modern, Westernized character. After 1948, more than half of the Jews immigrating to Israel were Sephardic Jews from countries in Southwest Asia, North Africa, and Asia. These Sephardic Jews were generally poorer and less educated than the rest of Israel's citizens. Most of them worked as unskilled laborers. They earned less money and had a lower standard of living than that of the European Jews. They also had less influence in the government. In recent years, however, the gap between the two groups has begun to close.

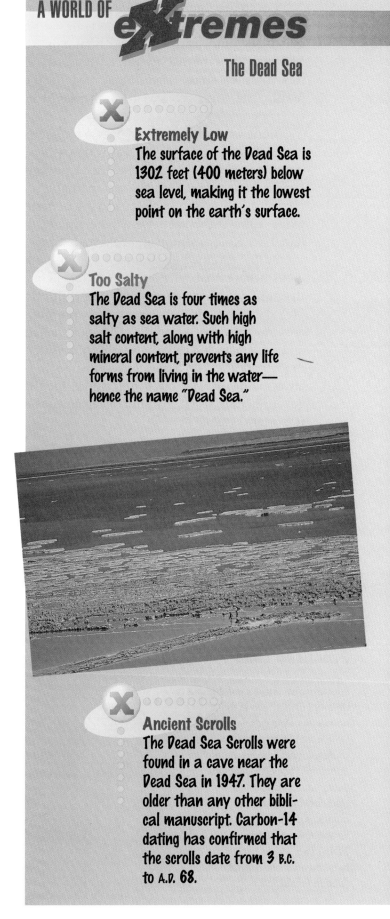

A WORLD OF eXtremes

The Dead Sea

X **Extremely Low**
The surface of the Dead Sea is 1302 feet (400 meters) below sea level, making it the lowest point on the earth's surface.

X **Too Salty**
The Dead Sea is four times as salty as sea water. Such high salt content, along with high mineral content, prevents any life forms from living in the water— hence the name "Dead Sea."

X **Ancient Scrolls**
The Dead Sea Scrolls were found in a cave near the Dead Sea in 1947. They are older than any other biblical manuscript. Carbon-14 dating has confirmed that the scrolls date from 3 B.C. to A.D. 68.

Most recent immigrants to Israel come from Ethiopia and the former Soviet Union. In the mid-1980s and early 1990s, thousands of Ethiopian Jews moved to Israel. Hundreds of thousands of Soviet Jews immigrated to the Jewish state when the Soviet Union relaxed its emigration policies in the 1980s.

Along with cultural differences among Jews in Israeli society, there are also wide political divisions. Representatives in the **Knesset**, Israel's democratically elected parliament, range from ultra-Orthodox Jews to the nonreligious. Ultra-Orthodox Jews adhere strictly to Jewish religious tradition and believe that Israel should be governed accordingly. The nonreligious believe that religion should not dictate the running of the state and interfere with people's daily lives. In between these two groups are a number of other groups. Divergent beliefs and goals have led to serious political conflicts in complicated, coalition governments. It is always difficult, and often impossible, for the government to reach any kind of agreement on important issues.

Israel's Arabs About 17 percent of Israel's population is Arab. It is a diverse population that includes Christians, Muslims, and Druzes (independent people who broke from Islam in the ninth century and live in villages in northern Israel). As a minority, the Arabs hold a very different place from that of the Jews in Israel.

Israeli Arabs are citizens of Israel. As such, they have full political rights. Arabs serve in the Knesset, enjoy the benefits of a free press, and in most cases are allowed to form political parties. Nevertheless, many Israeli Arabs complain that they are discriminated against in education, employment, and other areas. In recent years, Arabs in Israel have begun to demand a greater voice in Israeli society.

The Struggle for Peace

Along with building a strong economy and maintaining harmony among its diverse population, Israel faces another major challenge. It must build a lasting peace with the Palestinians and its other Arab neighbors. In the past fifty years, Israel and the Arab nations have gone to war four times.

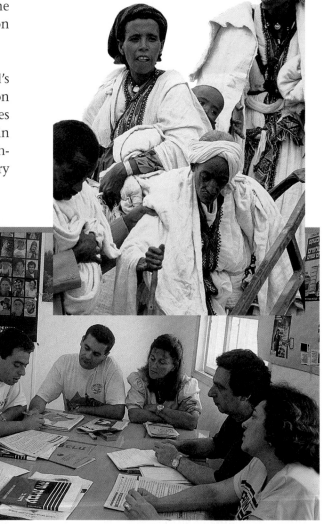

Adapting to the Promised Land

- **Movement** Israel's immigrants face different challenges in the Jewish homeland. Immigrants from former Soviet republics tend to be educated professionals who are unfamiliar with Judaism. Though Ethiopian Jews have strong religious traditions, many of their customs differ from those of Israeli Jews. **Critical Thinking** *What problems might new immigrants face in Israel?*

Land of Conflict

Regions Conflicts between Jews and Palestinians over land have plagued Israel since its creation in 1948. The Palestinians in this photograph plant a tree in observance of Land Day, a day Palestinians set aside to commemorate their losses. *What other sources of conflict are there between Israel's Arabs and Jews?*

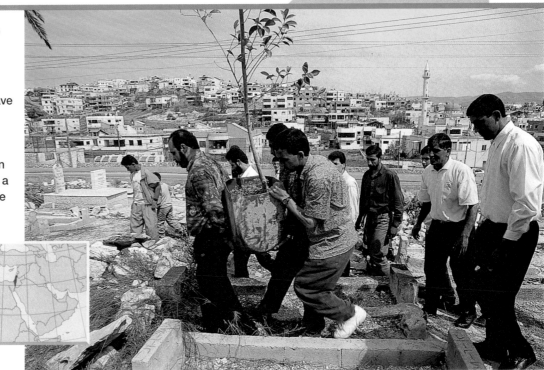

Palestinian Refugees The source of the conflict between the Israelis and the Palestinians goes back to 1947. That was the year when the United Nations voted to partition the British mandate of Palestine into two states—one Arab, one Jewish. Arab leaders refused to accept that decision. As a result, when Israel declared independence in May 1948, as the British left, a bitter war broke out between the new state of Israel and all its Arab neighbors.

By the end of the war in 1949, most of the Palestinians had lost their homes and property. As many as 500,000 people had fled to neighboring Arab countries. At the same time, an even larger number of Jews were expelled from Arab countries, most of whom were resettled in Israel. Societies across the Middle East were shattered.

The Palestinians took refuge in the Gaza Strip (ruled by Egypt), Jordan, Syria, and Lebanon. Provoked by these Arab countries, Israeli troops attacked in 1967 and took control of the West Bank in Jordan and the Gaza Strip. About 200,000 Palestinians fled from the West Bank to East Jordan. More than 1 million Palestinians remained in the West Bank under Israeli military rule, but Palestinians who had fled were not allowed to return to their homes.

By this time well over 1 million Palestinians were living permanently as refugees outside the area that was once Palestine. Some of these refugees eventually found jobs and housing in other Arab countries and resumed fairly normal lives. Others remained in crowded refugee camps in Lebanon, Syria, and Jordan. Palestinians everywhere dreamed of someday returning to their homeland and establishing an independent Palestinian state.

Bitter Enemies In the mid-1960s, many of these refugee camps became bases for the Palestinian Liberation Organization (PLO)—the Palestinians' government in exile. The PLO refused to recognize Israel as a country. It demanded that Palestine be liberated and the refugees be allowed to return to their homes. PLO extremists gained worldwide attention for their cause by hijacking planes, kidnapping and killing Israeli civilians, and conducting raids on Israeli communities.

GLOBAL issues

Pollution

Environmental legislation, combined with strict enforcement, has been successful in limiting water pollution from oil spills along Israel's Mediterranean coast.

Most Israelis viewed the PLO as terrorists whose goal was not only to destroy Israel but also Israeli Jews. Israel began to conduct raids on PLO bases in neighboring Arab countries. By the mid-1970s, most PLO activity was being conducted from Lebanon. The Israelis launched heavy attacks against Palestinian refugee camps situated near the Lebanese border that they suspected of supporting PLO guerrillas. In 1982, Israel invaded Lebanon in a final attempt to crush the PLO. After a long siege and a heavy bombardment, many Palestinian fighters left Lebanon.

Meanwhile, more and more Israelis were settling in the occupied territories—the West Bank and Gaza Strip. As Palestinians there increasingly despaired of ever gaining a homeland, support for the PLO grew. There were frequent demonstrations, strikes, and violence. In response, Israel tightened its control of the occupied territories, imprisoning or exiling thousands of suspected PLO supporters.

The Struggle for a Solution During the 1970s and 1980s, much blood was shed and many Palestinians and Israelis lost their lives. Various solutions to the challenge of creating a homeland for the Palestinians were proposed, but both sides viewed the possibility of peace with suspicion. In 1987, impatient Palestinians in Gaza began hurling rocks at Israeli soldiers. Soon the uprising, or intifada

Facts in BRIEF

Country	Population	Life Expectancy (years)	Per Capita GNP (in U.S. $)
Iran	61,300,000	67	2,239
Iraq	20,600,000	66	NA
Israel	5,500,000	77	13,760
Jordan	4,100,000	72	1,190
Kuwait	1,500,000	75	23,350
Lebanon	3,700,000	75	NA
Oman	2,200,000	71	5,600
Saudi Arabia	18,500,000	70	7,780
Syria	14,700,000	66	NA
Turkey	61,400,000	67	2,120
Yemen	13,200,000	52	NA
United States	263,200,000	76	24,750

Source: *Population Reference Bureau*   *NA indicates data not available.*

CHART SKILLS

● *Which two countries have the greatest populations?*

● **Critical Thinking** *How do you explain the fact that even though Saudi Arabia's oil reserves are much greater than Kuwait's, Saudi Arabia has a much lower GNP?*

APPEARED IN *NATIONAL GEOGRAPHIC*

Interns for Peace

Place Jewish children playfully welcome the newest arrival at a summer peace camp—a Palestinian Israeli citizen. Happily surprised at their own ability to work together, these young Interns for Peace offer Israel's future the possibility of peace. *What other moves toward peace have Israelis made in recent years?*

Historic Handshake

Regions In 1993 Israeli Prime Minister Yitzhak Rabin (left) and PLO Chairman Yasir Arafat (right) signed the historic Israeli-Palestinian Declaration of Principles in a White House ceremony. In his speech, Arafat said that "without peace in the Middle East, peace in the world will not be complete." **Critical Thinking** *How might the United States and other nations benefit from peace in the Middle East?*

(in-tee-FAH-dah) as it is called in Arabic, spread to the West Bank.

In 1991, peace talks resumed in Madrid, Spain. Israel talked to Palestinians from the occupied territories but refused to talk to the PLO. The talks proceeded haltingly. Finally, in 1993, via secret negotiations, Israel and the PLO exchanged two short letters formally recognizing each other and promising to begin negotiations.

After Israel handed over control of the Gaza Strip and several West Bank cities, the peace process stalled. Many Jews who settled in the West Bank opposed a Palestinian state, and a series of terrorist attacks damaged Israel's faith in the Palestinian government. A right-wing Israeli assassinated Prime Minister Yitzhak Rabin in November 1995, and Israel elected a new government which mistrusted the peace agreement. In July 2000, Israeli prime minister Ehud Barak and Arafat met in the United States with President Clinton, but these talks failed to reach a new agreement. You can read more about the history of the peace process in the Case Study on Global Issues on pages 450–451.

Section 2 Review

Vocabulary and Main Ideas

1. **Define: a. drip irrigation b. Knesset**

2. **How has Israel made use of technology in developing its land?**

3. **What are the main cultural, ethnic, and religious groups in Israel today?**

4. **Critical Thinking:** *Making Comparisons* **In what ways are Israel and the United States alike? In what ways are they different?**

learning LOCATIONS

5. Name the capital city of Israel.

6. Name the river that Israel shares with Jordan.

The Palestinians

The Issue

Lasting peace in Southwest Asia depends on Israel and the Palestinians reaching a permanent settlement regarding the future.

A Historic Breakthrough In 1993 there was a dramatic breakthrough in the Middle East peace talks. On September 13, Yasir Arafat, longtime leader of the PLO, and Yitzhak Rabin, the Israeli prime minister, signed an agreement in Washington, D.C. They agreed to establish limited Palestinian self-rule in the Gaza Strip and the ancient West Bank town of Jericho. The agreement also set the stage for negotiations on the status of the rest of the West Bank, as well as for peace talks with other Arab countries.

Dreams of a New Country Most of the over 2 million Palestinians living in the occupied territories strongly supported the new peace plan. One Palestinian said: "We have started on the road to establishing our state, independent and free. People can't quite grasp it yet, because the tragedy has been going on for decades. It's about time that both governments, Israeli and Palestinian, have stood up and thought about what's good for both people."

The Road to Self-Rule In 1995, the agreement made in 1993 was expanded to include more than 450 other Palestinian cities, towns, and villages in the West Bank. Large parts of the West Bank remained under Israeli control. These included areas where there were Israeli towns and cities with sacred Jewish religious sites. In addition, although Palestinians elected their own government, Israel kept control of foreign policy.

Bitter Opposition Some Palestinians called Arafat's agreement with Israel a sell-out. They demanded that the West Bank and Gaza Strip be completely independent. Radical Palestinian groups carried out suicide bombings and launched missile attacks against Israel. For these reasons, many Israelis remained deeply suspicious about the idea of Palestinian self-rule.

Global Impact The world is dependent on oil from the Middle East. In the past, fighting between Israel and its Arab neighbors erupted into major conflicts in the region, severely disrupting the world's oil supply. In addition, more and more governments around the world believed that the Palestinian people were entitled to an independent homeland.

Making Peace

Regions Yasir Arafat, Shimon Peres, and Yitzhak Rabin (left to right) received the 1994 Nobel Peace prize for their efforts to bring peace to the Middle East.

Some Solutions

By the late 1990s, many encouraging steps had been taken, although several difficult issues remained unresolved, even after talks in 2000.

An Independent State In the mid-1990s, some Israeli leaders considered the idea of an independent Palestinian state. These leaders realized, however, that many Israelis would feel that their security might be jeopardized.

Israeli Settlers When Israel took control of the West Bank, it allowed Israeli citizens to settle there. Some of these settlers claimed they had a historic right to the land. In addition, they opposed living under the authority of a Palestinian state.

Control of Holy Sites Religious sites that are important to both Jews and Muslims are located in Hebron and East Jerusalem. Many Jews and Muslims alike want to control those sites. A particularly difficult issue concerns East Jerusalem. Both sides are steadfast about it being included in their territory. One suggestion is that control of East Jerusalem might be shared between the two groups.

YOU DECIDE

1. What do you think are the greatest obstacles to achieving peace between the Israelis and the Palestinians?

2. What solutions would you propose to these obstacles?

3. Problem Solving You are appointed to negotiate a final peace treaty between the Israeli Jews and Palestinian Arabs. List five factors to be taken into consideration when designing a peace treaty that addresses the demands of both groups.

4. What You Can Do Learn more about conflict resolution. Find out how conflicts arise and how they can be resolved.

5. Internet Activity Visit the NewsHour Index of the Public Broadcasting System to learn about the current situation in the Middle East. Enter *Israel* and *peace* in the search area, then choose an article of interest. Write a paragraph summarizing what you read. Link to this site from:
• www.phschool.com

3 Jordan, Lebanon, Syria, and Iraq

Section Preview ....

Main Ideas

● Jordan and Lebanon have been greatly affected by wider conflicts in Southwest Asia.

● Syria is a rich agricultural land.

● Oil is important to Iraq's economy.

Vocabulary

militia, anarchy, embargo

Bedouin herders tend their flock.

Along with Israel, the land that is now the modern countries of Jordan, Lebanon, Syria, and Iraq made up the center of the ancient Middle East. An arc of rich land known as the Fertile Crescent ran through this area, where farming and the first civilizations developed. These countries remain at the center of Southwest Asia today, and are often the focus of political, economic, and social challenges that affect the entire region.

Jordan: A Fragile Kingdom

Notice on the map on page 453 that Jordan is bordered by Israel, Syria, Iraq, and Saudi Arabia. Its position between Israel and neighboring Arab countries puts it in the middle of political struggles in the region. Since 1948, Jordan has been greatly affected by conflicts in the area.

Changing Boundaries When Jordan was given its independence in 1946, almost all of its land was dry, rocky desert. However, after the 1948 war between the Arab countries and Israel, Jordan annexed the West Bank. The

addition of the West Bank to Jordan's territory supplied it with fertile land for growing crops. Workers built irrigation canals and farmers learned modern methods of growing vegetables, fruit, and wheat. Herders raised large flocks of sheep and goats. Jordan also opened industries in the area. By the mid-1960s, about one third of Jordan's gross national product came from the West Bank. Then in 1967 Jordan, Egypt, and Syria attacked Israel. Israel gained control of the West Bank. Jordan lost its second-largest city, East Jerusalem. The impact on Jordan's economy was devastating. Jordan lost a huge part of its agricultural production, its banking business, its tourism, and its industry.

Movement of Palestinians to Jordan The Arab-Israeli wars of 1948 and 1967 also had a significant effect on Jordan's population. After each of these wars, many Palestinian refugees fled to Jordan. Today about half of Jordan's population are Palestinian Arabs. Unlike other Arab countries, Jordan encouraged Palestinians to become part of its society. Most became Jordanian citizens. The Palestinians are a strong political force in Jordan. In the past, they have challenged Jordan's government, which is a constitutional monarchy. Palestinian political groups threatened to overthrow King Hussein if he did not support them in their struggle for a homeland.

A Modern Country Despite the economic and political challenges of the last decades, Jordan has established itself as a modern country. Since the late 1960s its economy has been steadily improving. In 1989, King Hussein began a process of political reform. The king hoped to unite his country's Islamic heritage with modern, democratic freedoms.

Lebanon: A Nervous Peace

The tiny country of Lebanon was looked upon for many years with a mixture of awe and envy by people from other Southwest Asian countries. Lebanon had a mild climate, beautiful beaches, and an open social and political atmosphere. It also had a thriving economy. Lebanon's capital, Beirut, was a center of international tourism, banking, and trade. A glamorous and free-spirited city, Beirut was often referred to as the "Paris of the Middle East." In recent years, however, a bloody civil war left the country in ruins. Today Lebanon struggles to rebuild itself.

The Beginning of the War The chaos in Lebanon grew out of a breakdown in the political system. Since Lebanon became independent of France in 1943, its many religious groups shared responsibility for governing the country. Power was divided among the Maronite Christians, Sunni Muslims, Shiite Muslims, Greek Orthodox Christians, and Druze based on the size of their populations. The Maronites, who were the largest group according to a census taken in 1932, held the most power.

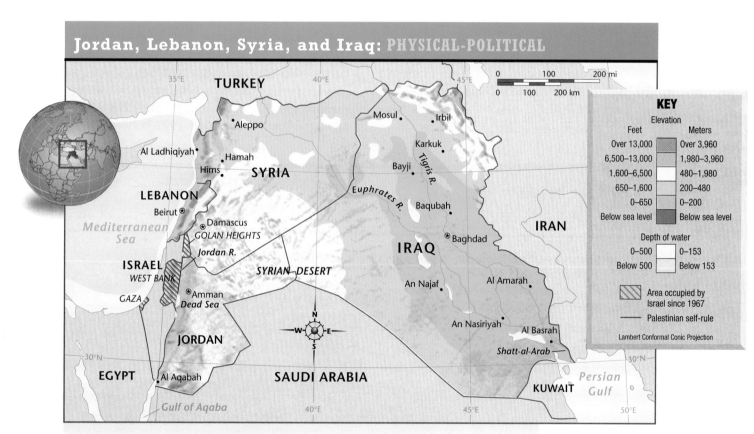

Jordan, Lebanon, Syria, and Iraq: PHYSICAL-POLITICAL

KEY

Elevation

Feet	Meters
Over 13,000	Over 3,960
6,500–13,000	1,980–3,960
1,600–6,500	480–1,980
650–1,600	200–480
0–650	0–200
Below sea level	Below sea level

Depth of water

0–500	0–153
Below 500	Below 153

Area occupied by Israel since 1967

Palestinian self-rule

Lambert Conformal Conic Projection

APPLYING THE GEOGRAPHIC THEMES

● **Location** *Where is the waterway known as the Shatt-al-Arab located? Between which two countries does it form part of the border?*

For many years this system of government worked well. But as the Muslim population grew, Muslims began to demand a greater share of power in the country's government. At the same time, growing economic inequality between groups in different parts of the country created disturbing social and political tensions. In southern Lebanon the Shiite Muslims felt that government policies particularly discriminated against them. A civil war erupted in 1958. Although a compromise was reached, the political system remained unchanged. In 1975 civil war broke out again.

A Kaleidoscope of Terror The situation had grown far more complicated by 1975. Thousands of Palestinian refugees had made their homes in Lebanon. The Palestinian Liberation Organization, or PLO, set up military bases in Lebanon from which they conducted raids across the border to Israel. The Israelis, in turn, struck back at PLO forces in Lebanon.

Because of the conflict between Israel and the PLO, other countries, including Syria, Iran, and the United States, became involved in Lebanon's civil war. In 1982 Israel invaded Lebanon to drive out the PLO. After destroying the PLO bases in Southern Lebanon, the Israelis advanced to Beirut. They bombed the city heavily for weeks.

An international peacekeeping force, including several thousand United States Marines, was sent in to establish peace in Beirut. In early 1983, an explosive-filled truck blew up the American embassy in Beirut killing more than sixty people. Then in October 1983, another truck loaded with explosives crashed through the gates of a marine barracks killing 241 Americans. By February 1984, all American troops had been withdrawn from Lebanon. The country slid further and further into chaos. Muslim and Christian groups split into different factions. Each faction had its own **militia**, or citizen army.

By the mid-1980s, Lebanon was in a state of **anarchy**, or lawlessness. No government, army, or police force could maintain order. Bands of militia roamed the streets kidnapping members of other groups and foreign citizens whom they held hostage. In the middle of the day, fights broke out between militias on crowded streets. Families installed steel doors on their houses and apartments and bought machine guns to protect themselves.

An Uneasy Calm Today Lebanon is in transition. In the late 1980s the Maronite Christians agreed to a plan that gave more political power to the country's Muslims. The militias stopped fighting each other in the early 1990s. The agreement reached in 1993 between Israel

War-torn Beirut

● **Place** As this archaeologist looks for clues to Lebanon's ancient Phoenician culture, Lebanon's recent history can be read in the surrounding destruction. *Why was Lebanon in a state of anarchy during the mid-1980s?*

and the PLO for limited Palestinian self-determination also brought hope to Lebanon. But the new peace was fragile. Israeli and Syrian armed forces remained in Lebanon and attacks on northern Israel brought with them the threat of renewed warfare.

Syria: A Troubled Land

Since the time of its earliest settlers, Syria has been a prosperous land. Its location on the eastern edge of the Mediterranean between Europe, Africa, and Asia has made cities like Damascus, the capital, and Aleppo busy centers of trade. For thousands of years, Syria's people have taken advantage of its rich farmlands and its thriving cities to make a living. They grow cotton, wheat, fruit, and vegetables on the fertile land.

In recent decades, more and more Syrians have left their farms to work in the cities. Although Syria is fortunate to have fertile farmland, many farming methods are out-of-date. Few farmers have modern machinery and only about one third of the farms are irrigated. Most of Syria's farmers depend on rainfall to water their crops. However, rainfall is unreliable. When droughts occur, farmers are unable to make a living.

The Syrian government is trying to improve farming methods in the hope of encouraging farmers to stay on their land. It has given money to farmers to help them buy modern machinery. In the last decade, Syria has also been focusing more attention on research to improve crop output. The government has also built dams in the northeast and northwest. The water in the lakes formed by these dams irrigates thousands of acres of land.

Changes upstream along the Euphrates may affect Syria's future. Turkey has built dams on the river that decrease the amount of water flowing downstream into Syria and Iraq. Syria has had to cut back on its use of electricity because there is less water available at the country's hydroelectric dams. More severe shortages could affect Syria's agriculture and its ability to feed its growing population.

In 1970 General Hafez al-Assad took power in Syria. Ruling until his death in 2000, Assad allowed little political freedom in his country.

Damascus

Place Damascus is Syria's major urban center and its capital. Syria's government is controlled by a harsh military regime that seized power in 1970. **Critical Thinking** *How is Syria's government reflected in this photograph?*

He made all key decisions regarding foreign policy, national security, and the economy.

For most of its recent history, Syria has been under a state of emergency. This has allowed the state wide latitude in dealing with suspects, detainees, and prisoners. Many human rights violations have been reported. One of the more notable events of Assad's long hold on power was his army's assault in 1982 on the city of Hama. This ancient Syrian city was a stronghold of the opposition Muslim Brotherhood group. Assad's forces killed thousands of Syrian civilians and destroyed Hama.

Iraq: The Spoils of War

Iraq is located in a fortunate place. A large part of the country lies on the well-watered plain between the Tigris and Euphrates rivers. Grains, fruits, and vegetables grow easily. For hundreds of years farming was the most important economic activity in this land. Then, in the late 1920s, large quantities of oil were discovered.

Iraq spent billions of dollars of oil money to develop the country. It built roads, airports, and hospitals. It opened new schools and universities. Dams and irrigation systems were built to increase agricultural output. Iraq even rebuilt its capital, the ancient city of Baghdad.

GEOfacts

There are 1,991 people per physician in Iraq. (U.S.=416)

War with Iran Since 1980, however, war has brought misfortune to Iraq. In 1980, Iraqi dictator Saddam Hussein took advantage of turmoil in Iran to occupy a disputed border area and then pushed deeper into Iran. Iran launched a counter-attack. Iraq used its superior weapons, tanks, airplanes, and even poison gas to stop the Iranian soldiers. When both sides attacked tankers and oil fields, the United States took steps to protect Persian Gulf shipping lanes by sending warships to the Gulf. Both the United States and the Soviet Union offered aid to Iraq, but the United States also secretly sold weapons to Iran. By 1988, despite enormous human and economic losses, neither Iran nor Iraq had accomplished its goal. Exhausted, they accepted a UN cease-fire. The eight-year war drained both sides and left Iraq heavily in debt.

The Persian Gulf War In 1990 Iraq, still under the leadership of Saddam Hussein, attacked its neighbor Kuwait. Amidst worldwide protest, it declared Kuwait a part of Iraq, thereby gaining control of a large percentage of the world's oil. War broke out in 1991 when armed forces, led by the United States and supported by the United Nations, attacked and liberated Kuwait in the Persian Gulf War.

Iraq suffered huge losses as a result of the war. More than 85,000 Iraqi soldiers were killed. Tens of thousands of civilians also probably died. The capital of Baghdad was badly damaged. Yet Saddam Hussein remained in power. Iraq refused to follow the terms of the UN cease-fire. An **embargo**, or a severe restriction on trade with

After the War

Place After the Persian Gulf War, Kuwait was a shambles. Its basic services, such as water and electricity, as well as schools and health care, were all but shut down. Its economy was in ruins, and environmental damage from hundreds of burning oil wells—allegedly set afire by the Iraqis— was substantial. Even libraries and art museums were robbed of their treasures. *Why did Iraq invade Kuwait?*

Iraqi Refugees

Movement According to the United Nations, the Persian Gulf War caused one of the largest displacements of civilian population in recent history. Fleeing Iraqi citizens, mostly Kurds, escaped into neighboring countries such as Turkey and Iran. The movement of such a large segment of Iraq's population into other countries threatened international peace in the region. **Critical Thinking** *Why might a country resent refugees from a neighboring nation? Why might a country want its fleeing refugees returned home?*

other countries, was imposed on Iraq by the UN. The goal of the embargo was to force Hussein to cease his chemical and nuclear weapons programs. Iraq was not allowed to sell its oil on the international market, which caused great suffering for the Iraqi people. In 1996, the UN had agreed to allow Iraq to sell limited quantities of its oil to pay for food and medicine. However, the discovery that Iraq may have used nerve gas in the Gulf War stopped the UN from lifting sanctions.

The Kurds The Kurds are the world's largest stateless minority. An estimated 25 million Kurds live in a region called Kurdistan that lies within the countries of Turkey, Syria, Iraq, Iran, and Armenia. For centuries the Kurds have fought to maintain their culture despite oppression. In 1988, Iraqi troops killed thousands of Kurds and destroyed hundreds of Iraqi villages. After the Persian Gulf War, Iraq crushed another Kurdish uprising and over one million Kurdish refugees fled to Turkey, Iran, and the mountainous areas in northern Iraq. The United Nations sent peacekeepers to northern Iraq to protect the Kurds. The Kurds' status in the region, despite this intervention, remains uncertain.

Section 3 Review

Vocabulary and Main Ideas

1. **Define a. militia b. anarchy c. embargo**

2. **What were the causes of Lebanon's civil war?**

3. **Describe the role that oil plays in Iraq's economy.**

4. **Critical Thinking:** *Cause and Effect* **How might Turkey's control of the waters of the Euphrates affect its political relationship with Syria?**

learning LOCATIONS

5. **Name four countries that border Jordan.**

6. **Name the capital city in Southwest Asia that is located on the Mediterranean Sea.**

4 Arabian Peninsula

Section Preview

Main Ideas

- Oil has brought great wealth to many countries on the Arabian Peninsula.

- The oil-rich countries of the region have used their oil wealth to pay for modernization.

- Oman and Yemen are the least developed countries in the region.

Vocabulary

desalination, infrastructure, *falaj* system

APPEARED IN *NATIONAL GEOGRAPHIC*

Oman's economy is heavily dependent on the bounty from its oil wells.

The Arabian Peninsula is a land of superlatives—of largests and leasts. Among the features that fall under the largest category is its desert, an enormous stretch of sand called the Rub' al-Khali, or the Empty Quarter. At 250,000 square miles (647,500 sq km), the desert is about the size of Texas. It is the world's largest sand desert. Among the leasts in the Arabian Peninsula is water. The peninsula, without one single body of fresh water, has the least amount of water of any large landmass. Instead it has the world's largest known petroleum reserves. Since oil is an important resource, the peninsula has seen the most change in the least amount of time of any place in the world.

Oil Changes a Region

In the early twentieth century, people in Saudi Arabia, Kuwait, Bahrain, Qatar, and the United Arab Emirates existed in much the same way as they had for centuries. Along the coasts, they fished and traded using *dhows*—Arab sailing ships. In the fertile oases of the desert, they lived in small towns and villages in houses made of sun-dried bricks. There they grew wheat, vegetables, and dates. They also tended small herds of camels, goats, and sheep. Groups of Bedouin herders roamed the deserts surrounding the oasis settlements.

Oil Pays for Modernization The discovery of oil in the Arabian Peninsula in the 1930s greatly changed traditional ways of life. It brought enormous wealth to the region. Money from oil was used to pay for modernization. Hospitals, schools, roads, airports, and apartment buildings were built. Health and other services were provided free or heavily subsidized by the government.

These countries also spent billions of dollars to create more of their scarcest resource—water. Industrial plants were constructed to remove the salt from sea water so that it could be used for drinking and irrigation. This necessary and expensive process is called **desalination**.

Today most of the people have moved to cities such as Riyadh, Saudi Arabia's capital, and Abu Dhabi, the capital of the United Arab Emirates. There many live in modern, air-conditioned houses and apartments. Some work in gleaming chrome-and-glass buildings as engineers, computer programmers, and executives of international corporations.

OPEC In 1960 Iran, Iraq, Kuwait, and Saudi Arabia joined with Venezuela to form the Organization of Petroleum Exporting Countries (OPEC). These countries met regularly to decide how much oil to produce and at what price to sell it. Their goal was to decrease the influence of western oil companies on their countries and to increase their profits. Between 1960 and 1980, and especially during the 1970s, oil prices soared. The impact of these soaring prices on the world economy was great. Developing countries had to cancel social programs in order to pay for oil. Companies in wealthier countries passed along their increased costs for fuel by raising prices. Runaway inflation resulted in many countries. OPEC has expanded to include more nations from Africa, Latin America, Southwest and Southeast Asia. As world demand for oil has increased, so too has OPEC's power.

Looking to the Future The countries of the Arabian Peninsula will not always be able to depend on oil to support their economies. Some experts believe that Saudi Arabian and Kuwaiti oil will last another fifty to sixty years. Qatar's and Bahrain's oil may last for only another twenty to thirty years.

Aware that they will one day run out of oil, these countries have invested large sums of money to develop other industries. Bahrain has

Arabian Peninsula: PHYSICAL-POLITICAL

KEY

Elevation

Feet		Meters
Over 13,000		Over 3,960
6,500–13,000		1,980–3,960
1,600–6,500		480–1,980
650–1,600		200–480
0–650		0–200
Below sea level		Below sea level

Depth of water

0–500		0–153
Below 500		Below 153

⊛ National capital

Lambert Conformal Conic Projection

APPLYING THE GEOGRAPHIC THEMES

🔵 **Movement** Many of the oil-producing countries of the Arabian Peninsula rely on the open passage of ships and oil tankers through the Persian Gulf to export their oil to countries around the world. Find the Strait of Hormuz on the map. *What two bodies of water does it connect?*

Desalination

DIAGRAM STUDY

● Many Middle Eastern countries turn to the sea for their water. Distillation is a common method of desalination, or the removal of salt from sea water. Salt water is heated and turned to steam in a low-pressure chamber. The steam condenses into fresh water on coils kept cool by incoming sea water. *Why has Saudi Arabia invested heavily in desalination?*

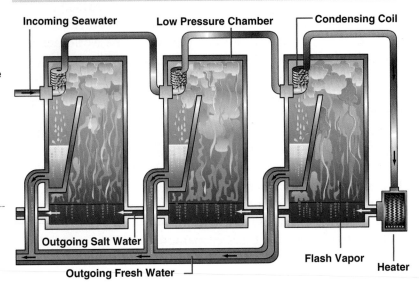

Incoming Seawater **Low Pressure Chamber** **Condensing Coil**

Outgoing Salt Water

Outgoing Fresh Water

Flash Vapor

Heater

---

established itself as an international banking center. Saudi Arabia, Qatar, and the United Arab Emirates have built steel and petrochemical industries.

Such massive development efforts require workers. But because their own populations are so small and often lack necessary skills, the oil-rich countries have had to hire huge numbers of foreign workers. In some countries on the Arabian Peninsula, foreigners outnumber citizens. As one author wrote:

> *My hotel [in Jiddah, a city on the western coast of Saudi Arabia] was typical. The receptionist was Lebanese. . . . Yemeni and Pakistani construction workers were building an extension to the hotel under a Palestinian foreman. When I came to leave, a Jordanian made up the bill. But it was a Saudi Arabian who drove me to the airport because taxi driving, like the army and police, is reserved for nationals.*

Saudi Arabia

Beginning in the late 1960s, the Saudi Arabian government spent billions of dollars of oil revenue to build the country's infrastructure. An **infrastructure** comprises a country's basic support facilities, including its roads, schools, airports, seaports, and communication systems.

Saudi Arabia opened schools throughout the country and provided children with free education. Universities began educating Saudi Arabians in engineering, science, and medicine so that one day they could run their own country.

Developing the Economy Two giant industrial cities—Yanbu on the west coast and Jubail on the east coast—were constructed in Saudi Arabia. There, oil and gas are collected, processed, and shipped. Besides petrochemicals, other new industries are being introduced and developed.

Saudi Arabia spent billions of dollars on irrigation and desalinization to increase agricultural production so that it would not have to rely on other countries for food. By the early 1980s, Saudi farmers were supplying much of the country's vegetables and poultry and most of its wheat.

Islam and Modernization In less than two decades, Saudi Arabia transformed itself from an ancient desert kingdom into a modern country. However, it did so cautiously. The government tried not to let modernization upset the Islamic and other traditions to which life in Saudi Arabia is rooted.

The family is still the most important social unit in Saudi Arabia. There are no public places of entertainment, such as movie theaters or nightclubs. Most people spend their free time at home with their families or visiting relatives.

Women, as wives and mothers, have an honored position in Saudi society. But they are limited members of society in other ways. Custom prohibits them from associating with men outside their immediate family. As a result, they must find professions where they are in contact only with other women, such as teaching in girls' schools or treating women patients. Some Saudi women would like the freedom to make more choices.

Saudi Arabia has tried to create a harmonious balance between change and tradition. Any radical changes in age-old traditions could upset more conservative members of society and cause social and political unrest. This balance between change and tradition can be seen in Saudi Arabia's role as guardian of Islam's most sacred cities, Mecca and Medina. Muhammad was born in Mecca, on the southwest coast of Arabia, around A.D. 570. Medina, which is about 200 miles (322 km) north of Mecca, is the city where Muhammad sought refuge after his departure, or *hegira*, from Mecca in A.D. 622.

Each year two million Muslims from all over the world visit Saudi Arabia for the hajj, or pilgrimage to Mecca. Pilgrims are greeted in modern airline terminals, then taken by bus to huge tent cities that have been set up especially for the hajj. Pilgrims to Mecca circle the cube-shaped holy shrine, known as the *Kaaba*, seven times reciting prayers. Inside the Kaaba is a black stone which they believe was sent by God. During the hajj, hundreds of thousands of people are provided with sanitation and medical facilities. Closed-circuit televisions monitor the crowds for emergencies. Saudi Arabia has used modern technology to support what Muslims believe to be the single most moving and meaningful religious ritual in Islam.

Oman and Yemen

Unlike other countries on the Arabian Peninsula, life for most people in Yemen and Oman has changed little since ancient times. Although Yemen has some oil deposits, it only

Change and Tradition

Place Saudi Arabia has sought a balance between its traditional culture and its attempt at modernization. *How has Saudi Arabia preserved its culture? How has it modernized?*

recently started to develop them. Oman began to use its oil revenues to improve life for its people in the early 1970s, but it has not undergone the large-scale modernization that countries like Saudi Arabia and Kuwait have.

Yemen is the poorest country on the Arabian Peninsula. It is also the newest. During the spring of 1990, the separate countries of North Yemen and South Yemen were merged into one unified nation. The new leaders hope the merger of the two countries will improve the economy and

GLOBAL issues

Desertification

More than six million trees have been planted near oases in the Saudi Arabian province of Al-Hasa to stop the advance of the desert.

Achieving Literacy

Place Thirty years ago Oman had only three schools, and illiteracy was common. Today Oman's school system supports around a half million students. The women pictured here are participating in an adult literacy program. *In what other ways is Oman trying to improve its standard of living?*

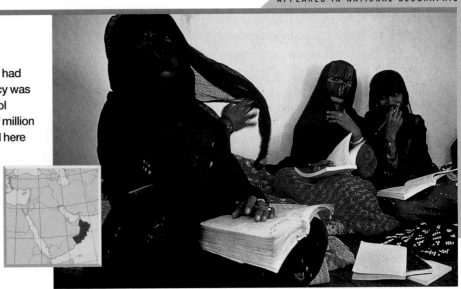

help Yemenis live a better life. In 1993 Yemen held its first parliamentary elections. It was the first election on the Arabian Peninsula in which women were allowed to vote.

Sanaa, the former capital of North Yemen, is the new political capital. However, it is the port city of Aden in what was formerly South Yemen that is the economic capital. It currently provides most of Yemen's income. As the map on page 459 shows, Aden is strategically located at the entrance to the Red Sea. Huge oil tankers and other ships on their way through the Suez Canal in Egypt use the port for refueling, repairs, and transferring cargo.

Most people in both Yemen and Oman make their living by farming and herding. It is a difficult existence as most of Oman is desert. Many farmers depend on an ancient system of underground and surface canals called the *falaj system* for water. These canals carry water from the mountains to villages miles away.

The government of Oman has used money from oil exports to improve its standard of living. It has updated irrigation systems and built roads, hospitals, and schools. But like the rest of the countries that depend on oil for most of their revenue, Oman is under pressure to diversify into other industries before its oil runs out.

Section 4 Review

Vocabulary and Main Ideas

1. **Define: a. desalination b. infrastructure c. *falaj* system**

2. **In what ways have the oil-rich countries of the Arabian Peninsula used their oil profits to improve their standard of living?**

3. **How are Yemen and Oman different from the other countries on the Arabian Peninsula?**

4. **Critical Thinking:** *Recognizing Ideologies* **In 1966, King Faisal told the people of Saudi Arabia, "We are going ahead with extensive planning, guided by our Islamic laws and beliefs, for the progress of the nation." What did the king mean when he said this?**

learning LOCATIONS

5. **Name the five countries on the Arabian Peninsula that lie on the Persian Gulf.**

6. **Name the sea that borders Saudi Arabia on the west.**

Focus on Skills

☐ Social Studies

☑ Map and Globe

☐ Critical Thinking and Problem Solving

Interpreting a Remote Sensing Image

For years, archaeologists have combed the world searching for evidence of lost civilizations. They often had to rely on legends or myths for hints about where to begin digging. Today archaeologists have a new tool to aid their research. Remote sensing allows them to quickly survey extensive areas for clues. The remote sensing image to the right was produced by combining space-shuttle radar data with satellite images of southern Oman. Use the following steps to help you analyze the image.

1. Understand the content of the image. It is often helpful to compare a remote sensing image with a map of the same area. Check the scale of the image and locate the major features shown in the map (inset), such as the region's main roads or rivers. (a) How many miles are shown looking north to south? East to west? (b) What is the major feature shown in the center of the image? (c) What feature makes up the yellow region in the upper left-hand corner of the image?

2. Look for unexplainable features. In this example, researchers were not able to explain the gouges that run from the lower right-hand corner of the image to almost the center of the map. These grooves were not visible on the ground or with conventional photography. They appeared only when infrared and radar images were combined. Researchers believe that the gouges are very old caravan routes that are no longer used.

The tracks converge inside the triangle created by the intersection of roads near the center of the image. What might you expect to find at the meeting point of old caravan routes?

3. Verify "ground truth." Once archaeologists hypothesized that the mysterious gouges were actually old caravan routes, their next step was to visit Oman to examine the tracks and the place where they converge. Verifying mapped data against true ground conditions —or checking the "ground truth"—is always recommended when attempting to explain the features of remote sensing images. The team that verified the ground truth in this example discovered the ruins thought to be that of the lost city of Ubar. The city is described by T. E. Lawrence—Lawrence of Arabia—as "the Atlantis of the sands." Archaeologists are excavating the site to confirm the existence of the city. Why do you think it is important to verify "ground truth"?

Remote Sensing Image

5 Turkey, Iran, and Cyprus

Section Preview

Main Ideas

- Turkey is a modern nation whose economy depends on industry and agriculture.

- Iran's Islamic revolution seriously affected the country's development.

- Ethnic unrest has divided Cyprus.

Vocabulary

secular, shah, ayatollah

APPEARED IN *NATIONAL GEOGRAPHIC*

Kurdish activists argue for an independent Kurdish state.

Turkey and Iran are different from the other countries in Southwest Asia. Although the majority of people in Turkey and Iran are Muslims, they are not Arabs. They speak different languages, and they trace their ancestors back to different roots.

Turkey

The Persians, the Greeks, and the Romans—at various stages in history—all controlled what today is Turkey. However, it is the Turks, the last empire builders in Southwest Asia, from whom most of the people in Turkey today trace their ancestry.

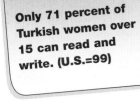

Only 71 percent of Turkish women over 15 can read and write. (U.S.=99)

The Turks originally came from central Asia. Scholars and merchants who traveled from Southwest to central Asia introduced them to Islam. When the Turks began conquering Southwest Asia, they came as Muslim warriors. Although they were Muslims, their language and culture were Turkish, not Arab.

The "Father of the Turks" When World War I ended in 1918, the victors broke up the Ottoman Empire. Turkey kept only Asia Minor—the peninsula south of the Black Sea—and the area around Istanbul. The Dardanelles were kept under international control. Many Turkish nationalists were furious that a weak sultan had given up so much of their territory. Mustafa Kemal, a fiery young army officer, began a movement to establish Turkey as an independent republic. In 1923 Kemal and his revolutionaries overthrew the sultan and declared Turkey a republic. Kemal was elected president.

Immediately Kemal set about making Turkey a modern country. He believed that Turkey would not survive without sweeping political and social reforms. One of his first changes was to break the bond between Islam and the government. Religious leaders were no longer involved in running the government. He replaced Islamic laws with laws based on European legal systems.

Many of Kemal's changes unraveled the fabric of social life. He outlawed the *fez*—a brimless, flat-topped hat worn by men—and he ridiculed the custom that required women to wear veils in public. After centuries of subservience, women were given the right to vote and hold office. And everyone was encouraged to attend school.

By the time Kemal died in 1938, Turkey was well on its way to becoming a modern country. Kemal had been such a force in establishing Turkey's identity after World War I that the Turks gave him the surname Atatürk, meaning "father of the Turks."

Turkey Today Turkey has faced challenges in its efforts to become a strong, modern nation. A large international debt and inflation have troubled the country since the late 1960s. In the 1970s and 1980s parties that believed Turkey's government should be **secular**, or that it should be run without religious influence, and Islamic parties fought one another for power. In the 1990s pro-Islamic and secular political parties continued to struggle for control of the government.

Another challenge facing Turkey is the Kurdish struggle. The Kurds, who make up about 10 percent of Turkey's population, live mostly in southeastern Turkey. Since the time of Atatürk, the Kurds have been harshly repressed. Today, the Turkish government is waging a war against Kurdish rebels, who want to form an independent state.

Despite these challenges, Turkey has made progress. Today, although agriculture is still important, Turkey is the most industrialized country in Southwest Asia. And Turkey's citizens are enthusiastic participants in their country's parliamentary government—one of the few freely elected governments in the region.

Islam Changes Iran

The Persians arrived in the area that is now Iran about 3,000 years ago. Today their descendants are the dominant cultural group in Iran. The Persians once ruled a vast empire that stretched west into what is now Libya and east to what is now the country of Pakistan. In 330 B.C.,

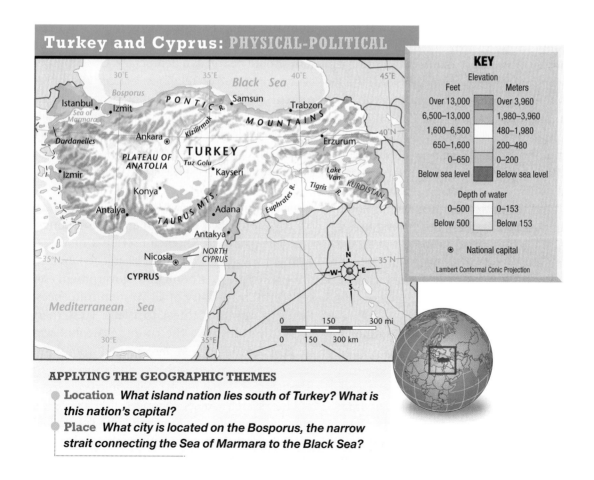

Turkey and Cyprus: PHYSICAL-POLITICAL

KEY

Elevation

Feet		Meters
Over 13,000		Over 3,960
6,500–13,000		1,980–3,960
1,600–6,500		480–1,980
650–1,600		200–480
0–650		0–200
Below sea level		Below sea level

Depth of water

0–500		0–153
Below 500		Below 153

⊛ National capital

Lambert Conformal Conic Projection

APPLYING THE GEOGRAPHIC THEMES

● **Location** *What island nation lies south of Turkey? What is this nation's capital?*

● **Place** *What city is located on the Bosporus, the narrow strait connecting the Sea of Marmara to the Black Sea?*

Ataturk Dam

Human-Environment Interaction
Turkey's Ataturk Dam is one of the world's largest volume embankment dams and has one of the largest capacity reservoirs. Look at the climate map on page 430. **Critical Thinking** *Why do you think Turkey has invested in the creation of such a large dam?*

Alexander the Great conquered the empire. Later, the Persians won back much of their territory. By the time conquering Arab armies reached them in the mid-600s, the Persian culture was well established in Iran.

For about six hundred years, Persia was part of the Islamic empire. Even though most of Persia's people converted to Islam, they were not Arabs. They maintained their links to their Persian past and continued to speak Farsi, the language of their ancestors.

Iran Becomes a Modern Country

In 1925, an army officer, Reza Khan, seized power and declared himself Iran's **shah**, or ruler. When he came to power most of Iran's people were either nomadic herders or farmers, barely able to make a living from Iran's dry land. In the years of the shah's rule, Iran began to change. Like Atatürk in Turkey, the shah opened schools, built roads and railroads, encouraged industry, and gave women more rights.

When his son, Mohammad Reza Pahlavi, took over during World War II, he was even more determined than his father to make Iran into a modern, Westernized nation. In a very short time, great changes took place in Iran. Profits from its huge oil industry were channeled into industrial and agricultural development. Teachers and medical workers traveled into the villages to improve literacy and health care. Women began to vote, hold jobs outside the home, and dress in Western-style clothing.

However, resentment against the shah's rule developed. Although many Iranians benefited from the shah's reforms, many more still lived in great poverty. Some Iranians believed that Iran should be run as a democracy. Others, especially conservative religious leaders known as **ayatollahs**, thought Iran should be governed in strict obedience to Islamic law. But the shah ran the country as a dictatorship. No one dared oppose the government for fear of being put in prison or exiled.

An Islamic Revolution

In 1979, the people of Iran revolted. The shah and his supporters fled. The Ayatollah Khomeini set up a new government and declared Iran an Islamic republic.

Immediately, Khomeini's government set out to rid the country of all Western influences, which it saw as a threat to Islam. Westerners were forced to leave the country. Alcohol was outlawed. Women were discouraged from wearing Western-style clothing and once again donned their long, black cloaks called *chadors*.

Iran's new rulers belonged to the Shiite branch of Islam, as do most Iranians. They called on Shiites everywhere in Southwest Asia to overthrow their governments and establish Islamic republics. Their appeal was particularly powerful to Shiites who lived in countries run by Sunni Muslims where the Shiites were an oppressed minority. In 1980, angered by Khomeini's attempts to provoke Shiites in Iraq to take such action, Iraqi leaders launched a war against Iran. Hundreds of thousands of Iranians were killed in the fighting, which lasted eight years.

Iran Today Since Ayatollah Khomeini died in 1989, Iran has begun to change. The revolution and the war with Iraq severely affected Iran's economy. Its radical position isolated it from the rest of the world.

Today Iran is taking a more moderate position. Some of the extreme changes imposed under Khomeini have been repealed. Iran has started to focus on increasing its export of oil instead of revolution. It is also working to renew other industries.

Cyprus

Cyprus is an island country in the eastern part of the Mediterranean Sea. Greek colonists came to this island as early as 1200 B.C. Today about four fifths of the Cypriot people speak Greek as their first language and are Greek Orthodox Christians. However, Cyprus was also part of the Ottoman Empire from the 1570s until the

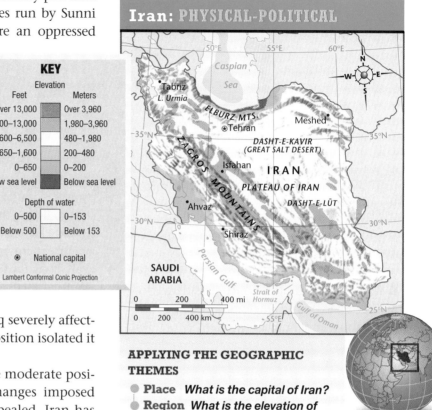

Iran: PHYSICAL-POLITICAL

KEY

Elevation

Feet		Meters
Over 13,000		Over 3,960
6,500–13,000		1,980–3,960
1,600–6,500		480–1,980
650–1,600		200–480
0–650		0–200
Below sea level		Below sea level

Depth of water

0–500		0–153
Below 500		Below 153

⊛ National capital

Lambert Conformal Conic Projection

APPLYING THE GEOGRAPHIC THEMES

- **Place** What is the capital of Iran?
- **Region** What is the elevation of the Plateau of Iran?

British occupied it in 1878. One fifth of the island's people trace their roots back to Turkey and follow Islam. In the 1970s, civil war split the island in two. Some Greek Cypriots wanted Cyprus to unite with Greece. In 1974, Turkey sent troops to Cyprus to prevent this. Turkey declared the northeastern part of Cyprus, which has a majority Turkish population, independent in 1983. This state is not recognized as such by most other countries.

Section 5 Review

Vocabulary and Main Ideas

1. Define: a. secular b. shah c. ayatollah

2. How did Atatürk change Turkey?

3. Why did Iranians revolt in 1979?

4. Critical Thinking: *Making Comparisons* How is the role of Islam in present-day Turkey different from its role in Iran?

learning LOCATIONS

5. Name the country that lies west of Iran.

6. Name the sea that forms Turkey's northern border.

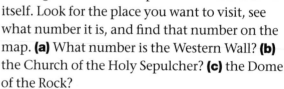

Map Skills
for Life

Skill: Reading a City Tourist Map
Setting: Visiting the Sites of Jerusalem

Tom Montoya, a student from Chicago, has traveled to Jerusalem, a city considered holy by three major world religions: Judaism, Christianity, and Islam. Like other visitors, Tom wants to see some of the many historic and religious sites of Jerusalem. Most are located in the crowded, hilly Old City, a walled area about a half mile square. Examples are:

★ the Western Wall, sometimes called the Wailing Wall, which is all that remains of the great Temple of the Jews in biblical times. Now it is part of the area known as the Temple Mount. (left)

★ the Church of the Holy Sepulcher, which is holy to Christians because it is believed to be built on the site where Jesus was crucified and buried. (top right)

★ the Dome of the Rock, a mosque built over the rock from which, in Islamic tradition, Muhammad rose to heaven. The building contains objects that are important to Jews and Christians as well. (bottom right)

Reading the Map

Follow the steps below to understand how Tom can use the tourist street map to find the three sites.

1. Check the key for the sites Tom wants to visit. Because space on maps is limited, maps such as this one help people find popular tourist sites by listing them in a separate key instead of labeling them on the map itself. Look for the place you want to visit, see what number it is, and find that number on the map. **(a)** What number is the Western Wall? **(b)** the Church of the Holy Sepulcher? **(c)** the Dome of the Rock?

2. Find the starting location on the map, and figure out the easiest way to reach the first site. (a) If Tom arrives in Jerusalem by train and takes a taxi to the wall of the Old City, which of the three sites is nearest? **(b)** To reach that site, which gate should he use to enter the Old City?

3. Use the map scale to determine distances between sites. The shortest distance between any two points is a straight line. But you can't always travel in a straight line, especially in old cities. Roads twist and curve to avoid buildings or natural barriers. To find out the distance between two sites, don't draw a straight line connecting them. Instead figure out the shortest practical route from one point to the other and then see how long that is. (If the route is full of turns, use a string or thread to help measure it.)**(a)** If Tom wants to see the archaeological excavations at the City of David, the oldest part of Jerusalem, where should he go? **(b)** What gate will he use? **(c)** Tom is willing to walk up to two miles in his sightseeing. Are the excavations close enough for him to go by foot?

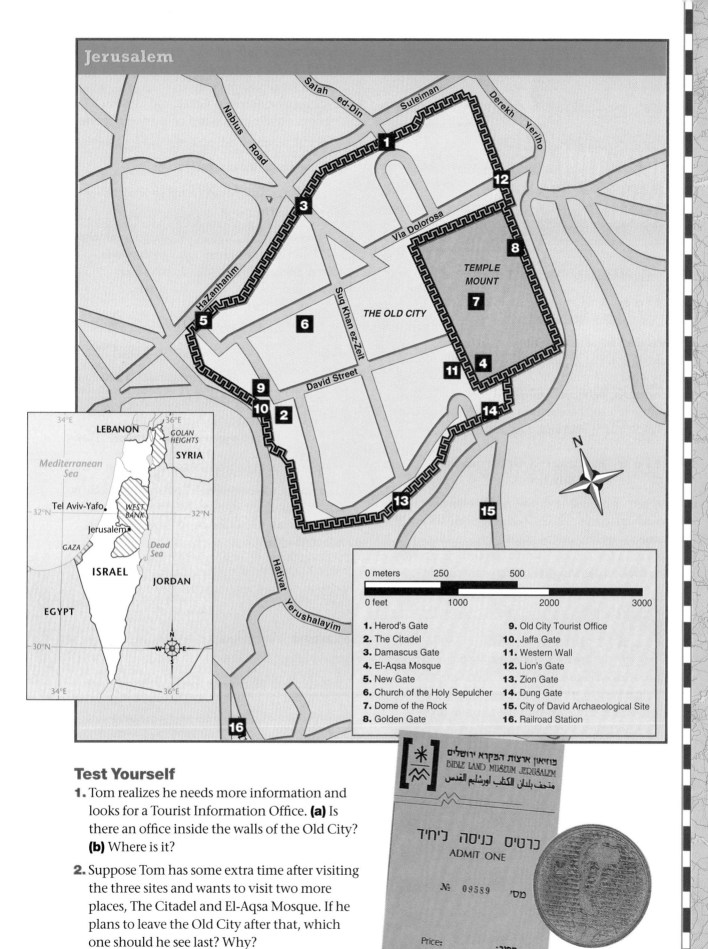

Jerusalem

THE OLD CITY

TEMPLE MOUNT

Via Dolorosa

Salah ed-Din
Suleiman
Derekh Yeriho
Nablus Road
HaZanhanim
Suq Khan ez-Zeit
David Street
Hativat Yerushalayim

Inset map:

LEBANON
GOLAN HEIGHTS
SYRIA
Mediterranean Sea
Tel Aviv-Yafo
WEST BANK
Jerusalem
GAZA
Dead Sea
ISRAEL
JORDAN
EGYPT

34°E 36°E
32°N
30°N

Scale:
0 meters   250   500
0 feet   1000   2000   3000

1. Herod's Gate
2. The Citadel
3. Damascus Gate
4. El-Aqsa Mosque
5. New Gate
6. Church of the Holy Sepulcher
7. Dome of the Rock
8. Golden Gate
9. Old City Tourist Office
10. Jaffa Gate
11. Western Wall
12. Lion's Gate
13. Zion Gate
14. Dung Gate
15. City of David Archaeological Site
16. Railroad Station

Test Yourself

1. Tom realizes he needs more information and looks for a Tourist Information Office. **(a)** Is there an office inside the walls of the Old City? **(b)** Where is it?

2. Suppose Tom has some extra time after visiting the three sites and wants to visit two more places, The Citadel and El-Aqsa Mosque. If he plans to leave the Old City after that, which one should he see last? Why?

מוזיאון ארצות המקרא ירושלים
BIBLE LAND MUSEUM JERUSALEM
متحف بلدان الكتاب اورشليم القدس

כרטיס כניסה ליחיד
ADMIT ONE

№ 09589   מס׳

Price: מחיר:

5

ש.ח.   IS

Summarizing Main Ideas

Section 1 Creating the Modern Middle East

- When the Ottoman Empire was defeated in World War I, the region was divided into many different countries.
- The struggle between Arabs and Jews over Palestine led to the creation of Israel and left the Palestinians without a homeland.

Section 2 Israel: A Determined Country

- Israel has created one of the most technologically advanced countries in the region since it became an independent country in 1948.
- Challenges facing Israel include political and social division among its citizens and achieving a lasting peace with the Palestinians and its Arab neighbors.

Section 3 Jordan, Lebanon, Syria, and Iraq

- Jordan and Syria are working to become modern countries.
- Although Iraq and Lebanon were once prosperous countries, war has brought great suffering to their people.

Section 4 Arabian Peninsula

- Countries on the Arabian Peninsula have used their oil wealth to modernize.
- Countries such as Saudi Arabia have not let modernization upset their Islamic way of life.

Section 5 Turkey, Iran, and Cyprus

- Turkey, the most industrialized country in the region, faces challenges to its stability.
- The 1979 Islamic revolution in Iran greatly affected its development.
- Ethnic unrest between Greek and Turkish Cypriots divides the island country of Cyprus.

Reviewing Vocabulary

Use each of the following terms in a sentence that shows its meaning.

1. **Zionist**
2. **self-determination**
3. **drip irrigation**
4. **Knesset**
5. **desalination**
6. **ayatollah**
7. **secular**
8. **shah**

Applying the Geographic Themes

1. **Regions** What role did World War I play in the creation of the modern Middle East?
2. **Human-Environment Interaction** How has technology been important to Israel?
3. **Place** How has warfare affected Iraq?
4. **Human-Environment Interaction** How has life changed on the Arabian Peninsula?
5. **Movement** Describe how Westernization affected Iran.

Critical Thinking and Applying Skills

1. **Analyzing Information** Water and oil are the two most important resources in Southwest Asia. Do you agree or disagree? Support your argument with examples from different countries in the region.
2. **Interpreting a Remote Sensing Image** Refer to the steps outlined in the skill lesson on page 463 to help you answer the following questions regarding the satellite images found on page 111.

   a. Which part of the river experienced the most flooding?

   b. How could images like these help city planners avoid future flood damage?

Journal Activity

Writing Across Cultures

▶ 1. Write two paragraphs that describe how the people of the Arabian Peninsula live from the point of view of a person who lives in the region.

▶ 2. "This world is for the powerful," says Omar Abu Gharbiyeh in a discouraged voice. Omar, 16, is a Palestinian. Originally from the West Bank, he now lives in Jordan, but dreams of returning to the land of his birth. Why do you think Omar feels so powerless? How might recent negotiations between Israel and the Palestinians affect Omar's future?

Take a virtual tour of Jerusalem. Link to this site from:

• www.phschool.com

When you've completed your tour, write a paragraph telling what you learned and what you'd most like to visit, and why.

The Countries of Southwest Asia

Number from 1 to 12 on a piece of paper. Next to each number, write the letter of the place on the map that corresponds to the place listed below.

1. Iraq
2. Iran
3. Israel
4. Jordan
5. Kuwait
6. Lebanon
7. Oman
8. Saudi Arabia
9. Syria
10. Turkey
11. United Arab Emirates
12. Yemen

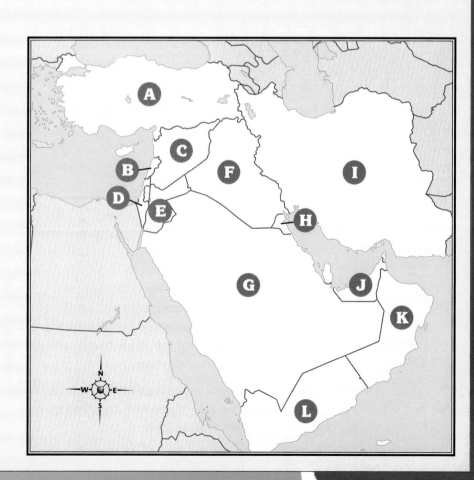

DESALINATION OF SEAWATER

Many regions of the world have limited water supplies and must rely on desalinated seawater for agriculture and drinking water. This lab uses a process called distillation to separate the salt from the water.

MATERIALS:

Ice

Water or seawater

Measuring cup

Small pan

Collecting cup

   (glass or ceramic)

Salt

Pyrex beaker

Funnel

Flexible

   tubing

Duct tape

Hot plate

Plastic wrap

PROCEDURES:

1. Make a cold water bath by adding ice and water to the small pan. Place the collecting cup in the cold water bath.

2. Add 1 cup (8 oz) of water and 2 teaspoons of salt to the Pyrex beaker. Swirl the beaker until the salt is dissolved. This is about the same salt concentration as seawater. (Use real seawater if it is available.)

3. Attach the tubing to the spout of the funnel. Then place the wide mouth of the funnel on the top of the beaker.

4. Secure the funnel to the beaker with duct tape.

5. Place the open end of the flexible tubing in the collecting cup and cover the cup with plastic wrap. Secure the wrap with tape.

6. Place the Pyrex beaker on the hot plate. **CAUTION:** *The beaker will become hot as it sits on the hot plate.* Observe what happens.

7. As the water in the Pyrex beaker boils down, it will get more concentrated and harder to boil. You will not be able to de-salt the entire cup (8 oz.) of water. Turn off the hot plate and allow the beaker to cool down.

8. Pour the water in the collecting cup into the measuring cup to see how much water you were able to desalinate.

OBSERVATIONS AND ANALYSIS:

1. How easy was it to desalinate water? Most desalination plants use other methods to treat water. Why do you think this is so?

2. What was your percent yield? Divide the amount collected by the amount you started with. (Number of ounces collected divided by 8 oz) x 100 = percent yield. The average family uses 360 gallons of water a day. How much seawater would you need to make 360 gallons of desalinated water by distillation?

3. Salt is a damaging substance to most plants. How could you dispose of or re-use the left-over salt to ensure that it would not come in contact with vegetation?

Water and PEACE

"If you want reasons to fight, water will give you ample opportunities," states a hydrology professor at a Middle Eastern university. "If countries here would share their resources and cooperate, everyone could have the water they needed," he adds, "but every country here wants to be independent."

One way that some countries have become independent is to desalinate, or remove the salt from seawater. However, desalinated water is extremely costly. A war over water is said to be unlikely, but experts claim that Southwest Asia has only 15 to 20 years before their natural fresh water resources run out.

Desalination plant in Saudi Arabia

taking Action

Less than 1% of the world's water supply is fresh and accessible for use. For this reason, fresh, clean water is a limited resource all over the world. Here are some ways that you can conserve this resource:

✔ Install water-saving faucets and shower heads— they can cut your water usage by 50%.

✔ If you water outdoors, do it only during the late evening after the sun sets to prevent evaporation.

✔ Plant gardens with native plants that are drought tolerant if you live in a dry area.

eight

Africa

CHAPTERS

A Global Perspective

Africa lies south of Europe and the Mediterranean Sea and is connected to Asia in the northwest by a mere strip of land. To its west are the waters of the Atlantic Ocean, and to its east is the Indian Ocean. Deserts and rain forests, mountains and plateaus, city dwellers and nomads can all be found in Africa. As you read this unit, you will discover the role that Africa's location, landforms, and climates play in shaping the lives of the many people who live in the region.

Robinson Projection

Tissisat Falls on the Blue Nile, Ethiopia

KEYS TO UNDERSTANDING THIS REGION

1 Countries and Cities *(pp. 476–477)*
European colonizers divided Africa into arbitrary regions that often did not reflect physical features or ethnic divisions. After the Europeans left, Africans worked hard to unite their nations. During this time, African cities grew at a tremendous rate.

2 Physical Features *(pp. 478–479)*
The most important feature of North Africa is the vast Sahara, a desert of rock and shifting sand. South of the Sahara, Africa is made up of a high plateau that drops sharply at the coastline. Powerful rivers run through the wide basins of Africa's interior.

3 People and Cultures *(pp. 480–481)*
Though a home of ancient and rich cultures, Africa has been troubled by conflict between ethnic groups, races, and political parties. Over the last decade, peaceful political changes have been made in several countries.

4 Climate and Vegetation *(pp. 482–483)*
On the African continent, the same climate regions—deserts, grasslands, and rain forests—mirror one another north and south of the Equator.

5 Economy and Resources *(pp. 484–485)*
Many African nations are too dependent on the export of a few raw materials and are working to vary their exports and to industrialize. They are also trying to improve agriculture so that they can feed their people.

VISUAL PREVIEW ACTIVITY

Each of the five keys above corresponds to a section of the Regional Atlas that follows. Number from 1 to 5 on a piece of paper. Use information from the maps, graphs, and photographs in the Regional Atlas to write one additional fact for each of the five keys above.

AFRICA

Use the Map, Graph, and Photo Studies in the Regional Atlas to gain a better understanding of the region's physical and cultural geography.

ATLAS VOCABULARY

escarpment	erg	leaching
cataract	rift valley	diversify

1 COUNTRIES AND CITIES

LARGEST CITIES

Cairo, Egypt
6,800,000

Alexandria, Egypt
3,380,000

Kinshasa, D.R. Congo
2,664,500

Casablanca, Morocco
2,263,500

Giza, Egypt
2,144,000

Abidjan, Côte d'Ivoire
1,929,000

Addis Ababa, Ethiopia
1,912,500

Cape Town, South Africa
1,911,500

Algiers, Algeria
1,740,500

= *1,000,000 people*
Source: *United Nations*

GRAPH STUDY

1 **Largest Cities** Nearly three quarters of the people who live in Africa south of the Sahara live in rural villages. However, country people have been steadily moving to cities over the years. In 1960 only a few cities in Africa had populations over 500,000. *What do all but one of the current largest cities listed on the graph have in common? Use the map on the next page to help find your answer.*

MAP STUDY
Applying the Geographic Themes

2 **Location** The equator passes through the middle of Africa. *Which nations does the equator cross?*

3 **Place** Find the following capitals: Cape Town, Monrovia, Freetown. *What do all these cities have in common?*

4 **Movement** The capitals of the Democratic Republic of the Congo and Congo take advantage of a major river transportation route. *On what river are these capitals located?*

Africa: POLITICAL

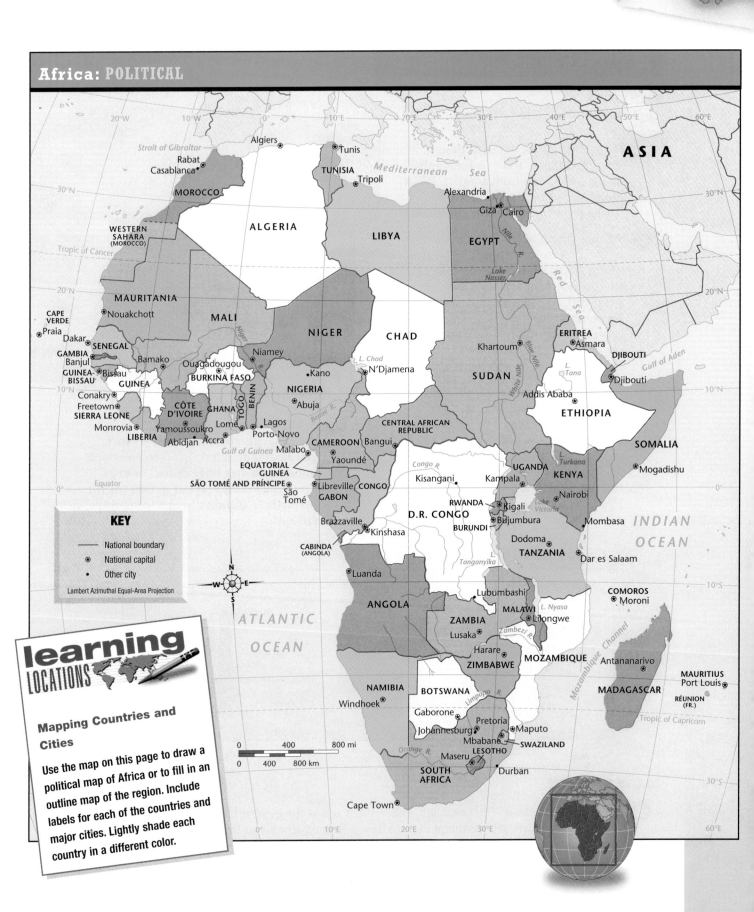

KEY

— National boundary
⊛ National capital
• Other city

Lambert Azimuthal Equal-Area Projection

learning LOCATIONS

Mapping Countries and Cities

Use the map on this page to draw a political map of Africa or to fill in an outline map of the region. Include labels for each of the countries and major cities. Lightly shade each country in a different color.

2 PHYSICAL FEATURES

MAP STUDY
Applying the Geographic Themes

1 Regions Africa has wide deserts, high mountains, and vast forests that divide one region from another. *What physical feature separates North Africa from the rest of the continent?*

2 Place South of the Sahara, Africa is a vast plateau interrrupted by basins. Along the coast, the plateau drops sharply down an **escarpment**, or steep cliff, to a narrow coastal plain. **Cataracts**, areas of the rivers that are broken by waterfalls and rapids, often prevent navigation up the rivers. *What basin is located in southern Africa?*

3 Human-Environment Interaction Great rivers like the Nile, the Niger, and the Congo flow thousands of miles through Africa, supplying water, electric power, and transportation. Humans change the ecology of African rivers as they dam them to provide irrigation or hydroelectric power. *In what part of Africa is the Nile River located?*

APPEARED IN *NATIONAL GEOGRAPHIC*

PHOTO STUDY

4 A Shifting Landscape Although the Sahara is covered mostly by rock, gravel, and boulders, in some areas drifting sand creates huge dunes, or **ergs**. *Critical Thinking* **What actions might people take if dunes began to cover a village?**

Cross Section: Africa

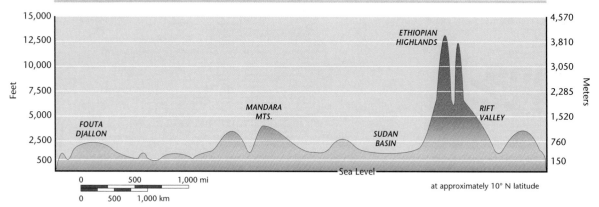

at approximately 10° N latitude

DIAGRAM STUDY

5 Physical Profile The Great Rift Valley slices across the eastern part of Africa. Scientists believe that a **rift valley** is formed when two tectonic plates move apart on the earth's surface. *What is the elevation of the portion of the Great Rift Valley shown in the diagram?*

AFRICA

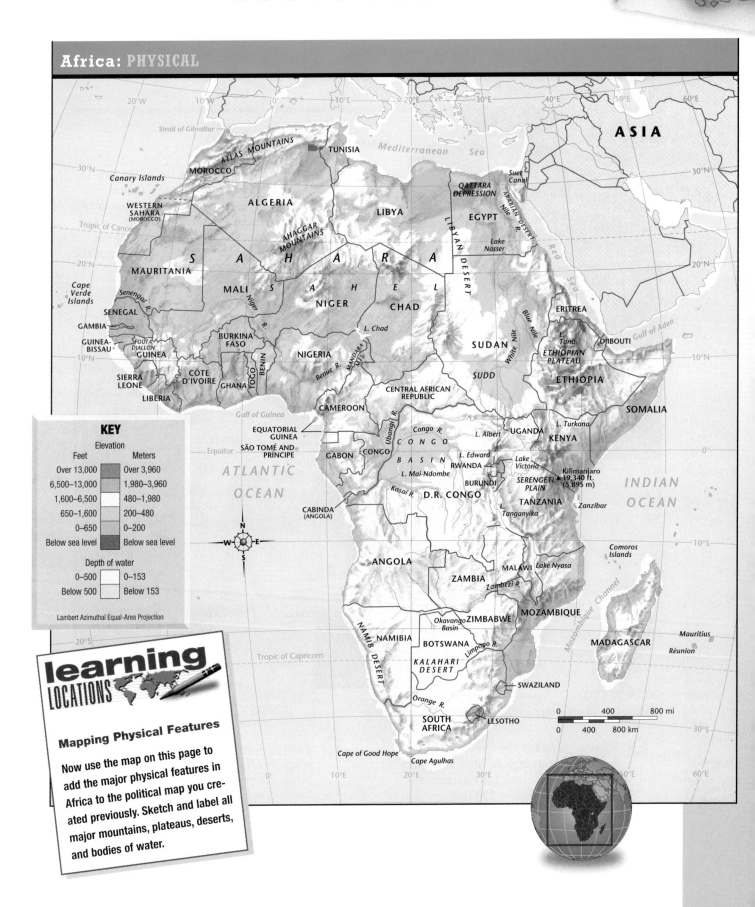

Africa: PHYSICAL

KEY

Elevation

Feet	Meters
Over 13,000	Over 3,960
6,500–13,000	1,980–3,960
1,600–6,500	480–1,980
650–1,600	200–480
0–650	0–200
Below sea level	Below sea level

Depth of water

0–500	0–153
Below 500	Below 153

Lambert Azimuthal Equal-Area Projection

learning LOCATIONS

Mapping Physical Features

Now use the map on this page to add the major physical features in Africa to the political map you created previously. Sketch and label all major mountains, plateaus, deserts, and bodies of water.

PHOTO STUDY

1 **Vast Ethnic Diversity** North of the Sahara, populations are less diverse than in the rest of Africa. Nearly 3,000 ethnic groups live south of the Sahara. They speak a total of more than 800 languages. *Critical Thinking Suggest ways in which ethnic groups can differ from one another besides language.*

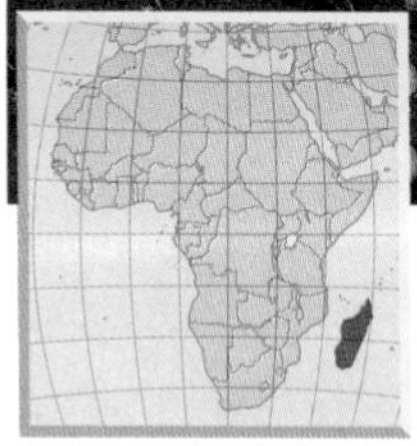

MAP STUDY
Applying the Geographic Themes

2 **Place** Africa is the world's second most populous region, after Asia, and is the fastest-growing continent in the world. Today almost 720 million people live in the region. *Explain why some areas are uninhabited.*

3 **Place** Keeping people healthy is a challenge in Africa. Life expectancy is only 55 years, lower than on any other continent. Many diseases that afflict Africans are carried by tropical insects and parasites. African's health is also weakened by poor diet due to constant problems of drought and famine. *Connections: Health How does poor diet contribute to disease?*

AFRICA

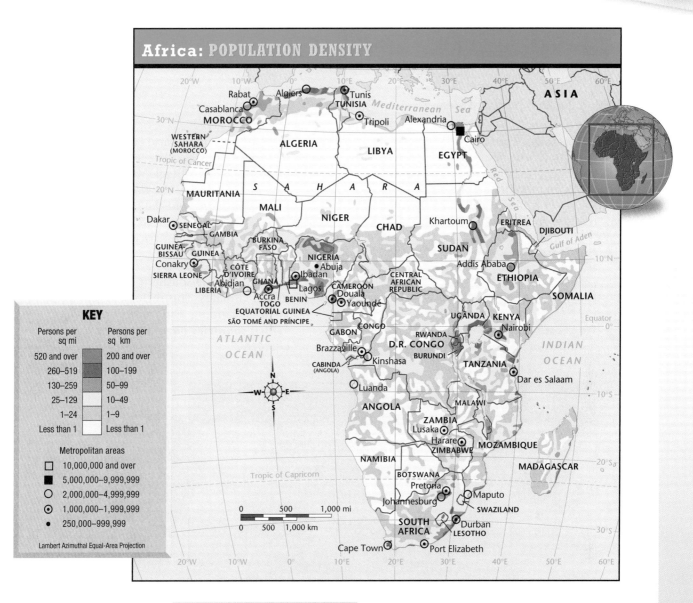

Africa: POPULATION DENSITY

KEY

Persons per sq mi	Persons per sq km
520 and over	200 and over
260–519	100–199
130–259	50–99
25–129	10–49
1–24	1–9
Less than 1	Less than 1

Metropolitan areas

☐ 10,000,000 and over
■ 5,000,000–9,999,999
○ 2,000,000–4,999,999
◉ 1,000,000–1,999,999
• 250,000–999,999

Lambert Azimuthal Equal-Area Projection

APPEARED IN *NATIONAL GEOGRAPHIC*

PHOTO STUDY

4 **African Women** Throughout Africa, women's work is important to the economic and social well-being of the community. Women such as the one shown here in the Democratic Republic of the Congo produce food, most of which is consumed within the country and not exported. *Critical Thinking* *Why is it vital that all family members work in African nations?*

A F R I C A

Chapter 24 ▪ Regional Atlas

4 CLIMATE AND VEGETATION

MAP STUDY
Applying the Geographic Themes

1 Location Much of Africa is tropical rain forest. The rain forest is always hot and rainy, with an average of 100 inches (254 cm) of rainfall each year. *Where is the main region of rain forest located in relation to the equator?*

2 Regions North and south of the rain forest, much of the land is savanna, an area of tall grasses with scattered trees. *What types of climate are found in these regions?*

3 Regions South of the desert that covers much of North Africa, the Sahara, lies a broad band of semiarid land known as the Sahel (suh HEL). The Sahel nations must constantly struggle with the approaching desert. *Use the climate and vegetation maps and the physical map on page 479 to locate and name two other arid regions in Africa.*

4 Human-Environment Interaction Parts of extreme southern Africa have milder climates. This region, which is good for farming, is heavily populated. *Which countries have these milder climates?*

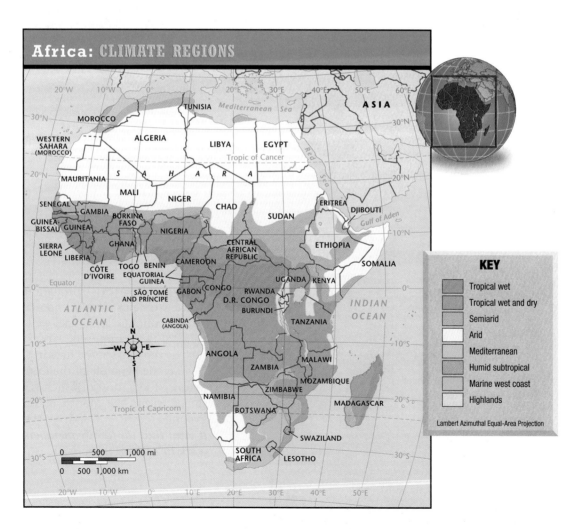

Africa: CLIMATE REGIONS

KEY
- Tropical wet
- Tropical wet and dry
- Semiarid
- Arid
- Mediterranean
- Humid subtropical
- Marine west coast
- Highlands

Lambert Azimuthal Equal-Area Projection

REGIONAL *atlas*

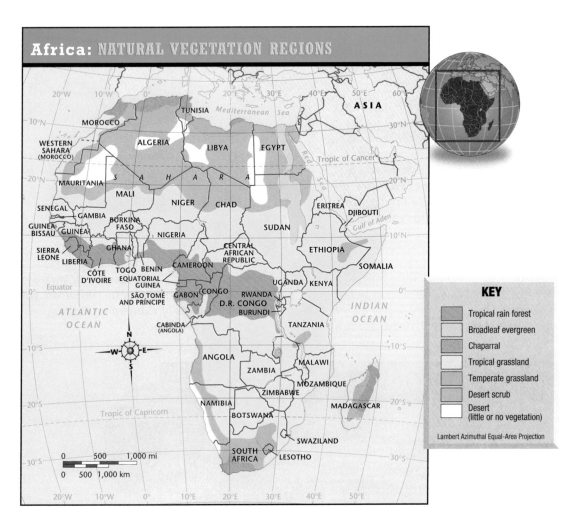

Africa: NATURAL VEGETATION REGIONS

KEY

- Tropical rain forest
- Broadleaf evergreen
- Chaparral
- Tropical grassland
- Temperate grassland
- Desert scrub
- Desert (little or no vegetation)

Lambert Azimuthal Equal-Area Projection

Linking Wind, Precipitation, and Vegetation

DIAGRAM STUDY

5 Prevailing Winds Wide bands of vegetation stretch across Africa. The colors on the diagram correspond to the vegetation key on the map above. *Critical Thinking How do prevailing winds influence Africa's precipitation and vegetation?*

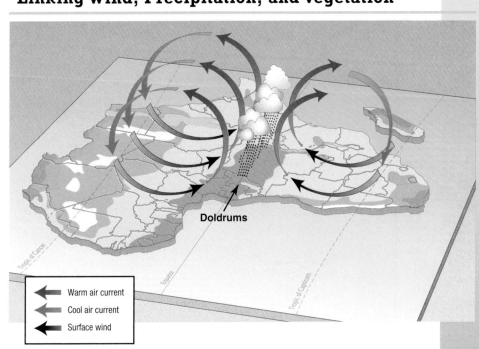

Doldrums

→ Warm air current
→ Cool air current
→ Surface wind

MAP STUDY
Applying the Geographic Themes

1 **Human-Environment Interaction**
Farming in Africa can be risky. In the tropical, wet climate of the rain forests, the soil is poor due to **leaching**—the dissolving and washing away of nutrients. In dry areas, frequent droughts cause crop failures. *What is the main kind of farming in Africa?*

2 **Regions** After winning their independence, many African governments borrowed large sums of money to pay for modernization. Loan repayments are now

a major part of many African national budgets. *Find economic activities on the map that might require loans in order to be developed.*

3 **Human-Environment Interaction**
Many African nations depend on one or two exports. If the world price drops, entire economies crumble. Thus governments are trying to **diversify**, or increase the variety of, their exports. *What are the main products of Cameroon, Gabon, Congo, and Angola?*

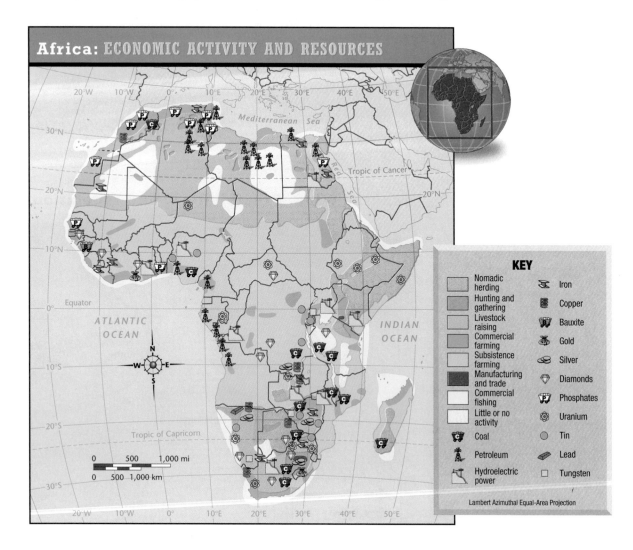

Africa: ECONOMIC ACTIVITY AND RESOURCES

KEY

Nomadic herding		Iron	
Hunting and gathering		Copper	
Livestock raising		Bauxite	
Commercial farming		Gold	
Subsistence farming		Silver	
Manufacturing and trade		Diamonds	
Commercial fishing		Phosphates	
Little or no activity		Uranium	
Coal		Tin	
Petroleum		Lead	
Hydroelectric power		Tungsten	

Lambert Azimuthal Equal-Area Projection

APPEARED IN *NATIONAL GEOGRAPHIC*

PHOTO STUDY

 A Desert Community
Wells and springs provide life-giving fresh water to North African oasis villages such as this one above in Algeria. The scarce water sustains plants, animals, and people.
Connections: Science Why are underground sources of water so important in North Africa?

atlas REVIEW

Vocabulary and Main Ideas

1. Define: **a.** escarpment **b.** cataract **c.** erg **d.** rift valley **e.** leaching **f.** diversify

2. What physical feature divides the continent into two major regions?

3. Why are African nations trying to diversify?

4. **Critical Thinking** Explain how the desire to modernize has created a problem for some African nations.

learning LOCATIONS

5. Which country is the largest in Central Africa?

6. What is the large island nation off Africa's eastern coast?

AFRICA

HISTORY shapes the present

Legacies of Colonialism

A century or more of European colonial rule has left modern African nations with many problems that work against their political stability. What are the legacies of colonialism in Africa?

European Nations Divide Africa

In 1884, delegates from twelve European countries, the Ottoman Empire, and the United States met in Berlin, Germany. All of them already had interests or claimed colonies in Africa. They wanted to set ground rules for taking over the continent without clashes among themselves. No representatives from Africa were invited, however.

The Berlin Conference was called because of a sudden expansion in European **imperialism**, or empire building, in the 1870s. National pride was strong in Europe, and ambitious nations wanted empires. Colonies and trading rights were also important because of the rapid growth of industries. Africa offered both rich resources and new markets for European goods.

The European Takeover

European nations carved up Africa to suit themselves. The slave trade in preceding centuries had weakened societies and economies in many parts of Africa. Still, some African rulers resisted strongly. The Ashanti kingdom battled British rule in a series of wars between

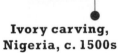

Ivory carving, Nigeria, c. 1500s

1824 and 1900. Mandinka warriors led by Samori Toure battled the French along the Niger River. Nonetheless, by 1914 (map, next page), only Liberia and Ethiopia remained free of European rule.

Wood carving, Congo, early 1900s

Types of Colonial Rule

Direct rule In most African colonies, European officials set up governments and laws like those in their home countries. They replaced local rulers with officials sent out from Belgium or Germany or Portugal. Africans were kept out of government and had few chances for education or professional training.

French colonial officials also took direct control, but they tried to make the local Africans into French citizens. They brought in French schools and political ways to replace African institutions.

Indirect rule In British colonies, African officials and local leaders were allowed to run local governments and community affairs. Final authority, however, rested with the local British residents.

The Past Challenges New Nations

In the 1950s and 1960s, most African colonies gained independence. But the years of colonial rule left many problems for the new nations. New national boundaries usually followed colonial borders, which had been drawn by Europeans who knew little about Africa. They often put together within one nation people from rival ethnic groups with different languages, religious beliefs, and traditions. These differences led to bloody violence and political unrest in a number of nations, such as Nigeria and present-day Rwanda.

Few Europeans were interested in Africa's long-term development. As a result, Africans gained no training as government workers or administrators. Education was not encouraged.

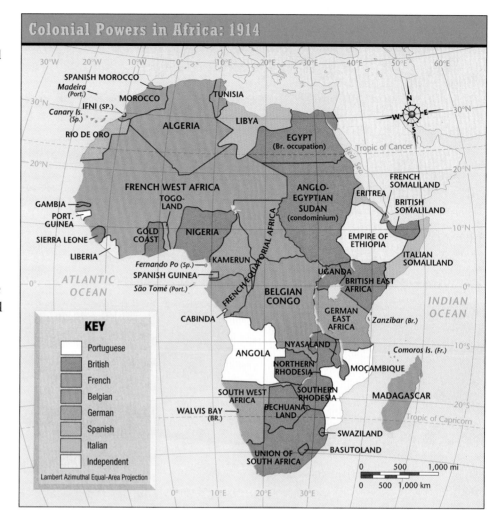

Colonial Powers in Africa: 1914

KEY
- Portuguese
- British
- French
- Belgian
- German
- Spanish
- Italian
- Independent

Lambert Azimuthal Equal-Area Projection

The economy, moreover, was run only to profit the colonizing country. Colonial industries stripped away valuable minerals and timber, while ignoring economic development in Africa itself.

Today African governments work to reverse these patterns. In many African nations, the struggle for true economic independence continues.

connecting
TO TODAY

1. **According to the map, what two European countries held the greatest amount of African territory in 1914?**

2. **What different styles did European nations adopt in ruling their colonies?**

3. Critical Thinking **What disadvantages did colonial rule have for Africans in colonies? What advantages might it have brought?**

4. **Hands-On Activity Trace the outlines of the map of Africa in 1914 and compare it with a map of Africa today. Label each present-day country with both its colonial name and its current name. (Redraw any national boundaries as necessary.) Color-code your map to show the colonial background of the modern nations.**

North Africa

SECTIONS

1 Egypt

2 Libya and the Maghreb

North Africa: POLITICAL

ATLANTIC OCEAN

Strait of Gibraltar

Tangier
Rabat
Casablanca
Marrakech
MOROCCO
Fès
Meknès

Oran
Algiers
Constantine
Annaba
Tunis
TUNISIA
Tripoli

Mediterranean Sea

Banghazi
Alexandria
Cairo
Giza

ALGERIA

LIBYA

EGYPT

Nile R.

Red Sea

WESTERN SAHARA (MOROCCO)

Tropic of Cancer

KEY

— National boundary
⊛ National capital
• Other city

Lambert Azimuthal Equal-Area Projection

0   300   600 mi
0   300   600 km

learning LOCATIONS

Mapping the Region
Create a map like the one above, shading
each country a different color. Then add
labels for countries and bodies of water
that are shown on the map.

Egypt

Section Preview

Main Ideas

Most Egyptians live in the Nile River valley, the Nile Delta, or the Suez Canal zone.

Urbanization and rapid population growth are major challenges in modern Egypt.

Although Egypt is still dependent on the export of raw materials, it is developing its industries.

Vocabulary

fellaheen, bazaar, pharaoh, basin irrigation, reservoir, perennial irrigation, capital

APPEARED IN *NATIONAL GEOGRAPHIC*

As the Nile approaches the Mediterranean Sea, it passes through Cairo, Egypt.

As the map on page 490 shows, the Arab nation of Egypt has a vital location: the northeast corner of Africa, where travelers and goods pass between two continents. It is large—about one-and-a-half times the size of Texas. It is also one of the most populous countries in the Arab world. These three factors—strategic location, size, and population—make Egypt a power to be respected in world affairs.

Location and Regions

Egypt is a land of wide, forbidding deserts divided by a single large river, the Nile. Without that river, all of Egypt would be desert. For this reason, Egypt is sometimes referred to as the "Gift of the Nile."

A Ribbon of Green The Nile is the world's longest river. It begins in Central Africa and flows northward for 4,145 miles (6,671 km) before it empties into the Mediterranean Sea. On its way it runs through Egypt from south to north.

As it nears the end of its course, the Nile forks into two major branches. Between these two branches is an area known as the Nile Delta. A delta is land formed by soil in the water that is dropped as the river slows and enters the sea. The delta, which has been enriched by the Nile for centuries, is astoundingly fertile. The **fellaheen**, as Egyptian farmers are called, grow impressive crops without the aid of modern machinery. Like other Egyptian farmers, they rarely even use plows. With a population of 61.9 million people, Egypt relies on human labor rather than machines to farm.

About 99 percent of Egypt's people live either in the Nile Valley or the delta region. Along the Nile's cultivated banks, population density averages about 5,000 people per square mile (1,900 per sq km). Egypt's two largest cities are Cairo, the capital, which straddles the Nile, and Alexandria, a major seaport and resort on the Mediterranean Sea.

The Desert Regions On either side of the Nile Valley are harsh wastelands. On the west is the Libyan Desert. On the east is a continuation of the Arabian Desert. The Sinai (SY ny) Peninsula, located in Asia to the east of the Suez Canal, is part of Egypt's eastern desert region.

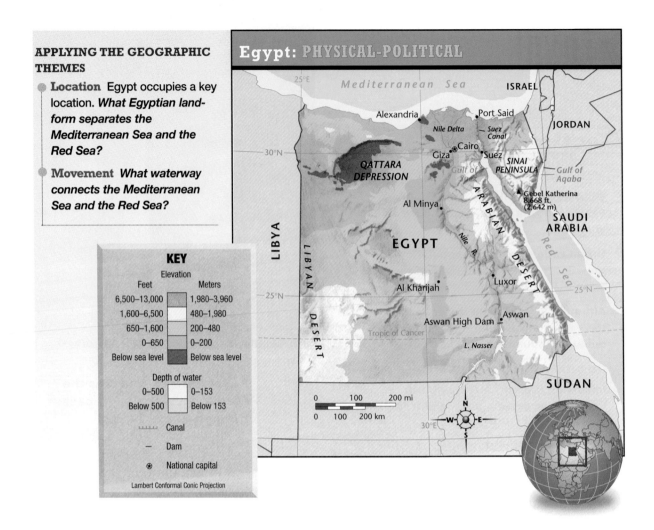

APPLYING THE GEOGRAPHIC THEMES

● **Location** Egypt occupies a key location. *What Egyptian landform separates the Mediterranean Sea and the Red Sea?*

● **Movement** *What waterway connects the Mediterranean Sea and the Red Sea?*

KEY

Elevation

Feet		Meters
6,500–13,000		1,980–3,960
1,600–6,500		480–1,980
650–1,600		200–480
0–650		0–200
Below sea level		Below sea level

Depth of water

0–500		0–153
Below 500		Below 153

······ Canal

— Dam

⊛ National capital

Lambert Conformal Conic Projection

Egypt: PHYSICAL-POLITICAL

Strong winds blow constantly across the Sahara. In the early summer a special wind, known in Egypt as the *khamsin* (kam SEEN), creates sandstorms. It blows hot air, dust, and grit into the Nile Valley. In bad years the *khamsin* blows so hard that the Egyptian sky turns orange with flying sand.

Oases are the only arable land in the desert. But the desert does hold some resources. Phosphates, for example, which are used to make fertilizer, are extracted from the desert, as is some oil.

Egyptian Life

Over half of Egypt's population lives in rural areas. Yet Egypt's urban areas have grown in recent decades, as more and more people have moved from rural villages to cities.

In some respects, village life in Egypt has remained unchanged for hundreds of years. The fellaheen live in small, low houses made of sun-dried mud bricks. These houses are often formed of rooms clustered around a central courtyard. If rural families can afford to, they keep domestic animals, such as chickens, goats, and donkeys, which provide food and transportation.

Life in the cities, however, has changed rapidly in recent times. After all, Cairo and Alexandria offer millions of people opportunities for jobs, schooling, culture, and entertainment. These opportunities constantly attract people from rural communities. Unfortunately, the cities cannot comfortably hold all the people who move to them. New arrivals from the countryside are often unable to find jobs or housing. Unwilling to return to their villages, they live in tents and other makeshift shelters. Cairo in particular has become a striking blend of new and old, rich and poor. Only blocks away from modern department stores that display the latest Paris fashions are the traditional Arab open-air markets, or **bazaars.**

Egypt's Past

Cities and their attractions have been a part of Egyptian life for well over 5,000 years. The civilization of the ancient Egyptians was unique and long-lasting. They were among the first people in the world to set up an organized government and religion and to invent a written language.

Ancient Egypt Among the accomplishments of the ancient Egyptians was the building of the world-famous pyramids, southwest of Cairo. The pyramids were built as tombs for the **pharaohs**, the rulers of ancient Egypt. Egyptians believed that a person's spirit might need to return to its body after death. Therefore they preserved the bodies of the pharaohs in a process known as mummification. Egyptians also believed that a person's spirit might need nourishment and assistance in the afterlife. They placed many useful objects, including food, furniture, jewelry, and gold in the pharaohs' tombs.

Invaders Rule The location of this rich kingdom at the crossroads of Asia, Africa, and Europe made it a tempting target for waves of invaders. Over the centuries, Egypt was ruled by the Greek Alexander the Great as well as by the Romans. They brought the Greek language and Roman customs to the ancient land.

When the Arabs conquered Egypt in A.D. 642, Arabic became Egypt's official language and Islam its official religion. Today more than 80 percent of Egyptians are Muslims. Most of the remaining minority are Copts, a very old Christian sect.

For more than one thousand years Egypt was ruled as part of various Muslim empires. The last of these was that of the Ottoman Turks.

European Interventions By the late 1700s, the Ottoman Turks' power was in decline, and European nations began to intervene in Egyptian affairs. The Suez Canal, which linked the Mediterranean and Red seas, opened in 1869 and made Egypt a vital link between Britain and its eastern colonies in Asia. In 1875, when Egypt's ruler faced heavy debts, Great Britain gladly purchased Egypt's share of ownership in the Suez Canal.

APPEARED IN *NATIONAL GEOGRAPHIC*

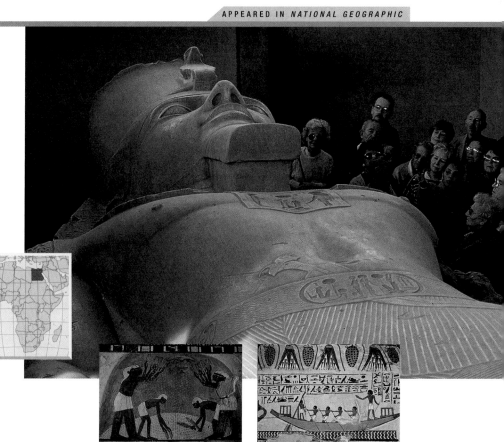

Egyptian Tombs

Place Through mummification, Egyptians preserved the bodies of their pharaohs, such as Ramses the Great (shown at right). Tombs of pharaohs and other important officials also contained paintings showing scenes of everyday life (below). **Critical Thinking** *Why do people today find mummies so fascinating?*

The list of cargoes carried through the Suez Canal has much to tell about trading relationships worldwide. Northbound ships often carry raw materials from less developed nations. Southbound ships often carry food and goods from industrial nations. Because the canal is not deep enough, oil tankers cannot use the route when returning northward with full tanks. Instead they must sail around the Cape of Good Hope.

In 1879 Egyptian nationalists revolted, determined to regain control of the canal. Nationalists are people who want to form an independent nation to protect their common culture and interests. Britain responded by invading Egypt and defeating the new government in 1882. British troops remained in Egypt for decades.

Following World War I, Egyptian nationalists again pushed for independence. In 1922 Britain agreed to their demands. But in effect the British continued to control Egypt, and Egyptian rulers had little power.

Independent Egypt In 1952 a group of nationalist army officers overthrew the government of Egypt. Colonel Gamal Abdel Nasser emerged as the new ruler. Nasser was determined to end Western domination of Egypt, modernize the country, and make it a major influence in world politics.

In 1956 Nasser seized control of the Suez Canal, creating an international crisis. Israel, Britain, and France jointly invaded Egypt in an attempt to retake the waterway. Both the United States and the Soviet Union supported a United Nations resolution demanding a cease-fire and the withdrawal of outside forces from Egyptian territory. This action forced the Western nations to call off the attack. Nasser held the canal, and the British left Egypt in 1957. For the first time in more than two thousand years, Egypt was ruled solely by Egyptians.

Nasser formed close ties with the Soviet Union, the major Communist nation at that time. Helped by Soviet money and experts, the Egyptians implemented Nasser's many modernization projects. Under Nasser, industry was developed, and Egypt's dependence on cotton, its main export crop, was reduced.

When Nasser died in 1970, Anwar Sadat became president of Egypt. Sadat ended Egypt's alliance with the Soviet Union and forged new ties with the West.

Egypt and Israel After World War II, Egypt developed closer links with the Arab Middle East. The main cause of this trend was the establishment of the state of Israel in 1948. The Arabs were united in their opposition to the existence of Israel. Egypt took a major role in the 1948, 1967, and 1973 wars with Israel, but suffered defeat in all three. In 1967 it lost control of the Sinai Peninsula to Israel.

When Egypt was defeated for the third time in 1973, Sadat decided to seek a permanent

Suez Canal

Movement Huge tankers and tiny rowboats share the Suez Canal. Completed in 1869, the canal links the Mediterranean and Red seas and is controlled by Egypt. *What happened when Egypt seized control of the canal in 1956?*

Aswan High Dam

● **Human-Environment Interaction**
The building of the Aswan High Dam
(at left of photo) created a giant
reservoir, named Lake Nasser. Water
from the reservoir is used to irrigate
Egypt's farmland, which no longer
receives yearly floods from the Nile.
Critical Thinking *How does the
Aswan High Dam show the costs
and benefits of changing the
environment?*

peace with Israel. In 1979 Egypt became the first
Arab nation to recognize Israel's right to exist. In
return, Israel agreed to return the Sinai
Peninsula to Egypt by 1982.

Sadat's peace treaty with Israel was harshly
criticized by other Arab nations, who believed that
he had betrayed the Arab cause. In 1981 Sadat was
assassinated. His successor, Hosni Mubarak, continues to honor the Egypt-Israeli peace treaty.

Controlling the Nile

Until recently, the Nile River flooded every
year, refreshing the fields with water and silt
that formed a rich, fertile soil. Egypt's farmers
have long built walls around their fields to trap
this water and silt. This form of irrigation,
basin irrigation, was good for growing
crops, but it did not work year round. And it
could not control heavy flooding, which often
brought disaster.

In 1959 President Nasser undertook an
enormous new water project. He started building a dam that would store Nile floodwaters in
a vast **reservoir**, or artificial lake. The waters of
Lake Nasser, as the reservoir was called, would
be the basis of a **perennial irrigation** system—one that provided water for agriculture all
through the year. The reservoir could also be
tapped to provide extra water for Cairo and to

generate electricity for the modern industries
Nasser hoped to develop in Egypt.

The Aswan High Dam was completed in
1970. It promptly ended flooding of the Nile
and permitted Egyptian farmers to plant two or

Country	Population	Life Expectancy (years)	Per Capita GNP (in U.S. $)
Algeria	28,400,000	67	1,650
Egypt	61,900,000	64	660
Libya	5,200,000	63	NA
Morocco	29,400,000	69	1,030
Tunisia	8,900,000	68	1,780
United States	263,200,000	76	24,750

Source: Population Reference Bureau — NA indicates data not available.

CHART SKILLS

● *What is the population of Egypt?*

● **Critical Thinking** *Note Egypt's per capita gross
national product (GNP). Why do you think it is so
low?*

three crops every year. Lake Nasser's irrigation water has also allowed more and more desert to be reclaimed for farming.

But the dam has also caused some problems. Floodwaters no longer carry silt to fertilize the land on the banks of the Nile. Farmers now are forced to use chemical fertilizers to make up for the lack of natural fertilization. Another problem caused by the dam is that perennial irrigation makes salt build up in the soil. Some 35 percent of Egyptian farmlands now suffer from a high salt content. Solving this new problem would involve installing huge drainage systems and would cost a great amount of money.

Changes in Egypt

As you have read, a key trend in Egypt today is urbanization—the movement of rural people to the nation's cities. For about the last forty years, the urban population has been growing at the rate of 4 percent annually. Cairo, for example, grew from 1.5 million in 1947 to more than 6.8 million in the early 1990s.

Population Growth A second key trend is rapid population growth throughout the nation. Egypt's overall population is growing at an annual rate of 2.3 percent, which means a doubling of the population every thirty-one years. Thus the Egyptian population increases by about a million people each year. Feeding, housing, educating, and providing other services for this fast-growing population strain the economy. But stemming population growth is not easy. Many Egyptians need the labor of every member of their large families. They resist government efforts to limit family size.

One of the major problems of Egypt's population growth is that it is outstripping the country's food supply. In 1960 Egypt produced nearly all its own food. Today, it imports more than one half of the food its people eat. The fertile land along the Nile is already intensively farmed. The Egyptian government has plans to increase the amount of arable land by irrigating farther into the desert, but this land will not be as naturally fertile as the soil in the Nile River valley. Large amounts of money will have to be spent on chemical fertilizers.

Egypt's Exports In the past, Egypt's economy depended on a single export: cotton. When international cotton prices were high, Egypt's economy prospered; when they fell, Egypt faced potential economic disaster. Now oil and petroleum products have taken first place among Egyptian exports.

Egypt's Future

Place Like many African countries, Egypt has a large percentage of young people. To train this growing population, Egypt offers free education through the university level. Shown here taking notes are students at the University of Cairo, which has some 100,000 students. **Critical Thinking** *What are the long-term benefits of education?*

Egypt's Major Exports

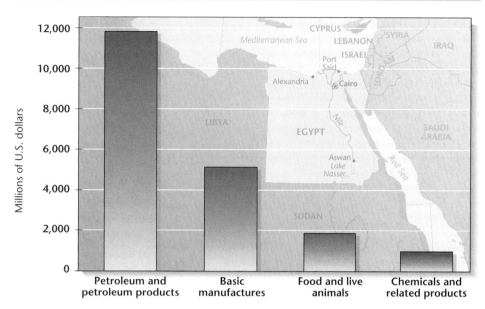

Millions of U.S. dollars

12,000 — 10,000 — 8,000 — 6,000 — 4,000 — 2,000 — 0

Petroleum and petroleum products | Basic manufactures | Food and live animals | Chemicals and related products

This change has not solved Egypt's economic problems. The country is still dependent upon the export of raw materials rather than manufactured goods. Most experts agree that to prosper, Egypt needs an industrial base that will provide much-needed jobs and produce goods for sale abroad.

Obstacles to Development Efforts to promote industrialization began in the late 1950s and increased in the 1960s. But several factors have limited the growth of industries. One factor is the country's limited number of skilled workers. Although Egypt has the largest pool of educated people in the Arab world, it frequently loses these professionals to wealthier countries, where salaries are much higher.

A second major challenge facing Egypt is lack of **capital**—money that is invested in building and supporting new industries. Average annual per capita GNP in Egypt is about $660, compared with about $7,780 in Saudi Arabia or $24,750 in the United States. With relatively low incomes, few Egyptians have money left over, after paying for their basic needs of food and housing, to invest in new factories or industries. Lacking the oil reserves of some of its more fortunate neighbors, Egypt depends heavily on aid from Western and other Arab nations.

Section 1 Review

Vocabulary and Main Ideas

1. Define: a. fellaheen b. bazaar c. pharaoh d. basin irrigation e. reservoir f. perennial irrigation g. capital

2. In what parts of Egypt do most Egyptians live?

3. What obstacles are slowing Egypt's attempts at industrialization?

4. Critical Thinking: *Perceiving Cause and Effect* How do you think life in Egypt might be different without the Nile River valley?

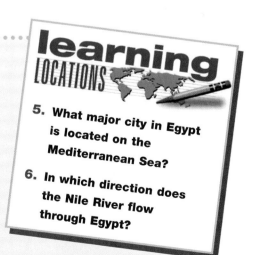

learning LOCATIONS

5. What major city in Egypt is located on the Mediterranean Sea?

6. In which direction does the Nile River flow through Egypt?

Focus on Skills

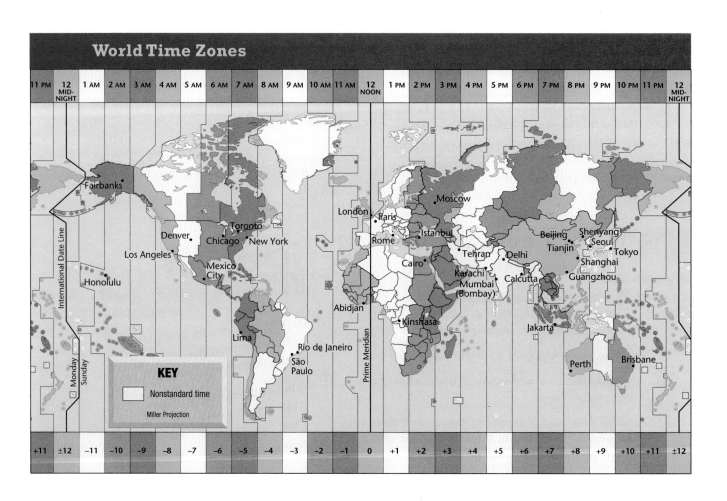

☐ Social Studies
☑ **Map and Globe**
☐ Critical Thinking
  and Problem Solving

Reading a Time Zone Map

In 1884, an international conference developed the present system of twenty-four time zones. Before the meeting, communities around the world calculated local time by the position of the sun. The International Date Line—located in the mid-Pacific Ocean at 180 degrees longitude—is the marker for where each day begins. So, if it is Sunday to the east of the line, it is Monday to the west. The following steps will help you to analyze a time zone map.

1. Study the information on the map. There are two sets of labels on this time zone map. At the top of the map is a sequence of hours labeled A.M. (before noon) and P.M. (after noon). The Prime Meridian at Greenwich, England, is labeled as "12:00 noon." Each colored band below the hour shares that hour's time. The sample hours shown express accurate readings only when the time is noon at the Prime Meridian. A second set of labels across the bottom of the map indicates the time difference in hours from the Prime Meridian. A value of +3 means a time three hours *later* than Greenwich time, and a value of -3 means three hours *earlier*. For example, if it is 2:00 P.M. in London, what time will it be in a zone bearing the label +7? If it is 3:00 P.M. in Cairo, what time will it be in a city six time zones to the west?

2. Pinpoint your zone and compare the time difference with other cities. Time zones make it easy to calculate global variations in time: If it is 2:00 P.M. in the time zone where you live, what time is it in Paris, France?

World Time Zones

| 11 PM | 12 MID-NIGHT | 1 AM | 2 AM | 3 AM | 4 AM | 5 AM | 6 AM | 7 AM | 8 AM | 9 AM | 10 AM | 11 AM | 12 NOON | 1 PM | 2 PM | 3 PM | 4 PM | 5 PM | 6 PM | 7 PM | 8 PM | 9 PM | 10 PM | 11 PM | 12 MID-NIGHT |

| +11 | ±12 | –11 | –10 | –9 | –8 | –7 | –6 | –5 | –4 | –3 | –2 | –1 | 0 | +1 | +2 | +3 | +4 | +5 | +6 | +7 | +8 | +9 | +10 | +11 | ±12 |

KEY

☐ Nonstandard time

Miller Projection

2 Libya and the Maghreb

APPEARED IN *NATIONAL GEOGRAPHIC*

For centuries, North Africans have used camel caravans to cross the Sahara.

Section Preview

Main Ideas

- North Africa's culture has been influenced by African, Arab, and European cultures.

- Urban and rural areas contrast sharply in Libya and the Maghreb.

- Libya and Algeria rely heavily on income from petroleum, but Tunisia and Morocco are beginning to rely on the export of manufactured goods.

Vocabulary

wadi, caravan, medina, souk

The North African countries west of Egypt are Libya and the Maghreb nations—Tunisia, Algeria, and Morocco. The word *Maghreb* comes from an Arabic term meaning "land farthest west." For a thousand years, these countries were the westernmost outposts of an Islamic empire that stretched across Asia, the Middle East, Africa, and into Europe. Today they retain close ties to other Islamic countries, especially those of the Middle East.

The North African nations are similar in many respects. The majority of the people are Arabic-speaking Muslims who live along the Mediterranean coast. Away from this narrow coast, their lands are arid, forming the northern margins of the Sahara. The shared presence of the desert and their similar history give the cultures of these four countries many things in common.

There are, however, important differences among these nations. For example, Libya is a large country with rich oil reserves and very little arable land. Tunisia is small and much more agricultural, but it has little oil.

The Landscape of North Africa

In the coastal areas of North Africa the climate is Mediterranean, with hot, sunny summers and cool, rainy winters. Away from the seacoast, the extremely dry climate of the Sahara prevails. But the landscape of the desert varies from area to area—sandy dunes flow into gravel and bare rock deserts. Dry riverbeds and sharp gullies, known as **wadis**, cut across the land, catching and temporarily holding water from sudden downpours. Low basins gradually rise to meet high, windswept plateaus and then mountains.

People who lived along the coast of North Africa found it easier to have contact with other countries than with interior regions of their own country. The people of the interior had limited contact with one another or with the outside world. No navigable rivers connected these places. The mountains and the desert were formidable barriers to travel and communication. For these reasons, the people of those interior regions have tended to maintain traditional ways.

A Blend of Cultures

Located on the southern coast of the much-traveled Mediterranean Sea, coastal regions of North Africa have been influenced by centuries of contact with other peoples. Today the region has a distinctive culture that is a blend of African, European, and Asian influences.

Early Movement Sometime after 5000 B.C. the Berbers—the original inhabitants of North Africa—became farmers and herders instead of nomads. They settled in villages along the Mediterranean coast and on the northern mountain slopes. Only a small portion of the population lived near oases. Over time, other groups came to power in the region, including the Carthaginians and the Romans.

During the period of Roman rule, camels imported from central Asia were introduced to North Africa. Camels have been called "ships of the desert." They are well adapted to desert conditions. Even in very hot weather, camels can travel for several days without water. Their large, flat feet allow them to walk over sand dunes much as snowshoes allow people to walk over snow.

Camels changed the geography of North Africa. For the first time, North Africans established regular trade with the people living south of the Sahara. They crossed the desert in **caravans**, large groups of merchants who have joined together to travel in safety. Southbound caravans carried salt, which was very valuable to people in tropical climates. Northbound caravans carried enslaved people as well as rich cargoes of ivory, gold, and feathers. They also transported wild animals such as hippopotamuses and elephants for the contests staged in Roman amphitheaters.

The Spread of Islam

A dramatic change occurred in Libya and the Maghreb during the mid-600s A.D., when Arab

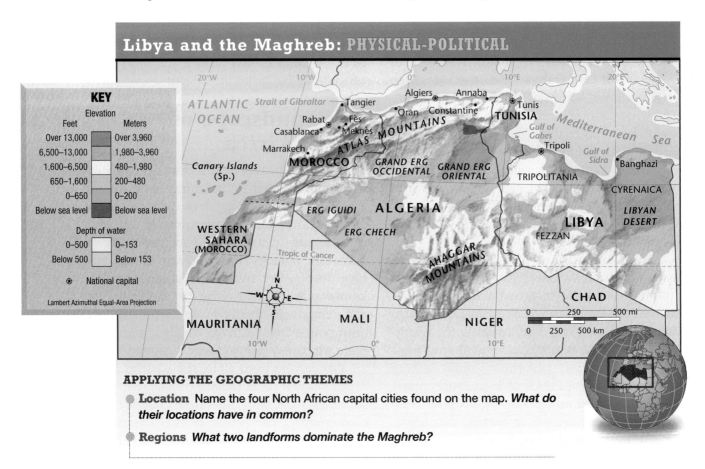

APPLYING THE GEOGRAPHIC THEMES

● **Location** Name the four North African capital cities found on the map. *What do their locations have in common?*

● **Regions** *What two landforms dominate the Maghreb?*

armies invaded North Africa. The Arabs' impact upon the region was tremendous. They brought with them a new religion, Islam, and a new language, Arabic. The Arab conquest was the start of a long golden age for North Africa. The region became a vital center of trade between Europe, Africa, and Asia and an important center of learning and scholarship.

Today, Arabs form the majority of the population in North Africa, with Berbers a substantial minority. Berbers in Algeria, for example, make up about 17 percent of the population.

European Influence In the nineteenth century some European powers sought to control North Africa. In 1830 France invaded Algeria. Algerian rebels battled French rule for more than fifty years, but were eventually defeated.

During the late 1800s, France extended its empire to Tunisia. European conquest of the area was completed in 1912, when France gained control of Morocco and Italy conquered Libya.

Following Italy's defeat in World War II, in 1951 the United Nations declared Libya an independent nation. However Algeria, Tunisia, and Morocco had to fight for their independence. In 1956 Morocco and Tunisia gained their freedom, followed by Algeria in 1962.

Rural vs. Urban

The most important cultural divisions in North Africa today are not between countries, but rather between rural and urban ways of life.

Rural Life Farmers living in Libya and the Maghreb still live in small rural villages, in mud or stone houses that may have only one room. For the sake of privacy, these houses usually do not have windows that face on the street. Instead, windows face the family's open courtyard. Water often comes not from a tap, but from a goatskin bag that hangs on a wall of the house. The family's supply of water must be carried from the village well each day.

People rise at dawn to begin their work. In the middle of the day, when temperatures are hottest, North Africans rest for several hours. Even in the cities, a three-hour midday break is the custom. When the sun's glare begins to lessen, people return to work until dusk. Some farmers own or

North African Traditions

● **Movement** This illustration, roughly 700 years old, shows two men traveling by camel. Today some North African peoples, such as the Tuareg, continue to follow their traditional nomadic way of life. *How have recent droughts in the Sahara affected the Tuareg nomads?*

rent small plots of land, raising wheat, barley, and livestock. The tools they use often are the same kind their ancestors used centuries ago. Wooden plows drawn by camels are not uncommon. Other villagers hire themselves out to work for someone else on larger, more modern farms.

Desert Nomads Some North Africans have always followed a nomadic way of life. One of the most distinctive nomadic groups is the Tuareg (TWAR ehg), who live in small groups throughout the southwest Sahara. The Tuareg speak their own language—the only Berber language that has a written form. They practice a unique form of Islam that preserves many elements of their previous religion.

The Tuareg's name for themselves means "free men." They have resisted giving up their nomadic ways and coming under the control of any government. Recently, severe droughts in the Sahara have forced many of the Tuareg to settle in villages and work on farms in order to survive. It is possible that their ancient way of life—and that of other remaining North African nomads—will soon disappear.

Urban Life Like Egypt, the rest of North Africa is undergoing rapid urbanization. Recent estimates show that half or more of the populations of Algeria, Libya, and Tunisia live in urban areas.

The older Arab sections of North African cities, called **medinas**, usually are centered around a great mosque. **Souks**, or market areas, wind out from the mosque in a maze of narrow streets and alleyways lined with shops and workrooms. One visitor recently described the streets of a medina:

> *You walk past endless walls shiny from having been polished by generations of human beings wedged into narrow alleys. . . . Exquisite and often sumptuous houses are hiding behind these walls amid scented gardens filled with the murmur of fountains.*

Like Cairo, the major cities of Libya and the Maghreb attract more rural people than they can absorb. Housing and jobs for unskilled laborers are scarce.

Since the 1950s, when European control of North Africa ended and oil wealth began, modern parts of cities have grown rapidly. Modern sections of North African cities look much like

Living in the City

● **Place** A street scene in Libya's capital city, Tripoli (upper right), contrasts with an open-air market in Morocco. **Critical Thinking** *What other kinds of variety can you see in these photos?*

APPEARED IN *NATIONAL GEOGRAPHIC*

Libya's Black Gold

Human-Environment Interaction
The fires visible in this photo of a Libyan oil field are caused by the burnoff of natural gas. Libya's economy depends heavily on money from exports of the country's large oil reserves. The United States, once a Libyan trading partner, has cut off oil imports from Libya to protest Libya's support for international terrorism. *What uses has the Libyan government made of oil revenues?*

cities in Europe or the United States, with broad avenues, modern skyscrapers, internationally known stores, and corporate offices.

North Africa Today

Since independence, the four nations of North Africa have taken different paths politically and economically.

Libya After years of Italian control, in 1951 newly independent Libya was one of the poorest nations in Africa. Its revenues came almost entirely from foreign aid and rent from British and American military bases. That situation changed abruptly with the discovery of oil. By 1961 Libya's first oil wells were in production. Today oil makes up 99 percent of Libya's exports.

Money from oil paid for roads, schools, housing, hospitals, and airports. It brought electricity and new water wells to rural villages. It provided farmers with modern machinery. It also dramatically increased the income of many Libyans, especially those who found jobs in construction and the new oil industry.

It is hard to say which has changed Libya more, oil wealth or the government of Colonel Muammar Qaddafi. In 1969 Qaddafi led a military coup that overthrew the pro-Western king and abolished the monarchy. Qaddafi established a unique form of socialism that combined strict adherence to Islamic traditions with some modern economic and political reforms. One of Qaddafi's goals was a more equal distribution of wealth in Libya. For example, he ordered that no Libyan could have more than one house or more than 1,000 dinar (about $3,400) in savings. The government seized the property of anyone who had more than it allowed.

Another of Qaddafi's goals was to root out Western influences, which he thought were unhealthy. His government closed bars and nightclubs. It banned blue jeans for men and any kind of pants or short skirts for women. To bring the country back to its Islamic traditions, Qaddafi established Islamic law as the law of the land.

In foreign policy, Qaddafi clashed both with Western nations and with Libya's neighbors. Libya used its oil revenues to buy billions of dollars worth of Soviet military equipment, which it then used in brief wars with Chad and Egypt during the 1970s and 1980s. Libya also supported terrorist groups around the world. In 1986 the United States launched an air strike against Libya

in response to Libyan involvement in a terrorist bombing. In 1992 the United Nations imposed sanctions on Libya for Libya's refusal to hand over two intelligence agents linked to another terrorist bombing. In addition, Libyan efforts to create an arsenal of chemical weapons alarmed many nations.

Algeria When Algeria won its war of independence from France, almost all of the 1 million French colonists who had lived in Algeria left the country. This flight was disastrous for Algeria. Algerians had no opportunities to educate themselves while under European rule, and they depended on educated French settlers to serve as teachers, doctors, lawyers, engineers, and government administrators. The new government began massive training and education programs so that Algerians could be adequately prepared to take over the positions abandoned by the French.

Oil and natural gas, which were first discovered in the 1950s, make up about 96 percent of the value of all Algerian exports. Like Libya, Algeria's oil revenues have raised the country's general standard of living. Yet Algeria still faces severe economic problems.

Although the oil industry produces most of Algeria's revenues, it employs few of the country's workers. With the population growing rapidly, too few jobs are available. Many Algerians have emigrated to Europe to work, especially to France.

The Algerian government is trying to encourage rural Algerians to continue farming instead of flocking to the cities. If it is successful in its efforts, it will accomplish three goals. First, fewer Algerians will be unemployed, because agricultural workers are in great demand. Second, Algeria will be able to reduce its expensive dependence on food imports. Today the country has to import more than one third of its food. And third, the severe problems of overcrowding in Algeria's coastal cities will be reduced. At present, two-room apartments house on average nine occupants.

The Algerian government has faced problems in the last few years. In 1988 economic discontent led to anti-government riots. Algerians began to demand an end to the one-party rule that had controlled the government since independence. In time, new local and national elections were scheduled.

In 1992 an Islamist party nearly won the national elections. Many Algerians were alarmed that this party would impose on them a government similar to the Islamic government in Iran. They were afraid that they would never attain the democratic freedoms they hoped for in the

Onion Fields

Place Near the Algerian capital of Algiers, farmers load a truck with onions. The Algerian government, hoping to reduce food imports and relieve overcrowding in the cities, has worked hard to strengthen the nation's farms. **Critical Thinking** *Why do people choose to leave the farm for the city?*

future. To prevent radical Islamists from coming to power, the army took over the government and postponed the elections. Radical Islamists responded with a wave of assassinations and other terrorist attacks to undermine the army-run government.

Tunisia and Morocco Unlike Libya and Algeria, Tunisia and Morocco do not have large oil reserves. Some inhabitants view this as a blessing. As one Tunisian business leader stated, "We are lucky we didn't find much oil. Otherwise we wouldn't have worked so hard to develop our people." Tunisia spends about 12 percent of its money on education, and education is free from the primary grades through the universities. One recent visitor to the Tunisian desert observed:

> *It is very touching to see groups of tiny children ... trudging sturdily to classes across a wide, dusty landscape in which, as far as the eye can see, there is no obvious sign of home or school.*

Aside from developing their human resources, Tunisia and Morocco have also begun to develop their manufacturing. Recently, both countries have increased their profits by manufacturing clothing for export. Another important resource for Tunisia and Morocco is minerals. Phosphates are exported by both countries. They

Traditional Methods

● **Place** This scene from the Moroccan city of Fès shows giant tubs made of earth. The tubs contain vegetable dyes used to color sheepskins and cowhides. Clothing exports, especially to nearby Europe, are an increasingly important part of Morocco's economy. *In what way does Morocco's economy differ from that of Libya or Algeria?*

have also built up their chemical industries in order to process phosphates before exporting them. As in other parts of the region, rural areas are declining in population as new industrial projects lure workers from the countryside to the cities.

Section 2 Review

Vocabulary and Main Ideas

1. Define: a. wadi b. caravan c. medina d. souk

2. What outside groups have influenced the North Africans during their long history?

3. What is the most important natural resource of Libya and Algeria? Of Morocco and Tunisia?

4. Critical Thinking: *Drawing Conclusions* How might North African governments encourage people to remain in rural areas instead of crowding into cities?

learning LOCATIONS

5. Which body of water do all the countries of North Africa border?

6. Which country of the Maghreb is farthest west?

Summarizing Main Ideas

Section 1 Egypt

- Because most of Egypt is harsh desert, most Egyptians live near water—in the Nile River valley and the Nile Delta.
- Rural Egyptians are surging to the nation's cities, where population has been growing at the rate of 2.3 percent annually.
- The Egyptian economy is still dependent upon the export of raw materials such as oil and petroleum products rather than manufactured goods.

Section 2 Libya and the Maghreb

- Coastal regions of North Africa have been influenced by centuries of contact with other peoples, including the Carthaginians, Romans, Arabs, French, and Italians.
- Urban and rural lifestyles differ greatly in Libya and the Maghreb.
- Oil has significantly helped the economies of Libya and Algeria, while Tunisia and Morocco have been slowly increasing their manufacturing.

Reviewing Vocabulary

Match the definitions with the terms listed below.

1. a system of irrigation in which walls are built around a field to trap the water and silt from a river overflowing its banks
2. money that is invested in building and supporting new industries
3. a system of irrigation that provides water throughout the year
4. a traditional Arab open-air market
5. ruler of ancient Egypt
6. an artificial lake
7. a large group of merchants who have joined together to travel in safety
8. a market district in an Arab community

a. **bazaar**	e. **reservoir**
b. **pharaoh**	f. **capital**
c. **basin irrigation**	g. **souk**
d. **perennial irrigation**	h. **caravan**

Applying the Geographic Themes

1. **Location** Why does the location of Egypt make it a power to be reckoned with in world affairs?
2. **Place** How did the Arab conquest change Egypt?
3. **Human-Environment Interaction** How has the environment of Egypt affected people's choice of where to live?
4. **Movement** How did the introduction of the camel affect movement in North Africa?
5. **Regions** What economic problems are shared by the nations of North Africa?

Critical Thinking and Applying Skills

1. **Expressing Problems Clearly** The Aswan High Dam has brought both benefits and disadvantages to Egypt. Explain why you think the dam should or should not have been built.

2. **Reading a Time Zone Map** Refer to the map on page 496 to answer these questions.
   a. When it is 7:00 A.M. in New York, what time is it in Tokyo?
   b. When it is 5:00 P.M. in Moscow, what time is it in Calcutta?

Journal Activity

Writing Across Cultures

▶ 1. When the Aswan High Dam was built, some spectacular ancient tombs were threatened with flooding. Write a conversation between an American archaeologist who opposes the dam and an Egyptian official who supports it.

▶ 2. Write a poem that might be composed by a Tuareg nomad describing his or her wandering life in the Sahara. Use facts about the Sahara you have learned in your study of Chapter 25. In the poem, comment on the possibility that you may soon be forced to end your wandering and live in a city.

INTERNET link

Look at Egypt's historic places on the Canadian Museum of Culture's Mysteries of Egypt site. Link to this site from:

• www.phschool.com

Read about a few sites. Choose one and describe how you think it could have been built in ancient times. How would you build it today? Describe the process.

learning LOCATIONS

North Africa

Number from 1 to 10 on a piece of paper. Next to each number, write the letter of the place on the map that corresponds to the place listed below.

1. Algeria
2. Algiers
3. Cairo
4. Egypt
5. Libya
6. Morocco
7. Casablanca
8. Tripoli
9. Tunis
10. Tunisia

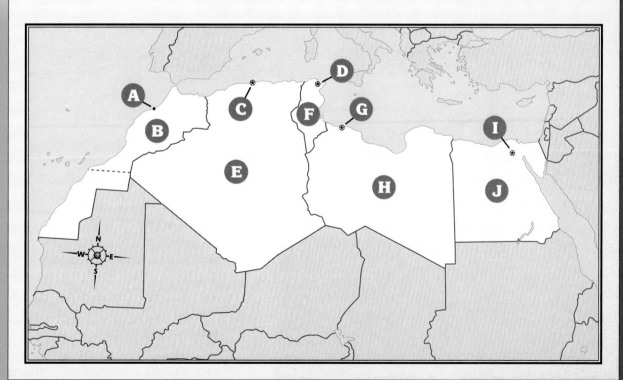

26

West and Central Africa

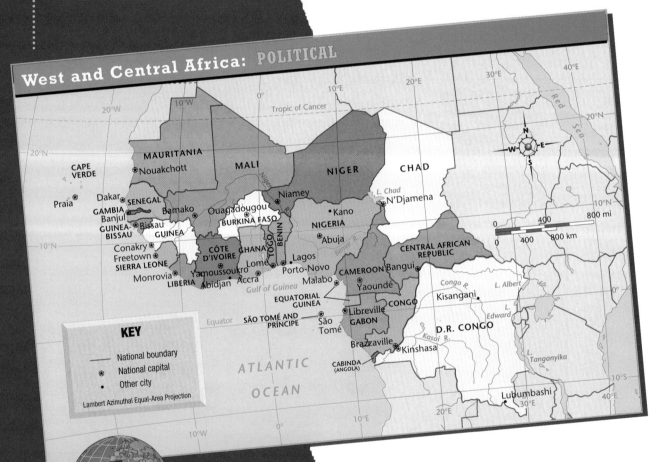

West and Central Africa: POLITICAL

CAPE VERDE
Praia ⊛
Dakar ⊛
SENEGAL
GAMBIA
Banjul ⊛
GUINEA-BISSAU
Bissau ⊛
GUINEA
Conakry ⊛
Freetown ⊛
SIERRA LEONE
Monrovia ⊛
LIBERIA
Abidjan

MAURITANIA
Nouakchott ⊛
MALI
Bamako ⊛
Ouagadougou ⊛
BURKINA FASO
CÔTE D'IVOIRE
GHANA
Yamoussoukro •
Accra ⊛
Gulf of Guinea

Niger
Niamey •
NIGER
NIGERIA
Kano •
Abuja ⊛
TOGO
BENIN
Lomé ⊛
Porto-Novo ⊛
Lagos •
Benue R.
EQUATORIAL GUINEA
SÃO TOMÉ AND PRÍNCIPE
São Tomé •
Malabo ⊛
CAMEROON
Yaoundé ⊛
Libreville ⊛
GABON

CHAD
L. Chad
N'Djamena ⊛
CENTRAL AFRICAN REPUBLIC
Bangui ⊛
Congo R.
CONGO
Brazzaville ⊛
Kinshasa ⊛
Kasai R.
D.R. CONGO
Kisangani •
L. Albert
L. Edward
L. Tanganyika
Lubumbashi •

CABINDA (ANGOLA)

Red Sea

Tropic of Cancer
20°W   10°W   0°   10°E   20°E   30°E   40°E
20°N
10°N
Equator   0°
10°S

0   400   800 mi
0   400   800 km

ATLANTIC OCEAN

KEY

— National boundary
⊛ National capital
• Other city

Lambert Azimuthal Equal-Area Projection

Mapping the Region

Create a map like the one above, shading each country a different color. Then add labels for countries and bodies of water that are shown on this map.

The Sahel

Section Preview

Main Ideas

- Many empires have flourished in the Sahel, a region defined by location, climate, and vegetation.

- The interaction between people and the environment in the Sahel has had negative consequences.

- The Sahel nations are making use of their natural resources in a continuing effort to be self-sufficient.

Vocabulary

shifting agriculture, forage, deforestation, desertification, refugee, landlocked, inland delta

APPEARED IN *NATIONAL GEOGRAPHIC*

In the Sahel, the threat of drought and famine is always present.

The Sahel, which extends across Africa, separates the Sahara to the north from the tropical rain forests to the south. Here is one journalist's description of the Sahel's many landscapes:

> *The forest thins out until it turns into the most characteristic of African landscapes, the savanna—undulating grasslands dotted with individual trees and occasional groves. . . . But this in turn shades off into sparser country, with scrubby trees and bushes and mottled patches of bare earth, and then into desert lands speckled only with thorn bushes and other tough growths and scarred by gullies and dry sand rivers; and at the final extreme, rocky, sandy, barren desert.*

Many people in the West think of the Sahel as an arid region. They believe, as well, that its history and culture are as barren as its climate. In fact, the Sahel was for centuries a busy crossroads and a meeting point for different cultures.

Today the area contains more than a dozen independent countries, each with its own vision of past, present, and future.

The Power of the Past

One of the many surprising facts about West Africa is that the Sahara was not always a desert. Rock paintings found there show that as recently as seven thousand years ago people hunted hippopotamuses in the region's rivers and chased buffalo on its wide, grassy plains. Over time, however, the climate grew drier. Some people of the Sahara moved north toward the Mediterranean Sea; others moved south toward the Sahel. Eventually, vast stretches of desert developed and separated them.

Trade Links and Empires The two groups never entirely lost touch with each other. Over the sea of sand came merchants from the north, bringing salt to trade. They sought ivory, slaves, and, most important of all, the gold that patient miners panned from the two great rivers of the Sahel region—the Senegal and the Niger.

◀ **Cattle grazing in Mali** *(photo left)*

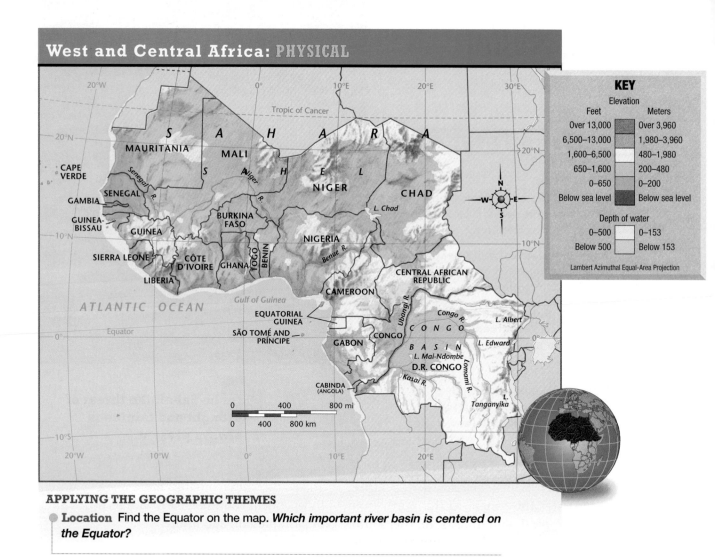

APPLYING THE GEOGRAPHIC THEMES

● **Location** Find the Equator on the map. *Which important river basin is centered on the Equator?*

Because of its central location, the Sahel's trade routes became a bridge between the Mediterranean coast and the rest of Africa.

The chiefs of the people of the Sahel found that they could grow wealthy by taxing the traders passing through their kingdoms. By A.D. 400 a great kingdom had emerged in the Sahel, then known as Ghana, the land of gold. By the year 800 its capital, Koumbi Saleh, had a substantial population. The Arab traveler and historian, al-Bakri, described the ruler of Ghana in these words:

> *When he gives audience to his people . . . he sits in a pavilion around which stand his horses . . . in cloth of gold; behind him stand ten pages holding shields and gold-mounted swords; and on his right hand are the sons of the princes of his empire, splendidly clad and with gold plaited into their hair.*

A Center of Learning Ghana was defeated by conquerors who swept in from the desert in 1076. But new empires soon took its place in the Sahel.

Mali (MAH lee) was just one of them. At its height in the early 1300s, Mali was one of the largest empires in the world. Its most famous emperor, Mansa Musa, made a triumphal journey to Mecca. Under his rule the capital of the empire, Tombouctou (TOM book TOO), became an important trading city. It also developed into a cultural center, rich in the knowledge and arts of Islam.

After Mali's decline, the Songhai Empire dominated the region. Under one of the Songhai rulers, Mohammad Askia, Tombouctou reached the height of its intellectual influence. One report stated, "In Tombouctou there are numerous judges, doctors, and clerics, all receiving good salaries from the king. He pays great respect to men of learning." The Songhai remained a great power in the Sahel until about four hundred years ago.

The Present

Today the Sahel is made up of independent countries. Mauritania (mawr i TAYN ee uh), Mali, named after the ancient kingdom, Niger (NY jer), Burkina Faso (boor KEE nuh FAH so), and Chad are the five northernmost countries of the Sahel. To their south lie eleven countries that fit like jigsaw pieces around the shore of the Atlantic Ocean. These nations are discussed mainly in the following section on coastal countries, but most of them have at least some savanna in the interior. They are, therefore, linked with the Sahel. In fact, one of them is named Ghana, after the ancient kingdom that lay deep in the Sahel.

Farming Many people of the Sahel support themselves by farming. The dry climate and the poor soil determine how they farm the region.

Farmers cope with the dry climate by growing crops during the short rainy season. They meet the challenge of poor soil by using **shifting agriculture**. Under this system a site is cleared, prepared, and used to grow crops. After a year or two the soil is stripped of its nutrients and no longer useful. Then the farmers move on to clear new areas of forest and do not return to the previously farmed land.

Two grains, millet and sorghum (SAWR guhm), are the vital crops that keep Sahel farmers alive. For cash they grow peanuts, which some sell to the distant cities of the coast for use there or for export.

Herding Instead of farming, many people in the Sahel herd camels, cattle, and sheep. The savannas of the Sahel might seem ideally suited to herding. They have low grasses and other edible plants, as well as trees such as the baobab (BAY o BAHB) and acacia (uh KAY shuh) with

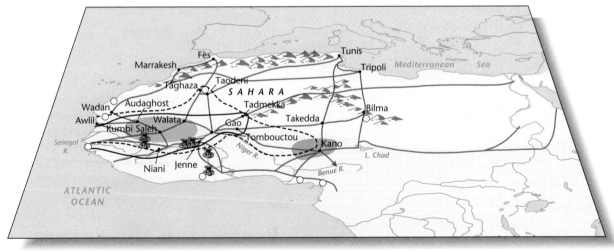

African Empires and Trade Across the Sahara, A.D. 900 to 1600

KEY

Empire boundaries:
- Ghana
- Mali
- Songhai
- Hausa states

Resources:
- Gold
- Salt
- Trade routes
- Desert

APPLYING THE GEOGRAPHIC THEMES

● **Movement** Mansa Musa, the Muslim king of the ancient kingdom of Mali, made Tombouctou a great commercial and cultural center. *According to the map, which regions of Africa were linked to Tombouctou by trade?*

leaves that provide **forage**, or food for grazing animals. Unfortunately, such animals can destroy plants and trees when they are crowded too closely onto the same range. Overgrazing by animals has had a grim impact on the environment.

Overgrazing harms the Sahel by destroying the plants that hold the sandy soil in place. Moreover, the endless search for firewood to use for cooking and the tremendous demand for charcoal by a growing, urban population have further damaged the environment. Overharvested land is stripped of its trees through a process called **deforestation**. When there is a drought, vast areas of the Sahel may suffer a loss of all vegetation, from grass to shrubs to trees, a phenomenon called **desertification**. In effect, the savanna turns to desert, and desertification is very difficult to reverse.

When a drought hits the Sahel region, desertification increases at a frightening pace. People throughout the Sahel flee to the cities, turning what would otherwise be modest, urban clusters into huge **refugee** camps. A refugee is a person who flees his or her home to escape danger or unfair treatment.

The more developed nations of the world can have difficulty aiding the Sahel, because all of the Sahel nations except for Mauritania are **landlocked**. A landlocked nation is cut off from the sea. Even the nations on the coast have poor transportation links. During one drought in Mauritania, the main road through the country could be kept open only by shoveling the sand off it every day.

GLOBAL issues

Famine

In the early 1980s, the worst drought in 150 years struck the Sahel, exposing 150 million Africans to the risk of starvation. The world rallied to the aid of the Sahel nations, and widespread famine was prevented. When the drought ended in 1985, aid efforts focused on preventing future disasters, but recurrent drought in the 1990s required more food aid.

Expanding Desert

Movement Like an approaching army, the sands of the Sahara advance on Nouakchott, the capital of Mauritania. Many of the city's residents are former nomads who moved to the city to escape Mauritania's recent droughts. **Critical Thinking** *How might the people of Nouakchott be forced to deal with the expanding desert?*

Protecting the Future

The nations of the Sahel are directing their energies toward three goals: withstanding the harsh environment; developing natural resources; and making the most of their current human resources and culture.

Holding On The Sahel countries need continuing foreign aid. Food, medicine, and technical help are always in demand. In Niger, for example, foreign aid has helped the country's people plant trees which form windbreaks for thousands of acres of land. In this way, the soil does not blow away during the dry season, and the crops have a better chance of growing when the rain does fall. The Sahel nations are trying to use their natural and human resources in a continuing effort to become self-sufficient.

Using Natural Resources One water resource has helped the people dwelling in the Sahel for thousands of years—the region's rivers. The Senegal and Niger rivers and their tributaries provide both transportation and water for irrigation.

The Niger's source is located in the mountains of the nation of Guinea only 150 miles (241 km) from the Atlantic Ocean, yet the river flows inland for 2,600 miles (4,183 km) before reaching the ocean. On its journey it brings water to countless villages within the Sahel. In Mali the Niger expands into an **inland delta**, an area of lakes, creeks, and swamps away from the ocean. Here people grow rice, cotton, corn, and vegetables.

The Sahel countries also possess valuable mineral resources that can be sold to buy food. Mauritania and Mali both have reserves of iron ore. Bauxite, the ore from which aluminum is made, is an important resource in Mali, as are Mauritania's huge reserves of copper in that country. Niger has one of the world's largest and most valuable deposits of uranium.

Facts in BRIEF

Country	Population	Life Expectancy (years)	Per Capita GNP (in U.S. $)
Burkina Faso	10,400,000	45	300
Chad	6,400,000	48	200
Mali	9,400,000	47	300
Mauritania	2,300,000	52	510
Niger	9,200,000	47	270
United States	263,200,000	76	24,750

Source: Population Reference Bureau

CHART SKILLS

● *Which country has the smallest population?*

● *Which country has the lowest life expectancy? How does this compare to the life expectancy in the United States?*

Using Human Resources The descendants of the people of the Sahel's ancient empires still dwell in the region today. One of the larger groups is the Mossi of Burkina Faso. In Niger and in other countries of the Sahel, many of the Fulani (FOO lah nee) live as herders, and the Hausa (HOW suh) are famous

River Traffic

● **Regions** The rivers of the Sahel provide much-needed water and transportation to the region's residents. This photograph shows boat traffic at Mopti, Mali. Since about two thirds of Mali is desert or semi-desert, most of the country's residents cluster near rivers. **Critical Thinking** *Mopti is located at the meeting point of the Bani and Niger rivers. Why do settlements often develop at points where rivers meet?*

Repair Shop

Place This Mali businesswoman is repairing hollow gourds, which are sold for use as containers. Though Mali remains one of the world's poorest countries, government reforms aimed at encouraging private enterprise have spurred economic growth. *How has the political system of Mali changed in recent years?*

as traders. In Mali, the Songhai people are known for their music and dance. The Mandingo (man DIN go) craft magnificent jewelry and the Bambara carve graceful objects of wood.

While much of Africa is struggling with repressive governments that simply do not work, one nation in the Sahel offers a model of how democracy and openness use human resources wisely. For 35 years, Mali was ruled by one political party. In 1992, Alpha Oumar Konare (AL fa OO mar ko NAR ay) was elected president in the first free and open elections. Under his leadership, the economy has been growing at a rate of 6 percent per year. Private companies are taking over state-owned businesses and running them better. Twenty newspapers have started to publish, and the exchange of ideas is free. "The single-party system was a total failure in all countries which practiced it," President Konare recently pointed out. "The logic of 'shut up and obey' gives immediate results, but offers no tomorrow."

Section 1 Review

Vocabulary and Main Ideas

1. Define: a. shifting agriculture b. forage c. deforestation d. desertification e. refugee f. landlocked g. inland delta

2. Why was the Sahel a key region in the ancient world?

3. Describe two ways in which people have contributed to the desertification of the Sahel.

4. Why is the Niger River important to the nations of the Sahel?

5. Critical Thinking: *Cause and Effect* Describe some of the ways that the people of the Sahel are directing their energies toward protecting the future of the region.

learning LOCATIONS

6. Name the nations of the Sahel in order from west to east.

7. Which Sahel nation is located north of Nigeria?

2 The Coastal Countries

Section Preview

Main Ideas

- The coastal nations of West Africa have long taken advantage of their location to trade with foreign nations.

- Power has shifted frequently in West African nations, with a trend toward democracy.

- West Africans are acting to improve their economies on the local level.

Vocabulary

coup, ancestor worship, animism

Many have suffered from Liberia's civil war.

Besides the five Sahel nations, West Africa contains eleven other countries. One, Cape Verde, is a small island nation. The others ring the coastline of West Africa, beginning in the west with Senegal and continuing along the Atlantic coast to Nigeria.

Location Leads to Trade

Because of their location, the coastal countries of West Africa have two advantages over those of the Sahel. First, they have a wetter climate. Adequate rainfall allows successful farming and the growth of valuable trees. Second, they have access to the sea. The natural harbors along the West African coastline offer great economic potential to the developing nations in this region. Freetown, in Sierra Leone, has one of the largest harbors in the world, though it does not rank as a leading port.

Resources for the World The coast of West Africa attracted European traders from the 1400s. They came for gold, ivory, palm oil, and enslaved people to use as laborers. This coastal trade made trade across the Sahara less important, and coastal kingdoms fought each other for control of the new foreign trade.

Today the nations on the West African coast export only a few products and raw materials. Senegal, Gambia (GAM bee uh), and Guinea-Bissau (GI nee bee SOW) export peanuts. Côte d'Ivoire (KOT dee VWAHR)—also called Ivory Coast—Ghana, Sierra Leone, and other nations largely depend upon the export of cocoa beans. Liberia exports iron ore.

Unequal Trade The economies of the West African countries suffer in part because their exports total less, in value, than their imports. Also, like many African countries, they are heavily in debt. Africa as a whole needs roughly 9 billion dollars every year just to pay the interest on its debts, and West Africa pays an enormous part of that.

Facts in BRIEF

Country	Population	Life Expectancy (years)	Per Capita GNP (in U.S. $)
Benin	5,400,000	48	420
Cape Verde	400,000	65	870
Côte d'Ivoire	14,300,000	51	630
Gambia	1,100,000	45	360
Ghana	17,500,000	56	430
Guinea	6,500,000	44	510
Guinea-Bissau	1,100,000	44	220
Liberia	3,000,000	55	NA
Nigeria	101,200,000	56	310
Senegal	8,300,000	49	730
Sierra Leone	4,500,000	46	140
Togo	4,400,000	58	330
United States	263,200,000	76	24,750

Source: Population Reference Bureau   NA indicates data not available

CHART SKILLS

● *Which country, aside from the United States, has the highest per capita GNP?*

● **Critical Thinking** *Which countries have the lowest life expectancy? What factors contribute to a low life expectancy?*

Struggles for Power

European colonial powers ruled most of Africa until the 1960s. When the African countries gained their independence, their economies were often in very weak condition. Few new governments in Africa have been able to overcome or recover from these economic burdens.

Shifts in Power When governments are weak, the army often steps in and takes over. Sometimes, different factions, or groups within the army, fight for power.

In Benin, six **coups**—sudden political takeovers—took place from 1963 to 1972. Major Ahmed Mathieu Kerekou (AKH muhd mat YUH ker uh KOO) stayed in control from 1972 until 1991. In that year, with Benin's economy failing, Kerekou was faced with

strikes and unrest. He then called for a new constitution that allowed others to share power. A president was elected, and the military government resigned.

Despite promising signs that one-man rule in West Africa was changing in the early 1990s, as the decade continued African trends toward democracy slowed. In Côte d'Ivoire, for example, the man who had ruled the nation for more than thirty years died, and a new president was elected in 1995. But he ran for office almost without opposition, and few citizens bothered to vote. By carefully rewriting the election laws, he had excluded the only candidate who might have defeated him.

Liberia's Agony More tragic was the case of Liberia. Founded in 1822 by freed American slaves, Liberia became independent in 1847 under an American-style constitution. The country began its slide into chaos in 1980, when a military coup overthrew the ruling government. Nine years later a civil war began, and in 1990 a new government forcibly took power. Fighting in Liberia continued into the 1990s. Peacekeepers from other West African nations proved unable to halt the violence, and attempts at a lasting cease-fire failed.

By the mid-1990s some 200,000 Liberians had been killed, hundreds of thousands had fled the country, and more than 1 million others had been left homeless. Armed gangs patrolled the streets while terrified civilians sought shelter. As one resident explained:

> *If I had the slightest opportunity to leave this country now, to go anywhere, even a slimy refugee camp, it would be better because I can expect a stray bullet or a direct bullet at any time. Nobody can guarantee my security.*

As the violence worsened, Oxfam, Save the Children, and other major humanitarian agencies pulled out of Liberia. Many feared for the lives of workers sent to help the suffering nation. Their earlier shipments of aid, in the form of food and medical supplies intended for civilians, had been stolen by soldiers. There were even suggestions that the United Nations make Liberia a trust territory—in effect, take over the country to prevent total collapse. Without some sort of foreign help, it appeared, Liberia could not save itself.

Hope in Sierra Leone Other West African countries appeared to offer more hope. In 1996, Sierra Leone held free elections for its first democratic government in three decades. Years of political violence seemed to be coming to an end. International observers of the election had great hopes that Sierra Leone would see a peaceful transition of power.

However, armed rebels overthrew the government in May 1997. In response to the rebel actions, troops from eleven of Sierra Leone's neighbors, including Nigeria, invaded and restored the democratic leaders to power. During the nine months of rebel control, hundreds of thousands of civilians fled their homes for refugee camps. President Ahmad Tejan Kabbah, who had been elected in 1997, returned from exile. Turmoil continued, however, and the economy was at a standstill.

In May 2000, rebels belonging to the Revolutionary United Front (RUF) took 500 UN peacekeepers hostage. Liberian president Charles Taylor, a supporter of the RUF, forced the rebels to free the peacekeepers. Still, instability and violence threatened the nation.

People Power West Africans have learned that their governments alone often can do little to improve depressed economic conditions. One writer described the consequences of this realization:

> *There are signs that some Africans already are taking matters into their own hands. As rural people have become disillusioned [disappointed] with outsiders and with their own governments, millions of them have begun grass-roots efforts . . . to organize local resources.*

The key to this new economic approach is its grass-roots beginnings. Grass roots means that the effort begins with people. In West Africa, increasingly, it is women who make grass-roots efforts work.

Democracy and Conflict

Regions In 1997, residents of Sierra Leone celebrated the nation's first free elections in three decades. Despite threats of political violence, some 60 percent of those eligible voted. *Why have many African countries experienced military rule?*

Traditional Roles

Many of the women of West African countries, just as in the rest of the continent, are front-line troops in a hard-fought battle: they grow crops in the war against hunger. In many West African countries women are establishing agricultural cooperatives to improve the economic conditions of their villages. In the village of Malon in Sierra Leone, more than 200 women work together to grow more crops. Women also run an important part of the economy—the markets where food is bought and sold. As Africa modernizes, women are constantly expanding their traditional roles and are becoming owners of small businesses.

Children are also valuable workers in West African countries, helping to grow and harvest crops. Children are important for another reason, as can be seen in the case of the Asante (ah SAHN tay), a group of people who live in southern Ghana.

The Asante, like many African peoples, believe that if their children continue to respect and honor them after death, they themselves will live on in the spirit world. An African chief once described his people as "a vast family, of which many are dead, few are living, and countless members are unborn." This belief in the spirits of the dead is called **ancestor worship**.

Ancestor worship is one aspect of the Asante religion; another is **animism**. According to this belief, ordinary things of nature—the sky, rivers, trees—all contain gods or spirits.

In Africa, as in other places, social custom, religious beliefs, and economic conditions sometimes translate into large families and a fast-growing population. The birthrate in Ghana—42 per 1,000 population—is nearly double the average birthrate for the world. In fact, the population of Africa is growing faster than populations anywhere else on earth.

Asante King

● **Place** The splendor of West African cultural tradition can be seen in this photograph of Asante king Koffi Yeebwa, shown at a festival with supporters. *What traditional roles remain important in West African life?*

Section 2 Review

Vocabulary and Main Ideas

1. **Define:** a. coup b. ancestor worship c. animism

2. How have the coastal nations of West Africa taken advantage of their location over the centuries?

3. What happened to the movement toward democracy in Côte d'Ivoire during the 1990s?

4. What new economic practice is finding success in West Africa?

5. **Critical Thinking:** *Making Comparisons* Compare women's roles in Africa with women's roles in the United States.

learning LOCATIONS

6. What coastal nation of West Africa is surrounded by another country, except for its seacoast?

7. What West African coastal nations border Nigeria?

Focus on Skills

☐ Social Studies

☐ Map and Globe

☑ Critical Thinking and Problem Solving

Perceiving Cause-Effect Relationships

Understanding the relationship between cause and effect is basic to an understanding of geography. Recognizing cause and effect means examining how one event or action brings about others. If you can understand how events or ideas relate to and affect each other, you can begin to find workable solutions to problems.

Use the following steps to practice identifying statements that tell about cause and effect.

1. Identify the two parts of a cause-effect relationship. A cause is an event or an action that brings about an effect. Authors usually indicate a cause-effect relationship by using key words. Words such as *because*, *due to*, and *on account of* signal causes. Words such as *so*, *thus*, *therefore*, and *as a result* signal effects. Read statements A through D at right and answer the following: (a) Which statements are cause-effect statements? (b) Identify the cause and the effect in each cause-effect statement. (c) Which word or words signal the cause-effect relationship?

2. Remember that an event can have more than one cause and more than one effect. Several causes can combine to create one event, just as one cause can bring about several different effects. Read statement E at right and answer the following questions: (a) What are the causes presented in the statement? (b) What are the effects of those causes?

3. An event can be both a cause and an effect. A cause can lead to an effect, which in turn can be the cause of a new event. In this way, causes and effects can form a chain of events. You can diagram such a chain as

follows: People relied on livestock as a food source. → Overgrazing of livestock destroyed vegetation. → Lack of vegetation led to soil erosion. Read statement F below and use arrows to draw a diagram of the causes and effects that show the chain of related events.

Statements

A. Because of heavy rainfall, a band of tropical rain forest covers the continent from the "bulge" of western Africa to the interior.

B. Africa is a huge continent of many countries and many different culture groups.

C. Rival chiefs were eager to make themselves monarchs of a great land. As a result, tribal warfare interfered with rebuilding the kingdom, and Ghana began to decline.

D. There are as many forms of African music as there are African languages.

E. Because European trade was expanding and African trade routes shifted from the Sahara to the coast, Saharan trade routes declined in importance, coastal communities became more powerful, and contact with Europeans increased.

F. In several African kingdoms, gold and the control of trade produced great wealth. With this wealth, the rulers built up their military might. Thus, each kingdom was able to conquer neighboring areas and demand payment from them. The demands for payment caused unrest in the conquered areas, and eventually the unrest led to the conquered areas breaking free.

3 Nigeria

Section Preview

Main Ideas

● Nigeria has the potential to become an economic powerhouse in Africa.

● Nigeria suffers from a lack of national unity.

● A repressive military government has brought difficult times to Nigeria.

Vocabulary

World Bank, International Monetary Fund, structural adjustment program

Nigeria is by far Africa's most populous country. This view is of the Nigerian city of Abeokuta.

Not long ago, Nigeria was seen as the hope for Africa's future. Though it depended too much on income from selling one product—oil—its economy was robust. A team of journalists summed up Nigeria's importance in this way:

> *The best hope for Africa is that the continent's two giant economies— South Africa and Nigeria—can be harnessed. . . . Together, they could become a giant market to absorb the rest of Africa's products.*

But ongoing problems have cast a shadow over that hope. The causes of Nigeria's problems are lack of unity and poor leadership by its military government.

Varying Regions

Nigeria's lack of unity stems from its varying regions. Of the coastal nations of West Africa, Nigeria, which is approximately twice the size of California, has the most varied climate and vegetation regions. A traveler going from south to north would find coastal swamps that give way to tropical rain forest, then a large area of savanna that gradually changes to desert scrub. Rainfall also varies widely over the country. Southern regions may receive up to 120 inches (305 cm) of rain a year, while the parched north gets only 20 inches (51 cm).

A variety of crops are grown throughout Nigeria. In the south, cocoa trees, oil palms, and rubber trees thrive. In the drier north, peanuts are cultivated. The middle belt of the country supports few crops because of its poor soil.

Settlement These variations affect where people live. Historically, the most powerful groups took control of the most valuable land. For example, the Yoruba (yaw ROO buh) settled in the southwest, the Ibo (EE bo) lived in the southeast, and the Hausa traders and Fulani herders controlled the most fertile areas of the north. Small, weak groups were left with the least fertile lands in the middle belt of the country.

Although English is the official language of Nigeria, more than 180 different languages are spoken in the middle belt—an area about the size of New Mexico.

Population Movement The many groups living in Nigeria total over 100 million people, giving Nigeria nearly one seventh of Africa's total population. Many of Nigeria's people migrate from one region to another, looking for work in the industries of the cities or on cocoa or rubber plantations. Though they all live together under one government, they frequently clash, often because of religious or political differences.

Military Leadership

Nigeria's governmental problems arose in the early 1980s. At that time, the sale of oil was providing most of the country's income, just as it does now. Unfortunately, countries that depend on selling only one crop, product, or resource often suffer economic disaster when prices fall on the world market. Such a disaster befell Nigeria when oil prices tumbled between 1981 and 1983.

As the economy broke down, the military staged a coup. Former government leaders who had stolen money were brought to trial. The new leaders promised to correct old economic problems. To do this, they turned for help to the **World Bank** and the **International Monetary Fund** (IMF), two agencies of the United Nations that give loans to countries for development projects. In 1986 Nigeria began to follow the **structural adjustment program** that the World Bank had suggested. A structural adjustment program is a set of guidelines that is supposed to make a country's economy work better. A country cannot borrow money from the World Bank and the IMF unless it agrees to follow the adjustment program guidelines.

During its structural adjustment, the Nigerian government sold state-run businesses to private companies, fired some government workers, and did not allow wages and prices to rise. But difficult times came with structural

Nigerian Oil

Human-Environment Interaction Nigerian oil workers prepare a drilling shaft. Oil exports earn Nigeria billions of dollars each year, but oil drilling has caused widespread environmental damage. Foreign governments condemned the Nigerian government's crackdown on environmental and human rights protesters. **Critical Thinking** *How did Nigeria's dependence on oil exports probably affect its environmental policies?*

adjustment, and students and workers often protested, keeping up pressure on the military and calling for democratic elections.

In 1993 the military seemed to be about to give up power. For a time the process of electing democratic leaders went forward. A candidate named Moshood Abiola (mow SHOOD a bee OH la) won several elections and was close to becoming president when the military suddenly declared the elections void. A new military ruler, General Sani Abacha (sAH nee a BAH cha), ruthlessly squashed all opposition. In 1994, he threw Abiola in jail. In late 1995, he executed many other political opponents, including a well-known environmentalist, Ken Saro-Wiwa. The international community expressed outrage over the continuing violence. Meanwhile, Abacha ended the structural adjustment program and delayed interest payments on Nigeria's enormous debt.

Following Abacha's sudden death in June 1998, General Abdulsalam Abubakar came to power. Hopes for a democratic government faded and anti-government riots broke out when, a few weeks later, Abiola died from a suspicious heart attack while still in prison.

In response to the unrest, Abubakar promised to dissolve the military government and hold free elections in 1999. With a turn in the right direction, Nigeria has a chance to become a vital leader on the African continent.

Fulani Cattle Herders

● **Place** Fulani herdsmen seek out grazing land for their cattle in the Sahel. Despite its abundance of natural resources, Nigeria must import large amounts of food to feed its people. *What is the size of Nigeria's foreign debt?*

Section 3 Review

Vocabulary and Main Ideas

1. Define: a. World Bank b. International Monetary Fund c. structural adjustment program

2. How could a strong Nigeria help all of West Africa?

3. What is the basic cause of Nigeria's lack of unity?

4. How did the international community react to government repression in Nigeria?

5. Critical Thinking: *Identifying Alternatives* What might Nigeria do about the problem of its huge debts?

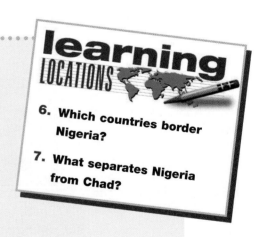

learning LOCATIONS

6. Which countries border Nigeria?

7. What separates Nigeria from Chad?

 Central Africa

Section Preview

Main Ideas

● **Movement in Central Africa is affected by the region's rivers, forests, and grasslands.**

● **Environmental damage results from the misuse of river and forest resources.**

● **The Democratic Republic of the Congo has tremendous resources, but is troubled by economic and political turmoil.**

Vocabulary

watershed, mercenary, barter

APPEARED IN *NATIONAL GEOGRAPHIC*

The Congo River provides transportation for the people of Central Africa.

East of Nigeria, the coast of Africa turns sharply to the south. Along this southward stretch lie the seacoasts of Cameroon, Equatorial Guinea, Gabon, Congo, and the Democratic Republic of the Congo. Offshore is the island nation of the Republic of Sao Tome (SOW tuh MAY) and Principe (preen SEEP), as well as five islands that make up the bulk of Equatorial Guinea. East of the coastal nations is the Central African Republic. Together these seven countries make up Central Africa. They range in size from the Republic of Sao Tome and Principe, a little larger than New York City, to the Democratic Republic of the Congo, which is as large as the part of the United States east of the Mississippi River.

A Region Built by Movement

Movement of people has affected this region possibly more than any other in Africa. The region's physical characteristics have, in turn, affected the ways in which that movement has taken place.

The Big River The largest river of the region is the Congo, also called the Zaire River. Like the Niger River, its source is only a short distance from the ocean, yet it flows inland for a great many miles. The Congo winds 2,900 miles (4,666 km) through a huge basin before finding its outlet in the Atlantic Ocean. The river and its many tributaries total about 9,000 miles (14,481 km) of waterway. The entire Congo River system is a great living highway that provides food, water, and transportation for much of the region.

Most of the Congo River is located in the Democratic Republic of the Congo. Boats can travel from Boyoma Falls in the northeast of the country to its capital, Kinshasa (kin SHAHS uh), located in the west. Below Kinshasa the course of the river is blocked by cataracts. Because boats cannot pass this stretch of the river, goods are carried overland by the railroad that links Kinshasa with the lower reaches of the Congo.

Through Forest and Savanna The basin that feeds the Congo River system is over 1 million square miles (2.6 million sq km) in area. In the center of the basin is a dense rain forest. It is easy to see why in the distant past people shied away from entering this dark and forbidding maze of trees.

If the forest presented a frightening barrier to movement, travel on the savannas was relatively easy. These grasslands stretch around the rain forests to the north, east, and south. From ancient times people of the savanna were able to conquer others, trade, or communicate without obstacles.

Today the forest is still a barrier to travel. Moreover, its valuable wood, such as mahogany, ebony, walnut, and iroko, can be easily harvested and exported only along rivers or where a railroad has been carved through the forest. And, in spite of the rich vegetation it supports, the forest soil is actually of little use for farming. Soil in the savanna lands, too, is often poor. People have migrated from both of these areas either to plantations located on more fertile soil or to great cities like Kinshasa or Brazzaville, the capital of Congo.

Movement to an Urban Area

Migration has turned Kinshasa into a major world city. Its population of 2.6 million is larger than that of either Paris or Vienna.

The city grew explosively in the second half of the twentieth century. Some of the people who moved to Kinshasa during those decades found wealth by working in the city's businesses or in the national government. They built expensive homes on Kinshasa's tree-lined avenues. Others continued the subsistence way of life they had known in the countryside, scraping together a living in Kinshasa's vast slums.

Rich and poor alike, however, take part in a culture that has grown from ancient African roots and has blended with the modern world. For example, Kinshasa has gained an international reputation for its popular music. A lively blend of African, rock, and pop rhythms, this music style known as Afro Pop is popular throughout the world.

Interdependence

Across the Congo River from Kinshasa lies Brazzaville. Although their two countries frequently disagree politically, these two cities share the river that forms the border between them.

Brazzaville, like Kinshasa, has a rail connection with the coast, and not surprisingly the route is dotted with industrial towns. The railroad also serves the inland nations of Chad and

Country	Population	Life Expectancy (years)	Per Capita GNP (in U.S. $)
Cameroon	13,500,000	58	770
Central African Republic	3,200,000	41	390
Congo	2,500,000	46	920
D. R. Congo	44,100,000	48	NA
Equatorial Guinea	400,000	53	360
Gabon	1,300,000	54	4,050
Sao Tome and Principe	100,000	64	330
United States	263,200,000	76	24,750

Source: *Population Reference Bureau*   NA indicates data not available.

CHART SKILLS

● *Which country, aside from the United States, has the highest per capita GNP?*

● *Which country, aside from the United States, has the largest population?*

the Central African Republic, which ship mineral resources down the Ubangi (yoo BANG ee) and Congo rivers to Brazzaville and from there to the Atlantic Ocean.

Many countries of West and Central Africa belong to an African financial community known as the CFA. The CFA countries use a currency, or form of money, called the CFA franc, which has solid value on international markets because it can be exchanged for the French franc. Use of this common currency promotes trade, travel, and general interdependence among countries in the region.

Rich Environmental Resources

The rivers and forests of Central Africa not only affect movement, they are resources in themselves. In theory, they are renewable—that is, if properly used, they can be maintained and never run out. Other resources are nonrenewable—once they are used up, they are gone forever. Sometimes, however, even renewable resources in Africa are destroyed as they are exploited.

Renewable Resources The continent of Africa consists of a group of basins set in a vast plateau. When the rivers that drain the basins cut through the edge of the plateau to the coastal plain, they drop sharply. At this escarpment, the rivers have great potential for creating hydroelectric power. The Democratic Republic of the Congo, for instance, is believed to be capable of producing 100,000 megawatts of hydroelectricity; at present it produces only about 2,500. Similarly, the Central African Republic lies on a **watershed**, or dividing ridge between two basins. About 80 percent of its electricity is produced by hydropower.

But, as you read in the case of the Nile River, a river does more than serve as a power source. It provides fish to eat. Its floods deposit fresh, fertile soil on farmland and sweep the riverbanks clear of disease-carrying insects. Once a river is dammed for hydropower, fishing and farming downstream are never the same. Diseases in the region increase as well. In short, the river is not allowed to renew itself.

Rain forests in Africa, too, are often treated like a nonrenewable resource. But deforestation has been less of a problem in Central Africa than in the coastal nations of West Africa, where loggers can get to forest areas more easily. In Côte d'Ivoire, for example, 85 percent of the rain forest has been destroyed since the 1940s. At this rate, the forests may be completely cut down early in the twenty-first century.

The rain forests are valuable for many reasons. In addition to supplying lumber, they provide habitats for thousands of animal species and shelter for thousands of plants. They also absorb carbon dioxide. Increasing amounts of carbon dioxide left unabsorbed in the atmosphere may lead to what scientists call global warming—a gradual rise in global temperatures.

The nations of Central Africa are still in a position to control logging within their borders. But planting new forests costs more than most

Kinshasa Marketplace

Location Kinshasa benefits from its location on the Congo River. Here women in the central market sell food fresh off the boat. *Why do goods travel from Kinshasa to the mouth of the Congo by rail rather than boat?*

African countries can afford. Instead, countries are looking at ways in which to practice conservation and still take economic advantage of their rain forests.

Nonrenewable Resources Central African nations have many other resources besides rivers and forests. The larger Central African nations have huge deposits of minerals. The Democratic Republic of the Congo has vast

GLOBAL issues

Rain Forests

Cameroon is practicing new conservation techniques in an effort to save its rain forests. In Korup National Park, special areas have been set aside where residents can practice small-scale hunting, fishing, farming, and forestry without harming protected land and wildlife. Officials are hoping that by rationing the use of resources now, long-term conservation will have a better chance of succeeding in the future.

copper reserves in the Shaba region in the south. It has more cobalt than any other country in the world, and one third of the world's industrial diamonds lie within its borders. Because of its resources, the Democratic Republic of the Congo once promised to be the same kind of economic giant in Central Africa that Nigeria was supposed to be in West Africa. But like Nigeria, the Democratic Republic of the Congo ran into economic and political troubles.

A Troubled Giant

The history of the Democratic Republic of the Congo is marked by periods of civil war and coups. Within a week of gaining independence from Belgium in 1960, it faced a revolt by its armed forces. At the same time, the province of Shaba chose to secede from the country.

A Country Divided The country was torn apart for four years as Belgian troops, United Nations forces, rebel armies, and **mercenaries**—hired soldiers—battled for power. Eventually a general who took the name Mobutu Sese Seko established himself as dictator and changed the country's name to Zaire.

Under Mobutu, Zaire won back the province of Shaba and improved its mining and industries. By the 1980s, however, the nation fell deeply into debt. Mobutu was forced to begin a structural adjustment program, but it did little good. By the early 1990s, Zaire owed foreign banks nearly 9 billion dollars. Mobutu's personal wealth was also estimated to be billions of dollars. The citizens of Zaire had little difficulty guessing where their wealth had gone.

Looking to the Future The wind of democratic change that swept over the world in the late 1980s seemed for a time to blow through Zaire as well. In April 1990, its dictator of twenty-five years announced that he was permitting the formation of other political parties and allowing a premier to rule in his place.

But even after a new premier was installed in office, supposedly to run the country, Mobutu refused to give up power. From a compound in his native village in northern Zaire, he controlled

APPEARED IN *NATIONAL GEOGRAPHIC*

Copper Mining

● **Place** The discovery of immense copper resources brought heavy industrial development to the Shaba region of the Democratic Republic of the Congo. *What were the cause and effect of violence in Shaba during the 1960s?*

Fighting Disease

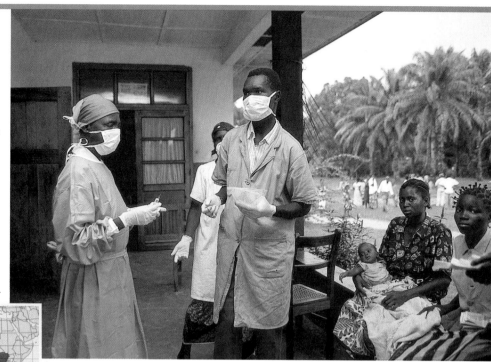

Place The deadly Ebola virus, named after a river in the Democratic Republic of the Congo, killed nearly 250 people in the Congolese city of Kikwit in 1995. International health organizations worked with local hospitals to bring the outbreak under control.
Critical Thinking *Why is it important for countries to work together to fight disease?*

the armed forces and police. His influence was so great that the premier found it impossible to bring about any changes that threatened Mobutu's wealth.

Mobutu's actions brought economic and political turmoil to Zaire. The World Bank estimated that Zaire's economy shrank 40 percent between 1988 and 1995. Industries, roads, and bridges broke down. People resorted to **barter**,

the exchange of goods without the use of money, to get the basic necessities.

In 1997, forces led by nationalist Laurent Kabila overthrew Mobuto's corrupt government. Kabila changed the nation's name to the Democratic Republic of the Congo. Despite the change in leadership, the country faced many challenges as it worked to recover from years of mismanagement.

Section 4 Review

Vocabulary and Main Ideas

1. **Define: a.** watershed **b.** mercenary **c.** barter

2. **How has the forest of Central Africa affected human movement in the region?**

3. **What kind of environmental damage is caused by hydroelectric dams?**

4. **Why has the Democratic Republic of the Congo failed to achieve its full economic potential?**

5. **Critical Thinking:** *Identifying Central Issues* **What advantages does interdependence bring to Central African countries?**

6. **Which nine countries border the Democratic Republic of the Congo?**

7. **What river forms a border between the Democratic Republic of the Congo and the Central African Republic?**

Summarizing Main Ideas

Section 1 The Sahel

■ The Sahel lies between the Sahara of northern Africa and the tropical rain forests of coastal West Africa and Central Africa.

■ It is mostly savanna with a semiarid climate. In ancient times important trading empires flourished in the region.

■ People have changed the environment through overgrazing and deforestation, and the region is in danger of desertification.

Section 2 The Coastal Countries

■ The location of these West African countries enabled them to trade with Europeans from the 1400s.

■ Social custom, religious beliefs, and economic conditions contribute to a high population growth rate.

Section 3 Nigeria

■ Nigeria's varied physical regions have each attracted different ethnic groups, leading to a lack of unity in the country.

■ Though Nigeria's economic potential is great, its political problems have prevented it from becoming a regional powerhouse.

Section 4 Central Africa

■ In recent times many people have moved away from areas with poor soil and into the region's cities.

■ Much of the wealth of the region is built on the environment and on mineral resources.

Reviewing Vocabulary

Match the following definitions with the terms they define below.

1. a belief in the spirits of the dead
2. an area of lakes, creeks, and swamps away from an ocean
3. a program to change the structure of an economy to make it work better
4. destruction of forest vegetation
5. a sudden takeover of a government
6. the practice of preparing and growing crops on a site for only a year or two
7. a loss of all vegetation
8. the exchange of goods without money
9. the belief that natural objects contain spirits or gods

a. **inland delta**
b. **ancestor worship**
c. **coup**
d. **deforestation**
e. **shifting agriculture**
f. **desertification**
g. **structural adjustment program**
h. **barter**
i. **animism**

Applying the Geographic Themes

1. **Human-Environment Interaction** What factor most affects life in the Sahel?
2. **Movement** Describe one problem concerning export trade from West African countries.
3. **Place** How has the diversity of groups in Nigeria affected that country?
4. **Location** How does the location of the Central African Republic promote the generation of electric power?
5. **Place** How does the Congo River affect life in Central Africa?

Critical Thinking and Applying Skills

1. **Testing Conclusions** Do you think African nations are beginning a slide into isolation? Explain your answer.
2. **Perceiving Cause-Effect Relationships** Restate this statement so that it expresses a cause-effect relationship: "There are many ethnic groups in Nigeria and much political unrest."

Journal Activity

Writing Across Cultures

► 1. Suppose you are applying for a grant (a gift of money) to study farming in the Sahel. The purpose of your study will be to help the people of the Sahel finds ways to farm that do not damage their fragile environment. Compose your application in your journal.

► 2. You have read about the blend of African, rock, and pop rhythms that can be heard in the streets of Kinshasa, Democratic Republic of the Congo. In your journal, write the lyrics of a song that could be set to this pop beat. Your song should be about life and times on the streets of Kinshasa.

Learn more about one Peace Corps volunteer and the place he or she visited. At the Peace Corps site, choose a volunteer who visited a West or Central African nation. Link to this site from:

• www.phschool.com

Write a short response to what you read. Then find a map of the country and locate the region the volunteer was in.

learning LOCATIONS

West and Central Africa

Number from 1 to 12 on a piece of paper. Next to each number, write the letter of the place on the map that corresponds to the places listed below.

1. Central African Republic
2. Congo
3. Côte d'Ivoire
4. Ghana
5. Lagos
6. Kinshasa
7. Liberia
8. Niger
9. Abidjan
10. Nigeria
11. D.R. Congo
12. Dakar

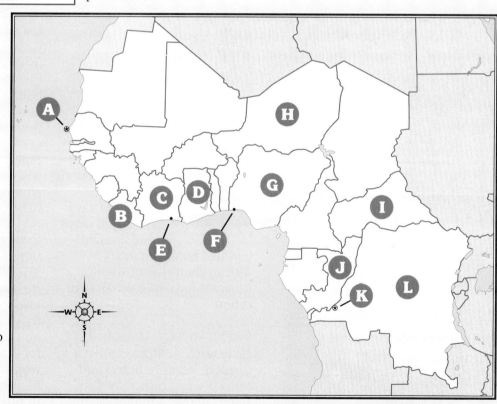

Water Use in Africa

The Issue

Much of Africa suffers from a severe shortage of water. This problem is a cause for concern on both local and international levels.

Lack of Clean Water More than half of all of Africa's people lack safe drinking water and live with inadequate sanitation. As the region's population grows, the situation gets worse. Aquifers, or underground reservoirs, and rivers that have been used as water sources for thousands of years are being drained. In some places renewable fresh water has dropped by more than 65 percent over the past 40 years. Many people are forced to use unclean water for both drinking and cooking.

Recurring Droughts Most farmers in Africa depend on rainfall to water their crops. But rainfall is unpredictable. Since the late 1960s, a series of droughts have destroyed crops and brought repeated famine to many African countries. In addition, droughts have sped up desertification.

Global Impact The scarcity of clean water in Africa is often a threat to health. Cholera and other diseases carried by dirty water kill over 5 million people a year. Many of the victims are children. Famine brought on by drought has also taken the lives of millions of Africans. Over the years, developed nations have sent billions of dollars in aid to suffering nations in Africa.

Some Solutions

Governments, international aid agencies, and individuals in different African nations have made some progress developing new water resources.

Large Scale Projects Governments in Africa and international donors have invested billions of dollars in building dams and desalination plants that provide fresh water for irrigation and drinking. In addition, giant pipelines are being built that will carry fresh water from aquifers in Libya and Lesotho to places that need water.

Success in the Villages Villages and towns across Africa are trying to improve their water supply by using low-cost technologies that they can manage and maintain themselves. In Zambia, for example, a group of women got together and financed the drilling of wells to supply their town with fresh water. In other places,

Well Water

Human-Environment Interaction This well in the Azadak region of Mali lies in the Sahel. Since water is scarce in the region, wells such as this one attract people and animals from the surrounding areas.

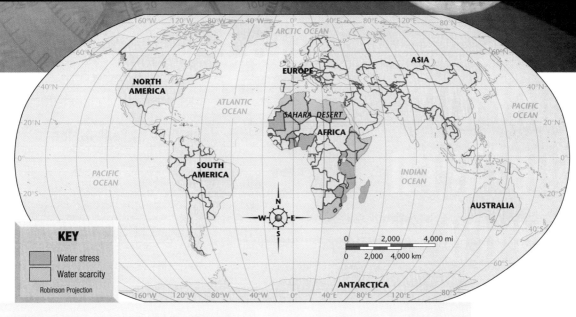

APPLYING THE GEOGRAPHIC THEMES

● **Human-Environment Interaction** The map above shows the African nations that are classified as having scarce water supplies, defined by fewer than 650 cubic yards (500 cubic meters) of water per person. Efforts to improve water supplies are being undermined by rapid population growth. **Critical Thinking** *How would an increase in population impact the available water supply?*

farmers operate their own simple irrigation systems.

Looking Toward the Future
Many experts say that a long-term solution to the water crisis depends less on securing water than on changing the way it is used. In the poorest countries 90 percent of the available water is used for irrigation. Much of it is wasted in the process. Alternative methods of irrigation, such as drip irrigation, can reduce the amount of water wasted. Some experts suggest it might be wiser for Africa's food to be grown in places that are rich in water. They support a movement that encourages Africa's people to develop other commodities that can be traded for water.

YOU DECIDE

1. What are some of the reasons why water is scarce in Africa?

2. What do you think is the best way to address Africa's water problem?

3. **Problem Solving** You are appointed to a panel of experts designing a policy for managing Africa's water resources. Draft a one-page policy with three to five proposals for how to meet the water needs of Africa's people.

4. **What You Can Do** Find out more about global water scarcity and what is being done around the world to address the problem.

5. **Internet Activity** Visit the site of an online journal called EcoNews Africa and read about Mali's plans to combat desertification. Then write a summary of the problem and Mali's plan of action. Link to this site from:
   • www.phschool.com

East and Southern Africa

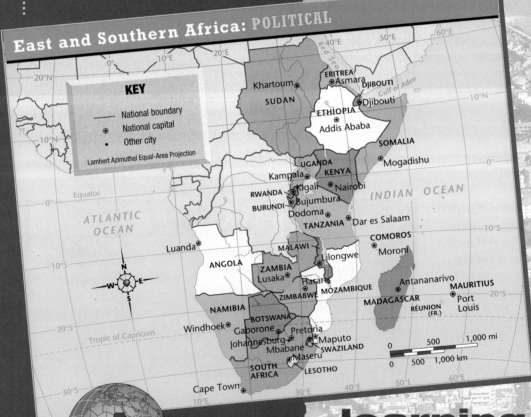

East and Southern Africa: POLITICAL

KEY

— National boundary

⊛ National capital

⊛ Other city

Lambert Azimuthal Equal-Area Projection

Khartoum ⊛
SUDAN
ERITREA
⊛ Asmara
DJIBOUTI
Djibouti
Gulf of Aden
ETHIOPIA
Addis Ababa
SOMALIA
Mogadishu
UGANDA
KENYA
Kampala ⊛
⊛ Kigali ⊛ Nairobi
RWANDA
BURUNDI
Bujumbura
Dodoma
TANZANIA Dar es Salaam
INDIAN OCEAN
COMOROS
⊛ Moroni
ATLANTIC OCEAN
Equator
Luanda ⊛
ANGOLA
MALAWI
Lilongwe ⊛
ZAMBIA
Lusaka ⊛
Harare ⊛
MOZAMBIQUE
ZIMBABWE
Antananarivo ⊛
MAURITIUS
Port Louis
MADAGASCAR
RÉUNION (FR.)
NAMIBIA
BOTSWANA
Windhoek ⊛ Gaborone ⊛ Pretoria ⊛
Johannesburg ⊛ Maputo ⊛
Mbabane ⊛ SWAZILAND
SOUTH AFRICA Maseru ⊛
LESOTHO
Cape Town ⊛
Tropic of Capricorn

0   500   1,000 mi
0   500 1,000 km

Mapping the Region

Create a map like the one above, lightly shading each country a different color. Then add labels for countries and bodies of water that are shown on this map.

Kenya

Section Preview

Main Ideas

- Kenya's most fertile land has been the focal point of activity in the area for centuries.

- After gaining independence, Kenyans built a healthy economy by working together.

- Kenya today is struggling to maintain its strong economy and sense of unity.

Vocabulary

harambee, pyrethrum, malnutrition

A Kenyan Masai, combining tradition with technology, checks cattle blood for disease.

Kenya has many features that have become symbols of Africa—rolling savanna lands, highland coffee plantations, the nomadic Masai (mah SY) people, and spectacular national parks where elephants, lions, and other protected wildlife roam freely.

Kenya is, of course, more than just these symbols. It is a vibrant country with a population of more than 28 million and a varied and beautiful landscape.

Lowlands vs. Highlands

Kenya is located on the east coast of Africa and extends deep into the interior of the continent. As the map on page 532 shows, the Equator runs right through the center of the country, so that parts of Kenya are bathed in steamy heat. In addition, the Great Rift Valley slices through Kenya's highlands, where elevation makes the climate cooler.

Most of Kenya's people live in the fertile highlands of the country's southwest region. Rainfall is uncertain in northern Kenya, making the area prone to drought. The plateau that leads toward the center of the country, gradually rising toward

the west, is the driest part of Kenya. In contrast, the highlands receive adequate rainfall, and forests and grasslands cover much of the area. In the westernmost corner of the region is magnificent Lake Victoria, the largest lake in Africa.

Seeking Fertile Land

The most fertile land in Kenya, found in the central highlands on either side of the Great Rift Valley, has been a main area of activity for centuries. When Kenya came under British rule in 1890, two groups occupied the highlands: a group of herders called the Masai, and another group, the Kikuyu (ki KOO yoo). Under the British, however, these groups lost their most fertile farmland and all political power.

The Railroad Arrives In an effort to encourage economic development and to gain access to the rich farmland in the central highlands, the British decided to build a railroad from the coast to Lake Victoria. It was an extremely difficult task that cost thousands of lives and millions of dollars. One writer described the hazards involved this way:

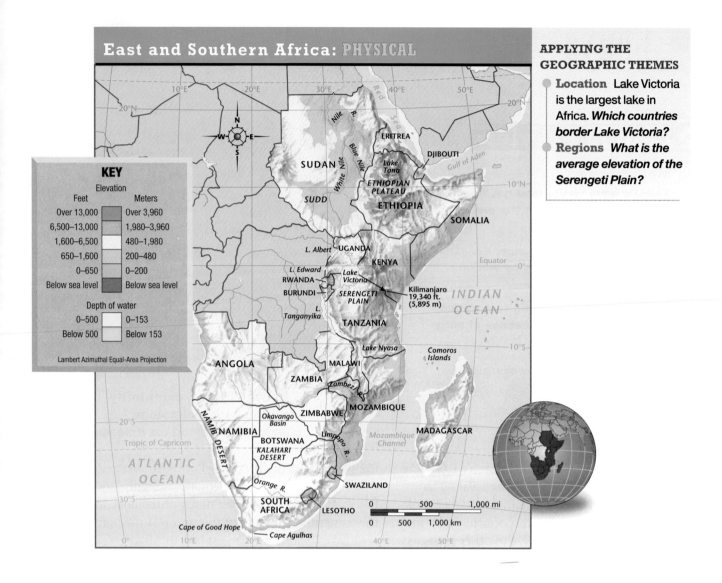

East and Southern Africa: PHYSICAL

KEY

Elevation

Feet	Meters
Over 13,000	Over 3,960
6,500–13,000	1,980–3,960
1,600–6,500	480–1,980
650–1,600	200–480
0–650	0–200
Below sea level	Below sea level

Depth of water

0–500	0–153
Below 500	Below 153

Lambert Azimuthal Equal-Area Projection

APPLYING THE GEOGRAPHIC THEMES

● **Location** Lake Victoria is the largest lake in Africa. *Which countries border Lake Victoria?*

● **Regions** *What is the average elevation of the Serengeti Plain?*

Waterless deserts, man-eating lions who preyed on and terrorized the [workers] . . . fever and sickness, the scaling of mountains, the spanning of valleys, the bridging of rivers that turned into swollen torrents in the rain—all these, and many more obstacles, had to be overcome.

Despite the challenges of the physical environment, the railroad was completed in 1903.

The new transportation link across Kenya brought changes. The British government encouraged its citizens and other Europeans to settle in Kenya and develop the highlands. White settlers, some from South Africa, were eager to move into the cool climate of the highlands. A new town was built on the railroad line. It was called Nairobi (ny RO bee) and it grew very rapidly.

Kenyans Challenge the British

The white settlers took over much of the land that the Kikuyu had traditionally considered their own. Many were forced to work on farms run by settlers.

In the 1950s, the Kikuyu went to war against the British settlers in Kenya in a fierce confrontation called the Mau Mau Rebellion. The rebellion was crushed, but one of the leaders of the Kikuyu, Jomo Kenyatta, became president when Kenya emerged from British rule in 1963. Under Kenyatta, the Kikuyu regained some of their farms in the central highlands.

Place Characteristics

Kenyatta encouraged all parts of the economy—the government, privately held companies, and individuals—to work together to strengthen

Kenya's economy. He called this working together "*harambee*," from a Swahili word that means "pulling together."

Harambee at Work *Harambee* grew as a grass-roots movement of people pulling together to help themselves and each other. Many foreign investors were pleased with Kenyatta's attitude and willingly pulled together with the Kenyans.

The result of this cooperation was solid economic growth. Because Kenya has little mineral wealth, the growth was based mostly on expanding agriculture. Kenyatta encouraged farmers to raise cash crops—coffee and tea—which grow well on the fertile central highland farms of the Kikuyu. Many government officials were Kikuyu, and they soon grew wealthy from their own farming.

Not Enough Food Rather than growing food, the government has concentrated on growing cash crops—especially certain flowers used to produce **pyrethrum** (py REE thrum), a pesticide, as well as luxuries like coffee and tea. As more land is used for cash crops, there is less land available for subsistence agriculture. For example, 30 percent of the country's wheat has to be imported, even while fresh flowers, fruits, and vegetables are rushed out of the country by air freight for sale in Europe. As a result, many Kenyans suffer from **malnutrition**, a disease caused by not having a healthy diet.

Politics in Kenya

Since independence, Kenya has been one of the most admired and stable countries in Africa. In the 1980s, however, Kenya began to face hard times. The population grew at an astounding rate, at times as much as 4 percent a year. Kenya was unable to supply its rapidly growing population with enough food or jobs. Social and political unrest developed, and ethnic groups that had lived in peace with one another since independence began to clash.

GLOBAL Issues

Conservation vs. Tradition

Kenya's wildlife reserves draw millions of tourists each year and bring the country much-needed revenue. But with one of the fastest-growing populations in Africa, Kenya suffers a severe shortage of land. The Masai need open rangeland in two of Kenya's biggest reserves to continue their traditional way of life. To offer them an alternative, the government is giving them a share of the profits from tourism.

Nairobi Skyline

● **Location** The city of Nairobi is Kenya's capital and main industrial center. Roads and railways connect Nairobi to the port of Mombasa on the Indian Ocean. *How did Nairobi's location help it grow?*

Kenyan Farmland

● **Place** The fertile soil in the Rift Valley is good for farming. Lush coffee plantations cover the hilly terrain. Yet because the government wants farmers to focus on cash crops for export, many Kenyans lack food. *How does concentration on cash crop production effect the health of Kenyans?*

Political Reforms Many Kenyans blamed the country's president, Daniel arap Moi, for their troubles. They accused him of corruption and mismanagement of the economy. Like citizens in other countries south of the Sahara, they demonstrated for democratic reforms in the government.

At first President Moi steadfastly refused to allow multiparty elections. He punished independent judges, threw critics in jail, and closed down newspapers that protested his policies. But Moi finally agreed to hold elections in 1992, when Western countries placed pressure on him by stopping loans to Kenya. Moi was reelected, but only by a small margin. In 1996, his supporters attacked and beat a world-famous Kenyan scientist, Richard Leakey, who was trying to organize an opposition party.

Search for Peace The struggle for unity and peace continues, despite setbacks. Ethnic violence has forced thousands of farmers in the Great Rift Valley off their land, which has further hurt food production. At times inflation has risen as high as 100 percent as Kenya struggles to pay off billions of dollars of foreign debt.

Still, Kenyans are hopeful of regaining their unity and prosperity, and they draw inspiration from the symbols of their nation. Kenya's flag has stripes of three colors: black, for the people of Kenya; red, representing their struggle for independence; and green, symbolizing the country's agriculture. The seal of the Republic of Kenya shows two lions leaning on a shield. Beneath them is the word *harambee*, reminding Kenyans of the importance of pulling together for their nation's future.

Section 1 Review

Vocabulary and Main Ideas

1. **Define:** a. *harambee* b. **pyrethrum** c. **malnutrition**

2. **What changes did the British railroad bring to the region?**

3. **How did *harambee* benefit Kenya?**

4. **Critical Thinking:** *Cause and Effect* **Explain why the highlands of Kenya are cool even though they are on the Equator.**

5. Describe the location of Kenya in East Africa.

6. Describe the location of Nairobi in Kenya.

Other Countries of East Africa

Section Preview

Main Ideas

- Several countries on the Horn of Africa are strategically located.

- Regional issues have caused lasting and bitter conflicts in several East African nations.

- Tanzania has changed its ideology to promote economic growth.

Vocabulary

strategic value, ethnocracy, villagization

UN workers help **Ethiopians rebuild a road destroyed by war.**

Kenya shares East Africa with many other countries. Several of these countries border the Indian Ocean, the Red Sea, or the Gulf of Aden, while others are landlocked. One of them, Ethiopia, is one of the oldest countries in Africa, while another, Eritrea, is the newest.

Key Locations

The region's coastal location gives some of its countries special opportunities for trade as well as **strategic value**—the value of the location to nations planning large-scale military actions. The countries of Ethiopia, Eritrea, Djibouti (ji BOO tee), and Somalia are located on a landform known as the Horn of Africa. These countries have particularly strategic locations. They lie near both the oil supplies of the Middle East and the shipping lanes of the Red Sea and the Gulf of Aden. These countries are also strategically located at the midpoint between Europe and Southeast Asia.

Djibouti Djibouti is a vital link between neighboring Ethiopia's capital city of Addis Ababa and the sea. Djibouti earns most of its income from its strategic ports. France pays large fees to Djibouti for the right to maintain a

military base in the country. When civil war broke out in 1991, France tried to bring the two sides to the negotiating table. The ruling party in the country agreed to a new constitution, and elections were held that were supposed to include the opposition, which was known as the Front for the Restoration of Unity and Democracy (FRUD). However, FRUD did not participate in the elections, and the fighting grew even more fierce after the voting.

Ethiopia Ethiopia has one of the longest histories of all the nations in Africa. Ruins and ancient Egyptian writings record the history of the Kushite civilization in Ethiopia about 3,500 years ago. The region's high, fertile plateaus, which enjoy temperate climates, rise like massive walls above the deserts of the Sudan to the west and Somalia to the east. In recent years, regional conflict and drought have brought this ancient nation almost to the edge of collapse.

A drought in 1984 caused famine and starvation in Ethiopia. In addition, war with neighboring Somalia, as well as civil war in the coastal province of Eritrea, caused grave crises. Other nations sent aid to Ethiopia, but the civil war prevented food from reaching those who needed it.

In 1991 the Ethiopian government was overthrown, and at about the same time, the Ethiopian army was beaten by Eritrean guerrillas. Ethiopia was forced to allow Eritrea its independence, and as a result Ethiopia's relative location changed. Once situated strategically on the Red Sea, Ethiopia is now landlocked. It is still badly torn by ethnic division: within the first few years of its new government, at least 100 political parties appeared, most based on ethnic grouping.

Eritrea After winning independence, the new nation of Eritrea found its economy was shattered. But the unity created in Africa's longest civil war lived on after the fighting was over. Said one Eritrean:

> There is almost a demonic [fierce] determination to get things done. It's one of those things I think comes out of suffering. The thirty years of war—one of the dividends ... was this tremendous sense of discipline.

By the mid-1990s the capital, Asmara, had become a handsome city in the European style, with bustling taxis and buses. A new steel plant had been built to melt down old military equipment for peaceful uses. Steam engines from the 1930s were being rebuilt to run again on the rail line to the main port. And a new $65 million housing complex was rising on the skyline. In making these improvements, the government had borrowed very little from other nations. Though democracy was not in sight and the government had been accused of repressing some minority groups, Eritrean willpower had brought about an economic miracle.

Country	Population	Life Expectancy (years)	Per Capita GNP (in US $)
Burundi	6,400,000	50	180
Djibouti	600,000	48	780
Eritrea	3,500,000	NA	NA
Ethiopia	56,000,000	50	100*
Kenya	28,300,000	56	270
Rwanda	7,800,000	46	200
Somalia	9,300,000	47	NA
Sudan	28,100,000	55	NA
Tanzania	28,500,000	49	100
Uganda	21,300,000	45	190
United States	263,200,000	76	24,750

Source: Population Reference Bureau   NA indicates data not available.
* Includes data on Eritrea

CHART SKILLS

- Which country, aside from the United States, has the highest per capita GNP?

- **Critical Thinking** Which countries do not have data available for per capita GNP? What are some possible reasons for the unavailability of data?

Somalia Since Somalia gained its independence in 1960, fighting between clans, border wars with Ethiopia, and drought have prevented it from becoming a strong, unified nation. In the late 1980s, full-scale, civil war erupted. By 1991, Somalia was in a state of anarchy.

To make the situation even worse, a severe drought struck the region in the early 1990s. Hundreds of thousands of Somalis were threatened with starvation. International relief agencies donated food, but the constant fighting within the country prevented food supplies from reaching the hungry people.

In 1992, the United Nations appealed to the world community for help in saving Somalia's people. The United States, along with several other countries, sent troops there to protect food supplies. A few years later, however, the United Nations, frustrated at its failure to bring peace to the nation, withdrew its forces.

The Sudan

The Sudan—the largest nation in area in all of Africa—is much like the Sahel nations discussed in Chapter 26. To the north the country is largely a desert of bare rock or ergs—shifting sand dunes; in the south are clay plains and an extensive swamp area called the Sudd, which means "the Barrier."

The people of the Sudan are divided. Muslim Arabs live in the north. In the south, the people belong to several different African ethnic groups, and they practice animism or Christianity. North and south have been at war almost continuously since independence in 1956, resulting in widespread suffering. During the 1990s, UN estimates of Sudanese in danger of starvation ranged into the millions, despite international aid missions.

Landlocked Countries

Along with Ethiopia, the three countries of Uganda, Rwanda, and Burundi are landlocked, or entirely surrounded by land. All three nations are heavily populated, agricultural countries. Coffee is the most important export crop, but Rwanda and Burundi lack the means to get their goods to foreign buyers.

Uganda Located to the west of Kenya, Uganda is for the most part a plateau with fertile soils. It prospered first by growing cotton, and then by raising coffee. But when the nation gained independence from Britain in 1962, civil war broke out and disrupted the country's prosperity. People in the north, who had won most of the military power, struggled against southern groups, which had most of the economic might. Under a ruthless dictator, Idi Amin (EE dee ah MEEN), as many as 300,000 Ugandans died or "disappeared" in the violent struggles that took place in the country during the 1970s. By the mid-1990s, Uganda was rebuilding itself and moving closer to a more democratic government. In 1996, an election was held for the president.

Rwanda and Burundi An **ethnocracy** is a government in which one ethnic group rules over others. Rwanda (roo AHN duh) and Burundi (boo ROON dee), two of the smallest African nations, are both ethnocracies.

In Rwanda, 90 percent of the population belongs to the Hutu (HOO too) group. Most of the remainder are Tutsi (TOOT see), sometimes called Watusi (wah TOO see). The Hutu remained firmly in power for 35 years after they successfully overthrew the Tutsi-controlled government in 1959, killing some 100,000 of the minority. In 1994, hundreds of thousands of Tutsi were murdered and 2 million Rwandans were driven from

Quitting Time

Movement This photograph shows a crowded bus station in Kampala, the capital of Uganda, at rush hour. Most Ugandans, however, are farmers rather than city dwellers. Uganda's economy depends heavily upon agriculture, especially coffee exports. *Critical Thinking Why does a country that exports farm products need good transportation as well as fertile soil?*

X ○○○○○○○

EXTREMELY LONG
Winding northward for over 4,145 miles (6,671 km), the Nile River is the longest river in the world. The White Nile originates in the mountains of Burundi. The Blue Nile starts in Ethiopia and joins the White Nile at Khartoum in Sudan.

X ○○○○○○○

WATERING THE DESERT
The Nile river flows through the desert lands of Sudan and Egypt before emptying into the Mediterranean Sea. Annual floods deposit rich soil causing the ancient Egyptians to refer to their land as "The Black Land."

their homes in a brief and horrifying civil war. Hutu and Tutsi currently share power in Rwanda.

In Burundi, on the other hand, the Tutsi are in power, although they are clearly a minority— only 14 percent of the population. They control the army, and they use it to maintain their power. In mid-1993, when Burundi held its first free elections, the people chose a Hutu president. Within months, the army staged a coup and overthrew him. Tens of thousands of Hutu have been massacred since Burundi received its independence in 1962.

Tanzania

To the east of Rwanda and Burundi lies Tanzania (tan zuh NEE uh). Like many African nations, it is a land of great potential wealth. Its soils are fertile in many areas. Its lands include the hot, humid coastal lands, the cool highlands, the varied terrain around Lake Victoria, and the dry central plains. Beneath its surface lie iron ore, coal, diamonds, and other minerals.

However, because of poor development, it remains the second poorest country in the world, after neighboring Mozambique. During an experiment in socialism between 1961 and 1985, Tanzania's rural people were subjected to **villagization**—forced to move into towns and to work on collective farms. The nation's economy ground to a halt. Not until socialism was abandoned did the economy turn around. The key to recovery was paying farmers a fair price for their crops. When they saw that they could profit by growing corn and cotton, they once again farmed land that had been idle for years.

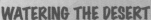

Section 2 Review

Vocabulary and Main Ideas

1. Define: a. strategic value b. ethnocracy c. villagization

2. Why does France maintain a military base in Djibouti?

3. Why did Tanzania change its political ideology?

4. Critical Thinking: *Cause and Effect* Explain how Ethiopia's relative location changed when it lost the province of Eritrea.

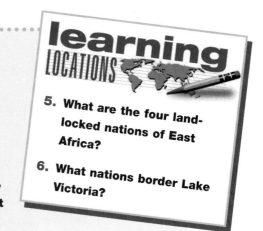

learning LOCATIONS

5. What are the four landlocked nations of East Africa?

6. What nations border Lake Victoria?

3 South Africa

Main Ideas

- For most of this century, a white minority has controlled the South African government and economy.

- The apartheid system, which was created in an attempt to preserve the power of whites in South Africa, was abolished in 1990 and 1991.

- In 1996, South Africa adopted a new, democratic constitution.

Vocabulary

apartheid, segregation, sanction

White South Africans control most of the nation's wealth.

The Republic of South Africa is one of the powerhouse economies of the African continent. In fact, it is the wealthiest, most highly developed nation in Africa. Yet it has not had an untroubled past. Black South Africans became equal citizens in their country only at the beginning of the 1990s, after years of protest and violence.

A Country Divided by Race

Much can be told about the Republic of South Africa with a few numbers. Some 76 percent of South Africa's population is black; less than 3 percent is Asian; about 9 percent is of mixed race; and 13 percent is white. Yet the white minority ruled South Africa for over a century.

Minority Rule Whites controlled not only the South African government, but about two thirds of the land in South Africa and most

of its highly paid jobs as well. The whites owned the gold mines, the diamond mines, and the mines where some seventy other minerals were dug from beneath the soil.

White South Africans owned the best farmland as well. The Republic of South Africa is mostly a high plateau. Around the edges of the plateau is an escarpment that drops to a narrow coastal plain. The plateau itself is generally dry, but in places where there is good rain, corn, wheat, and a wide variety of fruits grow abundantly. Whites also owned the thriving industries of South Africa, where the metals of the mines were manufactured into machines and other goods. In other words, the white population possessed nearly all of the country's wealth. How did this nation's minority come to possess so much wealth and power?

Movement into African Lands
The inequality of ownership in South Africa came about, first of all, through movement.

Europeans came to South Africa beginning in the 1600s—first the Dutch, then some Germans and a few French. Over time these groups together came to be known as Afrikaners (AF ri KAHN erz), or Boers. They spoke their own distinctive language, called Afrikaans (AF ri KAHNZ). The Afrikaners pushed the native Africans inland, gradually claiming the Africans' land by both treaty and by force. Then British settlers arrived in South Africa in great numbers. The Afrikaners continually moved inland to escape from the British, and the British moved after them repeatedly, reasserting British control.

An armed conflict called the Boer War broke out and raged for three years. In the end the Afrikaners accepted British rule. The final effect of this movement was a combined colony of Afrikaners and English-speaking settlers. The majority African population was driven into separate lands called reserves or put to work on plantations or in factories owned primarily by whites and Asians.

Movement into White Lands By the time South Africa left the British Commonwealth to become an independent nation in 1961, a new pattern of movement had appeared. Africans were moving out of the confining reserves into the cities. The reserves promised nothing but subsistence farming on arid land, while jobs were available in the cities.

From about 1950 until 1980 the economy of South Africa grew faster than that of any country on the continent, and faster than that of most nations in the world. There were four reasons for this growth.

First, South Africa had an inexpensive energy source from its abundant coal reserves. Second, the country also had capital, or money, to invest. Third, South Africa's excellent connections with Britain and the rest of Europe provided the technology, knowledge, and skills that South Africans needed to build productive factories and mills.

The fourth and most important element in South Africa's great expansion was the black South Africans themselves. They formed a vast pool of labor, and worked for low wages because they had little choice.

Artificial Regions

The white government was frightened by the movement of black South Africans toward the cities. Whites were afraid that the blacks who were crowding into the townships, or settlements near the cities, might claim a right to live there permanently.

Soweto Township

Place Soweto, shown here, is a large black township near the city of Johannesburg. Many black South Africans were once forced to live in townships. Many blacks remain there today, living in tin shacks like those in the foreground, because they are too poor to move. *What role did the townships play in opposing apartheid?*

Facts in BRIEF

Country	Population	Life Expectancy (years)	Per Capita GNP (in US $)
Angola	11,500,000	46	NA
Botswana	1,500,000	64	2,590
Lesotho	2,100,000	61	660
Madagascar	14,800,000	57	240
Malawi	9,700,000	45	220
Mozambique	17,400,000	46	80
Namibia	1,500,000	59	1,660
South Africa	43,500,000	66	2,900
Swaziland	1,000,000	57	1,050
Zambia	9,100,000	48	370
Zimbabwe	11,300,000	54	540
United States	263,200,000	76	24,750

Source: Population Reference Bureau   NA indicates data not available.

CHART SKILLS

● *Which country, aside from the United States, has the highest per capita GNP?*

● *Name the four countries that have a life expectancy lower than 50 years.*

Attempts at Control In order to control black South Africans, the South African government created arbitrary regions called homelands. Under the homelands plan, the blacks—about 75 percent of the total population—were forced to live on only 13 percent of the country's land. Every African in the nation was assigned to a homeland and was supposed to stay in it unless a pass had been issued allowing him or her to live somewhere else.

Along with the homelands plan, whites created a system of laws known as **apartheid** (uh PAR tate), which means "apartness." Under apartheid, black South Africans were **segregated**, or forced to live apart, from whites. By law blacks were required to use separate public facilities of all types, including schools and colleges. The facilities for black South Africans were never as good as those that were available to whites. For example,

in 1990 the average-size class in the black South African school system was forty-one, while the average size of white classes was only fifteen students.

International Backlash Apartheid and the homelands plan was an unjust system, and much of the world refused to let it continue without protest. In 1986, South Africa's major trading partners, Europe and the United States, placed economic **sanctions** against South Africa. Sanctions are actions that punish a country for behavior which the international community does not approve.

The United States sanctions prohibited Americans from investing in South Africa and banned the import of certain South African products. Imports from South Africa fell 40 percent in the first nine months. One expert estimated that sanctions were costing South Africa 2 billion dollars a year. Meanwhile, Africans in the townships kept up the pressure with protests that not even police violence could stop. Finally, South African whites began to admit that changes had to take place.

Winds of Change

In 1989 a new prime minister named F. W. de Klerk came to power in South Africa. He proved to be a reformer, and in spite of angry opposition from some whites, he started making changes.

Moving Toward Majority Rule One of de Klerk's most important actions was the release of prominent black South African activist Nelson Mandela from prison. Mandela had been held for twenty-seven years for his anti-apartheid activities.

As a leader of the African National Congress (ANC), Mandela entered into negotiations with the white government on behalf of blacks in

GLOBAL issues

Investment

After the peaceful transition to majority rule, it seemed that South Africa would not be able to attract investment money. In 1993, for example, fleeing whites took 15 billion rand (the South African currency) from the country. But one year later, the flow had reversed, and 5.2 billion rand in investment money was flowing into South Africa.

South African Peacemakers

● **Place** As prime minister, F. W. de Klerk (right) dismantled apartheid. His reforms led to South Africa's first all-race elections in 1994, which resulted in the selection of Nelson Mandela (left) as the first president of the new South Africa. De Klerk and Mandela received the Nobel Peace Prize for their work. *What was Mandela's career before becoming president?*

South Africa. In 1990 and 1991, apartheid and all the laws that supported it were repealed, or removed. A gradual transition of power to African majority rule ensued. In 1994 South Africa held its first truly free elections, in which blacks as well as whites were allowed to vote. Despite some violence, and despite fears that extremist whites and blacks would prevent the transition to majority rule, South Africans of all backgrounds went to the polls. This historic election paved the way for Nelson Mandela to become South Africa's first black president.

Looking Ahead In 1996 a new constitution was approved by the national assembly. Although some political parties protested the constitution, it laid the groundwork for a new South African future. In 1999, free elections brought Thabo Mbeki to the presidency in a peaceful transfer of power. Today, South Africa continues to face a number of social and economic problems. Yet within a decade, the nation of South Africa had gone from being a repressive police state to being a model for political change.

Section 3 Review

Vocabulary and Main Ideas

1. **Define: a. apartheid b. segregation c. sanction**

2. **How did the white minority come to gain power in South Africa?**

3. **Give two reasons for the change in the white South African government's policy toward black South Africans.**

4. **Critical Thinking: *Demonstrating Reasoned Judgment* Why do you think that economic sanctions are sometimes considered controversial?**

learning LOCATIONS

5. **Where is Pretoria located in relation to Cape Town?**

6. **Name two separate countries that lie within South Africa.**

Focus on Skills

☐ Social Studies

☐ Map and Globe

☑ Critical Thinking and Problem Solving

Drawing Conclusions

Drawing conclusions means figuring out information or finding an answer that is suggested but not stated directly. The ability to draw conclusions enables you to go beyond what is presented in the text and form new insights. Use the following steps to practice drawing conclusions.

1. Study the facts and ideas in the passage. Before you can draw conclusions, you must clearly understand the basic facts and ideas. Read the two passages below and answer the following questions: (a) How do most rural Kenyans support themselves? (b) Traditionally, who has benefited the most from government spending in South Africa?

2. Make a summary statement from the contents of the passage. After reading for facts and ideas, try to summarize the basic information in the passage. Answer the following questions: (a) From Passage A, what can you conclude about the nature of Kenyan agriculture? Are most Kenyan farmers able to support themselves through farming? (b) From Passage B, what can you conclude about the needs of Africans and white South Africans?

3. Consider whether or not you can draw a conclusion based on what is stated. Depending on the information in the passage, you may or may not be able to draw valid conclusions. As you read these questions, decide if you have enough information to draw conclusions. (a) Given what you read in Passage A, can you conclude that the number of small farmers in Kenya is more likely to grow or to shrink in the years ahead? (b) Given what you read in Passage B, what conclusion can you draw about future economic spending in South Africa?

Passage A

In the rolling countryside of Kenya, most people live in small villages. Here, families grow crops and raise livestock. Few people in this country can survive through farming alone. It is common for rural residents to hold part-time jobs to supplement their small, unreliable farm incomes. They may work as village carpenters or blacksmiths, or on large coffee and tea plantations.

The cities are a magnet for many Kenyans. Each year, thousands of rural Kenyans move to nearby cities in search of better-paying jobs—in factories, stores, and offices.

Passage B

White South Africans consider their country to be a first-world country. It has millions of rich white people, a good infrastructure, large companies, and famous hospitals and universities.

Africans of South Africa, who make up most of the population, fare little better than their neighbors in the developing countries of Zimbabwe and Botswana. Incomes are low, unemployment is high, and life expectancy is short. With the end of apartheid, South Africa began to shift the focus of its spending in order to meet the needs of its African majority.

4 Other Countries of Southern Africa

Section Preview

Main Ideas

- The countries of southern Africa are affected by the wealth and policies of the Republic of South Africa.

- Angola and Mozambique share a background of conflict and a potential for future prosperity.

- The current condition of Zambia and of Zimbabwe can be explained in part by their different attitudes toward farming.

Vocabulary

enclave, white flight, land redistribution

APPEARED IN *NATIONAL GEOGRAPHIC*

In Botswana, a woman shops at her local supermarket.

The Republic of South Africa is so powerful that it overshadows other nations in the region. Lesotho (luh SO to), for example, is an **enclave** of South Africa. That means it is completely surrounded by the larger country—and dependent on it. Swaziland, although richer in resources than Lesotho, is in much the same position. Namibia, on the west coast, was almost a colony of South Africa until recently. It even had its own version of apartheid, including African homelands. The rest of the southern African nations have dealt with their powerful neighbor in different ways.

Malawi and Botswana

Landlocked Malawi (muh LAH wee) and Botswana have worked to keep relations friendly with the Republic of South Africa because they have economic ties to the country. Malawi, a crowded nation on the western shore of Lake Nyasa in the Great Rift Valley, has many migrant workers who are under labor contracts in South Africa. Botswana is less dependent on

South Africa than Malawi only because Botswana is wealthier.

A comparison of Malawi and Botswana reveals the impact of physical geography on their economies. Malawi has fertile land and an excellent water supply, so that over time it has attracted a large population. Its resources must therefore be stretched to meet the needs of more people. Botswana, on the other hand, is an arid country that is sparsely populated. Its yearly profits from the sale of diamonds, copper, coal, and the millions of beef cattle it raises every year benefit a large part of its relatively small population.

Angola and Mozambique

Angola on the west coast and Mozambique on the east coast are separated from one another by the other countries of southern Africa. However, they share similar characteristics. Both coastal states were once Portuguese colonies. Both countries won their independence in 1975 after fighting long wars with Portugal. At the end of the wars, many Portuguese settlers fled, taking their wealth with them. This **white flight**, or departure of trained white administrators and technicians, made the task of the new government doubly difficult.

A Tangled Web Reacting to the problems that colonialism and capitalism had created in their countries, both governments committed themselves to a Communist economic system. This angered their capitalist neighbor, South Africa. In Angola a rebel group known as UNITA waged war against the new government. In Mozambique a group known as Renamo played a similar role. South Africa backed both rebel groups with weapons, money, and, in the case of Angola, troops.

The human cost of these wars was horrifying. Hundreds of thousands of people in Angola and Mozambique died in the fighting. Refugees fled the battle zones and packed themselves into urban areas, where they lived in terrible conditions. Under the stress of civil war, the economies of both nations fell apart. Disease and malnutrition were also widespread. In Angola, one child in four died before the age of five. Once able to feed its own people, Angola had to import most of its food.

Peace and Potential By the beginning of the 1990s, a glimmer of hope for peace began to emerge. South Africa and other nations ended their military involvement in Angola, which held its first free election in 1992. Although fighting erupted again between the new government and UNITA, the rebel group soon lost all international support because it would not agree to peace terms. In Mozambique, the civil war ended, and the government and the rebels worked out an agreement to join in a political settlement under United Nations supervision.

The political outlook for these countries is, therefore, more promising than it has been for decades. The economic outlook, however, is more difficult to predict. Although Mozambique is the world's poorest nation, it has a wealth of natural resources and a huge labor force. In 2000, however, Mozambique suffered devastating floods. The government reported that more than 490,000 people lost their homes as a result of the natural disaster. As for Angola, observers are hoping that it may soon again produce enough food for its population.

Zambia and Zimbabwe

Two countries in the region, Zambia and Zimbabwe (zim BAHB way), have tried with some success to keep themselves out of South Africa's long-reaching shadow. In spite of this shared goal, they have fared very differently.

On the Lookout

● **Place** In Angola, a long-running civil war between the government and UNITA rebels took many lives and devastated the economy. Here a government patrol searches for rebel troops. In 1992 Angola held its first free elections, raising hopes for a peaceful future. *How did events outside Angola help end the war there?*

Missed Opportunity

Zambia has over 880 million tons of copper reserves in an area adjoining the Democratic Republic of the Congo known as the Copperbelt. When Zambia achieved independence in 1964, the new president, Kenneth Kaunda, counted on copper to provide the country with a solid source of revenue.

Following independence, Zambia prospered. The government, certain that revenues from copper would always provide the nation with money to buy food, allowed Zambia's agricultural economy to decline.

In the long run, however, Zambia's reliance on copper proved to be a mistake. During the 1970s and 1980s, the price of copper on the world market plunged. Zambia could not get enough money to feed its people. The country became poor just as fast as it had become rich. President Kaunda tried to save the economy with a structural readjustment program, but he backed out of the program when Zambians rioted against the strict measures and their sudden poverty. In 1991 a new president was elected who clung stubbornly to structural readjustment. As the twenty-first century opened, economic recovery remained a long way off.

Making Farming Work The experience of Zimbabwe was different, in part because the country's citizens learned to work together. In 1965 the white minority government of Rhodesia—as Zimbabwe was then known—declared independence from Britain. But Britain and the United Nations demanded that Rhodesia's white leaders first respect the rights of the black majority. After years of conflict and negotiations, free elections were finally held in 1980. The same year, Rhodesia became the fully independent nation of Zimbabwe.

Hydroelectric Power

APPEARED IN *NATIONAL GEOGRAPHIC*

1. **Water tunnel** brings water into the power plant.
2. **Turbine wheel** turns as water is driven against blades.
3. **Water outlet** carries water out after passing through turbine.
4. **Turbine shaft** connects the turbine wheel to the generator.
5. The shaft turns the armature inside the **generator** to produce electricity.
6. **Transformer** boosts the voltage of electricity from the generator and transmits through high-voltage **power lines**.

DIAGRAM STUDY

● Water power is an important resource for many African nations. Hydroelectric plants are powered by rivers such as the Zambezi and by the rushing waters of Victoria Falls, shown at right. Examine the diagram. *How does water provide power for electricity?*

Zimbabwe's new leader, Robert Mugabe, was very cautious about making changes. At the time of independence, white farmers owned most of the nation's land. For this reason, Mugabe pursued a policy of **land redistribution**. Under such a policy, land is taken from those who have plenty and given to those who have little or none. According to Zimbabwe's constitution, white farmers had to be paid for their land, and they had to be willing to sell it.

Land redistribution took place slowly in Zimbabwe. This schedule gave the government more time to develop the necessary infrastructure for the new farmers. An infrastructure is a country's basic support systems, such as transportation, education, water, electricity, and other necessities.

As a result of Zimbabwe's cautious approach to land distribution, the nation's farmers continued to be among the most productive farmers in the world. In 2000, however, Zimbabwe's government abandoned caution. Veterans of the 1980 war of liberation began to occupy white-owned farms, and by July more than 1,600 farms had been seized without pay. In some instances, land owners were injured or killed. Although Mugabe initially supported the farm takeovers, political pressure forced him to change his stance. In August 2000, Mugabe promised to remove militants from farms they had occupied.

Farming Family

● **Place** Corn, tobacco, and cotton are among Zimbabwe's important crops. But less than 10 percent of the land is good for farming, and lack of rainfall can make even these areas unproductive. Here a family brings vegetables to market. **Critical Thinking** *Why are wealthier countries better able to deal with drought than poorer countries are?*

Section 4 Review

Vocabulary and Main Ideas

1. **Define: a. enclave b. white flight c. land redistribution**

2. **Why is Lesotho dependent on South Africa?**

3. **List three ways in which the southern African countries of Angola and Mozambique are similar.**

4. **Why did agriculture fail to develop in Zambia but did develop successfully in Zimbabwe?**

5. **Critical Thinking:** *Predicting Consequences* **How might the political and economic changes in the Republic of South Africa affect the other countries of southern Africa?**

learning LOCATIONS

6. Contrast and compare the locations of Angola and Mozambique.

7. How does Botswana's location make trade more difficult for that nation?

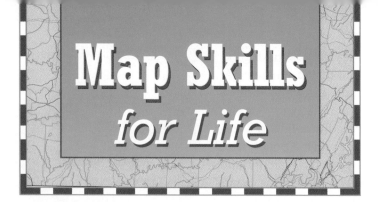

Map Skills for Life

Emma Hopkins and the other members of her Girl Guides troop in South Africa have become experienced hikers on many trips in the hilly regions near Johannesburg. Now they have saved enough to travel to Kilimanjaro National Park, in Tanzania, and make the trek to Kibo Peak, the summit of Mt. Kilimanjaro.

Emma's map shows roads and trails as well as huts for overnight shelter on the way up and down the mountain. She can tell how steep the climb will be by reading the contour lines on the map. These lines connect points at the same elevation; they are labeled with the elevation in feet or meters.

The highlights of the planned trek are:

★ the Marangu Trail, which is the trail that most visitors use. It begins at one of the entry gates to Kilimanjaro National Park.

★ the three huts for overnight stays:
Mandara Hut (2,700 m/8,858 ft)
Horombo Hut (3,720 m/12,200 ft)
Kibo Hut, nearest the summit (4,703 m/ 15,430 ft).

★ glaciers and icefields near Kibo Peak (5,895 m/19,340 ft).

Reading the Map

Follow the steps below to understand how Emma can use the contour map to guide their trek up Mt. Kilimanjaro.

1. Study the key to determine what each symbol on the map represents. Notice the symbols for each type of road or trail. **(a)** How far can Emma and her friends travel by truck or jeep up the Marangu Trail? **(b)** What buildings are at the end of the gravel road? **(c)** At about what elevation are they?

2. Use the map scale to determine distances between points on your trip. Remember that you must measure the actual distances along a trail, not a straight line between two points. **(a)** About how far will Emma have to walk from the Mandara Hut to the Horombo Hut? **(b)** About how much change in elevation is there between the two huts?

3. Use the contour lines to figure out how steep or difficult the trail will be. If contour lines on a map are close together, it means that the terrain is steep. A trail on a map shown crossing a series of contour lines close together is steep and usually difficult. A trail that follows a contour line or moves diagonally is easier because it stays at the same elevation or rises gradually. If Emma decides to take a different trail from Horombo Hut to the summit, which would be the easier route: to Kibo Hut or to the Barranco Hut?

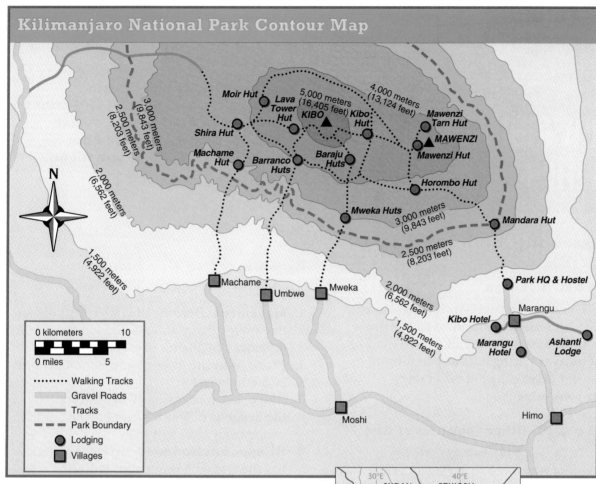

Kilimanjaro National Park Contour Map

Moir Hut

Lava Tower Hut

3,000 meters (9,843 feet)

2,500 meters (8,203 feet)

Shira Hut

5,000 meters (16,405 feet)

KIBO

Kibo Hut

4,000 meters (13,124 feet)

Mawenzi Tarn Hut

MAWENZI

Machame Hut

Barranco Huts

Baraju Huts

Mawenzi Hut

N

2,000 meters (6,562 feet)

Horombo Hut

Mweka Huts

3,000 meters (9,843 feet)

Mandara Hut

1,500 meters (4,922 feet)

2,500 meters (8,203 feet)

Machame

Umbwe

Mweka

2,000 meters (6,562 feet)

Park HQ & Hostel

Marangu

Kibo Hotel

1,500 meters (4,922 feet)

Marangu Hotel

Ashanti Lodge

| 0 kilometers | 10 |
| 0 miles | 5 |

········· Walking Tracks

Gravel Roads

Tracks

– – – Park Boundary

⬤ Lodging

■ Villages

Moshi

Himo

Test Yourself

1. One of Emma's friends suggests that the trail from Umbwe looks shorter and quicker. After the others look at the contour map, they say they would rather stay with the Marangu Trail. Why did they decide this?

2. Many hikers give up before they reach the actual summit of Kilimanjaro. If Emma and her friends do take the trail from Kibo Hut to the peak, what elevation will they reach?

30°E SUDAN ETHIOPIA 40°E

UGANDA KENYA SOMALIA

Nairobi

RWANDA

BURUNDI

Lake Victoria

▲ Mt. Kilimanjaro 19,340 ft. (5,895 m)

D.R. CONGO

Dodoma

Dar es Salaam

TANZANIA

ZAMBIA

30°E MALAWI 40°E

Summarizing Main Ideas

Section 1 Kenya

- Kenya's most fertile land is in the highland regions; it has been the focus of movement through the area for centuries.
- Kenya today is having difficulty feeding all its people and developing a sense of unity among competing groups.

Section 2 Other Countries of East Africa

- The Horn of Africa is a strategic location because of its closeness to oil routes on the Red Sea and the Indian Ocean.
- The nations of East Africa have been torn by bitter ethnic, religious, and political disputes that have caused suffering and famine.

Section 3 South Africa

- The apartheid system denied black South Africans equal rights.
- Apartheid was dismantled in the 1990s, and the black majority is gaining true political and economic power.

Section 4 Other Countries of Southern Africa

- Angola and Mozambique, torn by civil war, are working toward peace and prosperity.
- After independence, Zambia chose a risky dependence on its copper resources to fund its development, while Zimbabwe has been able to make its agricultural economy among the most productive in the world.

Reviewing Vocabulary

Use each of the following terms in a sentence that shows its meaning.

1. malnutrition
2. strategic value
3. ethnocracy
4. villagization
5. apartheid
6. sanction
7. land redistribution
8. segregation
9. harambee
10. white flight

Applying the Geographic Themes

1. **Movement** Describe the movement of various groups that wanted to exploit the fertility of Kenya's highlands over the centuries.
2. **Place** Why are Rwanda and Burundi considered ethnocracies?
3. **Place** List four reasons why the economy of the Republic of South Africa boomed in the period from 1950 to 1980.
4. **Human-Environment Interaction** How has the arid environment of Botswana actually helped that country?
5. **Region** Why did South Africa support rebels fighting against the Angolan and Mozambiquan governments?

Critical Thinking and Applying Skills

1. **Formulating Questions** Write two questions that a voter in Uganda might have had about the 1996 election.
2. **Drawing Conclusions** Refer to Passage B on page 543. What conclusions can you draw from the passage about the effect that a shift in economic spending will have on both white and black South Africans?

Journal Activity

Writing Across Cultures

▶ 1. Write a paragraph from the point of view of an American businessperson who took part in the sanctions against South Africa. In the paragraph, show how the businessperson feels about South Africa's new constitution.

▶ 2. As one diplomat has noted, "Africa never runs out of surprises. The lesson here is that things can always change for the better, and it is never too late to save a situation." Imagine you are a diplomat trying to help Africa become self-sufficient in food and settle its ethnic and religious differences. Propose a positive plan of action.

INTERNET link

Find out how students in a Pretoria, South Africa school are using the Internet. Visit the Micklefield School. Link to this site from:

- www.phschool.com

Look at some student projects. How are students in South Africa using the Internet? How does it compare with what you are doing? Write a paragraph with your thoughts on the subject.

learning LOCATIONS

East and Southern Africa

Number from 1 to 12 on a piece of paper. Next to each number, write the letter of the place on the map that corresponds to the places listed below.

1. Addis Ababa
2. Cape Town
3. Eritrea
4. Johannesburg
5. Kenya
6. Angola
7. Burundi
8. Nairobi
9. Ethiopia
10. Somalia
11. South Africa
12. Tanzania

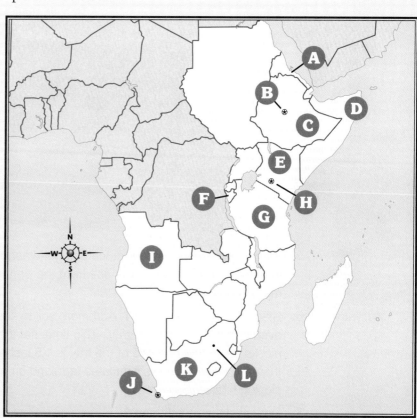

SOIL EROSION

Many factors can influence soil erosion, including wind, rain, the slope of the land, and intensive farming techniques. The following experiment will demonstrate how the slope of a field can affect the rate of erosion.

MATERIALS:

Loose topsoil

Tray (about 12" long)

Large, leak-proof pan

Wood blocks

One-gallon watering can

Water

Measuring cup

PROCEDURES:

Step 2

1. Spread soil evenly around the tray so that the soil level is even with the sides.

2. Set a few wood blocks in the pan so that the tray will rest evenly on top of them and place the tray on the wood blocks. This simulates farmland on level ground.

Step 3

3. Fill the watering can with one gallon of water and pour it all evenly over the soil. Some of the water will spill over the sides and wash some of the soil with it.

4. Take the tray out of the pan. Carefully pour off the water in the pan.

5. Estimate or measure how much soil got washed away into the pan by scraping the soil from the pan into the measuring cup.

6. Start over again with step 1. Add more soil to keep the level even with the sides of the tray. This time, set the wood blocks up so that one end of the tray is 1.5 inches higher than the other end. This simulates farmland on a mildly sloping hillside (5 degrees).

7. Repeat steps 3, 4, 5, and 6.

Step 6

GEOGRAPHER'S LAB

OBSERVATIONS AND ANALYSIS:

1. What was the amount of topsoil lost in each trial? How does the biggest loss of soil compare to the smallest loss?

2. How does slope affect soil erosion? Predict how much soil would be lost on a 15 and a 25 degree slope.

3. When land is prepared for farming, all of the trees and plants are cleared. What effect could trees and plants have on the rate of erosion?

4. One technique that farmers can use to prevent erosion is to plant strips of grass or shrubs around their fields. How do you think this might help?

FOOD CRISIS
in Africa

More than 27 countries on the African continent are below the world average for food available per person. Although many factors contribute to this situation, erosion is one of the main environmental causes of this problem. As existing farmland is worn out by intensive farming methods, growers must find new, fertile land. Unfortunately, many farmers are deforesting woodlands and hillsides in search of more fertile ground. This trend creates a dangerous downward spiral as more and more land is exhausted and abandoned.

taking Action

Throughout the world, topsoil is being lost at a rate of 25.4 billion tons per year. The United States loses 5.5 billion tons of soil each year. Here are some things you can do to help:

✔ Learn more about sustainable agriculture.

✔ Ask your local grocers to buy produce from farmers who practice responsible land management.

Sudanese field designed to prevent erosion

Soil erosion caused by overgrazing in Kenya

South Asia

CHAPTERS

A Global Perspective

South Asia looks like a giant triangle extending out into the Indian Ocean. Millions of years ago, the part of the earth's crust containing the subcontinent of South Asia collided with the rest of Asia. The force of this huge collision drove the earth skyward, creating the world's highest mountains, the Himalayas. These mountains formed a barrier that allowed the people of South Asia to develop their own unique cultures. Yet peoples and ideas did move into and out of the region, helping to transform South Asia and its neighbors.

Robinson Projection

KEYS TO UNDERSTANDING THIS REGION

1 Countries and Cities *(pp.556–557)*
India is the largest country in South Asia. The British ruled much of the region until 1947.

2 Physical Features *(pp. 558–559)*
The Himalayas, which rise about 5 miles (8 km) above sea level, are the highest mountain range in the world. They form a barrier between South Asia and the rest of Asia.

3 People and Cultures *(pp. 560–561)*
South Asia is one of the most densely populated regions of the world. The majority of people in the region practice Hinduism or Islam. Conflicts among religious groups have caused great turmoil in South Asia.

4 Climate and Vegetation *(pp. 562–563)*
South Asia's climate is heavily influenced by the monsoons. Half the year it is hot and dry; the other half it is hot with heavy continuous rains. Many of the region's farmers depend on rain from the monsoons to grow their crops.

5 Economy and Resources *(pp. 564–565)*
The majority of South Asia's people are farmers but jobs in industry are growing. India is one of the world's twelve leading industrial nations.

VISUAL PREVIEW ACTIVITY

Each of the five keys above corresponds to a section of the Regional Atlas that follows. Number from 1 to 5 on a piece of paper. Use information from the maps, graphs, and photographs in the Regional Atlas to write one additional fact for each of the five keys above.

APPEARED IN *NATIONAL GEOGRAPHIC*

Chapter 28

SOUTH ASIA

Use the Map, Graph, and Photo Studies in the Regional Atlas to gain a better understanding of the region's physical and cultural geography.

ATLAS VOCABULARY

subcontinent	"rooftop of the world"	monsoon
alluvial plain	Hindi	

1 COUNTRIES AND CITIES

MAP STUDY
Applying the Geographic Themes

1 **Place** The region of South Asia is a giant **subcontinent**, or large landmass, in the southern part of Asia. *Which country in the region lies north of Pakistan?*

2 **Location** The country in South Asia that lies farthest to the south is completely surrounded by water. *Name the country and its capital city.*

3 **Location** If you were to draw lines between the Indian cities of Mumbai, Calcutta, and New Delhi, you would form a triangle. *Which city is located at the northern tip of the triangle?*

4 **Location** The mountainous country of Nepal lies along the northern border of South Asia. *What is the capital of Nepal?*

APPEARED IN *NATIONAL GEOGRAPHIC*

PHOTO STUDY

5 **Capitals in South Asia**
The locations of South Asia's capitals reflect the dramatic variations of the region's physical geography. Look at the photograph of Thimphu, Bhutan, then locate this city on the map on page 557. *Critical Thinking How do you think the location of a capital city affects its country's image in the world?*

SOUTH ASIA

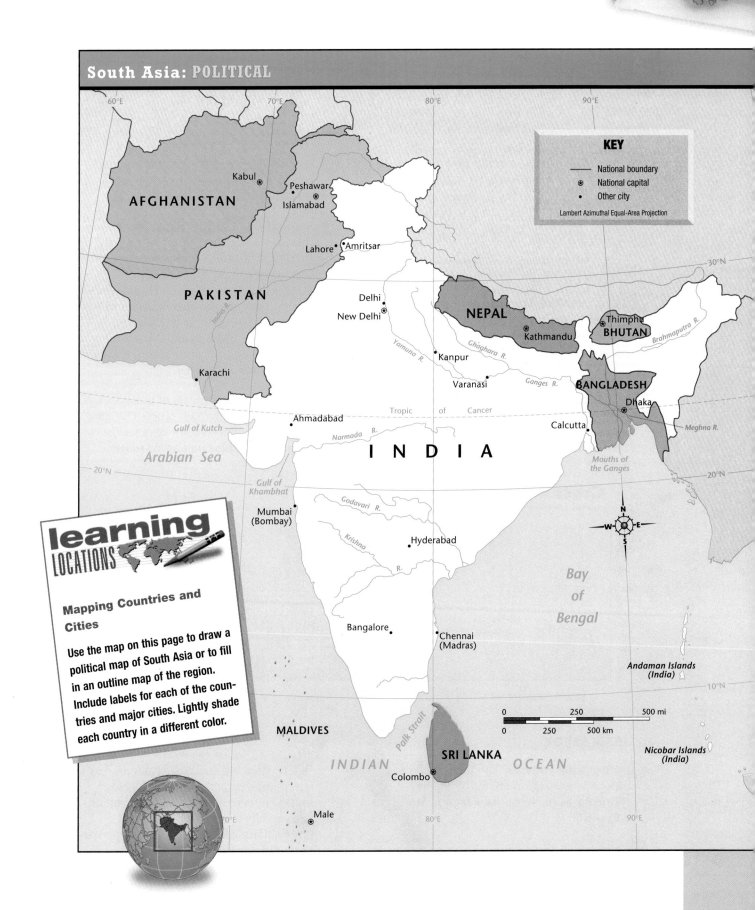

South Asia: POLITICAL

KEY
— National boundary
⊛ National capital
• Other city

Lambert Azimuthal Equal-Area Projection

AFGHANISTAN

Kabul ⊛

Peshawar •
Islamabad ⊛

PAKISTAN

Lahore • Amritsar

Karachi •

Indus R.

Delhi •
New Delhi ⊛

Yamuna R.

Kanpur •

Ghāghara R.

NEPAL

Kathmandu ⊛

Thimphu ⊛
BHUTAN

Brahmaputra R.

Varanasi •

Ganges R.

BANGLADESH

Dhaka ⊛

Ahmadabad •

Tropic   of   Cancer

Calcutta •

Meghna R.

Gulf of Kutch

Narmada R.

Mouths of
the Ganges

Arabian Sea

20°N

Gulf of
Khambhat

INDIA

20°N

Godavari R.

Mumbai
(Bombay) •

Krishna

R.

Hyderabad •

Bay
of
Bengal

Bangalore •

Chennai
(Madras) •

Andaman Islands
(India)

10°N

500 mi
250
0

0   250   500 km

MALDIVES

Palk Strait

SRI LANKA

Nicobar Islands
(India)

INDIAN

Colombo •

OCEAN

Male ⊛

learning LOCATIONS

Mapping Countries and Cities

Use the map on this page to draw a political map of South Asia or to fill in an outline map of the region. Include labels for each of the countries and major cities. Lightly shade each country in a different color.

2 PHYSICAL FEATURES

MAP STUDY
Applying the Geographic Themes

1 **Place** Three great rivers flow through the northern region of the Indian subcontinent: the Indus, the Ganges (GAN jeez), and the Brahmaputra (BRAM uh POO truh). These rivers begin their journey to the sea as trickles moving down the icy crags of the Himalayan slopes. *In which country is the mouth of the Indus River?*

2 **Human-Environment Interaction** As the Indus, Ganges, and Brahmaputra rivers travel through the low, flat land, they slow down and deposit rich silt that they picked up during their journey. When the rivers flood, they leave broad expanses of fertile land along their banks forming **alluvial plains**. *Name the plain the Ganges River flows through.*

3 **Place** The central part of the Indian subcontinent is made up of a huge plateau. *What is the plateau called?*

4 **Location** The Himalayan range includes more than thirty of the world's highest mountains and is often called the **"rooftop of the world."** Scientists believe that the Himalayas started pushing upward millions of years ago when the tectonic plate carrying what is now India collided with the Eurasian plate. *In what countries are the Himalayas located?*

5 **Place** The southern tip of India is shaped by two sets of mountain ranges that give the subcontinent its distinctive wedge shape. *Name these mountain ranges.*

Cross Section: South Asia

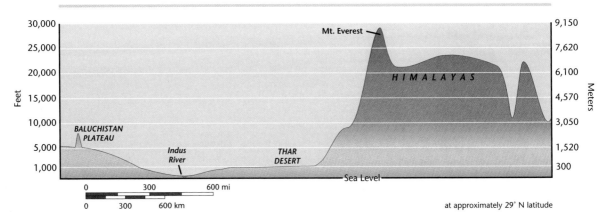

DIAGRAM STUDY

6 **Physical Profile** The highest elevations in the region are found in the Himalayas in Nepal. *How high is Mt. Everest?*

7 **Varied Landforms** The geographic landscape of South Asia varies greatly.

Deserts stretch throughout Pakistan. Lush rain forests spread across the slopes of India's west coast. Glacier-covered mountains overlook the villages of Nepal. *Connections: Math What is the approximate difference in elevation between the Indus River and the Baluchistan Plateau?*

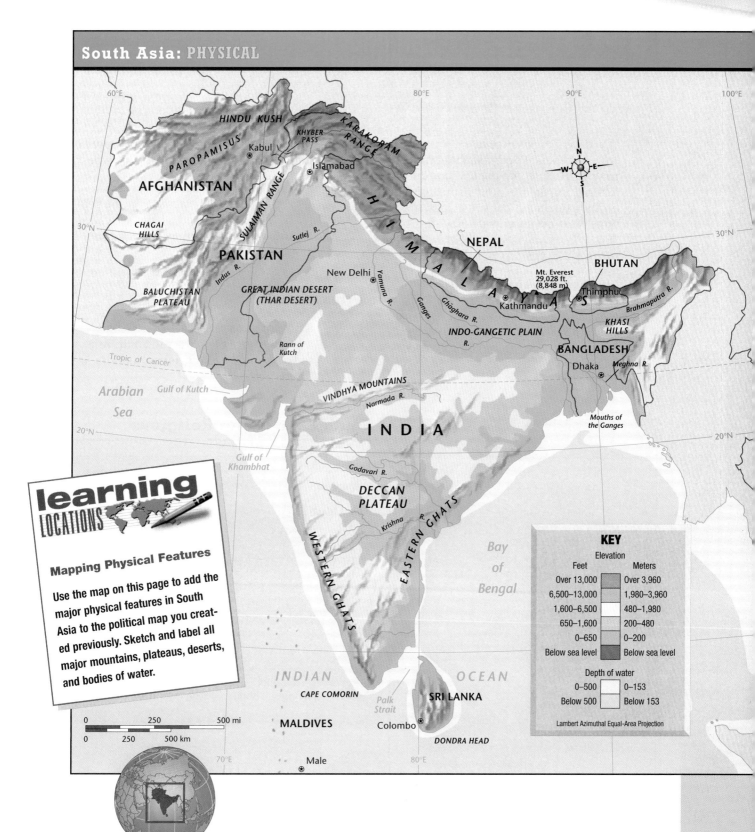

South Asia: PHYSICAL

60°E   80°E   90°E   100°E

HINDU KUSH

KHYBER PASS

KARAKORAM RANGE

PAROPAMISUS

Kabul ⊛

Islamabad ⊛

AFGHANISTAN

SULAIMAN RANGE

30°N   CHAGAI HILLS   30°N

PAKISTAN

H I M A L A Y A S

NEPAL

BHUTAN

Mt. Everest 29,028 ft. (8,848 m)

Thimphu ⊛

Indus R.

New Delhi ⊛

GREAT INDIAN DESERT (THAR DESERT)

Yamuna R.

Sutlej R.

Kathmandu ⊛

BALUCHISTAN PLATEAU

Ganges

Ghaghara R.

Brahmaputra R.

KHASI HILLS

INDO-GANGETIC PLAIN R.

BANGLADESH

Rann of Kutch

Dhaka ⊛

Meghna R.

Tropic of Cancer

Arabian Sea

Gulf of Kutch

VINDHYA MOUNTAINS

Narmada R.

Mouths of the Ganges

20°N   I N D I A   20°N

Gulf of Khambhat

Godavari R.

DECCAN PLATEAU

Krishna

EASTERN GHATS

Bay of Bengal

WESTERN GHATS

learning LOCATIONS

Mapping Physical Features

Use the map on this page to add the major physical features in South Asia to the political map you created previously. Sketch and label all major mountains, plateaus, deserts, and bodies of water.

I N D I A N   O C E A N

CAPE COMORIN

Palk Strait

SRI LANKA

MALDIVES

Colombo ⊛

DONDRA HEAD

0   250   500 mi
0   250   500 km

70°E   80°E

Male ⊛

KEY

Elevation

Feet	Meters
Over 13,000	Over 3,960
6,500–13,000	1,980–3,960
1,600–6,500	480–1,980
650–1,600	200–480
0–650	0–200
Below sea level	Below sea level

Depth of water

0–500	0–153
Below 500	Below 153

Lambert Azimuthal Equal-Area Projection

3 PEOPLE AND CULTURES

MAP STUDY
Applying the Geographic Themes

1 **Human-Environment Interaction** South Asia has one of the most densely settled populations on earth. Compare the most populated areas on the population density map to the same areas on the climate map on page 563. *What can you say about rainfall in areas of the greatest population density?*

2 **Movement** The lack of arable land due to a growing population is forcing more and more South Asians to move to cities in search of jobs. In India about 26 percent of the population live in cities. *Connections: Math If India's*

total population is 930 million, approximately how many people live in cities?

3 **Place** Although many languages are spoken in South Asia, about half the people in India understand a language called **Hindi**. *To what language family does Hindi belong?*

GRAPH STUDY

4 **The Impact of Religion** Religion is a major source of conflict in South Asia today. *What three religions dominate in the region?*

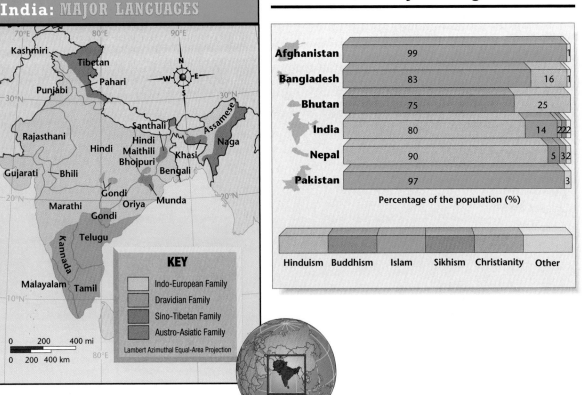

India: MAJOR LANGUAGES

Kashmiri
Tibetan
Pahari
Punjabi
Rajasthani
Santhali
Hindi
Maithili
Bhojpuri
Khasi
Assamese
Naga
Bengali
Gujarati — Bhili
Gondi
Marathi
Oriya
Munda
Gondi
Telugu
Kannada
Malayalam Tamil

KEY
Indo-European Family
Dravidian Family
Sino-Tibetan Family
Austro-Asiatic Family
Lambert Azimuthal Equal-Area Projection

0 200 400 mi
0 200 400 km

South Asia: Major Religions

Afghanistan	99		1
Bangladesh	83	16	1
Bhutan	75	25	
India	80	14	2 2 2
Nepal	90	5	3 2
Pakistan	97		3

Percentage of the population (%)

Hinduism Buddhism Islam Sikhism Christianity Other

SOUTH ASIA

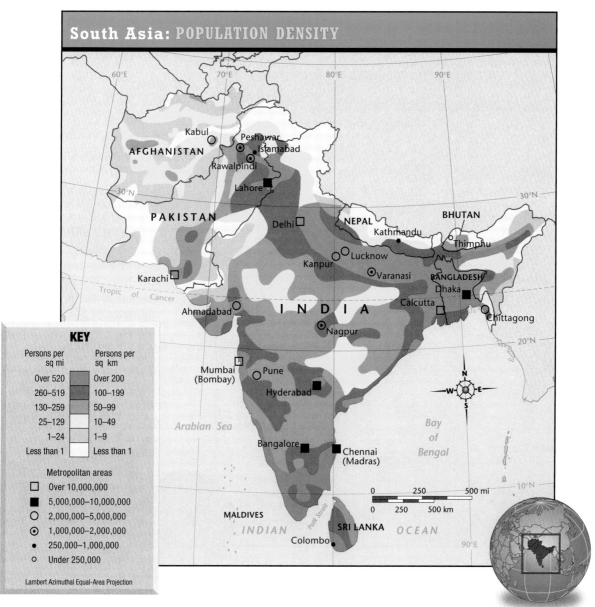

South Asia: POPULATION DENSITY

KEY

Persons per sq mi		Persons per sq km
Over 520		Over 200
260–519		100–199
130–259		50–99
25–129		10–49
1–24		1–9
Less than 1		Less than 1

Metropolitan areas
- ☐ Over 10,000,000
- ■ 5,000,000–10,000,000
- ○ 2,000,000–5,000,000
- ⊙ 1,000,000–2,000,000
- • 250,000–1,000,000
- ∘ Under 250,000

Lambert Azimuthal Equal-Area Projection

CHART STUDY

5 **Largest Cities** By the beginning of the twenty-first century, Calcutta and Mumbai were among the ten most populated cities in the world. Locate these six largest cities on the political map on page 557. *Critical Thinking* *What do most of these cities have in common? Why?*

LARGEST CITIES

Mumbai, India
12,572,000

Delhi, India
8,375,000

Karachi, Pakistan
5,180,500

Calcutta, India
10,916,000

Chennai, India
5,361,500

Lahore, Pakistan
2,952,500

❚ = 2,000,000 people
Source: United Nations

S O U T H   A S I A

4 CLIMATE AND VEGETATION

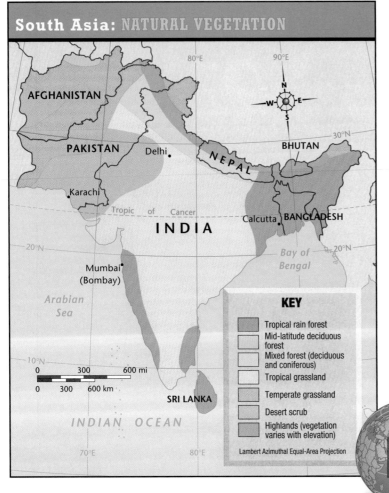

South Asia: NATURAL VEGETATION

AFGHANISTAN

PAKISTAN   Delhi

Karachi

NEPAL   BHUTAN

Tropic of Cancer

INDIA   Calcutta BANGLADESH

Mumbai (Bombay)

Bay of Bengal

Arabian Sea

INDIAN OCEAN

SRI LANKA

80°E   90°E   30°N   20°N   20°N   10°N   70°E   80°E

KEY

Tropical rain forest

Mid-latitude deciduous forest

Mixed forest (deciduous and coniferous)

Tropical grassland

Temperate grassland

Desert scrub

Highlands (vegetation varies with elevation)

Lambert Azimuthal Equal-Area Projection

0   300   600 mi
0   300   600 km

MAP STUDY
Applying the Geographic Themes

1 Regions Monsoons are seasonal shifts in the winds. In winter the winds blow from the northeast and bring dry air from Asia's mainland to much of South Asia. In summer the winds reverse direction, pick up moisture from the warm Indian Ocean, and drop heavy rains as they move over the land. *What countries in South Asia have tropical wet and tropical wet and dry climates?*

2 Regions When summer monsoon winds meet mountain ranges, they release their moisture as they are pushed upward. Because the Western Ghats block the rain, the land to the east is hot and dry. Compare the physical map on page 559 with the vegetation map. *What kind of vegetation grows there?*

PHOTO STUDY

3 Monsoons Much of South Asia is hot and dry for half the year (left). Farmers wait anxiously for the life-giving monsoons to arrive (right). However, if the rain hits too hard, lowland areas face the danger of floods. Other areas can be threatened by landslides. *Critical Thinking What might happen if the monsoons were late?*

APPEARED IN *NATIONAL GEOGRAPHIC*

SOUTH ASIA

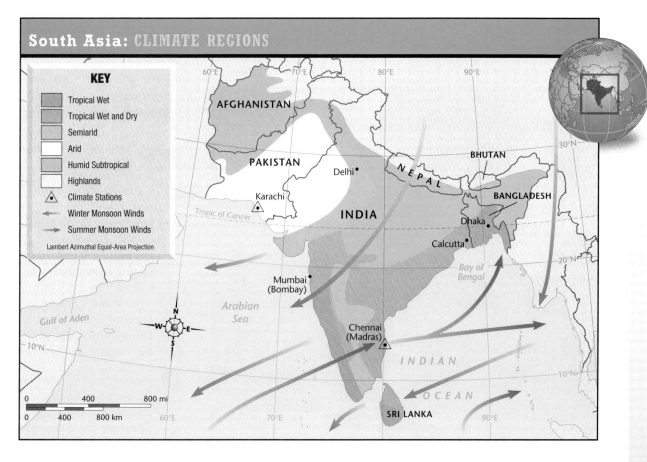

South Asia: CLIMATE REGIONS

KEY

- Tropical Wet
- Tropical Wet and Dry
- Semiarid
- Arid
- Humid Subtropical
- Highlands
- △ Climate Stations
- ← Winter Monsoon Winds
- → Summer Monsoon Winds

Lambert Azimuthal Equal-Area Projection

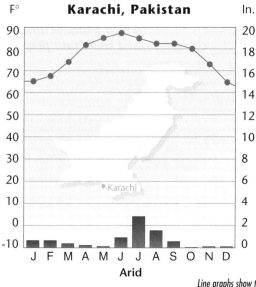

Karachi, Pakistan

F° / In.

Arid

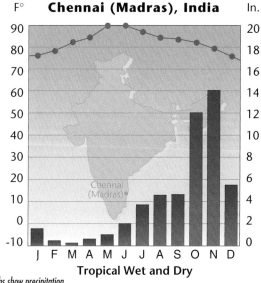

Chennai (Madras), India

F° / In.

Tropical Wet and Dry

Line graphs show temperature. Bar graphs show precipitation.

GRAPH STUDY

4 Temperature and Precipitation
Areas out of the path of the monsoon wind in South Asia receive little rain. In its wettest month Karachi, Pakistan, receives an average of only 2.5 inches of rain. But Chennai, India, receives 14 inches in its rainiest month. ***What are the wettest months in Chennai?***

S O U T H   A S I A

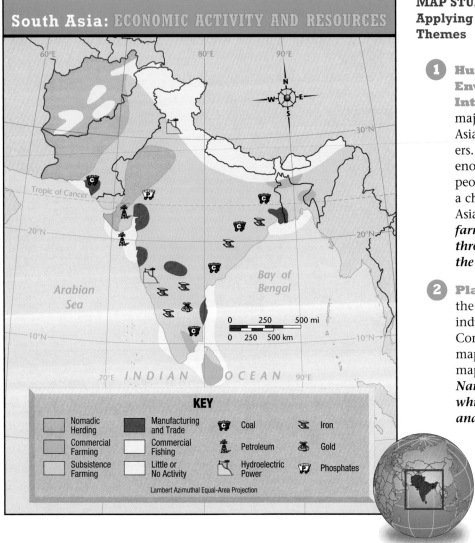

South Asia: ECONOMIC ACTIVITY AND RESOURCES

KEY

- Nomadic Herding
- Commercial Farming
- Subsistence Farming
- Manufacturing and Trade
- Commercial Fishing
- Little or No Activity
- **C** Coal
- Petroleum
- Hydroelectric Power
- Iron
- Gold
- **P** Phosphates

Lambert Azimuthal Equal-Area Projection

MAP STUDY
Applying the Geographic Themes

1 **Human-Environment Interaction** The majority of South Asia's people are farmers. Yet growing enough food to feed its people continues to be a challenge for South Asia. *What kind of farming takes place throughout most of the region?*

2 **Place** India is one of the world's leading industrial nations. Compare the economic map with the political map on page 557. *Name three cities in which manufacturing and trade take place.*

3 **Regions** Although most of South Asia has great amounts of precipitation, in some parts of the region there is an insufficient amount of water for farming. *In which regions of South Asia does nomadic herding take place?*

4 **Place** Very little economic activity occurs along the northern border of South Asia. Compare the economic activity map on this page with the physical map on page 559 and the population density map on page 561. *Critical Thinking* *What accounts for the lack of activity in this region?*

5 **Location** Separated from the Indian subcontinent by the Palk Strait, the small island nation of Sri Lanka has limited economic opportunities. *What activities contribute to the economy of Sri Lanka?*

PHOTO STUDY

6 **Industrial India** Many Indians are moving from rural areas to urban areas in search of employment opportunities (bottom). Despite this trend, agriculture still dominates South Asia's economy (left). About two thirds of the working population depend directly on the land for their livelihood. *Critical Thinking* **What impact do you think such movement has on urban planning and services?**

atlas REVIEW

Vocabulary and Main Ideas

1. Define: **a. subcontinent b. alluvial plain c. "rooftop of the world" d. Hindi e. monsoon**

2. **Why is the Indo-Gangetic Plain good for farming?**

3. **What are the two largest religions in South Asia?**

4. **Critical Thinking:** *Cause and Effect* **Explain why most of South Asia experiences hot, dry weather for half of the year and hot, rainy weather for the other half.**

learning LOCATIONS

5. Name the mountain range that divides South Asia from the rest of the Asian Continent.

6. Name the country that lies northwest of India.

S O U T H   A S I A

1500 B.C. *750* *0* *750* A.D. *1500* D *Today*

Religions of South Asia

Why is Pakistan officially a Muslim country, while nearby India is home to Hindus, Muslims, Christians, and others? How did South Asia come to be home to followers of many different beliefs?

Crossroads of Asia

For thousands of years geography has made South Asia a crossroads. The towering Himalayas protect the subcontinent on the north and east, but invaders have poured in through the mountain passes on the northwest frontier. Trade routes across the region brought merchants and missionaries.

Two major world religions began in South Asia and spread to other places. Another religion, brought by conquerors, had a great impact on society and politics.

The Roots of Hindu Culture

Much of the mainstream culture of modern India derives from long-ago invaders. About 1500 B.C., people known as Aryans crossed the mountains from the high plains of central Asia. The Aryans' language and culture soon drove those of the earlier inhabitants, the Dravidians, southward. The Dravidian traditions continued to survive in southern India.

The Aryans believed in many gods, who were related to

Shiva, one of the greatest gods of Hinduism

natural forces such as fire, water, and thunder. These beliefs became the basis of Hinduism, which has many gods who can take different forms. Aryan society was strictly divided along class lines. These divisions, in which class determined each person's life and work, eventually developed into the Hindu caste system. Brahmins, the priest class, had the most power and privilege.

Buddha, Tibeto-Chinese gilt brass sculpture

Birthplace of Buddhism

In the 6th century B.C., a very different religious leader was born in northern India (Nepal). Siddhartha Gautama, an Indian prince, underwent a number of experiences that sent him into a lifetime of teaching. Followers of the Buddha, as Siddhartha later was known, practiced his guidelines for living, the Eightfold Path, in order to reach enlightenment, or **nirvana**.

Buddhism appealed to people of all classes and spread throughout India. Missionaries and traders carried Buddhism eastward, and the religion took firm root across Asia. But since Hinduism was flexible enough to absorb most of its beliefs, Buddhism slowly disappeared as a separate religion in India.

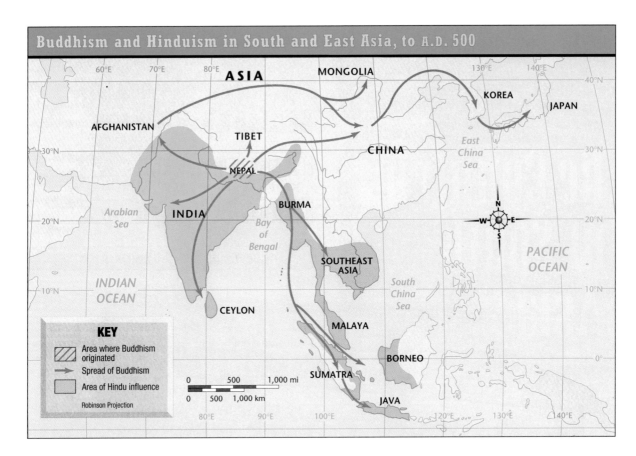

Buddhism and Hinduism in South and East Asia, to A.D. 500

KEY

- Area where Buddhism originated
- Spread of Buddhism
- Area of Hindu influence

Robinson Projection

0   500   1,000 mi
0   500 1,000 km

The map above shows the spread of Hinduism and Buddhism across East Asia.

lasting influence on India's culture and society, especially in the arts, architecture, and literature.

Muslims and Moguls

Soon after the religion of Islam emerged in Arabia in A.D. 622, some Muslims moved into northwest India. Over the next centuries four different groups of Muslims reached the peninsula. In the early 1500s, Muslims from Persia led by Babur conquered and united most of South Asia under the Mogul Empire. Mogul rule had a

Religion Divides South Asia

Differences between Islam and Hinduism were so deep that the two religions could not mix, as Hinduism and Buddhism had done. Devout Muslims, who believe in one God, could not tolerate the many Hindu deities. Attitudes toward class differences were also very different. Neither group could easily accept the other's ways. Deep and sometimes violent conflicts eventually led to the partition of South Asia into two modern nations: India, with a Hindu majority, and Pakistan, an Islamic state.

1. (a) **What two major religions originated in South Asia?**
   (b) **Which of those religions became more important in other parts of Asia? Where did it spread?**

2. **When and how did Islam become an important influence in South Asia?**

3. **Critical Thinking Why did Muslims and Hindus clash violently, whereas Buddhists and Hindus had been able to coexist?**

4. **Hands-On Activity Make a poster illustrating the three major religions associated with South Asia. Include pictures of art, architecture, statuary, symbols, and, if possible, a short quotation from the writings of each religion.**

The Countries of South Asia

South Asia: POLITICAL

KEY

— National boundary
⊛ National capital
• Other city

Lambert Azimuthal Equal-Area Projection

AFGHANISTAN
Kabul ⊛
Islamabad ⊛
PAKISTAN
Karachi •
Delhi •
New Delhi ⊛
Kathmandu ⊛
BHUTAN
Thimphu ⊛
BANGLADESH
Calcutta •
Dhaka ⊛
Tropic of Cancer
INDIA
Mumbai •
(Bombay)
Bay of
Bengal
Gulf of Aden
Arabian
Sea
Chennai •
(Madras)
MALDIVES
SRI LANKA
Colombo ⊛
INDIAN OCEAN

0   400   800 mi
0   400   800 km

learning LOCATIONS

Mapping the Region

Create a map like the one above, lightly shading each country a different color. Then add the labels for countries and water bodies that are shown on this map.

1 Road to Independence

Gandhi uses a charkha, or spinning wheel, which became the symbol of non-violent resistance in India.

Section Preview

Main Ideas

- Mohandas Gandhi used nonviolent methods to help India gain independence from Britain.

- When India became independent in 1947, it was divided into two countries, India and Pakistan.

- After a civil war in 1971, the eastern part of Pakistan became the nation of Bangladesh.

Vocabulary

nationalism, nonviolent resistance, boycott, partition

On August 14, 1947, thousands of Indians crowded outside the Assembly building in New Delhi to hear a dignified man speak these words:

At the stroke of the midnight hour, while the world sleeps, India will awake to life and freedom. A moment comes, which comes but rarely in history, when we step out from the old to the new, when an age ends, and when the soul of a nation, long suppressed, finds utterance.

The speaker was Jawaharlal Nehru (juh WAH huhr lahl NAY roo), the first prime minister of India, just hours before India's independence.

Indian Independence

Since the mid-1700s Britain had controlled India. The colonial rulers made many changes such as ending slavery, improving schools, and building a large railroad network that benefited India. Other changes, however, did not.

India once had a flourishing textile industry. The Indians were among the first people to grow cotton. Indian artisans spun the cotton into thread and wove new fabrics such as calico, cashmere, chintz, and muslin. The British, however, wanted to use India as a market for their own cheaper, machine-made textiles. The British colonial system imported raw cotton from India, made it into cloth, and shipped the finished product back to India for sale. As a result, millions of Indian textile workers lost their jobs.

In addition, the British did not treat their subjects as equals. For example, both the government and the army were organized with British officials in all of the positions of power. Indians were expected to take positions at the lower levels. This situation understandably angered some Indians.

Mohandas Gandhi During the late 1800s, Indians developed a strong sense of **nationalism**, or pride in one's nation. In addition, Western ideas of individual rights and self-government began to spread among the country's

Poverty

Religious communities have fought the effects of poverty in India and other countries. The Missionaries of Charity, founded by Mother Teresa of Calcutta, has opened centers around the world that care for orphans and the sick. Since its founding in 1948, the Missionaries of Charity have saved thousands of lives.

English-speaking middle class—its lawyers, doctors, and teachers. Many middle-class Indians traveled to England to study. One was a young law student named Mohandas Gandhi (moh HAHN dahs GAHN dee). It was Gandhi—later called Mahatma, meaning "the Great Soul"—who led India to independence.

Gandhi's belief in using **nonviolent resistance** against injustice was his most powerful weapon against the British. Nonviolent resistance means opposing an enemy or oppressor by any means other than violence. Gandhi also believed that peace and love were more powerful forces than violence. Everywhere he went, he won the hearts of the Indian people.

One way that Gandhi peacefully resisted British rule was to **boycott**—refuse to purchase or use—British cloth. Gandhi stopped wearing Western clothes, and instead wore clothes made from yarn he had spun himself. He devoted two hours each day to spinning his own yarn and urged other Indians to follow his example. The spinning wheel became a symbol of national pride. As a result of Gandhi's leadership and the boycott by the Indian people, the sale of British cloth in India fell sharply.

Gandhi's program of nonviolent resistance developed into a mass movement involving millions of Indians. In spite of Gandhi's pleas to avoid violence, however, some protests against British rule led to riots. Hundreds of people were killed or hurt.

Gandhi and his followers attracted support from other countries. In 1935 the British gave in to mounting Indian and international pressures and agreed to establish provinces that were governed entirely by Indians.

Religious Conflict

In the early 1940s the conflict between India's Hindus and Muslims deepened. For hundreds of years, the relationship between the two groups had often been hostile, but in recent years economic differences divided the two groups even further. The Muslims were generally the poorer peasants or landless workers, while the Hindus were often landowners.

For a time, Hindus and Muslims worked together for independence. But as they drew

Unrest in India

Place The conflict between Hindus and Muslims that led to the partition of India in 1947 continues today. In 1992, militant Hindus destroyed a historic Muslim mosque in northern India and sparked violence across the nation. *Critical Thinking Why didn't the partition of India bring a lasting peace?*

nearer to their goal, both groups began to fear being ruled by the other. In 1946 Britain offered independence to India on condition that Indian leaders could agree on a form of government. But Hindus and Muslims were unable to reach an agreement. Riots broke out in which thousands of people died.

Gandhi yearned for a united India, but the violence persisted. Finally, in 1947 British and Indian leaders agreed that the only solution to the conflict was to **partition**—divide into parts—the subcontinent into separate Hindu and Muslim countries. Part of the subcontinent became the mostly Hindu Republic of India. The northwestern and northeastern parts of the subcontinent, where most Muslims lived, formed the nation of Pakistan.

Violent Partition Independence came to India and Pakistan on August 15, 1947. The event brought joyous scenes of celebration. But independence also brought great confusion and suffering. In one of the greatest migrations in history, 12 million people moved. To avoid being ruled by a majority religion to which they did not belong, Hindus moved to India, where Hindus were in the majority, and Muslims moved to Pakistan, where Muslims were in the majority.

The journey was long and torturous. Ashwini Kumar, a young police officer who witnessed the migration, stated:

> *They passed in eerie silence. They did not look at each other. . . The creak of wooden wheels, the weary shuffling of thousands of feet, were the only sounds rising from the columns.*

Most of the refugees left their possessions along the road or traded them for lifesaving water. Many people, weakened by hunger, thirst, or exhaustion, died. In addition, an estimated one million were killed in the fighting between Hindus and Muslims.

Since independence, India and Pakistan have fought three wars. In 1965 India was forced to defend its northern border against Pakistan. The third war, in 1971, led to the creation of the new country of Bangladesh.

A Place of Worship

● **Place** The traditional Muslim place of worship is called a mosque. From the towers, or minarets, a crier calls the faithful to prayer five times a day. *How did religion play a role in the creation of Pakistan?*

Bangladesh When Pakistan became independent, it consisted of two regions—West Pakistan and East Pakistan—separated by 1,100 miles (1,770 km) of Indian territory. The boundaries of East and West Pakistan were not based on any physical landforms, but rather on the predominance of Islam in these two regions. In fact, Islam was the only thread that connected these two very different regions. The people of West Pakistan belonged to several ethnic groups, but most residents of East Pakistan were Bengalis (ben GAHL eez). Many people in West Pakistan spoke Urdu (OOR doo), which became the official language of the new country. This situation upset the East Pakistanis, who were proud of their Bengali language and their literary tradition.

Entrepreneurs

Place These Bangladeshi women are making baskets for the small business they created with the help of collateral-free loans offered by the Grameen Bank. Ninety-six percent of the bank's clients are women. **Critical Thinking** *Why do you think the Grameen Bank does not require collateral, which is property given to a lender as a pledge to repay a loan?*

Economics and politics further complicated the already difficult situation. West Pakistan contained some factories, while East Pakistan was largely agricultural. But despite being economically less developed, East Pakistan paid more taxes than West Pakistan. At the same time, more than half the national budget was spent in West Pakistan, where the government was located. Moreover, most positions of power in the government and the army were held almost exclusively by West Pakistanis.

Unrest continued to grow as many people in East Pakistan began to feel that their region was being treated merely as a colony of West Pakistan. Then, in 1970, more than 300,000 East Pakistanis died in a devastating flood caused by a cyclone and tidal wave. Many people in East Pakistan accused the government of deliberately delaying shipments of food and relief supplies to the victims.

The disaster touched off fighting between the two regions. India joined the conflict on the side of the East Pakistanis. In the face of such opposition, the West Pakistani forces surrendered and on December 16, 1971, East Pakistan became the independent country of Bangladesh, meaning "Bengali Nation." Bangladesh is shown on the map on page 557.

Section 1 Review

Vocabulary and Main Ideas

1. **Define: a. nationalism b. nonviolent resistance c. boycott d. partition**

2. **How did Gandhi use nonviolent resistance to oppose British rule?**

3. **How did Pakistan and Bangladesh gain their independence?**

4. **Critical Thinking:** *Making Predictions* **Do you think that other nations would have been as likely to support Indian independence if leaders like Gandhi had not practiced nonviolent resistance? Explain.**

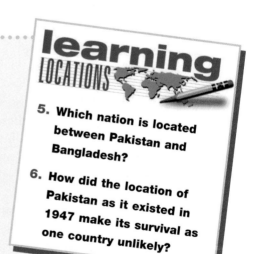

learning LOCATIONS

5. **Which nation is located between Pakistan and Bangladesh?**

6. **How did the location of Pakistan as it existed in 1947 make its survival as one country unlikely?**

Focus on Skills

- [ ] Social Studies
- [x] Map and Globe
- [ ] Critical Thinking and Problem Solving

Analyzing Cartograms

A cartogram is a special purpose map used to present statistics geographically. Countries on a cartogram are not drawn in proportion to their land area. Instead, some other feature—such as population growth, or GNP—determines the size of each nation. On the cartogram below, the size of a country's population determines its size on the cartogram.

Use the following steps to study and analyze the cartogram below.

1. Identify the kind of information represented on the cartogram. Look first for the title and the key that may help you interpret what you are looking at. You will need to compare a cartogram with a conventional land-area map—shown on pages 12–13—to assess the degree of distortion involved. Answer the following questions: (a) What kind of information does this cartogram show? (b) According to the key, how is population represented on the cartogram? (c) When compared to the land-area map, what countries appear to be very different on this map?

2. Practice reading the information shown on the map. Answer the following questions: (a) Which countries on the map show a very large population? (b) Which show very small populations? (c) Which two have the largest populations? (d) Name one country that appears about the same relative size on the cartogram and the land-area map.

3. Look for relationships among the data. Using information on the map, answer the following question. How would you explain the relatively large sizes of Japan, Taiwan, the Philippines, and Indonesia on the cartogram in contrast to the tiny size of Australia?

World Population Cartogram

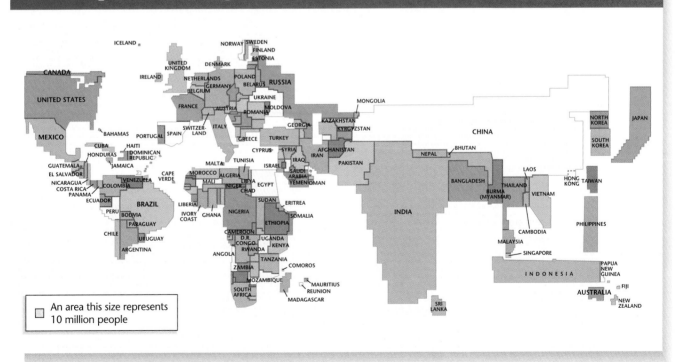

An area this size represents 10 million people

India's People and Economy

Section Preview

Main Ideas

- Most Indians live in rural villages, where traditional ways of life remain.

- The growth of cities and the rise of a middle class are major trends in modern India.

- India's government is working hard to raise the country's standard of living.

Vocabulary

reincarnation, caste system, charpoy, sari, purdah, joint family system, cottage industry

APPEARED IN *NATIONAL GEOGRAPHIC*

Traditional breads and a variety of spices are the hallmarks of Indian cuisine.

"The city air makes a man free," runs a medieval European saying. And, adds one modern journalist, "It is in the cities that twentieth-century India is casting off . . . the past." But most Indians still live in small, rural villages and carry on cultural traditions and religious customs.

Religious Life

The majority of people in India practice Hinduism, an ancient, polytheistic religion that teaches the unity of all life. Hindus believe that every living thing has a spirit, or soul, which comes from the Creator, Brahma. Because every creature possesses a soul, Hindus treat animals with great respect. Cows are especially sacred to Hindus and are allowed to wander freely through the city streets.

Hindus also consider the Ganges River to be holy. The Ganges is believed to purify the souls of people who bathe in it or drink its water. As a result, the banks of the Ganges often are lined with Hindus who have come there for healing.

According to Hinduism, the final goal of every living thing is unity with Brahma—a state of bliss without change or pain. In order to achieve this goal, the soul passes through cycles of **reincarnation**. Reincarnation is the belief that the souls of human beings and animals go through a series of births, deaths, and rebirths. Hindus believe that the soul does not die, but passes from body to body until it becomes pure enough to be united with Brahma.

The Caste System For hundreds of years, Hindu society has been organized according to the **caste system**. This system is a social hierarchy in which people are born into a particular group that has been given a distinct rank in society. Each caste has its own duties and obligations. Among these duties are obedience to caste rules as well as to moral laws. People can improve their position in the next life by carrying out their duties in this life.

At the top of the caste system are Brahmans—the priests, teachers, and judges. Beneath the Brahmans are the Kshatriyas

(SHAHT ree yuhz), or warriors. Below these two groups are the Vaisyas (VA ee syuhs), farmers and merchants. The fourth group are the Sudras, craftworkers and laborers.

A group called "untouchables," or outcasts, holds the lowest rank in the caste system. Traditionally, untouchables do the work that is considered "unclean," such as street sweeping and tanning hides.

Today the caste system continues to shape people's lives despite the fact that it has become less rigid. Although some people take up professions that follow the traditions of their caste, many do not. However, social relationships are often, though not always, confined to people within the same caste. Untouchables continue to have fewer educational and employment opportunities than citizens who belong to higher castes. Efforts are being made by the Indian government to offer greater opportunities to untouchables.

Other Religions Although the majority of Indians are Hindu, other religions practiced in India include Islam, Christianity, Sikhism (SEEK iz uhm), and Jainism (JY nihz uhm). Sikhism began as a movement to combine Hinduism and Islam. Sikhs are not divided into castes. Today many are farmers in their native province of Punjab in northwest India. Jainism, which developed in reaction to Hinduism, teaches that violence of any kind is wrong. Jains are taught to avoid harming any living creature.

Village Life

About seven out of ten Indians live in villages and farm for a living. Most Indian villages consist of a group of houses surrounded by fields. Dirt paths may lead to the village school, the pool used for washing clothes, and private vegetable gardens. A larger path may lead to the next village. Sometimes a bus goes by on its way to a larger town. Many people own bicycles; almost no one has a car. Each section, or social division, of the village shares a well.

Rural Housing Houses belonging to the more prosperous families in a village are often

The Caste System

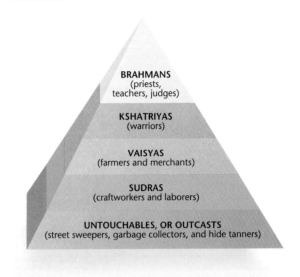

GRAPH STUDY

Untouchables have traditionally been denied common privileges and have lived bleak lives outside the social system. *Critical Thinking* *Why do you think "untouchables" traditionally have held the lowest rank in Indian society?*

built of brick and have tiled roofs and cement floors. Houses owned by poor villagers may be made of mud and thatched with dried grass. The floor is usually made of packed earth. Mud houses have no windows, which would only let in wind and rain.

Usually the only furniture is a **charpoy** (CHAR poy)—a wooden bed frame with knotted string in place of a mattress. Most families move the charpoy outside to the courtyard when the weather turns especially hot. The cooking is often carried out in the courtyard as well.

Food For both religious and economic reasons, Indians follow a mostly vegetarian diet. Hindus generally do not eat beef because the cow has religious importance, and Muslims are forbidden to eat pork. Some Indians do, however, eat goat meat and chicken. Those who live near rivers or the sea also eat fish.

Most Indians eat some form of rice every day. With it, they may eat a lentil soup called *dal* (DAHL). In northern India, the people make *rotis* (RO teez), or flat cakes of wheat or sorghum that are baked on an iron griddle. In

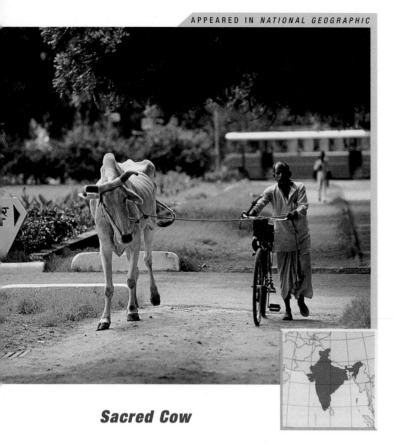

Sacred Cow

● **Place** India has the world's largest cattle population. Because of Hindu beliefs, India's cattle are considered sacred. Cows are as accepted in Indian cities as they are in the countryside. *Why do Hindus treat all animals with great respect?*

southern India, the people eat *idlis* (ID lees), or steamed pancakes of rice.

Clothing Because most of India is so hot and humid, clothing is light and loose. Many Indian women wear a **sari** (SAH ree)—brightly colored cloth that is draped over the body like a long dress. Some Indian women cover their faces with a veil when they are in public. This custom, called **purdah** (PUR duh), began among Muslims but is followed by Hindus as well.

Family Life Families in India are generally large. When a man marries, he usually brings his new wife to live in his parents' house. Often the household includes uncles and other relatives. This is known as the **joint family system**.

Everyone in the family has a role to play. Even the youngest children can take care of the

chickens, goats, or sheep. Older children carry water and help their parents in the fields. People who are too old to help in the fields do light jobs around the house, such as shelling peas or washing rice.

Life is very demanding for village women. Here is how one writer describes a typical day:

> *The women . . . work an 18-hour day, which begins at four in the morning with millet grinding–two women to a stone for more than two hours. After breakfast, the dung must be cleared and carried to the fields. . . . Then there is water to fetch and firewood to chop, the children to dress, and always a pile of clothes to wash and mend, not to mention the toil in the fields . . . planting, weeding, clearing stones, harvesting, gathering fodder and fuel. After a long day's work, there is still the rice to husk, the children to wash, and the supper to cook and serve.*

Signs of Change Some modern technologies have made their way into many Indian villages. Most villages now have electricity, and television reaches 75 percent of all Indians. Because illiteracy is still widespread, television, radio, and movies are more powerful media than newspapers for spreading new ideas to villagers. Indians are avid moviegoers, and the Indian film industry produces more than 800 films annually.

India's leaders hope that as villagers come to learn more about modern life and better farming techniques, they will be able to produce more food. The constant threat of a shortage of food in the face of an increasing population is a major concern of the Indian government.

Towns and Cities

India's urban areas are growing rapidly because of widespread immigration from rural villages. India's urban areas range in size from towns with 20,000 inhabitants to enormously crowded cities that swell with populations of more than 10 million.

Life in Towns Many of India's people live in small or medium-sized towns. India's towns are far more populated and lively than its rural villages. A writer who taught in India described a typical town:

> *Cows wander through the streets, washermen bang clothing against rocks in nearby streams, homes built of mud and tar paper and corrugated tin and planks and cardboard lean against one another, ready to be toppled by the first big storm. But the pace of the Indian town nearly terrifies the villager. The streets are often a wild free-for-all, with buses bearing down on pedestrians, dogs and goats scurrying out of the way of three-wheeled taxis and cars, bicycles weaving past the carters who wearily push their loads of flour sacks uphill.*

Life in Cities India's cities are even busier, because they are far more crowded. While New York City has 24,327 people per square mile (9,393 per sq km), the Indian city of Mumbai (Bombay) has an astonishing 127,461 inhabitants per square mile (49,213 per sq km)! The writer V. S. Naipaul described Mumbai's bulging population in this way:

> *In Bombay there isn't room for [the newcomers]. There is hardly room for the people already there. The older apartment blocks are full; the new skyscrapers are full; the small, low huts of the squatters' settlements on the airport road are packed tightly together.*

Despite the extreme crowding and poverty that exist, most families consider themselves better off in a city than in a village. Most people believe the cities offer far more opportunities for work and education than do rural areas. India's rural population therefore has been drawn to

India's Holy City

Place Varanasi contains hundreds of temples to accommodate the many Hindu as well as Buddhist pilgrims who travel to the holy city each year. The worshippers shown here are using ghats, the brick steps built into the riverbank, to wash away their sins in the sacred waters of the Ganges. *Critical Thinking* **Why do you think peoples of different religions make pilgrimages to holy sites?**

many of India's large cities. Mumbai, on India's west coast, is the country's busiest port and its financial center. Chennai and Calcutta (kal KUH tuh), both on the east coast, are also centers of commerce and shipping. New Delhi, India's capital and center of government, is located in the country's interior on the banks of the Yamuna River.

Because the city of Varanasi (vah RAH na see) is built on the banks of the Ganges, Hindus regard it as the holiest city in the world. Anyone lucky enough to die in Varanasi, Hindus believe, is released from the reincarnation cycle of birth, death, and rebirth. Devout Hindus hope to visit the city at least once within their lifetime to wash in the sacred Ganges River. Many pilgrims take bottles of Ganges water home to use in family worship.

Economic Improvements

India's government has tried to raise the standard of living for its people, whether they live in remote villages or teeming cities. It has been partially successful, but enormous challenges remain.

Advances in Farming One of India's main goals has been to feed its growing population. More land has been farmed. Better farming methods, increased irrigation, and higher quality seeds have produced more and better crops.

Despite these advances, only a few families own enough land to support themselves. Almost half of the farmers do not own any land at all.

To add to their income, many farmers have set up **cottage industries**. People in these industries make goods in their own homes, using their own tools and machines. They may spin yarn and weave cloth or make things like jewelry or pottery. These goods can then be sold in the cities and towns.

Expanded Industry Although about 65 percent of Indians are farmers, the country is one of the world's leading industrial nations. India has

APPEARED IN *NATIONAL GEOGRAPHIC*

A Village School

Place Education is compulsory in India until age 14. However, access to education remains a problem. Literacy rates in urban areas are much higher than in rural areas, and higher among males than among females. Only 50 percent of India's population is literate. *Why are many children unable to complete their schooling?*

made great advances in computers and in space research, and in recent years has placed several satellites in orbit. Another recent growth industry is consumer goods, such as televisions and video-cassette recorders.

Many of the new customers for these consumer goods are members of India's growing urban middle class. Traditionally, Indian society has been sharply divided between a wealthy minority and a poor majority. Over the past decades, however, teachers, doctors, and government workers have become part of an expanding middle class. Others have moved into the middle class after building their own successful businesses.

Education In 1950 only about 16 percent of Indians could read and write. By the mid-1990s the figure was nearly 50 percent and was still rising. As a result of intensive government efforts, almost every village now has a primary school. Yet many children still fail to complete their schooling. Often their families need them to work in the fields or to care for younger brothers and sisters.

Health Care The Indian government has also worked to improve people's health. In 1950 the average Indian's life expectancy was only 32 years. By the mid-1990s it had risen to 60 years, and the government aims to increase that figure to 64 years by the early twenty-first century. Yet many Indians cannot afford even basic medical care. In cities like Mumbai, many people live on the street. Millions of others live in slums, without healthy water or sanitation.

Availability of Electricity in India

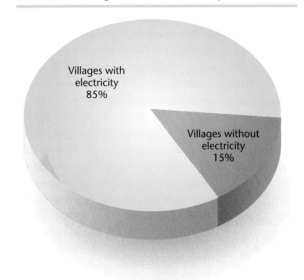

Villages with electricity 85%

Villages without electricity 15%

GRAPH STUDY

Rural electrification has put village people in touch with more of the world. *Critical Thinking How might the introduction of television, telephones, and movies have changed village life?*

Unhealthy water is also a problem in many rural areas. In the past, most Indians drank from open wells, which were breeding grounds for bacteria. Since the 1970s, the government has drilled hundreds of thousands of deep, machine-made wells with covers on them to reduce the risk of contamination. More villages than ever before now have a safe water supply. As a result, diseases such as malaria and cholera have become much less common.

Section 2 Review

Vocabulary and Main Ideas

1. Define: a. reincarnation b. caste system c. charpoy d. sari e. purdah f. joint family system g. cottage industry

2. Describe some differences between rural and urban life in India.

3. Describe the causes and effects of the growth of India's middle class.

4. Critical Thinking: *Cause and Effect* In what ways is education in India related to the country's economic improvement?

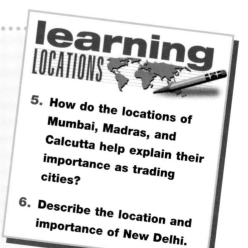

learning LOCATIONS

5. How do the locations of Mumbai, Madras, and Calcutta help explain their importance as trading cities?

6. Describe the location and importance of New Delhi.

India's Growing Population

The Issue

World population is growing rapidly. By the middle of the twenty-first century, it is expected to reach 10 billion people. Most of this growth will take place in developing countries like India.

India's Vast and Growing Population

India's population is nearing one billion people—about the population of the entire world in 1800. With a population growth rate of 1.9 percent, that figure will double in just thirty-

Controlling Growth

Place Murals such as this one in Jhardi, India encourage families to limit the number of children they have to two.

six years. Nearly two billion people will live on a land mass approximately one third the size of the United States.

A Tradition of Large Families

In rural India, children have meant security for their parents. Traditionally, parents depended on their children to help them farm or run the

family business. When parents grew old, they relied on their children to take care of them. Despite the fact that industrialization has altered Indian society, these long-held traditions are slow to change.

Global Impact

Overpopulation puts pressure on a country's resources and environment. As population grows, farms in India are overplanted, causing the land to lose its fertility. In many cases, forests are cut down to create more farmland and to provide wood for fuel. After a forest is cleared, there are no longer trees to stop rivers of mud from pouring down the mountainsides when the monsoon rains come. Tremendous landslides result. As India's forests disappear, its deserts expand and more land becomes unusable.

India: Population Pyramid

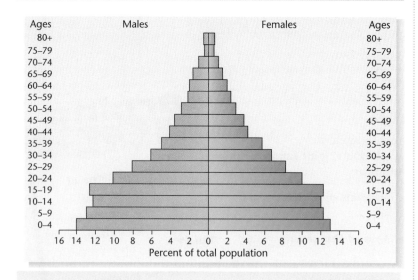

Ages	Males	Females	Ages
80+			80+
75–79			75–79
70–74			70–74
65–69			65–69
60–64			60–64
55–59			55–59
50–54			50–54
45–49			45–49
40–44			40–44
35–39			35–39
30–34			30–34
25–29			25–29
20–24			20–24
15–19			15–19
10–14			10–14
5–9			5–9
0–4			0–4

16 14 12 10 8 6 4 2 0 2 4 6 8 10 12 14 16
Percent of total population

Graph Study

● Population pyramids illustrate how a country's population is distributed. *What does the shape of this graph tell about India's population?*

World Population Growth

Some Solutions

Faced with the prospect of not being able to provide food for its citizens, the Indian government has taken steps to slow population growth.

Smaller Families The government encourages people to have smaller families. Government programs offer jobs, education, housing, and medical care to couples who have no more than two children. A public awareness campaign uses popular songs, billboards, and murals to promote the economic security and happiness of small families.

Improving Health Care Another strategy involves improving health services. The hope is that if children are healthier, families will not need the security of having many children in case some fail to survive.

Providing Education The Indian government is working to increase the level of basic education among women, as well as to expand opportunities for higher education. Research shows that birthrates are lower among better-educated women.

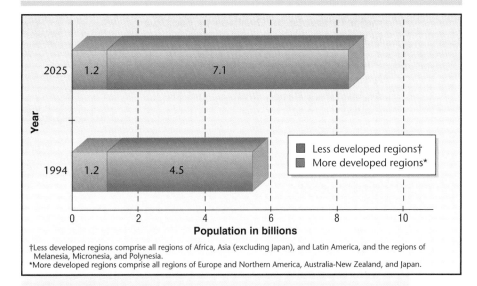

†Less developed regions comprise all regions of Africa, Asia (excluding Japan), and Latin America, and the regions of Melanesia, Micronesia, and Polynesia.
*More developed regions comprise all regions of Europe and Northern America, Australia-New Zealand, and Japan.

GRAPH STUDY

This graph compares the world's population in 1994 with the projected population growth for the year 2025. *What is the world's population expected to be in 2025?*

YOU DECIDE

1. Why does India have a tradition of large families?

2. Which of the Indian government's strategies described on these pages do you think is the most effective? Explain.

3. **Problem Solving** You are appointed to a government panel to investigate the issue of population growth in India. Draft a one-page policy statement with three to five proposals that balance tradition and change in India.

4. **What You Can Do** Find out about the World Health Organization (WHO), an agency of the United Nations, and its work in population in relation to world growth.

5. **Internet Activity** To find out more about current population trends, visit a publication of the World Resources Institute: World Resources 1996–97. Read the Population Trends section of Chapter 8: Population and Human Development. Then make a list of the main ideas of the section. Link to this site from:
   • www.phschool.com

3 Other Countries of South Asia

Section Preview

Main Ideas

- Water—too little or too much—has a major influence on the lives of people in Pakistan and Bangladesh.

- Physical geography has been a major factor in shaping the histories of Afghanistan, Nepal, Bhutan, and Sri Lanka.

Vocabulary

hydroelectric power, irrigate, embankment dam, buffer state, malnutrition, deforestation

APPEARED IN *NATIONAL GEOGRAPHIC*

Apricots have long been an important crop in Pakistan's Hunza Valley.

India's neighbors share many of India's challenges—poverty, overpopulation, and internal conflict between religious and ethnic groups. But from the crowded cities of Bangladesh to the remote mountaintop villages of Afghanistan, each country is physically and culturally distinct.

Pakistan

The physical map on page 559 shows that Pakistan is made up of three physical regions. Along its northern and western borders, one of the world's highest mountain ranges, the Hindu Kush, reaches majestically toward the sky. Several passes cut through the mountains, making transportation possible. The Khyber (KY ber) Pass allows movement between Peshawar (puh SHAH wuhr) in northwest Pakistan and Kabul (KAH buhl), the capital of Afghanistan.

Just as in India, the towering mountains keep the cold air from central Asia from penetrating the subcontinent during the winter. As a result, except at high elevations, temperatures in

Pakistan are generally warm or hot. Temperatures in the city of Islamabad average 60° F (16° C) in January and 90° F (32° C) in July.

Much of western Pakistan is covered by the rugged Baluchistan (bah LOO chi STAN) Plateau. To the east lie barren stretches of the Thar Desert and brown, dusty plains. Sandwiched between these two forbidding regions is the fertile valley created by the Indus River as it flows south out of the mountains to the Arabian Sea.

The Struggle for Water The Indus River is the lifeline of an otherwise dry country. Most Pakistanis live in the Indus River basin. The basin contains most of the country's agricultural areas, as well as its major **hydroelectric power** stations. Hydroelectric power is electricity produced by the movement of water.

Irrigation The government has devoted a fair amount of the nation's resources to developing agriculture. Since much of Pakistan receives less than 10 inches (25 cm) of rain each year, farmers must **irrigate** the land, or supply it with water. One of the keystones of the irrigation system is the Tarbela Dam, which was built to control the extreme seasonal changes of the Indus River. Completed in 1976, it holds more water than any other **embankment dam** in the world. An embankment dam is a wall of soil and rock built to hold back water.

The Tarbela Dam is one of the world's biggest producers of hydroelectric power. It has also turned millions of acres of arid desert into lush cropland, where wheat and cotton are grown in large amounts. The dam has created problems, however. The Indus River picks up silt as it flows through northern Pakistan, and this silt is slowly piling up behind the dam. Engineers estimate that within twenty years the dam will be unable to supply irrigation water.

Traditional Ways of Life As in India, most of the people of Pakistan live in farming villages. Almost all Pakistanis are Muslims, and prayers are an important part of daily life.

Tradition also plays an important role in their lives. For example, women generally have far fewer freedoms and opportunities than do men. Many women avoid contact with men outside the home and cover their faces with a veil in the presence of strangers.

National Challenges Islam is the tie that holds the people of Pakistan together. Yet differences among the Muslims have threatened to split the country apart. For example, only about 7 percent of Pakistanis speak Urdu, the national language. Almost 64 percent speak Punjabi, the language of the Punjab province. In addition, disputes among the country's various ethnic groups often turn violent.

Pakistan's literacy rate is lower than India's, while its rate of population growth is higher. Pakistan's leaders have a hard road ahead as they work to improve their people's standard of living and hold their nation together.

GEO *facts*
Afghanistan ranks 137, out of the 140 nations surveyed, in the category of infant mortality. (U.S.=21).

Afghanistan

In many ways, Afghanistan's history has been influenced by its location and terrain. The map on page 559 shows that the towering Hindu Kush forms the central backbone of the country. These mountains are nearly as high and certainly as rugged as the Himalayas. Indeed, the word *kush* means "death," and the mountains were

Strategically Located

Location The Khyber pass slices 33 miles (53 km) through the Safed Koh range of the Hindu Kush. It has a long history of military use. Over the centuries invaders slipped through the pass to invade India, and it was hotly contested during the Afghan Wars of the 1800s. *What role did the Khyber pass play in the Soviet war in Afghanistan in 1979?*

APPEARED IN *NATIONAL GEOGRAPHIC*

Displaced by War

● **Movement** This Afghan child is carrying freshly baked bread to her family in a refugee camp in Pakistan. *Critical Thinking How might continuing social unrest in Afghanistan affect the 5 million refugees?*

probably given this name because of the danger they posed to people crossing them. The Hindu Kush also marks the boundaries of three regions. The first region consists of the mountains themselves. At their feet lie several fertile valleys, where most Afghans live. North of the Hindu Kush is a region of semiarid plains. The land south of the Hindu Kush is mostly desert.

For centuries, merchants and soldiers crossed through Afghanistan on their way to or from China, the Middle East, and India. Although the Hindu Kush formed a barrier, it had many passes, the most well-known being the Khyber Pass.

A Diverse Population As a result of successive invasions and migrations, Afghanistan

today includes many ethnic groups. The country has two official languages, but the people speak many other languages as well. Over the centuries local groups isolated themselves in pockets of land as protection against invaders. Each group developed its own language and customs. As a result, some groups are unable to communicate with one another.

Despite their ethnic differences, however, the people are united by their Islamic faith. Religious holidays are national holidays. Mosques are educational and social centers as well as religious ones.

Buffer State Over the last two centuries, Afghanistan has been invaded several times. During the 1800s, Britain and Russia competed for influence in central Asia. Britain invaded Afghanistan from British-controlled India to the south. Russia invaded Afghanistan from the north.

When they failed to conquer Afghanistan, Britain and Russia agreed to leave it alone. In this way, Afghanistan became a **buffer state**— a country that separates two political enemies.

In December 1979, Soviet troops marched into Afghanistan to help put down a revolt at the request of the Afghan government. About 5 million people fled the country. Many of them crossed through the Khyber Pass and settled in refugee camps in or near Peshawar, Pakistan. Pakistan and the United States helped arm and train Afghan resistance fighters. The guerrillas slipped through the mountain passes to attack the Soviet and Afghan government forces.

Like earlier invaders, the Soviets were unable to conquer the Afghans. In 1989 the Soviets withdrew. Some refugees returned home, but new fighting among Afghan groups meant that Afghanistan was a long way from stability. Many Afghans remained in Pakistan.

Bangladesh

As the map on page 559 shows, most of Bangladesh is an enormous delta formed by three powerful rivers—the Ganges, the Brahmaputra, and the Meghna (MAYG nuh). As a result, the soil is very fertile. However, because the country is so close to sea level, floods occur regularly.

Challenging Climate The climate of Bangladesh is humid subtropical. Temperatures rarely drop below 80°F (27°C). Because of the monsoon winds, large amounts of rain fall within a four- to five-month period.

The climate and geography of Bangladesh create a delicate balance between prosperity and disaster. In good times, the warm temperatures, abundant water supply, and fertile soil enable farmers to plant and harvest three crops a year on the same land. In bad times, the raging rivers overflow and fierce, tropical storms sweep in from the Bay of Bengal, submerging the land in salt water.

Record monsoon rains lashed at Bangladesh in 1989 and 1990, causing severe flooding. Millions of people were rendered homeless and became ill from lack of food and clean drinking water. Power lines were knocked down, and roads, bridges, and railway lines were washed away. Transporting food and medicine from one part of the country to another proved almost impossible.

These successive disasters forced the government of Bangladesh to seek a lasting solution to the chronic flood problem. The first phase of a Flood Action Plan was launched in the early 1990s, funded with the help of the international aid community. The goal of the plan is to identify improved ways to lessen the effects of flooding and to improve future disaster management and relief.

Overpopulation Like India, Bangladesh is struggling with overpopulation. It is the ninth most populous country in the world and also one of the most densely populated. With about 119 million people, it has almost as many people as Mexico and Canada combined, squeezed into an area the size of Wisconsin.

Overpopulation and natural disasters have combined to create another problem: hunger. **Malnutrition**—a lack of food or an unbalanced diet—is an almost constant problem. The Green Revolution has helped to increase agricultural production. Despite larger harvests, however, the population keeps growing at a faster rate than the food supply.

To add to its problems, Bangladesh has few roads or bridges. Most travel is by boat along its many waterways. Without massive aid,

Keeping Business Afloat

Location Exhibiting the typical Bangladeshi pluck, this ricksha driver goes about business as usual, despite the monsoon waters. *Why are the streets of Bangladesh so often flooded?*

Bangladesh cannot improve its communications and transportation system. Bangladesh thus faces some of the greatest challenges of any country in the world.

eXtremes

Mount Everest

X ●●●●●●●●

Extremely Tall
The highest mountain peak in the world is Mount Everest, located in Nepal and Tibet.

X ●●●●●●●●

Head to Head
It would take 95 Statues of Liberty stacked head to toe to equal Mount Everest's height of 29,028 ft (8,848 m).

X ●●●●●●●●

First to the Top
Sir Edmund Hillary of New Zealand and Sherpa Tenzing Norgay were the first to successfully reach the summit in May 1953.

X ●●●●●●●●

Young and Old
The youngest person to make it to the top is Shambu Tamang of Nepal, who scaled the mountain when he was 19. Ramon Blanco Suarez of Venezuela was 60 years old when he reached the summit in October 1993.

X ●●●●●●●●

Deadly Climb
Everest expeditions have claimed the lives of more than 95 people, including 40 Sherpa guides.

Nepal and Bhutan

The countries of Nepal (nuh PAHL) and Bhutan (boo TAHN) span a great range in altitude, from a low elevation of about 600 feet (183 m) to that of the highest mountains in the world, the Himalayas. The tallest of the towering Himalayan peaks, Mount Everest in Nepal, towers 29,028 feet (8,848 m) high.

The southern lowlands of Nepal and Bhutan are hot and humid. Monsoon rains pour down every summer. Tropical crops flourish here, including citrus fruits, sugarcane, and rice. In the cooler, high areas, people grow wheat, millet, and potatoes. Most crops are grown in terraced fields built into the hillsides.

Nepal is about 90 percent Hindu, while Bhutan is about 75 percent Buddhist. Hinduism is more common in the lowlands, while Buddhism is the religion of the high areas. Yet each religion has influenced the other. For example, people often celebrate festivals honored by both religions.

Both high mountains and politics kept Nepal and Bhutan somewhat separated from the rest of the world until the middle of the twentieth century. Today, Bhutan continues to discourage contact with tourists and other foreigners in an effort to preserve its traditional culture. Nepal, on the other hand, welcomes those who come to hike in its mountains and enjoy its magnificent scenery. The Sherpas, who live high in the mountains of Nepal, are skilled mountaineers. Many of them make a living by guiding climbers through the challenging mountain terrain.

Sri Lanka

Sri Lanka, meaning "Magnificent Island," is located in the Indian Ocean 33 miles (53 km) southeast of the tip of India. Sri Lanka is often referred to as "a tear dropped off the subcontinent of India."

Environmental Challenge As the climate map on page 563 shows, Sri Lanka's climate is tropical, but is made cooler by ocean breezes. The heaviest rains fall in the southwestern part of the island, which contains plantations where crops like coconuts and rubber are grown for export. Another major crop is tea, which comes mainly from the higher slopes of the island's mountains. Sri Lanka produces about one eighth of the world's tea.

Sri Lanka was once covered with a thick rain forest. Today, almost two thirds of that forest is gone, cut down for farming and development. Scientists think that this **deforestation** may have helped change the island's weather and caused droughts. Restoring the rain forest is a major government challenge.

Social Unrest Another challenge is to keep the peace. About three fourths of Sri Lankans are Sinhalese (sin hah LEEZ), descendants of Aryans who migrated from northern India about 500 B.C. Later the Tamils (TAHM uhlz), a people of Dravidian origin, came to Sri Lanka from southern India. The Sinhalese and the Tamils often fought each other. Religion and language differences further split the two groups. The Sinhalese practice Buddhism, while the Tamils practice Hinduism. The two groups speak different languages and have different alphabets.

Since Sri Lanka gained its independence from Britain in 1948, the Sinhalese have controlled the government. But that government has faced serious obstacles. In 1971, a radical Sinhalese group tried to overthrow the government. In addition the Tamil minority has long felt that Sinhalese discrimination has denied them equal rights to education, jobs, and land ownership.

The Tamils have demanded the establishment of a separate Tamil state. The conflict has led to bloody fighting between government forces and Tamil guerrillas, and many civilians

have been caught in the crossfire. The economy has suffered because money has been diverted from agriculture to the military. About 45 percent of the population's labor force make a living from agriculture. But the fighting has disrupted farming and fishing, and a political solution does not seem likely in the near future.

Country	Population	Life Expectancy (years)	Per Capita GNP (in U.S. $)
Afghanistan	18,400,000	43	NA
Bangladesh	119,200,000	55	220
Bhutan	800,000	51	170
India	930,600,000	60	290
Nepal	22,600,000	54	160
Pakistan	129,700,000	61	430
Sri Lanka	18,200,000	73	600
United States	263,200,000	76	24,750

Source: Population Reference Bureau   NA indicates data not available.

CHART SKILLS

● *Which country in South Asia has the highest per capita GNP?*

● **Critical Thinking** *Which countries have the lowest life expectancy? What factors contribute to a low life expectancy?*

Section 3 Review

Vocabulary and Main Ideas

1. **Define: a. hydroelectric power b. irrigate c. embankment dam d. buffer state e. malnutrition f. deforestation**

2. **What effect does the Hindu Kush have on the climate of Pakistan?**

3. **What challenges do climate and landforms in Bangladesh create?**

4. **Critical Thinking:** *Analyzing a Statement* **Explain whether or not you think the following statement is accurate: "The monsoons bring life to the countries of South Asia."**

learning LOCATIONS

5. **Name and locate the capital city of Bangladesh.**

6. **Describe the relative location of Nepal and Bhutan.**

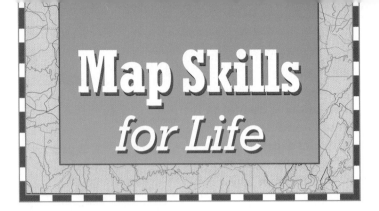

Map Skills for Life

Skill: Reading a Street Map

Setting: Visiting the Taj Mahal

Chitra Mehta has lived in the coastal city of Mumbai, India, all her life. She and her family are traveling to the historic city of Agra. Agra is a relatively small city near Delhi, India's capital, and is famous the world over for one building—the beautiful Taj Mahal.

On reaching Agra, the Mehtas find that Agra has other interesting sites as well. Looking at the street map, they decide to visit the following sites:

★ First, the goal of their visit: the Taj Mahal, built in the 1600s by the Mogul emperor Shah Jahan as a memorial to his well-loved wife.

★ The huge Agra Fort, with a moat and two great walls of rusty-red stone. It was also built by a Mogul ruler, Akbar the Great. Inside the walls of the Fort are palaces and other buildings. Visitors enter the fort at the Amar Singh Gate.

Reading the Map

Follow the steps below to understand how the Mehtas can use the street map of the city to find the places they want to visit.

1. Find the starting location on the map.
Look over the map and get a general idea of how the city is laid out. Notice major geographical features such as the Yamuna River. The Mehtas have arrived in Agra by bus from Delhi, and so they will begin their sightseeing from the bus station.

Some street maps, like this one, label a few major landmarks and, to save space, include a key for other sites. **(a)** What number is the bus station? **(b)** Find it on the map and notice its location in the town.

2. On the map, locate the places Chitra wants to visit.
The Taj Mahal and Agra Fort are two of the major sites of Agra and so are labeled on the map. **(a)** Are they generally in the same part of town? **(b)** What geographical or street landmarks can help Chitra find them? **(c)** Which site—the Fort or the Taj Mahal— is closer to the bus station?

3. Plan the route to follow to visit the selected places.
Notice street names, directions, and the places where one should turn from one street onto another. **(a)** When the Mehtas come out of the bus station, what road can they follow to walk to the Fort? **(b)** Which way will they turn to reach the visitors' entrance at Amar Singh Gate? **(c)** Because they are eager to see the Taj Mahal, the Mehtas may decide to take a taxi and see it first. As they leave the Taj, what direction should they turn to go back to the Fort?

4. Use the map scale to figure out distances between places.
Notice that the map scale is in both miles and meters. Knowing approximate distances can help decide whether to walk or use some other kind of transportation. Remember to measure the actual distance on the map, not a straight line between two places. If Chitra's family is tired after seeing the Taj Mahal, they may not want to walk more than a mile. Are they likely to walk back to the gate of the Fort?

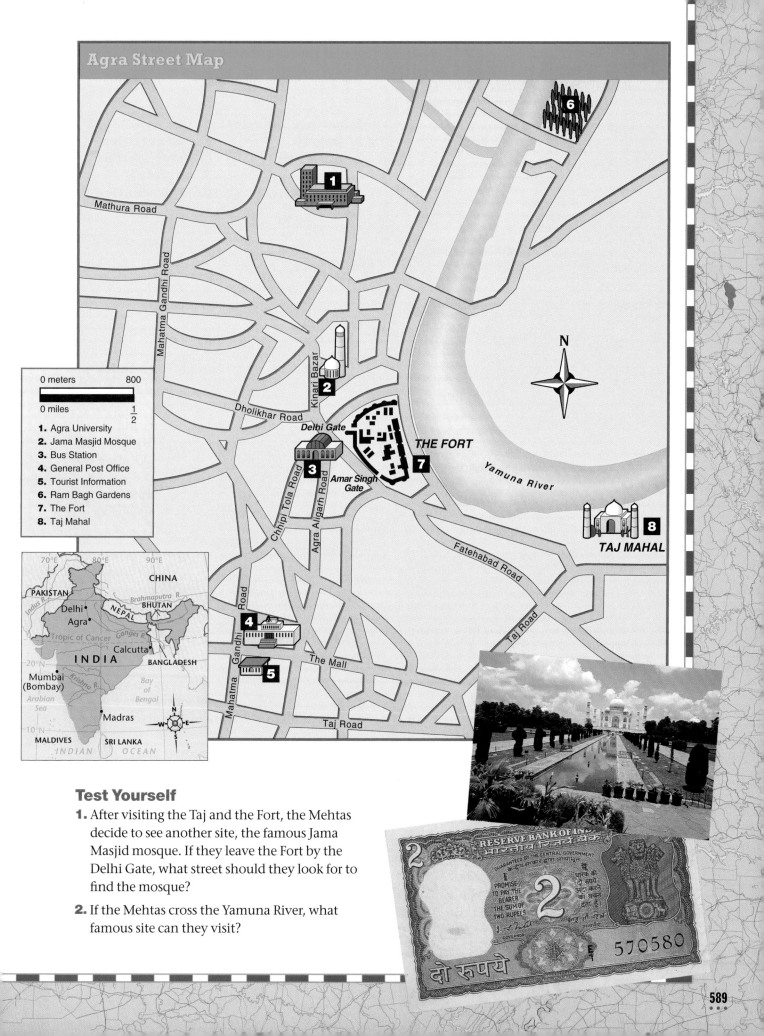

Agra Street Map

0 meters 800

0 miles 1/2

1. Agra University
2. Jama Masjid Mosque
3. Bus Station
4. General Post Office
5. Tourist Information
6. Ram Bagh Gardens
7. The Fort
8. Taj Mahal

Mathura Road

Mahatma Gandhi Road

Kinari Bazar

Dholikhar Road

Delhi Gate

Chhipi Tola Road

Agra Aligarh Road

Amar Singh Gate

THE FORT

Yamuna River

Fatehabad Road

Taj Road

Mahatma Gandhi Road

The Mall

Taj Road

TAJ MAHAL

N

India inset map:

70°E 80°E 90°E

PAKISTAN
CHINA
Delhi
Agra
NEPAL
BHUTAN
Brahmaputra R.
Indus R.
Tropic of Cancer
Ganges R.
Calcutta
INDIA
BANGLADESH
Mumbai (Bombay)
Krishna R.
Bay of Bengal
Arabian Sea
Madras
20°N
10°N
MALDIVES
SRI LANKA
INDIAN OCEAN
W N E S

Test Yourself

1. After visiting the Taj and the Fort, the Mehtas decide to see another site, the famous Jama Masjid mosque. If they leave the Fort by the Delhi Gate, what street should they look for to find the mosque?

2. If the Mehtas cross the Yamuna River, what famous site can they visit?

RESERVE BANK OF INDIA
2
GUARANTEED BY THE CENTRAL GOVERNMENT
I PROMISE TO PAY THE BEARER THE SUM OF TWO RUPEES
GOVERNOR
570580
दो रूपये

Summarizing Main Ideas

Section 1 Road to Independence

- The British established an empire in India in order to take advantage of resources and to find a market for their goods.
- Led by Mohandas Gandhi, Indians used non-violent resistance to pressure Britain into granting Indian independence in 1947.
- At the time of its independence, India was divided into two countries—a mostly Hindu India and a mostly Muslim Pakistan.
- In 1971 East Pakistan split off from Pakistan to become the country of Bangladesh.

Section 2 India's People and Economy

- Hinduism plays an important role in Indian life. People in rural areas of India live in traditional ways.
- Many villagers have migrated to cities, where a middle class is rapidly growing.
- The Indian government is working hard to improve the country's standard of living and its agricultural and industrial production.

Section 3 Other Countries of South Asia

- While the dry land of Pakistan requires irrigation for farming, Bangladesh receives plenty of rainfall and is vulnerable to devastating floods because of its low elevation.
- Afghanistan has served as a crossroads between East and West, as well as a buffer between India and Russia.
- The Himalayas isolated Nepal and Bhutan from much of the rest of the world.
- Divisions between the Sinhalese and the Tamils have brought violence to Sri Lanka.

Reviewing Vocabulary

Use each of the following terms in a sentence that shows their meaning.

1. cottage industry
2. irrigate
3. buffer state
4. partition
5. caste system
6. sari
7. malnutrition
8. deforestation
9. boycott
10. reincarnation

Applying the Geographic Themes

1. **Human-Environment Interaction** In what way was the building of the Tarbela Dam a response to Pakistan's climate?
2. **Place** Describe the two main peoples of Sri Lanka, including the places from which their ancestors migrated to Sri Lanka.
3. **Regions** How do the landforms and climate of Pakistan differ from those of Bangladesh?
4. **Location** Describe the relative location of Nepal.
5. **Movement** What was the reason for the great migration of people after India's independence?

Critical Thinking and Applying Skills

1. **Drawing Conclusions** Why do you think Gandhi's use of nonviolent resistance was successful in helping India to achieve independence?
2. **Demonstrating Reasoned Judgment** Although a majority of South Asians work the land, hunger is a major problem. How would you account for this contradiction?
3. **Analyzing Cartograms** Look again at the cartogram on page 573. Compare India on the world map on pages 14-15 with India on the cartogram. What does this comparison tell you about population density in that country?

Writing Across Cultures

▶ 1. Imagine that you are a young adult Indian who grew up in a rural village but then moved to a big city. Write a letter to your parents describing the benefits and drawbacks of life in the city compared to life in the village.

▶ 2. Write two paragraphs that describe the ethnic unrest in Sri Lanka, one from the point of view of a Sinhalese and one from the point of view of a Tamil.

INTERNET link

Find out more about current events in India. Visit the Indiatimes Web site. Link to this site from:

- www.phschool.com

Select one of the Web pages and read about an area that interests you. Were you surprised by what you read? Write a paragraph sharing new information you gathered.

learning LOCATIONS

South Asia

Number from 1 to 8 on your paper. Next to each number, write the letter of the place on the map that corresponds to the places listed below.

1. Afghanistan
2. Bangladesh
3. Bhutan
4. India
5. Islamabad
6. Nepal
7. New Delhi
8. Pakistan

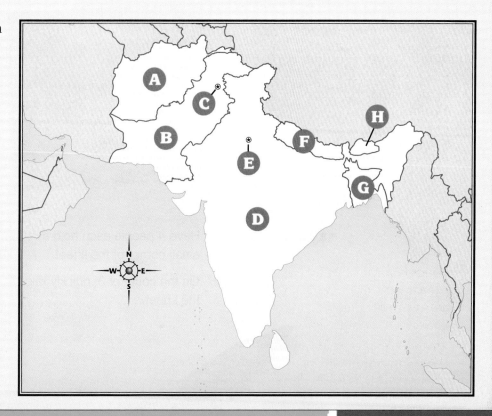

HOW MONSOONS ARE CREATED

The South Asian monsoon brings almost 3 feet (.9m) of rainfall over a four month period in the spring and summer. This activity will help you understand how monsoons form and how the changes we are making to our atmosphere could negatively affect this vital phenomenon.

MATERIALS:

Large map of India and surrounding seas (5' x 5')

Cloth sheet (3' x 5' with words "Hot Air" written on it)

Blue, latex balloons

Black permanent marker

PROCEDURES:

1. Place the map of India on the floor.

2. Blow up the balloons, tie them, and write "Cool, Moist Air" on them with the marker.

Step 2

3. Lay the cloth sheet over the map so that the seas are exposed on each side of the country. The words on the sheet should be facing up.

4. Place the balloons over the seas on the map.

Step 4

5. Have 4 people each hold a small corner of the sheet.

6. On the count of 3, quickly raise the sheet.

Step 6

OBSERVATIONS AND ANALYSIS:

1. Why does the air over the land rise?

2. What happens to the balloons? Where do they go? Why does this happen?

3. If the balloons represent cool, moist air, what do you think happens as they move over the land?

4. What season of the year do monsoons occur in? How might the monsoons be a blessing and a curse?

5. How could temperature changes in the atmosphere affect the monsoon season in India?

Air Pollution
Could Cause Monsoon Season TO SHRINK

Computer models of the atmosphere above India show that an increase of carbon dioxide and sulfur compounds could significantly alter the temperature difference between land and sea that creates the monsoon season. The development of a monsoon relies upon the difference between the high land temperatures and the cool sea temperatures. Scientists have demonstrated with a computer model how industrial air pollution could be equalizing the temperatures between land and sea and shrinking the monsoon season. Although the monsoon season can be destructive, it is also vital to the region's food and water supplies.

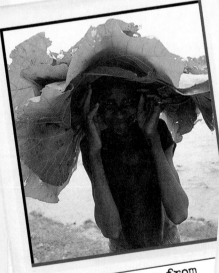
Seeking shelter from the monsoons

Herding oxen through the monsoons

taking Action

What we do in one place can greatly affect others far away. Global warming and rapid industrialization in China and India are the biggest factors that could be affecting monsoons. Here are some things you can do to slow this trend:

✔ Buy fewer goods made in countries that are experiencing unchecked, industrial growth.

✔ Reduce your activities that produce greenhouse gases. Ride your bike, walk, or carpool whenever possible.

East Asia and the Pacific World

CHAPTERS

A Global Perspective

Located partly in the Asian continent, the region known as Southeast Asia includes a host of island nations. The continent "down under," Australia, is itself an island. Its frozen neighbor to the south, Antarctica, anchors the world.

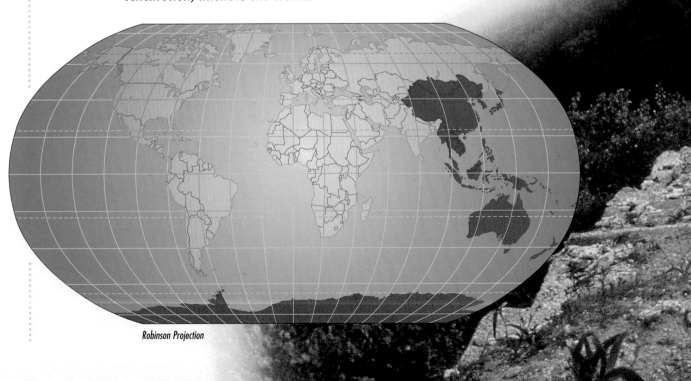

Robinson Projection

The Great Wall of China

1 Countries and Cities (*pp. 596–597*)
East Asia, located at the junction of the Pacific and Indian oceans, attracted colonizers and merchants from all over the world. Despite colonization, parts of the region remained proudly isolated until the last century.

2 Physical Features (*pp. 598–601*)
East Asia forms part of the "Ring of Fire," and is a tectonically active region. Australia and Antarctica are both mostly flat, though each has a single major mountain chain.

3 People and Cultures (*pp. 602–603*)
East Asia is a region of enormous ethnic diversity. One ethnic group—the Han of China—dominates the others numerically.

4 Climate and Vegetation (*pp. 604–605*)
The climate in East Asia ranges from cold and dry to hot and wet. Australia and Antarctica are largely dry deserts—one a desert of heat, the other a desert of cold.

5 Economy and Resources (*pp. 606–607*)
East Asia, as part of the highly populated Pacific Rim nations, is undergoing a vast economic boom. One of its main resources is its large working population.

VISUAL PREVIEW ACTIVITY

Each of the five keys above corresponds to a section of the Regional Atlas that follows. Number from 1 to 5 on a piece of paper. Use information from the maps, graphs, and photographs in the Regional Atlas to write one additional fact for each of the five keys above.

EAST ASIA AND THE PACIFIC WORLD

Use the Map, Graph, and Photo Studies in this Regional Atlas to gain a better understanding of the region's physical and cultural geography.

ATLAS VOCABULARY

seismic	intensive farming
aquaculture	terrace

1 COUNTRIES AND CITIES

LARGEST CITIES

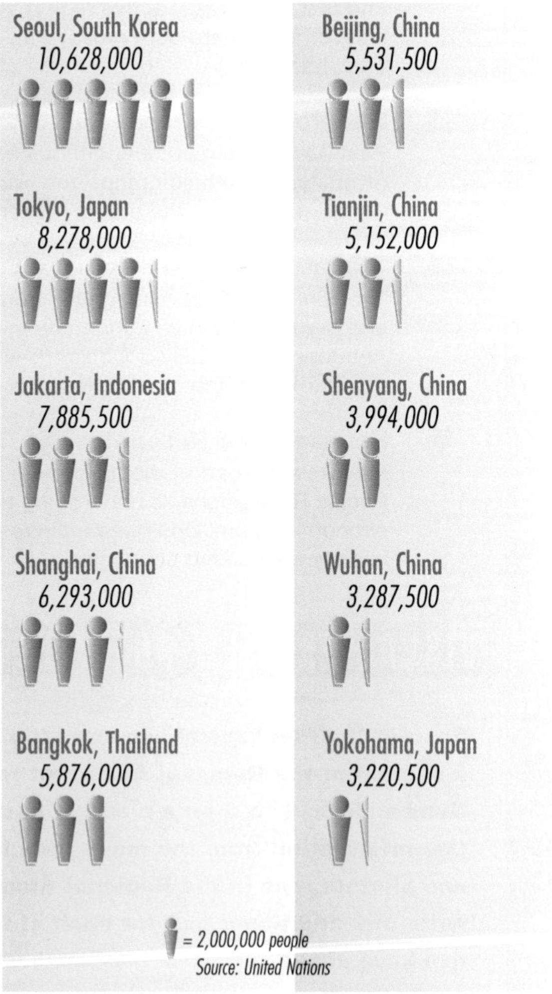

Seoul, South Korea
10,628,000

Beijing, China
5,531,500

Tokyo, Japan
8,278,000

Tianjin, China
5,152,000

Jakarta, Indonesia
7,885,500

Shenyang, China
3,994,000

Shanghai, China
6,293,000

Wuhan, China
3,287,500

Bangkok, Thailand
5,876,000

Yokohama, Japan
3,220,500

= 2,000,000 people
Source: United Nations

MAP STUDY
Applying the Geographic Themes

1 Place East Asia has long attracted the interest of traders and far-flung nations wishing to expand their power. The result is a patchwork region of nations, some of which are ancient and unified, and others of which are young and struggling to remain whole. *Which is the largest nation in the region?*

2 Location Though largely rural, East Asia can be said to be a region of cities because of the power and importance of its urban centers. Many of the region's cities are located near water. *Identify three major cities on the coast of East Asia.*

3 Movement Natural barriers of water and mountains have slowed the integration of the many nations of the region. *Name three island nations in the region.*

GRAPH STUDY

4 Largest Cities The East Asian region has 1.9 billion people—nearly a third of the world's population. It also is the location of some of the largest cities on earth. *Which country has the greatest number of cities with a population over 3 million?*

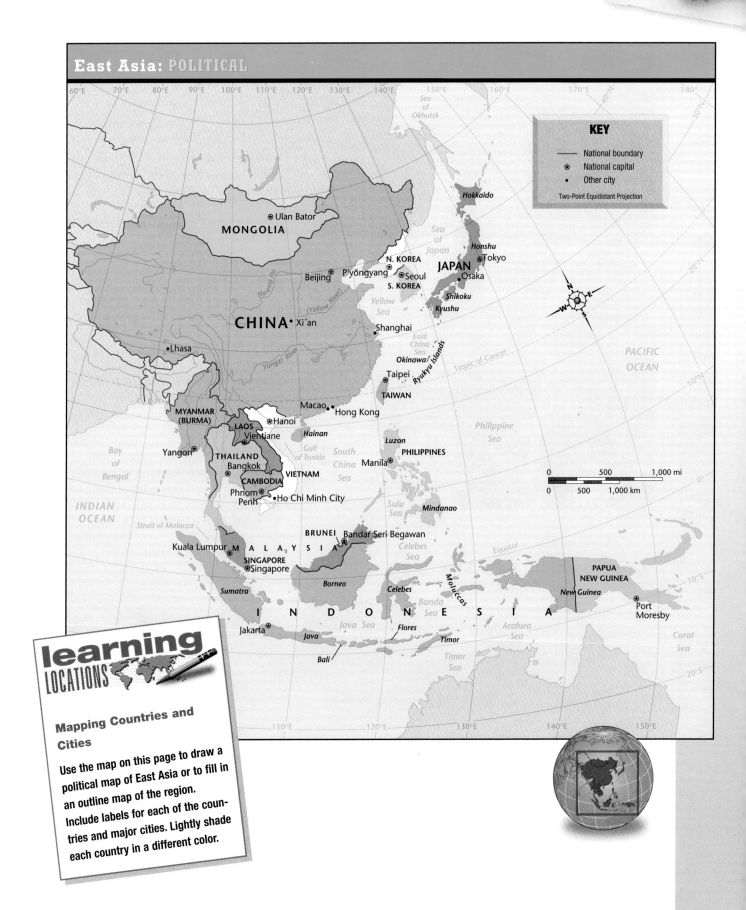

East Asia: POLITICAL

KEY

— National boundary
⊗ National capital
• Other city

Two-Point Equidistant Projection

MONGOLIA
Ulan Bator

CHINA
Beijing
Xi'an
Lhasa
Huang He
(Yellow River)
Yangzi River

N. KOREA
P'yŏngyang
Seoul
S. KOREA

JAPAN
Hokkaido
Honshu
Tokyo
Osaka
Shikoku
Kyushu

Yellow Sea

Sea of Japan

Sea of Okhotsk

Shanghai

East China Sea

Okinawa
Ryukyu Islands
Tropic of Cancer

Taipei
TAIWAN

Macao
Hong Kong

MYANMAR (BURMA)
LAOS
Vientiane
Hanoi
Hainan
Gulf of Tonkin

Yangon
THAILAND
Bangkok
CAMBODIA
Phnom Penh
VIETNAM
Ho Chi Minh City

South China Sea

Luzon
Manila
PHILIPPINES

Philippine Sea

PACIFIC OCEAN

Bay of Bengal

INDIAN OCEAN

Strait of Malacca

Mindanao
Sulu Sea

BRUNEI
Bandar Seri Begawan
Kuala Lumpur M A L A Y S I A
SINGAPORE
Singapore

Celebes Sea

Borneo

Celebes

Equator

Moluccas

PAPUA NEW GUINEA
New Guinea
Port Moresby

Sumatra

I N D O N E S I A

Banda Sea
Arafura Sea

Coral Sea

Jakarta
Java Sea
Java
Flores
Timor

Bali
Timor Sea

0 500 1,000 mi
0 500 1,000 km

learning LOCATIONS

Mapping Countries and Cities

Use the map on this page to draw a political map of East Asia or to fill in an outline map of the region. Include labels for each of the countries and major cities. Lightly shade each country in a different color.

PHOTO STUDY

1 **Earthquakes** Almost 20 percent of the world's earthquakes occur in Southeast Asia. In 1995, an earthquake in Kobe, Japan (left), took some 5,000 lives and caused $60 billion in damage. *Critical Thinking* **What measures can engineers and architects take to prevent earthquake damage?**

MAP STUDY
Applying the Geographic Themes

2 **Place** The collision of the Eurasian and Indo-Australian tectonic plates created much of East Asia's physical landscape, raising the Himalayas, the Kunlun Shan, the Altun Shan, and the Tian Shan. *Name two tectonic mountain ranges in Southeast Asia that extend in a north-south direction.*

3 **Regions** The Malay and Japan archipelagoes form part of the Ring of Fire—a circle of volcanic and **seismic**, or earthquake-related, activity that surrounds the Pacific Ocean. The island of Java, for example, has thirty-five active volcanoes. *In what nation is Java located?*

Cross Section: East Asia

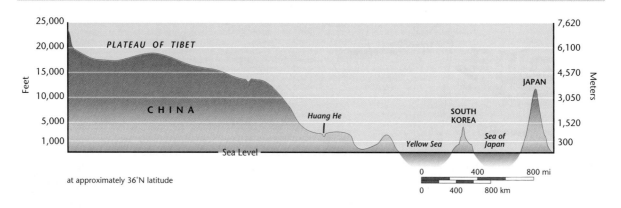

at approximately 36°N latitude

DIAGRAM STUDY

4 **Physical Profile** The Plateau of Tibet is a vast elevated region formed by tectonic forces. *What is the difference in elevation between the Plateau of Tibet and the highest area in Japan?*

EAST ASIA AND THE PACIFIC WORLD

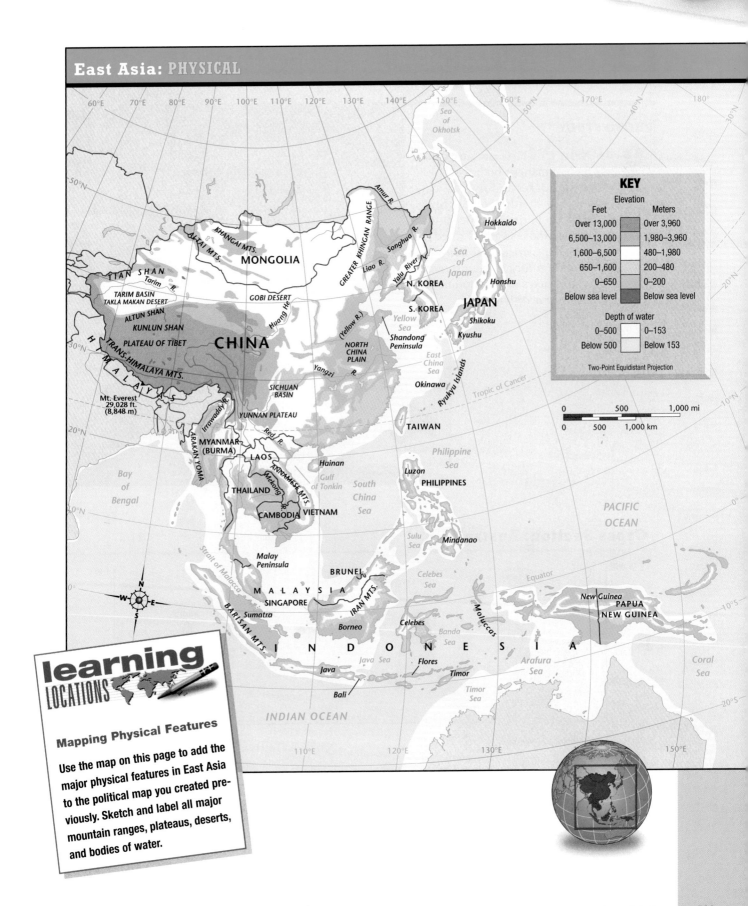

East Asia: PHYSICAL

KEY

Elevation

Feet		Meters
Over 13,000		Over 3,960
6,500–13,000		1,980–3,960
1,600–6,500		480–1,980
650–1,600		200–480
0–650		0–200
Below sea level		Below sea level

Depth of water

0–500		0–153
Below 500		Below 153

Two-Point Equidistant Projection

0   500   1,000 mi
0   500   1,000 km

Map labels:

Sea of Okhotsk, Hokkaido, Honshu, Shikoku, Kyushu, Sea of Japan, JAPAN, Okinawa, Ryukyu Islands, East China Sea, Tropic of Cancer, TAIWAN, Philippine Sea, Luzon, PHILIPPINES, Mindanao, Sulu Sea, Celebes Sea, PACIFIC OCEAN, Equator, New Guinea, PAPUA NEW GUINEA, Moluccas, Banda Sea, Celebes, INDONESIA, Arafura Sea, Coral Sea, Timor Sea, Timor, Flores, Java Sea, Bali, Java, INDIAN OCEAN, BARISAN MTS., Sumatra, SINGAPORE, MALAYSIA, BRUNEI, IRAN MTS., Borneo, Malay Peninsula, Strait of Malacca, Bay of Bengal, CAMBODIA, VIETNAM, THAILAND, Mekong, ANNAMESE MTS., LAOS, Hainan, Gulf of Tonkin, South China Sea, Red R., MYANMAR (BURMA), ARAKAN YOMA, Irrawaddy R., HIMALAYAS, Mt. Everest 29,028 ft. (8,848 m), TRANS-HIMALAYA MTS., PLATEAU OF TIBET, KUNLUN SHAN, ALTUN SHAN, TAKLA MAKAN DESERT, TARIM BASIN, Tarim R., TIAN SHAN, ALTAI MTS., KHANGAI MTS., MONGOLIA, GOBI DESERT, CHINA, Huang He (Yellow R.), Yangzi R., SICHUAN BASIN, YUNNAN PLATEAU, NORTH CHINA PLAIN, Shandong Peninsula, Yellow Sea, S. KOREA, N. KOREA, Yalu River, Liao R., Songhua R., Amur R., GREATER KHINGAN RANGE

60°E, 70°E, 80°E, 90°E, 100°E, 110°E, 120°E, 130°E, 140°E, 150°E, 160°E, 170°E, 180°
110°E, 120°E, 130°E, 150°E
50°N, 40°N, 30°N, 20°N, 10°N, 0°, 10°S, 20°S

N W E S

learning LOCATIONS

Mapping Physical Features

Use the map on this page to add the major physical features in East Asia to the political map you created previously. Sketch and label all major mountain ranges, plateaus, deserts, and bodies of water.

PHOTO STUDY

1 **An Arid Continent** Australia has few permanent bodies of water. Most lakes and rivers become full after heavy rains and then dry up in the burning sun, leaving behind a swath of dried mud (right). *Critical Thinking How would a lack of permanent rivers and lakes affect human activities in a region?*

Cross Section: Australia

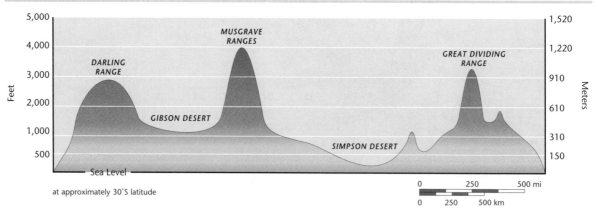

at approximately 30°S latitude

DIAGRAM STUDY

2 **Physical Profile** As the diagram above shows, Australia's landscape is characterized by broad deserts and low mountains. It is, in fact, the world's second driest continent and the flattest. *How do the Gibson and Simpson deserts differ?*

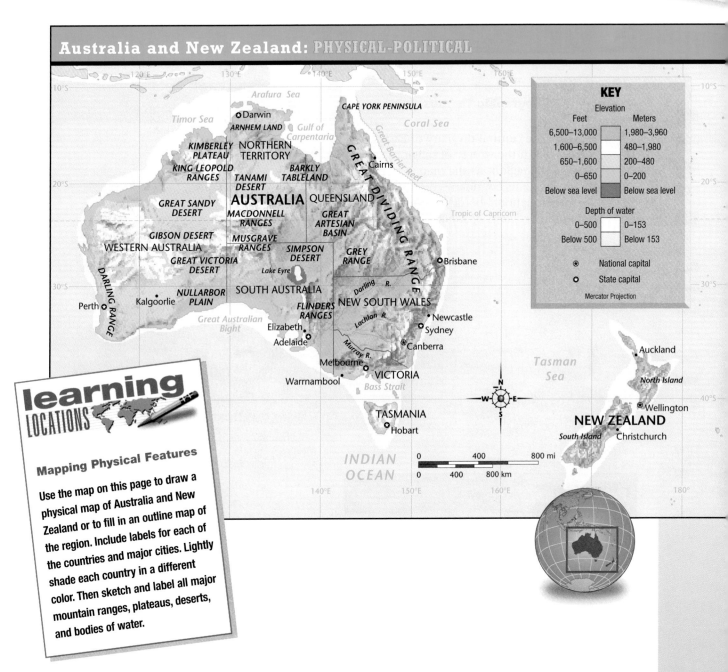

Australia and New Zealand: PHYSICAL-POLITICAL

KEY

Elevation

Feet		Meters
6,500–13,000		1,980–3,960
1,600–6,500		480–1,980
650–1,600		200–480
0–650		0–200
Below sea level		Below sea level

Depth of water

0–500		0–153
Below 500		Below 153

⊛ National capital

✪ State capital

Mercator Projection

learning LOCATIONS

Mapping Physical Features

Use the map on this page to draw a physical map of Australia and New Zealand or to fill in an outline map of the region. Include labels for each of the countries and major cities. Lightly shade each country in a different color. Then sketch and label all major mountain ranges, plateaus, deserts, and bodies of water.

MAP STUDY
Applying the Geographic Themes

3 Place Australia is the flattest continent. Along its eastern edge, however, stretches a line of hills and mountains. Nearly all of Australia west of this range is arid plain or dry plateau. East of the range the climate is moist. *Name this mountain range that prevents moisture from reaching most of the Australian interior.*

4 Location Australia's vast deserts are mostly uninhabited, although more and more people are now exploring the interior of the continent. The Great Sandy Desert and the Gibson Desert cover large parts of Australia. *Where are most of the deserts in Australia located?*

3 PEOPLE AND CULTURES

MAP STUDY
Applying the Geographic Themes

1 **Place** The cultural diversity of East Asia is reflected in the variety of religions practiced in the region. As the map at right shows, religious boundaries do not always align with national borders. *What are the major religions of Japan?*

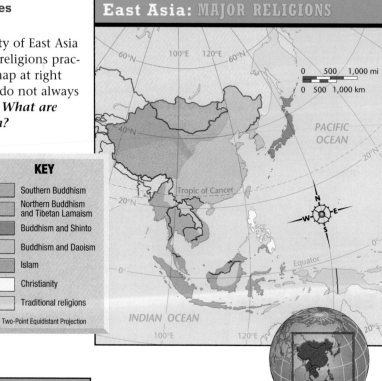

East Asia: MAJOR RELIGIONS

KEY

- Southern Buddhism
- Northern Buddhism and Tibetan Lamaism
- Buddhism and Shinto
- Buddhism and Daoism
- Islam
- Christianity
- Traditional religions

Two-Point Equidistant Projection

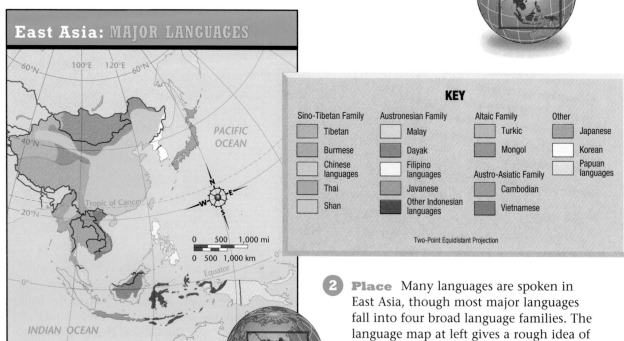

East Asia: MAJOR LANGUAGES

KEY

Sino-Tibetan Family
- Tibetan
- Burmese
- Chinese languages
- Thai
- Shan

Austronesian Family
- Malay
- Dayak
- Filipino languages
- Javanese
- Other Indonesian languages

Altaic Family
- Turkic
- Mongol

Austro-Asiatic Family
- Cambodian
- Vietnamese

Other
- Japanese
- Korean
- Papuan languages

Two-Point Equidistant Projection

2 **Place** Many languages are spoken in East Asia, though most major languages fall into four broad language families. The language map at left gives a rough idea of the great linguistic diversity in the region. *What are the major languages spoken in China?*

Chapter 30 ▪ Regional Atlas

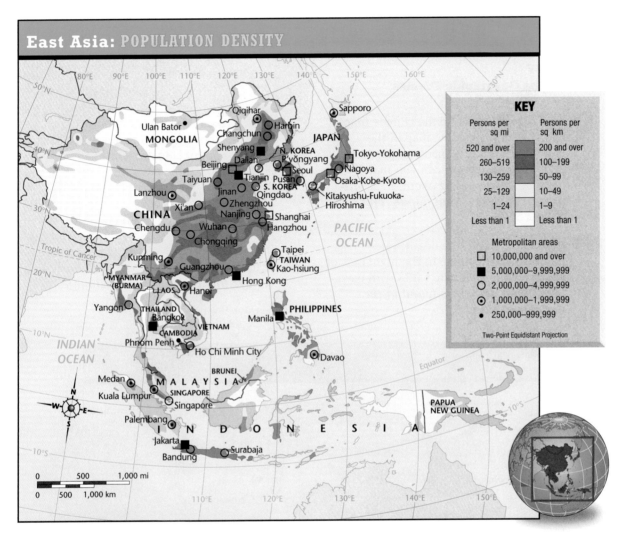

East Asia: POPULATION DENSITY

KEY

Persons per sq mi	Persons per sq km
520 and over	200 and over
260–519	100–199
130–259	50–99
25–129	10–49
1–24	1–9
Less than 1	Less than 1

Metropolitan areas
- ☐ 10,000,000 and over
- ■ 5,000,000–9,999,999
- ○ 2,000,000–4,999,999
- ◉ 1,000,000–1,999,999
- • 250,000–999,999

Two-Point Equidistant Projection

3 **Cause and Effect: Physical Geography and Population Density** Compare the population density map with the physical map on page 599 and the climate map on page 604. Notice how the areas of dense population match lowland areas that have mild and wet climates. *Why does much of western China have a low population density?*

PHOTO STUDY

4 **Urban Growth** In 1950, only about 15 percent of the population of Southeast Asia lived in urban areas. Now the figure is about 35 percent. *Critical Thinking Basing your reply on evidence in the photograph of Singapore (left), suggest some of the advantages and disadvantages of living in a city in East Asia.*

EAST ASIA AND THE PACIFIC WORLD

4 CLIMATE AND VEGETATION

MAP STUDY
Applying the Geographic Themes

1 **Location** Compare the climate map below with the climate map of the United States and Canada on page 120. *What generalization can you make about the climates at about 40°N latitude in Eastern China, Japan, and the United States?*

2 **Place** In Japan, the ocean waters help moderate the climate. In the highlands of western China, climate varies with elevation. *What climate is found in the Plateau of Tibet?*

3 **Regions** The southernmost tip of China and almost all of Southeast Asia have tropical climates. Only highland climates in some areas break this pattern. The Southeast Asian islands on and around the Equator have tropical wet climates. They receive rain about 200 days of the year for a total of about 60 inches (150 cm) per year. Their average temperatures are around 80°F (27°C). *What areas have tropical wet and dry climates?*

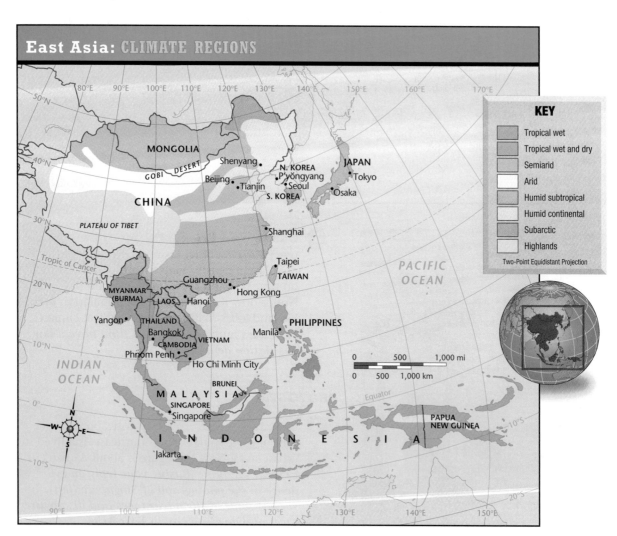

East Asia: CLIMATE REGIONS

KEY
Tropical wet
Tropical wet and dry
Semiarid
Arid
Humid subtropical
Humid continental
Subarctic
Highlands
Two-Point Equidistant Projection

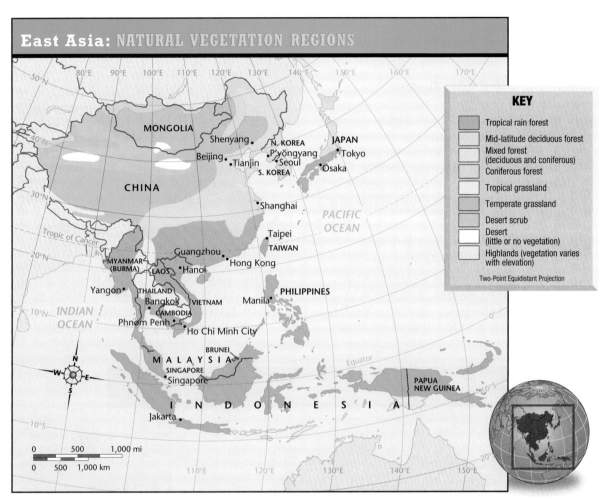

East Asia: NATURAL VEGETATION REGIONS

KEY

- Tropical rain forest
- Mid-latitude deciduous forest
- Mixed forest (deciduous and coniferous)
- Coniferous forest
- Tropical grassland
- Temperate grassland
- Desert scrub
- Desert (little or no vegetation)
- Highlands (vegetation varies with elevation)

Two-Point Equidistant Projection

MONGOLIA
Shenyang
Beijing · Tianjin
CHINA
N. KOREA
P'yŏngyang · Seoul
S. KOREA
JAPAN
Tokyo
Osaka
Shanghai
PACIFIC OCEAN
Tropic of Cancer
Taipei
TAIWAN
MYANMAR (BURMA)
Guangzhou
Hong Kong
LAOS · Hanoi
Yangon · THAILAND
Bangkok · VIETNAM
CAMBODIA
Phnøm Penh · Ho Chi Minh City
Manila
PHILIPPINES
INDIAN OCEAN
BRUNEI
MALAYSIA
SINGAPORE
Singapore
INDONESIA
Jakarta
Equator
PAPUA NEW GUINEA

0   500   1,000 mi
0   500   1,000 km

4 **Cause and Effect: Climate and Vegetation** By comparing the climate and vegetation maps on these pages, you can see the link between climate and vegetation in East Asia. *What is the most common type of vegetation in the highland and semiarid regions of China?*

PHOTO STUDY

5 **Tropical Rain Forests**
In some nations in East Asia hundreds of languages are spoken. The isolation of these languages is due in part to the difficulties of traveling through dense rain forest. *Critical Thinking How might communication problems change as rain forests are cut down and people move to cities?*

Chapter 30 ▪ Regional Atlas

MAP STUDY
Applying the Geographic Themes

1 **Place** East Asia, though largely agricultural, is rapidly increasing its industrial output. Japan, South Korea, Taiwan, and Singapore are all industrial powerhouses, and China is quickly taking its place beside them. *Where in China is industry most common?*

2 **Movement** Today East Asia has become a focus of world trade. Its nations' products are shipped from the many factories and workshops west to Europe and east to the Americas. Much new business is in the form of banking and finance. *Critical Thinking* *Why is banking growing in the region?*

3 **Place** Several nations in East Asia rely on sales of oil to fund development. *What nations in East Asia produce petroleum?*

4 **Place** In many areas of East Asia, people rely on fishing to supply their food and income. **Aquaculture**, or fish farming, contributes about one third of China's yearly catch. *What features of East Asia's physical geography explain why fishing is important to the region?*

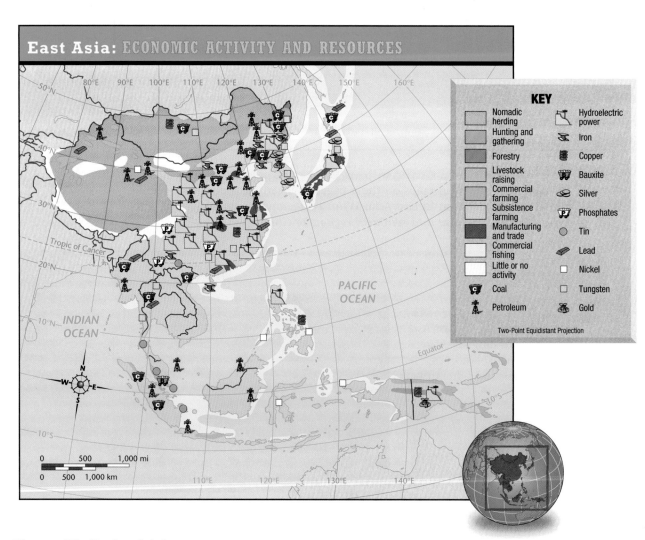

East Asia: ECONOMIC ACTIVITY AND RESOURCES

KEY

Nomadic herding
Hunting and gathering
Forestry
Livestock raising
Commercial farming
Subsistence farming
Manufacturing and trade
Commercial fishing
Little or no activity
Coal
Petroleum

Hydroelectric power
Iron
Copper
Bauxite
Silver
Phosphates
Tin
Lead
Nickel
Tungsten
Gold

Two-Point Equidistant Projection

EAST ASIA AND THE PACIFIC WORLD

PHOTO STUDY

5 **Using Every Inch of Land** East Asians use **intensive farming**, farming that requires great amounts of labor, to produce food. To use all available land, farmers in hilly areas have reshaped the land into **terraces**, or level, narrow ledges. *Critical Thinking* **What natural resources would terraced fields help conserve?**

atlas REVIEW

Vocabulary and Main Ideas

1. Define a. seismic b. aquaculture c. intensive farming d. terrace

2. Describe the population density, climate, and vegetation of western China.

3. What is the Ring of Fire?

4. Which East Asian countries are rapidly becoming industrialized?

5. Critical Thinking: *Cause and Effect* How might climate changes cause major food shortages in East Asia?

learning LOCATIONS

6. Where is Australia located in relation to New Zealand?

7. Where is Japan located in relation to South Korea?

People of the Pacific Islands

S cattered across the Pacific Ocean are nearly 800 islands, large and small, that are home to a variety of peoples. Who were the first inhabitants? How did other people reach these isolated spots?

Early Settlers

Though the Pacific islands are scattered over a vast area, some have been home to humans for many centuries. Archaeologists have shown that people were living in New Guinea, Australia, and parts of Melanesia more than 40,000 years ago. Other Pacific islands, though, have been settled for less than a thousand years.

Like the first people in the Americas, some Pacific islanders may have traveled across land bridges during the Ice Ages, when ocean levels were lower. New Guinea and Australia are believed to have been joined by dry land until about 8000 B.C. Other early migrants probably traveled by raft from the islands of Indonesia.

Peoples of Oceania

The first people in the islands included the native peoples of Australia, known as Aborigines, and the Melanesians. They were Australoids, one of the two main ethnic groups in Oceania. Their languages became the roots of modern Australian and Papuan.

Melanesian wood carving

Polynesians and Micronesians, the other group of island peoples, are more closely related to the people of mainland East Asia. They began their island-hopping migrations much later. Through history the two island cultures sometimes mixed, except for the isolated Australian Aborigines.

Melanesian wood carving

Ocean Travelers

The greatest explorers of the Pacific were the Polynesians. Although a few historians disagree, most think that they were expert sailors who could maneuver their canoes to sail eastward against the wind. They navigated by observing the sun and stars, winds, and currents. Until the European age of exploration began in the 1500s, the Polynesians were geographically the most widespread people on earth. Though scattered, they spoke related languages and lived in similar societies.

The Polynesian Triangle About 4,000 years ago, Polynesians began to migrate eastward from the islands of Southeast Asia. Pioneer Polynesians were living in Samoa, Tonga, and Fiji by about

1000 B.C. Later expeditions took them from one group of tropical islands to another.

As the map at right shows, Polynesian settlements eventually formed a huge triangle in the Pacific. About A.D. 300, some moved eastward to the Marquesas. From there, different groups went south to isolated Easter Island and north to the islands of Hawaii. The next stage, about 300 years later, took them to Tahiti and the other Society Islands. The final Polynesian expansion took Maoris to New Zealand about A.D. 800.

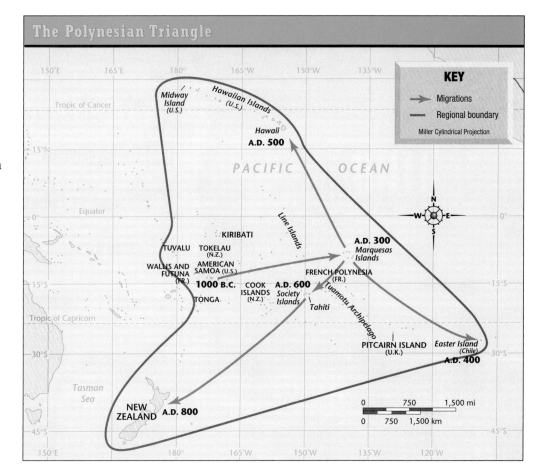

The Polynesian Triangle

KEY
→ Migrations
— Regional boundary
Miller Cylindrical Projection

PACIFIC OCEAN

Midway Island (U.S.)
Hawaiian Islands (U.S.)
Hawaii A.D. 500
KIRIBATI
Line Islands
TUVALU TOKELAU (N.Z.)
WALLIS AND FUTUNA (FR.) AMERICAN SAMOA (U.S.)
1000 B.C.
TONGA
COOK ISLANDS (N.Z.) A.D. 600 Society Islands
Tahiti
FRENCH POLYNESIA (FR.)
Tuamotu Archipelago
A.D. 300 Marquesas Islands
PITCAIRN ISLAND (U.K.) Easter Island (Chile) A.D. 400
NEW ZEALAND A.D. 800
Tasman Sea

0   750   1,500 mi
0   750   1,500 km

Polynesian Influence
As they moved across the Pacific, Polynesian settlers took their own foods and animals. Most of the major food plants and animals of Polynesia, including coconut, breadfruit, bananas, pigs, and chickens, are not native to the islands. It is likely that the Polynesians' arrival wiped out several native species of birds and reptiles in New Zealand.

The Polynesians also spread their language. Today people in many parts of the Pacific speak Polynesian languages, including Samoan, Tongan, and Tahitian. Some New Zealanders speak Maori. In Hawaii some people speak Hawaiian, another Polynesian language.

connecting
TO TODAY

1. (a) What was the ancient home of the Pacific island peoples?
   (b) How did they travel to the islands?

2. Name three Pacific islands or island groups settled by Polynesians.

3. **Critical Thinking** What effect can the arrival of new people, plants, and animals have on native species of plants and animals?

4. **Hands-On Activity** Choose any one of the island nations of Oceania and make a poster showing its flag and events in its history. Use travel articles to add pictures of native plants, animals, and scenery if possible.

SECTIONS

1 | The Emergence of Modern China

2 | Regions of China

3 | China's People and Culture

4 | China's Neighbors

China, Taiwan, and Mongolia: POLITICAL

MONGOLIA

Uliastay · Ulan Bator ⊛

Harbin ·

Sea of Japan

Beijing ⊛

Huang He (Yellow R.)

CHINA

Shanghai ·

Wuhan ·

PACIFIC OCEAN

Lhasa · Chongqing · Yangzi R.

Tropic of Cancer

Taipei ·
⊛
TAIWAN

Guangzhou · Hong Kong ·

INDIAN OCEAN

Macao ·

South China Sea

KEY

— National boundary
⊛ National capital
· Other city

Two-Point Equidistant Projection

learning LOCATIONS

Mapping the Region

Create a map like the one above, shading each country a different color. Then add labels for the countries, cities, and bodies of water that are shown on the map.

1 The Emergence of Modern China

Section Preview

Main Ideas

● **Mao Zedong (mow zhuh doong)** introduced many programs to construct a Communist state in China.

● The **Four Modernizations** changed the focus of China's economy.

● Calls for democratic reforms in China have met with a violent response.

Vocabulary

sphere of influence, abdicate, warlord, light industry, martial law

APPEARED IN *NATIONAL GEOGRAPHIC*

Families work the land together in rural China.

Since its birth along the Huang He in northern China around 3000 B.C., Chinese civilization has been deeply rooted in an agricultural way of life. Guided by the principles of Confucianism, the emperors of China ruled as if they were the fathers of their people. Their main responsibilities were to make sure their peoples' needs were met and to rule by setting an example of fairness.

Feeding China's large population has required large amounts of rice and other crops. One of the main duties of the Chinese emperors was to make sure that surplus food was stored for use in times of drought or flooding. The government also oversaw a system of trade among the different parts of the country. As a result, food shortages in one region could be met with surpluses from another region. This storage and distribution system worked well. Because China always had a large supply of agricultural workers, new technology did not come to be valued as it was in the West. In fact, according to the ideals of government in China, moral traits such as cooperation were more important than new technical knowledge.

Lack of military technology proved a serious disadvantage in the mid-1800s. The industrialized countries of Europe and the United States used their military strength to force their way into China. The changes forced on China by these Western powers upset the country's internal trade network. These changes, combined with a series of natural and other disasters, resulted in widespread famine. A series of rebellions then broke out across the country. China entered a period of turmoil that would last for decades.

The March to Communism

By 1900 the United States and a number of European powers had carved China into **spheres of influence**. These are areas in which these countries had some political and economic control, but did not directly govern.

Angered by the treatment they were receiving from the Western powers, many Chinese people called for changes. They disagreed, however, on what course to take. Some favored giving up their traditional ways and accepting the Western culture of their enemies. Others wanted to totally reject Western influences. A third group wished to take on parts of Western culture, like technology, as a means to defend and protect their own culture. During this struggle, a new political party emerged—the Nationalist People's party. Many Nationalists, although they disliked the foreign powers in China, were greatly influenced by Western ideas.

After a series of revolts in 1911, the Nationalists seized power, forcing the emperor to **abdicate**, or give up his throne. The Nationalists then declared China a republic, choosing Sun Yat-sen (soon yaht sen) as the country's first president. Sun, who had been educated in the United States, wanted China to adopt a government based on Western democratic principles.

A Struggle for Power The Nationalists found that seizing control was far easier than keeping it. As fighting broke out between the Nationalists and the former army, local **warlords**, regional leaders with their own armies, seized power in their own areas. The Nationalists realized that to gain control of the whole country, they would have to defeat the warlords.

In the mid-1920s Sun Yat-sen died and Chiang Kai-shek (ts yahng ky shek) took over the leadership of the party. Chiang, a trained soldier, quickly molded the Nationalist troops into a disciplined fighting force. In a two-year campaign, Chiang defeated one warlord after another, taking control of much of the country. By 1928 he had established himself as president of the Nationalist Republic of China.

The Long March In the 1920s a split developed in the Nationalist party. Some members of the party had adopted an ideology based on Karl Marx's communism. Marxism seemed to

The Long March

● **Movement** In 1934 the Communists, under the leadership of Mao Zedong (shown on horseback), left their stronghold in Jiangxi to evade a blockade by Nationalist forces. Their Long March, as it came to be known, was planned to engage Nationalist forces at their weakest points. *How many miles did the Long March cover?*

Route of the Long March

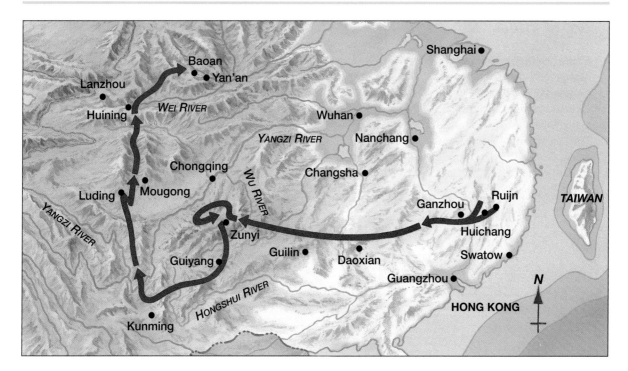

DIAGRAM STUDY

● One of the biggest challenges of the Long March was the difficult terrain.

What geographic obstacles did Mao and his troops face on their trek?

suggest an answer to the age-old problem of achieving prosperity for all Chinese. It also offered a means of defeating the imperialist powers in China through a revolution led by the working class.

To achieve these goals, Communists within the Nationalist party wanted to give more power to the workers and to give land to the landless peasants. But Chiang Kai-shek disagreed. In 1927 he ordered those who favored Communist ideas to be killed.

Some Communists survived Chiang's executions, fleeing to the mountainous region of south central China. There they built a stronghold in the province of Jiangxi (jyahng shee). Over the next six years, their numbers grew. Fearful that they would soon challenge his hold on the government, in 1933 Chiang sent a huge army to hunt them down and destroy them. After months of fighting, the Nationalists' superior numbers and resources began to prevail. In late 1934 the Communists left their positions in Jiangxi and started a year-long, northward journey known as the Long March.

The illustration on this page shows the long, winding route of the Long March. The Communists had to cross eighteen mountain ranges and more than twenty rivers on their 6,000 mile (9,700 km) journey. Hunger, disease, and almost constant attacks by Nationalist troops made the march even more hazardous. Of the 100,000 Communists who had left Jiangxi, only about 8,000 reached their goal—safety in the northern province of Shaanxi (shah ahn shee). There, in the mountain town of Yan'an (yahn ahn), they set up their new headquarters under the leadership of Mao Zedong (mow zhuh doong).

Communists Take Over

During the early 1930s, the Japanese took advantage of the fighting in China. They invaded the northern Chinese province of Manchuria. Then, in 1937, the Japanese attempted to take over other areas of China. This hostile invasion forced the Nationalists and Communists to unite against their common enemy.

Group Effort

Place In 1985, workers who lived along the 30-mile stretch of road between Chengdu and Guanxian widened the road on the orders of the Communist Party's Central Committee. The task was completed in a single week. **Critical Thinking** *How is this project reminiscent of Mao's Great Leap Forward?*

After the war ended in 1945, however, the two factions once again fought for control of China. But while fighting against Japan, the Communists had carried out major social reforms in the areas they controlled. These reforms included lowering the peasants' rents. Many of these peasants now joined the Communist struggle against the Nationalists. By 1949 the Nationalists had been defeated.

Chiang Kai-shek fled the mainland, seeking safety on the island of Taiwan. There he vowed he would one day reconquer China. In Beijing, Mao Zedong made a different statement. On October 1, 1949, he announced the establishment of a new Communist state: the People's Republic of China.

A Communist Nation

Much of China lay in ruins after years of war. Even so, Mao indicated that he had great plans for the nation. He wanted to increase agricultural productivity. He believed that improvements in farm production could be achieved only according to the Communist principle of replacing private ownership with common ownership. In 1953, therefore, he called for the establishment of collective farms. On a collective, people work together as a group and then share whatever they harvest. By 1956, 110 million families—about 88 percent of all Chinese peasants—were working on collective farms.

The Great Leap Forward Despite these economic changes, China still failed to meet Mao's goals. In 1958 he introduced yet another plan: the Great Leap Forward into Communism. Under this plan, the 700,000 collectives were combined into 26,000 People's Communes. These self-sufficient communal settlements, some of which had as many as 25,000 people, contained both farms and industries. Life in a People's Commune resembled life in the military. Communist party officials made all the decisions about what goods were made and who received them. The people's task was simply to work in the fields or factories.

Mao hoped that this new economic organization would, in a matter of years, increase China's production greatly. But the Great Leap Forward resulted, according to one Chinese official, in "a serious leap backward." Rather than increasing, production fell. The difficult life in the communes offered people no incentive to work hard. They received the same rewards regardless of the amount they produced. In addition, bad weather conditions hindered farm production. The harvests from 1958 to 1960 were among China's worst. The Chinese government abandoned its Great Leap Forward after only two years.

The Cultural Revolution Many political leaders criticized Mao Zedong for the failure of the Great Leap Forward. Even Mao's closest advisers charged him with making mistakes. Deng Xiaoping (dung shau ping), for example, felt that Mao had tried to do too much too quickly. "A donkey is certainly slow, but at least it rarely has an accident," Deng remarked.

Stung by this criticism, Mao responded that if the revolution was failing, then even more drastic measures were needed. In 1966, he called for a Great Cultural Revolution to smash the old order completely and establish a new, socialist society. Mao unleashed an army of radical young men and women, called Red Guards, to enforce his policies. Their job and command was to destroy the Four Olds: old ideology, old thought, old habits, and old customs.

No part of society was safe from the Red Guards. Communists who favored slower change, teachers, artists, writers—in fact, all those who disagreed with Mao—were publicly humiliated, beaten, and even killed. Those enemies who survived the wrath of the Red Guards lost their jobs and were imprisoned or sent to the country to work as peasants.

Farm production fell, factory work ground to a halt, and schools closed as the Red Guards moved through the country. Mao approved of their actions by saying, "To rebel is justified." The destruction was so great that Mao called for an end to the Cultural Revolution in 1969. He also ordered the army to disband the Red Guards.

Little Red Books

● **Place** During the Chinese cultural revolution, Mao's sayings were collected and distributed in what became known as Mao's little red book. In the frenzy of the Cultural Revolution, Mao was feverishly revered and his words were considered the final authority. *What were the "Four Olds" that Mao wished to destroy?*

The Cultural Revolution was an enormous failure for China. At its end the economy was almost completely ruined. Hundreds of thousands of innocent people were in jail or had been driven into remote, rural areas. An entire generation of young people had lost their chance for an education. This loss of talent alone made China's economic recovery very difficult.

The Four Modernizations

Mao Zedong died in 1976. A power struggle followed that pitted the Gang of Four—a group of politicians led by Mao's widow, who wanted to continue the Cultural Revolution—against a group led by Deng Xiaoping. Most people sided with Deng because they were tired of death and disorder. Deng took a more practical approach to solving China's problems than Mao.

To begin the changes needed to make China productive, Deng started a program called the Four Modernizations. The goals of the program were to improve agriculture, industry, science and technology, and defense as quickly as possible. To accomplish this, Deng said, any ideas would be considered, even if they approached the ideas of a free-enterprise economy. Said Deng, "It doesn't matter if a cat is black or white, as long as it catches mice."

Changes in Agriculture First, Deng took steps to repair the damage done to farm production during the Great Leap Forward. In place of the communes, he established the contract responsibility system. Under this arrangement, the government rented land to individual farm families. Each family then decided for themselves what to produce. The families contracted with the government simply to provide a certain amount of crops at a set price. Once the contract was fulfilled, they were free to sell any extra crops at markets for whatever prices they could get.

This chance to make more money by growing more crops led farmers to increase their production by about 8 percent more each year than

APPEARED IN *NATIONAL GEOGRAPHIC*

APPEARED IN *NATIONAL GEOGRAPHIC*

China's New Environment

● **Human-Environment Interaction** Home-grown industries, such as the ceramics-making business shown here (top photo), now exist side by side with international businesses. Deng Xiaoping's economic reforms include a new openness to the West. The Chinese have allowed U. S. soft drink makers to open bottling plants in China (right), in return for a share of the profits. *What were China's experiences with foreign trade at the turn of the century?*

they had in the previous year. In the first eight years, farmers' incomes tripled.

Industrial Development When the Communists came to power, they used most of China's resources to increase heavy industry. Heavy industries produce goods such as iron, steel, and machines that are used in other industries. At first, heavy-industry production grew rapidly. By the time Deng came to power, however, Chinese technology was outdated and inefficient.

Deng's program for industry had two goals. First, he wanted people to spend more money on consumer goods. Therefore he changed the focus from heavy industry to **light industry**. This refers to the production of small consumer goods such as clothing, appliances, and bicycles. He also wanted factories to step up production. Deng gave more decision-making power to factory managers. He started a system of rewards for managers and workers who found ways to make factories produce more.

In addition, Deng set up four Special Economic Zones along China's east coast. By locating the zones near Hong Kong and Taiwan, Deng hoped to attract foreign capital, companies, and technology from these offshore economic giants. As described in the next section, the zones have proven enormously successful. They have been so successful, in fact, that China now has not just four but hundreds of these special zones.

What Deng did not foresee, however, was the effect that his economic reforms would have on China. About 1.5 million industrial firms were in operation in 1978. Fifteen years later, that number had grown to over 20 million. This shift from agriculture to industry has changed the face of rural China in ways both good and bad.

Unexpected Results Unfortunately, China's rapid economic growth has taken place very unevenly. Spurred by the establishment of Special Economic Zones, the coastal cities have grown rich. The interior regions now lag far behind. As farmers realized they could get more money growing cash crops, China suddenly found itself short of staple foods, such as grains.

Country	Population	Life Expectancy (years)	Per Capita GNP (in US $)
China	1,218,800,000	69	$490
Hong Kong	6,000,000	78	17,860
Mongolia	2,300,000	64	400
Taiwan	21,200,000	74	NA
United States	263,200,000	76	24,750

Source: Population Reference Bureau   NA indicates data not available.

CHART SKILLS

- *Which country, aside from the United States, has the highest per capita GNP?*

- **Critical Thinking** *How do life expectancy and GNP seem to be related in this chart?*

The population has also shifted dramatically. About 120 million people have left their villages to make their fortunes in the booming cities. Rapid urban growth has resulted in an increase in crime that the weak and sometimes corrupt police force has trouble handling.

However, despite these negative effects, the economy is stronger than it has ever been. Since the start of Deng's reforms, China's economy has quadrupled in size. Some experts now predict that if China's economy continues to grow at its current rate, by 2025 it could be the largest economy in the world.

If you ask a Chinese person what is the most outstanding result of the economic growth, he or she will probably point to improvements in daily life. In the early 1980s, few households had any modern appliances. By the early 1990s, eighty percent of urban households owned washing machines.

GLOBAL issues

Trade and Human Rights

Although other nations threaten at times to stop trading with China if it does not liberalize its politics, few leaders put principle before profit. The United States gave up connecting human rights issues with trade with China during the 1990s.

An International Symbol

● **Movement** As global communications improve, the world's nations borrow ideas from each other. These student protestors adopted the symbol of the Statue of Liberty, sending an unmistakable signal to their government. *What was the "Fifth Modernization" that students demanded in 1989?*

More Political Upheaval

As they became accustomed to economic reform, many Chinese citizens began to demand a "Fifth Modernization"—political freedom. They were eager to enjoy democratic rights, such as the freedom to express their political beliefs openly and without fear. They also called for a voice in running the government.

Early in 1989, thousands of Chinese, mostly students, began a series of demonstrations in Beijing to demand democratic reforms. As many as 100,000 people crowded into Tiananmen Square in the center of the city. In May, the government decided to end the protests. The country's leaders imposed **martial law** and ordered demonstrators to leave the square. Martial law is law that is administered during periods of strict military control. Some demonstrators disobeyed the government's orders. On the night of June 3, the army moved in to disperse the few thousand people who remained.

The troops opened fire without warning, killing as many as 2,000 people and wounding hundreds more. In the days that followed, troops rounded up suspected leaders and killed many of them without a trial. When other nations expressed outrage at these actions, Chinese authorities accused them of wrongly interfering in China's internal affairs.

After the crackdown, leaders in China indicated their belief that economic growth can succeed only if the people are kept "in line" politically. Repression in China has continued.

Section 1 Review

Vocabulary and Main Ideas

1. Define a. sphere of influence b. abdicate c. warlord d. light industry e. martial law

2. How did the Communists gain control in China?

3. What was the purpose of the Great Leap Forward?

4. What were the goals of the Four Modernizations?

5. Critical Thinking: *Drawing Conclusions* Why do you think the Chinese authorities responded so violently to the pro-democracy demonstrations in Tiananmen Square?

learning LOCATIONS

6. Where is Beijing located in relation to Shanghai?

7. Describe the location of Taiwan.

2 Regions of China

Section Preview

Main Ideas

- The Northeast region serves as China's center of population, industry, and government.

- The Yangzi River in the Southeast is China's major trade route.

- The Northwest region has a stark, rugged landscape.

- Isolated by huge natural barriers, Tibet developed a distinct traditional society.

Vocabulary

double cropping, theocrat, autonomous region

APPEARED IN *NATIONAL GEOGRAPHIC*

Beijing's Imperial Palace lies within an enclosure known as the Forbidden City.

A journey through China's four major regions provides a vivid picture of the country's geographic diversity. Locate the regions of China on the map on page 620. Compare this map with the physical map on page 599. As you can see, China's regions are largely defined by geography. Each region has developed its own character. A densely populated area, the Northeast has served as the country's administrative and industrial center. However the Southeast, once China's major agricultural region, has become the center of its booming economy. China's frontier lies to the west and is characterized by two sparsely populated regions—the desert Northwest and the mountainous Southwest.

The Northeast

The Northeast region includes eastern China from the Amur River in the north to the North China Plain in the south. The region is bounded on the west by the Greater Khingan (shinj ahn) Range. China's major lowland areas are in the Northeast.

For centuries the Northeast formed China's core. It contains Beijing, the country's capital, and the greatest concentration of China's population. The Northeast was the site of one of the world's earliest culture hearths, centered on the Huang He. Each dynasty that ruled in China added more territory to its empire, extending Chinese influence far beyond the country's original boundaries. But no matter how far these empires extended, the capital remained in the Northeast.

Beijing Beijing continues to function as the seat of power for today's Communist government. Like other cities in the Northeast, Beijing is a major industrial center. But because the Southeast region has prospered so enormously with the establishment of the Special Economic Zones, Beijing may be losing its status as China's nerve center. Investment dollars are flowing south, and when people request permission from the government to change residence, they are often hoping to move south. A professor at Beijing Normal University explains the attraction this way:

China: REGIONS

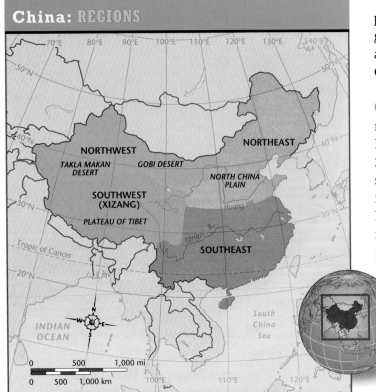

APPLYING THE GEOGRAPHIC THEMES

● **Regions** China's regions are divided between sparsely settled, dry, and mountainous lands in the west, and densely settled, well-watered lands in the east. *Name the regions of China. In which region is China's capital?*

Beijing was considered the best city in China [in which] to study, but that's changing. Now students want to stay in the south or be on the coast because they have more opportunities and can make more money.

Loess: Fertile Soil

In addition to having industrial centers like Beijing, the Northeast is also the site of a vast agricultural area. Here the soil has been made fertile by loess—a fine, yellow-brown loam deposited by seasonal dust storms. Strong winds blow the loess from Mongolia and the Gobi Desert, depositing it along the upper reaches of the Huang He. In fact, the Huang He, meaning Yellow River, takes its name from the color the loess gives the water. The loess is carried to the Huang He's lower reaches. During floods, it is deposited as silt across the lowland area of the North China Plain.

Loess, which is highly fertile, can become productive agricultural soil with the use of irrigation. As a result, the North China Plain is among the most intensely farmed areas in China.

China's Sorrow In addition to carrying rich, fertile soil to the lowland areas, the Huang He also serves as a transportation route. It flows 2,903 miles (4,670 km) on a tortuous path to the sea. Originating in the Tibetan Plateau, it makes its way north through the Gobi Desert to the North China Plain. At about 40ºN latitude it makes a sudden bend east and southward. It picks up the Wei River at around 35ºN latitude and turns east, coursing its way to the sea.

However, the river that helps transportation has also brought death and destruction to the region in the past. Some people call it "China's Sorrow."

In years when the spring thaw and rains were very heavy, the river's swollen waters spilled over its banks, flooding the surrounding areas. Countless numbers of people lost their lives in these destructive floods. Those who survived saw their homes and crops washed away or buried under thick layers of silt. In 1887 flooding along the Huang He resulted in history's greatest flood disaster, in which close to 1 million people died.

Incredibly, China now has a new problem with the Huang He. Because its water is used by some 120 million people in the region, it can dry up completely for months at a time. In the early twenty-first century, the region will need 20 percent more water than the river delivers. To solve this crisis, the Chinese government is considering projects that will divert water from the Yangzi River in the south to the Huang He in the north. The cost and the impact on people and the environment would be vast. However, as one Canadian expert put it:

They will go ahead with these schemes, because to them it will be the simpler solution to increase the supply of water rather than manage the supply through conservation. That is the typical Communist party solution.

The Southeast

Southeast China stretches from the North China Plain to the country's southern border, and from the eastern coast to the western highland areas. As the map on page 599 shows, the Southeast region is more mountainous than the Northeast. In addition, the Southeast has a warmer, wetter climate than the Northeast.

This climate, together with the fertile soil of the region's river valleys, makes the region excellent for farming. Farmers use a number of intensive farming methods to get the greatest yield from the land. In some areas, farmers practice **double cropping**—growing more than one crop a year on the same land. Elsewhere, farmers carve steplike terraces into the slopes of hills to increase the area of arable land. Rice, rather than wheat, dominates agriculture in the Southeast.

Movement on the Yangzi The valley of the Yangzi, or Ch'ang, River is the location of some of China's most productive farmland. With an average population density greater than 5,000 people per square mile (1,900 per sq km), the Yangzi valley ranks among the country's busiest and most crowded areas.

The Yangzi serves as China's east-west highway. Ocean-going ships can navigate some 700 miles (1,100 km) inland to the city of Wuhan. Small steamers travel even farther upstream, carrying goods to and from many towns deep in China's interior. Shanghai, located at the mouth of the Yangzi, illustrates the importance of the river to China's trade. Shanghai is China's major port. With a population of almost 7.5 million, it is also its largest city. Shanghai handles about 50 percent of the country's overseas cargo and close to 75 percent of its domestic trade goods.

Special Economic Zones One goal of the Four Modernizations was to spur economic growth by attracting foreign investment and technology to China. As discussed in Section 1, in the late 1970s the Chinese government created four Special Economic Zones in the Southeast. Three of the original zones, Zhuhai, Shenzhen, and Shantou, are located in Guangdong province, north of Hong Kong. The fourth, Xiamen, is in Fujian province just

Inland on the Yangzi River

Regions The Yangzi River connects China's vast interior with the coast. However, recent economic advances in the coastal regions have not reached far inland. Here the power of human physical effort is still as common as the power of modern engines is in modern cities. **Critical Thinking** *How does China's population size keep human power economically viable in some regions?*

across the Taiwan Strait from Taiwan. Hundreds of new economic zones have since been added. The government hoped to lure to these zones the foreign investment and technological expertise available from Chinese industrialists and financiers of Hong Kong and Taiwan. To entice these business people, the government set low tax rates. They also reduced the number of official forms and licenses required to operate a business in the economic zones. The strategy worked. By 1991, foreign investors had poured $22 billion into the special economic zones. Foreign investors from Hong Kong, Taiwan, and other countries from around the Pacific Rim have been racing to tap into the fastest-growing market in the world.

Evidence of the economic boom abounds. Scores of new apartment and office buildings have been constructed. Cars and electronic equipment, once considered luxuries, are now readily available. To take advantage of this wealth, hundreds of thousands of people have moved to the cities of the Southeast from other parts of China. (See the graph below.) Shanghai's population is expected to soar to 23.5 million by 2015. For more on China's urbanization crisis, see the Case Study on pages 630–631.

The Northwest

The landscape of China's Northwest region is stark, rugged, and barren when compared with the landscape of the country's eastern sections. The Gobi Desert forms China's northern boundary. Apart from leathery grasses that anchor the thin, sandy soil, very little grows in this rough, rock-strewn land. Few people find the region hospitable, and population is low. Mountains in this region surround and separate two large basins. The Takla Makan Desert occupies much of the western Tarim Basin. Steppe grasses cover most of the other basin.

The Silk Road, one of the great trade routes of ancient times, crossed the bare landscape of Northwest China. Along the road, way stations developed around oases fed by mountain

Population Growth in Southeast China

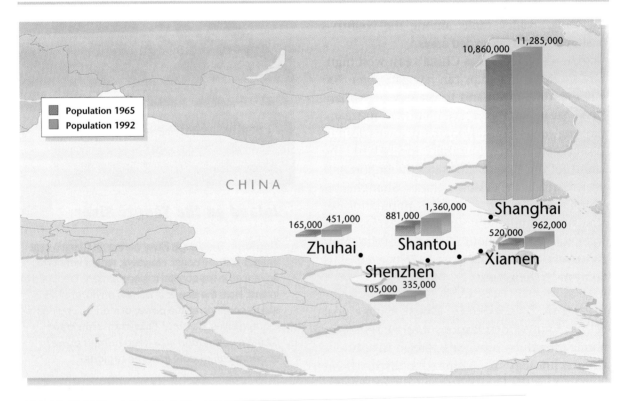

GRAPH STUDY

The establishment of Special Economic Zones has had a marked effect on the population of southeast China. *According to the graph, which of these cities has experienced the greatest growth in population?*

Effects of Erosion

● **Regions** The tortured landscape of this inland plateau shows the effects of erosion by wind and water. Yet this arid land near the Gobi Desert can support agriculture when irrigation brings life-giving water. **Critical Thinking** *How does an arid climate like that in northwestern China encourage a nomadic herding culture?*

streams. Over time, some of these way stations grew into large towns. For example, Kashgar, on the western edge of the Takla Makan, has a population of about 100,000. More than 1 million people live in Urumqi (oo room chi), in the foothills of the lofty Tian Shan Mountains (tyen shahn).

In these and other oasis towns, many people make a living through farming. For example, in Turpan (toor pahn), about 95 miles (150 km) southeast of Urumqi, a system of underground irrigation canals fed by streams flowing from the Tian Shan has helped to make grape growing an important occupation. Nomadic herding, however, is the major economic activity throughout the region. When spring arrives, herders drive their animals to higher elevations in search of fresh pastures. Then, with the onset of cold weather, they return their herds to their lowland meadows.

Tibet: The Southwest

If you look at the maps on pages 599 and 620, you will notice that one landform—the cold, dry Plateau of Tibet—dominates China's Southwest region. Its elevations exceed 14,000 feet (4,300 m) and surrounding mountains soar above 20,000 feet (6,100 m). Being the highest region in the world, the plateau is largely isolated from the rest of the world.

Occupying the plateau is Tibet—a distinct, traditional society based on the Buddhist religion. For most of their history the farmers and herders of Tibet lived quiet, simple lives ruled by Buddhist custom and the decrees of their theocratic leader, the Dalai Lama. A **theocrat** is someone who claims to rule by religious or divine authority.

In 1950 a Chinese invasion ended Tibet's isolation. The Chinese reduced Tibet's Buddhist monasteries to rubble and drove the Dalai Lama into exile in India.

GLOBAL issues

Exchanging Ideas

One of the main religions of Asia, Buddhism, has become increasingly popular in other nations, particularly the United States. According to a survey conducted at the beginning of the 1990s, American Buddhists number some 800,000. Tibetan Buddhism in particular has seen a sharp rise in interest.

The Rooftop of the World

● **Human-Environment Interaction** Tibet has been called the "Rooftop of the World" because of its altitude. Its average elevation is 16,000 feet (4,900 meters) above sea level. It is surrounded on the north, south, and west by the highest mountains in the world. These pilgrims have come to this remote temple to honor Buddha on the anniversary of his birth.
Critical Thinking *How has Tibet's physical geography protected the country's unique culture in the past?*

After an uprising in Tibet in 1959, the Chinese government instituted a policy designed to destroy Tibet's ancient culture. In 1965 China installed a Communist government and designated Tibet an **autonomous region**. An autonomous region is a political unit with limited self-government. The Chinese also gave Tibet a new name—Xizang (shee zahng), meaning "hidden land of the west." Even so, the Tibetans held on to their traditions and culture. After a series of reforms that relaxed limits on religion, the Chinese government clamped down on Tibet once again. This new Chinese interference in their affairs has only increased the Tibetans' desire to regain their independence.

Section 2 Review

Vocabulary and Main Ideas

1. Define a. double cropping b. theocrat c. autonomous region

2. Why has the Northeast region been considered the core of China in the past?

3. What natural feature promotes movement through the Southeast region?

4. How has Tibet been affected by Communist rule?

5. Critical Thinking: *Making Comparisons* What are the major differences between eastern and western China?

learning LOCATIONS

6. Identify and locate the two major river systems of China.

7. Name the desert that lies in north central China.

③ China's People and Culture

Section Preview

Main Ideas

- The Communist government has sought to control China's rapid population growth.

- The vast majority of the Chinese people share a common ethnic and cultural heritage.

- An ancient method of writing provides a vital means of unifying the Chinese nation.

Vocabulary

ideogram, atheism, acupuncture

APPEARED IN *NATIONAL GEOGRAPHIC*

Nearly 4 million commuters take to their bicycles each day in Shanghai.

Imagine standing on a street corner watching a parade in which the entire population of China marched by. If the people marched in rows of four, how long do you think it would take for the parade to pass? Would it take a few minutes, or would the time run into hours, or days? Actually, if the whole population of China took part in the parade, you would have to stand on that street corner for more than ten years to see all of the Chinese people pass by! With 1.2 billion people, China ranks as the world's most populous nation. Despite their numbers, the vast majority of China's people share a common language and culture.

A Huge Population

Mao Zedong, China's first Communist leader, believed that power lay in numbers. A huge number of people, he suggested, could never be overrun by outsiders. He urged the Chinese people to have more children. By the mid-1960s the population of China was growing annually by about 2.07 percent, a rate above that of most other countries. The growth rate in the United States, for example, stood at 1.46 percent.

For decades, Mao failed to recognize the problems his policy was causing. Demographers warned him that rapid population growth would mean serious shortages of food and shelter. By the 1960s, their predictions had come true. Overcrowding and hunger were a part of everyday life for many Chinese. The worst overcrowding was along China's eastern coast. Even today, population densities in this area rank among the world's highest.

Population Control Policies Finally realizing his country's predicament, Mao agreed to a new population policy. He called for families to have no more than two children. This policy slowed China's rate of growth a little. But overpopulation remained a social and economic problem.

When Deng Xiaoping came to power in the late 1970s, he argued that one sure way to improve the standard of living of the Chinese people was to reduce population growth still further. To achieve this goal, he set up a one-couple, one-child policy. Couples who followed this policy received special rewards, such as better housing and better jobs, or pay increases at

Population of China: 1950–2010

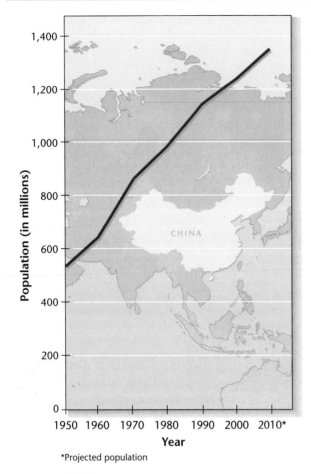

*Projected population

GRAPH STUDY

- Study the pattern in the line graph above. *How would you describe China's growth rate over the past 50 years?*

- Despite China's efforts to limit population growth, experts project that China's population will continue to rise. *What is the projected population for China in 2010?*

growth. The responsibility system shifted agricultural production away from communes and back to a system of family labor. As a result, rural couples began to have more children who would help in the fields. Children also represented security for parents, who eventually would become too old or sick to work. In rural areas, therefore, people simply had large families and accepted the punishments.

City dwellers, however, generally complied with the policy. By 1995, the annual population growth rate had slowed to 1.1 percent—a significant change. The new generation of only children, pampered by doting parents, were called the "little emperors." They posed a serious political question: Would they grow up to demand democratic reform, or fall in step with Communist nationalism? Even with the decline in the growth rate, slowing population growth remains a major challenge for China. As the graph at left shows, China's population is expected to reach nearly 1.4 billion by the year 2010.

Chinese Culture

Occupying a vast area and possessing a huge population, China is a land of great ethnic diversity. At the same time, the majority of the Chinese people share a common cultural background.

Ethnic Differences About fifty-five ethnic minority groups live in China, mostly in the frontier areas of western and northwestern China. Each of these groups has its own language, and the Chinese government officially recognizes no fewer than fifty-two separate languages. Different culture groups also have their own traditions, encompassing everything from the foods they eat to the clothes they wear. They practice many different religious faiths.

However, even the largest of these ethnic groups, the Mongols, Uygurs, Tibetans, and Kazakhs, are relatively small in number. Together, all the ethnic minorities represent only 6 percent

work. In contrast, couples who had more than one child faced the threat of fines, wage cuts, loss of their jobs, and the prospect of social disapproval.

Results To ensure the success of the new policy, the government started a large publicity campaign. It flooded the country with posters and billboards that listed the virtues of one-child families.

Propaganda did not convince people in rural areas. The contract responsibility system, the government's agricultural reform policy described in Section 1, was clearly at odds with government requests to limit population of China's population. The remaining 94 percent, more than 1 billion people, belong to the Han ethnic group. Taking its name from the Han Dynasty—established about 2,200 years ago—the Han have been the dominant ethnic group in China for centuries.

The Chinese Language The Han people speak Chinese. Written Chinese is unusual in that it is nonphonetic. Most other forms of writing use alphabets that give an indication of the sounds of words. The written form of Chinese, however, generally gives no clues to its pronunciation.

Written Chinese involves the use of **ideograms**—pictures or characters representing a thing or an idea. To perform a simple task like reading a newspaper, a person needs to master as many as 2,000 to 3,000 characters. To achieve a solid grasp of the entire written Chinese language, however, requires knowledge of at least 20,000 different characters.

Though these characters are pronounced in different ways in different parts of China, people throughout the nation can always communicate in writing. Why? Because they use the same characters. To help bridge the gap between spoken dialects, in 1956 the Chinese government declared Mandarin, the northern dialect, to be the official language. When students learn to read and write Chinese characters, they are taught Mandarin, whether or not they speak a different dialect locally.

APPEARED IN *NATIONAL GEOGRAPHIC*

The Art of Writing

Place Calligraphy is an important art form in China, but even basic literacy requires dedication and concentration. *How many characters, or ideograms, must one learn to master Chinese?*

The Chinese Family

● **Place** Confucian tradition encourages settled roles in families to promote a stable and harmonious society. Rural families rely on large families to do the farm work. **Critical Thinking** *How might Chinese philosophy and the needs of the rural poor make it difficult to convince people to limit the size of their families?*

广州市计划生育委员会 ·····广州··公司创作

继续大力··下抓好计划生育工作

Religions and Beliefs Ancient philosophies still have a great impact in China. The Chinese practice a variety of religions, but the traditional religions of Buddhism, Daoism, and Confucianism are the most popular.

Daoism is based on the teachings of Laozi (low DZEE), who lived from 604 to 531 B.C. According to Daoism, the path to true happiness lies in living in a harmonious relationship with the natural world. This path is called the right way, or Dao (dow).

Confucianism is the most widely practiced faith. It is a philosophy based on the teachings of Confucius, who lived from about 551 to 479 B.C. Confucius believed that society functioned best if every person respected the laws and behaved according to his or her position. For example, Confucius taught that parents should set good examples for their children and that children should obey their parents. Similarly, he stressed the importance of honoring one's ancestors.

Today many Chinese homes have altars where candles burn in memory of loved ones. Also, certain holidays are devoted to ancestors.

Although these philosophies, and religions such as Buddhism, still have a powerful effect on Chinese life, China is officially an atheist state. **Atheism** denies the existence of God. According to communism, religion is nothing more than a set of myths designed to keep workers under the domination of the ruling classes.

On coming to power in China, the Communists discouraged all religious practice. They seized churches, temples, and other places of worship, turning some of them into meeting halls, schools, and museums. During the Cultural Revolution a few years later, the Red Guards destroyed many of these buildings in order to tear down the Four Olds.

Still, neither laws nor the violent Red Guards could wipe out 2,000 years of tradition. Many Chinese people continued to practice

A Healthy Tradition

Place Many Chinese seek the health benefits of the ancient martial art Tai-chi (ty chee). *What other ancient practices are used to promote health in modern China?*

their religions. In the 1980s the government eased restrictions on religious practices. While not encouraging religion, it did not prevent people from following their chosen faith.

Traditional Medicine Many other old customs live on despite efforts by the Communist government to change and modernize Chinese society. People in both urban and rural areas still practice many forms of traditional Chinese medicine. This discipline, dating back 2,000 years, is based on the idea that

good health results from harmony between people and the environment.

Though Western medicine is also practiced in China, many people rely on traditional cures such as special diets and herbal remedies. They also use breathing exercises, massage, or **acupuncture**. Acupuncture is the practice of inserting needles at specific points on the body to cure diseases or to ease pain. Western scientists have proven that acupuncture does have a powerful effect on the body. However, they do not yet understand how it works.

Section 3 Review

Vocabulary and Main Ideas

1. Define a. ideogram b. atheism c. acupuncture

2. What steps did Deng's Communist government take to control China's rapid population growth?

3. Which ethnic group has dominated life in China for thousands of years?

4. Critical Thinking: *Expressing Problems Clearly* How does the government's contract responsibility system for farmers conflict with its efforts to reduce population growth?

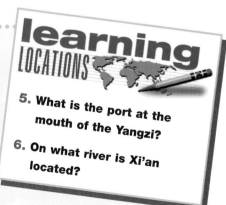

learning LOCATIONS

5. What is the port at the mouth of the Yangzi?

6. On what river is Xi'an located?

Urbanization in China

The Issue

Millions of people are migrating from the countryside to cities in China. Here are a few of the reasons why this is causing concern.

A Population Boom in the Cities
The population of China's cities is exploding. In recent years, as China's economy has improved, millions of people have left the countryside and moved to cities in search of jobs and a better life. Fifteen years ago, approximately 80 percent of China's population was rural. Today that figure is roughly 70 percent.

A River of Migrants
In Beijing an estimated 3.2 million migrants have streamed into the city. This is about one fourth of the city's population. The migrants cluster together on the outskirts of the city. They live in rundown buildings where some operate small businesses such as restaurants or workshops that make clothes and shoes. Most of them have no official residency papers, giving them permission to live in the city.

Global Impact
Social problems are widespread in overcrowded cities like Beijing and Shanghai. Many people are jobless. Crime is on the rise. In addition, city services, such as transportation systems, housing, schools, and sewerage are stretched to the limit. As a result, the air and water are polluted. Beijing's air pollution level, for example, is 16 times that of Tokyo's. In Shanghai, tons of waste are dumped daily into the Huangpu River. These conditions pose threats to public health and encourage epidemic diseases that thrive in crowded conditions.

Some Solutions
Government officials and urban planners have made some progress in developing policies and plans to handle the urban influx.

Controlling Migration
Officials in cities have taken steps to control migration.

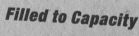

Filled to Capacity

Human-Environment Interaction Migration to urban areas in China has caused extreme overcrowding. The crowded neighborhood in the Chongwenmen district of Beijing (left) is overflowing its boundaries. New cities, like the one being built on Hainan Island (above right), are also quickly filling up to capacity.

China: Rural/Urban Population Balance

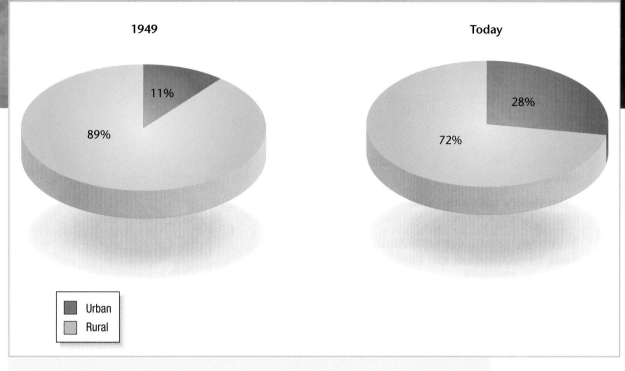

1949

11%

89%

Today

28%

72%

■ Urban
■ Rural

GRAPH STUDY

● **Human-Environment Interaction** China's population growth rate has caused a dramatic shift in the balance between rural and urban population. *What percent of China's population lives in an urban area today? How is this different from 1949?*

● *Critical Thinking* *What are some of the effects of a shifting population?*

They are enforcing residency requirements and checking job permits. In Beijing, migrants must pay a steep registration fee if they want to become residents.

Building New Cities Urban planners are designing new cities. If all goes as hoped, as many as 200 new cities will be built in China. Local governments will provide the basic infrastructure. The rest is up to private developers. One city on Hainan Island, one of China's special economic zones, is not even finished. Yet it already contains some 800,000 people—200,000 more than its planned population of 600,000.

YOU DECIDE

1. What do you think are the biggest problems that urbanization poses for China?

2. Do you think it is a better solution to redirect the rural-urban migration or stop it? Explain.

3. **Problem Solving** You are an official in Beijing. Draft a one-page proposal, including a brief analysis of the problem, with three to five ideas about how to solve the overcrowding caused by rural migration to your city.

4. **What You Can Do** Find out about the history of urbanization in the United States. Think about how the problems faced by China's cities compare to the problems in the United States in the late 1800s.

5. **Internet Activity** Visit the World Resources Institute to learn more about urban problems. Go to their publication *World Resources 1996-97*. From Part I of the publication, choose an urban problem of interest to you. Read the section and write a paragraph reporting on what you read. Link to this site from:

• www.phschool.com

4 China's Neighbors

Section Preview

Main Ideas

- Taiwan ranks as one of Asia's leading economic powers.

- Hong Kong's future freedom is uncertain.

- During the 1990s, Mongolia democratized its government and began to modernize its economy.

Vocabulary

buffer, provisional, exodus

APPEARED IN *NATIONAL GEOGRAPHIC*

Taiwanese soldiers bear portraits of Sun Yat-Sen in celebration of National Day.

The island state of Taiwan lies off China's southeastern coast. Hong Kong is part peninsula and part island, lying off China's southern coast. Mongolia fringes China's northern border, forming a **buffer**, or protective zone, between China and Russia. During the second half of the twentieth century, China cast a large shadow over its three smaller neighbors.

Taiwan: A World Apart

The small volcanic island of Taiwan lies 100 miles (160 km) off China's southeast coast. Mountains, its major landform, rise in tiers to an elevation of about 13,000 feet (3,960 m). This distinctive landscape gives the island its name. In Chinese, *Taiwan* means "terraced coastline."

The Emergence of Taiwan The Nationalists, led by Chiang Kai-shek, fled China and Communist rule and arrived in Taiwan in 1949. This new group of immigrants, primarily business people and military and government leaders, joined native Taiwanese living on the island. On their arrival, Chiang Kai-shek set up a **provisional**, or temporary, government.

Although repressive, Chiang's government allowed free enterprise to flourish. Meanwhile, on the mainland, Marxist collectivism was ruling political and economic life.

During the next few decades, a dispute raged between the Chinese and Taiwanese governments. The Nationalist government in Taipei (ty PAY), Taiwan's capital, claimed it represented all of China. The Communist government on the mainland claimed that it was the official government of China.

Much of the Western world backed the Nationalists in the hope that Chiang Kai-shek could oust the Communists. By the 1960s, however, many Western powers recognized that the Communists in China were there to stay. They began to seek better relations with the Beijing government. Then, in 1971, the United Nations accepted mainland China as a member. It voted to expel Taiwan, which had represented China at the United Nations since 1949. Immediately, most countries also recognized Beijing as the legal seat of government for China.

Since the 1970s, Taiwan has existed in an international limbo. Much of the world has refused to recognize it as a country. Yet many countries that do not recognize Taiwan still provide it with money and technical assistance. They also trade with Taiwan, helping make it one of the leading economic powers in Asia.

Taiwan's Economy When the Nationalist government arrived in 1949, it instituted a sweeping land-reform program that placed the land in the hands of tenant farmers. The government also encouraged farmers to use more fertilizers, plant more productive seeds, and practice intensive farming methods such as double cropping. As a result, Taiwan's farm production almost doubled.

The Nationalists also set in motion an industrial modernization program. With the help of foreign investment—especially from the United States—Taiwan quickly developed textile, food-processing, plastics, and chemical industries. This industrial growth was truly remarkable, given that nearly all the raw materials for these industries had to be imported.

In recent years Taiwan has pursued new industrial goals, concentrating on high-technology industries, such as electronics. Selling their products to huge markets in the United States and Europe, Taiwanese companies have greatly contributed to their country's rapid economic growth. This growth has allowed most Taiwanese to enjoy a high standard of living while holding on to their cultural heritage. In 1996, Taiwan's president noted:

> *Taiwan has been able in recent decades to preserve traditional culture on the one hand and to come into wide contact with Western democracy and science and modern business culture on the other.*

Taiwan's Future Until 1987, Taiwan had no official contact with China. In November of that year, the Taiwanese were finally permitted to visit relatives on the mainland. Soon bans on trade and investment were lifted. Taiwanese investors began pouring huge sums into China's Special Economic Zones.

China, however, still viewed Taiwan as a province, not an independent country. In 1996 it conducted war games in the Taiwan Strait,

APPEARED IN *NATIONAL GEOGRAPHIC*

Road Hazard

● **Human-Environment Interaction** Many people, even whole families, travel by motor scooter in Taiwan's crowded cities. Air quality, however, is a constant worry. **Critical Thinking** *How might Taiwan's rapid economic growth have contributed to air pollution?*

hoping to persuade Taiwan to vote against the pro-independence candidate, Lee Teng-hui. The tactic failed utterly, and Lee was elected. But Lee spoke softly on the topic of independence. He pointed out that Taiwan had "proved eloquently that the Chinese are capable of practicing

Taiwan's Export Economy

● **Movement** Taiwan's economy is based on foreign trade. It imports raw materials, like oil and basic metals, and exports manufactured goods, like the microchips shown here. *How has Taiwan's economic development changed its standard of living?*

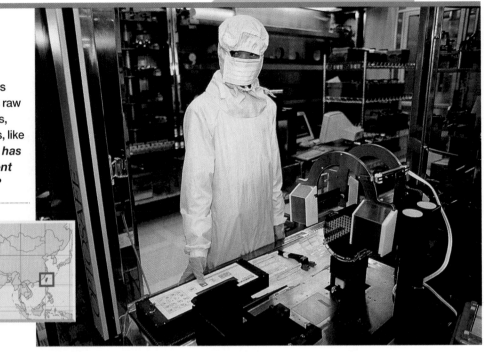

democracy." He hoped Taiwan could serve as a leader and model to China as it modernized and someday became a democracy as well. He said:

> *Taiwan is set gradually to exercise its leadership role in cultural development and take upon itself the responsibility for nurturing a new Chinese culture.*

Hong Kong Returns to China

Hong Kong faces an even more uncertain future. Located on China's southern coast, Hong Kong consists of the Kowloon Peninsula and several islands. It covers only about 400 square miles (1,000 sq km), yet it is home to 6 million people. With average population densities in excess of 15,000 people per square mile (5,800 per sq km), Hong Kong ranks as one of the most crowded places in the world.

The Growth of Hong Kong Hong Kong did not always bustle with human activity. Before the 1800s, it was largely uninhabited. During the 1800s, Britain used the site both as a naval base and as a way station for ships sailing to its far-flung Pacific empire. In 1898, the British forced China to agree to lease Hong Kong and other land in the area to them for ninety-nine years. During these years, Hong Kong enjoyed the benefits of free enterprise.

During the twentieth century, Hong Kong's deep, natural harbor and its central location on East Asian sea routes helped the port to become a leader in world trade. Hong Kong also became an important manufacturing center, specializing in textiles, clothing, and electrical appliances. In developing these industries, Hong Kong took advantage of a large pool of human resources. Following World War II, millions of people, fleeing war and political unrest elsewhere in Asia, sought a safe haven in Hong Kong. During the first fifteen years of Communist rule in China, Hong Kong took in more than 1 million Chinese refugees. It was these refugees who provided a vast supply of inexpensive labor for the factories of Hong Kong.

Hong Kong exports about 90 percent of the goods its factories produce. Recent estimates set the value of Hong Kong's trade—both imports and exports—at about $165 billion, about that of China, its giant neighbor to the north.

The End of the Lease Throughout its short history, Hong Kong developed with little interference from China. But the two places have developed an interdependence. Hong

Kong has long obtained most of its vital resources—fresh water, for example—from the mainland. Also, China has used Hong Kong as an exchange point for its trade with the West. Furthermore, since the establishment of the Special Economic Zones, Hong Kong has been a leading investor in the Chinese economy.

Hong Kong became part of China again on July 1, 1997. An agreement between Britain and China had provided that for the fifty years following that date, Hong Kong was to function as a Special Administration Region. It would be free to carry on as before, both economically and politically.

Events prior to the handover put the agreement in doubt, however. In 1992 the governor of Hong Kong introduced a plan for democratic reform. The plan called for an increase in the number of eligible voters, from 110,000 to 2.7 million. The Chinese were outraged. One Chinese official responded, "[The governor] cannot install Western-style democracy in Hong Kong designed to infect China." Soon after the July 1, 1997 handover, Hong Kong's new leader, Tung Chee-hwa, replaced the democratically-elected members of the assembly with pro-China lawmakers.

Hong Kong's worst fears did not come to pass. The local government permits modest protests and

GLOBAL issues

Sovereignty

Formerly controlled by Portugal, Macao was one of the oldest European settlements in East Asia. Macao consists of a peninsula and two small islands. It is only about 10 square miles (26 sq km) in area, but has about 432,000 inhabitants. Macao returned to Chinese rule in 1999.

APPEARED IN *NATIONAL GEOGRAPHIC*

Back to the Future

Location As Great Britain sailed out of Hong Kong's future, many wondered what would become of the former British colony as it reverted to Chinese rule. Many feared that the Chinese Communist government would bring an end to the free enterprise system to which Hong Kong owes its success. *How did Hong Kong's location help it become a leader in world trade?*

a free press. When limited elections were held in May 1998, many prominent democrats won seats in the new assembly.

In the late 1990s, Hong Kong's greatest worry was economic collapse. Recessions in other Asian countries lowered Hong Kong's exports and raised the cost of doing business in Hong Kong. Both China and Hong Kong have tried to avoid any actions that might shake confidence in Hong Kong's fragile economy.

Mongolia

Mongolia is a vast, dry land about the size of Texas. The Gobi Desert occupies the southern areas, while steppe vegetation covers much of the rest of the land.

In the thirteenth century, Mongolia was one of the world's great powers. The Mongols, under Genghiz Khan and his descendants, ruled an empire that extended from China in the east to Hungary and Poland in the west. In later centuries, however, Mongolia came under Chinese rule.

Mongolia remained a province of China until 1911 when, with the backing of the Soviets, the Mongols declared their independence. Ten years later, following Russia's example, Mongolia adopted communism. After Russia democratized its government in the early 1990s, Mongolia too held its first democratic elections. The winners were former Communists who had renounced communism and promised to create a free-market economy. Since the 1990s, people have been allowed to purchase state-owned businesses, and a stock exchange has opened its doors to investors.

Traditionally, the Mongols have made a living through nomadic herding. Even today, herding still ranks as the major economic activity on Mongolia's steppes, which are pasture for 30 million livestock. However, Mongolia has developed some industries. Among the most important rank coal and copper mining; food processing; and manufacturing leather goods, chemicals, and cement. With industrialization, Mongolia has become more urban. About 55 percent of the population now live in urban areas, many in Ulan Bator (oo LAHN BAH tawr), the capital.

Despite this modernization, in many ways the nation still falls far behind by Western standards. For example, in 1996, over 22 million acres of forest and grassland burned in forest fires—an area equal in size to the state of Colorado. The Mongolians literally had no way to fight these blazes. The total firefighting arsenal of the Mongolian nation included only 16 firetrucks, 10 chain saws, 34 shovels, 34 rakes, and 23 axes.

Section 4 Review

Vocabulary and Main Ideas

1. Define: a. buffer b. provisional c. exodus

2. How did Taiwan rise to economic power in Asia?

3. Why is the future so uncertain for Hong Kong?

4. What changes took place in Mongolia in the 1990s?

5. Critical Thinking: *Recognizing Ideologies* How do you think the Communist Chinese reacted to Taiwan president Lee Teng-hui's promise that Taiwan would lead China into democracy?

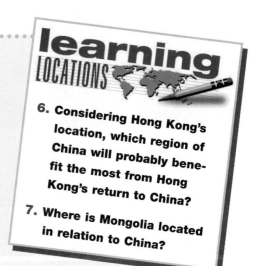

learning LOCATIONS

6. Considering Hong Kong's location, which region of China will probably benefit the most from Hong Kong's return to China?

7. Where is Mongolia located in relation to China?

Focus on Skills

☑ Social Studies
☐ Map and Globe
☐ Critical Thinking and Problem Solving

Analyzing Primary Sources

Historians often use primary sources in studying the past. A primary source is information produced during or soon after an event, usually by a participant or observer. Examples of primary sources are letters, journals, and eyewitness accounts. Primary sources may also include visual evidence, such as a news photo or a painting by an eyewitness.

Primary sources can convey a strong sense of an event or historical period. But the very fact that a writer is personally involved in the event may make the account biased or inaccurate. For that reason, you must analyze primary sources critically to determine their reliability.

In the boxes below are two primary-source descriptions of events that occurred when Chinese authorities used the army to end a mass protest in Beijing's Tiananmen Square in June 1989. Passage A is the statement of a student who was there. Passage B was written by a Chinese officer who helped direct the army. His statement, released in March 1990, was among the few given by Chinese leaders after the killings. Carefully read each passage below. Then practice analyzing primary sources by following these steps.

1. Identify the nature of the document. Primary sources often present one person's point of view, which may be biased. What is the main point of view of the author of each of the passages below?

2. Decide how reliable the source is. It is important to try to determine the purpose or goal of the author of a primary source, and to judge if the author's point of view is biased. Answer the following questions: (a) How convincing is the speaker in each passage? (b) Which speaker is more directly responsible for the events in Tiananmen Square? (c) Do you think the two speakers may have any interests that might lead them to conceal or distort the truth? (d) Would you say that Passage A is a reliable source? Is Passage B reliable? Give reasons for your answers.

Passage A

We expected tear gas and rubber bullets. But they used machine guns and drove over people with tanks . . . . It was like a dream. From where I was, the sound of crying was louder than the gunfire, but I kept seeing people falling. One line of students would stand up and then get shot down, and then another line of students would stand and the same thing would happen. There was gunfire from all directions. The soldiers were shooting everyone.

Passage B

The People's Liberation Army intervention in Tiananmen was a matter of necessity. . . . At the beginning, we stressed to our forces, "When beaten don't fight back; when scolded don't reply." First the PLA fired into the air as a warning. But a small minority shot at the PLA and snatched weapons. Under these circumstances, the PLA had to fire back in self-defense.

CHAPTER
31
Review and Activities

Summarizing Main Ideas

Section 1 The Emergence of Modern China

- Mao Zedong changed China into a Communist state.
- The Four Modernizations changed the focus of China's economy.
- When the Chinese people called for greater economic and political freedoms, the government cracked down.

Section 2 Regions of China

- China can be divided into four basic geographic regions—the Northeast, the Southeast, the Northwest, and the Southwest.
- The two eastern regions are the most densely populated and account for much of China's farming and manufacturing.
- The two western regions are dominated by mountains and have arid climates. They are home to most of China's ethnic minorities.

Section 3 China's People and Culture

- With about 1.2 billion people, China ranks as the world's most populous nation.
- Population growth has become such a problem that the government tries to limit the number of children couples may have.
- Most Chinese share a common culture.

Section 4 China's Neighbors

- Taiwan and Hong Kong are among Asia's leading economic powers.
- Taiwan and Hong Kong are reassessing their relations with China.
- Mongolia is gradually modernizing.

Reviewing Vocabulary

Use each term in a sentence that shows its meaning.

1. double cropping
2. ideogram
3. light industry
4. sphere of influence
5. martial law
6. theocrat
7. warlord
8. autonomous region
9. atheism
10. acupuncture
11. provisional
12. exodus

Applying the Geographic Themes

1. **Regions** Which region of China is booming economically? Why?
2. **Place** How did the Four Modernizations change China's economic focus?
3. **Human-Environment Interaction** Why is population growth a pressing problem for China?
4. **Human-Environment Interaction** How is China proposing to solve the problem of the drying up of the Huang He?
5. **Location** Why are Taiwan, Hong Kong, and Mongolia wary of China?

Critical Thinking and Applying Skills

1. **Identifying Alternatives** What alternative courses could the Chinese government have taken in dealing with the demonstrators in Tiananmen Square? How might a different response have affected China's relations with the West?
2. **Analyzing Primary Sources** Use library resources to locate two additional primary-source accounts of the events in Tiananmen Square, Beijing, in June 1989. Then, using the steps on page 637, analyze the sources and present a summary of your analysis to the class.

Journal Activity

Writing Across Cultures

▶ 1. Imagine you are a student in Shanghai. Write a letter to a friend in Beijing describing all the changes that have taken place in your city in your lifetime. Then write a letter in response, describing some of the problems of the Northeast Region.

▶ 2. Write a poem in which you explain the yearning for independence of the people in Tibet. In the poem, compare the situation in Tibet with events in American history.

INTERNET link

Learn more about Hong Kong by viewing the pictures in the Hong Kong Picture Archive. Link to this site from:

- www.phschool.com

Look at several types of pictures. Then list five things the pictures tell you about life in Hong Kong.

learning LOCATIONS

China and Its Neighbors

Number from 1 to 8 on a piece of paper. Next to each number, write the letter of the place on the map that corresponds to the places listed below.

1. Beijing
2. Hong Kong
3. Mongolia
4. Shanghai
5. Taipei
6. Taiwan
7. China
8. Ulan Bator

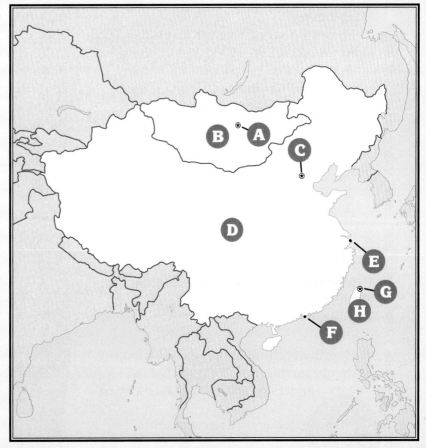

Map Skills
for Life

Bicycling is by far the most popular way to get around in Beijing and other cities in China. On his first trip to Beijing, Wang Jian is staying with his cousin, Xu Johong, who lives in the capital. They plan to take a number of bike tours around the city and see its parks, palaces, and other buildings.

Jian and Johong have a map that outlines a route across the center of the city. It includes symbols for some of the famous landmarks along the way.

These are three of the sights they will look for along the bike route:

★ the famous Tiananmen Gate on the north side of Tiananmen Square.

★ the modern marble and glass Arts and Crafts Exhibition Hall.

★ the Ancient Observatory, an astronomical observatory that dates back to the Ming Dynasty.

Reading the Map

Follow the steps below to understand how Jian and his cousin can follow the bike route map and see the sights of Beijing.

1. Find the starting location on the map. As they begin their ride, the boys check the street sign and discover they are on Sanlihe Road at Fuchengmen Street. Find that spot on the map. **(a)** What route should they ride to get to Tiananmen Square? **(b)** Where should they turn? **(c)** If they ride east on Fuchengmen Street instead, what landmark building will they come to?

2. On the map, locate the sights they want to see. Check their locations and where they are in relation to each other. At the same time, notice what other interesting sights or buildings are on their way. **(a)** For instance, what buildings can Jian and Johong see as they ride along the road to Tiananmen Square? **(b)** When they are at Tiananmen Gate, what else can they see in the square?

3. Keep the map available to check the route and location from time to time. If Jian and Johong make a mistake or take a wrong turn, the map can help them find their way back to where they want to be. Suppose that after leaving Tiananmen Square, Jian and Johong suddenly find themselves riding past the Forbidden City on Wangfujing Street. What should they do to get back to Chang'an Avenue?

Tiananmen Square

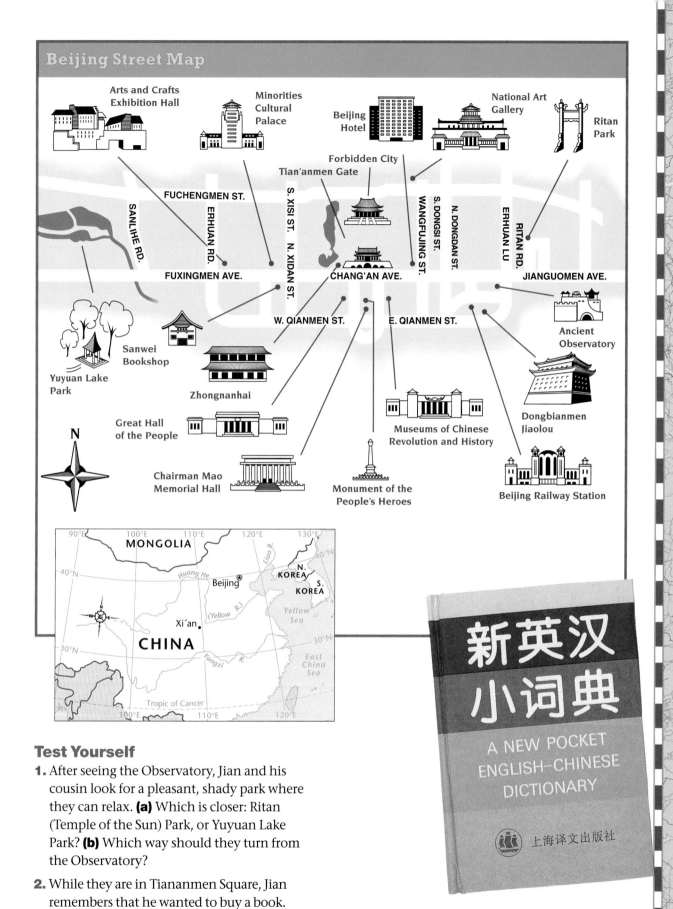

Beijing Street Map

Arts and Crafts
Exhibition Hall

Minorities
Cultural
Palace

Beijing
Hotel

National Art
Gallery

Ritan
Park

Forbidden City

Tian'anmen Gate

FUCHENGMEN ST.

SANLIHE RD.

ERHUAN RD.

S. XISI ST.

N. XIDAN ST.

S. DONGSI ST.

WANGFUJING ST.

N. DONGDAN ST.

RITAN RD.

ERHUAN LU

FUXINGMEN AVE.

CHANG'AN AVE.

JIANGUOMEN AVE.

W. QIANMEN ST.

E. QIANMEN ST.

Ancient
Observatory

Yuyuan Lake
Park

Sanwei
Bookshop

Dongbianmen
Jiaolou

N

Zhongnanhai

Great Hall
of the People

Museums of Chinese
Revolution and History

Beijing Railway Station

Chairman Mao
Memorial Hall

Monument of the
People's Heroes

MONGOLIA

90°E 100°E 110°E 120°E 130°E

40°N

Huang He

Beijing

N.
KOREA

S.
KOREA

Liao R.

(Yellow)

Huang He
(Yellow) R.

Xi'an

Yellow
Sea

CHINA

Yangzi R.

30°N

East
China
Sea

Tropic of Cancer

100°E 110°E 120°E

新英汉
小词典

A NEW POCKET
ENGLISH–CHINESE
DICTIONARY

上海译文出版社

Test Yourself

1. After seeing the Observatory, Jian and his cousin look for a pleasant, shady park where they can relax. **(a)** Which is closer: Ritan (Temple of the Sun) Park, or Yuyuan Lake Park? **(b)** Which way should they turn from the Observatory?

2. While they are in Tiananmen Square, Jian remembers that he wanted to buy a book. **(a)** How can they get back to the Sanwei Bookshop? **(b)** What public building is it near?

Japan and the Koreas

SECTIONS

1 Japan: The Land of the Rising Sun

2 Japan's Economic Development

3 The Koreas: A Divided Peninsula

Japan and the Koreas: POLITICAL

- Sea of Okhotsk
- *Hokkaido*
- Sapporo
- **NORTH KOREA**
- Sinŭiju
- P'yŏngyang
- Wŏnsan
- Namp'o
- Sea of Japan
- **JAPAN**
- Sendai
- Seoul
- Inch'ŏn
- **SOUTH KOREA**
- Taejŏn
- Taegu
- *Honshu*
- Tokyo
- Nagoya
- Yokohama
- Kyoto
- Kobe
- Osaka
- *Yellow Sea*
- Kwangju
- Pusan
- *Korea Strait*
- Hiroshima
- **PACIFIC OCEAN**
- *Cheju*
- *Shikoku*
- Nagasaki
- *Kyushu*
- *East China Sea*
- Ryukyu Islands (JAPAN)
- Okinawa
- *Philippine Sea*

KEY

— National boundary

⊛ National capital

• Other city

Lambert Conformal Conic Projection

learning LOCATIONS

Mapping the Region

Create a map like the one at left, shading each country a different color. Then add labels for countries, cities, and bodies of water that are shown on the map.

1 Japan: The Land of the Rising Sun

Japanese picnickers enjoy cherry blossom season.

Section Preview

Main Ideas

- The islands of Japan are part of the Ring of Fire, a region of tectonic activity surrounding the Pacific Ocean.

- Japan is one of the most densely populated countries in the world.

- Japan's population is both culturally and ethnically uniform.

Vocabulary

seismograph, typhoon, homogeneous

In ancient times, the Japanese knew of no people who lived to their east. They thought the sea was endless and that Japan was the land on which the rising sun first shed its light. According to legend, Amaterasu, the goddess of the sun, was the protector of Japan. The flag of modern Japan, a red circle on a white background, symbolizes Japan's special relationship with the rising sun.

A Country of Islands

Japan consists of an archipelago (AR kuh PELL uh GO), or chain of islands, that lies about 100 miles (160 km) off the coast of East Asia. The stormy Korea Strait and the Sea of Japan separate Japan from the mainland. The archipelago includes thousands of small islands, many of which are little more than large rocks. It also includes four large islands where almost all of Japan's people live. The largest, Honshu, is home to about 80 percent of Japan's population. South of Honshu are the islands of Shikoku and Kyushu. The farthest north of Japan's main islands is Hokkaido.

In the past, the seas surrounding Japan served to both isolate and protect it from invaders. The seas also provided links within Japan. Honshu, Kyushu, and Shikoku surround a body of water known as the Inland Sea. Sheltered from dangerous Pacific storms, the Inland Sea served as a major highway between islands.

The islands of Japan are actually the peaks of a great underwater mountain range. Millions of years ago these mountains began pushing up from the ocean floor when two tectonic plates collided in a subduction zone.

Because of its mountainous terrain, only about 13 percent of Japan's land is arable. Small and often inefficient farms are squeezed into small valleys between mountain ridges. To create more farmland, the Japanese carved terraces into hillsides and drained marshes, swamps, and deltas. Japan's best farmland has been created by the alluvial deposits of its rivers, including the Ishikari River, which cuts across the western half of the island of Hokkaido. These narrow plains, which make up only about one eighth of Japan's land area, hold most of its population.

The Ring of Fire Although Japan's islands are millions of years old, they are relatively new additions to the earth's surface. Japan is part of the Ring of Fire—a region of

◄ **Mt. Fuji, Japan** *(photo left)*

spectacular tectonic activity along the rim of the Pacific Ocean. Earthquakes and volcanoes are common in the region. In fact, Japan experiences more earthquakes than any other country in the world. Sensitive **seismographs**—machines that register movements in the earth's crust—record about 7,500 earthquakes in Japan each year. About 1,500 of these are strong enough to be felt by people.

The Japanese have learned to adapt to most of these mild earthquakes. About once every two years, however, Japan experiences an earthquake that causes serious damage and loss of life. If the epicenter of the earthquake is on land, the earth shifts and buckles, causing landslides in mountainous areas. Buildings, farmland, and whole villages may be destroyed. When an earthquake occurs offshore, the vibration can cause an enormous ocean wave, called a *tsunami*, which can devastate coastal lands.

As part of the Ring of Fire, Japan also has about 170 volcanoes, 75 of which are active. From time to time they erupt, sending showers of hot ash or molten lava down onto the surrounding countryside. The diagram on the next page shows how the region's tectonic forces result in Japan's volcanic activity.

Despite the dangers, volcanic activity has benefited Japan. In many places, volcanoes generate heat that warms underground water, creating hot springs. Resorts have been built up around these natural hot tubs.

Climate

If Japan were set along the east coast of the United States, it would stretch all the way from Maine to Florida. Japan's climates, like those of the eastern United States coast, vary according to latitude. The northern island of Hokkaido has

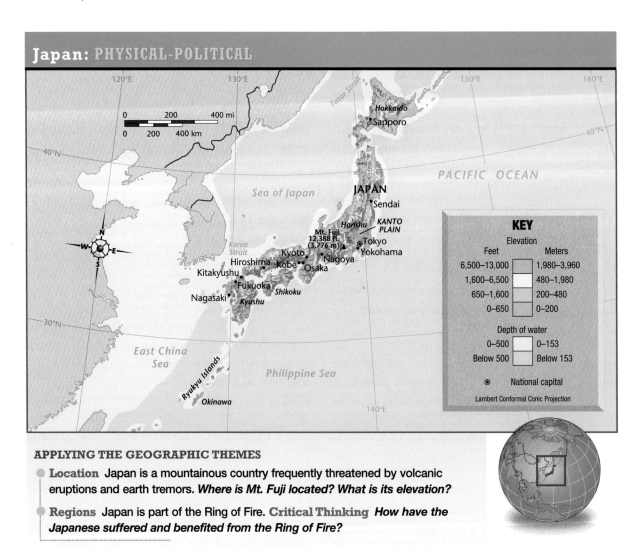

Japan: PHYSICAL-POLITICAL

KEY

Elevation

Feet		Meters
6,500–13,000		1,980–3,960
1,600–6,500		480–1,980
650–1,600		200–480
0–650		0–200

Depth of water

0–500		0–153
Below 500		Below 153

⊛ National capital

Lambert Conformal Conic Projection

APPLYING THE GEOGRAPHIC THEMES

● **Location** Japan is a mountainous country frequently threatened by volcanic eruptions and earth tremors. *Where is Mt. Fuji located? What is its elevation?*

● **Regions** Japan is part of the Ring of Fire. **Critical Thinking** *How have the Japanese suffered and benefited from the Ring of Fire?*

Volcano

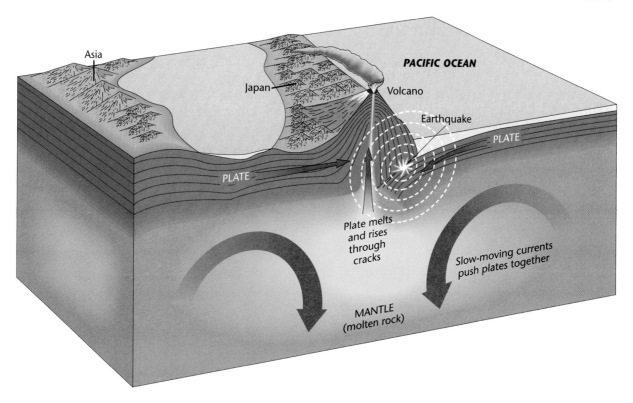

DIAGRAM STUDY

● The diagram above illustrates the shaky ground on which Japan stands.

Explain in your own words how the region's tectonic plate activity results in Japan's earthquakes and volcanic activity.

a climate like that of New England, with long winters and cool summers. Northern Honshū's climate is similar to that of the Mid-Atlantic states. In southern Honshū, the climate is similar to that of North Carolina, with hot summers and mild but sometimes snowy winters. Kyūshū and Shikoku, on the other hand, have climates more like that of Florida.

Monsoons Japan's seasons are affected by monsoons, or prevailing winds. In the summer, the monsoon blows onto the land from the east, bringing heavy rains and hot temperatures. From late summer to early fall is the season for **typhoons**. A typhoon is a tropical hurricane that forms over the Pacific Ocean, often causing floods and landslides. In winter the monsoon shifts, blowing in cold, dry air from the Asian mainland.

Ocean Currents Ocean currents also affect Japan's climate. The Japan Current, which flows northward from tropical waters along the southern and eastern coasts, warms the air. As a result, much of Japan has a long growing season that averages between 200 and 260 days. The cold Oyashio Current, on the other hand, flows southeastward along the east coast of Hokkaido and northeastern Honshu, cooling the air above it. (Review the ocean currents map on page 163.)

(Review the ocean currents map on page 163.)

GLOBAL issues

Globalization of Culture

What do you picture when you think of Japan? Probably not an American fast-food restaurant. But one restaurant chain, MacDonald's, has sold more hamburgers in a single day in its franchise in Enoshima, Japan, than in any of its franchises elsewhere in the world.

Capsule Hotels

● **Human-Environment Interaction** Space is tight in Japan, and highly valued. Shown here is a capsule hotel where patrons rent tiny rooms. In 1995 Japan had a population density of 857 people per square mile. At the same time the United States had 74 people per square mile. *What effect does Japan's high population density have on land prices?*

People and Culture

Japan is one of the world's most densely populated countries. Since the late 1800s, its population has more than quadrupled, climbing from 30 million to more than 125 million. Although Japan's entire area is about the size of California, it has nearly four times that state's population. Adding to the crowding is the fact that three quarters of the population live on the narrow coastal plain between Tokyo and Hiroshima. (See the population density map on page 603.)

Crowded Cities Population density has had far-reaching effects in Japan. For example, the shortage of space has driven up the prices of land and housing. Many families live in apartments in large high-rise buildings rather than in single-family homes. A family of four may share two or three small rooms.

This trend has had profound effects on the Japanese family. Traditionally, aging parents lived with their eldest son and his family. Now, older people often live by themselves or in special housing for the elderly. But great respect for the elderly is still part of the Japanese way of life.

Japan's large population and limited amount of land area also caused huge problems with pollution and waste disposal. In response, Japan has developed highly effective recycling and waste-treatment programs. Fifty percent of solid waste is now recycled in Japan, as compared with about eleven percent in the United States. In response to the oil crisis of the 1970s, the Japanese government enacted stringent pollution and energy efficiency laws. Japanese companies responded by developing technologies that used energy more efficiently and also decreased pollution. Over the past thirty years, the Japanese have made dramatic strides in cleaning up their crowded country.

Uniformity Japan's people share a common heritage. This shared ancestry makes

Japan's population **homogeneous**, or uniform. In fact, more than 99 percent of Japan's people have ancestors who lived in Japan thousands of years ago. Koreans are the only significant ethnic minority in Japan, and they make up only .5 percent of the population. Both ethnic and cultural similarities have enabled the Japanese to build a strong sense of national unity and identity.

Japan's isolated island setting helped to shape its society and its view of the world. From earliest times, the Japanese had a sense of their own separate, special identity. For years the Japanese actively tried to keep foreigners off their island.

A strong national identity has strengthened Japan but has also contributed to prejudice against the Ainu and the *burakumin*. The Ainu were the early native inhabitants of northern Japan who were excluded from Japanese society. The burakumin, although ethnically Japanese, are social outcasts and generally live in segregated communities. They are descendants of butchers and leather tanners who lived during feudal times. The Buddhist view against taking of life led to the negative feelings against the burakumin. The Koreans, the Ainu, and the burakumin all suffer from discrimination today.

Similar Religions Most of Japan's people also share similar religious beliefs and traditions. Japan's earliest people followed a religion known as Shinto. Shintoists worshiped the forces of nature and the spirits of their dead ancestors. Each household had an altar at which family members prayed and offered sacrifices. Today, while most of the holidays the Japanese celebrate are Shinto, the religion is no longer the focus of daily life. Nonetheless, it has had a great influence on Japanese culture, especially the Japanese people's great love of nature. To adapt this love of nature to crowded living conditions, the Japanese create miniature gardens that imitate nature. As one garden architect observed:

> *When I am arranging one stone after another, I am always entangling the stone with my dream and pursuing an ideal world of beauty.*

Zen Garden

● **Place** In "dry landscaping," the few elements of the Zen Buddhist rock garden represent nature. Individual rocks represent entire mountains, while the patterns raked into the bed of small stones represent water. **Critical Thinking** *How does such a garden reflect Japanese religion?*

The majority of Japanese also practice Buddhist traditions. Buddhism teaches that people should seek spiritual enlightenment or knowledge by overcoming selfishness and living modestly. The Japanese integrated or added Buddhist teachings into their Shinto beliefs.

Facts in BRIEF

Country	Population	Life Expectancy (years)	Per Capita GNP (in US $)
Japan	125,200,000	79	$31,450
North Korea	23,500,000	70	NA
South Korea	44,900,000	72	7,670
United States	263,200,000	75	24,750

Source: Population Reference Bureau   NA indicates data not available.

CHART SKILLS

● *Which country has the smallest population?*

● *Which country has the highest per capita GNP?*

● **Critical Thinking** *Which country has the highest life expectancy? What factors contribute to a high life expectancy?*

Shinto beliefs about the forces of nature and Buddhist teachings about the impermanence of life have both played a role in shaping the distinctive style of Japanese art. In accordance with Buddhist beliefs, artists suggest an idea, a thought, or a feeling with a minimum of detail. A few bold lines, for example, could suggest to the viewer the artist's impression of a mountain.

Japanese culture has also been greatly influenced by Confucianism, a philosophy that began in China. Confucianism stresses respect for the wisdom of older people and obedience to people in positions of authority, such as leaders, employers, parents, and teachers. Japanese society reflects the influence of Confucianism in its belief in the importance of the common good and in the high value it places on loyalty and respect for authority.

A Large Middle Class In most countries, modernization has gone hand in hand with the growth of the middle class. Nowhere is this more true than in Japan. Japan once had a small upper class of aristocrats and a large lower class of illiterate peasants. Today the vast majority of people belong to the middle class. This social and economic uniformity contributes to the homogeneity of the Japanese population.

Japanese popular culture is influenced by both Japanese traditions and ideas from the West. Like their Western counterparts, middle-class Japanese spend their leisure time watching television, going to the movies, or attending sports events. Styles and ideas travel both in and out of Japan. The Japanese have adopted many western sports, such as baseball, golf, and volleyball. On the other hand, sushi bars, architectural styles, and landscape gardening are all popular cultural "exports" to the West.

Section 1 Review

Vocabulary and Main Ideas

1. **Define: a. seismograph b. typhoon c. homogeneous**

2. **Name three of Japan's most important physical features.**

3. **How does Japan compare to the state of California in size and population?**

4. **What shared characteristics give Japan's people a strong sense of national unity?**

5. **Critical Thinking:** *Drawing Inferences* **Describe some ways in which you think a high population density might influence a region's culture.**

learning LOCATIONS

6. **Where is Osaka in relation to Tokyo?**

7. **What sea lies to the south of Japan?**

② Japan's Economic Development

Section **Preview**. . . . .

Main Ideas

- Japan was isolated from the West for centuries.

- Japan's limited supply of natural resources has influenced the country's history and economy.

- Several factors contributed to Japan's economic boom.

Vocabulary

militarism, downsize, tariff, quota

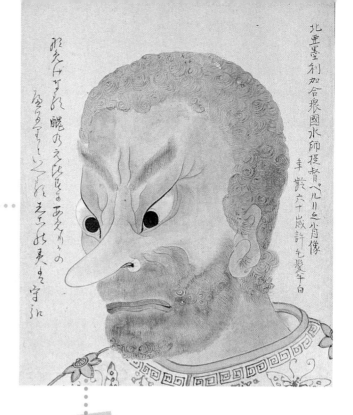

Portraits such as this showed the Japanese dislike of Commodore Perry.

A hundred and fifty years ago, Japan was an agricultural nation that had shut itself off from contact with other cultures. No one then could have foreseen that Japan would become one of the world's great industrial powers.

First Contacts

At the time of its first contact with the West, Japan had a highly developed civilization and was a prosperous nation. Trade between Japan and neighboring Korea, China, and Southeast Asia flourished. Its beautiful textiles were in great demand. From the court of the emperor in the charming city of Heian, now Kyoto, came impressive works of art and literature.

In 1543 the first Portuguese trading ships arrived in Japan. Traders were followed by Roman Catholic missionaries, who hoped to bring Christianity to Japan. At first, the Japanese welcomed the Europeans, but soon they began to worry that European nations might try to conquer them. As a result, in 1639 the government closed Japan's doors to the West, ordering most Europeans to leave the country.

A Forced Reopening

Japan's isolation lasted for more than 200 years. Then, in 1853, the United States government sent Commodore Matthew C. Perry to Japan to negotiate a trade agreement. Perry's request was backed up by a fleet of steam-powered warships. The Japanese knew that their weapons were no match for those of the United States navy, so they agreed to Perry's terms. In the next fifteen years, Japan was forced to sign treaties with other Western nations as well. These unequal treaties gave all the economic advantages to foreigners.

An Era of Reforms

In 1868 a new government took control in Japan. Its leaders were determined to modernize and industrialize the country so that it would no longer be at the mercy of foreign powers. The new emperor took the name Meiji (MAY jee), which means "enlightened rule."

During the period of the Meiji reforms, from 1868 to 1912, Japan underwent revolutionary changes. Meiji reformers sent hundreds of

The Meiji Era in Japan

Place One slogan from the Meiji era was, "Rich country, strong arms!" During the Meiji era, Japan industrialized rapidly. Industrialism and militarism were central to Japan's efforts to become competitive with the West in the late 1800s. **Critical Thinking** *How might this spirit have led to Japanese imperialism?*

Japanese to the United States and Europe to study Western institutions. Politically, the country became more democratic. A parliament, called the Diet, was created, and legal reforms made all Japanese men equal before the law. The government also established a new school system, so that all Japanese children could be offered a basic education. To promote rapid industrialization, the government paid for the development of railroads, mines, telegraph systems, and new industries. By 1900 Japan was strong enough to force an end to the unfair treaties and to deal with the West on equal terms.

Although Japan adopted many of the West's political and economic institutions, it did not wish to become a Western society. The Japanese practiced selective borrowing. They brought in only those ideas and innovations that seemed useful, adapting them to Japanese society. One of the Meiji leaders expressed his attitude in the following poem:

> *May our country,*
> *Taking what is good,*
> *And rejecting what is bad,*
> *Be not inferior*
> *To any other.*

Japanese Imperialism

Lack of natural resources was a serious obstacle to Japan's goal of becoming an industrial power. The two major resources needed for industry, iron ore to make steel and petroleum for energy, are almost nonexistent in Japan. These and other items needed by Japan's developing industries had to be imported. Following the Western example of imperialism, Japanese officials began efforts to gain control of weaker countries that were rich in natural resources.

At the turn of the century Japan fought and won wars with China and Russia, thereby gaining new territory and trading rights. The Russian defeat stunned Western nations. It was the first time in modern history that an Asian nation had defeated a major European power. The treaty ending the war gave Japan a foothold on the mainland in Manchuria. In 1910, Korea was forced to become part of Japan. During World War I, Japan joined the Allies. After the war, it was rewarded with control of Germany's former colonies in the Pacific Ocean.

The worldwide economic depression that began in 1929 took a terrible toll on Japanese industry. Many businesses were ruined, and unemployment soared. The government's inability to solve the crisis led to domestic troubles. Military leaders argued that the path to recovery was through more aggressive expansion in Asia. An overseas empire would provide Japan with markets, raw materials, and new land for its expanding population. As conditions grew worse, militarists were able to gain control of the government. In 1931 Japan invaded Manchuria, and in 1937, China. During the 1930s, Japan gradually became a military dictatorship. The new leaders promoted **militarism**, or the glorification of the military and a readiness for war. Military leaders encouraged people to believe that Japan's mission in the world was to free Asian nations from Western imperialism.

World War II

With the outbreak of World War II in Europe in 1939, Japan's leaders sided with Nazi Germany. When France and the Netherlands fell under Nazi occupation, Japan seized French and Dutch colonies in Southeast Asia.

On December 7, 1941, Japan attacked the United States naval fleet at Pearl Harbor, Hawaii, and the two countries went to war. Both suffered heavy casualties. The United States and its allies gradually destroyed Japan's ability to wage war. In August 1945, the United States dropped atomic bombs on the Japanese cities of Hiroshima and Nagasaki. Faced with the threat of this new superweapon, Japan quickly surrendered.

American Occupation

From 1945 to 1952, Japan was occupied by the United States army. It was the first time in Japanese history that the country had been ruled by a foreign power.

The United States introduced democratic reforms into Japan. The military leaders of Japan were removed from power. The Japanese emperor, who had been worshipped as a god, was stripped of his political powers. Finally, Japan's armed forces were disbanded, and Japan was forbidden ever to rebuild its military. The United States occupation forces introduced a democratic

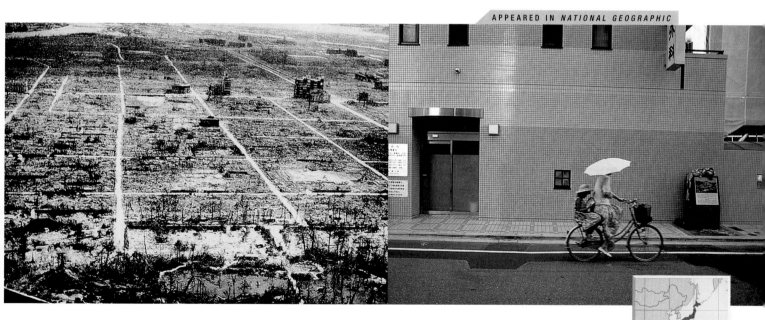

APPEARED IN *NATIONAL GEOGRAPHIC*

Ground Zero

● **Place** The unprecedented destructive force of the atomic bomb leveled three fifths of Hiroshima and killed 75,000 people in a matter of seconds (left). Today (right), little evidence of the destruction is evident in the city. The plaque to the right of the photo marks ground zero, the spot where the bomb exploded. *How was Japan able to recover so quickly from the devastation of World War II?*

constitution giving women legal equality with men. Large farms and businesses were broken up and sold to poor citizens.

The Economic Boom

In the years following World War II, the Japanese economy grew faster than any other economy in the world. Instead of seizing raw materials from conquered nations, Japan now obtained them through trade. Japan became known as the world's workshop because it imported raw materials and made them into finished goods for export.

At first, Japanese industries produced poorly made toys and novelties. Then the government encouraged a switch to expensive, high-quality goods such as cameras, electronic equipment, and motorcycles. By studying the methods used in Europe and the United States, the Japanese rapidly increased the efficiency of their factories. The quality of their goods gradually came to equal or surpass goods made anywhere. By the 1960s, Japan had become one of the most powerful industrial nations in the world.

Sources of Japan's Success

All over the world, people have admired Japan's economic success. Despite recent setbacks, Japan remains an economic superpower. How did this country, which began with so many seeming disadvantages, succeed so rapidly?

An Educated Workforce Japan's greatest natural resource has turned out to be its people. Education has always been very important in Japan. Today its people are among the most highly educated in the world. Almost all of its citizens attend high school, and a third go on to college.

Japanese schools have very high standards. The school day is long, and vacations are short. Students have a great deal of homework, and complete assignments during summer vacations.

To enter high school, students must take a special examination. To get into college, they must score well on another exam. Competition for places in the best schools is fierce, so many students take extra classes after school to help them perform better on these exams.

A Literate Nation

Place "Cram schools" like this calligraphy class give Japan's highly competitive students extra preparation for their exams. Japan's efforts in education are repaid by a literacy rate of 99.9 percent and have helped Japan keep a very low level of unemployment.
Critical Thinking
Why is education so important in an advanced economy like Japan's?

Women's Work

● **Place** Although women are represented in every sphere of the Japanese work force, only 1 percent of working women are executives. Tradition still pressures women to abandon their jobs when they marry. *In what ways have traditional work patterns begun to change in Japan?*

The Workplace Another reason for Japan's success during the boom years was the attitude and cooperative skills of its workers. Japanese employees worked hard and for long hours. They took pride in the success of their company and wanted to contribute to that success. In return for this dedication, Japanese companies provided many benefits for their employees.

During the growth years, large Japanese companies were frequently compared to families. Workers were often hired as soon as they graduated from high school or college. Once hired, Japanese workers were rarely fired or laid off, and very few workers ever quit their jobs.

Companies encouraged loyalty and team spirit in a variety of ways. Workers often assembled every morning to sing and exercise together. Many companies offered their employees low-cost apartments, making coworkers into neighbors. Coworkers often vacationed together on trips sponsored by the company. Companies also provided benefits like medical clinics, child care, and low-interest loans.

Today some of these traditional patterns are changing as the Japanese compete in the fierce international battle for profits. Like workers in the United States, Japanese workers now are finding themselves **downsized**, or fired, as their companies trim workers to save costs. Sometimes workers who refuse to retire early are given demeaning jobs to force them to leave.

Relative Location In recent years, Japan's growth was aided by shifts in patterns of global trade. Other Asian nations began to develop economically. As a result, Japan's relative location has changed. Instead of being far from the countries with which it trades, Japan is now at the center of active trade networks.

Government Planning In Japan, the government takes an active role in business. The Ministry of International Trade and Industry (MITI) is made up of leaders from business and government. MITI works to coordinate the efforts of Japan's many companies. For example, it sponsors

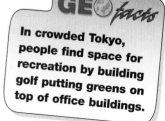

GEO *facts*

In crowded Tokyo, people find space for recreation by building golf putting greens on top of office buildings.

High Tech Robotics

Human-Environment Interaction The word robot comes from the Czech word *robota*, which means "drudgery." Robots, such as the ones pictured here in a Japanese car factory, are machines that are programmed to do routine, repetitive work in place of humans.

Critical Thinking *How might increased reliance on robots affect the Japanese work force?*

research to find out what kinds of products are wanted in foreign markets, then shares its findings with companies that might make these products. MITI plans far into the future, deciding what kinds of economic activity will bring the greatest benefit not to individual companies, but to Japan as a whole.

During the growth decades, the government aided businesses by controlling trade. For example, it passed laws requiring **tariffs**.

Tariffs are taxes on imports that make foreign goods more costly than their domestic equivalents. The government also sets **quotas**, or fixed total quantities, which limit the number of foreign-made cars or other goods that can be sold in Japan.

These policies have supposedly now ended. But old trading and consumer patterns linger on, making it difficult for foreign companies to sell their goods in Japan.

Section 2 Review

Vocabulary and Main Ideas

1. Define: a. militarism b. downsize c. tariff d. quota

2. Why did Japan cut off trade with the West in 1639? Why was trade reopened in 1853?

3. Why did Japan seek an empire in Asia?

4. What factors contributed to Japan's rapid economic growth after 1945?

5. Critical Thinking: *Synthesizing Information* What marketing problems would be encountered by an American film company selling its products in Japan?

learning LOCATIONS

6. What sea lies between Japan and the Koreas?

7. Where is Osaka located?

The Koreas: A Divided Peninsula

S ection Preview.............

Main Ideas

● Since 1945, the Korean Peninsula has been divided into two countries: North Korea and South Korea.

● Despite differences in political ideology, the people of North and South Korea share a common language, culture, and heritage.

● South Korea's economy has boomed under its capitalist system, while North Korea's economy has stagnated under communism.

Vocabulary

demilitarized zone, proliferation

APPEARED IN *NATIONAL GEOGRAPHIC*

With 21 percent of its land arable, South Korea produces many agricultural goods.

T he Korean Peninsula extends off the east coast of Asia between China and Japan. In area, the peninsula is about the same size as Minnesota. Though small, the peninsula is divided into two nations. North Korea, or the Democratic People's Republic of Korea, is a Communist country. South Korea, or The Republic of Korea, has a non-Communist government. Despite their political differences, the people of the Korean Peninsula share a common history and an ancient culture.

A Common Culture

Historians believe that the first people who lived in Korea came from the northwestern regions of Asia. Through the more than 2,000 years of Korea's recorded history, invading armies from Mongolia, China, and Japan have swept through the peninsula on numerous occasions.

Koreans adapted Chinese cultural ways to their own existing culture. They borrowed extensively from the Chinese writing system and adapted many Chinese words. The Korean language, however, is actually a branch of the Ural-Altaic group, which includes Finnish, Turkish, and Hungarian.

As did the Japanese, many Koreans accepted and integrated more than one religion and philosophy into their way of life. Daoism and Confucianism, for example, came from China. Later, many Koreans also adopted Buddhism, but they modified its teachings to fit their own existing culture. Today Buddhism is the most common religion among Koreans, though in the north, the Communist government discourages people from holding any religious beliefs.

The Korean War

In 1945, at the end of World War II, the Korean Peninsula became caught up in the Cold War struggle between Communists and non-Communists. The Soviet Union administered

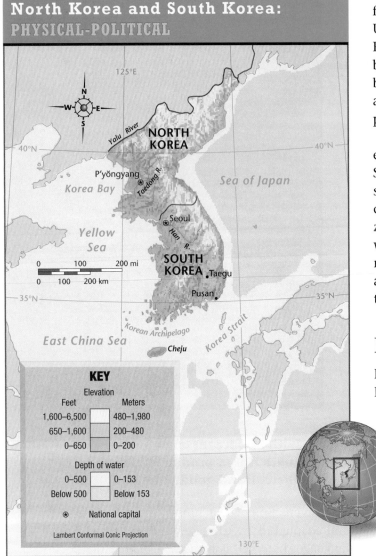

North Korea and South Korea:
PHYSICAL-POLITICAL

KEY

Elevation

Feet	Meters
1,600–6,500	480–1,980
650–1,600	200–480
0–650	0–200

Depth of water

0–500	0–153
Below 500	Below 153

⊛ National capital

Lambert Conformal Conic Projection

APPLYING THE GEOGRAPHIC THEMES

● **Place** *What kind of landform do the Koreas occupy? What is the capital of North Korea? What is the capital of South Korea?*

northern Korea, and the United States administered southern Korea. Both powers were expected to remove their troops as soon as Korea was able to govern itself. Instead, the Soviet Union established a Communist government in North Korea. In South Korea an election was held and American troops pulled out in 1949. Fearing life in a Communist state, more than 2 million Koreans fled to the south.

In 1950, the North Koreans launched a surprise attack on South Korea. Their objective was to unite the country under the rule of a single,

Communist government. United Nations forces from fifteen different countries, including the United States, came to the aid of South Korea. For three years the army of North Korea, helped by China, and the army of South Korea, helped by the United Nations, fought back and forth across the peninsula. An estimated 4 million people died in the fighting.

In 1953, a cease-fire agreement was signed establishing the division between North and South Korea near 38° N latitude—roughly the same as it had been before the fighting. The countries were separated by a **demilitarized zone**—a strip of land on which troops or weapons are not allowed. The Korean Peninsula remains thus divided today. More hostile forces are massed at this demilitarized zone, or DMZ, than at any other single place on the planet.

Different Environments

Beyond its political divisions, the Korean Peninsula is a land of opposites. The two countries that occupy its regions have different climates, landforms, and resources.

North Korea North Korea has about 23 million people and is less densely populated than South Korea. P'yŏngyang, the capital, is the only city with a population of more than 1 million.

Because it is located near the Asian mainland, North Korea is influenced by nearby continental climate regions. The climate is similar to that of southern Siberia, with short, cool summers and bitterly cold winters. The land itself is mountainous and rugged. Its fast-flowing mountain rivers have been harnessed to create hydroelectric power for its industries. North Korea also has some of the richest natural resources in East Asia, including coal, copper, iron ore, lead, tungsten, and zinc.

South Korea In contrast, South Korea, which is home to about 45 million people, is one of the most densely populated countries in the world. Almost a quarter of the population is concentrated in the capital city of Seoul.

South Korea is influenced by the moderating effects of the surrounding seas, and parts of

South Korea are actually subtropical in climate. It is less mountainous than North Korea and has wide, rolling plains. Because of its terrain and warmer climate, South Korea is better suited for agriculture than is its neighbor to the north.

A Changing Economy

At the time of the political division in 1953, South Korea was economically at a disadvantage. The best industries and hydroelectric plants were in Communist North Korea, and South Korea was overflowing with battle-weary refugees.

Communist states, such as China and the Soviet Union, became North Korea's new trading partners. South Korea, on the other hand, allied itself with the United States and Japan. With aid from its new economic partners, South Korea became industrialized. The government actively encouraged the development of both heavy and light industries. To solve its energy problems, South Korea built nuclear power plants. As a result, the country witnessed an impressive rate of economic growth in the ensuing years. South Korea also experienced the development of a new middle class, as well as an increase in its role in international trade and politics.

Today, South Korea is a major exporter of textiles, clothing, automobiles, and electronic goods. It is considered one of the new industrial powers of the region surrounding the Pacific Ocean.

Industrialization

Rapid industrialization has pulled at the social fabric of Korean culture. In an effort to compete economically with Japan and Western countries, family-owned businesses in South Korea have often treated workers unfairly. As a result of this conflict, massive labor strikes and political struggles have at times disrupted the country's economic growth.

Under Communist leadership, North Korea has continued to evolve from an agricultural to an industrial society. Despite the fact that it has greater natural resources than does South Korea, North Korea lags far behind its neighbor in its standard of living. Because the government alone decides what and how much to produce,

GLOBAL issues

Environmental Trade Barriers

In the early 1990s the United States placed an import ban on tuna fish caught by countries that use drift nets, including Japan and South Korea. Drift nets trap any living thing that swims in their path. The ban was credited with saving the lives of 130,000 dolphins in one year in the eastern Pacific.

A Consumer Society Takes Shape

● **Regions** The stores of Seoul, South Korea, are full of consumer goods. In recent years the nation has become a leading economy in the region, far outstripping North Korea's economy. *Has South Korea outperformed North Korea economically because its natural resources are richer? Explain your answer.*

Korea's Political Scene

- **Regions** This North Korean poster is promoting reunification of North and South Korea. *What are the political obstacles to reunification?*
- **Critical Thinking** *Why might North Koreans favor reunification?*

the North Korean economy has been in a prolonged decline.

Looking to the Future

Since 1953, North and South Korea have sometimes discussed reunification, but the two countries cannot agree on mutually acceptable terms. North Korea dreams of an exclusively Communist Korean Peninsula. As a successful capitalist state, South Korea will consider reunification only if both sides agree to cooperate peacefully, respect each other's system of government, and pledge not to use armed aggression.

In 1993 North Korea announced its withdrawal from the Nuclear Non-Proliferation Treaty. This treaty was designed to stop the **proliferation**, or increase in number, of atomic weapons around the world. The announcement from North Korea alarmed many nations, particularly South Korea. The crisis was patched over with help from the United States.

Later in the 1990s, however, a new crisis occurred as North Korea suffered flooding that severely damaged its ability to feed its people. As its economy staggered, some observers worried that North Korea might lash out at prosperous South Korea. When North Korea threatened to restart its nuclear program, the United States increased shipments of food and money.

Section 3 Review

Vocabulary and Main Ideas

1. **Define: a. demilitarized zone b. proliferation**

2. **How does the climate of the northern part of the Korean peninsula differ from that of the southern part?**

3. **What caused the division between North and South Korea?**

4. **Critical Thinking:** *Making Comparisons* **What cultural and economic factors do you think might encourage the people of North and South Korea to unite their countries? What factors might discourage unification?**

learning LOCATIONS

5. **Where is Seoul located in relation to North Korea?**

6. **Name three bodies of water that surround the Korean Peninsula.**

Focus on Skills

☐ Social Studies
☐ Map and Globe
☑ Critical Thinking and Problem Solving

Demonstrating Reasoned Judgment

Making connections between the things you know is the basis of reasoned judgment. This critical-thinking skill enables you to move beyond what is stated in a text and to reach your own conclusions. The statement below is followed by seven points of evidence that either support or contradict its message. Carefully read the statement about industry in Japan. Then use the following steps to practice using reasoned judgment about the statement and evidence.

1. Determine the main idea of the statement. Before you can evaluate any evidence, you must make sure that you understand the original statement. What is the main idea of the statement?

2. Examine the nature of the evidence. Before determining whether the evidence supports or contradicts the statement, it is necessary to determine the nature of the evidence. Answer the following questions: (a) Which of the points concern education? (b) Which points are related to social attitudes? (c) Which are concerned with national spending? (d) Which point concerns geography?

3. Look for relationships between the pieces of evidence. Analyze the evidence and try to infer information that may relate to the statement. (a) How would you describe the Japanese attitude toward education, based on points C and G? (b) What attitude toward women is suggested by points B and E?

4. Identify the relationship between the evidence and the statement. For each point of evidence ask yourself: Does this seem to prove or disprove the statement? Then decide whether the statement has been proven or disproven by all the evidence. (a) Which evidence seems to support the statement? (b) Which evidence seems to disprove the statement? (c) Based on the evidence here, do you agree or disagree with the statement?

Statement

Compared with industry in the United States, Japan's industry profits from a number of social and economic characteristics of Japanese life.

Evidence

A. Only about 1 percent of Japan's gross national product is devoted to military spending.

B. Women in Japan are discouraged from seeking jobs.

C. Japanese high school students attend class 220 to 240 days a year; in the United States, students attend for about 180 days.

D. Many company managers in Japan wear the company pin even when they're not working.

E. When they do find jobs, few Japanese women rise to positions of management.

F. Japanese industry must import most of its oil across great distances.

G. Teachers in Japan are highly respected and well paid.

Summarizing Main Ideas

Section 1 Japan: The Land of the Rising Sun

- The islands of Japan are part of the Ring of Fire—a region of tectonic activity surrounding the Pacific Ocean.
- Japan's high population density affects housing and family patterns.
- The Japanese people are united by a common ethnic heritage, a common language, and shared religious beliefs.

Section 2 Japan's Economic Development

- Japan was isolated from the West until 1543, and then again from 1639 to 1853.
- In the late 1800s Japan modernized and became a major industrial power.
- During the early twentieth century, lack of natural resources caused Japan to adopt imperialist policies. Its aggression in Asia led to war with the United States during World War II.
- Since 1945 Japan has enjoyed rapid economic growth.

Section 3 The Koreas: A Divided Peninsula

- The Korean War caused the death of nearly 4 million people. As a result of the war, the Korean Peninsula was divided into two countries: Communist North Korea and non-Communist South Korea.
- The people of both North and South Korea share an ancient history and culture.
- South Korea boasts a successful capitalist economy, but North Korea's Communist economy staggered.

Reviewing Vocabulary

Match each of the following definitions with one of the terms below.

1. to fire an employee to reduce costs
2. a strip of land free of troops and weapons
3. a tropical storm in the Pacific Ocean
4. a fixed number or quantity
5. a schedule of taxes on imports
6. an increase in the number of something
7. a machine that measures movements of the earth's crust
8. sharing the same characteristics

a. demilitarized zone   e. homogenous
b. tariff   f. typhoon
c. quota   g. downsize
d. seismograph   h. proliferation

Applying the Geographic Themes

1. **Location** Why does Japan experience many earthquakes?
2. **Movement** How did lack of movement between Japan and the West before 1853 affect that nation?
3. **Place** Why is the Japanese population described as homogeneous?
4. **Place** How has a limited supply of natural resources influenced Japan's history?
5. **Regions** What impact did the cold war have on the Korean Peninsula?

Critical Thinking and Applying Skills

1. **Drawing Conclusions** Why is education especially important to the success of Japan's economy?
2. **Demonstrating Reasoned Judgment** Look again at sentence A on page 659. Do you believe that the low percentage of gross national product devoted to military spending in Japan is an advantage or a disadvantage to Japanese industry? Explain your answer.

Journal Activity

Writing Across Cultures

▶ 1. Imagine you have a chance to win a scholarship to study for one year in Japan, South Korea, or North Korea. In your journal, write an essay in which you choose the country where you would like to study and explain the reasons behind your choice.

▶ 2. Write a letter from a resident of North Korea to a resident of South Korea, explaining why North Korea became a Communist country and describing everyday life in North Korea.

INTERNET link

Find out more about events in North and South Korea. Link to this site from:

- www.phschool.com

Choose one link of interest. Make notes on the information you read. Then pursue the same link for South Korea. Write a paragraph comparing and contrasting the information you gathered from both countries.

learning LOCATIONS

Japan and the Koreas

Number from 1 to 8 on a piece of paper. Next to each number, write the letter of the place on the map that corresponds to the places listed below.

1. Japan
2. North Korea
3. South Korea
4. Osaka
5. P'yŏngyang
6. Seoul
7. Tokyo
8. Kyoto

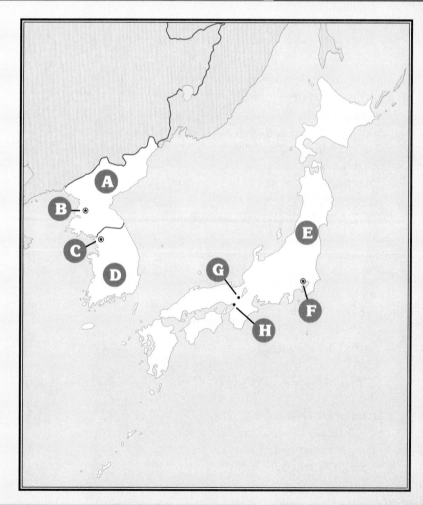

Southeast Asia

SECTIONS

1 **Historical Influences on Southeast Asia**

2 **The Countries of Southeast Asia**

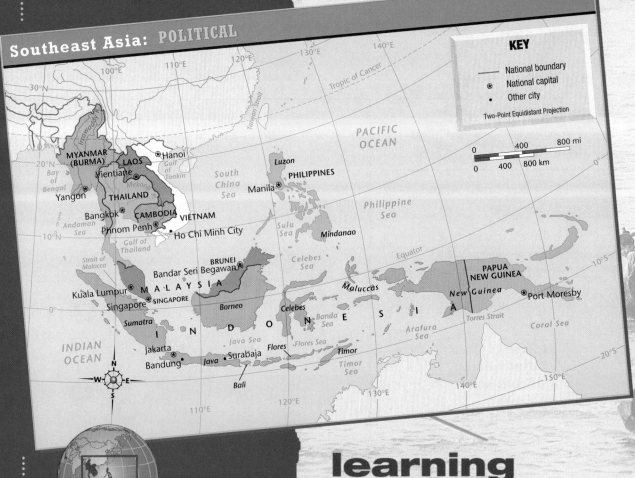

Southeast Asia: POLITICAL

KEY

— National boundary

⊛ National capital

• Other city

Two-Point Equidistant Projection

0   400   800 mi

0   400   800 km

PACIFIC OCEAN

Tropic of Cancer

MYANMAR (BURMA)

⊛ Hanoi

LAOS

Vientiane ⊛

Gulf of Tonkin

Luzon

PHILIPPINES

Manila ⊛

Bay of Bengal

Yangon

South China Sea

Taiwan Strait

THAILAND

Bangkok ⊛

CAMBODIA

Phnom Penh ⊛

VIETNAM

• Ho Chi Minh City

Andaman Sea

Philippine Sea

Mindanao

Sulu Sea

Strait of Malacca

Gulf of Thailand

BRUNEI

Bandar Seri Begawan ⊛

Celebes Sea

Moluccas

Equator

PAPUA NEW GUINEA

New Guinea

⊛ Port Moresby

Kuala Lumpur ⊛ M A L A Y S I A

Singapore • ⊛ SINGAPORE

Borneo

Celebes

I   N   D   O   N   E   S   I   A

Banda Sea

Torres Strait

Arafura Sea

Coral Sea

Sumatra

INDIAN OCEAN

Jakarta ⊛ •

Java Sea

Flores

Bandung • Surabaja

Java

Flores Sea

Timor

Bali

Timor Sea

learning LOCATIONS

Mapping the Region

Create a map like the one above, shading each country a different color. Then add labels for the countries, cities, and bodies of water that are shown on the map.

Historical Influences on Southeast Asia

Section Preview....

Main Ideas

- Many different groups of people settled in Southeast Asia.

- Hinduism, Buddhism, and Islam influenced the region's culture.

- European control greatly affected the physical and human geography of Southeast Asia.

Vocabulary

barbarian, paddy, indigenous

APPEARED IN *NATIONAL GEOGRAPHIC*

A Buddhist monk stands within view of the Cambodian temple Angkor Wat.

Southeast Asia's location makes it one of the world's great geographic crossroads. Many groups of people from distant regions have met here to trade. The cultures of India, China, Southwest Asia, and the West all influenced Southeast Asia. This rich variety blended with the cultures of native Southeast Asians to create a diverse and distinct region.

Early Movement

The earliest inhabitants of mainland Southeast Asia probably migrated to the region from southern China and South Asia. Over thousands of years, other people slowly moved south from central Asia and southern China into the region. Groups such as the Mons, Khmers (KMERz), and Thais eventually made their way down into the peninsula of Southeast Asia. They settled along the peninsula's rich river valleys and fertile coastal plains.

Indian Influence By the first century A.D., the Mons, Khmers, and other groups began to establish strongholds in Southeast Asia. No single group ever united the entire region, but various rich and powerful kingdoms did develop. Attracted by the wealth of these kingdoms, merchants from India sailed the coasts of Southeast Asia, bringing with them Hindu and Buddhist priests. Through their interaction with the people of Southeast Asia, these traders and priests greatly influenced life in the region.

Over the centuries, Indian culture and religion gradually blended with the culture of Southeast Asia. The people of Southeast Asia absorbed Hinduism and Buddhism into their existing religious beliefs. They adopted many Hindu myths and worshipped Hindu gods, but rejected other ideas such as the strict caste system. Southeast Asian rulers built palaces and temples in the Indian architectural style and dedicated them to Hindu gods. Others built Buddhist monasteries. Boys were encouraged to enter the monastery at an early age to learn to read and write. Although some became monks, the majority left the monastic life to marry.

Buddhist influences remain strong in much of Southeast Asia. Buddhist monasteries and temples are often at the center of village life. Farmers turn to Buddhist monks for advice on daily life and sometimes for political leadership.

Islam in Indonesia

● **Place** The Muslim influence in Southeast Asia can be seen in this Indonesian junior high school, which is run according to Muslim principles. *Which elements of the photograph show Islamic culture?*

● **Movement** *How did Islam first enter Southeast Asia?*

Muslim Influence Sometime between the 1200s and the 1400s, a new influence reached Southeast Asia. Traders from Arabia and India brought the Islamic religion to the region. Islam spread quickly along the trade routes. It reached the islands of Indonesia and spread as far east as the southern Philippines. Along with Buddhism and Hinduism, Islam became an important religion in the region. (See the religion map on page 602.) Islam created strong ties among the peoples of Malaysia, Indonesia, the southern Philippines, and other Muslim lands.

Chinese Influence Although many of the people who migrated to Southeast Asia came from China, the Chinese had little impact on the region. One reason was that the Chinese were not interested in exporting their culture. They viewed themselves and their civilization as superior, and they were not eager to share their culture with foreigners. They considered foreigners to be **barbarians**, or people without manners or civilized customs.

There was one exception. Around 100 B.C., China took control of what is today the northern part of Vietnam. For over 1,000 years Vietnam remained under Chinese influence. Vietnamese language, religious beliefs, art, government, and agriculture—all were affected by Chinese culture to some degree. But the Vietnamese never lost their identity. They kept their own customs, and although many Chinese words entered their vocabulary, they continued to speak Vietnamese.

Europeans Bring Change

Eager to gain access to the silks, spices, and precious metals in Southeast Asia, Portuguese traders arrived in Southeast Asia in the 1500s and set up trading posts. The Spanish, Dutch, British, and French soon followed. In the 1700s and 1800s, three changes in Europe caused these nation's colonies to expand deeper into Southeast Asia. First, Europeans acquired a taste for products such as coffee and tea that grew in tropical climates. Second, the rapidly expanding population in Europe led to an increased demand for these products. Third, the Industrial Revolution caused Europeans to look to Southeast Asia for not only the raw materials needed to produce factory-made goods, but for markets for these products as well. By the late 1800s, the Europeans had colonized all of Southeast Asia except for Thailand.

To take advantage of Southeast Asia's many natural resources, the Europeans drastically changed the region's physical and human geography. They cleared vast areas of forest and established plantations, or large farms, to grow cash crops such as coffee, tea, tobacco, and latex (raw rubber). They also encouraged rich, local landlords to grow rice for export. **Paddies**, the wet land on which rice is grown, spanned the deltas of the Irrawaddy, Chao Phraya, and Mekong rivers as far as the eye could see.

Southeast Asian farmers had traditionally tended their own small plots of land. However, they could not compete with the large landowners. Many small farmers were forced to leave their land and go to work on foreign-owned plantations and in the paddies of wealthy Southeast Asians.

The Europeans sold factory-made goods to their colonies. They undercut local crafts by

GLOBAL issues

Refugees

Starting in the mid-1970s, the forced migration of various Indochinese ethnic groups became a common occurrence in Southeast Asia. Changes in leadership in Cambodia, Vietnam, and Laos resulted in extensive ethnic purges. Hundreds of thousands of people from various Southeast Asian groups sought refuge in Thailand, the United States, and other countries.

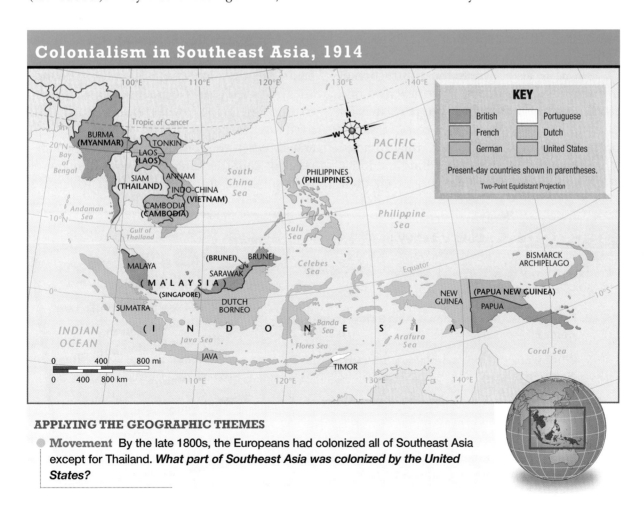

Colonialism in Southeast Asia, 1914

KEY

British — Portuguese
French — Dutch
German — United States

Present-day countries shown in parentheses.
Two-Point Equidistant Projection

APPLYING THE GEOGRAPHIC THEMES

● **Movement** By the late 1800s, the Europeans had colonized all of Southeast Asia except for Thailand. *What part of Southeast Asia was colonized by the United States?*

Asia's Key Crop

Human-Environment Interaction
No crop is more important for feeding humanity than rice, especially in Asia where 90 percent of the world's rice is grown. Rice is a single species of grass, but over 120,000 sub-species of rice are cultivated. *How did European intervention change the pattern of rice growing in Southeast Asia?*

selling cloth, tools, and other products more cheaply. Unable to compete with factory-made goods, local artisans were forced out of business. As a result, the economies of Southeast Asia became dependent on the industrialized nations for manufactured goods.

Europeans also financed the construction of inland roads and railroads. These new roadways carried crops and other goods to port cities for export to Europe. As these once slow, sleepy port cities began to grow rapidly, they attracted large numbers of people from China and India. Tensions sometimes developed between these new immigrants and **indigenous**, or native, Southeast Asians.

Colonization also greatly affected relations among different indigenous groups within Southeast Asia. When Europeans arrived in the region and carved out their own colonies, they paid little attention to existing ethnic boundaries. As a result, hostile groups often were united into one colony, while others, which had lived together peacefully for centuries, were separated. When the colonies finally became independent countries after World War II, many of them inherited deep ethnic conflicts.

Section 1 Review

Vocabulary and Main Ideas

1. Define: a. barbarian b. paddy c. indigenous

2. From where did Southeast Asia's first immigrants come?

3. What were the major religious influences on Southeast Asia?

4. How did Europeans change the geography of the region?

5. Critical Thinking: *Identifying Central Issues* What effect did location have on the development of cultures in Southeast Asia?

6. Which country in the region is located both on the Asian mainland and on an island?

7. What nation in Southeast Asia extends farthest north?

Focus on Skills

- ☐ Social Studies
- ☐ Map and Globe
- ☑ Critical Thinking and Problem Solving

Drawing Inferences

Drawing inferences means reading between the lines—forming conclusions that are suggested rather than directly stated. This skill is useful not only in evaluating passages in textbooks, but also in forming opinions about materials you read every day, such as newspaper and magazine articles. Inferences may be either limited or far-reaching in scope. Use the following steps to practice drawing inferences from the material you read.

1. Find the main idea of a sentence, paragraph, or longer passage. Before you can infer any conclusion, you must clearly understand what is stated. Read the passage below and then answer the following question: How can you summarize briefly the main idea contained in the passage?

2. Think about other facts you know about the same subject. Drawing inferences often requires you to draw upon information you have learned previously. (a) From which regions of the world, respectively, did the Buddhist, Muslim, and Christian religions first spread? (b) Historically, which regions have been among the primary sources of trade with Southeast Asia?

3. Infer conclusions from the text. Consider the main idea together with other facts that you know. Decide whether all of this information combined suggests additional facts or conclusions about the subject. Using the answers you gave in steps 1 and 2, answer the following question: What can you infer about the effects of trade and invasion on Southeast Asia?

Southeast Asia includes the mainland countries of Vietnam, Laos, Cambodia, Myanmar, and Thailand. It also includes the island archipelagoes of Indonesia and the Philippines, the Malay Peninsula, and the tiny island country of Singapore. Because landforms have kept most of the countries separated from one another, each country has developed its own traditions and its own way of life.

A thousand different languages and dialects are spoken in Southeast Asia, yet the people there follow only three main religions. Indonesia and Malaysia are mostly Muslim. Thailand, Myanmar, Vietnam, Cambodia, and Laos are mostly Buddhist. In the Philippines 92 percent of the people are Christian.

Southeast Asia is a vital crossroads for the trade and commerce of many nations. It's also a treasury of natural resources including tin, petroleum, latex, tea, spices, and kinds of fine wood. Southeast Asia's location and resources have made the region a target for frequent invasion.

The Countries of Southeast Asia

Citizens of Myanmar remain under the watchful eye of their military government.

Section Preview

Main Ideas

● Ethnic differences within countries in the region greatly complicate attempts to achieve national unity.

● Political repression is an ongoing problem in some Southeast Asian nations.

● Many of the nations of the region, including formerly Communist nations, are sharing in the Pacific Rim economic boom.

Vocabulary

insurgent, *doi moi*, heterogeneity

Most countries in Southeast Asia belong to the Association of Southeast Asian Nations (ASEAN). This organization, like the European Union, works to promote economic cooperation and peace among its members. Unfortunately, unity within many of these nations has often been hard to achieve. Although all of Southeast Asia is now independent, colonialism has left its mark on the region. In many cases, the factions that fought together to gain independence are having trouble learning to coexist and govern peacefully.

Myanmar's Struggle

Imagine a country about the size of Texas where more than 100 languages are spoken. That is the reality of Myanmar, formerly called Burma. About 69 percent of Myanmar's people are members of the Burman ethnic group and speak Burmese. The rest belong to a variety of ethnic groups and speak different languages. Sometimes people living in villages only miles apart may belong to completely different ethnic groups.

Throughout their history, these groups protected their cultural identities. When the British took control of the region in the late 1800s, they combined the people in Myanmar into a single political unit, but they made little attempt to unify them culturally. They allowed the people a great deal of autonomy. Partly for this reason, when Myanmar gained its independence in 1948, the new country lacked unity.

Since independence, various ethnic groups have fought against the government, some wanted to secede from the country; others tried to overthrow the government. Warfare with various ethnic **insurgents**, or people who rebel against their government, has greatly slowed Myanmar's economic growth.

Another cause of the weak economy is Myanmar's repressive military government. The leader in the fight for democracy in Myanmar is Daw Aung San Suu Kyi (daw awng sahn soo chee). She has led opposition to the government continuously for nearly a decade, even though she was under arrest from 1989 to 1995. In 1991, she won the Nobel Peace Prize for her efforts to bring change to Myanmar without violence. Pressing on with her struggle, she helped organize a meeting of opposition politicians in 1996. Though the government took harsh measures to try to stop the meeting, it went ahead as planned. Said Aung San Suu Kyi:

> *Giving in to bullying is not good. We must have the courage to face the bully's challenge. I am very pleased and satisfied to see the people have real courage.*

Thailand Prospers

The population of Thailand is not as divided as that of Myanmar. Though the population is made up of several groups, about 97 percent of the people speak Thai. Because of this cultural unity, as well as their long history as a free nation, Thailand's people have a strong national identity.

Preserving Independence Thailand is the one country in Southeast Asia that was not colonized by Europeans. Surrounded by colonial powers, Thailand's King Mongkut and his son, who ruled together from 1851 to 1910, made treaties with several European nations. The Thai say that they are like bamboo that bends in the wind: they have been flexible when dealing with foreigners in order to keep their independence.

Since World War II, Thailand has had close political ties to the United States. Threatened by the Communist revolution in China, it joined with the United States to stop Communist expansion in Southeast Asia. During the Vietnam War, Thailand allowed the United States to use its country as a base for air attacks against the Communists in Vietnam, Cambodia, and Laos.

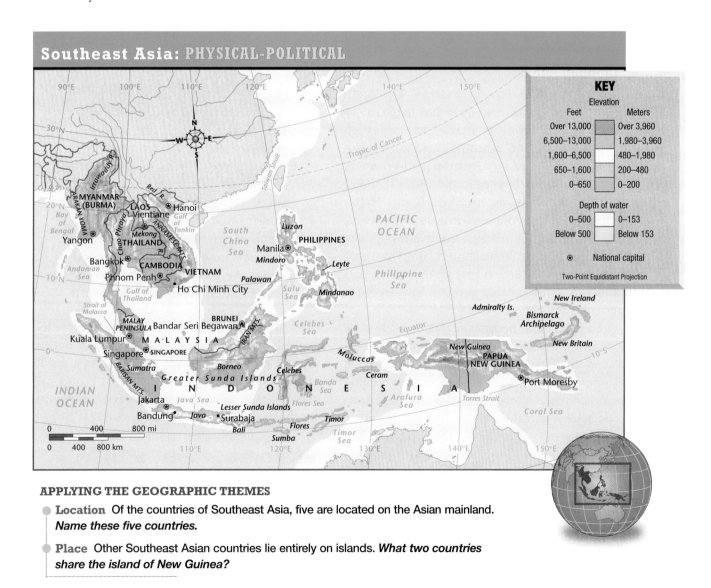

Southeast Asia: PHYSICAL-POLITICAL

APPLYING THE GEOGRAPHIC THEMES

Location Of the countries of Southeast Asia, five are located on the Asian mainland. *Name these five countries.*

Place Other Southeast Asian countries lie entirely on islands. *What two countries share the island of New Guinea?*

The New Thailand

● **Place** Bangkok, Thailand's capital and largest city, is also the center of the nation's flourishing economy. Once known for its leisurely pace, Bangkok has grown into one of the largest cities in the world, with a population of 6.6 million. *What are some of the important elements of Thailand's economic success?*

Progress Brings Change Thailand's ability to bend with the wind has helped it to build one of the strongest economies in Southeast Asia. Until recently, Thailand's economy was dominated by agriculture, and rice was its main export. However, in the 1960s Thailand began to diversify its economy. Today it has industries that produce cement, food products, paper, and textiles. Foreign companies operate plants that assemble machinery and electronic equipment. Manufactured goods now contribute more than twice as much to the economy as do agricultural products.

Tourism has become a major source of income for Thailand. In the last few decades, the tourist industry as grown significantly. Millions of foreign visitors flock to the country to enjoy its rich, varied culture, bringing with them nearly $5 billion annually.

Thailand's economic development has resulted in great changes. Bangkok, Thailand's capital, has become a transportation hub for the entire Southeast Asian region. Many international airlines serve this bustling city of skyscrapers, modern hotels, and noisy expressways. These modern structures stand in sharp contrast to the mysterious charm of traditional Bangkok, which one writer described in these words:

> *I still like Bangkok [because it is] a city of secrets. Not far from the railroad station, for example, stands a temple of ordinary exterior, Wat Trimit, containing an image of the Lord Buddha three meters high; it weighs five and a half tons—and is made of gold. Jewel merchants in simple shops may cover a desktop with a fortune in sapphires. . . . And behind the watery moat of the royal palace live the royal white elephants.*

Unlike Myanmar, Thailand has gladly opened its doors to the world, reaching out to interact with many other countries. As a result of this increased interdependence, Thailand has one of the most successful economies in Southeast Asia.

Vietnam, Laos, and Cambodia

Vietnam, Laos, and Cambodia are very different from one another ethnically. The overwhelming majority of the people in Vietnam are Vietnamese. In Cambodia, the vast majority belong to the Khmer ethnic group. Laos is ethnically more diverse. The country is home to Lao, Tai, Hmong, Yao, Mon, and Khmer, as well as Chinese and Vietnamese.

In other respects, Vietnam, Laos, and Cambodia have much in common. All of their cultures were influenced by India, and most of their people are Buddhists. As French colonies, the three countries together formed a region once known as French Indochina.

French influence in the area dates from the 1800s. By the early 1900s, Vietnam, Laos, and Cambodia had become French colonies. During World War II, from about 1940 to 1945, the Japanese took control of Indochina. But when the Japanese surrendered to the Allies in 1945, France was determined to regain its colonies.

Years of War France's attempt to return to power in Indochina marked the beginning of a series of long and bloody wars in the area. In 1945, Ho Chi Minh, a Vietnamese leader, declared Vietnam's independence from France. Ho Chi Minh's forces fought a bitter and fierce war with the French. In 1954, the French were defeated.

After the war, a peace conference was held in Geneva, Switzerland. Instead of ending the conflict, however, the conference laid the foundation for more fighting by dividing Vietnam into two parts. North Vietnam was left to the Communists under Ho Chi Minh. South Vietnam was headed by Ngo Dinh Diem (NGO DIN DEE em), a pro-Western ruler.

The Communists in North and South Vietnam wanted to reunite the two countries. Another war soon began which the United States entered, hoping to keep South Vietnam free of Communist control.

Neighboring Laos and Cambodia were also drawn into the fighting when Communists in those countries provided a supply line to the Communist insurgents in South Vietnam. The North Vietnamese set up bases in Cambodia, and the struggle between the Communists and non-Communists in Laos and Cambodia intensified.

The United States withdrew from the war in 1973 and South Vietnam fell to the Communists in 1975. Vietnam was reunited one year later. Communists also gained control

The Mekong River

Human-Environment Interaction
Putting the years of war behind them, Southeast Asians are trying to make use of resources offered by the Mekong. These wood-cutters are looking for trees to sell in foreign markets. **What other resources does a river offer?**

of the governments of Cambodia and Laos. In all three countries, the new governments killed huge numbers of non-Communists. In Cambodia, a brutal group called the Khmer Rouge (KMER ROUZH) murdered between 1 and 2 million people out of the total population of 7 million. Only an invasion by Vietnam in 1979 stopped the killings.

Facts in BRIEF

Country	Population	Life Expectancy (years)	Per Capita GNP (in US $)
Brunei	300,000	74	NA
Cambodia	10,600,000	50	NA
Indonesia	198,400,000	63	730
Laos	4,800,000	52	290
Malaysia	19,9000,000	71	3,160
Myanmar	44,800,000	60	NA
Papua New Guinea	4,100,000	57	1,120
Philippines	68,400,000	65	830
Singapore	3,000,000	74	19,310
Thailand	60,200,000	70	2,040
United States	263,200,000	75	24,750

Source: Population Reference Bureau   NA indicates data not available.

CHART SKILLS

- *Which country, aside from the United States, has the highest population?*

- **Critical Thinking** *Which country has the lowest life expectancy? How does it compare with that of the United States?*

Prospects for the Future Astounding changes have taken place since Communist forces swept over South Vietnam in 1975. In 1986, Vietnam began a program of economic change called *doi moi* (dwa mwah). The keystone of the program was attracting foreign investors. During the early 1990s, Vietnam's economy boomed, growing 8 percent each year. It went from a once-starving nation to the world's third largest exporter of rice. Even companies from its former enemy, the United States, were pouring money into the Vietnamese economy as they scrambled to compete with European businesses.

To encourage this effort, in 1995 the United States resumed official diplomatic relations with Vietnam. Also in that year, Vietnam joined ASEAN, which had originally been founded to counteract Communist aggression by Vietnam.

However, economic freedom in Vietnam has not yet brought about political freedom.

Laos and Cambodia have also turned away from strict government-controlled economies. Still, they have not attracted investment on the scale of Vietnam. Laos, more stable than Cambodia, joined ASEAN in July 1997.

Indonesia and the Philippines

Cultural **heterogeneity**, or lack of similarity, also challenges two other Southeast Asian nations. In Indonesia, more than 250 languages and dialects are spoken; in the Philippines, about 70 languages and dialects are spoken. These nations are also physically splintered. Indonesia has more than 13,660 islands, and the Philippines more than 7,100. What keeps countries with such variety united?

Indonesia Uniting Indonesia has required great effort. Indonesia has nearly 200 million people living on islands spread over 3,200 miles (5,100 km) of ocean. The government has been a very strong force in the lives of the people—some would say too strong. The military, under General Suharto, who celebrated thirty years of power in 1996, has sometimes enforced unity by violent means. It has often been criticized for failing to respect human rights, particularly in the region of East Timor. In 1999, after much violence, East Timor voted for independence and came under UN administration.

Strong government rule has had some advantages. Indonesia has achieved tremendous economic growth in the past thirty years. Annual per capita income rose from $50 to $960 between 1966 and 1996. Today Indonesia is racing to catch up with economic giants like South Korea and Singapore.

A good part of Indonesia's success can be linked to its oil resources. Indonesia, a member of OPEC, is a major producer of petroleum. Oil has given Indonesia money to spend on roads, airports, and schools. As a result of ample spending and planning, illiteracy dropped from 61 percent in 1960 to 23 percent in 1990. The government has also focused on developing the country's agriculture to ensure that the people could feed themselves.

The Philippines Unlike Indonesia, the Philippines experienced a long period of strong colonial rule. The Spanish ruled the Philippines for 333 years, until their defeat by the United States in the Spanish-American War in 1898. Independence from the United States came in 1946.

The people of the Philippines were strongly influenced by their colonial rulers. Spanish priests converted the Filipinos to the Roman Catholic religion. Today more than 90 percent of the current population of the Philippines is Roman Catholic. Many native Filipinos married Spanish people. This intermarriage spread the Spanish culture among various ethnic groups and helped to unite them.

The United States also had a great impact on the Philippines. It introduced a new educational system in which English was taught. Along with Pilipino, English is an official language of the Philippines. The United States also introduced democracy to the country. Western cultural influences and a shared Asian heritage help give the people of the Philippines a sense of national unity.

Today the Philippines is struggling with a high birth rate of about 30 per 1000 people, about twice the United States rate. The growth in population means that Filipinos do not have enough wealth, food, or work to go around. About 4.2 million Filipinos work overseas because they cannot find jobs at home.

Singapore

Represented by little more than a dot on world maps, Singapore is Southeast Asia's smallest country. It consists of a single city located on one main island and more than fifty smaller surrounding islands. But this tiny country casts a big shadow because of its political and economic power.

Singapore's physical features and relative location played an important role in its success. It has a deep, natural, sheltered harbor. Its location at the southern tip of the Malay Peninsula

GLOBAL issues

Conflicts and the Environment

Forests once covered approximately two thirds of Vietnam's land. The spraying of herbicides, such as Agent Orange, by the United States during the Vietnam War caused extensive destruction to Vietnam's vegetation. Today only about one third of Vietnam is forested.

The Pinatubo Effect

Place The 1991 eruption of Mt. Pinatubo, a volcano on the Philippine island of Luzon, had massive local and global effects. Heavy mudslides killed more than 800 Filipinos, and the cloud of volcanic ash from the eruption had a cooling effect on the global climate. *What other problems have the Philippines faced in recent years?*

places it in the center of an important trade route between Europe and East Asia.

From its beginning as a British trading post in 1819, Singapore prospered and attracted immigrants from Malaysia, China, and India. It became an independent country in 1965. Singapore's former leaders pushed through laws favorable to foreign investors. By keeping wages low, they attracted foreign companies eager to produce goods cheaply. Singapore actively courted high-tech companies and built a modern educational system to provide the highly skilled workers needed to work in high-tech industries.

Modern Singapore is a thriving center of international trade and an important manufacturing center. It is one of the world's busiest ports. Thousands of ships dock at Singapore each year carrying rubber, wood, petroleum products from Singapore's refineries, and many other goods.

Malaysia and Brunei

Like Singapore, Malaysia and Brunei have strong economies that are not based on agriculture. Malaysia and Brunei are two of the wealthiest countries in Southeast Asia.

About 50 percent of Brunei's wealth comes from its large reserves of oil and natural gas. Income from these natural resources enabled Brunei to modernize. Some remote villages now have electricity and running water. The government provides free schooling and medical care for its citizens.

Malaysia supports a wide variety of economic activities. Machinery and transport equipment, oil, and other raw materials are its

Tradition and Change in Malaysia

Human-Environment Interaction Malaysia has had one of the world's fastest growing economies over recent years. Yet traditional ways of life are still common in many parts of the nation. **Critical Thinking** *How might Malaysia benefit by retaining traditional cultures where possible?*

leading exports. As does Brunei, Malaysia uses its oil revenues to help develop manufacturing and improve agriculture.

Papua New Guinea

Like its larger neighbors, Papua New Guinea is ethnically diverse, with some 700 ethnic groups. It is actually part of two overlapping regions—Southeast Asia and Oceania. And it seems to straddle two worlds—one traditional, the other modern.

More than 80 percent of Papua New Guinea's 4.1 million people are engaged in agriculture. Villagers in the remote highlands still plant their crops with traditional tools. Communication is poor because there are no roads to many of the country's far-flung villages. Only one out of every fifty-nine people has a telephone. Electricity reaches only a small percentage of the nation.

In sharp contrast, modern machines are used to mine great quantities of gold and copper ore in Papua New Guinea. In village stores, you will find modern goods such as canned beef, rice, and sugar imported from Japan and Australia. The prospects are that early in the next century Papua New Guinea will become a more culturally integrated, modern consumer state.

Traditional Cultures of Papua New Guinea

● **Human-Environment Interaction** Papua New Guinea's forbidding physical geography has helped its traditional cultures survive. This woodcarver lives on Trobriand Island in the isolated Solomon Sea. *What is the most common occupation for the people of Papua New Guinea?*

Section 2 Review

Vocabulary and Main Ideas

1. Define: a. **insurgent** b. *doi moi* c. **heterogeneity**

2. What challenges do Indonesia and the Philippines have to work constantly to overcome?

3. Why was Daw Aung San Suu Kyi awarded a Nobel Peace Prize?

4. How has *doi moi* affected Vietnam's relations with other nations?

5. Critical Thinking: *Analyzing Information* Why would a Communist nation like Vietnam decide to invite investment by capitalist nations?

6. Where is Singapore located?

7. What two nations share the island of New Guinea?

Summarizing Main Ideas

Section 1   Historical Influences on Southeast Asia

- Early in its history, many different ethnic groups settled Southeast Asia.
- Because of its location at the center of an important trade route and its rich resources, the region was influenced by the cultures of India, China, Southwest Asia, and the West.

Section 2   The Countries of Southeast Asia

- Ethnic differences have hindered national unity in many nations in Southeast Asia. Some nations have hundreds of different ethnic groups and languages.
- Political repression continues in nations such as Myanmar, Vietnam, and Indonesia.
- With a few exceptions, the nations of the region are rapidly expanding their economies as part of the boom in trade that is taking place on the Pacific Rim.

Critical Thinking and Applying Skills

Drawing Inferences Read the passage below and then answer the questions that follow:

Singapore, which has one of the world's largest ports, is an independent nation. It boasts one of the highest per person incomes in Asia. While Singapore has become an economic "tiger," it also has developed an authoritarian government. The people do not enjoy many freedoms.

Reviewing Vocabulary

Choose the term in parentheses that best completes each sentence.

1. The wet land on which rice is grown is known as a **(paddy/swamp)**.
2. People who are native to a particular country or culture are **(immigrant/indigenous)**.
3. People who rebel against their own government are called **(insurgents/immigrants)**.
4. A person without civilized customs might be called a **(bohemian/barbarian)**.
5. Thailand has had more success in unifying its people because it has less cultural **(homogeneity/heterogeneity)** than other Southeast Asian nations.

Applying the Geographic Themes

1. **Movement** What religions spread to Southeast Asia from India, Southwest Asia, and Europe?
2. **Location** Why is Southeast Asia booming economically?
3. **Human-Environment Interaction** Why did the Europeans change the environment of Southeast Asia?
4. **Place** Why do the Thai people compare themselves to bamboo that bends in the wind?
5. **Location** How were Laos and Cambodia drawn into the Vietnam War?

a. Which factor mentioned in the passage explains Singapore's economic growth in terms of its geographical location?

b. Identify one economic advantage of living in Singapore as opposed to living in many other countries of the region.

c. What do you think the writer of the passage means by describing Singapore as an economic "tiger"?

Journal Activity

Writing Across Cultures

▶ 1. Interview someone who has strong memories of the Vietnam War era. Ask his or her opinion of the war and the changes it has brought to relations between Vietnam and the United States. Prepare for your interview by writing out a list of questions you intend to ask. After your interview, write up a complete, accurate account in your journal.

▶ 2. Write a short story in which you describe a journey through Southeast Asia by boat. Plan your story by consulting the map and listing the countries in the order in which you would be likely to visit them.

INTERNET link

Learn more about Daw Aung San Suu Kyi, the leader of the opposition in Myanmar who spent years under house arrest and was awarded the Nobel Peace Prize. Link to this site from:

• www.phschool.com

Follow a few links of interest, then write about your impressions of Suu Kyi.

learning LOCATIONS

Southeast Asia

Number from 1 to 12 on a piece of paper. Next to each number, write the letter of the place on the map that corresponds to the places listed below.

1. Cambodia
2. Ho Chi Minh City
3. Indonesia
4. Laos
5. Malaysia
6. Myanmar
7. Manila
8. Papua New Guinea
9. Thailand
10. Vietnam
11. Bangkok
12. Phnom Penh

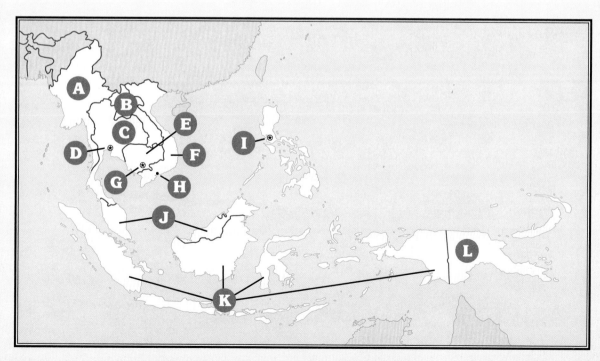

The Pacific World and Antarctica

Australia and New Zealand: POLITICAL

KEY

—— National boundary

⊛ National capital

✪ State capital

• Other city

Mercator Projection

Timor Sea · Arafura Sea · Coral Sea · Gulf of Carpentaria

Darwin

NORTHERN TERRITORY

Cairns · Great Barrier Reef

Tropic of Capricorn

AUSTRALIA · QUEENSLAND

Alice Springs

Brisbane

WESTERN AUSTRALIA · Lake Eyre

SOUTH AUSTRALIA · Darling R. · NEW SOUTH WALES · Newcastle

Kalgoorlie · Lochlan R. · Sydney

Perth · Great Australian Bight · Elizabeth · Adelaide · Murray R. · Canberra

Tasman Sea · Auckland · North Island

Melbourne · VICTORIA

Warrnambool · Bass Strait · Wellington

NEW ZEALAND

TASMANIA · Christchurch

Hobart · South Island

INDIAN OCEAN

0   400   800 mi
0   400   800 km

learning LOCATIONS

Mapping the Region

Create a map like the one above, shading each country a different color. Then add labels for countries, cities, and bodies of water that are shown on the map.

1 Australia

Section Preview

Main Ideas

- The population of Australia is small because the continent was considered remote in the past, and much of the climate is harsh.

- Australia's eight major cities lie along or near the coast.

- Australians have used the country's interior for mining resources and for raising sheep and cattle.

Vocabulary

Aborigine, lagoon, cyclone, outback, artesian well

Golfers play alongside kangaroos, one of the many animals found only in Australia.

Australia is both a continent and a country. In area, it is the world's sixth largest country and the smallest, flattest, and—except for Antarctica—driest continent. About 18 million people live in Australia. That's only about 2 million more than live in New York City. Yet Australia is nearly as large in area as the entire United States. Why is such a vast land so underpopulated? To answer this question, you must look at Australia's climate, natural vegetation, and the pattern of settlement and land use.

A History of Movement

Scientists think that the first Australians, known as **Aborigines** (ab uh RIJ uh neez), crossed a land bridge from Southeast Asia to Australia about fifty thousand years ago. The Aborigines were nomadic hunters and gatherers. They lived in small groups and spoke as many as 250 distinct languages. While customs varied from one group to another, they shared some things in common, including a deep respect for nature and the land.

At some point the land bridge connecting Australia to Southeast Asia sank under the sea, leaving the Aborigines isolated from the rest of the world for thousands of years. Australia's isolation ended in 1770, however, when Captain James Cook landed on the east coast of Australia and claimed it for Great Britain.

European Settlement The European settlement of Australia began in earnest eighteen years after Cook arrived. Britain quickly came to see Australia as a solution to the problem of its prisons, which were overcrowded with the poor. In 1787 the first group of prisoners boarded ships for the long journey to the southern continent. Many of them arrived in Sydney Harbor still wearing leg irons.

During the next eighty years, more than 160,000 men, women, and children were transported to Australia's distant shores. After their sentences ended, many prisoners stayed. Other settlers from Britain joined them, looking for land on which to raise sheep and grow wheat.

Meanwhile, the Aborigines suffered tremendous losses, killed by European diseases or weapons. The number of Australians who are completely Aborigine in ancestry sank from 300,000 in the 1700s to only about 50,000 today.

◀ **Sydney Harbor, Australia** *(photo left)*

Even while the Aborigine population was dwindling, the European population continued to grow, especially since the early 1900s. Until the end of World War II, most of Australia's immigrants came from Great Britain. After the war ended, large numbers of immigrants came from Greece, Italy, and other countries in southern and eastern Europe. Today many immigrants come from the nearby countries of Southeast Asia. They come because of Australia's location in the Pacific Ocean, and because of its high standard of living.

Land Use and Population

Australia's hot, dry climate and forbidding interior have greatly affected the country's settlement and land use patterns. As immigrants entered Australia, they sought out the areas that had the mildest climates. Look for these regions on the climate map on page 681. Notice that the moist and mild climates are along the eastern and southeastern coasts, while the interior of the continent is extremely hot and dry.

Now look closely at the population density map below. Notice that the vast majority of Australians live in cities located along the eastern and southeastern coasts—the so-called Urban Rim. In fact, 90 percent of Australia's population live within 100 miles (160 km) of the ocean. Commenting on the pattern of settlement in Australia, one author has noted:

In shape, Australia resembles a ragged square, but the real Australia where people live and work is a ribbon.

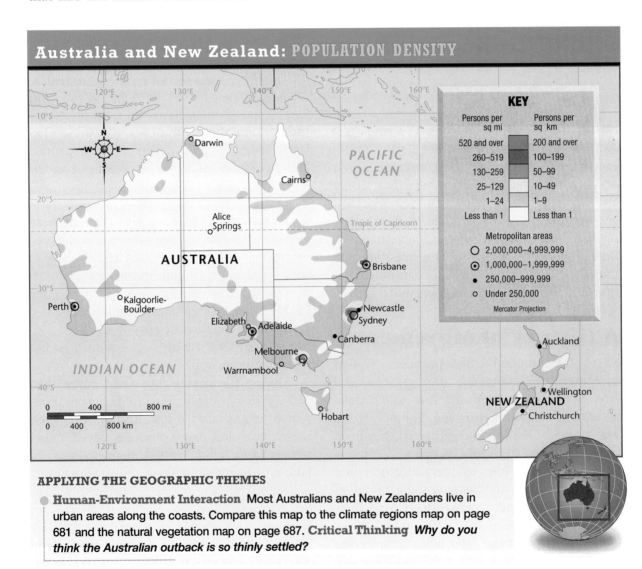

Australia and New Zealand: POPULATION DENSITY

KEY

Persons per sq mi	Persons per sq km
520 and over	200 and over
260–519	100–199
130–259	50–99
25–129	10–49
1–24	1–9
Less than 1	Less than 1

Metropolitan areas
○ 2,000,000–4,999,999
◉ 1,000,000–1,999,999
● 250,000–999,999
○ Under 250,000

Mercator Projection

APPLYING THE GEOGRAPHIC THEMES

● **Human-Environment Interaction** Most Australians and New Zealanders live in urban areas along the coasts. Compare this map to the climate regions map on page 681 and the natural vegetation map on page 687. **Critical Thinking** *Why do you think the Australian outback is so thinly settled?*

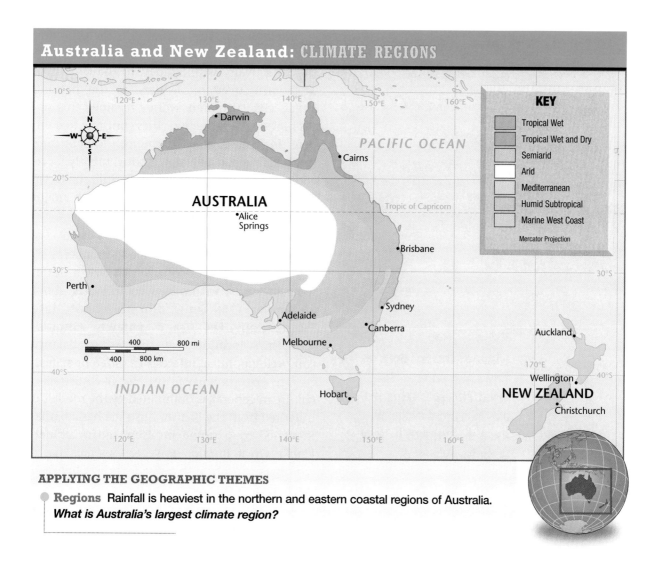

Australia and New Zealand: CLIMATE REGIONS

KEY
- Tropical Wet
- Tropical Wet and Dry
- Semiarid
- Arid
- Mediterranean
- Humid Subtropical
- Marine West Coast

Mercator Projection

APPLYING THE GEOGRAPHIC THEMES

● **Regions** Rainfall is heaviest in the northern and eastern coastal regions of Australia. *What is Australia's largest climate region?*

This, then, is the answer to the question about Australia's population. The population is small because relatively few people moved to the remote continent from other nations. And Australia's harsh climate discourages widespread settlement in the interior.

A Ribbon of Cities

Australia's population clusters in and around the eight largest cities. These cities include the capitals of Australia's seven states, plus Canberra, the national capital. Each city derives its own distinct flavor from its location, its landscapes, and its varied people.

Perth and Adelaide The huge state of Western Australia sits astride the Great Sandy, Gibson, and Great Victoria deserts. This region is very sparsely populated, with less than two persons per square mile (less than one person per sq

km). In this vast, empty area, Perth stands out as one of the world's most remote cities. Located on the western coast of Australia, Perth is more than 1,400 miles (2,300 km) from the next major city. If you flew east from Perth along Australia's southern coast, you would spend hours looking at barren land and small, isolated towns—until you reached Adelaide. A city of one million people, Adelaide is the capital and major city of the state of South Australia.

Australia's Urban Rim Three of Australia's most important cities—Sydney, Melbourne, and Canberra—lie within the Urban Rim. Moist winds from the Pacific Ocean and the Tasman Sea rise and cool as they approach the highlands, depositing their moisture in frequent rains. This weather pattern makes the Urban Rim one of Australia's best-watered and most fertile regions.

A WORLD OF eXtremes

Great Barrier Reef

Extremely Large
Stretching in a broken chain for 1,250 miles (2,000 km), Australia's Great Barrier Reef is the largest coral reef in the world.

Natural Formation
Made of the skeletons of tiny sea creatures, the Great Barrier Reef is the only structure made by animals that can be seen from the Moon.

A World of Diversity
Hundreds of varieties of coral grow on the reef. The staghorn is one of the most common types.

Sydney is the capital of the state of New South Wales, and is Australia's oldest and largest city. Sydney's splendid harbor is laced with small coves and crowned by the Sydney Opera House, which looks from the water like sails billowing in the wind.

Melbourne, the capital of Victoria and Australia's second-largest city, has a long-standing rivalry with Sydney. In the late 1800s Melbourne overtook Sydney as the nation's largest city. Although Sydney regained this status in the 1900s, the two cities continue to compete for trade and commerce. Melbourne's south-facing harbor is not as conveniently located for world markets as Sydney's. Still, the factories of the Melbourne area make it a major source of goods for Australia.

Canberra Australia's capital, Canberra, is the country's only major planned city. It lies in federal territory within New South Wales, about 100 miles (160 km) from the coast. Like Washington, D.C., and Ottawa, Ontario, Canberra's location was selected to balance competing political interests in different states.

The government of Australia, like Australian culture in general, is dominated by the models it inherited from the British. Australia has a parliament led by a prime minister and a cabinet. Unlike Great Britain, however, Australia has a written constitution that divides power between the federal government and the states.

Across the Bass Strait Hobart is the capital of the island state of Tasmania. This island hangs off the southeastern coast of Australia like a geographic punctuation mark. Tasmania was not always an island. About twelve thousand years ago, rising ocean levels covered the land that connected it to the mainland and created the Bass Strait.

The island of Tasmania is mountainous and heavily forested; Hobart is cradled in deep blue peaks. With only about 181,000 inhabitants, Hobart is much smaller than the mainland cities of Sydney or Melbourne.

The Sunshine Coast Showered with frequent rains from moist trade winds, the east coast of Queensland is Australia's wettest region. This region, which includes Queensland's capital city, Brisbane, is in the heart of Australia's vacation land. Known as the "Sunshine Coast," its humid subtropical climate and many lovely beaches attract millions of tourists to the region each year.

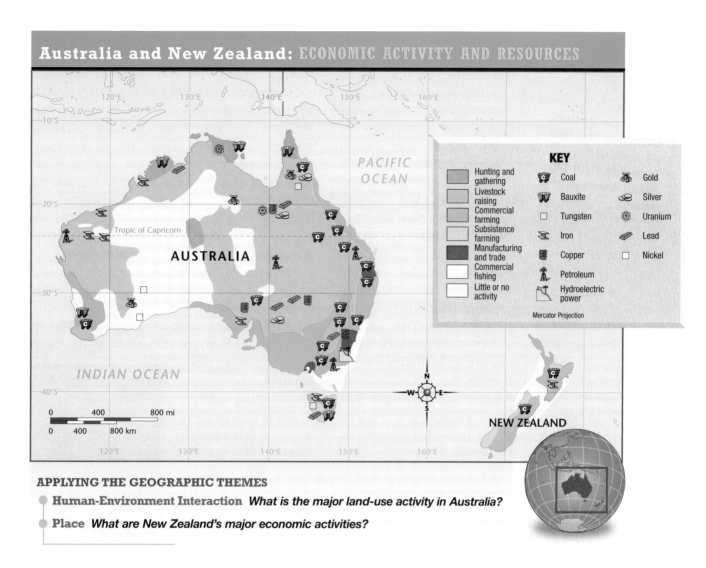

KEY

Hunting and gathering	Coal		Gold
Livestock raising	Bauxite		Silver
Commercial farming	Tungsten		Uranium
Subsistence farming	Iron		Lead
Manufacturing and trade	Copper		Nickel
Commercial fishing	Petroleum		
Little or no activity	Hydroelectric power		

Mercator Projection

PACIFIC OCEAN

INDIAN OCEAN

AUSTRALIA

Tropic of Capricorn

NEW ZEALAND

0 400 800 mi
0 400 800 km

APPLYING THE GEOGRAPHIC THEMES

● **Human-Environment Interaction** *What is the major land-use activity in Australia?*

● **Place** *What are New Zealand's major economic activities?*

North of Brisbane and the Sunshine Coast is the Great Barrier Reef, the largest coral reef in the world. The reef forms a **lagoon**, a shallow body of water with an outlet to the ocean, between itself and the mainland. The reef extends for 1,250 miles (2,010 km)—just about the length of the United States coast from Maine to North Carolina.

The Tropical North The sparsely populated Northern Territory is mostly too hot and dry to support human activities. The state's capital, Darwin, however, lies on the northern coast, where the climate is tropical, with wet and dry seasons. Darwin is the closest Australian city to Asia. As flights to other cities become more frequent, it continues to grow. Darwin's location has some disadvantages, however. The city was bombed by the Japanese in World War II. Moreover, it has twice been leveled by **cyclones**, the Australian term for hurricanes.

The threat of cyclones has influenced architecture in the area, with few buildings in Darwin rising higher than one or two stories.

The Outback

Nearly all of Australia west of the Great Dividing Range is arid plain or dry plateau. Australians often refer to the harsh wilderness region of the central and western plains and plateaus as the **outback**. The Aborigines were the first humans to live in the outback. They learned over time how fragile their environment was and felt a sacred obligation to protect it.

Aborigines and the Land The Aborigines had few possessions. But they did have a rich oral tradition that preserved their religious beliefs and explained how their ancestors created the world. Aboriginal creation stories teach that in a time long ago, known as the

Dreamtime, the ancestors of all living things moved across the formless earth and created the natural world. The ancestors were usually animals, but sometimes they took the form of human beings. Big Bill Neidjie (NAY jee), an Aborigine elder, says that when humans were created, the ancestors gave them responsibility for taking care of the earth: "Now we have done these things, you make sure they remain like this for all time. You must not change anything."

Over countless generations, the Aborigines took this responsibility to heart. They handed down ancient knowledge about the sacred sites of each ancestor from parent to child as a priceless gift. Aboriginal artists left records of these and other stories on rock paintings and carvings. The Aborigines learned to take from the land what they needed to survive without destroying their precious earth.

European Land Use The European settlers who came to Australia had a different view. They wanted to make the land produce something that could be sold for money. In 1851 gold was discovered in the outback of New South Wales and Victoria. In the gold rush that followed, Australians and new immigrants swarmed out of the cities, eager to join the search.

Today gold is only one of many mineral resources that are mined in various locations throughout Australia. Other resources include coal, iron ore, copper, zinc, uranium, and lead. Australia is the leading exporter of bauxite, which is used to make aluminum. The area also has fairly large deposits of oil and natural gas both in the interior and offshore. Some of these resources are shown on the map on page 683.

Many gold seekers stayed on in Australia to build farms and sheep ranches. Today huge sheep and cattle ranches, called stations, account for most of the economic activity in the outback. Many of these stations are enormous in area. For example, the Anna Creek cattle station in South Australia covers 12,000 square miles (31,000 square km), which is larger than many of the New England states. Ranchers round up livestock on the

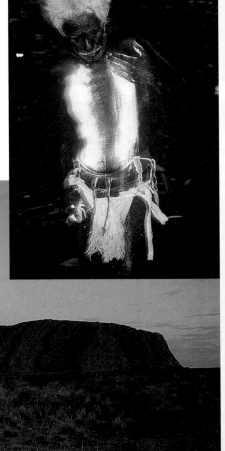

An Australian Symbol

Place Ayers Rock in Australia's interior desert is the largest monolith, or single stone, in the world. It looms 1,100 feet (335 m) above the floor of the desert and is four miles long. For many Aborigines Ayers Rock is a sacred site. *According to their customs, what relationship do the Aborigines have with the land?*

Land Use in the Outback

Regions Only 6 percent of Australia's land is arable, or suitable for planting row crops. Yet a great deal of land is suitable for grazing. Beef and wool taken from the nation's cattle and sheep are two of Australia's greatest exports. **Critical Thinking** *What conditions might make Australia's land non-arable?*

enormous stations by using helicopters to locate strays and then chasing them down with pickup trucks. Life on a station in the Australian outback can be difficult. Ranchers face dangerous working conditions, including high risk of heat exhaustion and dehydration in the hot, dry land.

Sheep, or "jumbucks," are raised in the cooler plains regions of southeastern and southwestern Australia. Some sheep and lambs are raised primarily for their meat, but the fine, curly wool of merino (muh REE noh) sheep is the most important product. Australia is one of the world leaders in wool production.

Cattle are raised in the hotter northern and central regions of Australia, where the native grasses and shrubs provide enough food. Water for these stations comes mainly from **artesian wells**. These wells are bored deep into the earth to tap a layer of porous material filled with groundwater.

Growth in the Australian cattle industry reflects changes in both the supply and demand for beef. New breeds of cattle that thrive better in hot, dry weather have increased beef yields, making Australia one of the world's leading producers of cattle.

Section 1 Review

Vocabulary and Main Ideas

1. **Define:** **a.** Aborigine **b.** lagoon **c.** cyclone **d.** outback **e.** artesian well

2. **Why does the population of Australia number only 18 million?**

3. **Why do the majority of Australia's cities lie along the coast?**

4. **How have European settlers made use of Australia's interior?**

6. **Critical Thinking:** *Demonstrating Reasoned Judgment* **Do you think it is fortunate or unfortunate that much of Australia remains unsettled? Explain your answer.**

learning LOCATIONS

7. **What body of water lies northeast of Australia?**

8. **Describe Sydney's location.**

2 New Zealand and the Pacific Islands

APPEARED IN *NATIONAL GEOGRAPHIC*

A Maori woman harvests sea urchins on the New Zealand shore.

Section Preview

Main Ideas

● New Zealand's population is mostly made up of people of European descent and the minority Maori group.

● New Zealand's economy is based primarily on agriculture.

● The Pacific Islands consist of two types—high islands and low islands— each with its own distinctive landscape.

Vocabulary

geyser, atoll, trust territory

British naturalist Charles Darwin wrote these words as he sailed across the Pacific from Tahiti to New Zealand in 1835:

> *It is necessary to sail over this great ocean to comprehend its immensity . . . . [F]or weeks together, we meet with nothing but the same blue, profoundly deep, ocean. Even with the archipelagoes, the islands are mere specks, and far distant one from the other. Accustomed to looking at maps drawn on a small scale, where dots, shading, and names are crowded together, we do not rightly judge how infinitely small the proportion of dry land is to the water of this vast expanse.*

The Pacific Ocean is indeed immense. At 64 million square miles (166 million sq km), the Pacific is more than twice the area of the Atlantic. Set in this watery expanse are the tiny islands of the Pacific. South of the Pacific Islands and east of Australia lie the two comparatively larger islands that make up New Zealand.

New Zealand

New Zealand lies about 1,000 miles (1,600 km) east of Australia across the rough and windy Tasman Sea. Although New Zealand is part of the Pacific Islands, its physical and human characteristics are very different from those of the other islands.

Two Islands The backbone of New Zealand is a string of volcanic mountains formed along the border between the Australian and Pacific tectonic plates. These mountains form two large islands, called South Island and North Island. The two islands are quite distinct geographically.

North Island is narrow and hilly. Spread across the center is a plateau and an active geothermal region. Volcanoes and **geysers** (GY sers), hot springs that shoot jets of steam and heated water into the air, fuel an active tourist industry.

New Zealand's highest mountains tower above South Island. Mystery novelist Ngaio (NY oh) Marsh, a native of New Zealand, described the scenery of these mountains— known as the Southern Alps—in this way:

At their highest, they are covered by perpetual snow. Turbulent rivers cut through them, you can see these rivers twisting and glittering like blue snakes through deep gorges, spilling into lakes and pouring across plains to the coast. The westward flanks of the Alps are clothed in dark, heavy forest. It rains a lot over there: everything is lush and green.

From Settlement to Today Perhaps referring to the rain and mist of the west, the first people to arrive in New Zealand called it Aotearoa—"Land of the Long White Cloud." The origin of these people, the Maori, is in dispute. Some scholars claim the Maori are a Polynesian people who came by canoe around A.D. 900. Others believe they came from the Malaysian Peninsula, or even from Peru.

Prior to European settlement of New Zealand in 1769, the Maori did not consider themselves a nation. They comprised many groups, each forming a highly ordered society with intricate rules of conduct and custom. Although they traded goods and shared a common culture, groups were fiercely territorial. Competition for choice cropland and fishing grounds often led to intergroup warfare. As time went by, however, more peaceful relations were established on the island. In 1840, the Maoris signed a treaty with the British. In exchange for certain land rights they agreed to accept British rule.

As European settlers moved onto their land, the Maori began to see themselves as a nation instead of individual competing groups. Though today the Maori number less than 10 percent of the population, they have their own political party, Mana Motuhake, which means "self-determination." They are currently attempting to reclaim lands that were once

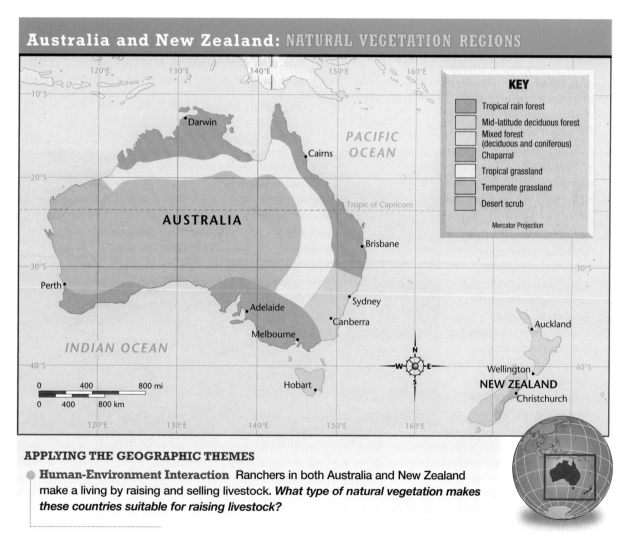

Australia and New Zealand: NATURAL VEGETATION REGIONS

KEY
- Tropical rain forest
- Mid-latitude deciduous forest
- Mixed forest (deciduous and coniferous)
- Chaparral
- Tropical grassland
- Temperate grassland
- Desert scrub

Mercator Projection

PACIFIC OCEAN

Darwin
Cairns

Tropic of Capricorn

AUSTRALIA

Brisbane

Perth

Adelaide
Sydney
Canberra

Melbourne

INDIAN OCEAN

Auckland

Hobart

Wellington
NEW ZEALAND
Christchurch

0   400   800 mi
0   400   800 km

APPLYING THE GEOGRAPHIC THEMES
● **Human-Environment Interaction** Ranchers in both Australia and New Zealand make a living by raising and selling livestock. *What type of natural vegetation makes these countries suitable for raising livestock?*

theirs in an effort to preserve their culture. In 1996, for example, the New Zealand government determined that a large area of North Island—nearly an entire province—had been taken from the Maori without any recognition of their rights.

Though the Maori are a vital force in New Zealand culture, they remain a minority. Some 74 percent of New Zealand's 3.5 million people are of European descent. The result of this mix of peoples is a national identity that is rooted in both its Polynesian and British past.

An Agricultural Economy The European settlers were largely responsible for developing the New Zealand economy, which is still in large part agricultural. Gentle plains slope down from the mountains on both islands of New Zealand. These plains have rich soils, and the marine west coast climate is ideal for farming. Dairy cattle graze on parts of North Island, and sheep are raised throughout the country.

Livestock are raised in New Zealand for many of the same reasons as in Australia. They are well suited to the local conditions, and their products can be shipped over thousands of miles to foreign markets. It is not practical to export milk from New Zealand. But butter and cheese can survive long journeys by boat or yield high enough prices to make the extra cost of air transportation worthwhile. Similarly, wool and frozen lamb and mutton from New Zealand reach buyers in Asia, Europe, and North America.

Kiwifruit are another New Zealand product commonly seen in American grocery stores. Today New Zealand produces one quarter of the world's kiwifruit.

Life in the Cities Despite the importance of agriculture, the great majority of the people live in large cities along the coast. Three out of four New Zealanders live on North Island. Auckland (AWK luhnd), New Zealand's largest city, is located there. Auckland's northern latitude places it closer to other nations than any other major New Zealand city. Its airport and ocean port are the country's busiest. Auckland has also developed as a manufacturing center, and nearby farms make it an agricultural trade center.

At the Heart of an Export Economy

● **Location** New Zealand's economy depends on exporting many of its agricultural and industrial products. Wellington's location makes it an important link in the nation's overseas trade. It has a superb harbor and sits near the middle of the country. *What are some of New Zealand's agricultural exports?*

The Pacific Islands

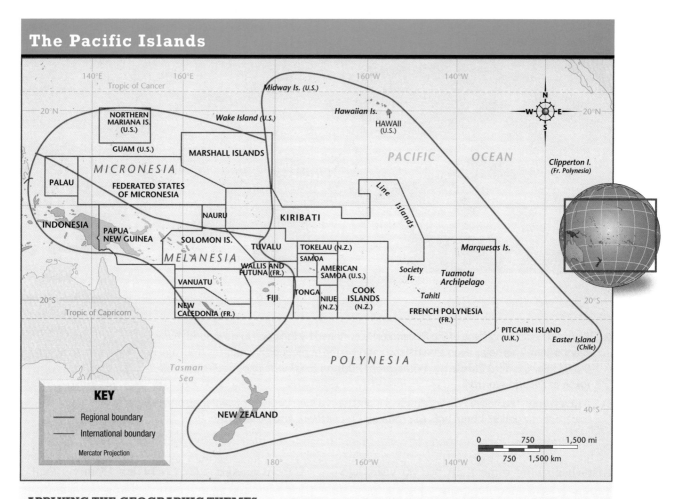

APPLYING THE GEOGRAPHIC THEMES

● **Regions** The Pacific Islands include Micronesia, Melanesia, and Polynesia. *In which region is the island of Tahiti? What country controls it?*

On South Island lies New Zealand's second-largest city, Christchurch. The national capital, Wellington overlooks Cook Strait, which separates North Island from South Island. Wellington symbolically unites the nation.

The Pacific Islands

Like the two islands that form New Zealand, many of the Pacific Islands are of a type called high islands. Imagine a huge chain of under-water mountains in the Pacific Ocean. Where the tops of these mountains break the surface of the water, they create high islands. Because many of these islands lie along the boundary of the Australian and Pacific plates, they are capped by volcanoes. On some islands, volcanic cones rise several thousand feet above the ocean's surface.

Other islands in the Pacific are known as low islands. On ring-shaped islands called **atolls** (AH tawlz), coral reefs surround an inner lagoon. Atolls form most of the Marshall Islands and the islands of Kiribati (KIR uh bas). An atoll begins as a fringing reef in the warm, shallow waters surrounding a volcanic island. When the volcanic cone falls below the ocean's surface, the coral continues to build up. Then, after millions of years, the volcano disappears, leaving only a ring of coral around a lagoon. Waves crashing over the coral break the top layer into sand. The sand piles up atop the coral and finally forms soil that can support plant and animal life.

Various Island Groups The Pacific Islands are divided into three groups: Micronesia, Melanesia, and Polynesia. Each group is shown on the map above. Melanesia was inhabited

Taming the Pacific

- **Place** The bruising force of the Pacific surf is softened by the coral reefs around many islands (left). This helps even small islands survive the hurricanes and storms that rage in the Pacific. **Critical Thinking** *What might happen to islands exposed to the full force of Pacific storms?*

- **Movement** The native Pacific Islanders (right) have a long tradition of seafaring and excellent navigation. *When was Micronesia first settled, and by whom?*

first—beginning more than 40,000 years ago— probably by people from Southeast Asia. Micronesia was settled between 3000 and 2000 B.C. by voyagers from the Philippines, Indonesia, and some of the islands north of New Guinea.

The distinct culture and physical characteristics of the Polynesians developed over a long period of time when they were isolated in the Tonga and Samoa islands. From this base, the Polynesians explored and settled a huge region of the Pacific, mostly to the north and west. (See the map on page 689.) Today, Fiji has large numbers of Melanesians, and Polynesians. About one half of its 800,000 residents are descended from East Indians who were brought to the islands in the late nineteenth century to work on sugar plantations.

GLOBAL issues

Global Warming

The rise in sea level predicted by some scientists as a result of global warming presents a particular problem to Pacific Islanders. A rise of only eight to ten inches could make some low-lying islands uninhabitable.

Economic Activities Many Pacific Islanders today make their living from farming or fishing. Coconut products, pineapples, bananas, skipjack (a kind of fish), and yellowfin tuna are some of the products exported from the Pacific Islands. Most people, however, live at a subsistence level. That is, they usually grow or catch only enough to feed themselves. Some high islands in Melanesia and Polynesia can support cash crops such as rubber, coffee, and sugar cane. Minerals are extracted on a few islands—a large gold mine operates on Fiji, and New Caledonia has a nickel mine. In 1995, Oceania officials rejected a proposal for a new kind of industry—storage of nuclear wastes—on Bikini Atoll. This atoll had been made radioactive by repeated United States nuclear tests in the 1940s and 1950s.

Pacific Island tourism is a growing industry. Vacationers in search of warm, sunny beaches and scenic beauty have increasingly headed for these islands as travel and communications have become faster and easier. Fiji, for instance, actively promotes tourism. Its airport is a stopping point for airplanes traveling between North

America and Australia. In Tonga—an archipelago of 169 volcanic and coral islands—tourism is the primary source of hard currency on the 45 islands that are inhabited. In contrast, Western Samoa is scenic and well-situated with respect to air routes. The government, however, does not want a large tourist industry. It fears that visitors might change the indigenous culture.

Toward Independence Most of the world paid little attention to the Pacific Islands until World War II. During the war, Japanese and United State forces fought many bloody battles on the islands. Afterward many islands were divided into **trust territories**, or territories supervised by other nations. The United States oversees Guam and American Samoa.

Most of the Pacific Islands were granted independence in the 1960s and 1970s. Independence helped renew interest in native cultures among the people. Many new national governments were based on traditional forms of leadership. Tonga, for example, chose to remain a kingdom. Western Samoa adopted a parliamentary system, but most representatives are selected by traditional village leaders. Other nations, such as Vanuatu (vahn uh WAH too), operate with fully representative democracies.

One Western nation that held on to its Pacific possessions is France. Its conduct in the region was a subject of controversy in 1995, when it provoked international outrage for using Mururoa Atoll as a site for atomic testing.

Facts in BRIEF

Country	Population	Life Expectancy (years)	Per Capita GNP (in US $)
Australia	18,000,000	78	17,510
Federated States of Micronesia	100,000	68	NA
Fiji	800,000	63	2,140
French Polynesia	200,000	70	NA
Guam	200,000	74	NA
Marshall Islands	100,000	63	NA
New Caledonia	200,000	74	NA
New Zealand	3,500,000	76	12,900
Palau	20,000	67	NA
Solomon Islands	400,000	61	750
Vanuatu	200,000	63	1,230
Western Samoa	200,000	65	980
United States	263,200,000	76	24,750

Source: Population Reference Bureau   NA indicates data not available.

CHART SKILLS

- Which country, aside from the United States, has the highest population?
- Which country has the highest life expectancy?

Section 2 Review

Vocabulary and Main Ideas

1. Define: a. atoll b. trust territory

2. What cultures served as models for New Zealand?

3. What are New Zealand's main economic activities?

4. What is the origin of the difference between the high islands and the low islands of the Pacific Ocean?

5. Critical Thinking: *Demonstrating Reasoned Judgment* How would you propose the New Zealand government repay the Maori for the land illegally taken from them?

learning LOCATIONS

6. Where is New Zealand in relation to the Pacific Islands?

7. Where is Micronesia in relation to Melanesia?

Interpreting a Topographic Map

A hiker poised at the start of an unfamiliar mountain trail needs a special kind of map tucked into his or her backpack: a topographic, or contour, map. This kind of map shows the changes in elevation that lie ahead—and how quickly these changes take place. Does the trail climb steeply for the next mile, or is the grade a slow and steady rise? Will there be serious climbing involved, or can the hiker cover the distance at an easy, arm-swinging pace? How far can the hiker expect to go in a single afternoon? A good topographic map can be used to answer all these questions and help ensure the success and safety of a hike.

Topographic maps are useful tools with many applications. Backpackers take them along when they set out on hiking, rock climbing, and camping trips. However, they are not the only people who use topographic maps. Engineers use them when deciding where to build highways and dams. Police and emergency medical personnel often consult topographic maps during search-and-rescue operations for people who are lost in the woods.

The topographic map at right shows the Pacific island of Tahiti. Use the following steps to study and analyze the map.

1. Understand what contour lines measure. The lines on a topographic map are called *contour lines*. A contour line connects all points where elevation is equal. If you were to hike along one of the contour lines shown on this topographic map, you would always be at the same height above sea level. Notice that the contour lines are labeled with numbers that tell the elevation in feet along that contour line. Now use the map to answer the following questions: (a) What elevation does the coastline represent? (b) What is the highest point on Tahiti? (c) Are Papeete and Mataiea at about the same or different elevations?

2. Interpret the relationships among contour lines. When a series of contour lines is close together, it means that the elevation of the land is changing rapidly—in other words, the terrain is steep. On the other hand, contour lines spread wide apart indicate that the elevation is changing slowly and the land is relatively flat. Answer the following questions: (a) Is the island generally steeper near the top of Mt. Orohena or near the coast? (b) Where is the steepest part of the Taiarapu Peninsula?

3. Put the data you have collected to use. Once you understand how to read a topographic map, you can use this skill to help plan a hike or a camping trip. Use the map to answer the following questions: (a) If you and a friend wanted to climb to the top of Mt. Orohena, how would you plot the most gradual ascent possible? (b) How would you plot a steeper climb?

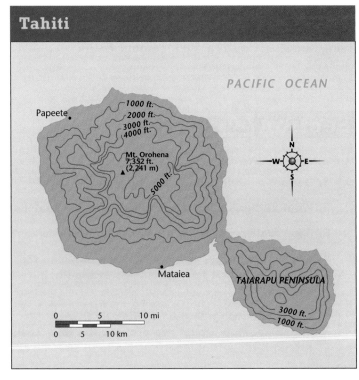

3 Antarctica

S ection Preview

Main Ideas

● Antarctica is a continent covered and surrounded by several different forms of ice.

● Antarctica's climate and terrain have made exploration slow and difficult.

● Scientific data is the greatest Antarctic resource.

Vocabulary

crevasse, ice shelf, pack ice, convergence zone, krill

APPEARED IN *NATIONAL GEOGRAPHIC*

"Pancake ice" forms in the seas around Antarctica.

On most world maps, Antarctica appears as a long, ragged strip of white stretching across the southern boundary. In reality, however, Antarctica is a large, mushroom-shaped continent that accounts for nearly one tenth of the world's land. To be seen clearly on a map, Antarctica must occupy a central position. Therefore, only a south-polar projection like the one shown in the map on page 694 provides a true picture of Antarctica's shape and size.

Following a visit to Antarctica in the early 1980s, environmental historian Stephen Pyne had this to say about Antarctica:

> *Ice is the beginning of Antarctica and ice is its end. . . . Ice creates more ice, and ice defines ice. Everything else is suppressed. This is a world derived from a single substance, water, in a single crystalline state, snow, transformed into a lithosphere composed of a single mineral, ice. This is earthscape transfigured into icescape.*

The Frozen Continent

As Pyne suggests, in a sense Antarctica *is* ice. Ice covers the continent's rocks, and it alters the climate. The ice affects Antarctica's wildlife, because few plants and animals can survive in its frigid conditions. And the ice has greatly limited human activity, leaving Antarctica as the only major landmass on the earth without permanent human settlements.

Dense Ice Sheets The ice covering Antarctica makes it on average the highest continent. It has an average elevation of 1.3 miles (2.1 km), compared to an average of 0.6 miles (1.0 km) for the rest of the world's land. The average thickness of the ice caps, or ice sheets, covering central regions of the South Pole ranges from 5,600 to 7,200 feet (1,700 to 2,200 m).

The weight of the Antarctic ice sheets is enormous. In many areas the ice creates so much pressure that the land surface actually sinks below sea level. If the ice were to melt, the land would rise 260 feet (80 m). In addition, the weight of the ice sheets on the South Pole gives the earth a slightly lopsided pear shape.

Ice and the Climate The Antarctic ice sheets have a significant effect on both the continent's own climate and on weather patterns throughout the Southern Hemisphere. The ice reflects most of the sun's rays back into space rather than absorbing their heat, making temperatures frigid. The average annual temperature at one research station is –71°F (–57°C). One of the coldest temperatures ever recorded on the earth was measured at the same site: –128.6°F (–89.3°C).

While even the glare of six months of summer sun cannot melt them, the Antarctic ice caps do not grow rapidly. This is because very little snow falls. Like high plateaus on other continents, the region is quite dry, because air loses its moisture as it rises. Air becomes even drier as it gets colder. As a result, the South Pole sees less than 2 inches (5 cm) of precipitation each year. Even the most arid deserts of Africa and Asia usually get more precipitation than Antarctica.

Glaciers Moister and warmer conditions near the coast and in the Transantarctic Mountains permit glaciers to flow over the land. Antarctic glaciers creep like giant, slow-moving frozen rivers, oozing down from the mountains and the edges of the ice sheet to the coast. The average annual glacial movement varies from about 360 to 3,600 feet (about 110 to 1,100 m). Glaciers provide the most convenient routes to the interior of the continent. However, travelers must beware of large cracks called **crevasses** that form in glacial ice.

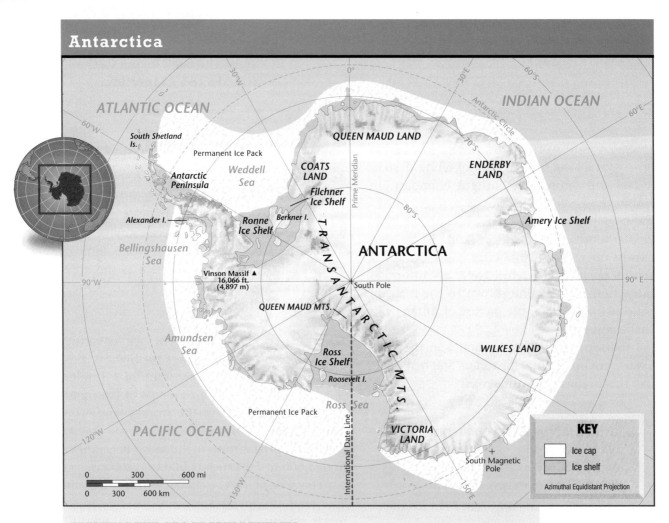

Antarctica

APPLYING THE GEOGRAPHIC THEMES
● **Place** Most of Antarctica lies south of 70° S latitude and is thickly covered with ice.
Which mountain range cuts across the middle of the continent from east to west?

Ice Shelves Antarctica's ice sheets and glaciers are so deeply frozen that the slowly creeping ice extends out over the ocean in several places and forms massive permanent extensions of ice called **ice shelves**. The larger shelves cover enormous areas of the Ross and Weddell seas; smaller shelves dot the coastline.

The ice on the shelves is more than 1,000 feet (300 m) thick in many places. The shelves thin out as they extend farther into the ocean, however. Near the edges, the ice often has many crevasses, and large blocks eventually break off and fall into the ocean as icebergs. Antarctic icebergs can be tremendous in size—sometimes five miles (8 km) long and 150 feet (45 m) high. They can travel thousands of miles over the course of a few years.

Pack Ice In the seas surrounding Antarctica, icebergs mix with ice formed in the superchilled waters to form **pack ice**. Pack ice fringes most of the Antarctic continent. During the long winter, when the sun shines for only a few hours each day, the pack ice can extend more than 1,000 miles (1,600 km). In the summer, the outer reaches of the ice melt, and the pack ice extends only about one tenth as far into the ocean.

The edge of the winter pack ice is close to the **convergence zone**. This is the area where the frigid waters around Antarctica meet the warmer waters of the Atlantic, Pacific, and Indian oceans. This clash of warm and cold waters causes severe storms along Antarctica's coastline. The contrast in temperatures also mixes different layers of water along the edge of the pack ice. Nutrient-rich, deep waters rise to the surface, feeding millions of small shrimp-like creatures called **krill**. The krill provide ample food for whales and fish. The fish, in turn, become food for seals, penguins, and other animals.

Interacting with the Land

Antarctica's unique physical geography makes its human geography different from that of any other continent. Because of its remote location and harsh natural conditions, it was the last of

Annual Ice Sheets

Regions Each winter the seas around Antarctica begin to freeze. By the end of the season this ice sheet covers an area twice the size of the United States. Then the Antarctic summer, weak as it is, melts the sheet away again. *What is the difference between these ice sheets and Antarctica's ice shelves? How do they both differ from pack ice?*

the world's continents to be discovered and explored. It remains uninhabited.

Antarctica was first sighted in the early 1820s by sailors from Russia, Great Britain, and the United States. Explorers reached the Ross Ice Shelf in the early 1840s. But the ice and cold prevented anyone from actually setting foot on the continent until 1895.

Roald Amundsen of Norway and Robert Scott of Great Britain each led major expeditions across Antarctica's ice sheets. Both reached the South Pole in the Antarctic summer of 1911–1912, but Scott and his four companions died on their return trip. Further exploration of the interior began in the late 1920s, when airplanes were built that could withstand Antarctica's high winds and cold temperatures.

GLOBAL issues

International Cooperation

In 1961, twelve countries, including those that had claimed portions of Antarctica, signed the Antarctic Treaty. The treaty provided for the peaceful use of the continent and the sharing of scientific research. When the treaty expired in 1989, the twelve original nations, and twenty-eight others, renewed it. They also added a section that prohibits any mining of Antarctica's mineral resources for fifty years.

Slicing the "Pie" Antarctica's unusual conditions also affected the ways in which nations tried to make territorial claims. Many early explorers made claims in the hope of protecting areas rich in whales and seals. But by the late 1880s, the world's most powerful nations agreed that land had to be occupied and actively governed for a national claim to be valid.

Through the first half of the twentieth century, Argentina, Australia, Chile, France, New Zealand, Norway, and the United Kingdom all claimed parts of Antarctica. Most of these countries' claims took the form of pie-shaped wedges that met at the South Pole. Two nations, the United States and the Soviet Union, refused to make any claims. They also refused to acknowledge the claims of other nations, arguing that actual settlement had not occurred.

Why did so many nations claim parts of Antarctica? One reason was national pride. Many countries wanted to expand their colonial empires to Antarctica's frontier or simply keep other countries from claiming large slices of the continent.

Antarctic Resources Another reason for territorial claims was to claim the ownership of resources. Demand for whales and seals had declined, but it was still possible to find valuable minerals under the ice. Geological discoveries in recent decades suggest that oil, gold, iron, and other minerals may well be present. Coal has already been found, but deposits remain untouched because it would cost too much to mine and transport them. Other minerals would cost even more to find and to exploit.

Sharing the Bounty By far the greatest resource Antarctica has to offer is its wealth of scientific information. Scientists worked to convince the world that Antarctica needed to remain open to all countries that wanted to conduct research there. In 1961, twelve countries

APPEARED IN *NATIONAL GEOGRAPHIC*

Open Water on an Icy Plain

● **Human-Environment Interaction** The ice sheets around Antarctica sometimes split open, exposing the open water just a few feet below. These gaps make a natural route for ice-breakers exploring the region. **Critical Thinking** *What forces might cause the ice to split open?*

Cutting Edge

Human-Environment Interaction Today's scientists meet the challenge of Antarctica's climate with cutting-edge technology. Early in this century, however, explorers struggled toward the South Pole on sleds pulled by dogs and Manchurian ponies. *Why is research on Antarctica so valuable?*

ratified the Antarctic Treaty. This treaty provided for the peaceful use of the continent and the sharing of scientific research. The treaty banned military activity, nuclear explosions, and the disposal of radioactive waste. A number of other countries later signed the treaty, and several countries set up research stations on the continent. Throughout the years, amendments have been added to protect wildlife.

The continent is the key to a vast store of knowledge that many countries are now exploring and sharing. For example, one team of scientists has drilled deep into the Antarctic ice, extracting a sample called a core as they proceeded. This core includes ice that was formed over 450,000 years ago, and gives clues as to what earth's environment was like during each of those years. Deeper still, on the bedrock of the continent, lie lakes of liquid water that have been sealed beneath ice for half a million years. Scientists dream of finding ancient microscopic lifeforms alive in those lakes.

Section 3 Review

Vocabulary and Main Ideas

1. Define: a. crevasse b. ice shelf c. pack ice d. convergence zone e. krill

2. Describe the discovery of Antarctica in the 1800s.

3. What has prevented the United States and other countries from claiming Antarctica?

4. What are some of Antarctica's resources?

5. Critical Thinking: *Formulating Questions* Imagine that you are planning an expedition to the South Pole. Create a list of questions that you would ask someone who had already completed such a trip successfully.

6. Suppose you were on another continent and were asked in which direction to travel to reach Antarctica. What direction could you give that would be correct, no matter where you were?

7. Where are the Transantarctic Mountains relative to the South Pole?

Review and Activities

Summarizing Main Ideas

Section 1   Australia

- Limited immigration has kept Australia's population low.
- Australia's seven state capitals are all located along the coast, and the national capital, Canberra, is not far inland.
- Aborigine culture is based on living in the difficult environmental conditions of the outback and respecting the land.
- European immigrants to Australia have used the land for farming, raising livestock, and mining.

Section 2   New Zealand and the Pacific Islands

- New Zealanders are mainly European in origin, but the indigenous Maori people form a large minority.
- New Zealand's economy is mostly agricultural, although Auckland is a modern industrial city.
- The Pacific Islands can be divided into two types—high islands and low islands.
- Tourism is a vital part of many island economies, since most islands have few mineral resources.

Section 3   Antarctica

- Antarctica is a large continent covered and surrounded by ice.
- Icebergs and pack ice around the continent made early exploration difficult.
- Nations have agreed not to make claims to Antarctica but to share scientific data instead.
- Antarctica has coal and other mineral resources, but it is not practical to exploit them.

Reviewing Vocabulary

Complete the following sentences with the correct term.

1. **(Crevasses/krill)** play an important role in the Antarctic food chain.
2. A shallow body of water with an outlet to the sea is called **(an artesian well/a lagoon)**.
3. Warm and cold waters mingle in the **(lagoon/convergence zone)**.
4. A **(trust territory/convergence zone)** is an area governed or held in trust by another nation.

Applying the Geographic Themes

1. **Regions** How is life along Australia's coast different from life in the outback?
2. **Place** What are some of New Zealand's main products?
3. **Movement** Who probably first settled the islands of Melanesia and Micronesia?
4. **Place** What are some of the different forms ice takes in Antarctica, and where is each found?
5. **Human-Environment Interaction** Why is no nation able to establish a legitimate claim to Antarctica?

Critical Thinking and Applying Skills

1. **Predicting Consequences** What might happen in Antarctica if a practical way were found to extract its mineral resources?
2. **Interpreting a Topographic Map** Refer back to the skill lesson on page 692 to answer the following questions.
   a. When a series of contour lines on a topographic map is close together, what information is being conveyed about elevation?
   b. What information is conveyed about elevation when contour lines are relatively far apart?

Journal Activity

Writing Across Cultures

▶ 1. Write a short story about one of the following: (a) the experiences of an Aborigine family traveling across the outback in the time before Europeans came to Australia; (b) the life of a family running a large cattle ranch in the outback today. You may need to do research to learn details to include in your story.

▶ 2. You read in the chapter how both the United States and France have used Pacific islands for atomic testing. Write a letter to the editor expressing your opinion for or against this practice and back up your opinion with logical arguments.

INTERNET link

Take a trip to Antarctica. Link to this site from:

• www.phschool.com

Follow the link to the Ship's Log and read one of the journals about the trip. Briefly state why you would or would not like to visit Antarctica.

learning LOCATIONS

Australia, Oceania, and Antarctica

Number your paper from 1 to 6. Next to each number, write the letter of the place on the map that corresponds to the places listed below.

1. Australia
2. Canberra
3. Sydney
4. New Zealand
5. Auckland
6. Wellington

EARTHQUAKE

Many urban areas are at a high risk for earthquakes. How can cities and towns be designed to resist severe earthquake damage and minimize the danger for people living there? Keep these questions in mind as you do the following experiment.

MATERIALS:

Cake pan

1 Piece of cloth (longer than cake pan)

Damp soil

Small model houses, trees, buildings, bridges, etc.

Scissors

PROCEDURE:

Step 2

1. Cut the piece of cloth in a jagged line close to, but not exactly in, the middle. This is the "fault line" for the earthquake. Lay the two pieces of cloth next to each other in the pan so that the "fault line" is along the bottom of the pan. Let the excess of both pieces hang over the sides of the pan.

2. Fill the pan with damp soil and pack it down firmly into the pan over the two pieces of cloth.

3. Place the model houses, buildings, trees, bridges, etc., on the soil to simulate a city or town. Lay down roads and railroad tracks. Designate the buildings as schools, police and fire departments, residential areas, and business districts.

Step 4

4. To create the "earthquake," pull the strips of cloth in *opposite directions* at the same time.

Step 4

OBSERVATIONS AND ANALYSIS:

1. Describe the damage that occurred to the "town" that you built. Be specific about what kind of damage you think occurred to the buildings.

2. Now that you know where the fault line is, how would you redesign the "town" to be more earthquake safe? Where would you relocate the school, fire, and police departments? What other buildings should be placed with careful consideration?

3. If an earthquake were to happen in your town, what would some of the most vulnerable areas be? What areas might be in danger of fire damage as well (for example, businesses and buildings contain flammable substances)? What buildings in your town have a large number of people in them?

EARTHQUAKE
Devastates Kansai

Railroads, roads, and buildings designed to be "quakeproof" crumbled as the worst earthquake in 50 years rocked through the Kansai region of Japan. Over 3,800 people have been pronounced dead and another 1,000 are missing and may be trapped under any of the 12,000 collapsed buildings. The center of the earthquake was located on a fault line near Kobe, a heavily populated city, and began at a depth of 12.4 miles. Rescue efforts have been delayed by the wreckage along major roads. Officials say it may be a month before power, gas, and water services are restored.

The 1995 earthquake in Kobe, Japan

Woman being rescued from Kobe earthquake

taking *Action*

Earthquakes can't be prevented. Here are some things you can do to keep safe if an earthquake occurs near you:

✔ Stand in a doorway away from large, loose objects that could fall.

✔ Shut off the main switches for gas. Don't turn on gas appliances.

✔ Be alert for aftershocks and don't walk near areas where there is a danger of falling debris.

Table of COUNTRIES

The following Table of Countries provides important geographic, economic, and political data for the countries of the world. Countries are listed alphabetically within regions, which are listed in the same order as they appear in the text.

When taken together, the data provide an overview of a country's standard of living, or general quality of life. The table includes the following information for each country:

- *Capital city* is the seat of government.
- *Land area* is given in square miles.
- *Population* estimate is given in millions. For example, a population of 26.3 means 26.3 million people.
- *Birth rate* is given for each 1,000 of population. For example, a birth rate of 36 means that for every 1,000 people, 36 babies are born each year.
- *Death rate* is given for each 1,000 of population.
- *Annual growth rate*, the speed at which a country's population is increasing per year, is given as a percentage. To find the actual number of people by which a population is increasing each

Country	Capital City	Land Area (sq. miles)	Population 1995 (millions)	Birth Rate	Death Rate
				(per 1,000 pop.)	
WORLD			5,771.0	24	9
MORE DEVELOPED			1,170.8	12	10
LESS DEVELOPED			4,600.2	27	9
LESS DEVELOPED (Excl. China)			3,382.6	31	10

The United States and Canada

Country	Capital City	Land Area (sq. miles)	Population 1995 (millions)	Birth Rate	Death Rate
Canada	Ottawa	3,560,220	29.6	13	7
United States	Washington, D.C.	3,539,230	263.2	15	9

Latin America

Country	Capital City	Land Area (sq. miles)	Population 1995 (millions)	Birth Rate	Death Rate
Antigua and Barbuda	St. John's	170	0.1	18	6
Argentina	Buenos Aires	1,056,640	34.6	20	8
Bahamas	Nassau	3,860	0.3	18	5
Barbados	Bridgetown	170	0.3	14	9
Belize	Belmopan	8,800	0.2	38	5
Bolivia	La Paz	418,680	7.4	36	10
Brazil	Brasília	3,265,060	157.8	25	8
Chile	Santiago	289,110	14.3	21	6
Colombia	Bogotá	401,040	37.7	27	6
Costa Rica	San Jose	19,710	3.3	26	4
Cuba	Havana	42,400	11.2	14	7
Dominica	Roseau	290	0.1	20	7
Dominican Republic	Santo Domingo	18,680	7.8	29	6
Ecuador	Quito	106,890	11.5	29	6
El Salvador	San Salvador	8,000	5.9	32	6
Grenada	St. George's	130	0.1	29	6
Guadeloupe (Fr.)	Basse-Terre	650	0.4	18	6

year, multiply the country's population by its annual growth rate.

- *Projected population* in 2025 is given in millions.
- *Infant mortality rate* refers to the number of infants out of every thousand born who will die before their first birthday.
- *Population* under age 15 is given as a percentage of the total population.
- *Population* over age 65 is given as a percentage of the total population.
- *Life expectancy* refers to the average number of years that a person can be expected to live.

- *Urban population* is the percentage of the population living in places considered urban, usually having at least 2,000 people.
- *Per capita GNP*, given in United States dollars, represents an average yearly income for each person.
- * Information not available

Source: 1995 World Population Data Sheet of the Population Reference Bureau, Inc.

Annual Growth Rate (percent)	Projected Population 2025 (millions)	Infant Mortality Rate (per 1,000 births)	Population Under Age 15 (percent)	Population Over Age 65 (percent)	Life Expectancy (years)	Urban Population (percent)	Per Capita GNP 1993 (U.S. dollars)
1.5	8,192.5	62	32	6	66	43	4,740
0.1	1,267.8	9	20	14	74	75	18,130
1.9	6,924.7	68	35	5	64	35	1,090
2.2	5,432.7	73	38	4	61	38	1,320
0.6	36.6	6	21	12	78	77	20,670
0.6	335.1	8	22	13	76	75	24,750
1.2	0.1	18	25	6	73	31	6,390
1.2	46.5	23	31	9	71	87	7,290
1.3	0.4	24	29	5	73	84	11,500
0.5	0.3	9	24	12	76	38	6,240
3.3	0.3	34	44	4	68	48	2,440
2.6	13.1	71	41	4	60	58	770
1.7	202.3	58	34	4	66	76	3,202
1.6	18.1	13	30	7	72	85	3,070
2.1	52.7	28	33	4	69	67	1,400
2.2	5.5	13	34	5	76	44	2,160
0.7	12.4	9	22	9	75	74	*
1.3	0.1	18	32	10	77	61	2,680
2.3	11.7	52	37	4	70	61	1,080
2.3	17.8	40	36	4	69	59	1,170
2.6	9.2	41	40	4	68	45	1,320
2.4	0.2	12	43	5	71	*	2,410
1.2	0.5	10	26	9	75	48	*

Country	Capital City	Land Area (sq. miles)	Population 1995 (millions)	Birth Rate	Death Rate
				(per 1,000 pop.)	
Guatemala	Guatemala	41,860	10.6	36	7
Guyana	Georgetown	76,000	0.8	25	7
Haiti	Port-au-Prince	10,640	7.2	35	12
Honduras	Tegucigalpa	43,200	5.5	34	6
Jamaica	Kingston	4,180	2.4	24	5
Martinique (Fr.)	Fort-de-France	410	0.4	15	6
Mexico	Mexico City	736,950	93.7	27	5
Netherlands Antilles (Neth.)	Willemstad	380	0.2	20	7
Nicaragua	Managua	45,850	4.4	33	6
Panama	Panama City	29,340	2.6	22	4
Paraguay	Asunción	153,400	5.0	34	6
Peru	Lima	494,210	24.0	29	7
Puerto Rico (U.S.)	San Juan	3,420	3.7	17	8
St. Kitts-Nevis	Basseterre	140	0.04	22	9
Saint Lucia	Castries	240	0.1	26	6
St. Vincent and the Grenadines	Kingstown	150	0.1	25	7
Suriname	Paramaribo	60,230	0.4	23	6
Trinidad and Tobago	Port-of-Spain	1,980	1.3	18	7
Uruguay	Montevideo	67,490	3.2	18	10
Venezuela	Caracas	340,560	21.8	26	5

Western Europe

Country	Capital City	Land Area (sq. miles)	Population 1995 (millions)	Birth Rate	Death Rate
Austria	Vienna	31,940	8.1	11	10
Belgium	Brussels	11,750	10.2	12	10
Denmark	Copenhagen	16,360	5.2	13	12
Finland	Helsinki	117,610	5.1	13	10
France	Paris	212,390	58.1	12	9
Germany	Berlin	134,930	81.7	9	11
Greece	Athens	50,520	10.5	10	9
Iceland	Reykjavik	38,710	0.3	17	7
Ireland	Dublin	26,600	3.6	13	9
Italy	Rome	113,540	57.7	9	10
Liechtenstein	Vaduz	60	0.03	12	7
Luxembourg	Luxembourg	990	0.4	14	9
Malta	Valletta	120	0.4	13	7
Netherlands	Amsterdam	13,100	15.5	13	9
Norway	Oslo	118,470	4.3	14	10
Portugal	Lisbon	35,500	9.9	11	10
San Marino	San Marino	20	0.03	11	8
Spain	Madrid	192,830	39.1	9	9
Sweden	Stockholm	158,930	8.9	12	11
Switzerland	Berne	15,360	7.0	12	9
United Kingdom	London	93,280	58.6	13	11

Eastern Europe

Country	Capital City	Land Area (sq. miles)	Population 1995 (millions)	Birth Rate	Death Rate
Albania	Tirana	10,580	3.5	23	6
Bosnia-Herzegovina	Sarajevo	19,740	3.5	13	7

Annual Growth Rate (percent)	Projected Population 2025 (millions)	Infant Mortality Rate (per 1,000 births)	Population Under Age 15 (percent)	Population Over Age 65 (percent)	Life Expectancy (years)	Urban Population (percent)	Per Capita GNP 1993 (U.S. dollars)
2.9	17.0	51	45	3	65	39	1,101
1.8	0.9	48	38	4	65	33	350
2.3	11.2	74	40	4	57	32	*
2.8	9.7	50	45	3	68	47	580
1.8	3.4	24	34	8	74	53	1,390
0.9	0.5	6	24	10	76	81	*
2.2	142.1	34	36	4	72	71	3,750
1.3	0.3	6	26	7	76	92	*
2.7	9.1	49	44	3	65	63	360
1.8	3.8	18	33	5	72	55	2,580
2.8	9.4	38	42	4	70	50	1,500
2.1	33.9	60	36	4	66	70	1,490
1.0	4.3	12	27	10	74	73	7,020
1.3	0.1	24	32	9	69	42	4,470
2.0	0.2	23	37	7	72	48	3,040
1.8	0.2	17	37	7	73	25	2,130
1.6	0.6	28	35	5	70	49	1,210
1.2	1.4	12	31	6	71	65	3,730
0.8	3.7	20	26	12	73	90	3,910
2.1	34.8	24	38	4	72	84	2,840
0.1	8.2	6	18	15	77	65	23,120
0.1	10.5	8	18	16	77	97	21,210
0.2	5.4	5	17	15	75	85	26,510
0.3	5.5	5	19	14	76	64	18,970
0.3	63.6	6	20	15	78	74	22,960
-0.1	79.3	6	16	15	76	85	23,560
0.1	10.0	8	18	13	77	72	7,390
1.0	0.3	3	25	11	79	91	23,620
0.5	3.8	6	25	11	75	57	12,580
0	54.4	8	15	16	77	97	19,620
0.5	0.03	6	19	10	72	*	*
0.4	0.4	5	18	14	76	86	35,850
0.6	0.4	9	22	11	75	89	7,970
0.4	17.4	6	18	13	77	61	20,710
0.4	5.0	5	19	16	77	73	26,340
0.1	10.0	8	18	14	75	48	7,890
0.3	0.03	8	15	15	76	91	*
0.1	34.6	7	18	15	77	64	13,650
0.1	9.6	4	19	18	78	83	24,830
0.3	7.5	5	18	15	78	68	36,410
0.2	62.5	6	19	16	76	90	17,970
1.7	4.6	33	33	6	72	37	340
0.6	3.9	*	23	7	72	*	*

Country	Capital City	Land Area (sq. miles)	Population 1995 (millions)	Birth Rate	Death Rate
				(per 1,000 pop.)	
Bulgaria	Sofia	42,680	8.5	9	13
Croatia	Zagreb	21,830	4.5	11	11
Czech Republic	Prague	30,590	10.4	10	11
Hungary	Budapest	35,650	10.2	11	14
Macedonia	Skopje	9,930	2.1	16	8
Poland	Warsaw	117,550	38.6	12	10
Romania	Bucharest	88,930	22.7	10	12
Serbia and Montenegro (Yugoslavia)	Belgrade	26,940	10.8	13	10
Slovakia	Bratislava	18,790	5.4	12	10
Slovenia	Ljubljana	7,820	2.0	10	10

Northern Eurasia

Country	Capital City	Land Area (sq. miles)	Population 1995 (millions)	Birth Rate	Death Rate
Armenia	Yerevan	11,500	3.7	14	7
Azerbaijan	Baku	33,400	7.3	21	7
Belarus	Minsk	80,200	10.3	10	13
Estonia	Tallinn	17,410	1.5	9	15
Georgia	Tbilisi	26,900	5.4	11	9
Kazakstan	Almaty	1,049,200	16.9	18	9
Kyrgyzstan	Bishkek	76,600	4.4	25	8
Latvia	Riga	24,900	2.5	9	16
Lithuania	Vilnius	25,210	3.7	12	12
Moldova	Chisinau	14,170	4.3	14	12
Russia	Moscow	6,592,800	147.5	9	15
Tajikistan	Dushanbe	55,300	5.8	28	7
Turkmenistan	Ashkhabad	188,500	4.5	32	8
Ukraine	Kiev	233,100	50.2	10	15
Uzbekistan	Tashkent	172,700	22.7	29	7

Southwest Asia

Country	Capital City	Land Area (sq. miles)	Population 1995 (millions)	Birth Rate	Death Rate
Bahrain	Manama	260	0.6	29	3
Cyprus	Nicosia	3,570	0.7	16	8
Gaza	*	*	0.9	55	5
Iran	Tehran	631,660	61.3	36	7
Iraq	Baghdad	168,870	20.6	44	7
Israel	Jerusalem	7,850	5.5	21	6
Jordan	Amman	34,340	4.1	32	6
Kuwait	Kuwait	6,880	1.5	26	2
Lebanon	Beirut	3,950	3.7	25	5
Oman	Muscat	82,030	2.2	53	4
Qatar	Doha	4,250	0.5	18	2
Saudi Arabia	Riyadh	830,000	18.5	36	4
Syria	Damascus	71,070	14.7	44	6
Turkey	Ankara	297,150	61.4	23	7
United Arab Emirates	Abu Dhabi	32,280	1.9	23	4
West Bank	*	*	1.5	45	5
Yemen	Sanaa	203,850	13.2	53	21

Annual Growth Rate (percent)	Projected Population 2025 (millions)	Infant Mortality Rate (per 1,000 births)	Population Under Age 15 (percent)	Population Over Age 65 (percent)	Life Expectancy (years)	Urban Population (percent)	Per Capita GNP 1993 (U.S. dollars)
-0.4	7.9	16	19	15	71	68	1,160
0.0	4.2	10	20	12	70	54	*
-0.1	10.6	8	19	13	73	75	2,730
-0.3	9.3	12	18	14	69	64	3,330
0.8	2.3	24	24	8	72	58	780
0.2	40.5	14	23	11	72	62	2,270
-0.2	21.2	24	21	12	70	55	1,120
0.3	10.6	19	22	11	72	57	*
0.3	6.1	11	23	11	71	57	1,900
0.0	2.0	7	19	12	73	50	6,310
0.7	4.1	15	31	7	71	69	660
1.4	10.3	25	33	5	71	53	730
-0.3	11.2	13	22	12	69	69	2,840
-0.5	1.4	15	20	13	70	70	3,040
0.2	6.0	18	24	10	73	55	560
0.9	20.5	27	31	6	69	56	1,540
1.6	7.0	29	38	5	68	35	830
-0.7	2.3	19	21	13	68	69	2,030
-0.1	3.9	14	22	12	71	68	1,310
0.3	5.1	23	27	9	68	47	1,180
-0.5	153.1	18	21	12	65	73	2,350
2.1	13.1	47	43	4	70	28	470
2.4	7.9	46	41	4	66	45	1,380
-0.5	54.0	14	20	14	69	68	1,910
2.3	42.3	28	41	4	69	39	960
2.6	0.9	19	32	2	74	88	7,870
0.9	1.0	9	25	11	77	53	10,380
5.0	3.8	32	51	3	69	94	*
2.9	106.8	57	44	3	67	58	2,230
3.7	52.6	67	47	3	66	70	*
1.5	8.0	7	30	9	77	90	13,760
2.6	8.3	34	42	3	72	78	1,190
2.3	3.4	12	29	1	75	96	23,350
2.0	6.1	28	33	7	75	86	*
4.9	5.5	24	36	3	71	12	5,600
1.6	0.9	11	30	1	73	91	15,140
3.2	50.3	24	43	2	70	79	7,780
3.7	31.7	44	49	4	66	51	*
1.6	91.8	47	33	5	67	63	2,120
1.9	3.0	23	32	15	72	82	22,470
4.0	3.4	33	48	4	68	*	*
3.2	36.6	83	52	3	52	23	*

Country	Capital City	Land Area (sq. miles)	Population 1995 (millions)	Birth Rate	Death Rate
				(per 1,000 pop.)	

Africa

Country	Capital City	Land Area (sq. miles)	Population 1995 (millions)	Birth Rate	Death Rate
Algeria	Algiers	919,590	28.4	30	6
Angola	Luanda	481,350	11.5	47	20
Benin	Porto-Novo	42,710	5.4	49	18
Botswana	Gaborone	218,810	1.5	38	11
Burkina Faso	Ouagadougou	105,710	10.4	47	19
Burundi	Bujumbura	9,900	6.4	46	16
Cameroon	Yaoundé	179,690	13.5	41	12
Cape Verde	Cidade de Praia	1,560	0.4	27	8
Central African Republic	Bangui	240,530	3.2	42	17
Chad	N'djamena	486,180	6.4	44	18
Comoros	Moroni	860	0.5	47	11
Congo	Brazzaville	131,850	2.5	40	17
Côte d'Ivoire	Abidjan	122,780	14.3	50	15
Djibouti	Djibouti	8,950	0.6	38	16
Egypt	Cairo	384,340	61.9	30	7
Eritrea	Asmara	48,260	3.5	43	15
Equatorial Guinea	Malabo	10,830	0.4	41	15
Ethiopia	Addis Ababa	376,830	56.0	46	16
Gabon	Libreville	99,490	1.3	29	14
Gambia	Banjul	3,860	1.1	48	21
Ghana	Accra	88,810	17.5	42	12
Guinea	Conakry	94,930	6.5	44	20
Guinea-Bissau	Bissau	10,860	1.1	43	21
Kenya	Nairobi	219,960	28.3	40	13
Lesotho	Maseru	11,720	2.1	38	12
Liberia	Monrovia	37,190	3.0	44	12
Libya	Tripoli	679,360	5.2	45	8
Madagascar	Antananarivo	224,530	14.8	44	12
Malawi	Lilongwe	36,320	9.7	50	20
Mali	Bamako	471,120	9.4	52	20
Mauritania	Nouakchott	395,840	2.3	39	14
Mauritius	Port Louis	710	1.1	20	7
Morocco	Rabat	172,320	29.2	29	6
Mozambique	Maputo	302,740	17.4	45	19
Namibia	Windhoek	317,870	1.5	37	11
Niger	Niamey	489,070	9.2	53	19
Nigeria	Lagos	351,650	101.2	43	12
Réunion (Fr.)	St. Denis	970	0.7	21	6
Rwanda	Kigali	9,530	7.8	44	17
São Tomé and Príncipe	São Tomé	370	0.1	35	9
Senegal	Dakar	74,340	8.3	43	16
Seychelles	Victoria	100	0.1	23	8
Sierra Leone	Freetown	27,650	4.5	46	19
Somalia	Mogadishu	242,220	9.3	50	19
South Africa	Pretoria	471,440	43.5	31	8
Sudan	Khartoum	917,370	28.1	42	12
Swaziland	Mbabane	6,640	1.0	43	11
Tanzania	Dar-es-Salaam	342,100	28.5	43	14
Togo	Lomé	21,000	4.4	47	11
Tunisia	Tunis	59,980	8.9	23	6

Annual Growth Rate (percent)	Projected Population 2025 (millions)	Infant Mortality Rate (per 1,000 births)	Population Under Age 15 (percent)	Population Over Age 65 (percent)	Life Expectancy (years)	Urban Population (percent)	Per Capita GNP 1993 (U.S. dollars)
2.4	47.2	55	40	4	67	50	1,650
2.7	26.6	137	45	3	46	32	*
3.1	12.3	86	47	3	48	36	420
2.7	3.0	41	43	5	64	46	2,590
2.8	20.9	94	48	3	45	15	300
3.0	12.2	102	46	4	50	6	180
2.9	29.2	65	44	4	58	41	770
1.9	0.7	65	45	6	65	44	870
2.5	5.2	97	43	3	41	39	390
2.6	12.9	122	41	3	48	22	200
3.6	1.4	80	48	3	58	29	520
2.3	4.2	109	44	3	46	58	920
3.5	33.4	88	47	2	51	46	630
2.2	1.1	115	41	2	48	77	780
2.2	97.6	62	40	4	64	44	660
2.8	7.0	105	44	3	*	17	*
2.6	0.9	103	43	4	53	37	360
3.1	129.7	120	49	3	50	15	100
1.5	1.8	95	34	5	54	73	4,050
2.7	2.1	90	45	2	45	26	360
3.0	38.0	66	45	3	56	36	430
2.4	13.2	139	44	3	44	29	510
2.1	2.0	140	43	3	44	22	220
2.7	49.1	62	48	3	56	27	270
2.6	3.8	79	41	5	61	16	660
3.1	6.8	113	44	3	55	44	*
3.7	14.4	63	45	3	63	85	*
3.2	34.4	93	46	3	57	26	240
3.0	18.5	134	48	3	45	17	220
3.1	23.7	106	48	3	47	26	300
2.5	4.4	101	45	4	52	39	510
1.3	1.5	18	29	6	69	44	2,980
2.2	40.7	57	38	5	69	47	1,030
2.7	35.1	148	46	2	46	33	80
2.7	3.1	57	42	5	59	32	1,660
3.4	22.4	123	49	3	47	15	270
3.1	246.0	87	45	3	56	16	310
1.6	0.9	8	31	6	73	73	*
2.7	13.7	110	48	3	46	5	200
2.6	0.3	51	47	4	64	46	330
2.7	16.9	68	45	3	49	43	730
1.5	0.1	13	31	7	70	50	6,370
2.7	8.7	143	44	3	46	35	140
3.2	21.3	122	48	3	47	24	*
2.3	70.1	46	37	5	66	57	2,900
3.0	58.4	80	43	3	55	27	*
3.2	2.5	93	46	2	57	30	1,050
3.0	56.3	92	47	3	49	21	100
3.6	11.7	89	49	2	58	30	330
1.7	13.5	43	37	5	68	60	1,780

Country	Capital City	Land Area (sq. miles)	Population 1995 (millions)	Birth Rate (per 1,000 pop.)	Death Rate (per 1,000 pop.)
Uganda	Kampala	77,050	21.3	52	19
Western Sahara	El Aaiún	103,000	0.2	47	19
Zaire (D.R. of the Congo)	Kinshasa	875,520	44.1	48	16
Zambia	Lusaka	287,020	9.1	45	15
Zimbabwe	Harare	149,290	11.3	35	9

South Asia

Country	Capital City	Land Area	Population	Birth Rate	Death Rate
Afghanistan	Kabul	251,770	18.4	50	22
Bangladesh	Dhaka	50,260	119.2	31	11
Bhutan	Thimphu	18,150	0.8	39	16
India	New Delhi	1,147,950	930.6	29	10
Maldives	Malé	120	0.3	43	7
Nepal	Kathmandu	52,820	22.6	39	12
Pakistan	Islamabad	297,640	129.7	39	10
Sri Lanka	Colombo	24,950	18.2	20	5

East Asia

Country	Capital City	Land Area	Population	Birth Rate	Death Rate
Brunei	Bandar Seri Begawan	2,030	0.3	27	3
Cambodia	Phnom Penh	68,150	10.6	45	16
China	Beijing	3,600,930	1,218.8	17	7
Hong Kong	Victoria	380	6.0	12	5
Indonesia	Jakarta	705,190	198.4	24	8
Japan	Tokyo	145,370	125.2	10	7
Korea, North	Pyongyang	46,490	23.5	24	6
Korea, South	Seoul	38,120	44.9	15	6
Laos	Vientiane	89,110	4.8	43	15
Macao	Macao	10	0.4	15	3
Malaysia	Kuala Lumpur	126,850	19.9	28	5
Mongolia	Ulan Bator	604,830	2.3	22	8
Myanmar	Yangon	253,880	44.8	31	12
Philippines	Manila	115,120	68.4	30	9
Singapore	Singapore City	240	3.0	16	5
Taiwan	Taipei	13,900	21.2	15	5
Thailand	Bangkok	197,250	60.2	20	6
Vietnam	Hanoi	125,670	75.0	30	7

The Pacific World

Country	Capital City	Land Area	Population	Birth Rate	Death Rate
Australia	Canberra	2,941,290	18.0	14	7
Federated States of Micronesia	Palikir	270	0.1	38	8
Fiji	Suva	7,050	0.8	25	5
French Polynesia (Fr.)	Papeete	1,410	0.2	26	5
Guam (U.S.)	Agana	210	0.2	30	4
Marshall Islands	Majuro	70	0.1	26	4

Annual Growth Rate (percent)	Projected Population 2025 (millions)	Infant Mortality Rate (per 1,000 births)	Population Under Age 15 (percent)	Population Over Age 65 (percent)	Life Expectancy (years)	Urban Population (percent)	Per Capita GNP 1993 (U.S. dollars)
3.3	37.4	115	47	3	45	11	190
2.8	0.4	152	*	*	46	*	*
3.2	107.6	108	48	3	48	29	*
3.0	18.5	107	47	3	48	42	370
2.5	17.3	53	45	3	54	31	540
2.8	45.3	163	41	3	43	18	*
2.0	175.8	88	40	3	55	16	220
2.3	1.6	121	39	4	51	17	170
1.9	1,384.6	79	36	4	60	26	290
3.6	0.6	50	47	3	65	26	820
2.6	43.5	98	42	4	54	10	160
2.9	232.9	91	41	3	61	28	430
1.5	23.2	18	35	4	73	22	600
2.4	0.4	7	35	3	74	67	*
2.9	22.8	111	46	3	50	13	*
1.1	1,492.0	44	27	6	69	29	490
0.7	8.1	5	19	9	78	*	17,860
1.6	276.5	66	35	4	63	31	730
0.2	125.8	4	16	15	79	78	31,450
1.8	32.1	28	29	4	70	61	*
0.9	50.8	11	23	6	72	74	7,670
2.9	9.8	102	45	3	52	19	290
1.2	0.6	6	24	7	69	97	*
2.4	34.5	11	36	4	71	51	3,160
1.4	3.6	61	40	4	64	55	400
1.9	72.2	49	36	4	60	25	*
2.1	113.5	34	38	4	65	49	830
1.1	3.6	4	23	7	74	100	19,310
1.0	25.5	5	24	7	74	75	*
1.4	75.1	35	30	4	70	19	2,040
2.3	118.8	42	40	5	65	19	190
0.8	23.1	6	21	12	78	85	17,510
3.0	0.2	52	43	3	68	26	*
2.0	1.1	19	38	3	63	39	2,140
2.1	0.4	13	36	3	70	57	*
2.6	0.2	10	30	4	74	38	*
2.2	0.5	63	51	3	62	65	*

Country	Capital City	Land Area (sq. miles)	Population 1995 (millions)	Birth Rate (per 1,000 pop.)	Death Rate (per 1,000 pop.)
New Caledonia	Noumea	7,060	0.2	26	6
New Zealand	Wellington	103,470	3.5	16	8
Palau	Koror	190	0.2	22	8
Papua-New Guinea	Port Moresby	174,850	4.1	34	10
Solomon Islands	Honiara	10,810	0.4	39	5
Vanuatu	Port-Vila	4,710	0.2	38	9
Western Samoa	Apia	1,090	0.2	31	8

Land Area Comparison Maps

United States and Canada

United States
= 3,539,230 sq. miles
Canada
= 3,560,220 sq. miles

United States and Latin America

United States
= 3,539,230 sq. miles
Latin America
= 7,750,910 sq. miles

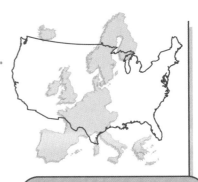

United States and Western Europe

United States
= 3,539,230 sq. miles
Western Europe
= 1,383,010 sq. miles

United States and Southwest Asia

United States
= 3,539,230 sq. miles
Southeast Asia
= 2,378,010 sq. miles

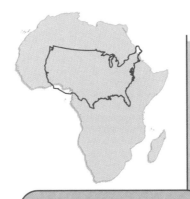

United States and Africa

United States
= 3,539,230 sq. miles
Africa
= 11,444,670 sq. miles

United States and South Asia

United States
= 3,539,230 sq. miles
South Asia
= 1,843,660 sq. miles

Annual Growth Rate (percent)	Projected Population 2025 (millions)	Infant Mortality Rate (per 1,000 births)	Population Under Age 15 (percent)	Population Over Age 65 (percent)	Life Expectancy (years)	Urban Population (percent)	Per Capita GNP 1993 (U.S. dollars)
2.0	0.3	8	33	5	74	70	*
0.9	4.3	7	23	12	76	85	12,900
1.4	0.02	25	30	6	67	69	*
2.3	7.5	63	42	2	57	15	1,120
3.4	0.8	28	47	3	61	13	750
2.9	0.3	45	44	4	63	18	1,230
2.3	0.3	21	41	4	65	21	980

United States and Eastern Europe

United States
= 3,539,230 sq. miles
Eastern Europe
= 431,030 sq. miles

United States and Northern Eurasia

United States
= 3,539,230 sq. miles
Northern Eurasia
= 8,601,890 sq. miles

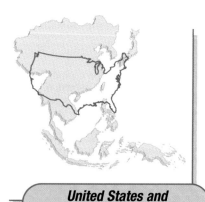

United States and East Asia

United States
= 3,539,230 sq. miles
East Asia
= 6,133,520 sq. miles

United States and The Pacific World

United States
= 3,539,230 sq. miles
The Pacific World
= 3,252,480 sq. miles

GAZETTEER

Berlin (53°N, 13°E) The capital city of Germany, p. 269

Bern (47°N, 7°E) The capital city of Switzerland, p. 269

Bhutan A country in South Asia, p. 557

Biscay, Bay of A part of the Atlantic Ocean bordered by France to the north and east, and Spain to the south, p. 271

Black Sea A landlocked sea between Europe and Asia, connected to the Mediterranean Sea by the Bosporus, pp. 14–15

Bogotá (5°N, 75°E) The capital and largest city of Colombia in South America, p. 189

Bolivia A country in South America, p. 189

Bombay (see **Mumbai**)

Bosnia and Herzegovina A country in Eastern Europe, p. 349

Bosporus A narrow strait between the Black Sea and the Sea of Marmara, p. 427

Boston (42°N, 71°W) The capital and largest city of Massachusetts, p. 115

Bothnia, Gulf of An arm of the Baltic Sea, extending between Finland and northern Sweden, p. 271

Botswana A country in southern Africa, p. 477

Brahmaputra River A major South Asian river, flowing from the Himalayas through Bangladesh and into the Bay of Bengal, p. 559

Brasília (16°S, 48°W) The capital city of Brazil, p. 189

Bratislava (48°N, 17°E) The capital city of Slovakia (Slovak Republic), p. 349

Brazil The largest country in South America, p. 189

British Columbia A western province of Canada, along the Pacific coast, p. 166

Brunei (Negara Brunei Darussalam) A country on the northern coast of the island of Borneo in Southeast Asia, p. 597

Brussels (51°N, 4°E) The capital city of Belgium, p. 269

Bucharest (44°N, 26°E) The capital and largest city of Romania in Europe, p. 349

Budapest (48°N, 19°E) The capital city of Hungary, p. 349

Buenos Aires (34°S, 59°W) The capital city of Argentina, p. 189

Bulgaria A country in Eastern Europe, p. 349

Burkina Faso A country in West Africa, p. 477

Burma (*see* **Myanmar**)

Burundi A country in Central Africa, p. 477

C

Cairo (30°N, 31°E) The capital city of Egypt, p. 477

Calcutta (22°N, 88°E) One of the largest cities in India, located by the Bay of Bengal, p. 557

Calgary (51°N, 114°W) A major city in Alberta, Canada, p. 115

California The most populous state in the United States, located on the Pacific Ocean coast, p. 126

Cambodia A country on the Indochina Peninsula in Southeast Asia, p. 597

Cameroon A country in Central Africa, p. 477

Canada A country in North America, consisting of ten provinces and two territories, p. 115

Canadian Shield A large horseshoe-shaped formation of exposed bedrock around the southern end of Hudson Bay, p. 117

Canberra (35°S, 149°E) The capital city of Australia, p. 601

Cape of Good Hope (34°S, 18°E) Cape in the Republic of South Africa, p. 479

Cape Horn (56°S, 67°W) Cape in Tierra del Fuego, Chile, the southern extremity of South America, p. 191

Cape Town (34°S, 18°E) A major city in the nation of South Africa, p. 477

Cape Verde A chain of fifteen islands in the Atlantic Ocean, off the west coast of Africa, p. 477

Caracas (10°N, 67°W) The capital and largest city of Venezuela in South America, p. 189

Caribbean Sea Part of the southern Atlantic Ocean, p. 191

Carpathian Mountains A major mountain system of Central and Eastern Europe, a continuation of the Alps, p. 351

Casablanca (34°N, 8°W) The largest city in the North African nation of Morocco, p. 477

Cascade Range A mountain range extending from northern California in the United States into southern British Columbia, Canada, p. 117

Caspian Sea A landlocked salt-water sea, which lies in Northern Eurasia, p. 389

Caucasus Mountains A mountain range in Northern Eurasia and Turkey, p. 389

Central African Republic A country in Central Africa, p. 477

Central America The part of Latin America that comprises the seven republics of Guatemala, Honduras, El Salvador, Nicaragua, Costa Rica, Panama, and Belize, p. 216

Central Siberian Plateau A major plateau in Siberia between the Lena and Yenisei rivers, p. 389

Chad, Lake A large freshwater lake in north central Africa, p. 479

Chad A country in Central Africa, p. 477

Chicago (42°N, 88°W) A major city in Illinois in the midwestern United States, p. 115

Chile A country in South America, p. 189

China A country occupying most of the mainland of East Asia, p. 597

Coast Ranges A series of mountain ranges along the Pacific coast of North America, extending from Baja California in the south to Alaska in the north, p. 117

Colombia A country in South America, p. 189

Colorado A mountainous state in the western part of the United States, p. 126

Colorado River A major river in western North America, flowing from central Colorado into the Gulf of California, p. 117

Comoros An island nation between the East African coast and the island of Madagascar, p. 477

Congo A country in Central Africa, p. 477

Congo (Zaire) River A major river of central Africa, flowing into the Atlantic Ocean, p. 477

Connecticut A state in the northeast region of the United States, p. 126

Copenhagen (56°N, 12°E) The capital city of Denmark, p. 269

Coral Sea An arm of the Pacific Ocean, located between Australia and the Solomon Islands, p. 601

Corsica A French island in the Mediterranean Sea west of Italy, p. 271

Costa Rica A country in Central America, p. 189

Côte d'Ivoire A country in West Africa, p. 477

Crete A Greek island in the Mediterranean Sea, p. 271

Croatia A country in Eastern Europe, p. 349

Cuba An island country that is the largest of the Caribbean islands, p. 189

Cyprus An island country in the eastern Mediterranean Sea, off the coast of Turkey, p. 425

Czech Republic A country in Eastern Europe, p. 349

D

Dakar (15°N, 17°W) The capital and largest city of the West African nation of Senegal, p. 477

Dallas (33°N, 97°W) A major city in Texas, in the southern United States, p. 115

Danube River A river in Central and Eastern Europe, flowing from Germany east to the Black Sea, p. 351

Darling River A major river in eastern Australia, p. 601

Dead Sea A salt-water lake on the border of Israel and Jordan, the lowest point on the earth's surface, p. 427

Deccan Plateau The plateau in southern India between the Eastern and Western Ghats, p. 559

Delaware A small state in the northeastern United States, p. 126

Delhi (29°N, 77°E) A major city located in northwestern India, p. 557

Denmark A country in northern Europe, p. 269

Denver (40°N, 105°W) The capital and largest city of Colorado, in the western United States, p. 115

District of Columbia Identical to the city of Washington, D. C., located on the Potomac River between Maryland and Virginia, p. 115

Djibouti A country in East Africa, p. 477

Dnieper River A major river of eastern Europe that flows into the Black Sea, p. 389

Dniester River A major river of southeastern Europe that flows through Moldova and into the Black Sea, p. 389

Dominican Republic A country in the Caribbean Sea on the island of Hispaniola, p. 189

Don River A major river of European Russia that flows into the Black Sea, p. 389

Dublin (53°N, 6°W) The capital city of the Republic of Ireland, p. 269

E

East China Sea An arm of the Pacific Ocean east of mainland China and north of Taiwan, p. 599

Eastern Ghats A mountain chain in southern India on the eastern side of the Deccan plateau, p. 559

Ecuador A country in South America, p. 189

Edinburgh (56°N, 3°W) The capital city of Scotland, p. 282

Egypt A country in northern Africa, p. 477

El Salvador The smallest country in Central America, p. 189

England (*see* **United Kingdom**)

English Channel A strait between England and France, connecting the Atlantic Ocean and the North Sea, p. 271

Equatorial Guinea A country in Central Africa, p. 477

Erie, Lake One of the Great Lakes of the United States, p. 117

Eritrea A country in East Africa, p. 477

Estonia A country in Northern Eurasia, p. 387

Ethiopia A country in East Africa, p. 477

Euphrates River A river flowing from Turkey south through Syria and Iraq, p. 427

Europe The world's second-smallest continent, a peninsula of the Eurasian landmass bounded by the Arctic Ocean, the Atlantic Ocean, the Mediterranean Sea, and Asia, pp. 14–15

European Plain A broad plain in eastern Europe, extending through parts of Russia, Belarus, and Ukraine, p. 389

Everest, Mt. The world's tallest mountain, in the Himalayas, p. 559

F

Fiji A country consisting of an island group in the southern Pacific Ocean, p. 689

Finland A country in northern Europe, p. 269

Florida A populous state in the southern part of the United States, p. 126

France A country in Western Europe, p. 269

French Guiana (Department of Guiana) An overseas department of France in South America, p. 189

French Polynesia A country in the South Pacific Ocean roughly midway between Australia and South America, pp. 12-13

G

Gabon A country in Central Africa, p. 477

Gambia A country in West Africa, p. 477

Ganges River A river in northern India and Bangladesh, flowing from the Himalayas to the Bay of Bengal, p. 559

Gaza Strip A strip of land at the southeastern end of the Mediterranean Sea, formerly part of Egypt, occupied by Israel from 1967 until 1994, p. 425

Gdansk (54°N, 19°E) A seaport city in northern Poland, p. 349

Genoa (44°N, 10°E) A major seaport city in northwestern Italy, p. 333

Georgia A state in the southern United States, p. 126

Georgia, Republic of A country in Northern Eurasia, p. 387

Germany A country in Europe, p. 269

Ghana A country in West Africa, p. 477

Gibraltar A British colony at the southern tip of Spain, p. 326

Gibraltar, Strait of The narrow passage of open water connecting the Mediterranean Sea and the Atlantic Ocean, p. 271

Glasgow (56°N, 4°W) The largest city in Scotland, p. 269

Gobi Desert A desert in Mongolia and northern China, p. 599

Great Barrier Reef The long series of coral reefs running along the northeastern coast of Australia, p. 601

Great Indian Desert A large desert in northwestern India, p. 559

Great Lakes A group of five large lakes— Superior, Michigan, Huron, Erie, and Ontario—in central North America, p. 117

Great Plains The broad fertile plain descending east from the base of the Rocky Mountains in central North America, p. 117

Great Rift Valley A long depression running from Jordan in southwestern Asia to Mozambique in southeastern Africa, p. 23

Great Salt Lake A large, salty lake in the Great Basin region, p. 117

Great Sandy Desert A desert in western Australia, p. 601

Greater Antilles A group of islands in the Caribbean Sea, p. 191

Greece A country in Mediterranean Europe, p. 269

Greenland A large, self-governing island in the northern Atlantic Ocean, part of Denmark, p. 117

Greenwich The place in England through which the Prime Meridian runs

Guatemala A country in Central America, p. 189

Guinea, Gulf of A part of the Atlantic Ocean along the western coast of Africa, p. 479

Guinea A country in West Africa, p. 477

Guinea-Bissau A country in West Africa, p. 477

Gulf of Mexico An arm of the Atlantic Ocean, east of Mexico and south of the United States, p. 115

Guyana A country in South America, p. 189

H

Hague, The (52°N, 4°E) A city in the Netherlands, headquarters of the International Court of Justice, p. 269

Haiti A country in the Caribbean Sea on the island of Hispaniola, p. 189

Hamburg (54°N, 10°E) A major seaport city in Germany, p. 310

Hanoi (21°N, 106°E) The capital and one of the largest cities of Vietnam, p. 597

Havana (23°N, 82°W) The capital city of Cuba, p. 189

Hawaii A state in the United States made up of several islands in the central Pacific Ocean, p. 126

Helsinki (60°N, 25°E) The capital city of Finland, p. 269

Himalayas A mountain system of south central Asia, extending along the border between India and Tibet and through Pakistan, Nepal, and Bhutan, p. 559

Hindu Kush A mountain range in Afghanistan, p. 559

Hiroshima (34°N, 132°E) A seaport city in Japan, on the island of Honshū, p. 644

Hispaniola An island in the Caribbean Sea, divided between Haiti on the west and the Dominican Republic on the east, p. 191

Ho Chi Minh City (11°N, 106°E) Formerly called Saigon, the largest city of Vietnam, p. 597

Honduras A country in Central America, p. 189

Hong Kong (22°N, 115°E) Formerly a British crown colony in East Asia, it became part of the People's Republic of China in 1997, p. 597

Honolulu (21°N, 158°W) The capital and largest city of Hawaii, in the United States, p. 115

Hormuz, Strait of A narrow passage of water between the Persian Gulf and the Gulf of Oman, p. 427

Huang He River A river in northern China, p. 599

Hudson Bay An inland sea in the Northwest Territories, Canada, p. 117

Hungary A country in Eastern Europe, p. 349

Huron, Lake One of the Great Lakes of central North America, p. 117

I

Iberian Peninsula A peninsula in southwestern Europe, shared by Spain and Portugal, pp. 14–15

Iceland An island country in the northern Atlantic Ocean, close to the Arctic Ocean, p. 269

Idaho A state in the western United States, p. 126

Illinois A state in the midwestern region of the United States, p. 126

India A large country occupying most of the Indian subcontinent in South Asia, p. 557

Indian Ocean The world's third-largest ocean, lying between Africa, Asia, and Australia, pp. 14–15

Indiana A state in the midwestern part of the United States, p. 126

Indochina Peninsula The southeastern peninsula of Asia, surrounded by the South China Sea and the Andaman Sea, p. 25

Indo-Gangetic Plain A major plain of South Asia, in northeastern India, p. 559

Indonesia A country in Southeast Asia consisting of many islands, including Sumatra, Java, Sulawesi (Celebes), Bali, and the western half of New Guinea, p. 597

Indus River A river in South Asia, starting in Tibet and flowing through India and Pakistan to the Arabian Sea, p. 559

Ionian Sea An arm of the Mediterranean Sea, between Greece and southern Italy, p. 351

Iowa A state in the midwestern region of the United States, p. 126

Iran A country in southwest Asia, p. 425

Iran, Plateau of A major plateau of Southwest Asia, east of the Zagros Mountains, p. 427

Iraq A country in southwest Asia, p. 425

Ireland A country in northern Europe, occupying part of an island lying west of Great Britain in the Atlantic Ocean, p. 269

Irrawaddy River A major river of southeastern Asia, running south through Myanmar, into the Andaman Sea, p. 599

Irtysh River A major Siberian river, starting in the Altai Mountains and flowing into the Ob River, p. 389

Islamabad (33°N, 73°E) The capital of Pakistan, p. 557

Israel A country in southwest Asia, p. 425

Istanbul (41°N, 29°E) A seaport city in northwestern Turkey on the Bosporus; formerly Constantinople, p. 425

Italian Peninsula The European peninsula in the Mediterranean Sea, surrounded by the Adriatic and Tyrrhenian Seas, p. 21

Italy A boot-shaped country in southern Europe, including the islands of Sicily and Sardinia, p. 269

J

Jakarta (6°S, 110°W) The capital and largest city of Indonesia, p. 597

Jamaica An island country in the Caribbean Sea, p. 189

Japan An island country in the Pacific Ocean off the east coast of Asia, consisting of four main islands—Honshū, Hokkaidō, Kyūshū, and Shikoku, p. 597

Japan, Sea of An arm of the Pacific Ocean between Japan and the Asian mainland, p. 599

Java Sea A sea among the islands between the Indian and Pacific Oceans, south of Borneo, p. 599

Jerusalem (32°N, 35°E) The capital city of Israel, holy to Jews, Christians, and Muslims, p. 425

Johannesburg (26°S, 28°E) The largest city in the Republic of South Africa, p. 477

Jordan A country in southwest Asia, p. 425

Jordan River A river in southwest Asia, starting in Syria and flowing to the northern end of the Dead Sea, forming the border between Israel and Jordan, p. 427

K

Kabul (34°N, 69°E) The capital and largest city of Afghanistan, p. 557

Kalahari Desert A desert plateau in Southern Africa, p. 479

Kamchatka Peninsula A peninsula of northeastern Asia pointing into the Pacific Ocean, p. 389

Kansas A state in the midwestern United States, p. 126

Karachi (25°N, 67°E) The largest city of Pakistan, p. 557

Karakoram Range A major chain of mountains at the meeting point of Pakistan, India, and China, p. 559

Kara Kum Desert A desert of central Eurasia, south of the Aral Sea and east of the Caspian Sea, p. 389

Kathmandu (28°N, 85°E) The capital and largest city of Nepal, p. 557

Kazakhstan A country in Northern Eurasia, p. 387

Kenya A country in East Africa, p. 477

Kentucky A southern state in the United States with a long northern border on the Ohio River, p. 126

Kiev (50°N, 31°E) The capital and largest city of Ukraine, p. 387

Kilimanjaro, Mt. The highest mountain of Africa, located in Tanzania, p. 479

Kinshasa (4°S, 15°E) The capital and largest city of the Democratic Republic of the Congo, p. 477

Kirgiz Steppe A plain of Northern Eurasia, north of the Aral Sea, p. 389

Korean Peninsula A peninsula of eastern Asia, surrounded by the Sea of Japan and the Yellow Sea, p. 599

Kuril Islands A chain of islands running north from Japan toward the Kamchatka Peninsula, p. 389

Kuwait, State of A country in southwest Asia, p. 425

Kuwait City (29°N, 47°E) The capital and seaport city of Kuwait, p. 425

Kyrgyzstan A country in Northern Eurasia, p. 387

L

Lagos (6°N, 3°E) The capital and largest city of Nigeria, p. 477

Laos A country on the Indochina Peninsula in Southeast Asia, p. 597

Latin America The culture region that includes Mexico, Central America, South America, and some of the Caribbean Islands, p. 186

Latvia A country in Northern Eurasia, p. 387

Lebanon A country in southwest Asia on the eastern end of the Mediterranean Sea, p. 425

Lena River A major Siberian river, flowing north into the Arctic Ocean, p. 389

Lesotho A country in Southern Africa, completely surrounded by the Republic of South Africa, p. 477

Lesser Antilles A group of islands in the Caribbean Sea, p. 191

Liberia A country in West Africa, p. 477

Libya A country in northern Africa, p. 477

Liechtenstein A country in Central Europe, p. 269

Lima (12°S, 77°W) The capital and largest city of Peru, in South America, p. 189

Lisbon (39°N, 9°W) The capital and seaport city of Portugal, p. 269

Lithuania A country in Northern Eurasia, p. 387

London (52°N, 0°) The capital city of the United Kingdom of Great Britain and Northern Ireland, p. 269

Los Angeles (34°N, 118°W) A seaport city in California in the southwestern United States, p. 115

Louisiana A southern state in the United States with a long border on the Gulf of Mexico, p. 126

Luxembourg A country in Central Europe, p. 269

M

Macao (22°N, 114°E) A major city on the east coast of mainland Asia, p. 597

Macedonia A former republic of Yugoslavia, p. 349

Mackenzie River A major river of Canada, flowing through the Northwest Territories and into the Arctic Ocean, p. 117

Madagascar An island country off the southeast coast of Africa in the Indian Ocean, p. 477

Madras (11°N, 78°E) A major city of India, located on the southeast coast, p. 557

Madrid (40°N, 4°W) The capital city of Spain, p. 269

Magellan, Strait of A narrow passage of water between Tierra del Fuego and the South American mainland, p. 191

Maine One of the northeastern states in the United States, p. 126

Malacca, Strait of A narrow passage of water between the Malay Peninsula and the island of Sumatra, p. 599

Malawi A country of southeastern Africa, p. 477

Malay Peninsula A peninsula in Southeast Asia, comprising west Malaysia and part of Thailand, p. 599

Malaysia A country in Southeast Asia, p. 597

Maldives A country consisting of a chain of islands in the Indian Ocean southwest of India, p. 557

Mali A country in West Africa, p. 477

Malta An island country in the Mediterranean Sea, p. 269

Manila (15°N, 121°E) The capital of the Philippines, p. 597

Manitoba A province of Canada, located between Saskatchewan and Ontario, p. 166

Marseille (43°N, 5°E) A major seaport city in southeast France, p. 269

Marshall Islands An island nation in the central Pacific Ocean, p. 689

Maryland A state on the Atlantic coast of the United States, p. 126

Massachusetts One of the New England states in the United States, p. 126

Mauritania A country in West Africa, p. 477

Mauritius An island nation in the Indian Ocean, east of Madagascar, p. 477

Mecca (21°N, 40°E) Islam's holiest city, in western Saudi Arabia, p. 425

Medina (24°N, 40°E) Islam's second-holiest city, in western Saudi Arabia, p. 425

Mediterranean Sea A large sea separating Europe and Africa, p. 271

Melbourne (38°S, 145°E) Australia's second-largest city, p. 601

Mekong River A major river of southeastern Asia, flowing through Indochina and into the South China Sea, p. 599

Mexico A country in North America, p. 189

Mexico City (19°N, 99°W) Capital and largest city of Mexico; largest urban area in the world, p. 189

Miami (26°N, 80°W) The largest city in Florida, in the southern United States, p. 115

Michigan A state in the midwestern United States, p. 126

Michigan, Lake One of the Great Lakes of central North America, p. 117

Micronesia A nation of many islands in the central Pacific Ocean, pp. 12–13

Middle East (*see* **Southwest Asia**)

Midway Islands Two islands, Eastern and Sand, in the central Pacific Ocean, administered by the United States, p. 26

Milan (38°N, 15°E) A city in northwestern Italy, p. 269

Minneapolis (45°N, 93°W) The largest city of Minnesota and a major city of the Midwest region of the United States, p. 115

Minnesota A state in the midwestern region of the United States, sharing a border with Canada, p. 126

Minsk (54°N, 28°E) The capital and largest city of Belarus in eastern Europe, p. 387

Mississippi A southern state in the United States with a border on the Gulf of Mexico, p. 126

Mississippi River A river in the central United States, flowing from Minnesota south into the Gulf of Mexico, p. 117

Missouri A state in the midwestern part of the United States, p. 126

Missouri River A river in the central United States, p. 117

Moldova A country in Northern Eurasia, p. 387

Monaco A country in Western Europe, p. 269

Mongolia A country in East Asia, p. 597

Montana A large western state on the Great Plains of the United States, p. 126

Montenegro A former republic of Yugoslavia, p. 349

Montreal (46°N, 74°W) A city in the province of Quebec in eastern Canada, p. 115

Morocco A country in northern Africa, p. 477

Moscow (55°N, 37°E) The capital city of Russia, p. 387

Mouths of the Ganges The delta region of the Ganges River in eastern India and Bangladesh, p. 559

Mozambique A country in Southern Africa, p. 477

Mumbai (Bombay) (19°N, 73°E) The largest city in India, p. 557

Munich (48°N, 12°E) A city in southeastern Germany, p. 269

Murray River A major river of Australia, p. 601

Myanmar A country in Southeast Asia; formerly Burma, p. 597

Nairobi (1°S, 36°E) The capital and largest city of Kenya, p. 477

Nagasaki (33°N, 130°E) A seaport city on the west coast of Japan, p. 644

Namib Desert A desert in southern Africa, p. 479

Namibia A country in southern Africa, p. 477

Narmada River A river in South Asia, flowing into the Arabian Sea, p. 559

Nebraska A state in the Midwest of the United States, p. 126

Nepal A country in south Asia, p. 557

Netherlands A country in Western Europe, p. 269

Netherlands Antilles Two groups of islands in the Caribbean Sea, p. 191

Nevada A western state in the United States, largely in the Great Basin, p. 126

New Brunswick A maritime province of Canada, located south of the mouth of the St. Lawrence River, p. 166

New Delhi (29°N, 77°E) The capital city of India, p. 557

New Hampshire One of the northeastern states in the United States, p. 126

New Jersey The most densely populated state in the United States, p. 126

New Mexico A western state in the United States, p. 126

New Orleans (30°N, 90°W) A major seaport city in Louisiana in the southern United States, p. 115

New York The second most populous state in the United States, p. 126

New York City (41°N, 74°W) A major seaport city in the state of New York in the northeastern United States, p. 115

New Zealand A country in the southwest Pacific Ocean, consisting of two major islands, p. 601

Newfoundland One of the maritime provinces of Canada and the farthest east of Canada's provinces, p. 166

Nicaragua, Lake A lake in the Central American nation of Nicaragua, p. 191

Nicaragua A country in Central America, p. 189

Niger A country in West Africa, p. 477

Niger River A river in West Africa, flowing from Guinea into the Gulf of Guinea, p. 479

Nigeria A country in West Africa, p. 477

Nile River A river in east and northeast Africa, the longest in the world, flowing north into the Mediterranean Sea, p. 479

North America The world's third-largest continent, consisting of Canada, the United States, Mexico, and many islands, pp. 14–15

North Carolina A southern state along the Atlantic coast of the United States, p. 126

North Dakota A state in the Midwest of the United States, p. 126

(North) Korea A country in East Asia, p. 597

North Sea An arm of the Atlantic Ocean between Great Britain and the European mainland, p. 271

Northern Ireland (*see* **United Kingdom**)

Northwest Territories A northern territory of Canada, bordered in part by Hudson's Bay and the Arctic Ocean, p. 166

Norway A country in northern Europe, p. 269

Nova Scotia One of Canada's maritime provinces, located east of New Brunswick, p. 166

Nyasa, Lake A major lake in southeastern Africa along the borders of Malawi, Tanzania, and Mozambique, p. 479

Ob River A major Siberian river, flowing from the Altai Mountains and into the Arctic Ocean, p. 389

Ohio A state in the midwestern part of the United States, with a long border on the Ohio River, p. 126

Ohio River A major North American river, flowing from the Allegheny Mountains into the Mississippi River, p. 117

Okeechobee, Lake A large lake in Florida in the southern United States, p. 148

Okhotsk, Sea of An arm of the Pacific Ocean between the Kamchatka Peninsula and the Asian mainland, p. 389

Oklahoma A state in the Midwest of the United States, p. 126

Oman, Gulf of An arm of the Indian Ocean between mainland Asia and the southeastern tip of the Arabian Peninsula, p. 427

Oman A country in southwest Asia on the Arabian Peninsula, p. 425

Ontario The most populous of Canada's provinces, located between Quebec and Manitoba, p. 166

Ontario, Lake One of the Great Lakes of central North America. p. 117

Orange River A river in southern Africa, flowing west into the Atlantic Ocean, p. 479

Oregon A western state on the Pacific coast of the United States, p. 126

Orinoco River A South American river, flowing through Venezuela and into the Atlantic Ocean, p. 191

Osaka (35°N, 135°E) One of the largest cities in Japan, p. 597

Oslo (60°N, 11°E) The capital city of Norway, p. 269

Ottawa (45°N, 76°W) The capital city of Canada, located in the province of Ontario, p. 115

P

Pacific Ocean A large body of water, bounded by North and South America on the east and Asia and Oceania on the west, and stretching from the Arctic to the Antarctic, pp. 14–15

Pakistan A country in South Asia, p. 557

Palestine (32°N, 35°E) A historical region at the eastern end of the Mediterranean Sea, p. 425

Pamirs Mountains A mountainous area in southeastern Tajikistan, p. 389

Panama, Isthmus of A narrow strip of land linking South and Central America and separating the Atlantic and Pacific oceans; site of the Panama Canal, p. 191

Panama, Republic of A country in Central America, p. 189

Panama Canal An important shipping canal across the Isthmus of Panama, linking the Caribbean Sea (hence the Atlantic Ocean) to the Pacific Ocean

Panama (9°N, 80°W) The capital and seaport city of the Republic of Panama, p. 189

Papua New Guinea A country in Southeast Asia, p. 597

Paraguay A country in South America, p. 189

Paraguay River A major river of South America, rising in Brazil and flowing south into the Atlantic Ocean, p. 191

Paraná River A river of South America, flowing into the Paraguay River, p. 191

Paris (49°N, 2°E) The capital city of France, p. 269

Pennsylvania A state in the northeastern part of the United States, p. 126

Persia The historical name for the region around present-day Iran

Persian Gulf An arm of the Arabian Sea, p. 427

Peru A country in South America, p. 189

Philadelphia (40°N, 75°W) A city in Pennsylvania in the northeastern United States, p. 115

Philippine Sea A part of the Pacific Ocean east of the Philippines and north of New Guinea, p. 599

Philippines An island country in Southeast Asia, p. 597

Phnom Penh (12°N, 105°E) The capital and largest city of Cambodia, p. 597

Phoenix (33°N, 112°W) The capital and largest city of Arizona in the United States, p. 115

Pindus Mountains A range of mountains in central and northern Greece, p. 271

Poland A country in Eastern Europe, p. 349

Portugal A country in southwestern Europe, p. 269

Prague (50°N, 14°E) The capital city of the Czech Republic, p. 349

Prince Edward Island One of Canada's maritime provinces and the smallest of the provinces, p. 166

Puerto Rico An island commonwealth of the United States in the Caribbean Sea, p. 189

Pyongyang (39°N, 126°E) The capital and largest city of North Korea, p. 597

Pyrenees A mountain range in southwestern Europe forming the border between France and Spain, p. 271

Q

Qatar A country in southwest Asia on the Arabian Peninsula, p. 425

Quebec The largest of Canada's provinces, located in the eastern part of the country, p. 166

Quebec City (47°N, 71°W) The capital city of the province of Quebec in eastern Canada, p. 115

Quito (1°S, 79°W) The capital of Ecuador and one of its largest cities, p. 189

R

Red Sea A narrow sea separating northeastern Africa from the Arabian Peninsula, connected to the Mediterranean Sea by the Suez Canal and to the Indian Ocean by the Gulf of Aden, p. 427

Réunion An island in the Pacific Ocean east of Madagascar, p. 477

Rhine River A river in Central Europe, starting in Switzerland and flowing north through Germany to the Netherlands, p. 271

Rhône River A river in Western Europe, starting in Switzerland and flowing

south through France into the Mediterranean Sea, p. 271

Rhode Island The smallest state in the United States, located in the Northeast, p. 126

Riga (57°N, 24°E) The capital and largest city of Latvia, p. 387

Rio de Janeiro (23°S, 43°W) A major city in Brazil, p. 189

Rio Grande A major river of North America, flowing from the Rocky Mountains in Colorado to the Gulf of Mexico, p. 117

Rocky Mountains A mountain system in North America, p. 117

Romania A country in Eastern Europe, p. 349

Rome (42°N, 12°E) The capital city of Italy, p. 269

Rub' al-Khali (Empty Quarter) A desert on the Arabian Peninsula, p. 427

Russia A country in Northern Eurasia, p. 387

Rwanda A country in East Africa, p. 477

S

Sahara A desert in northern Africa, p. 479

St. Lawrence River A major North American river, flowing from Lake Ontario into the Atlantic Ocean, p. 117

St. Louis (38°N, 90°W) A major city of Missouri in the midwestern United States, p. 115

St. Petersburg (60°N, 30°E) Formerly called Leningrad, one of the largest cities of Russia, p. 387

San Francisco (38°N, 122°W) A seaport city in California in the western United States, p. 115

San Juan (18°N, 67°W) The capital and largest city of Puerto Rico, p. 189

San Marino A country in north central Italy, p. 269

Santiago (33°S, 71°W) The capital city of Chile, p. 189

São Francisco River A river of eastern Brazil, rising in the Brazilian Highlands and flowing into the Atlantic Ocean, p. 191

São Paulo (23°S, 46°W) The largest city in Brazil, p. 189

São Tomé and Principe An island nation off the coast of western Africa, p. 477

Sarajevo (44°N, 18°E) The capital city of Bosnia and Herzegovina, p. 349

Sardinia An Italian island in the Mediterranean Sea west of Italy, p. 271

Saskatchewan A province on the Great Plains of Canada, p. 166

Saudi Arabia A country in southwest Asia occupying most of the Arabian Peninsula, p. 425

Scandinavia A region in northern Europe consisting of Norway, Sweden, Denmark, and sometimes Finland, Iceland, and the Faroe Islands, p. 271

Scandinavian Peninsula A peninsula of northwestern Europe surrounded by the Baltic, North, and Norwegian Seas, p. 21

Scotland (see **United Kingdom**)

Seattle (48°N, 122°W) The largest city in Washington, one of the western United States, p. 115

Seine River A river in northern France, flowing through Paris and emptying into the English Channel, p. 271

Senegal A country in West Africa, p. 477

Senegal River A river in West Africa, p. 479

Seoul (38°N, 127°E) The capital and largest city of South Korea, p. 597

Serbia A former republic of Yugoslavia, p. 349

Seychelles An island country in the Indian Ocean, northeast of Madagascar, p. 22

Shanghai (31°N, 121°E) A large city in eastern China and one of the world's leading seaports, p. 597

Siberia A resource-rich region of Russia, extending east across northern Asia from the Ural mountains to the Pacific coast, p. 389

Sicily An Italian island in the Mediterranean Sea, p. 271

Sierra Leone, Republic of A country in West Africa, p. 477

Sierra Madre A rugged mountain system in Mexico, including the Sierra Madre Oriental (East), the Sierra Madre Occidental (West), and the Sierra Madre del Sur (South), p. 191

Sierra Nevada A mountain range in California in the western United States, p. 117

Singapore An island country in Southeast Asia, p. 597

Slovakia (Slovak Republic) A country in Eastern Europe, p. 349

Slovenia A country in Eastern Europe, p. 349

Solomon Islands A nation of islands in the South Pacific, north of the Coral Sea, pp. 12–13

Somalia A country in East Africa, p. 477

South Africa A country in southern Africa, p. 477

South America The world's fourth-largest continent, bounded by the Caribbean Sea, the Atlantic Ocean, and the Pacific Ocean and linked to North America by the Isthmus of Panama, pp. 14–15

South Carolina A southern state on the Atlantic coast of the United States, p. 126

South Dakota A state in the Midwest of the United States, p. 126

Southwest Asia The region that includes southwest Asia and sometimes part or all of northern Africa, pp. 425

(South) Korea A country in East Asia, p. 597

Spain A country in southwestern Europe, p. 269

Sri Lanka An island country off the southeast coast of India, p. 557

Stockholm (59°N, 18°E) The capital city of Sweden, p. 269

Sudan A country in East Africa, p. 477

Suez Canal A shipping canal across the Isthmus of Suez, connecting the Mediterranean Sea and the Indian Ocean through the Gulf of Suez and the Red Sea, p. 427

Superior, Lake The largest of the Great Lakes in central North America, p. 117

Suriname A country in South America, p. 189

Swaziland A country in Southern Africa, p. 477

Sweden A country in northern Europe, p. 269

Switzerland A country in Western Europe, p. 269

Sydney (34°S, 151°E) The capital of New South Wales, a state of Australia, p. 601

Syria A country in southwest Asia, p. 425

Syrian Desert A desert in southwest Asia, p. 427

Taipei (25°N, 121°E) The capital and largest city of Taiwan, p. 597

Taiwan An island country off the southeast coast of the People's Republic of China, p. 597

Tajikistan A country in Northern Eurasia, p. 387

Takla Makan Desert A large desert in western China, p. 599

Tallinn (59°N, 25°E) The capital and largest city of Estonia, p. 387

Tanganyika, Lake A lake in eastern Africa, along the borders of Tanzania, Burundi, and Zaire, p. 479

Tanzania A country in East Africa, p. 477

Tashkent (41°N, 69°E) The capital and largest city of Uzbekistan in central Eurasia, p. 387

Tasman Sea An arm of the Pacific Ocean, located between Australia and New Zealand, p. 601

Taurus Mountains A mountain chain in southern Turkey, p. 427

Tbilisi (42°N, 45°W) The capital and largest city of Georgia, in southeastern Europe, p. 387

Tehran (36°N, 52°E) The capital city of Iran, p. 425

Tennessee A state in the southern part of the United States, p. 126

Texas A large state in the southern part of the United States, located along the Rio Grande, p. 126

Thailand A country in Southeast Asia, p. 597

Tian Shan A mountain system in central Asia, p. 599

Tigris River A river in Turkey and Iraq, p. 427

Togo A country in West Africa, p. 477

Tokyo (36°N, 140°E) The capital and largest city of Japan, on the island of Honshū, p. 597

Toronto (44°N, 79°W) The largest city in Canada and capital of the province of Ontario, p. 115

Tripoli (34°N, 36°E) The capital and largest city of Libya, p. 477

Tunis (37°N, 10°E) The capital and largest city of Tunisia, p. 477

Tunisia A country in northern Africa, p. 477

Turkey A country in Europe and southwest Asia, p. 425

Turkmenistan A country in Northern Eurasia, p. 387

Tyrrhenian Sea An arm of the Mediterranean Sea, west of the Italian Peninsula, p. 271

U

Uganda, Republic of A country in East Africa, p. 477

Ukraine A country in Northern Eurasia, formerly a republic of the Soviet Union, p. 387

United Arab Emirates A country in southwest Asia on the eastern coast of the Arabian Peninsula, p. 425

United Kingdom of Great Britain and Northern Ireland An island country of Western Europe, consisting of England, Scotland, Wales, and Northern Ireland, p. 269

United States of America A country in North America, consisting of forty-eight contiguous states, the District of Columbia, and Alaska and Hawaii, p. 115

Ural Mountains A mountain system in Northern Eurasia, forming part of the border between Europe and Asia, p. 389

Uruguay A country in South America, p. 189

Utah A western state in the United States, p. 126

Uzbekistan A country in Northern Eurasia, p. 387

Vancouver (49°N, 123°W) A major seaport city in western Canada, p. 115

Vanuatu A nation made up of many islands, formerly called New Hebrides, in the Pacific Ocean, east of the Coral Sea, pp. 12-13

Vatican City The capital city of Holy See, an independent state contained within Rome, Italy; headquarters of the Roman Catholic church, p. 269

Venezuela A country in South America, p. 189

Venice (45°N, 12°E) A seaport city located on more than one hundred islands in the Lagoon of Venice in northern Italy on the Adriatic Sea, p. 333

Vermont A state in the New England region of the United States, p. 126

Victoria, Lake The largest lake in Africa, located along the Tanzania-Uganda border, p. 479

Vienna (48°N, 16°E) The capital city of Austria, p. 269

Vietnam A country in Southeast Asia, p. 597

Vilnius (55°N, 25°E) The capital and largest city of Lithuania, p. 387

Virginia A southern state along the Atlantic coast of the United States, p. 126

Vladivostok (43°N, 132°E) A port city on the Pacific coast and Russia's largest city in the far East, p. 387

Volga River A river in Russia, rising near Moscow and flowing into the Caspian Sea, p. 389

Wales (see United Kingdom)

Warsaw (52°N, 21°E) The capital city of Poland, p. 349

Washington A northwestern state along the Pacific coast of the United States, p. 126

Washington, D.C. (39°N, 77°W) The capital city of the United States, p. 115

West Virginia A mountainous state in the eastern part of the United States, p. 126

Western Dvina River A river flowing from Russia, west through Belarus and Latvia, into the Baltic Sea, p. 389

Western Samoa An island nation in the South Pacific, pp. 12–13

Western Siberian Lowland A major lowland between the Ural Mountains and the Central Siberian Plateau, p. 389

White Sea An arm of the Arctic Ocean in far northwestern Russia, p. 389

Wisconsin A midwestern state in the United States, p. 126

Wyoming A western state in the United States, p. 126

Y

Yangzi River A major river in China, p. 599

Yellow Sea An arm of the Pacific Ocean between the Korean Peninsula and mainland China, p. 599

Yemen A country in southwest Asia on the Arabian Peninsula, p. 425

Yenisei River A major Siberian river, flowing north into the Arctic Ocean, p. 389

Yeravan (40°N, 44°E) The capital and largest city of Armenia, p. 387

Yucatán Peninsula A low, flat peninsula in southeastern Mexico, p. 191

Yukon River A major North American river, flowing from the Yukon Territory of Canada, through Alaska and into the Bering Sea, p. 117

Yukon Territory Located in the far northwest of Canada, bordered in part by Alaska and the Arctic Ocean, p. 166

Z

Zagreb (46°N, 16°E) The capital city of Croatia, p. 349

Zagros Mountains A mountain system in southern and western Iran, p. 427

Zaire (Democratic Republic of the Congo) A country in Central Africa, p. 477

Zambezi River A river in southern Africa, flowing east into the Indian Ocean opposite Madagascar, p. 479

Zambia A country in southern Africa, p. 477

Zimbabwe A country in Southern Africa, p. 477

GLOSSARY

PRONUNCIATION KEY

Symbol	Key Words
a	asp, fat, parrot
ā	ape, date, play, break, fail
ä	ah, car, father, cot
e	elf, ten, berry
ē	even, meet, money, flea, grieve
i	is, hit, mirror
ī	ice, bite, high, sky
ō	open, tone, go, boat
ô	all, horn, law, oar
oo	look, pull, moor, wolf
ōō	ooze, tool, crew, rule
yoo	use, cute, few
yōō	cure, globule
oi	oil, point, toy
ou	out, crowd, plow
u	up, cut, color, flood
ʉr	urn, fur, deter, irk
ə	a as in ago e as in agent i as in sanity o as in comply u as in focus
ər	perhaps, murder
zh	azure, leisure, beige
nj	ring, anger, drink

A

abdicate To relinquish power or responsibility formally; to surrender one's office, throne, or authority, p. 612

Aborigine (ab´ə rij´ə nē´) An original inhabitant; one of the original inhabitants of Australia, p. 679

absolute location The position on the earth in which a place can be found, p. 35

acculturation The process of accepting, borrowing, and exchanging traits between cultures, p. 85

acid rain Rain whose high concentration of chemicals, usually from industrial pollution, that pollutes water, kills plant and animal life, and eats away at the surface of stone and rock; a form of chemical weathering, p. 49

acupuncture The ancient Chinese practice of inserting fine needles at specific body points to cure disease or to ease pain, p. 629

alluvial plain A broad expanse of land along riverbanks, consisting of rich, fertile soil left by floods, p. 558

altiplano (äl´ tē plä´nō) A Spanish word meaning "high plain"; a series of highland valleys and plateaus located in the Andes of Bolivia and Peru, p. 252

anarchy Political disorder and violence; lawlessness, p. 454

ancestor worship The belief that respecting and honoring one's ancestors will cause them to live on in the spirit world after death, p. 516

animism The religious belief that such things as the sky, rivers, and trees contain a spirit, or soul, p. 516

annex To formally incorporate into a country or state the territory of another, p. 292

apartheid (ə pärt´hāt) An Afrikaans word meaning "apartness"; formerly in the Republic of South Africa, the policy of strict racial segregation and discrimination against nonwhites, p. 541

aquaculture Fish farming; the raising of fish for food in enclosed environments such as tanks, reservoirs, ponds, sheltered bays, and river estuaries, p. 606

aqueduct A large pipe or channel designed to transport water from a remote source over a long distance, usually by gravity, p. 160

arable Capable of being farmed, or cultivated, p. 432

archipelago (ärk´ə pel´ə gō´) A group of islands, p. 224

artesian well A well that is drilled deep enough to tap a layer of porous material filled with ground water, p. 685

atheism The belief that God does not exist, p. 628

atmosphere A multilayered band of gases, water vapor, and dust above the earth, p. 59

atoll (a´tôl) A ring-shaped coral island surrounding a lagoon, p. 689

authoritarian Descriptive of a system of government in which one person, perhaps a dictator, holds all political power, p. 94

autonomous region A political unit with limited self-government, p. 624

ayatollah A religious leader among Shiite Muslims, p. 466

B

balkanize To break up into small, mutually hostile political units, as occurred in the Balkans after World War I, p. 372

barbarian A person without manners or civilized customs, p. 664

barter The exchange of goods without money, p. 525

basin An area drained by a river and its tributaries, p. 190

basin irrigation An old system by which water and silt was controlled by embankments and time-released to irrigate farmlands, p. 493

bauxite A mineral used in making aluminum, p. 248

bayou A marshy inlet or outlet of a lake or a river, p. 148

bazaar An open-air market; a street lined with shops and stalls, p. 490

bedrock Solid rock underlying all soil, gravel, clay, sand, and loose material on the earth's surface, p. 170

birthrate The number of live births each year per 1,000 people, p. 83

blight A plant disease, p. 293

bog An area of wet, spongy ground, p. 286

boycott To refuse to purchase, sell, or use a product or service as an expression of disapproval, p. 570

buffer A protective zone between two countries, p. 632

buffer state A country that separates two or more hostile countries, p. 584

C

campesino (käm´pe sē´nō) A Spanish word meaning "rural or rustic; a peasant"; in Latin America, a tenant farmer or farm worker, p. 250

canopy The uppermost spreading branchy layer of a forest, p. 195

canton A political division or state; one of the states in Switzerland, p. 318

capital Wealth in the form of money or property owned or used in business; wealth, in whatever form, used to produce more wealth, p. 495

capitalist Descriptive of an economic system (capitalism) in which the means of production are controlled by private individuals or corporations; also called a market economy in which people, as consumers, help determine what will be produced by buying or not buying certain products, p. 95

caravan A large group of merchants who join together to travel in safety, p. 498

cardinal direction One of the four points of the compass: north, south, east, and west, p. 4

cartographer A person who makes maps or charts, p. 6

cash crop A farm crop grown for sale and profit, p. 209

caste system A social hierarchy in which a person possesses a distinct rank in society that is determined by birth, p. 574

cataract A large waterfall; any strong flood or downpour of water, p. 478

caudillo A Latin American military dictator, p. 222

cay (kā, kē) A small, low island or coral reef, p. 190

census The systematic counting of a population, p. 2

chaparral A type of natural vegetation that is adapted to Mediterranean climates; small evergreen trees and low bushes, or scrub, p. 74

charpoy A wooden bed frame with knotted string in place of a mattress, p. 575

chemical weathering The process by which the actual chemical structure of rock is changed, usually when water and carbon dioxide cause a breakdown of the rock, p. 49

chernozem The Russian word for fertile soil, meaning "black earth," p. 395

climate The term used for the weather patterns that an area or region typically experiences over a long period of time, p. 59

collective farm A state-owned farm in the former Soviet Union managed by workers who shared the profits from their produce, p. 367

Columbian Exchange Two-way trade between the Americas and Europe that began with the arrival of Christopher Columbus in the "New World," p. 198

command economy An economic system in which the government dictates what goods will be manufactured, p. 402

commercial farming The raising of crops and livestock for sale in outside markets, p. 107

communism A system of government in which the government controls the means of production, determining what goods will be made, how much workers will be paid, and how much items will cost, p. 95

confederation A system of government in which individual political units keep their sovereignty but give limited power to a central government, pp. 93, 318

coniferous Cone-bearing; a type of tree able to survive long, cold winters, with long, thin needles rather than leaves, p. 74

continent Any of the seven large landmasses of the earth's surface: Africa, Antarctica, Asia, Australia, Europe, North America, and South America, p. 41

continental climate The type of climate found in the great central areas of continents in the Northern Hemisphere; characterized by extreme temperatures—cold, snowy winters and warm or hot summers, p. 65

continental divide A boundary or area of high ground that separates rivers flowing toward opposite sides of a continent, p. 116

continental drift theory The idea that continents slowly shift their positions due to movement of the tectonic plates on which they ride, p. 43

convergence zone An area of severe storms where the frigid waters circulating around Antarctica meet the warmer waters of the Atlantic, Pacific, and Indian oceans, p. 695

coral reef A marine ridge in shallow, tropical seas, formed primarily from skeletal fragments of certain marine organisms and the limestone resulting from their compaction, p. 190

cordillera (kôr´ dil yer´ə) A related set of separate mountain ranges, pp. 116, 250

core The earth's center, consisting of very hot metal that is dense and solid in the inner core and molten, or liquid, in the outer core, p. 40

cottage industry A small-scale manufacturing operation in which people produce goods in their own homes using their own tools, p. 578

coup (kōō) Also called coup d´état (kōō´ dā tä) The sudden overthrow of a ruler or government, often involving violent force or the threat of force, p. 514

crevasse (kri vas´) A deep crack in glacial ice, p. 694

crust The solid, rocky, surface layer of the earth, p. 40

culture The way of life that distinguishes a people, for example, government, language, religion, customs, and beliefs, p. 81

culture hearth A place in which important ideas begin and thereafter spread to surrounding cultures, p. 90

customs Duties, or taxes, charged by a government on imported goods; a government agency authorized to collect duties on imported goods, p. 179

cyclone The Australian term for hurricane; a violent, rotating windstorm, similar in intensity to a hurricane, p. 683

czar An emperor of Russia, p. 387

death rate The number of deaths each year per 1,000 people, p. 83

decentralize To transfer government power to smaller regions, p. 317

deciduous Leaf-shedding; a type of tree that sheds its leaves when winter approaches, p. 73

deforestation The process of stripping the land of its trees, pp. 510, 587

demilitarized zone A strip of land on which there are no troops or weapons, p. 656

democracy A system of government in which the people are invested with the power to choose their leaders and elected representatives, and determine government policy based on the will of the majority, p. 94

demography The study of human populations, including their size, growth, density, distribution, and rates of births, marriages, and deaths, p. 81

desalination The process of removing salt from seawater so that it can be used for drinking and irrigation, p. 458

desertification The loss of all vegetation; the transformation of arable land into desert either naturally or through human intervention, p. 570

developed country A modern industrial society with a well-developed economy, p. 106

developing country A country with relatively low industrial production, often lacking modern technology, p. 106

dialect A variation of a spoken language that has its own distinct pronunciation or vocabulary and is unique to a region or community, p. 307

dictatorship A system of government in which absolute power is held by one person, p. 94

diffusion The process of spreading cultural traits from one person or society to another, p. 85

dike An embankment of earth and rock built to hold back water, p. 315

diversify To expand; to give variety to, p. 484

Doi moi The economic change begun by Vietnam in 1986, p. 672

double cropping In farming, growing more than one crop a year, p. 621

downsize To fire an employee in order to reduce costs, p. 653

drainage basin The entire area of land that is drained by a major river and its tributaries, p. 116

drip irrigation A process by which precisely controlled amounts of water drip directly onto plants from pipes, thus preserving precious water resources in dry areas, p. 444

ejido (e hē´dō) A Spanish word describing farmland owned collectively by members of a rural community, p. 209

El Niño A warm ocean current off South America's northwestern coast that influences global weather patterns, p. 194

emigrant A person who leaves a country to live elsewhere, p. 83

embankment dam A wall of soil and rock to hold back water, p. 583

embargo A severe restriction of trade with other countries, pp. 456–457

enclave A country completely surrounded by another country, p. 544

entrepreneur A go-getter individual who starts and builds a business, p. 373

environment The physical conditions of the natural surroundings, p. 71

Equator An imaginary line that circles the globe at its widest point (halfway between the North and South poles), dividing the earth into two halves called hemispheres; used as a reference point from which north and south latitudes are measured, p. 35

equinox Either of the two times each year (spring and fall) when day and night are of nearly equal length everywhere on earth, p. 61

erg A great expanse of shifting sands; a sand dune, p. 478

erosion The movement of weathered materials, including gravel, soil, and sand, usually caused by water, wind, and glaciers, p. 50

escarpment A steep cliff that separates two level areas of differing elevations, pp. 233, 478

estuary A flooded river valley at the wide mouth of a river; an inlet, or arm of the sea, where freshwater river currents meet saltwater, pp. 258, 283

ethnic minority A cultural subgroup, not of the dominant culture, p. 409

ethnocracy A system of government in which one ethnic group rules others, p. 537

Eurasia The name some geographers suggest should be used for the landmass of Europe and Asia, p. 386

exodus A mass migration from a region, p. 636

falaj **system** In the Arabian Peninsula, an ancient system of underground and surface water canals that carry water many miles from mountains to desert villages, p. 462

fault A fracture, or break, in the earth's crust, p. 42

favela A Portuguese word meaning "poor community," p. 235

federal Relating to a union of states that recognize a single central government but retain certain powers for themselves, p. 93

fellah An Egyptian farmer; a peasant or farm laborer in Arab countries (pl. fellaheen), p. 486

fertile Able to produce abundantly, rich in resources, p. 281

fjord (fyôrd) A narrow valley or inlet from the sea, originally carved out by an advancing glacier and filled by melting glacial ice, p. 294

fold A bend or buckle in the earth's crust, pp. 41–42

forage Food for grazing animals, p. 510

formal regions Places that have similar attributes; for example, political regions, p. 37

fossil fuel Any one of several nonrenewable mineral resources—coal, oil, natural gas—formed from the remains of ancient plants and animals and used for fuel, p. 101

free enterprise An economic system based on capitalism that allows individuals to own, operate, and profit from their own businesses, p. 131

front The boundary between two masses of air that differ in density or temperature, p. 64

functional regions Places connected by movements; for example, rail systems, p. 38

G

gasohol A fuel mixture of gasoline and ethanol, p. 240

gaucho (gou´chō) A cowboy who herds cattle in the Pampas of Argentina and Uruguay, p. 259

genocide The intentional destruction of a people, p. 413

geography The study of the earth's surface and the processes that shape it, the connections between places, and the complex relationships between people and their environments, p. 33

geology The study of the earth's physical structure and history, p. 40

geothermal energy Energy from the earth's intense interior heat, which transforms underground water to steam that can be used to heat homes or to make electricity, pp. 103, 294

geyser (gī´zər) A natural hot spring that shoots a column of water and steam into the air, p. 686

ghetto A section of a city in which a particular minority group is forced to live as a result of either economic or social pressures, p. 362

glacier A huge, slow-moving mass of snow and ice, formed over many years from layers of unmelted snow pressing together, thawing slightly, and refreezing, p. 52

glasnost A Russian word meaning "openness"; in the former Soviet Union, a policy allowing citizens to do and say what they wished, p. 404

glen A narrow valley, p. 287

graben (grä´ bən) A long, narrow area that has dropped between two faults, p. 338

grain elevator A tall building equipped with machinery for loading, cleaning, storing, and discharging grain, p. 155

grain exchange A place where grain is bought and sold as a commodity, p. 155

great circle Any imaginary line that circles the earth and divides it into two equal halves, p. 6

gross national product (GNP) The total value of goods and services produced by a country in a year, pp. 106, 127

growing season In farming, the average number of days between the last frost of spring and the first frost of fall, p. 153

guerrilla (gə ril´ə) A member of an armed force that is not part of a regular army; relating to a form of warfare carried on by such an independent armed force, p. 221

H

hacienda (hä´sē en´də) A large Spanish-owned estate in the Americas, often run as a farm or a cattle ranch, p. 208

Hajj (haj) In Islam, a pilgrimage or religious journey to the holy city of Mecca, birthplace of Muhammad, p. 428

Harambee A policy of cooperation adopted in Kenya after independence to encourage economic growth, p. 533

heavy industry The production of goods such as steel and machinery used by other industries, p. 402

hemisphere A half of the earth; the Equator divides the Northern and Southern hemispheres. The Prime Meridian divides the Eastern and Western hemispheres, p. 35

heterogeneity A lack of similarity, p. 672

hierarchy Rank according to function; a group of persons or things arranged in order of rank, grade, or class, p. 135

Hindi A language spoken by half the people of India, p. 560

hinterland The area served by a metropolis, p. 135

Holocaust The execution of 6 million Jews in Nazi concentration camps during World War II, p. 362

homogeneous (hō´mə jē´nē əs) Having a similar nature; uniform in structure or quality; identical, p. 646

hub A center point of concentrated activity and influence, p. 329

hurricane A destructive tropical storm that forms over the Atlantic Ocean, usually in late summer and early fall, with winds of at least 74 miles (119 km) per hour, p. 194

hydroelectric power Electricity that is generated by moving water, pp. 122, 582

I

ice shelf A massive extension of glacial ice over the sea, often protruding hundreds of miles, p. 695

ideogram In written language, a character or symbol that represents an idea or thing, as in the Chinese language, p. 627

immigrant A person who moves into a country, p. 83

Impressionism A style of art where painters try to catch visual impressions made by color, light, and shadows, p. 307

indigenous Native to or living naturally in an area or environment, p. 666

inflation A sharp, widespread rise in prices, p. 310

infrastructure An underlying foundation; the basic support facilities of a country, such as roads and bridges, power plants, and schools, p. 460

inhabitable An area that is able to support permanent residents, p. 340

inland delta An area of lakes, creeks, and swamps away from the ocean, p. 511

insurgent A person who rebels against his or her government, p. 668

intensive farming A farming method that requires a great deal of labor, p. 607

International Monetary Fund An agency of the United Nations that provides loans to countries for development projects, p. 519

irrigation The artificial watering of farmland, often by means of canals that draw water from reservoirs or rivers, pp. 203, 582

isthmus (is´məs) A narrow strip of land having water on each side and joining two larger bodies of land, p. 217

J

joint family system In India, the custom of housing all members of an extended family together, p. 576

K

karst A landform made of soft limestone that is easily dissolved by wind and water, thus producing protruding rock and caverns, p. 350

Knesset The parliament of Israel, p. 446

krill Small, shrimplike creatures; food for whales and fish, p. 695

L

lagoon A shallow body of water separated from the sea by coral reefs or sandbars, p. 683

land redistribution A policy by which land is expropriated from those who own large amounts and redistributed to those who have little or none, pp. 209, 547

landlocked Almost or entirely surrounded by land; cut off from the sea, p. 510

latifundio (lat´ə fun´dē ō) A Spanish word describing a large commercial farm owned by a private individual or a farming company, p. 209

latitude One of the series of imaginary lines, also called parallels, that circle the earth parallel to the Equator; used to measure the distance north and south from the Equator in degrees, p. 35

lava Magma, or molten rock from the earth's mantle, that breaks through the surface of the earth during volcanic activity, p. 41

leaching The dissolving and washing away of nutrients in the soil, p. 484

leeward Situated on the side facing away from the direction from which the wind is blowing, p. 225

light industry The production of small consumer goods such as clothing and appliances, p. 617

lignite A soft, brownish-black coal having a slightly woodish texture, p. 312

literacy The ability to read and write, p. 118

Llanos A plains region in southeastern Venezuela, p. 249

lock An enclosed section of a canal, in which a ship may be raised or lowered by raising or lowering the level of the water in that section, p. 169

loess (les, lō´es) Fine-grained, mineral-rich loam, dust, or silt deposited by the wind, p. 51

longitude One of the series of imaginary lines, also called meridians, that run north and south from one pole to the other; used to measure the distance east and west from the Prime Meridian in degrees, p. 35

M

malnutrition Disease caused by lack of proper food; inadequate nutrition resulting from an unbalanced diet or insufficient food, pp. 533, 585

mandate A commission from the League of Nations authorizing a nation to govern a territory, p. 439

mangrove A tropical tree that grows in swampy ground along coastal areas, p. 148

mantle A thick layer of mostly solid rock beneath the earth's crust that surrounds the earth's core, p. 40

manufacturing The process of turning a raw material into a finished product, p. 105

map projection A way of showing the round earth on a flat surface such as paper; each of the various types of map projections produces some distortion of the earth's surface, p. 6

maritime Bordering on or near the sea; relating to navigation or shipping, p. 167

martial law The law administered during a period of strict military control, p. 618

mechanical weathering The actual breaking up or physical weakening of rock by forces such as ice and roots, p. 48

medina The old section of a North African city, usually centered around a mosque, p. 500

megalopolis (meg´ə läp´ə ləs) A very large city; a region made up of several large cities and their surrounding areas, considered to be a single urban complex, p. 145

mercenary A person who works as a soldier purely for financial gain; a professional soldier hired by a foreign country, p. 524

mestizo (mes tē zō) A person of mixed European and Native American heritage, p. 192

migrant worker A worker who travels from place to place, working where extra help is needed to cultivate or harvest crops, p. 210

militarism The glorification of the military and a readiness for war, p. 651

militia An army; also, the private army of a particular fighting faction, p. 454

minaret A tall, slender tower attached to a mosque, p. 428

mixed economy A system combining different degrees of government regulation, p. 296

monarchy A system of authoritarian government headed by a monarch—a king, queen, shah, or sultan—whose position is usually inherited, p. 94

monotheism The belief in one God, p. 428

monsoon A seasonal shift in the prevailing winds that influences large climate regions, p. 562

moor Broad, treeless, rolling land, often poorly drained and having patches of marsh and peat bog, p. 286

moraine (mə rān´) A ridgelike mass of rock, gravel, sand, and clay carried and deposited by a glacier, p. 52

mosque An Islamic house of religious worship, p. 428

muezzin (myoo ez´in) In Islam, a crier who calls the faithful to prayer five times each day from a minaret, p. 428

mulatto (mə lat´ō) A person of mixed ancestry, p. 248

multiethnic Composed of many ethnic groups, p. 352

multilingual Able to speak several languages, p. 272

multiplier effect The effect an investment has in multiplying related jobs throughout the economy, p. 373

Muslim A follower of Islam, p. 428

N

national identity A people's sense of what makes them a nation, p. 361

nationalize To bring a business under state control, p. 308

nationalism Devotion to the interests or culture of a nation; the desire for national independence to promote a common culture or interests, pp. 413, 569

natural resource A material that humans take from the natural environment to survive and to satisfy their needs, p. 101

natural vegetation The typical plant life that abounds in areas where humans have not significantly altered the landscape, p. 71

navigable Deep or wide enough to allow the passage of ships, p. 328

nonrenewable resource A natural resource that cannot be replaced once it is used—for example, minerals such as fossil fuels, iron, copper, aluminum, uranium, and gold, p. 101

nonviolent resistance The policy of opposing an enemy or oppressor by any means other than violence, p. 570

nuclear energy A type of energy produced by fission—the splitting of uranium atoms in a nuclear reactor, releasing stored energy, p. 103

O

oasis (ō ā´ sis) A place where a supply of fresh water makes it possible to support life in a dry region, p. 431

ore A rocky material containing a valuable mineral, p. 284

outback Remote, sparsely settled, arid, rural country, especially the central and western plains and plateaus of Australia, p. 683

P

pack ice Floating sea ice formed by a mix of icebergs with other ice formed in superchilled ocean waters, p. 695

paddy Irrigated or flooded land on which rice is grown, p. 665

pampas A grasslands region in Argentina and Uruguay, p. 259

páramos (par´ə mos´) A series of highland valleys and plateaus in the Andes of Ecuador, p. 253

partition A division into parts; a separation; to divide into parts, p. 571

peat Spongy material containing waterlogged and decaying mosses and plants, sometimes dried and used as fuel, p. 291

peninsula A strip of land that juts out into an ocean, p. 201

per capita GNP The gross national product of a country divided by the country's total population, p. 106

perennial irrigation An irrigation system that provides necessary water to the land throughout the year, p. 493

perestroika (p´ə ru stroi´ kə) A Russian word meaning "a turning about"; in the former Soviet Union, a policy of economic restructuring, p. 404

perishable good A product that does not stay fresh for long, p. 319

permafrost A layer of soil just below the earth's surface that stays permanently frozen, pp. 76, 399

pharaoh A ruler of ancient Egypt, p. 490

piedmont A region of rolling foothills, p. 258

plant community A mix of interdependent plants that grow naturally in one place, p. 71

plate tectonics The theory that the earth's outer shell is composed of a number of large, unanchored plates, or slabs of rock, whose constant movement explains earthquakes and volcanic activity, p. 42

polder An area of low-lying land that has been reclaimed from the sea by encircling the area with dikes and pumping the water into canals, p. 315

politically neutral Not taking sides in disputes, p. 296

population density The average number of people living in a given area, p. 81

prairie A temperate grassland characterized by a great variety of grasses, p. 120

precipitation All the forms of water that fall to earth from the atmosphere, including rain and snow, p. 63

prevailing westerlies The constant flow of air from west to east in the temperate zones of the earth, p. 274

Prime Meridian An imaginary line of longitude that runs from the North Pole to the South Pole through Greenwich, England; it is designated 0° longitude and is used as a reference point from which east and west lines of longitude are measured, p. 35

privatization The process of selling government-owned industries and businesses to private owners who can run them more efficiently, p. 366

proliferation An increase in the number of something, p. 658

prophet A person whose teachings are believed to be inspired by God, p. 428

province A territory governed as a political division of a country, p. 167

provisional Temporary; pending permanent arrangements, p. 632

purdah (pʉr´də) The practice among Hindu and Muslim women of covering the face with a veil when outside the home, p. 576

pustza An area in the Hungarian Basin that was once covered with grasses but is now farmland, p. 355

pyrethrum A pesticide produced from certain flowers, p. 533

quota A fixed quantity; a proportional share assigned to a group or to each member of a group; the number of immigrants allowed to enter a country in a given period, p. 654

recession An extended decline in general business activity, p. 308

refugee A person who flees his or her country to escape invasion, oppression, or persecution, p. 510

reincarnation The belief that the soul of a human being or animal goes through a series of births, deaths, and rebirths, p. 574

relative location The position of a place in relation to another place, p. 36

relief The differences in elevation, or height, of the landforms in any particular area, pp. 8, 41

remote sensing A method by which airplanes and satellites can produce photographs or computer-generated images of sections of the earth's surface, p. 2

Renaissance The revival of art, literature, and learning that took place in Europe during the 14th, 15th, and 16th centuries, p. 335

renewable resource A natural resource that the environment continues to supply or replace as it is used, p. 101

reparations Money paid for war damages, p. 310

reservoir A body of water collected in a natural or artificial lake, p. 493

revolution One complete orbit of the earth around the sun. The earth completes one revolution every 365¼ days, or one year, p. 60

rift valley A large split along the crest of an underwater mountain system where small earthquakes and volcanic eruptions frequently occur, p. 478

Ring of Fire A ring of volcanic mountains surrounding the rim of the Pacific Ocean, p. 45

roof top of the world A common name for the Himalaya Mountains, p. 558

rotation The spinning motion of the earth, like a top on its axis, as it travels through space, p. 60

rugged individualism The willingness of an individual to stand alone and struggle to survive and prosper, relying on his or her own personal resources and beliefs, p. 131

rural Of, or characteristic of, the countryside, p. 84

sanction An action taken by the international community to punish a country for unacceptable behaviors and to bring pressure on that country to reverse its policy, p. 541

sari A brightly colored cloth, worn by many Indian women, that is draped over the body like a long dress, p. 576

savanna A tropical grassland with scattered trees, located in the warm lands nearest the Equator, pp. 74, 190

secede To withdraw formally from membership in a political or religious organization, p. 177

secular Worldly, not relating to religion, p. 465

sediment Small particles of soil, sand, and gravel carried and deposited by water, p. 50

segregation The act of imposing the social separation of races, p. 541

seismic Descriptive of earthquakes or earth vibrations, p. 598

seismically active A region having many earthquakes and volcanic eruptions, p. 332

seismograph An instrument that measures and records movement in the earth's crust, such as earthquakes and other tremors, p. 644

self-determination The right to decide one's political future, p. 440

selva (sel´və) A Spanish word meaning "forest" or "jungle"; in Ecuador, Peru, and Bolivia, a forested region, p. 253

separatism The cause of winning political, religious, or ethnic independence from another group, p. 176

sertao A region in Brazil with poor soil and little rain, p. 238

service industry A business that provides a service, such as hotels and restaurants, p. 240

shah The ruler of Iran, p. 466

shifting agriculture A type of agriculture in which a site is prepared and used to grow crops for a year or two, at which point the farmer moves on to a new site, p. 509

silo A tall, round, airtight building used for the storage of grain, p. 153

sinkhole A hole formed when limestone is dissolved, causing the land above to collapse, p. 204

sirocco A hot, dry wind from northern Africa, p. 328

socialism A system in which the government owns, manages, or controls the production, distribution, and exchange of goods in such basic industries as transportation, communications, and banking, p. 95

solar energy Energy produced by the sun, p. 103

solstice Either of the two times a year when the sun appears directly overhead at noon to observers at the Tropics of Cancer and Capricorn, p. 61

souk A market in an Arab community, p. 500

sovereignty A country's freedom and power to decide on policies and actions, p. 92

soviet In the former Soviet Union, any one of various governing councils that made decisions at various levels, p. 401

sphere of influence An area or country that is politically and economically dominated by, though not directly governed by, another country, p. 611

standard of living A person's or group's level of material well-being, as measured by education, housing, health care, and nutrition, p. 118

steppe (step) A temperate grassland, often lightly wooded, found in Europe and Asia, p. 388

strategic value Importance of a place or thing for nations planning military actions, p. 535

structural adjustment program A program to reform the structure of an economy, p. 519

subcontinent A large landmass; a major subdivision of a continent, p. 556

subsidence A geological phenomenon in which the ground in an area sinks, p. 334

subsistence farming Farming that provides only enough for the needs of a family or a village, pp. 106, 209

suburb A usually residential area or community on the outer edge of a city, p. 134

summit The highest point of a mountain or similar elevation, p. 270

Sunbelt The southern and southwestern states of the United States, from the Carolinas to southern California, characterized by a warm climate and, recently, rapid population growth, p. 150

taiga Thinly scattered, coniferous forests found in Europe and Asia, p. 392

tariff A duty or tax imposed by a government on imported goods, p. 654

telecommunications Communicating by electronic means, p. 130

terrace In farming, a flat, narrow ledge of land, supported by walls of stone and mud parallel to the natural slope of the land, usually constructed in hilly areas to increase the amount of arable land, p. 607

theocrat The ruler of a theocracy; someone who claims to rule by religious or divine authority, p. 623

timber line The boundary in high elevations above which continuous forest vegetation cannot grow, p. 253

totalitarianism A system of government in which a central authority controls all aspects of society, subordinating individual freedom to state interests, p. 94

tributary A river or stream that flows into a main river, p. 116

tropical storm A storm with winds of at least 39 miles (63 km) per hour, p. 194

trust territory A dependent colony or territory supervised by another country or countries by commission of the United Nations, p. 691

tsunami (tsoo nä´mē) A huge wave caused primarily by a disturbance beneath the ocean, such as an earthquake or a volcanic eruption, p. 340

tundra A region where temperatures are always cool or cold and only specialized plants can grow—either alpine tundra, in high elevations, or arctic tundra, in high latitudes, pp. 76, 392

typhoon A destructive tropical storm occurring in the western Pacific Ocean or the China Sea; similar to a hurricane, p. 645

unitary A system of government in which one central government holds most of the political power, p. 93

urbanization The growth of city populations; the change from a rural, or countrylike society, to one that is urban, or citylike, in character, p. 84

velvet revolution A revolution without bloodshed, p. 366

villagization A political movement by which rural people are forced to move to towns and work on collective farms, p. 538

W

wadi (wä´dē) A gully, or usually dry riverbed, cut in the earth by running water after a downpour in arid regions of the Middle East and North Africa, p. 497

warlord A local leader with a military following, p. 612

watershed A dividing ridge between two basins, p. 523

weather The condition of the bottom layer of the earth's atmosphere in one place over a short period of time, p. 59

weathering The chemical or mechanical process by which rock is gradually broken down, eventually becoming soil, p. 48

white flight The departure of trained white administrators and technicians from a region, p. 545

windward Situated on the side facing toward the direction from which the wind is blowing, p. 225

World Bank An agency of the United Nations that provides loans to countries for development projects, p. 519

Y

yurt A round tent made of wooden framework and covered with felt or skins, p. 414

Z

Zionist A member of a movement known as Zionism, founded to promote the establishment of an independent Jewish state, p. 440

INDEX

The index includes references not only to the text but to maps, pictures, and charts as well. A page number followed by *m*, such as 477*m*, refers to a map. Page numbers with *p* and *c* after them refer to pictures and charts.

A

developing countries, 106
dhows, 458
diagrams, 10, 10*c*, 11, 11*c*
diamonds, 395, 400, 524
dictatorship, 94
Diet (Japanese parliament), 650
diffusion, cultural, 85, 90
dikes, 315
Dinaric Alps, 338, 350
direct rule, colonial, 486
diseases, in Africa, 528; in South America, 236, 255
displaying information, 3, 6*m*, 6–7, 7*m*
District of Columbia, 147, 152
Djibouti, 535, 536*c*
Dnieper River, 396
doi moi, 672
doldrums, 63
Dominica, 228*c*
Dominican Republic, 223, 224, 227, 228*c*
double cropping, 621
drainage basin, 116
Dravidian language family, 85–86
Dravidian people, 566, 587
Dreamtime, 684
drip irrigation, 444
drought, in Africa, 528; in West Africa, 510; in Zimbabwe, 546
drug trade, 250
Druze, 446, 453
dry climate, 66*m*, 66–68, 68*c*
dust bowl, 51

E

earth, effect of sun on, 59–63; erosion of, 50–53; geologic history of, 42–47; greenhouse effect, 60; internal forces of, 41–42; rotation and revolution, 60*c*, 60–61; structure of, 40–41, 41*c*; weathering of, 48–50
earthquakes, 42, 45, 164, 698–699, 699*p*, 700–701; in East Asia, 598; in Italy, 332; in Japan, 644, 645*c*; in Mexico, 201
East Africa, 530*m*, 531–538; religion in, 537
East Asia, cities of, 596, 597*m*; climate of, 604, 604*m*; countries of, 596, 597*m*; culture hearth of, 90; culture of, 602, 602*m*, 603, 603*m*; economy of, 606, 606*m*; farming in, 607, 607*p*; during Ice Ages, 124–125; landforms of, 598, 598*c*, 599*m*; language of, 602*m*; natural resources of, 606, 606*m*; population of, 84, 603*m*; refugees from, 177; religion of, 602*m*; vegetation of, 605, 605*p*, 605*m*
East Australian Current, 63
East Germany, 311
East Pakistan, 571
East Siberian Highlands, 388
East Timor, 672

Easter Island, 609
Eastern Churches, 88–89
Eastern Europe, 346–377, 349*m*, 351*m*, 360*m*; cities of, 348–349, 349*m*; climate of, 354*m*, 354–355; communism in, 356; countries of, 348–349, 349*m*, 360–377; economy of, 356*m*, 356–357, 357*c*; ethnic groups of, 352–353, 353*m*; landforms of, 350*p*, 350–351, 351*m*; languages of, 352, 352*m*; natural resources of, 356*m*, 356–357, 357*c*; people of, 352*m*, 352–353; population of, 348*c*, 353*m*; refugees from, 375; vegetation of, 354*m*, 354–355
Ebola virus, 525*p*
economic activity, in India 578–579; in South Asia, 564*m*, 564–565; in United States, 122*m*, 131, 155
economic activity maps, 9, 9*m*, 104, 104*m*
economic development, 106
economic systems, 94, 94*c*, 95
economy, of Africa, 484, 484*m*; of Albania, 374; of Australia, 9*m*, 683*m*; of Austria, 321; of Brazil, 233, 234, 238–241; of Brunei, 674; of Canada, 172; of Caribbean Islands, 227–228; of Central America, 220; of Chile, 256; of China, 617, 621–622; of East Asia, 606, 606*m*; of Eastern Europe, 356*m*, 356–357, 357*c*; of Ecuador, 254; European Union, 276; of France, 308, 308*c*; of Germany, 310–311; of Great Britain, 283–285; of Guianas, 248; of Indonesia, 672; of Italy, 333; of Japan, 650–651, 652–654; of Kazakstan, 414; of Latin America, 196*m*, 197; of Malaysia, 674; of Mexico, 210–211; mixed, 296; of New Zealand, 683*m*, 688, 688*m*; of Norden, 296–297; of North Korea, 657; of Northern Eurasia, 394*m*, 394–395; of Pacific Islands, 690–691; of Paraguay, 259; of Peru, 254; planned, 95; of Poland, 363; of Romania, 372–373; of Russia, 401–403; of Scotland, 287; of South Africa, 540; of South Korea, 657; of Spain, 328–329; of Switzerland, 319; of Taiwan, 633, 634*p*; of Thailand, 670; tropical rain forests and, 244–245; of Vietnam, 672; of Wales, 289; of Western Europe, 276*c*, 276–277, 277*m*, 300–301
ecosystems, 31
Ecuador, 254, 254*c*
Edmonton, Alberta, Canada, 171
education, in Canada, 173*p*; in India, 578*p*, 579; in Japan, 652*p*, 652–653. *See also* literacy
Egypt, 82, 442, 489–496; exports, 494, 495*c*; Great Britain and, 491–492; gross national product, 493*c*, 495; history of, 490–492; industry in, 494–495; Israel and, 492; landforms, 489*p*, 489–490, 490*m*; life

expectancy, 493*c*; life in, 490; natural resources of, 490; population, 489, 493*c*, 494; religion of, 491; Soviet Union and, 492
Eightfold Path, 566
ejidos, 209
El Nino, 194
El Paso, Texas, 148
El Salvador, 220*p*, 222*c*, 223*c*; ethnic groups of, 219, 225*c*; political unrest in, 221
Elbe River, 312
electricity, 118*m*, 122, 579*c*
elevation, 41, 59; climate and, 66
Elias, Jorge Serrano, 222
embankment dam, 583
embargo, 456–457
emigration, 83
Empty Quarter, 458
enclaves, 544
encomienda system, 208
energy resources, 102–103, 128*c*
engineering, natural disasters and improved, 164–165
England. *See* Great Britain
English Channel, 283, 285*p*
English language, 176–177, 278–279
entrepreneurs, 373
environment, 71; changes to the, 123; energy resources, 102–103; natural resources and the, 101–102; population density and, 81–82; in Soviet Union, 403–404
Equator, 5, 5*m*, 35, 61, 62, 72–73
Equatorial countercurrent, 63
Equatorial Guinea, 521, 522*c*
equinox, 60, 61
Erie Canal, 133
Eritrea, 535, 536*c*
erosion, 50–53, 552–553, 553*p*
escarpment, 478
Eskimo-Aleut language family, 85–86
Estonia, 386, 409*p*, 409–410, 412*c*
estuary, 258, 283
ethanol, 240
Ethiopia, 446*p*, 486, 535*p*, 535–536, 536*c*
ethnic cleansing, 375, 378
ethnic groups, of Africa, 480–481, 481*m*; of Bulgaria, 373; of Caribbean Islands, 225*m*, 226; in China, 626–627; of Eastern Europe, 352–353, 353*m*; of former Yugoslavia, 375*p*, 375–376; of Guianas, 247–248, 248*c*; in South America, 253; of Southeast Asia, 670–671; of Switzerland, 318. *See also* culture
ethnic minorities, in Northern Eurasia, 409, 410*m*
ethnocracy, 537
Euphrates River, 426, 434*m*, 435, 455, 456
Eurasia, 44*m*, 102, 386
Eurasian Plate, 43, 45, 338
Eurodollar, 300
Europe, African colonies of, 486–487, 487*m*; forests of, 74; languages of,

H

I

multilingual, 272
multiplier effect, 373
Mumbai, India, 561, 577
Munich, Germany, 268, 313
Mururoa Atoll, 691
music, of Austria, 321, 321p; of Brazil, 235; in Caribbean Islands, 226, 226p; of Scotland, 286p
Muslims, 375, 376, 428, 461, 466–467, 567; in the Balkans, 359; in Central Asia, 413; in East Africa, 537; in Egypt, 491; in India, 570p, 570–571; in Lebanon, 454; in Pakistan, 583; in Southeast Asia, 664, 664p; in Turkey, 464. See also Islam; Shiite Muslims; Sunni Muslims
Myanmar, 668p, 668–669

N

NAFTA. See North American Free Trade Agreement; North American Free Trade Agreement (NAFTA)
Nagasaki, Japan, 651
Nairobi, Kenya, 532
Namibia, 541c, 544
Naples, Italy, 336
Napoleon Bonaparte, 307
NASA. See National Aeronautics and Space Administration
Nashville, Tennessee, 136
Nasser, Gamal Abdel, 492, 493
Natchez people, 127, 149
National Aeronautics and Space Administration (NASA), 151
National Geographic Society, xx, 1
national identity, 361
National Water Carrier (Israel), 444
nationalism, 413, 569
Nationalist People's Party (China), 612
Native Americans, in Canada, 173, 175, 175p, 176–177; in Central America, 219; creation stories, 198; cultivation and, 127–128, 149; in Latin America, 188; in Mesoamerica, 198; Paleo–Indians, 124–125
natural disasters, 164p, 164–165, 165m
natural gas resources, 101–102; of Canada, 172; in Siberia, 395; in United States, 128–129, 159
natural resources, 92; of Africa, 484m, 484–485; of Antarctica, 696–697; of Australia, 9m, 683m; of Austria, 320p, 321; of Canada, 122m, 167, 170, 172, 179; of Central Africa, 523–524; of Côte d'Ivoire, 523; of East Asia, 606, 606m; of Eastern Europe, 356m, 356–357, 357c; of Egypt, 490; of Germany, 312; of Latin America, 196m, 197; of New Zealand, 683m; nonrenewable, 101–102; of Northern Eurasia, 394–395, 395m; of Poland, 361; renewable, 101; of Romania, 372; of

Russia, 399–400; of the Sahel, 511; of South Asia, 564m, 564–565; of Southeast Asia, 665; of United States, 122m, 127–129, 144, 149, 155–156, 158–159; of Western Europe, 276c, 276–277, 277m; of Zaire, 523, 524, 524p
Nazca Plate, 43, 45
Nazi Party, 362
Nebraska, 154m, 155, 156
Negev Desert, 444
Nehru, Jawaharlal, 569
Nepal, 555p, 556, 557m, 558, 586; religions of, 566, 567m
Netherlands, 272, 307c, 315p, 315–316, 316m; Caribbean Island colonies of, 227; Latin American colonies and, 192; Southeast Asia and, 665
Netherlands Antilles, 224, 227, 228c
neutrality, political, 297
Nevada, 159m
Nevado del Ruiz, 250
New Brunswick, Canada, 167
New Caledonia, 690, 691c
New Delhi, India, 578
New Guinea, 608
New Hampshire, 144m, 145, 146
New Jersey, 134p, 144m
New Mexico, 159m
New Orleans, Louisiana, 133, 135, 151
New South Wales, Australia, 682
New Spain, 207–208
New Testament, 428
New York, 52, 114, 134, 135, 144, 144m, 145p, 146, 146p, 228
New York City, 114, 133, 134, 135, 145p, 146, 146p, 228
New Zealand, 103, 609, 679m; climate, 681m; economy of, 683m, 688, 688m; landforms of, 600c, 601m, 686–687; natural resources of, 683m; population of, 680m; vegetation of, 687m
Newark, New Jersey, 134p
Newfoundland, Canada, 167, 177
Ngo Dinh Diem, 671
Niagara Falls, 144, 180p
Nicaragua, 221p, 222c; ethnic groups of, 219, 225c; landforms of, 219; political unrest in, 221
Niger, 509, 510, 511, 511c
Niger-Congo language family, 85–86
Niger River, 478, 508, 511
Nigeria, 486p, 487, 516c, 518p, 519p, 520p; cultures of, 518–519; farming in, 518; government of, 519–520; landforms, 518
Nile Delta, 489
Nile River, 82, 434m, 435, 478, 489, 523, 538; controlling the, 492p, 492–493, 493p
Nilo-Saharan language family, 85–86
nirvana, 566
nomads, 414, 499–500, 564; in China, 623; in Mongolia, 636

nonviolent resistance, 570
Norden, 294–297
Norgay, Tenzing, 586
North Africa, 488–503; cultures of, 498; France and, 499; landforms of, 497–498, 498p religion of, 498–499; urbanization of, 500p, 500–501
North America, 38; cities of, 115m; climate of, 65; countries of, 115; forests of, 74; landforms of, 116–117; languages of, 279; population of, 84; Ring of Fire and, 45; temperate grasslands of, 75. See also Canada; Mexico; United States
North American Free Trade Agreement (NAFTA), 180, 210
North American Plate, 42, 43, 45, 201
North Atlantic Current, 63, 65
North Atlantic Drift, 274
North Atlantic Treaty Organization (NATO), 338, 375, 376, 377p
North Carolina, 51, 148m, 149
North China Plain, 619, 620
North Dakota, 154m
North Equatorial Current, 63
North European Plain, 270, 276, 303, 350, 354, 354p, 361
North German Plain, 312
North Island, New Zealand, 686
North Korea, 656m, 656–658
North Pacific Current, 63
North Pole, 35, 61, 62
North Sea, 315
North Vietnam, 671
Northeast region, of United States, 135, 143–146
Northern Eurasia, cities of, 386–387, 387m; climate of, 65, 392–393, 393m; countries of, 386–387, 387m; cultures of, 390–391, 391p, 391c; economy of, 394m, 394–395; energy resources of, 102; landforms of, 388–389, 389m; languages of, 391c; natural resources of, 394–395, 395m; people of, 390m, 390–391; population of, 386, 390, 409, 410m; steppe region of, 37; vegetation of, 392m, 392–393
Northern Hemisphere, 35, 61, 62; climate of, 65; weathering and, 49–50
Northern Ireland. See Ireland
Northern Territories, of Canada, 173–174
Northwest Territories, of Canada, 173–174
Norway, 283c, 294, 294p, 295m, 296, 297
Nova Scotia, Canada, 167p, 168
Novgorod, Russia, 396
Novosibirsk, Rusia, 386
nuclear energy, 103
Nuclear Non-Proliferation Treaty, 658
nuclear power, 411, 411p
nuclear waste, 416p, 416–417, 417p
Nunavut, Canada, 176

ACKNOWLEDGMENTS

Photo Research: Linda L Rill

Editorial Services: Ed Hagenstein, Dotti Marshall, Jean C. Thomas

Design Services: Mark MacKay, David Maurand, Bonny Pope, Carolyn Langley

Page Production: Todd Christy, Christine LeGoff

Cover Design: Bruce Bond and Martucci Studio

Cover, Title Page Photos: Satellite photos, EROS Data Center; Mount Everest National Park by Nicholas DeVore; Sailing on the Nile River by Ary Diesendruck, both Tony Stone Images.

Cartography and Technical Illustration

GeoSystems Global Corporation
(unless otherwise noted)

Creative Illustrated Maps

Function Thru Form Inc.: xviii, 57, 141, 215, 371, 469, 549, 589, 641(top).

Illustrations

Steve Hetzel: 155, 460, 546.
Matthew S. Pippin: 42, 64, 65, 149, 208, 416, 613.
Precision Graphics: 46, 285, 645.

Photographs

Frequently cited sources are abbreviated as follows: NGIC, National Geographic Image Collection; NGS, National Geographic Society; WC, Woodfin Camp & Associates; TS, Tony Stone Images; MP, Magnum Photos; RL, Russ Lappa; MT, Mark Thayer.

Key to position of illustrations: T, top; C, center; B, bottom; L, left; R, right.

v B, © Robert Knight/TS; v T, © Cotton Coulson/WC; vi L, © Peter Pearson/TS; vi B, B. Anthony Stewart/NGIC; vi T, Bruce Dale/NGS; vii T, Bruce Dale, © NGS; vii B R, © Chris Reid/Aurora; vii L, James P. Blair/NGIC; viii T, Sam Abell/NGIC; viii C, William Albert Allard/NGIC; viii B, © Courau/Explorer/Photo Researchers, Inc.; ix T, Tass/Sovfoto/Eastfoto; ix C, © Joan Iaconetti; ix B R, James L. Stanfield/NGIC; ix B L, © Ed Kashi; x T, James L. Stanfield/NGIC; x T C, © Georg Gerster/Comstock; x B C, © Trevor Wood/TS; x B, © David Sutherland/TS; xi T, Jodi Cobb/NGIC; xi C, Robert Harding Picture Library, Ltd.; xi B, © Jennie Jones/Comstock; xvi B R, © Oshihara/Sipa Press; xvi B L, James P. Blair/NGIC; xvii B R, Robert W. Madden, © NGS; xviii B L, Gordon Gahan © NGS; xviii T, Petit Palais, Paris [Photo: Bulloz]; xx–1 B, © Stuart Franklin/MP; xx–1, background Maria Stenzel/NGIC; xx L, Tomasz Tomaszewski © NGS; xx C, Thomas J. Abercrombie © NGS; xx T, © Steve McCurry/MP; 1 B R, Frank & Helen Schreider/NGIC; 1, Sam Abell/NGIC; 1 T R, James P. Blair/NGIC; 2 L, © Brian Gordon Green/NGIC; 2 R, Maria Stenzel/NGIC; 3 T R, © 1993 W. T. Sullivan, III; 3 T L, Satellite image data processing by the Environmental Research Institute of Michigan (ERIM), Ann Arbor, Michigan; 30–31, Bates Littlehales/NGIC; 32, George F. Mobley/NGIC; 33, Vince Streano/TS; 34, Thomas J. Abercrombie, © NGS; 35, Steve Raymer/NGIC; 36, Satellite image data processing by the Environmental Research Institute of Michigan (ERIM), Ann Arbor, Michigan; 37, © Ken Biggs/TS; 38, Michael E. Long © NGS; 39, Winfield I. Parks/NGIC; 40, Steve Raymer/NGIC; 45, © Georg Gerster/Comstock; 47, © Nicholas DeVore III/Photographers Aspen; 48, © Paul Chesley/Photographers Aspen; 49, © Kurgan-Lisne/Gamma Liaison Network; 50 T, © Cameron Davidson/Comstock; 50 B, © Gilles Rigoulet/Cosmos/Matrix; 51, © Steven C. Wilson/Entheos; 52–3, © Robert Knight/TS; 56–57, Ph. by RL; 58, NOAA/NGIC; 59,

© Cotton Coulson/WC; 61 L, Dean Conger/NGIC ; 61 R, Dean Conger/NGIC; 69, Edward H. Kim/NGS; 71, Paul A. Zahl, Ph.D./NGIC; 74, Thomas J. Abercrombie © NGS; 75, © Paul Chesley/Photographers Aspen; 76–7, © Michael Medford/The Image Bank; 80, © Rich Iwasaki/TS; 81, Thomas Nebbia © NGS; 90, © Thomas Nebbia/WC; 92, © Marvin E. Newman/The Image Bank; 93, © C. Renault/Gamma-Liaison Network; 98, James L. Amos/NGIC; 100, James P. Blair/NGIC; 101, James L. Amos/NGIC; 102 B, George F. Mobley/NGIC; 102 T, Jodi Cobb/NGIC; 105, Frank & Helen Schreider/NGIC; 106, © David Austen/WC; 107, © Cotton Coulson/WC; 110, Ph. by MT; 111 L, Earth Observation Satellite Company; 111 R, Earth Observation Satellite Company; 112–13, © Bill Ross/WC; 118 T, © 1993 W. T. Sullivan, III; 118 B, © Katie Miller/Frozen Images; 123 L, © Peter Essick/Aurora; 123 R, James P. Blair/NGIC; 124, [Detail]: North American, Salado region, Mimbres Culture, from a cache of ritual figures, wood, cotton, feathers, fiber, black, blue, yellow, red and white earth pigments, c. 1150–1400, 63.5 x 17.1., Major Acquisitions Centennial Fund, 1979.17.1–11, photo © 1993, The Art Institute of Chicago. All Rs Reserved. 125, © Lee Boltin/Boltin Library; 126, Doris De Witt/TS; 127, © Sarah Leen/Matrix; 129, © Ted Spiegel/Black Star; 130, Property of AT&T Archives., Reprinted with permission of AT&T; 131, The Granger Collection; 132, © Peter Pearson/TS; 133, © Maggie Steber/Aurora & Quanta Productions; 134, © Don Spiro/TS; 140–141, Ph., by RL; 142, © Eastcott/Momatiuk/WC; 143, B. Anthony Stewart/NGIC; 145, © Nicholas DeVore III/Photographers Aspen; 146, © Louis Psihoyos/Matrix; 147, Bruce Dale/NGS; 150, David A. Harvey/NGS; 151, © Stuart Cohen/Comstock; 152 B, Postcards: Ph. by RL; 152 T, Sisse Brimberg/NGIC; 153, © Georg Gerster/Comstock; 156, James L. Stanfield/NGIC; 158, Gordon Gahan/NGIC; 160, © Larry Ulrich/TS; 161, Steven L. Raymer/NGIC; 164, John Lopinot/Post Beach Post/Post Stock; 166, George F. Mobley/NGIC; 167, Gordon Gahan © NGIC; 170, © David Hiser/Photographers Aspen; 171, David Alan Harvey/NGS; 172, George F. Mobley/NGIC; 173, © David Hiser/Photographers Aspen; 174 R, Todd Buchanan/NGS; 174 L, © Al Harvey/Masterfile; 175, © David Hiser/Photographers Aspen; 176 L, George F. Mobley/NGIC; 176 R, Sisse Brimberg/NGIC; 178, © Georg Gerster/Comstock; 179, Todd Buchanan/NGS; 180, James P. Blair/NGIC; 184 R, Ph. by MT; 185 L, Bruce Dale/NGIC; 185 R, © Chuck Nacke/WC; 186–87, © Mireille Vautier/WC; 192, Comstock Photography; 198, Ph., by RL; 200 © Peter Menzel; 201, Kenneth Garrett/NGIC; 204, Kenneth Garrett/NGIC; 205, © Annie Griffiths Belt; 207, © David Hiser/Photographers Aspen; 209, Bruce Dale, © NGS; 210, Kenneth Garrett/NGIC; 211, Joel Sartore/NGIC; 214, Ph. by, RL; 216, Jodi Cobb/NGIC; 217, Joseph J. Scherschel/NGIC; 219, © Chris Reid/Aurora; 220, Tomasz Thomaszewski, © NGS; 221, © Peter Menzel; 224, Bruce Dale, © NGS; 226 B,© Joe Viesti/Viesti Associates, Inc.; 226 T, © Joel Simon/TS; 227, James P. Blair/NGIC; 229, © Tony Pacheco/Sygma; 232, © Loren McIntyre; 233, © Loren McIntyre; 236, © Loren McIntyre; 238, © Stephanie Maze/Material World; 239, Stephanie Maze/NGS; 240, © Bernard Bourtrit/WC; 241, © Jose Azel/Aurora; 244 T, James P. Blair/NGIC; 244 B, Ph., by RL; 246, © Hans Strand/TS; 247, © Jose Azel/Aurora; 249, Robert W. Madden, © NGS; 251, Sam Abell/NGIC; 252, © Loren McIntyre; 253, © Loren McIntyre; 255, William Albert Allard/NGS; 256, © Peter Menzel; 258, © Loren McIntyre; 259, © Loren McIntyre; 260, © Stephanie Maze/WC; 261, James P. Blair/NGIC; 264, Ph. by MT; 266–67, © Paul Chesley/TS; 273, © Adam Woolfitt/WC; 278, Petit Palais, Paris [Photo: Bulloz]; 280, © Janet Gill/TS; 281, © Mike Yamashita/WC; 284, © Annie Griffiths Belt; 285, © Mike McQueen/TS; 286, © Yann Layma/TS; 287, Winfield I. Parks, Jr./NGIC; 288, Sam Abell/NGIC; 289, © A. Howarth/WC; 291, © J. Langevin/Sygma; 292, Sam Abell/NGIC; 293, Sam Abell/NGIC; 294, Andrew H. Brown/NGIC; 296, Emory Kristof/NGIC; 297, Tomasz Tomaszewski © NGS; 301, © Kessler/Sipa Press; 302, Volkmar Wentzel/NGIC; 303, William Albert Allard/NGIC; 304, © Michael Busselle/TS; 306, Bruno de Hogues/TS; 309, © P.Habans/

748